VIOLENCE AGAINST WOMEN AND CHILDREN

A Christian Theological Sourcebook

CAROL J. ADAMS AND MARIE M. FORTUNE,
Editors

CONTINUUM • NEW YORK

SCI

1995

The Continuum Publishing Company
370 Lexington Avenue
New York, NY 10017

Printed in the United States of America

Library of Congress Cataloging-in-Publication Data

Violence against women and children : a Christian theological
  sourcebook / edited by Carol J. Adams and Marie M. Fortune.
       p.   cm.
    Includes bibliographical references.
    ISBN 0-8264-0830-3 (pbk. : alk. paper)
      1. Women—Crimes against—Religious aspects—Christianity.
  2. Violence—Religious aspects—Christianity.   3. Children—Crimes
  against—Religious aspects—Christianity.   4. Feminist theology.
  I. Adams, Carol J.   II. Fortune, Marie M.
  BT704.V56   1995
  261.8'32—dc20   95-17449
                                                              CIP

Proceeds from this book benefit the Center for the Prevention of Sexual
and Domestic Violence.

The traumatic event challenges an ordinary person to become a theologian, a philosopher, and a jurist. The survivor is called upon to articulate the values and beliefs that she once held and that the trauma destroyed. She stands mute before the emptiness of evil, feeling the insufficiency of any known system of explanation. Survivors of atrocity of every age and every culture come to a point in their testimony where all questions are reduced to one, spoken more in bewilderment than in outrage: Why? The answer is beyond human understanding.

Beyond this unfathomable question, the survivor confronts another, equally incomprehensible question: Why me? The arbitrary, random quality of her fate defies the basic faith in a just or even predictable world order. In order to develop a full understanding of the trauma story, the survivor must examine the moral questions of guilt and responsibility and reconstruct a system of belief that makes sense of her undeserved suffering. Finally, the survivor cannot reconstruct a sense of meaning by the exercise of thought alone. The remedy for injustice also requires action. The survivor must decide what is to be done.

As the survivor attempts to resolve these questions, she often comes into conflict with important people in her life. There is a rupture in her sense of belonging within a shared system of belief. Thus she faces a double task: not only must she rebuild her own "shattered assumptions" about meaning, order, and justice in the world but she must also find a way to resolve her differences with those whose beliefs she can no longer share.

—Judith Herman, *Trauma and Recovery*

To those who survived and
in memory of those who did not.

Contents

Preface

Sexual and domestic violence provoke spiritual as well as physical crises, especially for victims: Where was God and why did God allow this to happen to me? Is my sinfulness the cause of this? Do I need to forgive my abuser? What is justice and how is it achieved? Whom can I tell? Victims of sexual and domestic violence often turn to their religious institutions in seeking help to answer these questions. In the midst of a faith crisis such as this, Christian victims want to turn to Christian churches. They want to turn to the church because they want to understand the meaning of their experience and because they want the abuse to stop and/or the abuser brought to justice. But as Judith Herman acknowledges in the epigraph to this book, survivors experience a rupture in their sense of belonging within a shared system of belief. How do they rebuild their own shattered assumptions and resolve their differences with those whose beliefs they can no longer share? How does Christianity aid or impede this process?

When we first began educating church leaders about sexual and domestic violence in the late 1970s, their most common response was: "*But no one ever comes to me with this problem.*" We knew that this was true, but we also knew that the reason that no one was coming to them was that the battered women, incest survivors, rape victims, and others in their congregations were afraid to come to them because they did not trust that they would be treated appropriately. At that point, there was still very little media attention devoted to the issues of sexual and domestic violence, and many church people who suffered with memories or current critical situations did so in silence.

It was troubling to realize how resistant many clergymen were to information that would increase their awareness and expand their pastoral resources for their people. Their denial was fed by many sources: they concluded erroneously that if their people were not coming to them with "these problems" then they did not have "these problems." They also bought into the belief that "these problems" happen to other people, not to them or to people they know. In other words, the Episcopalians could believe that it is a Methodist problem, the Methodists could believe that it is a Baptist problem, and they all could believe that it is a Roman Catholic problem. Invariably, race and class also shaped their beliefs that battering, incest, rape, sexual harassment, and other forms of sexual violation happen to people unlike them.

But clergywomen were having a different experience as they began to pastor in congregations. They were finding that a significant portion of their time was being spent in pastoral care and crisis intervention with battered women, incest victims/survivors, rape victims/survivors, and victims of sexual harassment in the workplace. In other words, they had no question that their people were struggling with these experiences. And they had no question that as pastors, they were ill-prepared to respond.

Seminary had not trained them for what they would surely encounter in
the first year of parish ministry or institutional chaplaincy. A United Church of
Canada pastor, after describing the multiple cases of abuse to which she had
attempted a pastoral response, concluded: "I look out my window at the blue
sky and the green leaves, the traffic and the pedestrians, and it hardly seems
possible that there's a war on. But I really believe that there is, and that this
quiet little church is a MASH unit." Another student returning from his first
parish to visit his ethics professor exclaimed in desperation, "Why didn't you
tell us that the most common thing we would see in the parish was incest?"
She had not told him because she did not know that would be the case. During
the 1980s, regardless of gender, there was at least some agreement that semi-
nary-trained ministerial leaders were not prepared to deal with the reality of
personal violence and abuse that was happening in their congregations.

Slowly and painfully, individual pastors began to see the need to learn
more about sexual and domestic violence. For many male pastors, it took a crisis to wake them up. One Presbyterian pastor acknowledged that he had never
considered the problem of battering until his daughter was abused by her husband who finally tried to kill her and him. Now he is a strong advocate for the
church and its leaders to attend to the problem of violence in the family. Some
male pastors accidentally discovered the problems in their midst. An Episcopalian priest, in the midst of a four-week training seminar on sexual and
domestic violence, announced to his congregation that he was taking this seminar and as a result would be away from the office on Wednesday mornings for
these four weeks. Immediately, he was confronted with two incest survivors
and a rape survivor from his small congregation. He was initially very distressed
by what seemed to be a sudden outbreak of violence. But as he began to reflect
on his situation, he began to see that none of these cases was "new" but had all
been long-standing. These three people now had permission to seek him out for
pastoral care because he announced that he was getting training and therefore
might be of some use to them. He was learning the lesson that we do not *hear*
about sexual and domestic violence in our congregations until we *speak* about
it. His experience has been repeated many times over in other churches.

In 1985, the first Theological Education and Domestic Violence Conference
was held in San Antonio, Texas. This event, sponsored by the Center for the
Prevention of Sexual and Domestic Violence and with strong support from a
number of Protestant denominations, brought together faculty, administrators, and students who shared a concern for increased attention to domestic
violence in seminary curricula. This event served to focus concern and to provide support for those faculty, administrators, and students who were working on these issues in their own seminaries. They understood that no one
should graduate from seminary without being at least alerted to the facts that
(1) they will encounter sexual and domestic violence, that (2) when they do,
they need to identify it and use community resources to assist in responding,
and that (3) they need to provide an informed pastoral response that focuses
on ending the violence rather than supposedly "keeping the family together."

But we were few in number, about 125, and although participants felt support for their efforts, we all realized that the need was much greater than one conference could address. One of the concrete areas identified by the conference was the need for critical scholarship in all disciplines. We wanted to find ways to support research and writing in order to begin to develop a body of literature within theological education. We raised these questions: What would a theological education look like if it took the common experiences of sexual and domestic violence seriously? What if theological education were actually in dialogue with the insights arising out of the growing secular literature on domestic and sexual violence? What issues would the various disciplines encounter? How might students be better prepared for their vocations in ministry and teaching? Given the facts of sexual and domestic violence, there is no area of the theological curriculum that does not need to be re-examined.

While the issues of sexual and domestic violence are definitely issues associated with the practice of pastoral care, and while the pastoral care field has perhaps shown more attention to the issues, this is not sufficient because these are not only pastoral issues. They are also hermeneutical, exegetical, liturgical, theological, ethical, and historical issues because all of these areas profoundly affect the lives of congregants and students. The need to address sexual and domestic violence in the seminaries should not be passed along to pastoral care and counseling, but rather should be examined in every discipline.

In the years following the 1985 conference, additional concerns have arisen. We began to realize that not only were there serious concerns about the adequacy of training for seminarians, but also they were experiencing sexual and domestic violence while in the seminary community. Again, this reality was not new, but it was newly apparent as students and others began to discuss their experiences more openly. On seminary campuses, the problems of battering between intimate partners, the issues of young adults remembering incest experiences, and the sexual harassment of students (or faculty or staff) by faculty, administrators, or other students were becoming apparent. So in recent years, a new level of awareness has pushed many seminaries to attend to their own house as well as to try to better prepare their students to attend to others. A discussion which focused this concern took place on a panel at the American Academy of Religion in 1992 (see Baker-Fletcher and Fortune articles). This awareness has dramatically presented the need for an institutional response at the level of policy and practice which remains a major challenge for most seminaries today.

This anthology draws upon the discussions at the 1985 conference and subsequent discussions at the American Academy of Religion and on many campuses throughout North America. It represents the current as well as some of the early efforts to examine critically the Christian tradition, scriptures, doctrines, and teachings in order to support and encourage a greater awareness of the experiences of sexual and domestic violence which are pandemic in North American life today. In it you will find articles that were written specifically for this volume as well as articles that have appeared elsewhere. The previously published articles, we believe, reveal both the development in the field as well as the fact that, as yet, nothing has superseded them. (As a result of this pulling of material from a variety of sources, the anthology features two different citation systems.)

In this volume we intentionally limit our discussion to Christian sources. Although all religious traditions struggle with interpretations and distortions that may be used to justify sexual or domestic violence, we do not presume to address traditions other than our own. In addition, because Christianity is the dominant religious tradition in North America, it shapes public consciousness beyond those persons who identify as Christians and thus necessitates an in-depth, focused discussion.

We have organized the anthology by discipline to convey the message that these issues not only need to be incorporated into each discipline, but they can and have been. This anthology is not exhaustive, though it attempts to be comprehensive in the sense that it incorporates a number of different approaches on a number of different issues in the fields of sexual and domestic violence. We wanted to demonstrate how the disciplines could be absorbing and responding to this information. We are therefore offering a *model* as much as a *resource*. For instance, the historical analyses contained in this volume do not attempt grand reviews, but instead offer specific analyses that provide models for the kind of historical work that is still necessary.

Nor is the anthology exhaustive of the issues before us. But our task here is to point forward within a framework that is multidisciplined, in dialogue with secular discussions, that takes the particularities of gender, race, and class seriously, and calls our churches to incorporate new awarenesses of sexual and domestic violence into every aspect of ministry and teaching.

This book focuses on violence against women and children. Why? Why not violence against persons? In a patriarchal society, if we are to understand the particulars of personal violence, we must utilize a gender analysis. Using the lens of gender will reveal some very important aspects to us. Physical and sexual violence against women, usually committed by men, is pandemic in our culture and the high rates of violence against women and girl children make it clear that we who are female are particularly vulnerable to violence simply due to our gender. We live with the reality that theologian Mary Hunt has described: violence is the *context* of our lives rather than separate, individual episodes in our lives.

This is the biggest difference between women's and men's experiences: for men, personal violence is episodic. It occurs occasionally to individuals. It occurs more frequently to men who, by virtue of their occupation, are at great risk, e.g., in the military, professional sports, or police work. Their occupations may require them to be in harm's way. But as women, we live in harm's way: everyday, everywhere. There is no respite. And we are statistically more at risk at home than in public. Physical and sexual violence is the context of our lives. We get up in the morning and go to work or to school in spite of this knowledge. In other words, we utilize denial to help us cope with the reality around us. But the knowledge of our vulnerability dramatically shapes our lives: our decisions about what job to take, what hours to work, what school to attend, what movies to see, whom we spend time with, how we relate to our families, whether and where to jog, hike, or walk.

The point of this is to help us recognize that violence against women is a social problem, not merely an individual one. It is a reality that is congruent with the patriarchal culture and values of our society. And so it is important to address it in its particularity as a deeply rooted problem in our social, cultural, and religious contexts. At the same time, we must remember that violence and the threat of violence are common experiences in women's *individual* lives and must also be addressed pastorally and individually.

This sourcebook documents pain and in the reading it can evoke pain. In the past, many Christians who have been victims of sexual or domestic violence have had to choose between their faith and coming to terms with their victimization. We believe that it is the church's responsibility to offer something other than this debilitating choice. To do this, theological education must be transformed.

It is our hope that this text not only will encourage attention within theological education but also will help to shape the future directions of theological education so that those who partake of its offerings will be adequately prepared for the tasks of ministry or teaching ahead of them. When adequately prepared, our ministers and teachers can respond not only to the individual victim/survivor or perpetrator but can also address and change the structural foundations of our churches which have allowed the violence to go unchallenged for so long.

Acknowledgments

Thanks to Mary Pellauer who began the process of creating an anthology such as this, identifying potential contributors, and working with them in creating appropriate and valuable essays. She has believed in the importance of this anthology for many, many years, and through her commitment to it helped to bring it about. Peggy Halsey, too, has been steadfast in her support, staying abreast of developments and setbacks, and helping to turn setbacks into progress; as a result, more than anyone, she worked to keep the project alive. She insured funding for the project from its inception, and we thank Ministries with Women and Families of the General Board of Global Ministries of the United Methodist Church for its financial support. Kathy Nickerson, another midwife to this anthology, over many years maintained a commitment to making this anthology a reality, and helped to secure the support of people who could insure that this commitment was realized. Marjorie Procter-Smith has lived with the joys and concerns of this anthology more intimately than she ever expected to, and has done so with grace and wit. Thanks to all of these women, pioneers who have helped shape the field and this anthology.

Thanks for the understanding, patience, and support through the years of Bruce A. Buchanan, Anne L. Ganley, and Evander Lomke who have helped us believe that the anthology could be finished. Mary Hunt offered a listening ear and reasoning mind during the final months; we thank her for her tenacity. Thanks, too, to Frances Wood, Maryviolet C. Burns, Thelma Burgonio-Watson, Elizabeth Stellas-Tippins, Rebecca Voelkel-Haugen, Sandra Barone, and Jean Anton for ongoing support of work such as this. Charles Sprague gave counsel and support at a critical time, and we thank him for that. We appreciate the financial support of Caroline Rose Hunt and the Sands Foundation in keeping the anthology alive. We are grateful for the support and efforts of Rob Baker and the staff of Watersign Resources.

We acknowledge the work of the contributors in striving to stop violence and in offering their support of this project. Their generosity of spirit and caring buoyed the editors along the way. The editors also appreciate each other's work and commitment which made this project and the process of collaboration itself an enriching and stimulating experience.

This anthology represents the desires of many in the church who offered much moral support along the way. We cannot necessarily name each person who believed in the importance of this anthology during the past ten years and offered counsel and blessings. Thanks, though, to all named and unnamed who helped to bring this anthology into being.

Part I

Theological Foundations

Toward a Feminist Theology
of Religion and the State

CAROL J. ADAMS

You become what you do not resist.
—Catharine MacKinnon (1990, 5)

Introduction

Sexual victimization affects every woman's life. Women and children are considerably less safe in the home than anywhere else. Battering is the major cause of injury to adult women. Marital rape is among the most common kind of sexual assault there is. One in three American girls before eighteen years and one in seven boys are sexually abused. Every six minutes a woman is raped in the United States according to estimates based on reported cases. When the high rate of underreporting is taken into account, the FBI estimates that a rape occurs every two minutes. Woman-battering is a major cause of homelessness for women and their children. At least forty percent of homeless women are women who were abused by their partners, and left. They now face rape on the street rather than battering in the home.[1] They also face sexual harassment from landlords and building superintendents in seeking apartments. More than ninety percent of women in paid employment surveyed had been sexually harassed on the job. Sexual harassment and rape of domestic workers, mainly women of color, has been well documented; Patricia Hill Collins refers to it as sexual extortion. Women seminarians must often choose between their call or telling the truth about the sexual harassment to which they have been exposed at seminaries and in internships.

We are learning from historians that a major reason for Black women's exodus to the North of the United States at the turn of the century was to escape sexual harassment, rape, and battering in the South;[2] abusers of documented immigrant women often threaten to destroy the documentation if they leave, and without such documentation the women could be deemed "illegal aliens" in United States government parlance and deported; married immigrant women (for instance, Asian "mail-order" brides and political prisoners from Latin or Central America) in this country often stay married to their abuser for fear of losing their right to stay in this country. We are learning of women raped by Serbian troops, the prostituting of women and girl refugees in Zagreb by United Nations peacekeeping troops, the rapidly growing sex tourism business in Asia, and now in Russia. Byllye Avery, founder of the Black Women's Health Network, argues that we must connect the issue of Black teenage pregnancy to incest.[3] Patricia Collins points out that according to statistics, Black women are more likely to be victimized than white women (Collins 1990, 178), and Angela Y. Davis has demonstrated how sexual violence is central to the economic and political subordination of African Americans.

We know that when we teach this material, we must anticipate personal reaction from our students: "It happened to me" (Reineke 1992, 3). We know that researchers studying "women's way of knowing" had to redesign their research questions because of the overwhelming number of women self-reporting forms of sexual victimization (Belenky et al. 1986, 58, 59).

I have been involved in responding to the trauma and carnage that results from sexual victimization since the mid-1970s. When I started a Hotline for Battered Women in 1978 and throughout some of the 1980s, I held what I would now call a liberal theological view of the subject. This meshed nicely with the secular material of the time, such as Lenore Walker's theory of learned helplessness and a cycle of violence with a honeymoon period.[4] This liberal theological view tends toward therapeutic analyses, toward differentiating between sex and violence, and sees sexual violence as an abuse of power. But as I have continued reading and being involved in the issue, as I have taught a course at a seminary on theological and pastoral issues associated with domestic and sexual violence, as I have clipped—almost daily—from the *Dallas Morning News* stories about women's brutal murders by their abusive male partners, about women's rape, about sexual abuse of children, I have discovered the foundation of the liberal theological/therapeutic view shaken. In addition, I have searched during this time for an understanding of the systematic nature of animals' oppression. For all of these reasons and more, I have turned to the writings of Catharine MacKinnon. The title of my essay clearly and purposely echoes one of her books. Now, after working through the many implications of her thought, it might also be called "A feminist metatheory for theology and sexuality."

Catharine MacKinnon's work in the wider feminist circle is more disputed than refuted, simplistically engaged with by many critics rather than systematically encountered. A recent article in *Hypatia: A Journal of Feminist Philosophy* argued that feminist philosophy has failed to respond directly to MacKinnon's important work (Bernick 1992). Many of her critics think they understand her and offer only a superficial reading of her. And when I turn to theology I find little engagement with MacKinnon's work.

The purpose of this essay is to describe MacKinnon's theory, indicate how MacKinnon's theory critiques much liberal theological work on the subject of sexual victimization, and conclude with some thoughts on the implications of MacKinnon for theology. MacKinnon's devastating analysis of how things are, right now, leads to a series of questions about theology in general and feminist theology in particular. I raise these questions as part of my resistance to our dominating society. I do not raise them in any way to dispute the justice-seeking thoughtfulness of the theologians whom it will appear I am explicitly or implicitly critiquing. There is much we share and I have intense respect for their work. But if MacKinnon's analysis of "what is" is correct, our collective justice-seeking work must engage itself with her analysis.

MacKinnon's Theory of Sex Inequality

Though MacKinnon clearly states that she is working *toward* a feminist theory of the state, her work offers a metatheory for theology. Currently, there is a proliferation of standpoints from which the issues of sexual violence and victimization can be discussed. I offer MacKinnon as a lightning rod through which the energy around this issue must be grounded.

MacKinnon explains that she is describing "what *is*, the meaning of what is, and the way what is, is enforced" (1989, xii). For the purposes of this essay I will highlight seven specific areas of insight that MacKinnon offers.[5]

Gender Is Not Difference but Dominance

MacKinnon says gender is "a material division of power" (1989, 58). Gender is a hierarchy, a matter of domination and subordination. The concept of gender is not biologically based, but part of social construction:

> This is not to say that all men have power equally. For example, American Black men have substantially less of it. But to the extent that they cannot create the world from their point of view, they experience themselves as unmanned, castrated. This observation supports rather than qualifies the sex specificity of the argument. (1989, 275n. 45)

Consider, for example, the way Clarence Thomas's reference to "hi-tech lynching" definitively brought the unmanning issue forward, since one of the tactics of white racists when lynching African-American men was literally to attack the victim's penis.

Gender Inequality Is Sexualized

"As sexual inequality is gendered as man and women, gender inequality is sexualized as dominance and subordination" (1989, 241). In other words, gender is a systematic inequality of power. Sexuality is a form of its practice. Sexuality is predicated on the domination of women. "Men dominate women, this domination is sexual." "Sex inequality is what creates what we interpret to be sex difference and thus what so many find to be sexually desirable" (Olsen 1158). What we have is "sex as inequality and inequality as sex" (1989, 241). Vulnerability and enforced silence is made sexy: "Sexuality as a social construct of male power: defined by men, forced on women, and constitutive of the meaning of gender" (1989, 128). "Misogyny *is* sexual. . . . As a result, sexuality, as socially organized, is deeply misogynist. . . . [S]exuality is premised on sex *in*equality" (1990, 13). "Sexuality for MacKinnon isn't anything at all. It is a social process that eroticizes dominance and submission and that creates men and women as the social creatures as we know them" (Bernick 1992, 6). We experience the social reality of domination made into sex through rape, incest, pornography, sexual harassment, captivity in the home.

"The Line between Sex and Violence Is Indistinct and Mobile in a Society in Which Violence Means Violation of That Worthy of Respect, and Women Are Not"

We have to talk about women's rapability. Women's rapability is intrinsic to the practice of the sexual, women's sexual identity: we learn to accept the coercive as normative. One is raped as a member of a socially subordinated group: "Women are raped because we are women: neither individually or at random, but because of gender." "The sexiness of inequality, a part of the eroticization of domination and subordination, that is a part of sex, is the eroticization of violence, that is rape." "Rape is a sex-specific violation. Not only are the victims of rape overwhelmingly women, perpetrators overwhelmingly men, but also the rape of women by men is integral to the way inequality between the sexes occurs in life. Intimate violation with impunity is an ultimate index of social power. Rape both evidences and practices women's low status relative to men" (1989, 245). "Sexual violation is both a practice and an index of inequality between the sexes, both a symbol and an act of women's subordinate social status to men" (1991).

The Concept of Consent Assumes a Gender-Neutral World That Does Not Exist

First, we live "in a society of sex inequality—where sex is what women *have* to sell, sex is what we are, sex is what we are valued for, we are born sex, we die sex" (1990, 10). Gender neutrality ignores what is distinctively done to women and ignores who is doing it (1990, 6). Second, "when force is a normalized part of sex, when no is taken to mean yes, when fear and despair produce acquiescence and acquiescence is taken to mean consent, consent is not a meaningful concept" (1990, 4). In other words, "As long as women are thought to falsely or ambiguously deny wanting sex, men may be confused regarding consent. From MacKinnon's perspective, 'consent' is meaningless as long as society fails to hear or believe a woman's refusal of sex" (Olsen, 1157).

Women's Words about Sexual Victimization Become Oral Pornography

Women are "heard only when mouthing a sexual script" (1989, 196). When women's words about sexual violence circulate, they do so in contaminated, patriarchal space. When victims of sexually violent men and sexually harassing men report their experiences, these accounts of sexual violation are a form of sex. This understanding may help to account for the reason so many instances of sexual abuse by clergy and therapists occur against women who have reported to them instances of sexual victimization. The woman who speaks about sexual harassment is experienced as part of a pornographic narrative:

> Perhaps men respond sexually when women give an account of sexual violation because sexual words are a sexual reality, in the same way that men respond to pornography, which is (among other things) an account of the sexual violation of a woman. Seen in this way, much therapy as well as court testimony in sexual abuse cases is live oral pornography. (MacKinnon 1989, 152)

Describing the Clarence Thomas hearings, MacKinnon said:

> The more silent he is, the more powerful and credible. But the moment she opens her mouth, her credibility founders. Senators said they were offended by her; President Bush said he felt unclean. The dirt and uncleanliness stuck to her. When she spoke truth to power, she was treated like a pig in a parlor. He said these things, but she was blamed.

> Once you are used for sex, you lose your human status. Your own testimony becomes live oral porn in a drama starring you. (quoted in Landsberg 1992, 3)

Incest Functions to Inculcate Normative Male Sexual Expectations

Child sexual abuse is a way of initiating girl children into the practice of the sexual based on their own rapability. A chilling example of this observation is found in a psychotherapist's report of a conversation he had with a pimp. The pimp explained what he looks for in a woman he is considering to make one of his prostitutes:

> Beauty, yes. Sexual expertise, somewhat. That can be taught easier than you think. What is important above all is obedience. And how do you get obedience? You get obedience if you get women who have had sex with their fathers, their uncles, their brothers—you know, someone they love

and fear to lose so that they do not dare to defy. Then you are nicer to the woman than they ever were, and more dangerous as well. (Kluft, 25)

MacKinnon reminds us, "Recall that more than one-third of all girls experience sex, perhaps are sexually initiated, under conditions that even this society recognizes are forced or at least unequal" (1989, 147). One-half of all rape victims are under eighteen years of age; 25 percent of rape victims are under twelve years of age.

The adult survivor *is* at great risk of repeated victimization in adult life: "The risk of rape, sexual harassment, or battering, though high for all women, is approximately doubled for survivors of childhood sexual abuse" (Herman 1992, 111). The explanation for this is not the patriarchal answer of women's masochism but that

> repeated abuse is not actively sought but rather is passively experienced as a dreaded but unavoidable fate and is accepted as the inevitable price of relationship. Many survivors have such profound deficiencies in self-protection that they can barely imagine themselves in a position of agency or choice. (Herman, 112)

It is what Ellyn Kaschak calls "sensitivity to the aggressor" (Kaschak 1992, 125). Also a dissociative coping style "leads survivors to ignore or minimize social cues that would ordinarily alert them to danger" (Herman 112).

Pornography Is a Central Factor in Women's Subordination

Finally, the most controversial aspect of MacKinnon's theory: "Gender is sexual. Pornography constitutes the meaning of that sexuality" (1989, 197). Pornography "makes harm to women invisible by making it sex" (1990, 11). "Compare victims' reports of rape with what pornography says is sex. They look a lot alike" (1989, 146). Moreover, "Pornography is masturbation material. It is used as sex. It therefore is sex" (1993, 17).

A Critique of Liberal Theological Presumptions Following MacKinnon

Dominance or Difference?

To treat gender as a difference is to cover disparities of power; instead men's dominance and women's subordination account for many so-called differences. Responding to feminist discussions of the possibility that women share a care-based, rather than a rights-based, ethic, that draw on the work of Carol Gilligan, MacKinnon observes:

> By establishing that women reason differently from men on moral questions, [Carol Gilligan] revalues that which has accurately distinguished women from men by making it seem as though women's moral reasoning is somehow women's, rather than what male supremacy has attributed to women for its own use. When difference means dominance as it does

with gender, for women to affirm differences is to affirm the qualities and characteristics of powerlessness. (1989, 51)

Since difference is the result of domination, it is a mistake to reclaim difference as a good thing .

Sex as the Locus of Domination or the Erotic as a Source of Identity?

The difference formulation states that the erotic is the opposite of sexual violation, what one feminist calls "erotic faith" (Sands 1992). The domination formulation, on the other hand, considers the erotic as the locus of the enacting of sexual domination. MacKinnon observes, "Most people see sexuality as individual and biological and voluntary; that is, they see it in terms of the politically and formally liberal myth structure" (1987, 60). People want to believe that

> sexuality is part of the natural world first, the social world incidentally, the political world only when the state gets involved. Audiences want to affirm that the sexuality for which we need what we do not have—a society of sex equality—already exists and merely needs to be unearthed. (1987, 218)

But sexuality is not part of the natural world first; it is part of the political world. We cannot escape that fact.

If the erotic is sexualized dominance how can the erotic be something we can "have" or possess as power as Carter Heyward suggests? MacKinnon says sex is what men say it is. But instead Sands argues that the "hermeneutical privilege of the oppressed" can be overcome (that is, we need not develop theory solely from the voices and experience of the sexually victimized): "Though the interests of victims must certainly be protected within an adequate sexual theology, sex also carries mystical and aesthetical valences which deserve acknowledgment on their own terms" (Sands 1992, 15). Sands, like many theologians, including feminists, is still positing sex as something essential, something we possess rather than something we are. She defines sex as "an elemental power which can carry a variety of goods but which is fundamentally characterized by intensity. Cruelty, betrayal and humiliation all evoke intense responses, and these responses are easily sexualized. Sexual desire and satisfaction can be painful or pleasurable, or can defy one's usual distinctions between pleasure and pain" (Sands, 14). MacKinnon's reply might be "It is interesting that, in spite of everything, many women who once thought of their abuse as self-actualizing come to rethink it as a violation, while very few who have ever thought of their abuse as a violation come to rethink it as self-actualizing" (1989, 287 n. 74). Moreover, MacKinnon would say that we cannot use our own experience of pleasure as a bellwether for our politics: "To see the personal as the political did not mean that what turns you on grounds the policies you promote" (1990, 5).

The comments of Kwok Pui-lan are a helpful counterpoint to the feminist theological claim that posits the erotic as liberatory:

Ever since the Afro-American poet and writer Audre Lorde published
the classic article "The Uses of the Erotic: The Erotic as Power" feminist
theologians such as Rita Nakashima Brock and Carter Heyward are
excited about the possibility of talking about God and the power of the
erotic. But strangely enough, the language of the erotic is noticeably
missing in the theological construction of Afro-American women, and
feminist theologians from other parts of the world also find it difficult to
speak about the power of female sexuality. . . .

Asian women find it embarassing to talk about sex and the erotic not
only because decent women are not supposed to raise those issues in
public, but also because many of our sisters are working as prostitutes in
the hotels, nightclubs, bars, disco joints, and cocktail lounges in the big
cities like Manila, Bangkok, Taipei, Hong Kong, and Seoul. . . . The
magnitude of the international flesh trade and the courageous action of
these women's groups challenge us to rethink the connection between
the language of the erotic, the control of the female body, and power
over women in its naked and symbolic forms. (Pui-Lan 1992, n.p.)

Sex and Violence Fused, or Rape Is Violence, Not Sex?

Here our ontological viewpoints come crashing down. Is this a case of a bad
piece in a good pie or a totally bad pie? Olsen points out that a beneficial
change in awareness occurred by the argument that rape is violence and not
sex. Now we can comprehend that rape is (also) sex, (which is why people
now take seriously date rape and marital rape). Olsen believes this "change
would not have been possible before the public became aware of the serious
harm rape causes, an awareness that was facilitated by the assertions of rape
being a crime of violence, not of sex" (Olsen, 1157). But we have to shift our
perspective to see that sexual victimization is to be expected, rather than that
sexual victimization is the exception, not the rule. In this shift, we come to
perceive not that men who commit sex crimes must be "sick" but that this is
exactly how male sexuality is constructed. In fact, "most rapists continue to
live in society undetected, unreported, unpunished, and unrehabilitated"
(MacKinnon 1991). As Judith Herman notes in her chapter on Captivity in
Trauma and Recovery, the batterer's "most consistent feature . . . is his
apparent normality" (1992, 75). From this perpsective, we can see that the
very, very few men who are prosecuted for acts of sexual victimization may
be the "failures," that is, those who get "caught," and therefore it is not accurate to build our understanding of sex crimes on this pool of individuals.

Political Language or Therapeutic Language?

I will give a few examples of the wrong answers we are being given by the
choice of therapeutic language instead of political language in theologizing
about sexual victimization.

A. A POWER ANALYSIS OF MALE CONTROL OR ABUSE AS A RESULT OF STRESS?
First fact: abuse works. One feminist theologian, Susan Thistlethwaite, proposed

that the feminization of the ministry has produced stress because of the accompanying professional loss of status. Sexual harassment is the result of this stress. She queried, "Are male pastors who sexually abuse numerous women in their churches acting out their unstable and insecure sense of what it means to be a man and a pastor?"(see Thistlethwaite 1991, 329). I think this is not the question or the cause. There is an *a priori* male sexual identity that male ministers and seminary professionals possess along with other males. This male sexual identity is one of dominance; maleness in our society continues to have privileges and rights that femaleness does not. This situation of dominance/subordination is then enacted through one's professional role which provides further reinforcement of gender stratification. *Whatever else it is, sexual violation is also a sexual practice.* To propose an explanation of stress is to propose a therapeutic analysis for what is actually a political issue and problem of justice—unequal power relations and sexualized domination. If there is any lesson from the movement against woman-battering it is that *abusive men know what they are doing, to whom they are doing it, and what it is they are doing* (see Adams 1994). We can apprehend the faulty reliance on therapeutic analysis in the explanation that post-traumatic stress disorder is sometimes identified as a *cause* of battering, yet it is curious that when women develop post-traumatic stress disorder as a *consequence* of battering they do not then turn around and express this through battering.

B. MALE SEXUAL IDENTITY OR ABUSE OF POWER? We see a trend in pastoral care these days to focus on sexual harassment and sexual abuse as "the abuse of power" (Poling 1991). MacKinnon's explanation of the problem with this renaming and refocusing is extremely helpful:

> The way the analysis of sexual harassment is sometimes expressed now (and it bothers me) is that it is an abuse of power, not sexuality. This does not allow us to pursue whether sexuality, as socially constructed in our society through gender roles, is *itself* a power structure. . . . It seems to me that we haven't talked very much about gender *as* a hierarchy, as a division of power, in the way that's expressed and acted out, primarily I think sexually. And therefore we haven't expanded the definition according to women's experience of sexuality, including our own sexual intimidation, of what things are sexual in this world. So men have also defined what can be called sexual about us. They say, "I was just trying to be affectionate, flirtatious and friendly," and we were just all felt up. We criticize the idea that rape comes down to her word against his—but it really *is* her perspective against his perspective, and the law has been written from *his* perspective. If he didn't mean it to be sexual, it's not sexual. If he didn't see it as forced, it wasn't forced. Which is to say, only male sexual violations, that is, only male ideas of what sexually violates us as women, are illegal. We buy into this when we say our sexual violations are abuses of power, not sex. (1987, 89–90)

After all, sexuality itself is a power structure.

C. THE USE OF LANGUAGE THAT ELIDES AGENCY. The tendency in theological and pastoral discussion is to elide agency. Thus we encounter terms such as "family violence," (as though what was happening was a free-for-all), "violent relationships," "incestuous families," "battering couples," or "spouse abuse" instead of terms that establish agency such as male violence, abusive men, battering men, and the like.

D. RELIANCE ON ALICE MILLER INSTEAD OF MACKINNON. Facing the information, we turn to a different interpreter. MacKinnon herself says she is reporting on what is. It is as though liberal theology gravitated to Alice Miller rather than MacKinnon for conceptualizing the *why* of violence, rather than understanding MacKinnon on the *what* of sexual violation. MacKinnon and Miller at times are talking about the same victims in a very different way, one has a gender analysis, the other does not. Miller is sweeping, and this sweeping nature to her writing is acceptable. MacKinnon is sweeping but more threatening in her analysis, arguing for the cathexis of sexuality, maleness, control. Embracing Miller and avoiding MacKinnon raises a question about whether we have some unarticulated theoretical gate-keeping systems for what circulates in theology.

It is instructive therefore, that many in the battered women's movement have turned to Mary Daly and Paulo Friere to help them explicate the problem with the use of the therapeutic in responding to the situation of women abused by their male partners. Bonnie Mann (1987) demonstrates how the political statement "You have a foot on your neck" is transformed into the therapeutic response "How do you feel about having a foot on your neck?"

After Hearing MacKinnon: Implications for Theology

MacKinnon's arguments raise specific theological issues, and while these issues are more acute for feminist theology, they are relevant to many theological efforts concerned with gender, sexuality, violence, and relationships.

First, there can be no gender-neutral theologizing; our experience of the world includes our experience of either maleness or femaleness, and this filters our experience of dominance and subordination.

Second, while some theologies propose that sexuality comes to us pure and unadulterated, a natural phenomenon we come to know through our body, unmediated by social forces and gender, sexuality cannot be posited as a part of our life energy separate from social construction. MacKinnon reveals exactly how it is socially constructed. Theologies that place sexuality as central to spirituality, and to how we know God and each other—without such acknowledgments—presume a theological anthropology, but are actually reifying a male dominant ontology.

Theological concern with responses to evil encounters many pitfalls when the issue is sexual victimization. Surely, this, the violation of another, is evil. Yet, the often troubling responses of theological institutions to sexual victimization in their midst suggest that this evil is seen somehow to be qualitatively different from other forms of evil. Often religious communities fail to adopt even the inadequate prevailing legal standards concerning sexual victimization, adopting instead the abuser's perspective. Is this one form of evil in which the perpetrator is more identified with than the victim?[6]

MacKinnon argues that the term "male"

> has nothing whatever to do with inherency, preexistence, nature, inevitability, or body as such. Because it is in the interest of men to be male in the system we live under (male being powerful as well as human), they seldom question its rewards or even see it as a status at all. (1987, 264, n. 6)

John Stoltenberg proposes that men must choose between justice and maleness (1989). In the Hill–Thomas hearings, Senators chose maleness instead of justice. This dilemma faces men in power throughout the country when confronting the issue of sexual harassment in theological, religious, or academic communities. They are more likely to see the harm against the individual male and the corporate group (defined by race, sex, institution, and so on) who will be affected by giving justice to the harmed woman.

So in the Hill–Thomas hearing, Hill was defined as having violated Black solidarity by telling the world about Thomas's behavior, but Black feminists and womanists responded by asking why abuse of Black women by Black men is not seen as violating Black solidarity? As Evelyn Hammonds wrote:

> The message was sexual harassment is not important; Black women must always put duty to the race first. No mention was made of how Clarence Thomas had failed in *his* duty to the race, especially to Black women. The deeply held ethic, that Black women have a duty to the race while Black men are allowed to have a duty only to themselves, can only be challenged by a Black feminist analysis that emphasizes the importance of Black women's lives. (Hammonds 1992)

Similarly, women speaking up about violence are thought to violate the sanctity of marriage, or the church, or some other institution; the women's violation is presumed and normative.

Many who hear the story of sexual abuse actually experience it through the eyes of the abuser. The tendency to identify with the abuser, especially if he is in a respected position, instead of the victim, occurs when his actions become excused because of his excellent reputation or track record. The focus is on the abuser's believability and his normalcy (he's just like you and me). We may be told, "It was an aberration, not a practice, not an ongoing problem." The tendency to identify with the perpetrator is evident whenever the seriousness of the charges is dismissed. I have known of instances where the administrative personnel to whom victims appealed may protect the offender and seek ways to avenge him against his accusers and their mentors. Pastors and professors—especially those who thrive on power—elicit strong loyalties, and often demand unconditional loyalty. Moreover, professors and administrators in seminary may see the future of the church in the Pastor Donovan-types described in Marie M. Fortune's book *Is Nothing Sacred?* Since these responses are not framed theologically, they reveal that somehow sexual victimization is not pertinent to the prevailing theologies of evil and the incumbency of responding to evil.

How do we speak about the integrity of the individual self who has been victimized in the light of a group of persons who are consistently harmed, who are constructed precisely as violable? Speaking of Linda Marchiano ("Linda Lovelace"), MacKinnon states:

> It is apparently difficult to carry on about the ultimate inviolability of the person in the face of a person who has been so ultimately violated. . . . If it happened and it hurt her, she deserved it. If she didn't deserve it, either it didn't happen or it didn't hurt her. If she says it hurt her, she's oversensitive or unliberated. (1987, 13)

What results is the double standard of harm: "the degradation of women stigmatizes women to the point where that degradation is taken as evidence that there was nothing of value to which harm could be done; a raped or pornographed person is damaged goods hardly worth the respect a recognition of her harm would bring" (Bartlett, 1562).

The failure to regard sexual victimization as evil has one further influence: "The fact is, anything that anybody with power experiences as sex is considered ipso facto not violence, because someone who matters enjoyed it. And power, of which violence is merely an extreme expression, is apparently very sexy" (1987, 233 n. 19). Judith Herman offers a confirmation of this: if "the normative social definition of sexuality involves the erotization of male dominance and female submission, then the use of coercive means to achieve sexual conquest might represent a crude exaggeration of prevailing norms, but not a departure from them" (Herman 1988, 696). Or as another feminist has put it: "violence *is* sex to those who practice it *as* sex" (Annie McCombs quoted in MacKinnon 1987, 233 n. 23).

Finally, theological discussions about the nature of intimate relating and the importance of consent require re-examination given the role of sex in sexual inequality and sexual victimization. Is consent a meaningful concept given women's current status? For instance,

> Women and low-income people were most likely to have risky sexual partners, and about 71 percent of those with such partners reported not using condoms.

> Women either don't recognize the risk or they are not in a position where they can really enforce safe sex practices. (Recer, 1992)

Judith Herman concurs: "Because of entrenched norms of male entitlement, many women are accustomed to accommodating their partners' desires and subordinating their own, even in consensual sex" (Herman 1992, 65). Individually we may focus on the need to treat the victims, but not see their experience as instructing us about gender hierarchy and the problem that such hierarchy presents to achieving any true mutual consent.

Judith Herman, confirming MacKinnon, tells us that "When the victim is already devalued (a woman, a child), she may find that the most traumatic events of her life take place outside the realm of socially validated reality. Her experience becomes unspeakable" (1992, 8). Given how much we do not know about the violence in women's and children's lives because there is no space in which to speak it, given, that is, that less than ten percent of all sexual assaults are reported to police, our theological gestures at discussing violence against women and children may be epistemologically suspect.

What Are the Implications of MacKinnon's Theory for Feminist Theologies?

Like MacKinnon, feminist theologians are concerned with what she calls the "crunch"—in MacKinnon's case it is the noise the law makes when it collides with somebody's life (see Strebeigh, 30); for us it is the noise theology and religion make when they collide with somebody's life.

We say that women's reality is the source of theologizing for feminists. MacKinnon offers us a compelling description of what that reality is. Given this description of women's reality, feminist theologies will need to examine several overlapping and interrelated theological discussions. I will briefly identify a few of these.

God-Language and Male Dominance

MacKinnon's articulation of a feminist theory of male dominance, in which dominance is sexualized, helps to elucidate problems with any gendered language about God as well as the resistance to changing male language for God. In a male dominant culture, substituting male language for God with female language for God may be an inadequate response. As Mary E. Hunt queries: "Why not think of the divine in feminine terms to balance the centuries of masculinist religion? Of course, but by the same token if it is dominance and not difference we are dealing with, why further reinforce the stereotypes and hence exacerbate the dominance by insisting on 'gendering' the concept of the divine?" (Hunt 1995, 206). Moreover, thinking of the divine as feminine encounters great resistance precisely because of the sexualizing of dominance. Since dominance over women is sexualized, women's bodies have been weighted with representing wanton, shameful, yet unavoidable carnality. The representation of the female body's erotic nature is directly related to a sexuality that is constructed through dominance. As Margaret R. Miles observes, "In Christianity the body scorned, the naked body, is a female body. . . [T]he female body [is] a cipher for male desire" (1989, 185, 179). References to femaleness no matter how metaphorical (such as God language which is metaphorical to the core) are experienced as references to female bodies, female bodies that are seen as sexually available through the lens of male dominance. As a result, women's bodies carry so much baggage regarding carnality that imputing divinity to femaleness becomes difficult and arouses great resistance. Associating femaleness with God "debases" the Godhead because women's bodies represent sex. Language about God is metaphoric, but introducing talk about women irrevocably moves the focus from the metaphoric to the carnal. This will inevitably be considered blasphemous in a male dominant culture.

The Women's Movement and Ontology

In her classic book, *Beyond God the Father*, Mary Daly argued that the women's liberation movement was an ontological movement, a movement about women's Be-ing. Indeed it has been. But in the 1980s, Catharine MacKinnon argued that the ontological is constructed by the epistemological: "In life, 'woman' and 'man' are widely experienced as features of being, not constructs of perception, cultural interventions, or forced identities. Gender, in other words, is lived as ontology, not as epistemology. Law [ditto theology] actively participates in this transformation of perspective into being" (MacKinnon 1989, 237). MacKinnon argues that the women's liberation movement is even more centrally about knowing and perspective than it is about being. As MacKinnon explains, "If the shift in perspective from gender as difference to gender as dominance is followed, gender changes from a distinction that is ontological and presumptively valid to a detriment that is epistemological and presumptively suspect. The given becomes contingent" (1989, 243). She explains further:

> Through legal mediation, male dominance is made to seem a feature of life, not a one-sided construct imposed by force for the advantage of a dominant group. To the degree it succeeds ontologically, male dominance does not look epistemological: control over being produces control over consciousness, fusing material conditions with consciousness in a way that is inextricable short of social change. Dominance reified becomes difference. Coercion legitimated becomes consent. Reality objectified becomes ideas; ideas objectified become reality. Politics neutralized and naturalized becomes morality. (1989, 238)

Rather than refocusing on the epistemological in which social construction occurs, feminist theologies may keep the focus on the ontological level, and accept or misread it. We then mistake ontology for epistemology. For instance, do we want to bring together sexuality as it is currently lived ontologically and the sacred? As we have seen, the erotic has been postulated by some feminist theologians as the source of beingness, as a life force that connects us to the divine. But this accepts a certain ontological givenness of the erotic, and thereby absolutizes it, while also disembodying male sexual agency. Those who challenge the work of feminists who have attempted to insure that appropriate boundaries between therapists, counselors, and ministers are maintained, often do so by adhering to an ontological faith in the erotic (see Heyward, 1993).

Control over beingness (and consequently our bodies) controls consciousness. Thus, body-mediated knowledge, a valuable concept introduced by feminist ethicist Beverly Harrison, must be reconsidered: how do our ontologized bodies convey, communicate, and experience knowledge when that ontology has been determined by a patriarchal culture? When placed within the context of the coping mechanisms of disassociation that incest survivors and survivors of their male partner's battery and captivity rely on, body-mediated knowledge is further problematized. Disassociation reveals that there is some body-knowledge we do not want to know, that consciousness and beingness have often become so disconnected that we do not know what our bodies experienced. Perhaps if the way epistemology constructs ontology were more widely understood, the memories of sexual assault survivors would be more easily acknowledged and the backlash against these memories would not have received the attention it currently has.

Debating the appropriate gender for God-language is an ontological strategy that presumes some sort of relationship between anthropocentric metaphors for God and the human condition. However, as MacKinnon argues, ontological debates may prevent us from inquiring into the underlying epistemological positions.

Consciousness Raising and Hearing to Speech

MacKinnon asserts:

> The point of view of a total system emerges as particular only when confronted, in a way it cannot ignore, by a demand from another point of view. This is why epistemology must be controlled for ontological dominance to succeed, and why consciousness raising is subversive. It is also why, when law sides with the powerless, as it occasionally has, it is said to engage in something other than law [ditto theology]—politics or policy or personal opinion—and to delegitimate itself. When seemingly ontological conditions are challenged from the collective standpoint of a dissident reality, they become visible as epistemological. Dominance suddenly appears no longer inevitable. (1989, 239–40)

But how does a collective standpoint such as feminism evolve?

MacKinnon sees consciousness raising as the important method for feminism in deconstructing our ontological subjugation and achieving subjectification. Consciousness raising, Nelle Morton and many after her have argued, is inherently a theological task. "Hearing women into speech" shifts the episteme and intersects with a basic feminist theological tenet of starting with women's experience (Morton 1985, 202–10).

> From the feminist point of view, the question of women's collective reality and how to change it merges with the question of women's point of view and how to know it. What do women live, hence know, that can confront male dominance? What point of view can question the code of civil society? The answer is simple, concrete, specific, and real: women's social inequality with men on the basis of sex, hence the point of view of

women's subordination to men. Women are not permitted fully to know
what sex equality would look like, because they have never lived it. It is
idealist, hence elitist, to hold that they do. But they do not need to. They
know inequality because they have lived it, so they know what removing
barriers to equality would be. (1989, 241)

Marjorie Procter-Smith in her forthcoming work, *Praying with Our Eyes
Open*, builds on MacKinnon's insights concerning consciousness raising and
consent. She believes that the notion of consent as it is problematized by
MacKinnon must be considered in terms of corporate prayer, in which consent to the content of the prayer is presumed. For instance, specifically with
prayers of confession, and generally in other prayers, congregants are not
asked if they accept the words that they are asked to pray. Yet, often for
women, especially those who have experienced sexual and domestic violence,
the appropriate response to the content of these prayers would be "no, I do
not consent to the content of these prayers." The prayer's function is inimical
to the needed consciousness raising that would validate a woman's reality.

Pornography and Salvific Suffering

If you grant MacKinnon's position on pornography, the association of
women's bodies with sex reveals not only why feminist challenges to God-language are so problematic and seen as blasphemous, but also why salvific
images associated with women, especially, but not exclusively, crucified images
of women, are so risky. Certainly the model of a suffering servant is problematic to women who are socially constructed to be suffering servants.[7] But
pornography specifically eroticizes this suffering as it eroticizes women's sub-
missiveness, passivity, and willingness to suffer. Edwina Sandy's *Christa*, in
which a woman hangs crucified on a cross, is greeted by many who see it as
pornographic. This is understandable, because this is how women are depicted
in pornography. As Margaret Miles explains, pornography "fetishizes suffering women. The naked and tortured female body has been appropriated by a
media culture and cannot therefore be arbitrarily assigned religious meaning"
(Miles 177). The point of pornography is not only that we women cannot save
ourselves, that we cannot protect ourselves, but that we actually do not want
to save ourselves.[8] Our suffering only has (erotic) meaning for others.

MacKinnon argues that "Politics neutralized and naturalized becomes
morality." How true that it is with the pornography debate, whose terms are
often set by the religious right as one being about obscenity and morality; as a
result the criminalization of pornography is encouraged. Rather, feminists
concerned about pornography argue for recognizing the harm that pornography does and want it to be actionable through civil, not criminal, law.

Instead of the glorification and eroticization of salvific suffering by women
that saves others, Christians need to affirm more centrally that women should
be assured minimally of their own personal safety. A dream I had before I presented an earlier version of this paper at the 1992 annual meeting of the
American Academy of Religion insisted on this. Before I went to sleep I had

been reading "Victims Again: Homeless Women in the New York City Shelter System" by the Homeless Women's Rights Network. I read of women turned away from shelters because they had arrived after curfew, being harassed by men in the street, and the security guards of the shelter watching but not intervening. I read of one shelter where residents were paid for sex. I read of women being thrown out of the women's shelter at night into dangerous neighborhoods. As the report explains "Shelter residents put out on the streets at night are in acute danger of rape and assault by men who are aware of the location of these women's shelters" (Homeless Women's Rights Network 1989, 3). After reading this chilling information, I fell asleep.

In my dream I was at the AAR. I was a part of a panel on social action. I followed two well-respected and well-published white men. The first had lectured on the theological implications of involvement in the peace movement and being involved in social protests. His paper did not acknowledge any issues associated with gender and peace. Another man spoke and said "Now that we have heard women's voice, we can get back to regular theology." (Recall MacKinnon: when theology sides with the powerless it is said to engage in something other than theology.) I got up and said that the primary theological issue that feminism presents to the theological community is salvation: will women be safe (saved) from violence or not? Everything else derives from this basic question.

Salvation must incorporate the meaning of safety and then address ways to insure that women are safe; this requires both a transformation of the material reality of women's lives and a transformation of theology.

🌺

Notes

Thanks to Pat Davis, Millie Feske, Marie Fortune, Mary Hunt, Marjorie Procter-Smith, and Alison Webster for their support of this inquiry.

1. Golden (1992) argues that many women survive homelessness by accepting rape as the cost of homeless life. For instance, consider the situation of a homeless woman who even reports a rape. A homeless woman was in a Dallas soup kitchen and saw the man who had raped her a year earlier. It turned out that when she had filed the police report she had not provided them with a permanent address since she did not have one. Without a permanent address, most police departments treat rape cases as unprosecutable. If rapes are not prosecuted unless there is a permanent address, then de facto homeless women are not "rapable" in a legal sense as they become agonizingly more "rapable" ("rapable" to others besides the abusive partner they probably left) in the material sense.

2. "The combined influence of rape (or the threat of rape), domestic violence, and economic oppression is key to understanding the hidden motivations informing major social protest and migratory movements in Afro-American

history" (Hine 1989, 913). "I believe that many Black women quit the South out of a desire to achieve personal autonomy and to escape both from sexual exploitation from inside and outside of their families and from the rape and threat of rape by white as well as Black males" (Hine 1989, 914).

3. "When you talk to young people about being pregnant, you find out that most of these girls did not get pregnant by teenage boys. Most of them got pregnant by their mothers' boyfriends or their brothers or their daddies. We've been sitting on that. We can't just tell our daughters, 'Just say no.' We need to talk to our brothers. . . . We need men to stop giving consent, by their silence, to rape, to sexual abuse, to violence" (Avery 1990, 79–80).

4. Lenore Walker developed this in her classic 1979 book *The Battered Woman*. But this theory has been challenged recently. Battered women are not evidencing "learned helplessness" but are always developing survival mechanisms, and for many, there is no such thing as a honeymoon period (see Gondolf and Fisher 1988; and Dobash and Dobash 1979).

5. Space does not allow me to address the many misreadings of MacKinnon. However, let me flag those issues that are most frequently raised. First, it is claimed that she has no understanding of race and ethnicity. Yet in her analysis of why the McRae decision that denied women federal funding for abortion is consistent with the Roe v. Wade decision about privacy, she recognizes that it is "poor women and women of color whose sexual refusal has counted for especially little" (1985, 32). Furthermore, the first pornography ordinance arose from the the fact that the city of Minneapolis was attempting to control pornography by zoning it into particular neighborhoods—mostly poor and minority ones. She also argues that "parallels which converge and interact (such as race and gender) are not parallels" (1989, 288 n. 82). This observation is akin to the argument that identity is intersectional, not additive, for instance, one is not a woman + Black + poor.

Second, it is charged that she believes all men are rapists and all intercourse rape, that she is anti-male, but "a critique of male supremacy is only 'anti-male'. . . if you equate maleness with male supremacy" (1986, 70). "To say that rape is not just violence but is also sex is not, however, the same thing as saying that all sex is rape" (Olsen, 1157). It is claimed that she is ahistorical, but

> MacKinnon and other feminists do not deny that the meaning of womanhood, femaleness, and/or femininity has changed and will change again. The claim is that unless the change is liberating for women, it is merely a modification in the mechanisms of oppression; a particular form of womanhood might disappear from the face of the earth without it being the case that any woman has ceased being oppressed. (Bernick 1992, 11)

Bernick explains further:

> What MacKinnon wants women to be able to have is something like integrity, something like selves of our own. She says, for example, "Women have been deprived not only of terms of our own in which to express our lives, but of lives of our own to live" (1987, 15). If a life is

understood as the project of a self, then we are pushed into consideration of how this concept of self is deeply tied to Western ideas about the value of the individual, and, indeed, to Western individualism. The postmodern, postliberal reply to this demand is that having an integral self is impossible for anyone, not just women—just when women (and others) have begun to articulate what it means to be limited in the kind of self one can have, why and how we have been denied selves, and the cost to human beings of being denied a self. (Bernick 1992, 10)

Finally, it is charged that she denies that women ever enjoy sex with men or that she disapproves if they do. In response, Bernick argues:

Other than the move of redefining terms, there are at least two other approaches that might be taken. The first is to claim that sex, sexuality, and perhaps even gender are natural, and, in their natural state, can or do exist in nonoppressive forms. This approach is usually considered politically dangerous for a variety of reasons, not the least of which is that women do not control research into "nature." It is also considered false by large numbers of feminists, and so objectionable for that reason. A second alternative is to develop a competing theory of sexuality. The challenge for any such theory is that it must do at least as well as does MacKinnon's in accounting for the prevalence of sexual abuse without making it women's fault. If some account of women's sexual agency is desired (the lack of possibility under MacKinnon's account is the most common complaint lodged against it), the new theory must give an account of how such agency is theoretically possible. Merely asserting its existence or even its possibility is insufficient, especially since MacKinnon has some powerful arguments for how such agency is theoretically impossible. (Bernick 11)

6. MacKinnon would argue that this inability to respond to the evil of sexual victimization may be linked to use of pornography: "As pornography consumers, teachers may become epistemically incapable of seeing their women students as their potential equals and unconsciously teach about rape from the viewpoint of the accused" (1993, 19).

7. See discussion in Adams 1994, 103–14.

8. Insight of Marjorie Procter-Smith; this section is indebted to conversations with her.

Works Cited

Adams, Carol J. 1994. *Woman-Battering*. Minneapolis: Fortress Press.

Adler, Emily Stier. "'It happened to me': How Faculty Handle Student Reactions to Class Material." *Feminist Teacher*. 3/1: 22–26.

Avery, Byllye. 1990. "A Question of Survival/A Conspiracy of Silence." In *From Reproduction to Reproductive Freedom: Transforming a Movement*, ed. Marlene Gerber-Fried. Boston: South End Press.

Bartlett, Katharine T. 1987. "MacKinnon's Feminism: Power on Whose Terms?" *California Law Review* 75: 1559–70.

Belenky, Mary Field, et al. 1986. *Women's Way of Knowing: The Development of Self, Voice, and Mind*. New York: Basic Books.

Bernick, Susan E. 1992. "The Logic of the Development of Feminism; or, Is MacKinnon to Feminism as Parmenides Is to Greek Philosophy?" *Hypatia*. 7/1: 1–15.

Collins, Patricia Hill. 1990. *Black Feminist Thought: Knowledge, Consciousness, and the Politics of Empowerment*. Boston: Unwin Hyman.

Davis, Angela Y. 1981. *Women, Race, and Class*. New York: Vintage Books.

Dobash, R. Emerson and Russell Dobash. 1979. *Violence against Wives: A Case against Patriarchy*. New York: The Free Press.

Fortune, Marie M. 1989. *Is Nothing Sacred? When Sex Invades the Pastoral Relationship*. San Francisco: Harper & Row.

Golden, Stephanie. 1992. *The Women Outside: Meaning and Myths of Homelessness*. Berkeley, Calif.: University of California Press.

Gondolf, Edward W. with Ellen R. Fisher. 1988. *Battered Women as Survivors: An Alternative to Treating Learned Helplessness*. Lexington, Mass: Lexington Books.

Hammonds, Evelyn. 1992. Comment on the testimony of Anita Hill during the Clarence Thomas hearings. *Sojourners*. November

Harrison, Beverly. 1985. *Making the Connections: Essays in Feminist Social Ethics*, ed. Carol S. Robb. Boston: Beacon Press.

Herman, Judith Lewis. 1988. "Considering Sex Offenders: A Model of Addiction." *Signs: Journal of Women in Culture and Society*. 13/3

——. 1992. *Trauma and Recovery*. New York: Basic Books.

Heyward, Carter. 1989. *Touching Our Strength: The Erotic as Power and the Love of God*. San Francisco: Harper & Row.

——. 1993. *When Boundaries Betray Us*. San Francisco: HarperSanFrancisco.

Hine, Darlene Clark. 1989. "Rape and the Inner Lives of Black Women in the Middle West: Preliminary Thoughts on the Culture of Dissemblance." *Signs: Journal of Women in Culture and Society*. 14/4: 912–20.

Homeless Women's Rights Network. 1989. "Victims Again: Homeless Women in the New York City Shelter System."

Hunt, Mary E. 1995. "Lead Us Not Into Temptation." In *Rattling Those Dry Bones: Women Changing the Church*, ed. June Steffensen Hagen. San Diego: Lura Media.

Kaschak, Ellyn. 1992. *Engendered Lives: A New Psychology of Women's Experience*. New York: HarperCollins.

Kluft, Richard P., M.D. 1990. "On the Apparent Invisibility of Incest." In *Incest-Related Syndromes of Adult Psychopathology*, ed. Richard P. Kluft, M.D. Washington, D.C.: American Psychiatric Press, Inc.

Landsberg, Michelle. 1992. "Demanding Power and Parity: Feminists Vow to Take Back Politics." *New Directions for Women* (July-August), 3.

MacKinnon, Catharine. 1987. *Feminism Unmodified: Discourses on Life and Law*. Cambridge: Harvard University Press.

——. 1986. "The Male Ideology of Privacy: A Feminist Perspective on the Right to Abortion." *Radical America* 23–35.

——. 1987. "Reply by MacKinnon." *Radical America* 69–70.

——. 1989. *Toward a Feminist Theory of State*. Cambridge: Harvard University Press.

——. 1990. "Liberalism and the Death of Feminism." In *The Sexual Liberals and the Attack on Feminism*, ed. Dorchen Leidholdt and Janice G. Raymond. New York: Pergamon Press.

——. 1991. "The Palm Beach Hanging." *The New York Times*. December 15, op-ed page.

——. 1993. *Only Words*. Cambridge: Harvard University Press.

Mann, Bonnie. 1987. "Working with Battered Women: Radical Education or Therapy." *In Our Best Interest: A Process for Personal and Social Change*. Ellen Pence et al. Minnesota Program Development, Inc.

Miles, Margaret R. 1989. *Carnal Knowing: Female Nakedness and Religious Meaning in the Christian West*. Boston: Beacon Press.

Morton, Nelle. 1985. *The Journey Is Home*. Boston: Beacon Press.

Olsen, Frances. 1989. "Feminist Theory in Grand Style." *Columbia Law Review*. 89: 1147–78.

Poling, James. 1991. *The Abuse of Power: A Theological Problem*. Nashville: Abingdon Press.

Pui-Lan, Kwok. 1992. "The Future of Feminist Theology: An Asian Perspective." *The Auburn News*. Fall.

Recer, Paul. 1992. "Forgoing 'safe sex' leaves millions at risk for AIDS, report finds." *Dallas Morning News*. November 13.

Reineke, Martha J. 1992. "Tales of Terror: On Building a Course around the theme of Women, Christianity, and Abuse." *Religious Studies News: Spotlight on Teaching*. November 3–4.

Sands, Kathleen M. 1992. "Uses of the Thea(o)logian: Sex and Theodicy in Religious Feminism." *Journal of Feminist Studies in Religion*. 8/1: 7–33.

Sheffield, Carole J. 1984. "Sexual Terrorism." In *Women: A Feminist Perspective*, ed. Jo Freeman. Palo Alto: Mayfield Publishing, 1984.

Stoltenberg, John. 1989. *Refusing to Be a Man: Essays on Sex and Justice*. Portland, Oregon: Breitenbush Books, Inc.

Strebeigh, Fred. 1991. "Prof. Catharine A. MacKinnon: Defining Law on the Feminist Frontier." *The New York Times Magazine*. October 6: 28–31, 52–56.

Thistlethwaite, Susan. 1991. "Sexual Harassment: to Protect, Empower." *Christianity and Crisis*, October 21: 328–330.

Walker, Lenore. 1979. *The Battered Woman*. New York: Harper & Row.

Zahirovic, Ajsa. 1992. "An International Appeal: Word out of Bosnia." *off our backs*. 22/10 (November): 2–3.

For God So Loved the World?

Joanne Carlson Brown and Rebecca Parker

Women are acculturated to accept abuse. We come to believe that it is our place to suffer. Breaking silence about the victimization of women and the ways in which we have become anaesthetized to our violation is a central theme in women's literature, theology, art, social action, and politics. With every new revelation we confront again the deep and painful secret that sustains us in oppression: We have been convinced that our suffering is justified.

Theology and Abuse: Women's Experience

Our acculturation to abuse is manifested in the difficulty we have acknowledging the near-constant repression of our power, our rights, and our lives that occurs in most cultures. In North America many women agree with the men who say that women are not oppressed. They do not see the brutal murders of thirty-six young women in Seattle as a sign of the culture nor understand that the federal government's cutting $7 billion from food stamp programs is evidence that women are not valued since 85 percent of the recipients of food stamps in the United States are women and children. In many parts of the world, cultural tradition dictates that women are second-class citizens: men eat first, are educated first, and make decisions for women. Kumari Jayawardene, a Sri Lankan political scientist and feminist, has commented, "Actually, you know, women really don't understand that they are exploited. When I talk with women's groups I realize this. One day an old woman spoke up and said that she agreed with everything I had said about the situation of women, but that women 'must still have fear and shame, for such are their qualities.'"[1] While we may recognize and reject situations in which there are layers of oppression—as there are for ethnic minority women in North America and poor women in Third World countries—we may still find ourselves so accepting of our own place as helpmate that we cannot see that we are denied our full humanity because we are women. Our acculturation to abuse leads us to keep silent for years about experiences of sexual abuse, not to report rape, to stay in marriages in which we are battered, to give up creative efforts, to expend all our energy in the support of other lives and never in support of our own, to accept it when a

man interrupts us, to punish ourselves if we are successful, to deny so habitually our right to self-determination that we do not feel we have an identity
unless it is given to us by someone else.

　　Christianity has been a primary—in many women's lives *the* primary—
force in shaping our acceptance of abuse. The central image of Christ on the
cross as the saviour of the world communicates the message that suffering is
redemptive. If the best person who ever lived gave his life for others, then, to
be of value we should likewise sacrifice ourselves. Any sense that we have a
right to care for our own needs is in conflict with being a faithful follower of
Jesus. Our suffering for others will save the world. The message is complicated further by the theology that said Christ suffered in obedience to his
Father's will. Divine child abuse is paraded as salvific and the child who suffers "without even raising a voice" is lauded as the hope of the world. Those
whose lives have been deeply shaped by the Christian tradition feel that self-
sacrifice and obedience are not only virtues but the definition of a faithful
identity. The promise of resurrection persuades us to endure pain, humiliation, and violation of our sacred rights to self-determination, wholeness, and
freedom. Throughout the Scriptures is the idea that Jesus died for our sins.
Did he? Is there not another way for sins to be forgiven? Why an idea of original sin? Christianity has functioned to perpetuate the Fall, for without it
there is no need for a saviour. Mary Daly argues that imitation of this saviour
is exactly what is desired:

> The qualities that Christianity idealized, especially for women, are also
> those of a victim: sacrificial love, passive acceptance of suffering, humil-
> ity, meekness, etc. Since these are the qualities idealized in Jesus "who
> died for our sins," his functioning as a model reinforces the scapegoat
> syndrome for women.[2]

That victimization is precisely what is perpetuated by this theology can be
seen particularly in women's experiences in both the church and society,
where women have been assigned the suffering-servant role. Our full personhood as well as our rights have been denied us. We have been labelled the sinful ones, the other; and even when we are let in, so to speak, we are
constantly reminded of our inferior status through language, theological concepts of original sin, and perpetual virginity—all of which relate to sex, for
which, of course, women are responsible.

　　In order for us to become whole we must reject the culture that shapes
our abuse and disassociate ourselves from the institutions that glorify our suffering. This leads to the conclusion that in order to be liberated we must leave
the church, make our exodus from the halls of the oppressor.

　　Many women, however, even when conscious of the church's contribution to our suffering, do not leave. We stay in the institution. Feminist theologians who attempt to rework the tradition by finding feminist undercurrents
and countercultures, doing new quests for the historical feminist Jesus, and
writing women back into the Bible and the tradition (the *Inclusive Language
Lectionary* is a good example) are trying valiantly to "fix" the institution so

that they can remain in it. They enter the ordained ministry in order to "redeem" the church, but they pay so high a personal, emotional, and psychological price that they begin to resemble the very people they want to redeem. All the while, they call to their crucified lord to understand their suffering and support them in their times of trial and martyrdom.

The women who stay in the church are victimized and abused. The reasons given by women who stay in the church are the same as those coming from women who remain in battering situations: they don't mean it; they said they were sorry and would be better; they need me/us; we can fix it if we just try harder and are better; I'd leave but how can I survive outside; we have nowhere else to go. Despite all the correctives taught by liberation theology on how to interpret suffering, this Christian theology with atonement at the center still encourages martyrdom and victimization. It pervades our society. Our internalization of this theology traps us in an almost unbreakable cycle of abuse. Our continuing presence in the church is a sign of the depth of our oppression.

The only legitimate reason for women to remain in the church will be if the church were to condemn as anathema the glorification of suffering. Only if the church is the place where cycles of abuse are named, condemned, and broken can it be a haven of blessing and a place of peace for women. That the church is such a place is not clearly evident. Whether Christianity in essence frees or imprisons is the issue that must be considered.

This essay will explore the question, Can the case be made that it is contrary to the gospel to maintain that suffering is redemptive? Our approach is theological, not biblical, and focuses on the issue of the atonement. Classical views of the atonement have, in diverse ways, asserted that Jesus' suffering and death is fundamental to our salvation. Critical traditions have formulated the issue of redemption in different terms but still have not challenged the central problem of the atonement—Jesus' suffering and death, and God's responsibility for that suffering and death. Why we suffer is not a fundamentally different question from why Jesus suffered. It may be that this fundamental tenet of Christianity—Christ's suffering and dying *for us*—upholds actions and attitudes that accept, glorify, and even encourage suffering. Perhaps until we challenge and reject this idea we will never be liberated. And if this glorification of suffering is so central to Christianity itself, perhaps our redemption and liberation, particularly as oppressed people, will be obtained only by leaving.

The Classical Tradition

Jesus died on the cross to save us from sin. This is what the penal theory of the atonement affirms. In classical orthodox theology, the death of Jesus is required by God to make God's plan of salvation effective. Doctrinal standards assert that there was no way more effective, perhaps even no alternative to Jesus' death. Without the death of Jesus we would not be saved. Though there are many different interpretations of *how* we are saved by the death of Jesus, there is no classical theory of the atonement that questions the necessity of Jesus' suffering. And, though the way in which suffering gives birth to redemption is diversely understood, every theory of the atonement commends suffering to the disciple. The Christian is to "be like Jesus"—and imitation of Christ is first and foremost obedient willingness to endure pain.

Three strands of tradition are usually identified as being at the core of the classical views of the atonement. The "Christus Victor" tradition sees the death of Jesus as a mortal confrontation with the powers of evil that oppress human life. Jesus' death represents the apparent triumph of evil, but his resurrection from the dead reveals that God is the greater power whose purpose will finally prevail. Redemption is liberation from evil forces that is brought about by the force of God. The "satisfaction" theory of the atonement says that Jesus died to "pay the price" or "bear the punishment" for human sin. He dies in our place to satisfy God's sense of justice. By his death, a satisfactory payment or sacrifice is offered to God and the barrier of God's wrath is removed. Redemption is accomplished when God is freed from the requirements of "his" honor and is able to relate to human beings with mercy without, so to speak, compromising "his" principles that the sinner should suffer. The "moral influence" theory of the atonement places the barrier to our redemption not in God's nature but in human nature. People's hearts are hardened against mercy; they are unable to see or accept it. Jesus' death on the cross is a divine demonstration of the magnitude of God's mercy. God loves us so much "he" is even willing to die for us. We are to behold the cross and be moved to faith and trust in God, persuaded to accept mercy and dedicate ourselves to obedience to God's will. Each of these theories of the atonement needs to be examined for what it says about suffering, what it counsels the believer to do with regard to his or her own exposures to suffering, and what it says about the nature of God.

The Christus Victor Tradition

The Christus Victor theory of the atonement says that suffering is a prelude to triumph and is in itself an illusion. In some early forms of this view of the atonement, Jesus is imagined as bait for Satan, who seeks to devour human beings. When death swallows up Jesus he gains entrance into the underworld. Confronted with God in hell, Satan is overwhelmed, and the divine light casts darkness from its throne. Gregory of Nyssa, for example, explains:

> Since the hostile power was not going to enter into relations with a God present unveiled or endure his appearance in heavenly glory therefore God . . . concealed himself under the veil of our nature, in order that, as happens with greedy fishes, together with the bait of the flesh the hook of the Godhead might also be swallowed and so through life passing over into death and the light arising in the darkness that which is opposed to life and light might be brought to nought.[3]

As a mythic drama this atonement story is a tale of hope, with antecedents in Greek stories about Persephone's escape from the evil lord of the underworld bringing Spring with her, and of Orpheus's journey to the underworld to rescue Eurydice. But its charm ends here. By incorporating the actual death of Jesus into a mythic framework, his suffering and death are retold as divine trickery, part of a larger plot to deceive the deceiver. The death of Jesus is merely a ploy, a sleight of hand, an illusion.

More sophisticated theologies that have their roots in this dramatic framework spiritualize the struggle. The journey to the underworld becomes the believer's journey into the dark night of the soul, where God is eclipsed. But this soul journey is part of what is necessary for salvation: all the evil, unfaith, and barrenness in the self must be encountered with the trust that the light of God's presence will finally triumph. Jesus' death becomes a paradigm for a stage in a psychological process that is to be patiently endured. Matthew Fox, discussing the spiritual journey through darkness, writes, "Salvation, we learn from the Via Negativa, is not a salvation *from pain* but *through pain*."[4] He continues:

> All sinking usually has a note of panic about it, and the Via Negativa, which calls us to the deepest sinkings of all, is no exception. Here the refusal to trust, to trust the buoyancy of the water, of the darkness, of the pain, of the nothingness . . . all this is sinful because it stifles our spiritual growth.[5]

When whatever psychological value exists in facing one's inner darkness on the path to greater wholeness and healing is equated with the real death of Jesus, the meaning of suffering is obscured. Fox gives Jesus' actual death as an example to inspire spiritual "letting go" and goes on to blur the distinction between psychological struggle and the sufferings of the poor "who must face their darkness more directly than the comfortable."[6] In a theological effort to show evil and darkness as not ultimately true, the death of Jesus becomes not ultimately real.

The believer whose thoughts and feelings have been shaped by a tradition that teaches or ritualizes in liturgy the Christus Victor view may interpret her or his suffering in this light. In response to suffering it will be said, Be patient, something good will come of this. The believer is persuaded to endure suffering as a prelude to new life. God is pictured as working through suffering, pain, and even death to fulfill "his" divine purpose. When suffering comes it may be looked upon as a gift, and the believer will ask, Where is God leading me? What does God have in store for me? In this tradition, God is the all-powerful determiner of every event in life, and every event is part of a bigger picture—a plan that will end with triumph. When people say things such as, God had a purpose in the death of the six million Jews, the travesty of this theology is revealed.

Such a theology has devastating effects on human life. The reality is that victimization never leads to triumph. It can lead to extended pain if it is not refused or fought. It can lead to destruction of the human spirit through the death of a person's sense of power, worth, dignity, or creativity. It can lead to actual death. By denying the reality of suffering and death, the Christus Victor theory of the atonement defames all those who suffer and trivializes tragedy.

The Satisfaction Tradition

The satisfaction theory of the atonement as formulated by Anselm says that "the Father desired the death of the Son, because he was not willing that the world should be saved in any other way."[7] Because of sin, humanity owed a debt to God which it could not pay. Only by the death of God's own Son could God receive satisfaction. In Anselm's view, God's desire for justice and God's desire to love are in conflict. While there is value in Anselm's claim that love and justice cannot be separated, his view of justice is not that wrong should be righted but that wrongs should be punished.

> Let us . . . consider whether it were proper for God to put away sins by compassion alone, without any payment of the honor taken from him. To remit sin in this manner is nothing else than not to punish: and since it is not right to cancel sin without compensation or punishment: if it be not punished, then it is passed by undischarged. It is not fitting for God to pass over anything in his kingdom undischarged. It is therefore not proper for God thus to pass over sin unpunished.[8] . . . So then, everyone who sins ought to pay back the honor of which he has robbed God and this is the satisfaction which every sinner owes to God.[9]

God's demand that sin be punished is fulfilled by the suffering of the innocent Jesus, whose holiness is crowned by his willingness to be perfectly obedient to his father's will. God is portrayed as the one who cannot reconcile "himself" to the world because "he" has been royally offended by sin, so offended that no human being can do anything to overcome "his" sense of offense. Like Lear, God remains estranged from the children God loves because God's honor must be preserved. God's position is tragic, and it is to free God that the Son submits to death, sacrificing himself, it is imagined, out of overwhelming love for the two alienated parties: God and the human family.

The idea that justice is established through adequate punishment has been questioned by theologians from Anselm's time to the present, though the satisfaction theory has remained the dominant theory of the atonement. The primary criticism is that this theory presents God as a tyrant. Walter Rauschenbusch comments, "The worst form of leaving the naked unclothed, the hungry unfed, and the prisoners uncomforted, is to leave people under a despotic conception of God and the universe; and what will the Son of Man do to us theologians when we gather at the day of doom?"[10] As Rauschenbusch asserts, "Our universe is not a despotic monarchy with God above the starry canopy and ourselves down here; it is a spiritual commonwealth with God in the midst of us."[11]

Anselm uses medieval forensic categories in his construction of a theology that reflects the existing social order—one that operated through coercion and terror. As Rauschenbusch rightly critiqued, "A conception of God which describes him as sanctioning the present order and utilizing it in order to sanctify its victims through their suffering, without striving for its overthrow, is repugnant to our moral sense."[12] But it is precisely this sanctioning of suffering which is the legacy of the satisfaction theory of atonement.

Suffering is sanctioned as an experience that frees others, perhaps even God. The imitator of Christ, which every faithful person is exhorted to be, can find herself choosing to endure suffering because she has become convinced that through her pain another whom she loves will escape pain. The disciple's role is to suffer in the place of others, as Jesus suffered for us all. But this glorification of suffering as salvific, held before us daily in the image of Jesus hanging from the cross, encourages women who are being abused to be more concerned about their victimizer than about themselves. Children who are abused are forced most keenly to face the conflict between the claims of a parent who professes love and the inner self which protests violation. When a theology identifies love with suffering, what resources will its culture offer to such a child? And when parents have an image of a God righteously demanding the total obedience of "his" son—even obedience to death—what will prevent the parent from engaging in divinely sanctioned child abuse? The image of God the father demanding and carrying out the suffering and death of his own son has sustained a culture of abuse and led to the abandonment of victims of abuse and oppression. Until this image is shattered it will be almost impossible to create a just society.

Yet another dimension of the satisfaction theory of the atonement needs to be addressed. Though Anselm's formulation of the satisfaction theory is influenced by medieval legal concepts, the theory has deep roots in biblical images of sacrifice. In the liturgy, hymnody, and practical piety of the church, these images are continually evoked. While the biblical view of the power of blood sacrifice is complex, four major themes may be identified:[13]

1. Blood protects. Blood circumcision and the blood of the passover lamb are seen as having power to ward off the destroyer (see Exod. 4:24–26; 12:27).

2. Blood intercedes. In the Book of Genesis, Abel's blood is said to "cry out to God" (Gen. 4:10); and this idea that spilled blood has a power greater than language to attract God's attention is taken up in Heb. 12:24: "But you have come . . . to Jesus, the mediator of a new covenant, and to the sprinkled blood that speaks more graciously than the blood of Abel" (see also Isa. 56:7, in which sacrifice is associated with prayer).

3. Blood establishes covenant. The covenant with Abraham (Genesis 15), the Covenant at Sinai (Exod. 24:3–11), and the "new Covenant" (Matt. 26:28; 1 Cor. 10:16, 11:25; Heb. 9:16–18) are all sealed or established with the letting of blood. Further, membership in the house of Israel is established for men by the letting of blood that occurs in the circumcision ritual.

4. Blood makes atonement. The ritual sacrifice of whole and unblemished animals at the altar serves to make peace between God and the sinful community. The prophets emphasized that true or effective sacrifice has to do with the right attitude on the part of the one who offers. Sacrifice as magic was rejected, and "spiritual" sacrifice began to replace ritual sacrifice. Through the prophetic critique of false sacrifice it became clear to the religious imagination of Israel

that righteousness was the only true sacrifice. But who is righteous enough to offer completely effective sacrifice? The significance of Jesus as the one true sacrifice must be understood in this light. Jesus' death was, in the biblical tradition, God's gracious offering of the perfect sacrifice, which none of us was capable of presenting.

Through all these varied images of the "power of let blood," the questions must be asked, Why does blood have the power to protect life, establish relationship, restore life, speak with silent eloquence? The answer to such a question lies in the history of ritual practices and in the grounding of symbolic elements in life experience. The holy power of blood comes from the understanding of blood as essential to life. Its power is the power of life. Beyond this, however, the power of *let* blood—flowing, released, spilled blood—has an additional source in human experience. The slaughter of animals means food that will nurture human life; this is one form in which let blood is a sign that life will be sustained. But there is another form of flowing blood and birth blood.

Ironically, in the biblical tradition menstrual blood is a sign of ritual uncleanness. Here, the student of religious symbolism must pause. Studies have revealed that various forms of ritual bloodletting are imitations, by members of a male cult, of women's bodily experience. Circumcision, for example, occurs in many cultures, not only the ancient Hebrew, and is often spoken of as "men's menstruation."[14] This would indicate that the notion of "flowing blood" has its roots in cultural efforts by men to take unto themselves power that belongs to women. The imitation by men of women's bodily power has almost universally been accompanied by the subjugation of women.[15] Ritual exclusion of menstruating women and women who have given birth is a sign that sacred imagery has been stolen. This analysis suggests that the religious imagery of the atonement is founded upon the robbery and subsequent defamation/degradation of women's experience.[16] The religious imagery of Jesus' blood carries an implied, silent devaluation of women. Jesus becomes the true mother who gives us new birth through his body and feeds us with his flesh. In medieval mysticism, this symbolism becomes blatant. Jesus is imaged as a mother: "His outspread arms will invite you to embrace him, his naked breasts will feed you with the milk of sweetness to console you."[17] And his wounded body becomes a womb to which the believer can crawl back:

> Those unsearchable riches of your glory, Lord, were hidden in your secret place in heaven until the soldier's spear opened the side of your Son, our Lord and Savior on the cross, and from it flowed the mysteries of our side, like Thomas, but through that open door may enter whole, O Jesus, even into your heart.[18]

While many may argue that the primitive origins of blood sacrifice are not relevant, they do continue to hold power over us. Their subtle influence is pervasive in women's experience. Having an understanding of Jesus as our new mother, who gives life through death, serves to devalue our natural mothers, who give life through life, and communicates to every woman that she is inferior to man. Can an image offer redemption while perpetuating devaluation? Or can it speak of justice when its symbolic origins involved subjugation? The symbol itself is a form of abuse.

The Moral Influence Tradition

The moral influence theory of the atonement began with Abelard questioning the satisfaction theory:

> If [the] sin of Adam was so great that it could be expiated only by the death of Christ, what expiation will avail for the act of murder committed against Christ, and for the many great crimes committed against him or his followers? How did the death of his innocent Son so please God the Father that through it he should be reconciled to us?[19]

In answering this question Abelard rejected the satisfaction theory of the atonement in favor of saying that the barrier preventing reconciliation between God and human beings is not in God but in human beings. The problem is that we need to be persuaded faithfully to believe in God's overwhelming mercy. The evidence that should persuade us is that Jesus was willing to die for us. He has shown that he holds our souls in such high esteem that we should recognize our forgiven and loved condition and in gratitude commit ourselves to obedience like his.

The moral influence theory is founded on the belief that an innocent, suffering victim and only an innocent, suffering victim for whose suffering we are in some way responsible has the power to confront us with our guilt and move us to a new decision. This belief has subtle and terrifying connections as to how victims of violence can be viewed. Theoretically, the victimization of Jesus should suffice for our moral edification, but, in fact, in human history, races, classes, and women have been victimized while at the same time their victimization has been heralded as a persuasive reason for inherently sinful men to become more righteous. The suffering of ethnic minorities and the poor has been graphically described, along with the suffering of Jesus, in sermonic efforts to move the powerful to repentance and responsibility. Sometimes this amounts to using the victims for someone else's edification. But, most perniciously, it is the victimization of women that is tied to a psychology of redemption.

Christian ethicist Helmut Thielicke provides a particularly clear example of how theories of atonement find expression in sexual politics. His view is that woman's sexuality is by nature holistic and vulnerable. He images women as holy and sees women as intrinsically good in their sexual nature, in which sexual desire is completely integrated with the heart and with a desire for faithfulness. He also sees woman as intrinsically vulnerable because her integrated sexual nature is such that if she is sexually intimate with a man she becomes bonded for life with that man. He sees men, on the other hand, as intrinsically destructive in their sexuality—originally sinful, you might say. Men's sexual energy is energy to violate and destroy. It is unfaithful, also, because the man's sexual feeling is an alienated, unintegrated part of himself, making him tend toward polygamy. In Thielicke's view, men are saved from their inherent destructiveness when they are moved by the suffering of victimized women. When a man sees the holiness and fragility of woman, he may be persuaded to repent of his destructive behavior, discipline himself to be obedient to love's demand, and thereby become a saved, holy, good human being himself.[20]

In this twentieth-century formulation of Christian ethics, woman is cast as a Christ figure; she is imagined to be a victim who does not deserve the suffering that comes to her. Thielicke writes of a woman, "She can exist and be herself only as long as the other person who has become the one and only for her preserves the bond in which she has invested her being."[21] Man's faithfulness is required or she will cease to exist. In this pattern of relationship, communion is maintained through the threat of death. The actual deaths or violations of women are part of the system just as necessarily as the death of Jesus is part of the system that asks for us to be "morally persuaded" to be faithful to God. The burden is on the believer to redeem Jesus's death from tragedy. This is the kind of double bind in which women find themselves in Christian culture. We must be viewed as vulnerable to victimization and loved not because of who we are but to save another from the guilt of being himself with us. If a man is himself, he destroys us. If he saves us, he must contradict his own nature. The hostility that pervades such a view of women is intense and hidden. But it is similar to the hostility that this form of Christian theology creates in the relationship between human beings and God. We can protect God from our violent rejection by disciplining ourselves, but it is the vulnerable holy One who is to blame for our having to construct rigid systems of self-control. God must be hated—just as women are hated. The moral influence theories of the atonement sanctify love/hate relationships. Redemption is not to be found in intimate relationships; only vicious cycles of violence may be found. Holding over people's heads the threat that if they do not behave someone will die requires occasional fulfilment of the threat. The threat of death, however, should not be called moral persuasion but should be identified as the most pernicious and evil form of coercion and terror.

How can we explain the condition of women, and others who are the chosen victims in a society, who live in constant fear of rape, murder, attack, verbal assault, insult, and the denial of rights and opportunities except as a condition of terrorization? To glorify victims of terrorization by attributing to them a vulnerability that warrants protection by the stronger is to cloak the violation. Those who seek to protect are guilty. Justice occurs when terrorization stops, not when the condition of the terrorized is lauded as a preventive influence.

The Critical Tradition

Many theologians of the modern and postmodern period have directed severe criticism at the traditional atonement concepts. Biblical concepts of suffering

as traditionally interpreted have been reexamined and found not only wanting but also contributing to oppression. These critical theologians have
claimed that classical atonement theories have been used to maintain the status quo and exonerate the purposes of a tyrannical God. They have seen that
their task is to free God from the charge of Divine Oppressor and then join
with this liberated God in laying the ax to the root of oppression, that is, to
end the suffering that is at the heart of oppression. This has been done by
insisting that all suffering must be regarded as negative and not ordained by
God. All, that is, except Jesus'! This is where the critical traditions fall short
of pushing the challenge to its logical conclusion.

Three trends in the twentieth-century critique of classical atonement theories may be identified. One trend criticizes the traditional view of God as
impassive and asserts that God suffers with us. A second interprets suffering
as an essential and inevitable part of the historical process of the struggle for
liberation. A third trend radically critiques the notion of redemptive suffering
but insists on retaining the cross as an image of liberation.

The Suffering God

Ronald Goetz has suggested that the notion of the "Suffering God" is becoming a new orthodoxy in the twentieth century.[22] He says that until this century
the orthodox position affirmed again and again the doctrine of God as
immovable and impassible, but twentieth-century theologians from even radically diverse schools of thought have forwarded the image and concept of God
as one who suffers passionately what the world suffers. Goetz lists those he
would characterize a modern theopaschite thinkers: "Barth, Berdyaev,
Bonhoeffer, Brunner, Cobb, Cone and liberation theologians generally, Kung,
Moltmann, Reinhold Niebuhr, Pannenberg, Ruether and feminist theologians
generally, Temple, Teilhard and Unamuno."[23] We would add to this list Edgar
Sheffield Brightman and the personalists, and process theologians in general.

In our view the emergence of the notion that God suffers with us is theological progress. God as one who experiences, feels and knows life, as one
intimately bound up with the creation in all its tragedy and turmoil, resur-
rects God from the grave of stony impassibility. To live is to experience, and,
finally, the doctrine of an impassible God cannot be reconciled to the doctrine of a *living* God. To see God as the "fellow sufferer who understands" is
to draw God close to all those who suffer and give divine companionship to
the friendless.

We would not reject the image of God as a Suffering God and would
welcome the demise of that distant, impassive patriarch in the clouds who is
beyond being affected by the turmoil below. The advent of the Suffering God
changes the entire face of theology, but it does not necessarily offer liberation
for those who suffer. A closer examination of one form of Suffering God theology will reveal that this apparently new image of God still produces the
same answers to the question, How shall I interpret and respond to the suffering that occurs in my life? And the answer again is: patiently endure; suffering
will lead to greater life.

Edgar Sheffield Brightman, a Boston personalist[24] of the 1920s and 1930s, proposed one of the clearest doctrines of a Suffering God. His definition of God is captured in this passage:

> God is a conscious Person of perfect good will. He is the source of all value and so is worthy of worship and devotion. He is the creator of all other persons and gives them the power of free choice. . . . There is within him, in addition to his reason and his active creative will, a passive element which enters into every one of his conscious states, as sensation, instinct, and impulse enter into ours, and constitutes a problem for him. This element we call The Given. The evils of life and the delays in the attainment of value, insofar as they come from God and not from human freedom, are thus due to his nature, yet not wholly to his deliberate choice. His will and reason acting on The Given produce the world and achieve value in it.[25]

This definition may be put more concisely in the following terms:

> God is a Person supremely conscious, supremely valuable, and supremely creative, yet limited both by the free choices of other persons and by restrictions within his own nature.[26]

In Brightman's view God has limited power, and this limitation is not the result of divine free choice but is imposed by God's very nature. It is the tension within God's self as God responds to the "Given" within Godself. Gradually God is working out God's purpose, as God responds to the Given in a way that will transform/transcend all evil. The reason there is evil is because things just do not fit together. Evil is inherent in the nature of things, what Brightman calls the "cosmic drag." God is unfinished. Suffering occurs because of the conflict between what is and what could be within God. Hence, God participates in the suffering of all the creation, groaning together with the creation in the travail of perfection coming to birth. Brightman says of God:

> He is supreme goodness conquering all obstacles, although slowly and with round about and painful methods. He is a God who suffers and who redeems. He is a finite God, working under the conditions given by his own eternal nature. He is not free to emancipate himself wholly from these conditions, although he is able to accomplish his purpose of achieving good in every situation and is never finally baffled by any problems. He is not responsible for causing the evils of life; he is responsible for dealing with them.[27]

Brightman's identification of the origin of suffering in the conflict between what is and what could be views all suffering as a byproduct of God's progressive creativity. It must be criticized as inadequate for explaining those forms of suffering that are the consequence of blatant injustices committed by human beings, such as slavery, abject poverty, or violence against women.

Brightman's answer to oppressed peoples struggling to interpret their suffering is: God suffers with you, knows, and understands your pain. God suffers actively, not passively, a suffering that knows a change is needed. So must we all become active sufferers.

> One [who is] moved by pity and love, uses every ounce of strength he possesses in fighting disease and disaster, pain and woe of every kind; but he has the insight to see that lamentations over the imperfection of the result would only add to the sufferings of life and consequently he is patient even when his efforts are most unsuccessful. Patient submission to the inevitable is a virtue only when one has gained the right, by one's attitude, to call it inevitable. To ascribe war, crimes, and lawlessness to fate is a cheap and irresponsible patience.[28]

Brightman challenges patient acquiescence before suffering and provides a way to continue to work against oppression when success is not immediate. The atonement is to be understood as support for this struggle. It is in the struggle of Christ on the cross that we see and know that God struggles and suffers for the world's salvation.[29]

Brightman, with critical theologians in general, uses God's suffering with us to call human beings to suffer with one another for liberation, suggesting that "suffering with" is itself a redeeming action. The identification in Suffering God theology of solidarity with redemption should be questioned. Bearing the burden with another does not take the burden away. Sympathetic companionship makes suffering more bearable, but the friendship between slaves, for example, does not stop the master from wielding the lash. Goetz also makes this observation:

> There is a certain immediate psychological comfort in the notion that God does not require of us a suffering that he himself will not endure. However, if this comfort is to be any more than a psychological prop, it must show how God's suffering mitigates evil. This explanation has been, to date, curiously lacking the theodicy of divine self-limitation.[30]

The challenge of how to claim that a suffering God offers not only comfort and companionship but also redemption is perhaps met by the argument that the cross makes relationship where relationship has been lost. It breaks down the dividing wall between suffering humanity and an impassive God and calls disciples to cross the barrier that separates oppressor from oppressed, rich from poor, healthy from sick, into a new humanity in which each takes on the burdens and joys of all in a fellowship of mutual openness and support. Such a passage into community involves being open to one's own pain and the pain of others. Thus it involves being willing to face reality, to feel, to see, instead of to repress feeling and hide from the truth or insulate oneself and ignore the realities of injustice. Such commitment to *live* establishes new community, and it is the establishment of community in which the alienation caused by rejection of suffering is overcome through mutuality that creates justice. The vision of such a community commends itself to all people. The creation of such a community surely does involve individuals choosing to see their intimate connection with those they may have rejected or ignored and choosing to admit those others into the circle of their concern and commitment. Indeed, such commitment involves facing the fact that an image of the self as impassible and immutable to pain blocks a person from being in relationship to others. A God who cannot feel cannot be alive and intimately related to other lives. So also a human being who idealizes the transcendence of emotion and seeks freedom from "being affected" by others cannot be fully alive or intimately related to others. Life is changed by the decision to feel, to be involved, to care, and not to turn away out of offense at or fear of another's suffering. The new community that is brought into being by God's intimate connection to us and by our openness to the life in ourselves and in others claims our attention and indeed has a right to be called redemption.

But a question arises: Even if the creation of communities of just relationship mitigates the evils of oppression, abuse, injustice, and alienation, that is, even if the establishment of *right relationship* is the meaning of *redemption*, how is it that the torturous death of Jesus can be spoken of as initiating this new community? Do we need the death of God incarnate to show us that God is with us in our suffering? Was Jesus' suffering and death required for revelation to occur? Was God not with us in our suffering before the death of Jesus? Did the death really initiate something that did not exist before?

It is true that fullness of life cannot be experienced without openness to all truth, all reality; fullness of life involves feeling the pain of the world. But it is not true that being open to all of life is the equivalent of choosing to suffer. Nor is it right to see the death of Jesus as a symbol for the life-giving power of receptivity to reality.

It is not acceptance of suffering that gives life; it is commitment to life that gives life. The question, moreover, is not, Am I willing to suffer? but Do I desire fully to live? This distinction is subtle and, to some, specious, but in the end it makes a great difference in how people interpret and respond to suffering. If you believe that acceptance of suffering gives life, then your resources for confronting perpetrators of violence and abuse will be numbered.

Jurgen Moltmann, for example, fails to make this distinction and hence continues the traditional presentation of Jesus as one who chose to suffer. He writes, "Jesus himself set out for Jerusalem and actively took the expected suffering upon himself."[31] Moltmann explicitly rejects the interpretation of Jesus' death that says Jesus died because of the "deep rooted evil of other people"[32] and speaks instead of Jesus *inciting violence against himself.*

> Jesus did not suffer passively from the world in which he lived, but incited it against himself by his message and the life he lived . . . . By proclaiming the righteousness of God as the right of those who were rejected and without grace to receive grace, he provoked the hostility of the guardians of the law, . . . he incited the devout against him.[33]

Moltmann's view amounts to blaming the victim. Jesus is responsible for his death on the cross, just as a woman who walks alone at night on a deserted street is to blame when she is raped.

Moltmann's intent is to distinguish between what he calls "active suffering" (i.e., chosen suffering) and acquiescence to suffering viewed as fate. But by continuing a theology that cloaks the perpetrator of violence and calls the choice *for life* a choice *to suffer*, he fails to present a theology capable of moving beyond suffering as fate to be endured.

At issue is not what we choose to endure or accept but what we refuse to relinquish. Redemption happens when people refuse to relinquish respect and concern for others, when people refuse to relinquish fullness of feeling, when people refuse to give up seeing, experiencing, and being connected and affected by all of life. God must be seen as the one who most fully refuses to relinquish life. Lust for life—the insistent zest for experiencing and responding—is what has the power to create community and sustain justice. The ongoing resurrection within us of a passion for life and the exuberant energy of this passion testifies to God's spirit alive in our souls.

By confusing "suffering with" with action that does something about evil instead of asserting that testifying for life is what sustains justice, the Suffering God theologies continue in a new form the traditional piety that sanctions suffering as imitation of the holy one. Because God suffers and God is good, we are good if we suffer. If we are not suffering, we are not good. To be like God is to take on the pain of all. In this form of piety, pain becomes attractive—the more we suffer the more we can believe we approach God. By interpreting Jesus' suffering as a sign that chosen suffering is salvific, the Suffering God theology baptizes violence done by people resistant to grace and abundant life, and uses Jesus' death to invite people to be open to all of life. This theology is offensive because it suggests that acceptance of pain is tantamount to love and is the foundation of social action.

There is another motivation for our commitment to live in solidarity with others. It is found in the rightness of the claim that burns in every human heart that we are created for life and life abundant. Life calls us to not abandon one another to the grave, and it is the claim of life that should inspire us to remain faithful to one another—not the glorification of pain.

The Necessity of Suffering

The second major trend in twentieth-century critiques of classical atonement theories is that suffering is an essential part of the process of liberation. A version of this is seen in Brightman's theology: God is unfinished, and the creation is slowly moving toward a final harvest of righteousness. More recent theologians have not shared the Social Darwinism of early twentieth-century optimistic, progressive theology, but in a different form have insisted, nevertheless, that suffering be understood within the larger context of historical processes of change. Returning to biblical themes of hope, they interpret the crucifixion of Jesus as a sign that before the dawn of a new age a period of struggle, violence, sacrifice, and pain will inevitably occur. In liberation and critical theologies the suffering of Jesus becomes a symbol for the conflicts that occur when people fight for new and more just social forms. The old must pass away before the new comes, and in its death throes the old lashes out against the new. The martyrs of the revolution are the sign that the beast is dying. Their blood gives hope, because it reveals the crisis that is at hand. Furthermore, violence against the vanguards of a new age is to be accepted. Acceptance witnesses against the perpetrator of violence and ennobles the victim. Martin Luther King, Jr., for example, accepted the inevitability of the violence directed against the civil rights movement and saw it as the responsibility of people in the movement to bear the suffering in order to transform the situation.

> Suffering can be a most creative and powerful social force. . . . The non-violent say that suffering becomes a powerful social force when you willingly accept that violence on yourself, so that self-suffering stands at the center of the nonviolent movement and the individuals involved are able to suffer in a creative manner, feeling that unearned suffering is redemptive, and that suffering may serve to transform the social situation.[34]

King's view is similar to the "moral influence" theory of the atonement: unjust suffering has the power to move the hearts of perpetrators of violence. The problem with this theology is that it asks people to suffer for the sake of helping evildoers see their evil ways. It puts concern for the evildoer ahead of concern for the victim of evil. It makes victims the servants of the evildoers' salvation.

King sees suffering as necessary because the very suffering of the victims of injustice will cause change by inspiring evildoers to change. Archbishop Oscar Romero reflected similarly:

> The only violence that the Gospel admits is violence to oneself. When Christ lets himself be killed, that is violence—letting himself be killed. Violence to oneself is more effective than violence against others. It is very easy to kill, especially when one has weapons, but how hard it is to let oneself be killed for love of the people![35]

This martyrdom theology ignores the fact that the perpetrators of violence against "the faithful" have a choice and, instead, suggests to the faithful that when someone seeks to silence them with threats or violence, they are in a situation of blessedness. Romero wrote,

> To each of us Christ is saying: if you want your life and mission to be fruitful like mine, do like me. Be converted into a seed that lets itself be buried. Let yourself be killed. Do not be afraid. Those who shun suffering will remain alone. No one is more alone than the selfish. But if you give your life out of love for others, as I give mine for all, you will reap a great harvest. You will have the deepest satisfactions. Do not fear death or threats. The Lord goes with you.[36]

Instead of making the straightforward observation that those in power resist change by using violence to silence and terror to intimidate any who question an unjust status quo, these theologians are saying that suffering is a positive and necessary part of social transformation. The violence of those who resist change becomes mythologized as part of a divinely ordained process of transformation, exemplified through Jesus' death and resurrection. In this mythologizing, historical realities are clouded, as Jon Sobrino rightly observes:

> There has been a tendency to isolate the cross from the historical course that led Jesus to it by virtue of his conflicts with those who held political religious power. In this way the cross has been turned into nothing more than a paradigm of the suffering to which all human beings are subject insofar as they are limited beings. This has given rise to a mystique of suffering rather than to a mystique of following Jesus, whose historical career led to the historical cross.[37]

The Negativity of Suffering

The third trend in twentieth-century critical traditions' view of the atonement is perhaps the most radical. It rejects the concept that human suffering can have positive or redemptive aspects. This trend is represented by such people as Jon Sobrino, William R. Jones, and Carter Heyward. Their critique is radical in the sense of the questions raised regarding theodicy.

> The whole question of God finds its ultimate concretion in the problem of suffering. The question rises out of the history of suffering in the world, but it finds its privileged moment on the cross: if the Son is innocent and yet put to death, then who or what exactly is God?[38]

In his book, *Is God a White Racist?* Jones searches for the answer to the how and why of suffering, particularly ethnic suffering. He recognizes four features of ethnic suffering: maldistribution, negative quality, enormity, and noncatastrophic character. From these he postulates what he terms "divine racism." The question of divine racism arises when this ethnic suffering is joined with a particular interpretation of God's sovereignty over human history. Is God responsible for evil and suffering, and does this responsibility fit in with our traditional concept of a benevolent God? Some feminist theologians have challenged the traditional understanding and interpretation of the suffering servant and the suffering and death of Jesus. Most reject the traditional use of the crucifixion to bless the victimization of women.

> Women are particularly sensitive to the way in which the suffering servant image has functioned in the Christian tradition, for we have invariably played that role within the family and vis-a-vis man in the larger society. . . . And in carrying the sins of the male half of the world on their shoulders, women are discovering that they have allowed men to escape from the responsibility of bearing their own burdens and coming to terms with their own sin and guilt. . . . Thus the suffering servant role model, a product of the patriarchal consciousness, has functioned to perpetuate that very dichotomy and alienation between human beings that

the tradition claims to overcome. In accepting that particular interpretation of the Christ event as normative for their lives, women have participated in their own crucifixion. As feminists, we must exorcise that image from our midst in order to discover the roots of that true reconciliation which can only come about between equals.[39]

But even while recognizing the link between Jesus' suffering and theirs, most feminist theologians have been reluctant to criticize the idea of the atonement. Carter Heyward, in her book *The Redemption of God*, comes closest to this type of critique by challenging and rejecting a notion of a sadistic God. But even with all these radical critiques and theodicies, these theologians continue to save the cross as a viable and meaningful, indeed necessary, part of what Christianity is.

Jon Sobrino, in *Christology at the Crossroads*, best represents this idea, especially among Latin American liberation theologians. He radically critiques traditional views of the cross, which have spiritualized the impact and taken away the scandal. He asks what justification there is for a God who allows the sinfulness of the world to kill his son and, by implication, other human beings as well.[40] But Sobrino goes on to point out the positive aspect he sees in the cross:

> On the positive side the cross presents a basic affirmation about God. It says that on the cross God himself is crucified. The Father suffers the death of his Son and takes upon himself all the sorrow and pain of history. This ultimate solidarity with humanity reveals God as a God of love in a real and credible way rather than in an idealistic way. From the ultimate depths of history's negative side, this God of love thereby opens up the possibility of hope and a future.[41]

This idea is closely related to the suffering God idea discussed above, but it carries the concept a bit further. The cross and the suffering and death of Jesus are necessary for God to have any solidarity with the poor and oppressed of the world. Without it God cannot be the compassionate, loving God we have posited. Without the cross there is no Christianity.

Latin American liberation theologians have focused on the cross as an example of commitment to justice and liberation. It is the result of working for justice. It is the example of love and hence of life. It enables us to endure. These ideas encompass each of the trends of the critical tradition, and, in a time of severe persecution such as Christians in Latin America are currently experiencing, it is understandable. There is a need to understand a situation of senseless suffering and death and to remain courageously committed to the struggle in the face of the despair and grief such suffering brings. But to sanction the suffering and death of Jesus, even when calling it unjust, so that God can be active in the world only serves to perpetuate the acceptance of the very suffering against which one is struggling. The glorification of anyone's suffering allows the glorification of all suffering. To argue that salvation can only come through the cross is to make God a divine sadist and a divine child abuser.

William R. Jones has a stronger critique of the cross than does Sobrino. His critique begins with the suffering servant motif, which he sees involved in many Black justifications of Black suffering. Jones states that the suffering servant motif cannot deal with noncatastrophic suffering, such as has faced the Black race, because an exaltation-liberation event must occur for the interpretation of deserved punishment to be dismissed. The suffering must cease, the suffering servant must be vindicated, and the suffering must be replaced by liberation.[42] This, says Jones, has clearly not happened in the Black situation. He expresses this especially in terms of the crucifixion-resurrection event, which is traditionally viewed by Christians as *the* liberation event.

> To speak of the cross, in the Christian tradition, has been to speak of human redemption, their salvation and deliverance. But the fact of oppression after the occurrence of the normative event of reconciliation raises special questions.[43]

Hence Jones insists on viewing all suffering as negative, for if we define an instance of suffering as positive or necessary for salvation, we are persuaded to endure it. This has been used too long by the oppressors both to justify their positions and release them from any responsibility for the oppressed's condition and suffering. Jones states that a theology of liberation must provide persuasive grounds for removing the sanctity and hallowed status from those it seeks to challenge.[44] Any attempts to eliminate or reduce suffering or to challenge one's condition is, by that very act, a direct challenge to the appropriateness of that suffering and condition.[45] It is to challenge God, if one believes in God's responsibility for all things in this world. It is to call God a white racist.

How can we judge God's motive or character at this point? Jones looks at the approach of the Hebrew Scripture writers to this critical issue. He finds that their convictions about the nature of God's future acts were grounded in the character of God's past and present acts.[46] What conclusions can be drawn about God by looking at past and present persistent and ruthlessly enforced suffering of the oppressed? Unrelieved suffering is explicable if (1) there is no God; (2) God exists but is not active in human affairs; or (3) God exists and is active in certain sectors of human history but is absent from the struggle for liberation. The elimination of oppression is not a priority item on God's agenda, if it is found there at all. God is clearly an oppressor, a white racist.[47] This view is theologically impossible if one posits a universally benevolent God. If one assumes God's intrinsic goodness and justice, one must do one of two things: (1) adopt a theodicy based on God's benevolence (Jones sees this as question begging and ultimately skirting the issues or desperately attempting to justify God's position) or (2) opt for atheism or, as Jones presents his solution, humanocentric theism. This humanocentric theism stresses the functional ultimacy of humans by virtue of their creation and eliminates God's responsibility for the crimes or errors of human history. This ultimacy is in total conformity with the sovereignty, purpose, and will of God.[48] It is in respect for human free will, which God created, that God acts as a persuader rather than a coercer. By becoming human in Jesus of Nazareth, God affirmed that God's activity in human history from then on would be carried out in the activity of particular people.

In this view of God, this humanocentric theism, God is not for the oppressed, in terms of their being "unique objects of God's activity in a manner that differs from persuasion."[49] It is essential for Jones's system that human activity be decisive for one's salvation or liberation. History is open-ended, "capable of supporting either oppression or liberation, racism or brotherhood."[50] This, he argues, does not remove hope from theology; it restores responsibility to humanity. He challenges some of the traditional beliefs of Blacks as being, in fact, part of their oppression.[51]

Jones's critique comes closest to naming the problem. He labels all suffering as negative, asserts that the crucifixion is not liberating without the resurrection, and suggests that our cherished beliefs may, in fact, be part of our oppression. But he, too, fails to make the connections among all these ideas. Why is the crucifixion necessary? Does God demand this suffering and death as payment for sin or even as a condition for the forgiveness of sin? Is the question not, Is God a racist, but rather, Is God a sadist? And is the identification Black people, particularly Black women, felt with the suffering Jesus part of their oppression? Again, Jones does not intend to denigrate the suffering and oppression of Black people. Jesus is clearly seen as a political messiah for Blacks. The condition of Black people today signifies Christ's crucifixion. His resurrection signifies Black hope.[52] The suffering that Jesus experienced is not being questioned. God's demand, the sacralizing of the suffering, is at issue and is not addressed by Jones.

Carter Heyward makes the most radical departure from traditional views of the atonement. She does so because she approaches the question free from some theological trappings. First, she asserts that Jesus is important if he is only and fully human. She also implies that there is no original sin in the classical sense, hence nothing from which humanity needs to be redeemed. For Heyward, Jesus' death was an evil act done by humans. It was unnecessary, violent, unjust, and final.[53] This leads her to condemn the glorification of suffering found in traditional Christian theology:

> Any theology which is promulgated on an assumption that followers of Jesus, Christians, must welcome pain and death as a sign of faith is constructed upon a faulty hermeneutic of what Jesus was doing and of why he died. This theological masochism is completely devoid of passion. This notion of welcoming, or submitting oneself gladly to, injustice flies in the face of Jesus' own refusal to make concession to unjust relation.[54]

Jesus died because he was a radical who challenged the unjust systems under which he lived. Jesus challenged the theological idea of a sadistic God:

> The image of a Jesus who, in the prophetic tradition of Israel, despised the blasphemous notion of a deity who likes sacrifice, especially *human* sacrifice, can assure us that we are not here to give ourselves up willingly

to be crucified for anyone's sake, but rather to struggle together against the injustice of all human sacrifice, including our own.[55]

Heyward, by rejecting the notion of a sadistic God, argues very effectively that this notion is blasphemy. But she fails to identify the traditional doctrine of the atonement as the central reason for the oppressiveness of Christianity. Despite her many unorthodox beliefs, Heyward still locates herself firmly in the Christian tradition and struggles to stay there. It is precisely this struggle that prevents her from labeling Christianity as essentially an abusive theology. She struggles to redeem the doctrine of the atonement. Despite her reimaging of a Jesus who "redeems" by showing us that "salvation" consists in being in an intimate, immediate love relationship with God, has she merely reworked the traditions and called them blasphemous when in reality that blasphemous God, the God who demands sacrifice, that patriarchal God, is the one to be found in the text, is, in fact, the God upon which the entire Christian tradition is built?

Conclusion

Christianity is an abusive theology that glorifies suffering. Is it any wonder that there is so much abuse in modern society when the predominant image or theology of the culture is of "divine child abuse"—God the Father demanding and carrying out the suffering and death of his own son? If Christianity is to be liberating for the oppressed, it must itself be liberated from this theology. We must do away with the atonement, this idea of a blood sin upon the whole human race which can be washed away only by the blood of the lamb. This bloodthirsty God is the God of the patriarchy who at the moment controls the whole Christian tradition. This raises the key question for oppressed people seeking liberation within this tradition: If we throw out the atonement is Christianity left? Can we call our new creation Christianity even with an asterisk?

We do not need to be saved by Jesus' death from some original sin. We need to be liberated from the oppression of racism, classism, and sexism, that is, from patriarchy. If in that liberation process there is suffering it will be because people with power choose to use their power to resist and oppose the human claim to passionate and free life. Those who seek redemption must dare to live their lives with passion in intimate, immediate love relationships with each other, remembering times when we were not slaves.

Our adventure into freedom is empowered by rejecting and denying the abuse that is the foundation of the throne of sacrifice. We choose to call the new land we enter Christianity if

- Christianity is at heart and essence justice, radical love, and liberation.
- Jesus is one manifestation of Immanuel but not uniquely so, whose life exemplified justice, radical love, and liberation.
- Jesus chose to live a life in opposition to unjust, oppressive cultures. Jesus did not choose the cross but chose integrity and faithfulness, refusing to change course because of threat.

- Jesus's death was an unjust act, done by humans who chose to reject his way of life and sought to silence him through death. The travesty of the suffering and death of Jesus is not redeemed by the resurrection.

- Jesus was not an acceptable sacrifice for the sins of the whole world, because God does not need to be appeased and demands not sacrifice but justice. To know God is to do justice (Jer. 22:13–16). Peace was not made by the cross. "Woe to those who say Peace, Peace when there is no peace" (Jer. 6:14). No one was saved by the death of Jesus.

- Suffering is never redemptive, and suffering cannot be redeemed.

- The cross is a sign of tragedy. God's grief is revealed there and everywhere and every time life is thwarted by violence. God's grief is as ultimate as God's love. Every tragedy eternally remains and is eternally mourned. Eternally the murdered scream, Betrayal. Eternally God sings kaddish for the world.

- To be a Christian means keeping faith with those who have heard and lived God's call for justice, radical love, and liberation; who have challenged unjust systems both political and ecclesiastical; and who in that struggle have refused to be victims and have refused to cower under the threat of violence, suffering, and death.

- Resurrection means that death is overcome in those precise instances when human beings choose life, refusing the threat of death. Jesus climbed out of the grave in the Garden of Gethsemane when he refused to abandon his commitment to the truth even though his enemies threatened him with death. On Good Friday, the Resurrected One was Crucified.

Notes

1. Perdita Huston, *Third World Women Speak Out* (New York: Frederick A. Praeger, 1979), 36.

2. Mary Daly, *Beyond God the Father* (Boston: Beacon Press, 1973), 77.

3. Gregory of Nyssa, *The Great Catechism*, chap. 24.

4. Matthew Fox, *Original Blessing* (Santa Fe: Bear & Co., 1983), 162.

5. Ibid., 159.

6. Ibid., 164.

7. Anselm, *Cur Deus Homo*, chap. 9.

8. Ibid., chap. 12.

9. Ibid., chap. 11.

10. Walter Rauschenbusch, *A Theology for the Social Gospel* (New York: Abingdon Press, 1917), 174.

11. Ibid., 49.

12. Ibid., 184.

13. From John Driver, *Understanding the Atonement for the Mission of the Church* (Scottdale, Pa.: Herald Press, 1986), 129–46.

14. Judy Grahn, "From Sacred Blood to the Curse and Beyond," in *The Politics of Women's Spirituality*, ed. Charlene Spretnak (Garden City, N.Y.: Anchor Books, 1982), 265–79.

15. Nancy Jay ("Sacrifice as Remedy for Having Been Born of Women," in *Immaculate and Powerful*, ed. C. W. Atkinson, C. H. Buchanan, and M. R. Miles [Boston: Beacon Press, 1985], 283-309) shows the relationship between blood sacrifice and the subordination of women.

16. Mary Daly, *Gyn/Ecology* (Boston: Beacon Press, 1978), 82.

17. Alfred of Rievaulx, quoted by Caroline Walker Bynum in *Jesus as Mother* (Berkeley: University of California Press, 1982), 123.

18. William of St. Thierry, quoted by Bynum, *Jesus as Mother*, 120.

19. Peter Abelard, "Exposition of the Epistle to the Romans," in Gerhard O. Forde, "Caught in the Act: Reflections on the Work of Christ," in *Word and World* 3/1: 22.

20. Helmut Thielicke, *The Ethics of Sex*, trans. John W. Doberstein (New York: Harper & Row, 1964), 79-98.

21. Ibid., 88.

22. Ronald Goetz, "The Suffering God: The Rise of a New Orthodoxy," *The Christian Century* (April 16, 1986): 385.

23. Ibid.

24. Personalism is the name of any theory that makes personality the supreme philosophical principle; idealistic personalism makes persons (and selves) the only reality. E.g., Edgar Sheffield Brightman, *An Introduction to Philosophy* (New York: Holt & Co., 1951), 218.

25. Edgar Sheffield Brightman, *The Problem of God* (New York: Abingdon Press, 1930), 113.

26. Ibid.

27. Edgar Sheffield Brightman, *The Finding of God* (New York: Abingdon Press, 1930), 113.

28. Ibid., 140.

29. Brightman, *Problem of God*, 94.

30. Goetz, "Suffering God," 389.

31. Jurgen Moltmann, *The Crucified God* (New York: Harper & Row, 1974), 51.

32. Ibid.

33. Ibid.

34. Martin Luther King, Jr., quoted in *A Testament of Hope*, ed. James Washington (New York: Harper & Row, 1986), 47.

35. Quoted in *The Church Is All of You*, ed. James Brockman (Minneapolis: Winston Press, 1984), 94.

36. Ibid., 69.

37. Jon Sobrino, *Christology at the Crossroads* (Maryknoll, N.Y.: Orbis Books, 1978), 373.

38. Ibid., 224.

39. Sheila Collins, *A Different Heaven and Earth* (Valley Forge, Pa.: Judson Press, 1974), 88–89.

40. Sobrino, *Christology at the Crossroads*, 371.

41. Ibid.

42. William R. Jones, *Is God a White Racist?* (New York: Anchor Press, 1973), 81.

43. William R. Jones, "Reconciliation and Liberation in Black Theology: Some Implications for Religious Education," *Religious Education 67* (Sept.-Oct. 1972): 386.

44. Jones, *Is God A White Racist?*, 68.

45. Ibid., 55.

46. Ibid., 13.

47. Ibid., 29.

48. Ibid., 188.

49. Ibid., 201.

50. Ibid., 196.

51. Ibid., 202.

52. Remarks made by Jacqueline Grant in a panel discussion entitled, "Women's Issues in the Development of Black Religion," American Academy of Religion, Nov. 26, 1985.

53. Carter Heyward, *The Redemption of God* (Washington, D.C.: University Press of America, 1982), 54–57.

54. Ibid., 58.

55. Ibid., 168–69.

Washed in
the Grace of God

EMILIE M. TOWNES

to be called beloved
is to be called by God
to be called by the shining moments
be called deep within deep

to be called beloved
is more than one plus infinity
more than the million breaths of loving
than the sounds of tomorrow's horizon

to be called beloved
is the marvelous yes to God's what if
the radical shifting of growth
mundane agency of active faith

to be called beloved
is to ask the question
what would it mean
what would it look like if we actually believed
that we are washed in God's grace

to be called beloved
is to answer the question
we are not dipped
we are not sprinkled
we are not immersed
we are washed in the grace of God

to be called beloved
is to listen to the words of Baby Suggs
holy
who offered up to them (us) her great big heart

—emt

"Here," she said, "in this here place, we flesh; flesh that weeps, laughs; flesh that dances on bare feet in grass. Love it. Love it hard. Yonder they do not love your flesh. They despise it. . . . Love your hands! Love them. Raise them up and kiss them. Touch others with them, pat them together, stroke them on your face 'cause they don't love that either. *You* got to love it, *you*! . . . This is flesh I'm talking about here. Flesh that needs to be loved. Feet that need to rest and to dance; backs that need support; shoulders that need arms, strong arms I'm telling you. . . . So love your neck; put a hand on it, grace it, stroke it and hold it up. And all your inside parts that they'd just as soon slop for hogs, you got to love them. The dark, dark liver—love it, love it, and the beat and beating heart, love that too. More than eyes or feet.

More than lungs that have yet to draw free air. More than your life-holding womb and your life-giving private parts, hear me now, love your heart. For this is the prize."[1]

This admonishment/sermon to love one's heart is an individual and a communal call to question the radical nature of oppression and devaluation of the self and the community in the context of structural evil. This line of questioning can and should take a multitude of directions because it addresses the nature of *systemic* evil, not individual sin alone. My aim is to consider what it means for one community, the African-American community and culture to love our heart, to be called beloved. I invite you to make your own cultural and religious translations.

To Be Called Beloved Is to Shatter the Silence

To pay heed to Baby Sugg's words requires that we be willing to confront—to face together. To take the risk of learning about the weak spots and places we need to work on as well as the riches within us. We must be willing to face *our* own lack of understanding, the stereotypes *we* have within us, *our* unwillingness to change, *our* comfort with the status quo. It also means that we draw on our faith, the ability we have to hope, our unwillingness to let go of loving, and our accepting responsibility to do justice.

We must learn to struggle not only within ourselves, but within our community as well. *We* are the harvest, we are each others' tomorrows, todays, and yesterdays. *We* are the ones who need healing from dis-ease and infirmity. We suffer from the disease of racism. Sometimes we fool ourselves that the off-color (literally) joke is harmless. We don't really mean it or that the person we're talking to knows that we really were just kidding.

We suffer from the infirmity of sexism. We try to fit into predefined roles that bear no relation to whom we really are and how we really feel about others and about ourselves. Each of us battles the disease of heterosexism—straight, gay, lesbian, bisexual. We all fear within us that which is the erotic,

which is the powerful. We have been taught to separate ourselves into parts
that do not interact. We are told that we live in a mind/body, a sacred/profane,
a male/female, a dominant/submissive world—and we have to conform to that
world. We suffer from the infirmities of classism, militarism, ageism, and dis-
criminate against the disabled. We find ourselves among those who remain
insensitive to the rich diversity of creation. To be part of the *living* body of this
culture, this nation, this church means that we have to start with ourselves.

We have to surrender much that is familiar and warm and loving and step
out into uncharted seas with only those strange things we call convictions,
principles, faith, and integrity. This is difficult for us to do. For many, there
can be no security in life apart from being surrounded by the broad expanse
of a country in which all landmarks are clear and the journey takes us along a
well-worn path. Day after day, we draw comfort in being able to look up at
any moment and know exactly where we are. We are stuck on the familiar.
We have grown comfortable with and are comforted by the status quo.

We do this with social issues as well. Once we get a grasp of the dynamics involved within a given issue, it's hard for us to look beyond the issue for
the connections to other issues that are just as hard and problematic—that
will challenge our horizons again and that will call us to grow anew. And so I
want to share with you *a few* of the elements that I am convinced we must
address if we are, as Black folk in the United States, to speak beyond the
silences and confront and then work against sexual and domestic violence as
a community of faith.

Racism

To be called beloved is to shatter the silence.

One aspect of racism is that it has structured dominant and subordinate
roles and relationships between Blacks and whites. African Americans are
placed within a relatively closed system that labels us as manifesting deviant
behavior. Some of us have succumbed to the double consciousness that
W.E.B. DuBois wrote of in 1904. And we have done new turns and twists on
the theme of our alleged deviancy.

Recent neo-conservative and conservative African-American theorists
splinter the silence rather than shatter it. Shelby Steele's *The Content of Our
Character* is a case in point. Steele argues that the 1954 Civil Rights Bill was
passed on the understanding that equal opportunity wouldn't mean racial
preference. He believes that affirmative action moved from anti-discrimina-
tion enforcement to social engineering. For Steele, the imposition of affirmative action goals and time tables creates a false sense of pluralism and equality
inside college campuses because most Blacks are not culturally or intellectu-
ally prepared to compete with whites on an equal basis.

What we achieved, according to Steele, was a type of cosmetic diversity
that did not address the roots of African-American deprivation. All in all,
affirmative action has caused whites to draw the inaccurate conclusion that
all Blacks, regardless of their talent, achieve due to their race. Steele tells us

that preferential treatment translates into a lowering of standards to increase Black participation. This spawns debilitating doubt that then undermines African-American performance in the public realm.

Steele should have stood in the Clearing with Baby Suggs and the other women, men, and children. And listened again to the words that followed from Baby Suggs' big heart.

> "Here, . . . in this here place, we flesh; flesh that weeps, laughs; flesh that dances on bare feet in grass. Love it. Love it hard. Yonder they do not love your flesh. They despise it."[2]

The lesson for African Americans in the Clearing is that we have learned to hate ourselves without even realizing the level of our self-contempt. In loving ourselves, in shattering the silence, we must become our own best critics and our greatest cheerleaders for justice and hope. Such arguments as Steele's fail to consider the nature of structured social inequality. They represent modernist notions of individualism and an ease with systems that promise diversity, but are structured to deny diversity's concrete demands for change.

Sexism

To be called beloved is to shatter the silence.

Black folk have watched, observed, and studied the larger culture. And without even realizing it, we have taken as our own, ways of relating which are often not true to our African, Native American, and Indian, and Caribbean roots. Still in 1993, too many of us think and act as though it's "natural" if not "normal" for men to dominate due to their participation in public life and that women are relegated to the private or domestic sphere. This assignation of place gives rise to universal male authority over women and a higher valuation of male over female roles.

The public realm contains the institutionalized rules and practices that define the appropriate modes of action. It is the political, economic, legal, cultural and social institutions in which we live as a society. In addition, it is the wide range of actions and practices covered by law. The public realm is the arena of paid work and ideas. It is the world of men. This country's laws, values, education, and morality are debated and shaped in this sphere. Despite the gains made in recent years, men, not women, remain the primary participants in this sphere.

The private realm is that place of individual actions and interpersonal relations. It is the home. It is the arena where the dominant cultural norms of our society place women. Each woman lives with this split and participates in its existence and maintenance—African American and white.

We take separate paths when we reach the juncture of the systematic exclusion of African-American men (and the majority of men of color) from the public sphere of the dominant white culture. This exclusion suggests that sex-role relationships between people of color cannot be explained fully by the structural oppression between the domestic and public spheres or the differential participation of men and women in the public sphere. Therefore, it is necessary to distinguish between the public life of the dominant and the dominated societies. The public life of the dominated society is *always* subject to the stresses put upon it by the dominant society. The private life of the dominated society suffers even more so than that of the dominant society's.

The sad irony is that African-American women and men were never meant to participate as full members of this public/private split. African-American women have been forced to play a highly functional and autonomous role within the family and Black society due to economic and social conditions that have devalued and ill-defined African-American men and women historically.

Black women and men are warehoused, as are other women and men of color and white women, into images of womanhood and manhood imposed by a larger society. Black women also know that they will never reach this model due to the constraints of race and class.

Black women have been called matriarchs, Sapphires, and castrators. This is due largely to the active role many Black women have had to play in the support of children, husbands, and Black society. All have usually assumed the Black woman's capabilities. This legacy differs considerably from where the majority of white women begin. White culture, by and large, does not assume that white women are capable. Black women who have the legacy of clearing the fields, caring for the children of others as well as their own, and functioning in marginalized roles—while being called on to provide the moral center of Black values—are considered a deviation from the norm and an anomaly.

This is more than a cruel joke of sexism. For what this does is set up a system of inequalities that stunt the mental, spiritual, emotional, social, economic, and physical growth of African-American children, men, and women. We end up fighting each other and putting forth such lopsided and misogynistic views as Shahrazad Ali's *The Blackman's Guide to Understanding the Blackwoman*. The pity of this, is that Ali, a Black woman, condones emotional, physical, and spiritual battering, abuse, and violence against Black women by Black men. All this in the name of some misbegotten notion of building up African-American manhood and womanhood.

Among her many observations:

> It has been proven that a Blackman is capable of taking a woman and making her beautiful, intelligent and wise. She is not able to create this same effect by herself.

> A good woman. The kind of woman who is in submission to her man and loves it. The kind of woman who obeys because she wants to obey and not because she is forced into doing so.[3]

Much of what Ali advocates in her book condones violence against women and children in the name of a renewed communal solidarity among Black folk. She, too, would do well to listen to the words of Baby Suggs.

And no, they ain't in love with your mouth. Yonder, out there, they will see it broken and break it again. What you say out of it they will not heed. What you scream from it they do not hear. What you put into it to nourish your body they will snatch away and give you leavins instead. No, they do not love your mouth. *You* got to love it.[4]

Ali says that she has come to her conclusions based on information obtained through interviews and/or participant observation. What she does not tell us is the number of women interviewed, their socio-economic status, the questions asked, or the method of interview. We, as African Americans, have often been the victims of extensive negative stereotyping and conclusions about our alleged pathology that have been based on "reports." It is no better when we are the ones who do it to ourselves. There is no future in setting up our *own* system of subjugation.

Concepts of African-American manhood and womanhood have biological roots *and* emerge from acculturation. If we fail to see that we take in the culture around us in our breathing, if we miss that we are picking up all sorts of cues about what it means to be a "real" man or a "womanly" woman or a "whole" people through institutions, if we miss that we are socialized along gender lines, then we fall victim to racism and sexism.

When we lash out at each other, what we commit is horizontal violence, not nation-building. We destroy pieces of our selves, and we cut short hope for shattering the silence of sexism in the African-American community. What we commit, in blackface, is a pale mimicry of what too many white folks do to each other. It has functioned well to create a society built upon injustices. But it reflects neither King's dream nor Malcolm's nightmare. It reflects a broken, dispirited people who grasp at the rods of injustice rather than the branches of community.

Heterosexism

To be called beloved is to shatter the silence.

We live in a sexually repressive culture. I say this although the media, the church, and even our personal observations may indicate that we are promiscuous. We are sexually repressed in the sense that we have made all kinds of compromises regarding our sexuality to live on this planet and in our society and to survive in the church.

I say that we live in a sexually repressive culture because even in the face of a life-denying disease like AIDS, countless folk remain ignorant of how it is transmitted, how to protect ourselves from spreading or catching HIV, or even realize that everyone needs to take precautions.

I was stunned when a young woman told me that before this "AIDS thing" she had no animosity toward gays, but now she thinks *they* are a menace to society. When I asked if she were practicing safe sex, she did not know what that was. She was not aware of the need for condoms, avoiding oral contact with the penis, vagina, or rectum. She was not aware that the use of intravenous drugs by her sexual partner who shares needles or even her sharing needles put her in the risk group for AIDS. She was unaware of the risk she runs in being sexually active without proper precautions, even in light of the growing number of heterosexuals contracting the virus.

We are sexually repressed while at the same time being sexually active and this is a dangerous combination. We don't understand how our bodies function or how the bodies of our sexual partners function. We fumble in the dark regarding subjects like teenage pregnancy. Time and again children repeat the all too familiar litany, "I never thought it would happen to me," and when asked if they were using any form of birth control the answer is a resounding "No." That is a manifestation of sexual repression.

We separate our body from our spirit in this sexual repression. We have inherited this separation from years of church doctrine and theological treatises. The history of our society and the church is one that neglects, ignores, or denigrates the body. The history is that the body is lower than the mind that represents spirit. To be religious means living and acting in split bodies. Therefore, sexual activity is equated with sexuality. And we are only to express our sexuality within the bounds of marriage.

This is a false equation. Our sexuality is how we are as thinking, feeling, and caring human beings. It is our ability to love and nurture. To express warmth and compassion. It is not only our gonads. Heterosexism encourages the objectification of our bodies—male and female. One of its strongest underlying premises is that the emotion expressed in same-sex relationships is only that of pure sex. Too often we are blinded from seeing or wanting to discover the care and nurture that lesbians and gay men can and do have for each other. We must raise some exacting questions about an ethic that insists that homosexuals should either try to engage in heterosexual relationships unhappily or remain celibate. I am always suspicious of an ethic that allows some to impose on others obligations that they are unwilling to accept for themselves.

As we begin to recognize that we are fighting history and tradition it is easier to see that much of the response we have as well as others have to gay men and lesbians comes from a subtle and deadly unwillingness to reexamine everything. Heterosexism's continued presence means the devaluation of people. It permits the social, political, economic, and theological systems that encourage us to deny parts of our being for the sake of others, to continue to destroy all of us.

It prevents us from addressing fully racism and sexism. The 1992 report from the President's Commission on AIDS alarmed many. The idea that 21 percent of the total population accounts for 46 percent of the people in the United States with AIDS caught many off guard. The 1994 numbers continue to rise with Blacks and Hispanics/Latinos accounting for 50 percent of the reported AIDS/HIV cases. However, in 1987 the statistics were already alarming. Then, Blacks and Hispanics made up 20 percent of the population. At a conference, I raised the concern that the Black community was under siege with AIDS because even then, 37 percent of the male AIDS sufferers and 73 percent of the female sufferers were Black or Hispanic. I was told by several Black folk in attendance that using such statistics was detrimental to the Black community. Their concern was the *perception* that the folks who had contracted the HIV virus were gay men or prostitutes. They could not hear that the disproportionate rise of AIDS in our communities is due to intravenous drug use. Yes, there are gay men like my uncle who contract the AIDS virus and die. But there are men and women like Arthur Ashe and Ruby Johnson who die of the complications of AIDS. Fear of an image or images *will* literally kill us if we do not address the realities.

The heterosexism in our communities continues to allow too many to believe that if they are not gay men, then they do not have to worry. Meanwhile, there is still no systematic, structural, and effective anti-drug program in communities of the dispossessed in this nation.

Justice

To be called beloved is to realize that when we shatter the silences, we are called to make justice. For it is justice that tells us each of us has worth, each of us has the right to have that worth recognized and respected, each of us has a right to be known for whom we are. Justice holds us accountable to and with each other.

> And O my people they do not love your hands. Those they only use, tie, bind, chop off and leave empty. Love your hands! Love them. Raise them up and kiss them. Touch others with them, pat them together, stroke them on your face 'cause they don't love that either. *You* got to love it, *you!*[5]

If Black folk cannot live into justice or help create it, then we have consigned ourselves to worthlessness. For to continue in pathways in which we condone or ignore the violence we do to our minds, bodies, and souls is to allow racism, sexism, heterosexism, classism, ageism, colorism, nationalism, and any other "ism" you can image to dictate to us our values and our aspirations. We must make it personal and communal, our struggle for justice.

It is out of this context that African Americans must begin to have open and honest conversations about how sexual and domestic violence destroys the fabric of a community that is literally holding on for dear life in this nation. Too many of us carry within us the scenes of battering and pillage to our souls and bodies. Too many of us have been there or heard about the times someone thought "No" meant "Yes." Too many of us have shaken our heads when we heard sounds during the night or during the day. Too many of us have been at the checkout counter and chatted with a checker who was wearing a black eye for the fourth or fifth time. And in our souls we wanted to say something, but we saw in her eyes, "Don't ask."

This *is* flesh we are talking about here. "Flesh that needs to be loved. Feet that need to rest and to dance; backs that need support; shoulders that need arms, strong arms . . ."[6] But make no mistake about what sexual and domestic violence does to the soul and spirit. For much of what spawns the ability to commit violence to a physical body is also that which holds racism, sexism, and heterosexism in place. It is a deep and abiding desire and then ability to dominate, to control, to dehumanize, to devalue. It is an abomination to the very fiber of existence.

African Americans must take this into the communal context. Our self-respect, our self-esteem, our future as a people are under assault. And in too many cases and all too often, we are leading our attackers. It is not only what racism has done to us, it is not only what sexism has done to us, it is not only what heterosexism and all the other "isms" have done to us. When Baby Suggs talks about the flesh, our flesh, she is telling us it's what we do to ourselves, it is how we respond to the structural injustices of this day. We need to get clear on why and how we permit and commit sexual and domestic violence on Black folk. We need to decide how we are going to love ourselves and each other rather than rely on popular culture, even our own popular culture, to tell us who we have been, who we are, and where we are heading, and how we are to behave with each other in justice and hope.

We need to hear again "separate but equal." And this time, expand the notion of what it means to be separate in this culture. Too often when we talk about separating ourselves, we are actually setting someone up as a target. When cast in the context of sexual and domestic violence, it means to beat someone into invisibility, into silence, into despair. There is no equality here. There is no justice. There is no equity. There is no fairness.

We must shatter the silence of our ignorance about ourselves. For far too long, the Black community had to battle the image that sexual and domestic violence were confined to our communities. Years ago, I remember quite clearly having to repeat the litany that violence of this sort is not confined to folks living in poverty or to specific communities of racial ethnic folk. What we did, unwittingly, was not focus enough on what *was* and *is* going on that condones and commits sexual and domestic violence among Black people.

Shattering the silence means that we proclaim our identities as African Americans in the United States *for ourselves.* Yes, we are male and female, young, middle-aged, old, conservative, neo-conservative, liberal, radical, nationalist, patriotic, anarchist. Yes we come in a variety of colors and shapes, we have diversity of sexualities, we are a variety of religions, we have a multitude of ways to express ourselves in the arts. What we cannot afford is to have no clue about whom we are. For you can be sure, that someone or some industry will be more than happy to define us to suit their purposes, their gain, their profit—not ours. We must do this for ourselves as individuals and our collective selves as a people. If we can do this, we will begin to look at the structural and emotional roots of violence in our community.

We have a responsibility for our future. We must decide if we are going to live in an uneasy, destructive, but comfortable acquiescence or in communal accountability. Are we going to live with some of us filling the role of colonized victims? Or are we going to realize the great gift of whom we are as African Americans and begin to love hard our inside parts and "the dark, dark liver."

To be called beloved is not only to shatter the silence, but to get rid of it altogether. We owe one another respect and the right to our dignity as people of God. If we deny justice, we are telling those who go without that they are worthless. Perhaps this is one of the reasons that the first Rodney King verdict cuts so deep in our souls. For it didn't seem to matter to some folks that no one in creation deserves to be beaten like that—not in the line of duty, not because you have the power to do so. Many of us got a deep message with that verdict: Black men, children, and women are worthless. And it is no better nor should it be more acceptable or more understandable when it is Black folk doing it to other Black folk.

So we must teach and live justice. We must engage in community-building work that ministers to our souls, lifts our spirits (individually and collectively), assures our connection with each other and to God, pulls us beyond ourselves. The Black religious community needs to create large spaces of welcome, understanding, and confrontation from the pulpit to its religious programming. Folk need to hear the church say in a clear and unequivocal voice that sexual and domestic violence are not acceptable behaviors but they are lethal values.

Black folk need to work with Black folk to help create positive images of male and female that are not dominated by some one else's version of who we are. We must become each other's harvest and in doing so, we will begin to recognize the gift of life we have in each other and turn away from battering ourselves into victimage. One place to begin to gain these new images is in the life of a church that no longer condones business as usual or transmits religiousized versions of domination and subordination.

Justice holds us accountable to the demands of living in a community of responsibility and one that fosters self-worth and self-esteem for others and for itself. Every time we walk into a dessert shop and see gigantic chocolate breasts complete with nipples and think of how funny this is and how good the chocolate must be, every time we watch *School Daze* or *Boyz N the Hood* and miss *Daughters of the Dust* or *Losing Ground*, every time we hear the sounds during the night or day, every time we feel someone we know or don't know is in trouble, every time we see injustice and treat it as just, we have done violence and mayhem to the body and soul. We have pushed ourselves away from the pulse of morning and condemned ourselves to "the gloom of dust and ages."[7]

"... in this here place, we flesh; flesh that weeps, laughs; flesh that dances on bare feet in grass. Love it. Love it hard. ... and the beat and beating heart, love that too. More than eyes or feet. More than lungs that have yet to draw free air. More than your life-holding womb and your life-giving private parts, hear me now, love your heart. For this is the prize."[8]

To be called beloved is to answer the question: we are not dipped, we are not sprinkled, we are not immersed, we are washed in the grace of God.

Notes

1. Toni Morrison, *Beloved* (New York: Alfred A. Knopf, 1987), 88–89.
2. Ibid.
3. Shahrazad Ali, *The Blackman's Guide to Understanding the Blackwoman* (Philadelphia: Civilized Publications, 1989), 11, 40, 75.
4. Morrison, 88–89.
5. Ibid.
6. Ibid.
7. Maya Angelou, "On the Pulse of Morning." Inaugural poem for President William Jefferson Clinton, January 20, 1993.
8. Morrison, 88–89.

Ending Innocence
and Nurturing Willfulness[1]

RITA NAKASHIMA BROCK

Introduction

From 1974 until 1988 I worked as a volunteer staff member of a youth education program called Brotherhood/Sisterhood USA (BSUSA) sponsored by the Los Angeles National Conference of Christians and Jews. The summer camps we facilitated brought together a multiracial group of 150–200 Southern California high school students and 30–40 adult staff, in either June or August, for a week of examining, both personally and socially, racism, sexism, homophobia, substance abuse, and family and community violence. Throughout the year the adult staff received a half dozen weekends of training in which we were expected to struggle with the same issues, methods, and experiential exercises we used with the campers. My specific roles in the program were usually to be the Protestant Chaplain, to lead a small support group, to co-facilitate a group meeting of all the females, and to work with Asian-American and mixed-parentage youth.

During those summer weeks, I listened to young people, ages thirteen to nineteen, talk about the tragedy in their lives, about sexual molestation, incest, rape, alcoholism, racial attacks, drug abuse, gangs in their neighborhoods, and physical violence in their families, neighborhoods, and cities. I wondered about the state of the American family and its neighborhoods and schools. These were ordinary young people, recruited from Southern California schools and religious organizations, not overtly "troubled" youth. In fact we sent home anyone who seemed too psychologically unstable to handle the intense emotional demands of the week's experiences (which on rare occasions meant adult staff also).

I learned several important lessons from the experiences I had in BSUSA. These lessons were based in my growing awareness of what people are capable of doing to children, how little accountability there is for adults who inflict the equivalent of torture on the most helpless and defenseless members of families, and how private, isolated, and unsupported parenting is in our society, especially for parents of color for whom social support services are either nonexistent, alienating, or inadequate. Windows opened on horrifying evil through the stories I heard over the years—windows I wished sometimes had never been opened. I sometimes sensed the parental despair, desperation, and self-hatred that lurked under the abuse I heard described by their children. And I felt their anguish at being unable to protect their children from the terrors of a racist and sexist society.

These windows helped me see the power of evil in human life, the regularity of its occurrences, its banality, its deep embeddedness in the most intimate corners of life, the scarcity of means for social accountability in minimizing evil, and the length of its legacies. For many youth, our one week together was the only time in their lives they had been given permission to tell the truth of the sometimes unimaginable horrors of those lives. I grew to understand why gangs were important to them, why some turned to drugs or alcohol, why they were sometimes sexually promiscuous, and why a few had been to jail—and I learned to withhold judgment on behaviors I knew I could not understand. Often a young person's annoying, self-destructive, or hostile behavior would suddenly become coherent and transparent when I heard them tell of the pain they were carrying. And I learned that if I did not rush to judgment but reached out, despite my annoyance, and listened instead, I could touch them heart to heart.

In those moments when we connected, I was made startlingly aware of the remarkable resiliency of human beings. Most of the youth arrived at camp appearing carefree and happy. In three to four days those persona changed dramatically as we made ways for them to share their pain and suffering. Those ways were strongest when the adult staff shared our own pain and suffering. As I watched, listened, and participated, I was amazed at how much we all wanted to be able to trust and love others, how much we yearned to reach out to each other, and how deeply ran our passions for integrity and wholeness. I learned important lessons about the power of emotional courage, and I became aware that I, too, needed to examine my experiences as a child, the roots of my fears and hostilities, and my pain. For if I had not had to do so, I could not have survived in the program so long. I learned that every time I used the authority of my staff role to protect myself and to mask my fears or sense of inadequacy, I created barriers that destroyed the safe space I sought to create. I struggled against what I had experienced and understood as authority and tried to create a different way to use power.

Rethinking how I understood and used power was not easy. I was raised, after the age of five, in a U.S. Army family, as the military "dependent" of my stepfather. I was born in Fukuoka, Japan, to a Japanese mother and a Puerto Rican father who left after I was six months old. When I was almost three my mother married my step-father, Roy Brock, from rural Mississippi, who had lied about his age to fight in the Second World War. When I was six, we emigrated to Kansas. My step-father was raised a Southern Baptist, but he did not like being a Southern Baptist, and in the South, I am told, Southern Baptists who wished to declare themselves heretics said they were Methodists—so he called himself a Methodist, although I doubt he had any idea what that meant.

Like many good Southern men, he believed that physical punishment was the way to discipline children. I do not remember at what age I started being physically punished, but I know I thought it was wrong. I remember thinking carefully that if I actually changed my behavior because of this treatment by my father he would get the mistaken idea that it was effective. So I refused to change my behavior. If he talked to me, I was willing to listen to reason, but if I was physically punished for something, then I refused to change. And as my sister said, I spent a lot of time in trouble for minor things, such as not adhering to the decorum of a Southern lady, which was not important to me. I was unwilling to give in, and would tell my father that I felt what he was doing to me was wrong. I could tell him because we were emotionally close; he was my friend and emotional support system far more than my mother. To his credit, I was not punished for speaking up and telling him what I thought, even when it made him angry. Talking back was not a crime in my family. Spunkiness was OK.

I believe my willfulness served me well, because it made me resistant to coercion, both physically and theologically. I lived in rural Mississippi for a year, in seventh grade, as the only non-white person in the junior high school I attended. I remember sermons of fire and brimstone, to which I listened and thought, "Maybe I should go forward to be saved, whatever that means," but it never felt right to this Japanese-raised child to make such a spectacle of herself in public. I remember when I made a clear decision not to be saved at a revival meeting. Unlike other revivals that required a long march forward up the center aisle, we were asked to close our eyes and raise our right hands to be saved. The preacher went on and on and said, "I'm not going to stop until everyone's saved." With my eyes closed, head bowed, hands firmly in my lap, I thought "I'm not that bad, I'm not going to raise my hand, I don't need this." I kept my hands in my lap, and for years I thought I was the only one in the room without my hand up.

Since that revival, I have had an allergic reaction to that kind of emotional coercion from fanatics of the left as well as the right. I was willing to take responsibility for my own behavior. There is an enormous difference between guilt and healthy self-criticism. I think I received enough fair criticism as a child to know the difference.

During those fourteen years I worked at BSUSA, I had to examine the other side of power—the way I had learned to use coercion myself when I felt helpless or defensive about my power. As I struggled to use my authority and power to listen, to open space for honest sharing, and to touch brokenness, I became acutely aware of how little the world encouraged that way of using power. As I worked in the program, I also attended seminary and graduate school. The cognitive and emotional dissonances were intense. Self-sacrificing love was upheld as the ideal, an ideal which felt to me increasingly misguided and abusive as I saw how it worked to aggravate suffering. The theologies I was required to read (none by women) and the structure of authority in the classroom I experienced seemed to reinforce patterns of passivity, guilt, false gratitude, and dependency. I listened for but could not find a voice that made sense of my experiences in BSUSA. I heard words of comfort and kindness sometimes, but not of empowerment. Nor did I hear an echo of my own voice.[2]

I was reminded, in those summer camp experiences, of the differences in human behavior produced by different uses of power in a community. In communities that value prestige, status, and competition, posturing, self-protection, rationalization or denial of feelings, and struggles for attention and supremacy often determine patterns of behavior. In those that value authenticity, community good will, and empowerment, listening to others, self-disclosure, and generosity were often in evidence. These two ways of handling power are often mixed, and they were in BSUSA, but the weight went toward the latter. That made all the difference.

I found nothing in my formal education that spoke theologically from the perspective of those who had experienced family violence, child abuse, gang violence, racism, sexism, or chemical addiction, that encouraged outrage and self-preserving action, that deconstructed hierarchies of power, and that taught a healthy suspicion of authority. I found those voices, of course, outside of my classes in feminist communities and writings and in liberation theology—work never assigned in my classes.

Karen and Asian-American Women

I share the above autobiographical material because I want to discuss the situation of Asian-American women, and I do not want to leave the impression either that we are all similar or that I know nothing about the experiences of Asian-American women. My early experiences as an immigrant to this country are not totally dissimilar to those of many one-and-a-half generation Asian Americans, those born overseas and brought to the United States young enough that we have become more familiar with the society and its language than those who come as adults.

I must admit I have some personal ambivalence talking about these issues because even though I am a first generation Asian American, I grew up with a white step-father. Though I came from Japan, I am as American as whites are. One aspect of racism against Asian Americans in this society is that we get confused with Asians because people automatically assume that Asian-looking faces make us foreigners. We may have been here four and five generations, but we are regarded as foreign guests and called exotic "Orientals." The question an Asian American often gets from someone who is not is "Where are you from?" If we say, "I'm from Cincinnati, Ohio," they say, "But where are you *really* from?" *Really* is the code for foreigner. The assumption is that we do not belong here.

It is a touchy thing in the Asian-American community, this getting confused with Asians. I have been at scholarly gatherings, such as the American Academy of Religion, where the issue of race was discussed in the American context, and an Asian, not an Asian American was asked to speak. This would be like inviting a Swede to represent a white perspective on racism in America. I have studied Asian culture because it seemed important to me to know what my own ancestry was. But every time I talk about Asian culture I know I am treading a thin political line because my political orientation is Asian-American, and no, we are not interchangeable. And yes, we are connected culturally to our lands of origin, just as many European-Americans are connected to theirs.

My work with Asian-American women has forced me to re-think my own theological conceptualities, and look to what I would call "Asian ways." I have come to appreciate the wisdom of some Asian traditions, the role of ambiguity, and a tolerance for tension and complexity. So in the following reflections, I want to discuss two directions my thoughts have taken; one is the re-thinking of innocence, and the second is the meaning of nurturing willfulness. The theorists I discuss on these topics below are white middle-class feminists, but my first insights into these questions came from reading works by writers such as Gish Jen, Cynthia Kadohato, Maxine Hong Kingston, Joy Kogawa, and Amy Tan.

One of the stories of an Asian-American woman from that BSUSA program continues to haunt me. A fifteen-year-old Korean woman, who called herself Karen because Americans could not say her real name correctly, had been in the United States a year with her family. She was fairly isolated because her language skills were poor. She was not especially likable. She was sullen, intense, emotionally cold, and, by Northern European standards, histrionic. She had two parents and an older brother who was, I think, seventeen. She had few friends outside of her family. We heard from one of the youth leaders, who spoke Korean, that she was talking about killing herself, which we took very seriously, given her obviously troubled emotional state. An adult staff woman, who spoke Korean, attempted to find out why she was threatening suicide—to no avail. Finally, through the youth leader, we learned that she was pregnant, and she wanted to kill herself because she was pregnant by her older brother who had been molesting her for two years. She was positive that if her parents found out she was pregnant, that they would assume she was a whore and disown her. If she told them the truth, that their darling, only son was molesting her, they would call her a liar and disown her anyway. And she preferred to be dead than to be alone. She had nowhere to turn.

We were forced to tell her that, because we knew about this abuse, we were legally obligated in California to report it to the authorities, which made her more intent on killing herself for bringing disgrace on her family. The only reassurance that we could give her about this reporting was that the California system on child abuse was overburdened with complaints, and it would probably be two or three years before they got to her case. We said we would insist that someone who spoke Korean be assigned to the case, which would delay the process even further. By that time her older brother would probably be in college and she would legally be an adult.

According to the last census report, two-thirds of the Asian Americans in this country are, like Karen, first-generation. They have come here as immigrants or as traumatized refugees. They are often overeducated for the kind of work they can find, and they are disproportionately poor. Sixty-five percent of the Laotian population in the United States live under the poverty line. And because there are few people that speak Asian languages in any area of the service sector, they are vastly underserved by health care professionals and by social service workers, who rarely understand the scope of the problems they face. They are silenced and marginalized by American culture.

The history of immigration by Asian-American women to the United States is laced with suffering, betrayal, endurance, and hope. Some came as girls to serve as prostitutes for the many Chinese men whom the government did not want to encourage to stay here. Others came as picture-brides for men they had never seen to an inhospitable land where they worked very hard to care for their families—many of these women were bold adventurers, looking for a new life. Most first generation Asian-American women came alone. My mother, like many who married soldiers, had families, but their children are enigmatic cultural hybrids. Some women today come from poor countries, such as the Philippines, as mail-order brides because there are American men who find American women too assertive and think, if they get an Asian wife, they will have an obedient, devoted, and docile wife. The women they marry often lack survival skills for this culture and find themselves trapped in abusive marriages from which there is no escape. Some Asian-American women, since the Vietnam war, have come from Southeast Asia, from Vietnam, Cambodia, and the hill tribes, like the Hmong, where there is a strong Shaman culture and women are married very young. Other Asian-American women come from South Asia which is a mixture of Muslim, Hindu, and Theravadan Buddhist, all of which are religions that do not value women, any more than Christianity does. Still another group comes from West Asia and is called Arab, Iranian, or Semitic. Asian women are also trafficked to North America for the sex industry here. Visit the red light district around any military base if you have any doubts, or a brothel in an Asian area of a major city.

Few women's shelters offer a cultural climate hospitable to Asian-American women. When we tried to help Karen, we knew of no shelters for a pregnant Korean teen who spoke little English. There are vast cultural gaps between first generation Asian Americans and the American White Protestant individualistic culture we find when we come here. If we come from East Asia, Confucian values are the bedrock of the culture. Confucian cultures value sons, family duty, and age, not young daughters. If we come from Southeast Asia, we are largely Buddhist, which itself has its own history of not valuing women and projecting sexuality onto women as problematic. St. Paul, Minnesota, has the second largest Hmong community in the United States, and one of the issues that we are struggling with in the Asian-American community is what to do with the child marriage customs. In Hmong society, the children are married at nine or ten or twelve years old by kidnapping. This is against State law. But does it help to say that it is against the law and put people in jail? What happens to the young girls? How can we educate a community about what it means to live in the United States under its laws in one breath and talk about valuing cultural diversity in another breath?

Asian Americans often experience a major conflict in this society between traditional Asian values of family and society, and the American values of individualism and personal achievement. For Karen, to leave her family environment would have been to leave the language that she knew, the structure of meaning that she understood as the only personal value that she had, and to enter what to her was a very unsafe culture. For her to leave her family would be to jump out of the frying pan into the fire. She was unwilling to do that. Feminist separatism, the safe space that is talked about in feminist circles and shelters, does not work for Asian-American women. We do not feel safe because family is the place of language and meaning, of personal worth, of financial support, and even of emotional support, abusive as it can be. It is also often the place of resistance to racism. A family is a place of both love and sorrow, of both terror and hope, of pain and companionship, and of despair and meaning. They are all there—brokenness and healing inextricably bound together in daily doses.

Other tensions among family, society, and the individual appear in the orientation toward justice in this society, which is especially focused around individual rights and power. The West paints issues in dualistic ways so that race is talked about along Black and white lines, as polarized aspects of good and evil. Asian, Latin, and Native Americans get lost in that dialogue, because we are somewhere else outside the dualism. Those of us who are mixed-race are even more marginalized in the conversation because there is no language of race to talk about our struggles. Most census and affirmative action forms ask us to fill in one category, assuming we all are monoracial or monoethnic. How does one have an undivided loyalty to anything when one's life is so complex?

The Western orientation toward justice in terms of individual rights is distinct from Asian-based cultures that value harmony, that have what I would call an aesthetic orientation to reality, in which is embedded an ethical orientation. Well-being is not focused around rights and personal freedoms, but is focused around affiliation, loyalty, social harmony, and wisdom.

The Ending of Innocence

Many Asian-American women are familiar with oppressive factors such as race, economics, and gender, but the illuminating power of our lives and the theological impact of our stories lie in how we are more than the politics of our lives. Through this "more", we have survived destructive circumstances that inhibit and traumatize us. There is, I believe, no greater witness to the sacred live-giving Spirit in the world than the survival of those who are not meant to endure—those who are meant to be ground under by forces of oppression and destruction, but who defeat those principalities and powers, and live on.

Perhaps because the cultural roots of many Asian Americans lie, to some extent, in Confucian values which respect the wisdom and sophistication of age, rather than the innocence of children, innocence is understood in many Asian-American women's writing differently than in the West.

Innocence is something one outgrows, or else one risks remaining superfluous and disempowered, which is, of course, the state in which women and children are supposed to be. By innocence, I mean the sense that our actions are not willfully chosen, that we are doing what we do by instinct, by our very inborn nature, or because we do not know anything else. Jesus' innocence is often depicted this way—as an extension of his perfect nature, such that he knew no evil.

Innocence may be appropriate to babies, but innocence maintained in adults is dangerous. Hence, innocence in many Asian-American stories is not described as lost so much as it is described as rejected, because it leads to victimization. Innocence is not a survival skill. It does not nurture and empower life, or pass it on. Survival skills emerge with the rejection of innocence and the capacity to make wise, willful choices.

As I was talking about this issue of innocence with a close friend of mine who is a survivor of childhood molestation, she said, in fact, that she spent most of her life using innocence as a way to protect herself from remembering. She could not think her way out of that innocence because sexuality terrified her. And so she maintained an aura of child-like innocence into adulthood, disassociating herself into mystical experiences during sex. Her innocence protected her from pain, but it also prevented any willful action on her part to heal it. As the memories of her molestation surfaced, she went through therapy and began to come to terms with it. Her whole persona changed. Her self-presentation changed from sweet innocence into mature womanliness in a couple of years. In reflecting on her strategy, she realizes that innocence and disassociation were how she both protected herself from the harm she experienced and also kept herself from remembering.

This immobilizing quality of innocence is developed in Nel Noddings' analysis of the entrapment of women into a false innocence.[3] She argues that women, in order to be regarded as good and worthy of protection, must be seen to rely on an unconscious feminine nature from which wells forth our maternal instinct and benevolent nurturing abilities. That nature may come from an archetype or from the power of God. In any case, the power of women to be good rests in an innocence of choice and a passive acceptance of this female nature. Any sign from a woman that her behavior is consciously chosen, that she could have acted otherwise, and that she knows her own agency and power are reasons to denounce her as unfeminine and, therefore, not good. The ability to think ethically and to act as an agent of ethics is reserved for men, so that the woman who claims such skills becomes a man.

Noddings argues that this whole dichotimization of good and evil in Western society and the understanding that the point of being ethical is to defeat evil, itself favors what she calls masculine virtue—the need to defeat others, to win control, to dominate, which, of course, only men can do. If a woman tries to do so, she has lost the ability to rely on her unconscious nature or her faith. And since she can not be a man, she becomes morally unreliable—that is, evil. Hence, woman's only moral voice comes from innocence, the paradigmatic virtue for honorable victims.

To be allowed to take responsibility for both good and evil in ourselves, rather than to defeat evil or to rely on a savior to overcome it, Noddings suggests we redefine evil non-dualistically so that evil becomes whatever increases human helplessness. Evil is whatever reinforces intractable pain. And evil is what creates separation from relationships of love and nurture. Those three things—helplessness, pain, and separation—define evil.

Such evil permeates human life inevitably to some degree. In fact, the need to control, dominate, and defeat evil creates pain, separation, and helplessness. Hence, to confront evil, I suggest we ask what increases or decreases the amount of evil in our lives, rather than what will defeat or end evil. The redemptive task is our ability to minimize evil in human life to the best of our ability by increasing human efficacy and ethical action, alleviating or preventing pain, and enabling and enhancing relationships. This is the work of fighting evil, and it requires willful behavior and the right use of power. No adult is totally innocent of the power to make another helpless, to inflict pain, or to destroy relationships just as no one has the knowledge and power to prevent all occurrences of helplessness, pain and separation in human life.

Systems of abuse destroy fabrics of human community and afflict everyone by their demands for obedience to the good, a good defined by the powerful who want control. Could it be that as long as we believe that the suffering of the innocent demands our outrage and compassion, we reinforce the idea that suffering is deserved by the guilty and the knowledgeable? If we maintain that disobedience must be punished, we must identify who is to blame for the evil. And we perpetuate the mechanisms of domination and oppression which are not seen as inherently wrong, but as serving the protection of goodness. We defend the divine mandate to punish the wicked no matter what structures and methods do this. The relationship of innocence and passivity to goodness, and of knowledge and action to evil, escalates the premium on innocence, which I believe is highly problematic. Innocence makes for passive scapegoats.

In the years that I worked in the BSUSA summer program, I struggled with being in between structures of power. While I needed to be aware of my own childhood experiences in order to empathize with the youth I counseled, and to refrain from working out unresolved conflicts with them, I could not simply identify with them and lose myself in mirroring their feelings. As adult staff I had responsibilities and with them came power. I had to guide youth through thinking about survival strategies and to be a source of firm support so that when they broke down emotionally, I would not. I was also responsible for protecting them from each other, to help them see how their behavior and attitudes affected others by allowing those who were hurt to speak. If I identified too strongly with one victimized group, which I often did, my reactions interfered with their being able to speak for themselves, to think through their own strategies for survival. At moments of my failure to empower, I became ideological, refusing to listen to experience.

In addition to working with the youth, I was also responsible for working with Anglo and male staff. I was expected to confront issues of racism and sexism, and that expectation sometimes placed me in a defensive, self-protective position in relation to Anglo women and men of color. I was also aware, however, that I was better educated formally and theologically than most of the other staff. With that education came middle-class values and structural power. I sometimes found myself in the position of giving guidance or help to Anglo staff and men of color which I needed to do for the less-experienced staff to handle their assignments, even when the same people sometimes used their power against me. I also spent time discussing religion and theology as a Christian with Jewish, Buddhist, and Muslim staff. And finally, I was a straight Asian woman working with gays and lesbians of every racial group.

Because of the political nature of the program, I was aware of the ambiguities of power in which I was enmeshed. And I found myself, more often than I wanted, taking the safe road by protecting my status as victim, and ignoring my misuses of power or defending them when challenged.

American society and its social justice structures tend to give moral voice to those who claim victimization and innocence. The importance of this mentality is not something I want to minimize. The concern for victims has allowed women, the disabled, the poor, people of color, gays and lesbians, and abused children to demand justice. I suspect that this mentality is rooted in prophetic Judaism and in christological doctrines of the atonement. But they have permeated the secular culture. Paying attention to victims of oppression has been, and is, a major contribution of Jewish and Christian thinking to many, especially in pricking the consciences of those with power and status. I am not arguing that those subject to abuse do not have a unique lesson to teach others about oppression. Rather, I think something is missing. Something beyond moral proclamation and denunciations of oppression. Something that opens doors of conversation at least among groups differently victimized.

Moral high ground goes to innocent victims. A ground from which one can make demands. There is danger, however, in this structure of morality and victims. If a victimized group can be proven to lack innocence, the implication is that the group no longer deserves justice. Any hint of moral ambiguity, or the possession of power and agency, throws a shadow across one's moral spotlight. Maintaining one's status as victim becomes crucial for being acknowledged and given credibility.

Exploring one's experiences of victimization is crucial to any possibility of healing, and to avoiding inflicting similar pain on those we love. But most of us are not just victims. It is not clear to me that those who have remembered and struggled to come to terms with childhood abuse, or who have experienced oppression are automatically able to move beyond this identification with victims. What brings us to a point from which we are able to see the power we gain from the hegemonic structures of status-oriented societies? What shows us the ways we may misuse our own power? Without such awarenesses it is difficult for us to see how we misuse what power we have.

A great deal of energy can be generated from a morally unambiguous sense of outrage at abuse and injustice. At times, such energy and outrage are important and necessary for fueling social change. But we should be clear that such energy is usually reactionary. As reactionary energy it can imitate the power it opposes, and it can carry serious misuses of power because it cannot admit an understanding of the ambiguities within which people live their lives. A person's complex and sophisticated understanding of oppression and exploitation, and a willingness to stand up to and condemn misuses of power does not automatically translate into behavior that is liberating of others.

For example, the failure, until recently, of male liberation theologians to take gender oppression into account, or the amount of domestic violence in the homes of peace activists, point to how easily oppressive behavior is perpetuated. Reactionary energy does not make room for confronting the complex relationships we must examine in order to build understanding and coalitions among differently oppressed groups. Perhaps this is, in part, why discussions of racism and classism seem so difficult in feminist circles, why discussions of sexism and homophobia seem so difficult among men of color, and why discussions of gender justice are so difficult in peace groups.

This tendency to identify with innocent victims, and to avoid discussions of the moral ambiguities of life continues to place responsibility for abuse on the victims of the system. Abuse is wrong not because victims are innocent, but because abuse, even by good people for a good cause, dehumanizes the abuser and abused. Hence, we need to focus not on innocence, but on what is wrong with abusive behavior.

The Nurturing of Willfulness

To know our own victimization is a necessary but not sufficient means for coming to terms with the complex and difficult relationships of power and love in which we find ourselves enmeshed. Sufficient means would include our attention to a multiplicity of voices that allow us to see where we are accountable and take responsibility, and enable us to use our voices strategically for change, while avoiding doing harm. Sara Ruddick, in her work on mothering, explores the shifting sands of such complex experiences from her life as a middle-class, well-educated, white feminist.[4] She attempts to understand what mothering can teach us about those who straddle worlds between the helplessness and suffering that come with attempting to mother a male-dominated society, and the immense potential for power and control that resides with having virtually sole responsibility for caring for children.

Ruddick explores the behavior and values that create nurturing, empowering ways to raise children. She does this by discussing important principles which are thoroughly grounded in acknowledgement of the ambiguity of parent-child relationships, and the necessity of maternal honesty and ethical reflection. And she calls it maternal thinking because it's something that people of both genders can do, or I would say all the genders since there are more than two.

In exploring the experiences, actions, and thinking behind adequate mothering, Ruddick does not set up a moral code of mothering, but examines nurturing for what it can tell us about ethical adult behavior in a culture that does not support mothering. She notes that "there is much about children that provokes anger, and maternal feelings about children involve a great deal of ambiguity. Some children are far more difficult to nurture than others regardless of the reasons why."[5] Ruddick explores the highly charged nature of such mother-child relationships. And using examples of moments when children are difficult, and mothers feel rage or despair, Ruddick points to how we can learn appropriate uses of power and authority to preserve through love, to foster growth, and to teach conscience.

Ruddick is not concerned with the guilt or innocence of children. She understands that even tiny infants make demands that are often quite difficult to meet, especially in a society such as ours which gives so little support to mothering. Infants are capable of provoking highly ambiguous feelings in their caretakers, even in those who love them deeply. Instead of focusing on the nature or state of children, Ruddick explores the ethics, behaviors and responsibilities of mothering. She argues that regardless of the behavior of a child, mothering requires certain commitments that must be held even under the most trying of circumstances, and even through the most conflicted feelings.

One of those commitments which carries ambiguities is to nurture willfulness—to create the capacity in a child to gain the knowledge and self-confidence that enables her or him to assert her or his will in the world, sometimes in opposition to a parent's desires. The paradox of mothering is to have used one's power to nurture an individual who becomes independent of that power, and to take satisfaction from having used one's power to give it away. In this paradox, to be happy, a child is not always good, and instead sometimes acts willfully against a mother's wishes.

Ruddick describes the ambiguous irony of parenting that is trustworthy, so that a healthy suspicion of authority is encouraged. She says:

> If, when mothers fail them as they inevitably do, children deny their hurt and rage so that they can continue "trusting," they are in effect giving up on their mothers. By contrast, when they recognize and protest betrayal, they reaffirm their expectation that their mother has been and can again become worthy of their trust. . . . Proper trust is one of the most difficult maternal virtues. It requires of a mother clear judgment that does not give way to obedience or denial. It depends on her being reliably goodwilled and independent yet able to express and to accept from her children righteous indignation at trust betrayed.[6]

Such willfulness and trusting is enhanced not by attempting to maintain innocence in children, but by encouraging them to gain greater knowledge of both good and evil in others, including their own mothers, and by mothers supporting the right of their children, at times, to be disobedient. This is less a process of protecting the innocent, and more a process of empowering wisdom. To enable such a process, a mother must possess self-knowledge and the ability to accept personal responsibility for her behaviors, because she pays attention to the conflicted feelings and concerns that all mothers feel. Mothers who are good nurturers learn to manage their behavior through ethical reflections upon their deepest commitments in the midst of a series of competing voices. Ruddick insists that maternal choices are highly sophisticated decisions involving both attention to feeling and intense intellectual thought. Her work opens doors for examining the multiple voices that allow us both to identify with those who are vulnerable, and to accept responsibility for our power, because mothers sit on the fulcrum of power and powerlessness, of hope and despair, and of abuse and empowerment.

Persons in hegemonic systems must learn to empower others even when the choices of those they empower are frustrating, and Ruddick shows us how it is possible to allow the greatest possible freedom to choose for everyone within the limits of what is safe for all when that can be determined. While Ruddick is careful not to recommend maternal thinking as a model for all human relationships because adults must relate as peers, she argues that the values maternal thinking teaches are crucial to the creation of just and peaceful societies.

Through maternal thinking we can explore how the infliction of pain can be avoided, and the willful expression of anger at or resistance to pain encouraged. Ruddick breaks open the dilemmas of the choices that face us when we are both subject to oppressive powers and possess the power to hurt others. We must see that all adults, like mothers, are capable of learning to minimize and manage evil by nurturing life forces, by being empathetically attuned to the physical and emotional lives of others, by choosing cooperation over competition, and by loving others.

Conclusion

In that BSUSA summer program, when my friends and I sat down to discuss what we could do about Karen, we struggled with our feelings of helplessness, and also with our feelings about Karen. She was withdrawn and defiant, but we saw in her intense desire to die a passion that might be used to live. She was not innocent, for that had been taken from her already. And we could not protect her from herself or her family, for she chose her family over herself. But her willfulness made us hopeful for her.

We explained to her what the choices were and let her decide. We told her that we could help her find a shelter where she could have her child, if that was what she wanted to do. We suggested we might be able to get some emergency family services intervention and have her placed in a foster home to protect her. Or, because California was a pro-choice state and did not have a parental consent law, we could assist her in getting an abortion and put her on the pill. She chose the last option.

One of the staff members who was a school nurse at a high school helped her arrange for her abortion and for the birth control pills. I do not know what happened to her. She did not stay in touch with any of us. But I am hopeful that her willfulness served her well—that she chose to live. I hope, too, she has been able find a safe place for herself and to heal at least a little. I have no certainty, only hope, but sometimes hope is all we have, and sometimes, it's enough, if our hope is lived out in making services and safety for women like Karen. Let it be so.

❧

Notes

1. A version of this essay was delivered in May 1993 at a conference in Chicago sponsored by the Center for the Prevention of Sexual and Domestic Violence, Seattle, Washington.
2. See "The Other Half of the Basket: Asian-American Women and the Search for a Theological Home," by myself and Naomi Southard, *Journal of Feminist Studies in Religion* 3/2 (Fall 1987): 135–49, for a discussion of the alienation from theology many Asian-American women feel.
3. In Nel Noddings, *Women and Evil* (Berkeley: University of California Press, 1990).
4. See Sara Ruddick, *Maternal Thinking: Toward a Politics of Peace* (Boston: Beacon Press, 1988).
5. Ibid., 104.
6. Ibid., 119.

The Transformation of Suffering: A Biblical and Theological Perspective

MARIE M. FORTUNE

A religious person who is victimized by rape, battering, or child sexual abuse frequently faces the questions, Why do I suffer in this way? and, Where is God in my suffering? These profound theological questions cannot be answered simply with platitudes and then dismissed. The question of why there is suffering at all is one of classic theological debate, that is, the question of theodicy, to which there is no completely satisfactory answer. Human suffering in the midst of a world created by a compassionate and loving God is a dimension of human experience which is most disturbing and disquieting. The particular experience of suffering that accompanies victimization by sexual and domestic violence raises particular issues in regard to theodicy.

Why Suffering?

People struggle with two fundamental aspects of the experience of suffering when they ask, Why do I suffer? First is the question of cause, that is, the source of the suffering. The second aspect involves the meaning or purpose of suffering.

Why is there suffering? It suffices to say that some suffering results from arbitrary, accidental sources such as natural disasters. However, much suffering is caused by human sinfulness: sinful acts by some bring suffering to others. These acts can generally be understood as acts of injustice. God allows such sinfulness because God has given persons free will and does not intervene when they choose to engage in unrighteous, unjust acts. Other people suffer from the consequences of these acts. This explanation may be adequate for situations clearly caused by human negligence or meanness, intended or not: for example, a fatal car accident caused by a drunk driver, chronic brown lung disease in textile workers who are denied protection from occupational hazards, birth defects in families living near toxic waste dumps, or incestuous abuse inflicted by a father upon his children. Yet it is still not a wholly satisfactory explanation. Those who suffer search further for answers, or at least for someone to blame.

Victims of sexual or domestic violence have a strong tendency to hold God or themselves responsible for the abuse even though there is clearly a perpetrator whose actions resulted in the victim's suffering. While his/her sinful acts may be understood as a consequence of his/her own brokenness and alienation (sometimes rooted in his/her own victimization), he/she is nonetheless responsible for actions that bring suffering to others. Self-blame or God-blame for one's experience of victimization simply avoids acknowledging that a particular person is responsible for the abusive acts.

Another explanation that is frequently utilized by victims is really old-fashioned superstition. It seeks to explain a current experience of suffering in terms of a previous "sinful" act on the part of the victim: the current suffering is God's punishment for the preceding "sin" which God has judged. Hence a battered woman now being abused by her husband can "explain" why this is happening by remembering that when she was sixteen, she had sexual intercourse once with her boyfriend. She knows this was a "sin" and that God was displeased with her, so God must now be punishing her teenage indiscretion. Or she may have been "disobedient" and not submitted to her husband. She understands the situation to reflect God's acting to bring about her suffering for a justifiable reason; she blames herself and accepts her battering as God's will for her. At least she can "explain" why this happened to her; unfortunately, her explanation leaves no room for questioning her suffering or for confronting her abuser with his responsibility for it.

If God is to blame for the misfortune, one can direct anger at God for causing the suffering. For whatever reason, it is argued, God has singled out the victim of sexual or domestic violence to suffer. Two things result. First she/he is driven away from God by the pain and anger; second, no one is held accountable for what he/she has done to the victim. The suffering of the victim is exacerbated by the feeling that God has sent this affliction to him/her personally and has abandoned her/him in the midst of it. Harold Kushner offers a valuable reframing of this assumption:

> We can maintain our own self-respect and sense of goodness without having to feel that God has judged us and condemned us. We can be angry at what has happened to us, without feeling that we are angry at God. More than that, we can recognize our anger at life's unfairness, our instinctive compassion at seeing people suffer, as coming from God who teaches us to be angry at injustice and to feel compassion for the afflicted. Instead of feeling that we are opposed to God, we can feel that our indignation is God's anger at unfairness working through us, that when we cry out, we are still on God's side, and He [sic] is still on ours.[1]

God is not only *not* the cause of injustice and suffering but is instead the source of our righteous anger at the persons or circumstances that do cause suffering as well as our source of compassion for those who suffer.

The second aspect of the experience of suffering involves the attribution of meaning or purpose. What meaning does this experience of suffering hold for the victim? People have great difficulty accepting the irrational and often arbitrary nature of sexual and domestic violence. Instead of realizing that these things happen for no good reason, they attempt to manufacture a good reason or seek a greater good; for example, suffering "builds character" or is "a test of one's faith." The purpose of suffering is then the lesson it teaches, and the result should be a stronger faith in God. Purposefulness somehow softens the pain of the suffering. If some greater good is salvaged, then perhaps the suffering was worth it.

An understanding of the meaning of one's suffering begins with the differentiation between voluntary and involuntary suffering. Voluntary suffering is a painful experience which a person chooses in order to accomplish a greater good. It is optional and is a part of a particular strategy toward a particular end. For example, the acts of civil disobedience by civil rights workers in the United States in the 1960s resulted in police brutality, imprisonment, and sometimes death for these activists. These consequences were unjustifiable but not unexpected. Yet people knowingly chose to endure this suffering in order to change the circumstances of racism, which caused even greater daily suffering for many. Jesus' crucifixion was an act of unjustifiable yet voluntary suffering; in 1 Peter it is viewed as an example:

> For to this you have been called, because Christ also suffered for you, leaving you an example, that you should follow in his steps. He committed no sin; no guile was found on his lips. When he was reviled, he did not revile in return; when he suffered, he did not threaten; but he trusted to [the one] who judges justly. (1 Pet. 2:21–23)

But it is an example not of simply being a sacrificial doormat but of choosing, in the face of the violence and oppressive authority which threatened him, to suffer the consequences of his commitment. It was a witness to his love, not his suffering. Beverly Wildung Harrison further reframes Jesus' suffering on the cross:

> But those who love justice, and have their passion lovingly shaped toward right relation act not because they are enamored of sacrifice. Rather, they are moved by a love strong enough to sustain their action for right relation, even unto death. . . . Jesus' paradigmatic role in the story of our salvation rests not in his willingness to sacrifice himself, but in his passionate love of right relations and his refusal to cease to embody the power-of-relation in the face of that which would thwart it. It was his refusal to desist from radical love, not a preoccupation with sacrifice, which makes his work irreplaceable.[2]

Jesus' crucifixion was the tragic consequence of his faithfulness and refusal to give up his commitment in the face of Roman oppression. He voluntarily accepted the consequence, just as did civil rights workers, in order to bring about a greater good.

Like voluntary suffering, involuntary suffering is unjustifiable under any circumstance. However, unlike voluntary suffering, involuntary suffering is not chosen and never serves a greater good; it is inflicted by a person(s) upon another against their will and results only in pain and destruction. Sexual and domestic violence are forms of involuntary suffering. Neither serves any useful purpose; neither is chosen by the victim; neither is ever justified. Yet both cause great suffering for large numbers of people.

Many victims of involuntary suffering respond with the question: Why did God send *me* this affliction? In the face of the personal crisis of violence, one's deepest need is to somehow explain this experience, to give it specific meaning in one's particular life. By doing this, victims begin to regain some control over the situation and the crisis. If one can point accurately to the cause, perhaps she/he can avoid that circumstance in the future; if one can ascribe meaning, then she/he can give it purpose, can incorporate the experience more quickly and not feel so overwhelmed by it.

Neither superstition nor the search for a greater meaning necessarily encourages the victim of violence to deal with the actual source, that is, the abuser's behavior. Neither encourages the victim to question the abuse she/he is experiencing. Neither motivates the victim to act in seeking justice. Neither is theologically adequate for the person who is struggling to comprehend his/her experience of abuse in light of faith.

In Jesus' encounter with the man born blind (John 9:1–12), he is confronted with the question about the cause of suffering.[3] "And his disciples asked him,'Rabbi, who sinned, this man or his parents, that he was born blind?'" (v. 2). Jesus answers their question in terms of the meaning rather than the cause of his suffering: "It was not that this man sinned, or his parent, but that the works of God might be made manifest in him. We must work the works of [the one] who sent me while it is day; night comes, and no one can work" (vv. 3–4).

Jesus proceeds to make a medicine and heal the man's blindness. He dismisses the request for a superstitious cause and restates the search for meaning. The blind man's suffering is a fact. Where is God in this suffering; what can God do in this situation; and what are we called to do? Jesus acts to relieve suffering rather than discuss its cause. He is teaching that the responsibility belongs to us to act regardless.[4] The question for us is not who sinned (in cosmic terms) or how can God allow women to be beaten and raped but how can *we* allow this to go unchallenged? In challenging this victimization, the question is, Who is accountable for this suffering and how can justice be wrought here?

What Jesus does not address in this parable is the situation in which there is clear responsibility for the suffering of another. A more current reading of this story might include the information that the man's father beat his mother during her pregnancy with him, and the child's blindness resulted. In this case, when asked the question who sinned, Jesus might have said, "The one who beat his mother is accountable for his acts. Rebuke him. If he repents, forgive him. [See Luke 17:1–4.] Here we must work the works of the one who sent me." Part of that work,which is clearly expected in the prophetic tradition of Hebrew and Christian theology, is that of calling to repentance and accountability and making justice in order to accomplish forgiveness, healing, and reconciliation. These responses to experiences of suffering at the hands of another are requisite if the suffering is to be more than simply endured.

Endurance

In both the explanation of superstition and the attribution of greater meaning, God is held responsible for the suffering itself. This presupposes a belief in God as omnipotent and omniscient. If God is in control and choosing to exercise that control by bringing suffering upon the afflicted as punishment or in order to teach them something, then both cause and meaning are clearly determined to be in God's hands.

In the face of this interpretive framework, most victims accept endurance as the means of dealing with this suffering. Deciding that being battered or molested is justifiable punishment, one's lot in life, cross to bear, or God's will, sets in motion a pattern of endurance that accepts victimization and seeks ways to coexist with it. Victims are encouraged to endure when support and advocacy to get away from the violence are not provided, when they are told to go home and keep praying, and when they are expected to keep the family together even though the violence continues and they are in danger. This "doormat theology" teaches that it is God's will that people suffer and the only option is to endure it. There is no space to question or challenge the suffering that comes from this injustice, to feel anger, or to act to change one's circumstance. The result of this theology is that a victim remains powerless and victimized and her/his physical, psychological, and spiritual survival are jeopardized. This understanding of the meaning of suffering comforts the comfortable and afflicts the afflicted but ignores the demands of a God who seeks justice and promises abundance of life.

There is no virtue in enduring suffering if no greater good is at stake. Certainly, being battered or sexually abused is such a situation. There is *no greater good* for anyone—certainly not for the victim and the children and others who witness the violence, but also not for the abuser. Endurance that merely accepts the violence ignores the abuser's sinfulness and denies him a chance for repentance and redemption which may come from holding him accountable for his acts. Endurance in order to "keep the family together" is a sham because the family is already broken apart by the abuse. There is no virtue to be gained in this situation where everyone loses; there is no virtue in encouraging a victim of abuse to accept and endure it.

Transformation

For the Christian, the theology of the cross and the resurrection provides insight into the meaning of suffering and transformation. God did not send Jesus to the cross as a test of his faith, as punishment for his sin, or to build his character. The Romans crucified Jesus and made him a victim of overt and deadly anti-Semitic violence. It was a devastating experience for Jesus' followers who watched him murdered. They were overwhelmed by fear, despair, and meaninglessness. They left the scene of the crucifixion feeling abandoned and betrayed by God. The resurrection and subsequent events were the surprising realization that in the midst of profound suffering, God is present and new life is possible.

This retrospective realization in no way justified the suffering: it transformed it. It presented the possibility of new life coming forth from the pain of suffering. Sometimes Jesus' crucifixion is misinterpreted as being the model for suffering: since Jesus went to the cross, persons should bear their own crosses of irrational violence (for example, rape) without complaint. But Jesus' crucifixion does not sanctify suffering. It remains a witness to the horror of violence done to another and an identification with the suffering that people experience. It is not a model of how suffering should be borne but a witness to God's desire that no one should have to suffer such violence again. The resurrection, the realization that the Christ was present to the disciples and is present to us, transformed but never justified the suffering and death experience. The people were set free from the pain of that experience to realize the newness of life among them in spite of suffering.

Personal violence presents a victim with two options: endurance and acceptance of continued suffering, or an occasion for transformation. Endurance means remaining a victim; transformation means becoming a survivor.

In order to become a survivor and transform one's suffering, persons must use their strength and all available resources within themselves and from others to move away from a situation in which violence continues unabated. God is present in this movement as a means to transformation. A young woman, raped at age eighteen, reflected on her rape experience in light of her faith. As she recovered, she observed that her prayer life had shifted dramatically after the assault. Prior to the rape, she recalled that her prayers most often took the form of "Dear God, please take care of me." As she recovered from the rape, she realized that now her prayers began, "Dear God, please help me to remember what I have learned." She moved from a passive, powerless position of victim in which she expected God to protect her to a more mature and confident position of survivor in which she recognized her strength and responsibility to care for herself with God's help. In addition, her compassion and empathy for others increased and she was empowered to act to change things that cause violence and suffering. She was able to transform her experience and mature in her faith as she recovered from the assault with the support of family and friends.

One of the most profound fears experienced by one who suffers is that God is literally abandoning her/him. The experience of suffering and the resulting righteous anger in the face of that suffering need not separate us from God. Paul gives witness to this in Romans.

> For I am sure that neither death, nor life, nor angels, nor principalities, nor things present, nor things to come, nor powers, nor height, nor depth, nor anything else in all creation, will be able to separate us from the love of God in Christ Jesus our Lord. (Rom. 8:38)

God is not responsible for suffering; God is not pleased by people's suffering; God suffers with us and is present to us in the midst of the pain of sexual and domestic violence; God does not abandon us even though everyone else may. This is the promise of the Hebrew and Christian texts—that God is present in the midst of suffering and that God gives us the strength and courage to resist injustice and to transform suffering.

Just as God does not will people to suffer, God does not send suffering in order that people have an occasion for transformation. It is a fact of life that people do suffer. The real question is not, Why? but, What do people do with that suffering? Transformation is the alternative to endurance and passivity. It is grounded in the conviction of hope and empowered by a passion for justice in the face of injustice. It is the faith that the way things are is not the way things have to be. It is a trust in righteous anger in the face of evil which pushes people to action. Transformation is the means by which, refusing to accept injustice and refusing to assist its victims to endure suffering any longer, people act. We celebrate small victories, we chip away at oppressive attitudes cast in concrete, we say no in unexpected places, we speak boldly of things deemed secret and unmentionable, we stand with those who are trapped in victimization to support their journeys to safety and healing, and we break the cycle of violence we may have known in our own lives. By refusing to endure evil and by seeking to transform suffering, we are about God's work of making justice and healing brokenness.

Notes

1. Harold S. Kushner, *When Bad Things Happen to Good People* (New York: Schocken Books, 1981), 45.

2. Beverly Wildung Harrison, *Making the Connections* (Boston: Beacon Press, 1985), 18–19.

3. "It is assumed that sin, by whomsoever committed, was the cause of the blindness. This was the common belief in Judaism; see e.g., *Shabbath* 55a: There is no death without sin (proved by Ezek. 18:20) and no punishment (i.e., sufferings) without guilt (proved by Ps. 89:33). When a man has been blind from birth, the sin must be sought either in the man's parents, or in his own ante-natal existence" (C. K. Barrett, *The Gospel According to St. John* [London: SPCK, 1955], 294).

4. In light of the Holocaust some have asked, Where was God? and many Jews have reframed the question to, Where were the people who could have stopped this?

Part II

Reconsidering Biblical Concepts

Reading Adam and Eve: Re-Visions of the Myth of Woman's Subordination to Man

CHARLES ESS

Introduction: Eve, Myth, and Re-Visioning Woman

If we are concerned with violence against women, we must carefully consider the story of Eve in Genesis 2–3. This story—more precisely, a later, especially Christian interpretation of this story—establishes an image of woman which mythically justifies male violence against her. To attack the problem of violence against women requires us to attack the mythic justification of such violence.

To see how this is so, I begin in Section I with a discussion of myth as defining basic images and values, and hence as justifying given behaviors in a culture shaped by myth. Susan Brooks Thistlethwaite points to the Genesis story as a legitimating myth of domestic violence. I examine and expand on her account so as to uncover what I argue to be a fundamental image of woman in Western cultures—namely, woman as "chaos agent," as threatening to disrupt patriarchal order. In both ancient and contemporary story, this mythic image justifies violence against the female for the sake of preserving the hierarchies which define patriarchal conceptions of order. Reading Eve as such a chaos agent hence provides the mythic foundation for violence against women.

But such a reading, as Rosemary Radford Ruether and others point out, is at best a later, especially Christian, *interpretation* of the Genesis story. In Section II, I examine more closely how this interpretation emerges in the West, culminating in Augustine's reading of Genesis and what Phyllis Trible identifies as "the standard account" of the woman in Genesis 2–3. Again, the standard account works as a mythic justification for male violence against women. But by examining how this interpretation emerges historically, we will see that this standard account is at best a severe distortion of the original story, a distortion forced by the later social and political conditions which shape the standard account. (Readers less historically oriented may elect to omit this section.)

In Section III, I examine the standard account of the woman in Genesis in light of recent scholarship on the text and archaeologically supported understandings of the social and political conditions in which the Genesis story first emerges. This examination reinforces the insight of Section II—namely, that the standard account, especially as it functions mythically to legitimate female subordination and male violence against women, cannot be supported by a careful reading of the Genesis story in its original context. At the same time, these re-readings replace the standard account with (re)new(ed) visions of Eve.

These re-visions thus demolish the standard account, an account which legitimates violence against women, and then replace that account with a more original myth—one which now affirms the intelligence and powers of the woman. In short, the myth that legitimated violence against women for two millennia in the West is uncovered as an empty excuse, and such violence is in fact countermanded by the new image of woman lifted up in contemporary re-visions of woman in Genesis.

By better understanding the history of the interpretation of Eve which works to excuse violence against women, and by examining recent re-visions of the Genesis texts, workers in the domestic violence movement will be better equipped to dissolve the myth of Eve exploited by batterers to excuse their behavior.[1] Indeed, by taking up these re-visions of her story, we may construct a new myth, one closer to the original sense of the story—one which makes clear that violence against women is unacceptable.

I: Eve as Myth: Woman as Chaos Agent, Domestic Violence, and the Need to Re-View Genesis 2–3

Who is Eve?

This question is crucial for those of us concerned with violence against women. Our understanding of Eve establishes an archetype for our culture: "Eve" stands as a primordial definition of "woman as such," of the nature or essence of woman *per se*. In more philosophical terms, our understanding of Eve constitutes a fundamental, culturally shared assumption regarding the nature or character of woman as such—and thereby, the nature and character of all women.

To say it still another way, our understanding of Eve makes up a fundamental *myth* about the nature of woman. Myth, as I use it here, means an accepted story or image which expresses a kind of conceptual vocabulary: this includes our fundamental concepts regarding the basic nature of things (such as the nature of male and female), and correlated ethical and political values. For example, some myth suggests that males and females are essentially *different* from one another, and values the abilities and characteristics of males above those of females. Such myths, as we will see, further value an *ethic* of male control and female submission, as it further values a *political* order of hierarchy. Other myths, by contrast, assert that male and female are *by nature* the same. Correlatively, these myths value the characteristics and abilities of both male and female as equal, as complementary to one another. They hence value an ethic of cooperation and a political order of equality.

Such myth defines a culture. If a story or image is accepted by most members of a culture, it then defines the mythic vocabulary, the basic assumptions and values of that culture. And, because myth defines basic assumptions and values—what is good, what is bad—the *behavior* of the members of specific culture largely follows from the myths central to that culture, from the understanding of things and the values that myth expresses. Specifically, these myths are crucial as they define a culture's beliefs about gender roles and the valued and disvalued behaviors for male and female in the culture. The myth thus shapes a culturally-shared landscape, a world of agreed-upon values, concepts, and behaviors in which the members of a culture live.[2]

If myth works this way, then our understanding of Eve, as it forms in our culture our most basic assumptions and beliefs about the nature of woman, will powerfully shape men's behaviors towards women, as it will also shape women's acceptance of male behavior towards them. In particular, if we accept a prevailing version of the Eve myth, the myth works to justify male violence against women. That is, the myth defines the nature of woman in such a way that male violence against her may be perceived as legitimate.

Rosemary Radford Ruether makes this point by way of the interpretation of Genesis 2–3 found in 1 Tim. 2:12–14. This passage in the Christian Scriptures ("New Testament") takes the *order* of creation in Genesis 2–3 (man first, woman last) to signal the inferiority of the woman. This passage then singles out the woman as the one primarily to blame for an act of disobedience further seen to bring death and evil into the world. As we will see, this interpretation of Genesis, as a story of especially the woman's disobedience which then issues in death, is later taken up and expanded by Augustine in his development of the doctrine of Original Sin (1989, 32).

If this is our story, if this is our myth, it establishes a conceptual vocabulary which ultimately legitimates male violence against women. It does so by first establishing woman's *nature*: the woman is second and thus (read as) inferior to man; and, by presenting the woman as the first to disobey, the story suggests that woman is *intrinsically* disruptive or disorderly—a "chaos agent." The story further values an ethical and political order—namely, a hierarchy defined by the authority of God and the male, and the subordination of the woman. The mythic nature of the woman as chaos agent thus clashes with the valued ethical/political order: the woman disobeys the authority of God. Finally, the story values a specific ethic, a specific behavior in response to the woman's disobedience: she is punished—most drastically, as she and the man are expelled from the Garden, an expulsion reinforced with the threat of a flaming sword.

In this way, the story provides the conceptual vocabulary which legitimates violence against women. When woman disobeys the higher authority (God's injunction against eating from the tree of knowledge), she is properly punished for such disobedience (by being set below her husband, by forceable expulsion from the Garden). By implication, if the woman disobeys the man, her master, she may likewise be legitimately punished and corrected by violence. The story, understood in this fashion, thus lays the mythic foundation for violence against woman as she threatens to evade male dominance and control (cf. Ruether, 1989, 31; Bledstein, 44).

In fact, Susan Thistlethwaite has documented how the Genesis story was used by a husband to legitimate his violence against his wife.[3] As well, by recalling the historical antecedents of the story, she further highlights the way in which the story serves as a foundational myth legitimating violence against women. Thistlethwaite reaches back to an earlier Middle-Eastern myth—the story of Marduk and Tiamat in the Babylonian creation myth, the *Enuma Elish*. In this story, Tiamat is the salt-waters; out of her mingling with Apsu, the fresh waters, the first generation of gods and goddesses emerge. Through a complicated series of conflicts, however, Tiamat becomes the primordial agent of chaos, as she threatens to destroy the younger gods and goddesses. The warrior-hero Marduk rises up to defend the younger gods and goddesses: he does so by killing his Grandmother Tiamat. He then splits her body into two pieces, creating the world as sky and waters. This new order of things is reflected in a new social order—a patriarchal hierarchy ruled by Marduk. In this way, the *Enuma Elish* establishes what Rosemary Radford Ruether sees as "the essential dualism of patriarchal religion" (Ruether 1975, 194, in Thistlethwaite 1989b, 63).

More carefully, the story establishes on the level of *myth* a fundamental chaos/order theme characteristic of patriarchal religion. Simply, the primordial female Tiamat is now portrayed as a source of chaos which threatens an emerging order—an order that will quickly become defined as the patriarchal/hierarchical social system of kingship. Moreover, violence is central to establishing this order: specifically, male violence against chaos—represented by Marduk's murder and dissection of the "monstrous" and uncontrollable Tiamat, the primordial female and creatrix—is justified for the sake of establishing this order. Indeed, as the story continues, Marduk establishes guardians at the boundaries of the newly created world to prevent the salt-waters from rushing back in. That is, the feminine remains as the chaos agent who threatens the (patriarchal) order of things: should this continued threat to (patriarchal) order emerge, violence against the feminine will once again be called for.

As Thistlethwaite observes (following the analysis of Catherine Keller), this *mythic* chaos/order theme then functions as a story which is used to legitimate *real* violence: as myth, the *Enuma Elish* justifies first of all the political violence of the Sumero-Akkadian kingdoms (represented by Marduk in the story) against indigenous peoples (represented by Tiamat and the threat of chaos). Again, such violence is mythically justified as it is necessary to establish and preserve (hierarchical) order against the threat of chaos (Thistlethwaite 1989b, 64). In short, as the story establishes the chaos/order theme characteristic of Middle-Eastern myth, it thus works on the social and political level to legitimate "the patriarchal culture of violence" (1989b, 64). Simply, order (mythically defined as the patriarchal/hierarchical social system of kingship) is threatened by the feminine as chaos (represented by Tiamat, the primordial female). The male warrior-hero attains his position of dominance through violence against the female, and the threat of further violence against her should she unleash chaos against his order again. *The mythic image of the female as* essentially *chaos agent is hence crucial if the story is to justify violence*: the myth justifies male violence for the sake of preserving order (in the form of patriarchal/hierarchical kingship), over against the disorder threatened by the female as primordial chaos agent.

This image of the female as chaos agent who threatens male hierarchies, and the validation of violence against her, inhabits the myth of both the ancient and modern worlds. In the ancient *Gilgamesh* epic, for example, Ishtar (goddess of love and war) is attracted to the warrior-hero Gilgamesh and wants him as her husband. Gilgamesh rebuffs her, citing a litany of her lovers whom she has abandoned and destroyed. In her anger, Ishtar threatens vengeance in the form of chaos: she will bring famine, and overturn the boundaries between the dead and the living. She unleashes the Bull of Heaven, a beast whose very snort destroys hundreds of men. Gilgamesh and his companion Enkidu meet this threat with violence: they kill the Bull of Heaven with their swords (Tablet VI, pp. 51–55). In short, Ishtar, the erotically-charged chaos agent, can only be controlled through male violence.[4]

Similarly, in Homer's *Odyssey* the goddess Kalypso and the "witch" Kirke are primary obstacles to Odysseus in his effort to return home. In particular, Kirke attempts to seduce Odysseus, as part of her plan to castrate him and then magically transform him into an animal; in response, Odysseus draws his sword on her, forces her to swear an oath to do him no harm, and only then enters her bed (Bk. X, ll. 292–379., pp. 173–76). The erotically aggressive Kirke—the chaos agent who threatens the order of male dominance—is hence mastered only by the threat of male violence.

In the same way, Klytaimnestra is pictured in Greek myth as the primordial bad wife, the one whose adulterous liaison with Aigisthos and murder of her returning husband Agamemnon signals the end of "the day of faithful wives" (Bk. XI, l. 504, p. 200). Over against this absolute violation of patriarchy, Klytaimnestra (and her lover Aigisthos) in turn must be killed by her son Orestes, just so as to restore patriarchal order. Again, the erotically aggressive female functions as a chaos agent—one whose violation of male control can only be answered with violence.

This image of the female as the chaos agent who threatens male control —and the violence against women it justifies—continues to appear in the literatures of Western cultures and thrives in contemporary culture. As but one example, the sea-witch Ursula in *The Little Mermaid* is the source of chaos who directly threatens the rule of King Triton; her threat is ended only as Prince Eric impales her with the (phallic) bowsprit of a ship. This destruction of the female chaos agent then makes possible Triton's transformation of his daughter Ariel into a human wife for Prince Eric, thus firmly establishing her under the control of her male. The same image of the female—especially the Ishtar/Kirke image of females as "erotically charged," as taking sexual initiative and thus threatening the control and dominance of males—drives films such as *Fatal Attraction*.

Given the prominence of this feminine chaos/male violence-order theme throughout Western tradition and in contemporary culture, it is not surprising to see this theme in the Eve myth as well, as Thistlethwaite and others suggest (cf. Phillips, chap. 1; Sarna, 21–22). On this reading, patriarchal order is established from the beginning in the form of a God who creates the man, a garden, the animals, and then the woman. A fledgling hierarchy is suggested by God's prohibition against eating of the fruit of the tree of knowledge: that is, God will retain the knowledge of good and evil, over against the humans who lack it. The disruption of this hierarchy is suggested by the serpent, who informs the woman that upon eating the fruit, "you will become like gods, knowing both good and evil" (Gen. 3:5). The woman does so: she emerges as a chaos agent who blurs the hierarchical boundary between divine knower and the now-knowing humans. Indeed, God acknowledges that "the man has become like one of us, knowing good and evil, and now, lest he put forth his hand and take also of the tree of life, and eat, and live for ever" (Gen. 3:22). That is, God appears to fear the possibility of the hierarchical boundary between divine and human dissolving entirely if the humans acquire the second divine characteristic, that of everlasting life. In the face of this threat to (hierarchical) order, God acts decisively to preempt such a complete collapse of hierarchy: God banishes the couple from the Garden, and reinforces the ban with the threat of (male) violence, with the threat of "a flaming sword" (Gen. 3:27).

The near Middle-Eastern context of Genesis 2–3 may suggest that we understand the story of Eve as a chaos/order myth which directly justifies male violence against women. Read in this way, the story mythically defines the primordial woman—and hence all women—as agents of chaos who threaten the male order of hierarchy and patriarchy. The story further portrays violence against the primordial woman—and hence all women—as justified, precisely as such violence is intended to preserve hierarchy and patriarchy against the chaos threatened by the female.

Understood in this way, the story can directly serve to excuse the batterer's use of violence to maintain control and order—understood precisely as male control over a subordinate female. Understood in this way, the story directly supports batterers' "patriarchal belief system [which] grants them the privilege and power to enforce their expectations on their partners, using violence if necessary."[5]

But as Ruether points out, the myth of Eve which legitimates violence against women is *not* necessarily the story of Genesis 2–3, so much as it is an *interpretation* of that story by much later, especially Christian, writers. In fact, a cluster of interpretations of Genesis 2–3 have emerged in the West which, like the reading in 1 Timothy and the view of the Garden as a chaos/order story, both define our understanding of woman, and provide fundamental justifications for violence against women. Those of us concerned with the problem of violence against women must then ask: is Genesis 2–3 best understood as a legitimating myth of patriarchy and violence against women—or does the text support different readings, readings which may in fact work to condemn such patriarchy and violence?

In the following, I pursue two ways of seeing central flaws in the interpretations of Genesis 2–3 which support violence against women. One, the history of these interpretations makes clear that much of these readings results from additions to and revisions of the story drawn from much later cultural beliefs and political contexts. In particular, we will see that the image of woman as chaos agent—the image found in early Middle Eastern story—is overlaid on the woman in Genesis 2–3 by later interpreters, precisely in order to develop a reading which mythically justifies the social and political subordination of women in their day. This history suggests, then, that such readings may not be well grounded in the story itself (Section II).

Two, these later, especially Christian, interpretations are countered by recent archaeology and biblical scholarship. Indeed, these contemporary revisions of Eve provide a much different understanding of Eve and of her relationship to the man than is portrayed in later interpretations: this Eve emerges as intelligent and productive, as the equal and complement of the man. On these readings, patriarchal submission and violence are exceptions to and distortions of the rule of equality. In light of these re-visions, to use the myth of Eve to justify violence against women emerges as an unjustifiable *misuse* of the texts.

II. Genesis 2–3 and Its Interpretations

Early History

In her extensive effort to understand the Genesis story in the context of ancient Near Eastern myth and society, Carol Meyers begins by emphasizing the *mythic* function of the story—that is, how the character of Eve works to define our understanding of woman: "Portrayed as the first woman, Eve in fact symbolizes all women. She stands alone of her sex, signifying to all others in times to come the essence of female existence" (3).[6]

At the same time, however, our received understanding of Eve, shaped as it is over millennia by diverse social conditions and requirements, is at odds with the Genesis narrative itself. Meyers begins to develop this point by observing that

Her story is so well known that it is somewhat surprising to find that in the rest of the Hebrew Bible, the story of Eden is not a prominent theme. Neither are the actions of Adam and Eve ever cited as examples of disobedience and punishment, although the long story of Israel's recurrent rejection of God's word and will provides plentiful opportunity for drawing such analogies. (3)

In particular, Meyers points out that

Apart from the early chapters of Genesis, there is in the Hebrew Bible no mention of Eve. Other figures or events, such as the Patriarchs or the Exodus, are often mentioned subsequent to the original narration of their stories. But Eve does not resurface at all in Hebrew scripture and is certainly not a dominant figure in the Israelite canon. (74)

In fact, the story attains prominence only in early Judaism and Christianity—specifically, Rabbinic material, the Christian Scriptures (New Testament), and the Apocryphal and Pseudepigraphical writings.

More carefully, Eve first reappears in the Apocryphal work Ecclesiasticus (Wisdom of Ben Sira). Apparently referring to Eve, Eccles. 25:24 reads: "From a woman was the beginning of sin, / And because of her we all died." Meyers observes that "In associating sin with Eve, Ben Sira was probably taking a minority position because his contemporaries tended to ascribe sin either to Adam or, on the basis of Gen. 6:1–4, to the fall of evil angels and their cohabitation with women" (75). This interpretation, as it identifies sin and death as the negative consequences of the woman's act (75), clearly recasts the woman in the role of a chaos agent: she is the one who is responsible for the entrance of sin and death into the world. While at the time this reading of the woman as such a chaos agent stands as a minority view, it nonetheless provides the foundation for what will become a widely shared—and, in Christian tradition, orthodox—interpretation of the narrative.

From here, the reading of Eve as the sole agent in bringing about sin and suffering into creation is expressed in Jewish pseudepigraphical works (*The Books of Adam and Eve* and the *Apocalypse of Moses*,) dating from the first century B.C.E. This reading—reinforced by a Greek (specifically Orphic and Platonic) conception of a "Fall"—then enters the conceptual vocabularies of early Christian communities, as can be seen in the now familiar passage from 1 Tim. 2:12–14 (Meyers, 74–75). As Meyers points out, however, the "imported" (my phrase) Greek notion of a "Fall" of heavenly beings who shed their divine perfections in order to be born as human beings runs entirely counter to the Genesis narrative, "where the first pair are creatures of earth and not of heaven. Thus, it is more appropriate to drop the term 'Fall' from any reference to the story in its Hebraic context" (77).

Nonetheless, this intrusion of Greek thought into the interpretation of the narrative directly contributes to the foundational myth of domestic violence. As this putative "Fall" is further conjoined with an image of the woman as temptress, the woman comes to represent a "cluster" of negative values—sin, sexuality, and lust; the woman hence emerges even more clearly as a threaten-ing, now erotically-charged chaos agent. As with her mythic cousins Ishtar and Kirke, this Eve justifies male dominance, control, and, by implication, violence. As Meyers puts it, ". . . the more Eve is identified as the source of sin, the more urgent becomes the need to control, subdue, and dominate her. Eve is seen as representative of her sex, and thus all women are regarded as requiring subjugation to wiser and superior male figures" (76).

But this re-vision of Eve into the erotically-charged chaos agent, who thereby stands as the mythically legitimate victim of male violence, emerges only in a much different time and place than the context of the original story. As Meyers notes, "nearly a thousand years after the original shaping of the Eden story, Eve's role is recast by the beliefs and needs of the nascent Jewish and Christian communities in the Roman world" (3). This reading of the story, in fact, squares precisely with the social condition of women in the Israel of first century B.C.E. through the Diaspora. Briefly, Meyers argues that the Genesis narrative bespeaks "egalitarian values and pat-terns" (188) marking the condition of women in Israel prior to the monar-chy (tenth century B.C.E.). By contrast, the interpretation which reads the Genesis narrative as a story of female inferiority and sinfulness (tied to sex-uality and lust) reflects the condition of women brought about by the monarchy, the Babylonian Exile (sixth century B.C.E.)—and the absorption of a Greco-Roman culture, which includes such notions as a "Fall" and associated dualisms which aligned good with male and soul, and evil with female and body.[7] Eve as the mythic archetype, Meyers concludes, is

> . . . the victim of this alignment: female was linked with body and evil. Relegated to a position of decreasing power as the household lost its prominence, she then became associated with negative aspects of life. . . . A new concept of Eve associated with sin, death, and suffering is superim-posed so indelibly on the assertive and productive figure of the Eden nar-rative that we can hardly see the original woman of Genesis 2–3. (196)

This reading, she goes on to describe, is further embedded in both transla-tions of the Hebrew Bible (beginning with the Latin Vulgate) and the works of Milton (76–77).

Perhaps the single most important source in Western tradition for the image of Eve as (sexual) temptress and cause of sin is Augustine, the fourth-century theologian whose work powerfully shapes and defines Christian belief in both Roman Catholic and Protestant traditions. Augustine both develops the interpretation of the woman in Genesis 2–3 as the primary source of sin, and makes this interpretation a foundational element of what becomes the orthodox doctrine of Original Sin. In this way, Augustine embeds in Christian orthodoxy an image of the primordial woman which serves as a myth justifying the subordination of the female—especially as the female functions as a chaos agent who threatens male hierarchies.

At the same time, however, the Augustinian reading of Genesis 2–3 emerges only in conflict with alternative views held by other significant

Christian theologians. By examining how Augustine's interpretation further develops the image of the woman which justifies her subordination, and how this interpretation contrasts with competing Christian views, we will see how the Augustinian reading is an interpretation of Genesis 2–3 open to debate within Christian circles. This debate over the interpretation of Genesis 2–3 will then prepare us to turn to contemporary readings of Eve which expose the Augustinian interpretation as indeed an interpretation shaped more by the social and political context of Augustine's day than by the contexts of the original text. Both the debate over the Augustinian reading of Eve in the fourth century, and contemporary re-readings of Genesis 2–3 work together to suspend the reading of Eve as properly subordinate to man, as the legitimate victim of male violence as she threatens male control; indeed, this interpretation will be replaced by contemporary readers who see in Genesis 2–3 a story which powerfully *contradicts* the Augustinian reading—and thereby eliminates the myth of Eve which can be used to justify male violence against women.

Augustine and the Doctrine of Original Sin

It is worth noting that in the Christian Scriptures, Jesus refers to the Genesis narrative only once—and that in order to criticize the Mosaic law as it permitted men to divorce their wives (Matt. 19:4–6). In the larger context of Jesus' other teachings and encounters with women, Jesus' move here can be seen as part of his critique of patriarchy and the liberation of women into standing and roles equal to those of men (see Carmody, 163–64). On this view, the Jesus movement and the early Christian communities exemplified "radically egalitarian" attitudes and practices, which eroded only as Christianity began to appropriate the hierarchical and patriarchal arrangements of the larger Hellenistic world (Carmody, 166, with reference to Schüssler Fiorenza).

Three centuries later, Augustine appropriates both Paul—including 1 Tim. 2:12–14[8]—and Manichean dualism (Pagels, 99, 106) so as to read the Genesis story in ways very different from both Jesus and even Augustine's contemporary Christians. Augustine's reading is then woven into his doctrine of Original Sin—where this doctrine tightly associates the woman, as the primary agent responsible for introduction of sin and suffering into the world, with temptation and sexuality (Ruether 1974, 156; Ralph, 146–64).

Elaine Pagels carefully examines Augustine's doctrine of Original Sin, especially in light of the larger social and political contexts of fourth century Christianity. Briefly, Pagels points to John Chrysostom's reading of the Genesis story, as it stresses that human beings—both male and female—are not *intrinsically* sinful, as Augustine would have it. Rather, we are each individually responsible for our own sinful acts, where these sins may further be forgiven. Such a reading appears to reflect the understanding of the Genesis story in early Christianity, when Christianity existed primarily in *opposition* to the larger culture—for example, in its apparent practice of gender equality (see Carmody, 160; Gritz, chap. 4). Such a Christianity thus stressed the importance of individual freedom and autonomy, including the ability to oppose the larger culture by disobeying its norms and expectations (including obedience to a monarch in a hierarchical, militaristic empire). Such a reading, moreover, closely follows earlier Jewish understandings of the story (see Plaut, 38).

By contrast, Augustine's reading more neatly fits the social and political context of Christianity in the fourth century, when Christianity becomes endorsed by now-Christian emperors, beginning with the conversion of Constantine in 313 C.E. That is, Augustine's teaching of Original Sin emphasizes the intrinsically sinful nature of human beings, beginning with the woman as the primary agent responsible for the introduction of sin into the world—first of all, in the example of her *disobedience* to the authority of God. In addition, what Pagels characterizes as the "alarmingly autonomous" passion of male sexuality, as experienced (and regretted) by Augustine, becomes both the primary *example* and *metaphor* of disobedience and rebellion (in a dualistic fashion, as the rebellion of the body against reason and soul), and the primary *punishment* for disobedience in the Garden (see Pagels, 107; for a still more careful consideration of Augustine's reading of the Genesis story, see Clark, 353–85). Augustine's teaching, by lifting up *disobedience* as the primary sin, thus renders *obedience* to *authority* as the highest virtue, whether the authority in question is God, monarch, or husband. Rather than stressing human freedom in ways consistent with especially the gender equality practiced by Christian communities in the first generation (as in the reading of Chrysostom and earlier Christians), Augustine's reading of the story, as incorporated in the doctrine of Original Sin, thus serves as a foundational myth which sacralizes both a patriarchal relationship between the sexes (justified by the woman's responsibility for sin and suffering, and her apparent inferiority and subordination to the man in the order of creation) and the hierarchical politics of monarchy and empire.[9] Indeed, Augustine largely assumes the late Roman understanding of the father as the center of power and authority in the family—an understanding which entails the use of corporal punishment, including whipping children and slaves (Shaw, 11–18, 23–24, 28–32). While Augustine himself may have opposed wife abuse, his teaching on Original Sin nonetheless serves as a primary source for the patriarchal myth which portrays the woman as a threatening chaos agent, who must hence be controlled by violence for the sake of preserving patriarchal authority and domination.

III: Contemporary Scholarship and the Re-Vision of Eve

These readings of Genesis—of woman as chaos agent, associated with sexuality and sin, who requires male control—establish a myth defining woman which dominates contemporary culture. Phyllis Trible has articulated the elements of this contemporary myth, of what she takes to be "the standard account" of Genesis 2–3 for both those who affirm and those who oppose the myth. Those elements most pertinent to a mythic foundation for domestic violence include:

(1) Woman is created for the sake of man: a helpmate to cure his loneliness (2:18–23).

(2) Woman tempted man to disobey and thus she is responsible for sin in the world (3:6); she is untrustworthy, gullible, and simpleminded.

(3) A male God creates first man (2:7) and last woman (2:22); first means superior and last means inferior or subordinate.

(4a) Woman's desire for man (3:16) is God's way of keeping her faithful and submissive to her husband.

(4b) God gives man the right to rule over woman (3:16).

(5) Man names woman (2:23) and thus has power over her.[10]

Trible's analysis of the story argues that "not one of these elements are accurate and most of them are simply not present in the story itself" (1978, 73). For Trible, the Genesis story is centrally "a love story gone awry," one concerned with the discovery of human sexuality and the adverse consequences of the disobedience intertwined with that discovery (139). She then turns to the Song of Songs, where the "tragedy" of human sexuality—bound up with the woman's *desire* in Gen. 3:16—is redeemed in another "garden of Eros" (144; cf. Meyers, 110–11).

More generally, we can examine each of these elements in light of contemporary scholarship—primarily, the work of Trible, Meyers, Tikva Frymer-Kensky, and Ilana Pardes. We will find that Meyers, Frymer-Kensky, and Pardes reiterate Trible's contention that each of these elements (as the history of the reinterpretation of Genesis 2–3 suggests) is at best an *interpretation*—an interpretation, moreover, not grounded in the text. And, as these elements of the standard account are refuted, they are replaced by more accurate readings of the story—by re-visions of the character of Eve as more originally understood in the story. We will see that this "new/old" Eve is *not* presented as the chaos agent who must be tamed and controlled into submission by her husband/master. Rather, she emerges as the intelligent and productive counterpart to the man, with whom she is to stand in egalitarian and complementary relationship. In this light, the foundational myth of domestic violence—of Eve as the erotically-charged chaos agent, whom the myth thus justifies as the legitimate victim of male violence for the sake of preserving hierarchical order—has no ground in the original story. In this light, the use of such a reading of Eve to excuse domestic violence is shown to contradict the original context and sense of the story.

(1) WOMAN IS CREATED FOR THE SAKE OF MAN: A HELPMATE TO CURE HIS LONELINESS (2:18–23). Over against this interpretation, Trible and Meyers point out that when the "earthling" (so Trible's suggestion for 'adam: see below) is divided into male and female, the female element is created as 'ezer. Translating this term as "helper" easily falls (!) into the Augustinian reading, insofar as "helper" may be thought to be a subordinate or inferior. But such a translation, in Trible and Meyers' view, is not required by either the term or the context. Rather, 'ezer is also used in the Hebrew Bible to speak of God as "helper" to those in distress (e.g., Ps. 121:1–2). As well, the prepositional

phrase *neged* which joins *'ezer* in Gen. 2:18 and 20 is taken to connote equality, so that the phrase more precisely means "a helper who is a counterpart" (Trible 1992, 75; Meyers, 85).[11]

(2) WOMAN TEMPTED MAN TO DISOBEY AND THUS SHE IS RESPONSIBLE FOR SIN IN THE WORLD (3:6); SHE IS UNTRUSTWORTHY, GULLIBLE, AND SIMPLEMINDED. We have already seen that this reading emerges only in the Apocryphal and Pseudepigraphical writings. Meyers further observes that there is no mention of the term "sin" in Genesis 3, nor does the Hebrew Bible ever associate later sins with the acts of the man and the woman in the Garden (87–88). Rather, if we attend to the fact that "perhaps the most prominent theme word in the Eden tale is . . . the root *'kl*, 'to eat'," the story primarily reflects "the Israelite struggle for sustenance as a dominating concern of daily life" (89).

Frymer-Kensky counters this interpretation even more powerfully. On her reading, the Bible—including the story of Adam and Eve—is remarkable for its *failure* to attribute to women the "several strategies and powers that became associated with women in Western cultural tradition" (140). These include precisely the notion of woman as an erotically-charged chaos agent—one who uses her beauty and sexuality as a weapon of power. Beauty, Frymer-Kensky points out, is never presented as a woman's weapon, but only as "a mark of divine favor, as is the beauty of men" (140). Similarly,

> The biblical tales of women's persuasion also ignore erotic attraction. There are no stories of sexual enticement, no femmes fatales, no figures like Mata Hari who use sex to seduce and then deceive men. . . . The Bible never considers eros a tool of women, as something against which men should guard. The Bible does not present beauty and lust—both of which might tend to emphasize the differences between male and female and to codify the woman as "other"—as part of a woman's toolkit at all. (140–41)

In contrast with the later reading which would have the woman marked as *different* from the man, as her putative beauty and eros distinguish her from him, Frymer-Kensky sees the Bible "homogenizing" gender. In particular, she sees the creation of Eve as a story expressing "the essential similarity between male and female in biblical thought. . . ." (141) As she points out, this essential similarity echoes the first story of Creation in Genesis 1, where both male and female are created as the image of God. Moreover, she emphasizes that this notion of gender equality distinguishes the biblical story from other Mesopotamian story, which stresses the difference between male and female by establishing gods and goddesses for whom the only appropriate companions are divine beings of the *same*, not different, gender (i.e., the male Enkidu for the male Gilgamesh in the *Epic of Gilgamesh*, and the female Saltu for the female Ishtar in "The Hymn of Saltu": 142). Indeed, Frymer-Kensky argues that the gender equality of the biblical story is appropriate to the radical monotheism of Israel: the conception of one God excludes the gender differentiation represented by diverse male and female divinities (142–43).

On Frymer-Kensky's reading, then, the later efforts we have seen to read Mesopotamian motifs onto the woman of Genesis 2–3—including precisely the Ishtar image of the female as erotically-charged chaos agent, who is thus radically differentiated from the male as agent of (violent) control and (hierarchical) order—obliterate crucial differences between the biblical story and its Middle-Eastern counterparts. Such readings, simply, impose images of gender differentiation, tied to polytheism, onto a story of monotheism and gender equality.

(3) A MALE GOD CREATES FIRST MAN (2:7) AND LAST WOMAN (2:22); FIRST MEANS SUPERIOR AND LAST MEANS INFERIOR OR SUBORDINATE. We have already seen this reading of the story, as reflected in the passage from 1 Timothy, countered by Ruether and Gritz. Meyers and Trible attack this point in two additional ways.

To begin with, contrary to the reading that *man*—in the sense of a person of male gender—was created first (and thus somehow stands in a position of superiority), Meyers emphasizes that the Hebrew term '*adam* is better translated as a generic term, such as "humanity," which is understood to incorporate *both* male and female (81). In particular, '*adam*, as a pun with '*adamah* ("ground" or "earth"), reflects the origin and essence of humanity as made from the earth (suggesting "earthling" as a still better translation for '*adam*: 81; cf. Trible 1978, 76–81).

Secondly, the *order* of creation by no means connotes a movement from superior to inferior. Rather, as an *inclusio* or ring composition commonly used in Hebrew literature, the beginning and end are presented as parallels or complements (Trible 1992, 75). Meyers expands on Trible's suggestion this way:

> In Genesis 2 the ring, or cyclic, structure of creation is completed by the differentiation of human life into complementary female and male beings. Only now do specifically gendered words appear in the narrative, and only now are the creative acts of Yahweh complete. The creation of humanity in its sexually nuanced form brings to an end the sequence of creation begun when God took up a formless clod of earth and formed a human being. (85)

In light of these and other considerations, Meyers sees Genesis 2 as establishing complementary male and female roles in a marital relationship (85–86).

Finally, Mieke Bal counters the Pauline reading of Genesis 2–3 sketched out in 1 Tim.: 2:11–15, by closely attending to the "construction of character" in the Yahwist account. Like Trible, Bal sees in '*adam* a sexless "earth creature," a "character-to-be" (112; Pardes, 29). From the viewpoint of semiotics, sexual differentiation takes place in the story as the *woman* is formed first, then the man. And, as Pardes paraphrases, "Although man is the first to speak and differentiate, the woman is the first to be differentiated" (30). This issues in what Bal sees as an "equalizing dialectic," in which "man and woman mutually constitute one another, and in this respect they are created at the same time" (Pardes, 30). On this reading, the Yahwist account hence narrates events echoing the equality implied in the Priestly account (Gen. 1:26–31), as it observes that "God created them male and female" (Bal, 119; Pardes, 30).

As the narrative continues:

> When woman finally chooses to disobey and eats from the fruit of the
> tree of knowledge, she performs the first independent act, promoting her
> status in the narrative. The feature this act entails for the woman (and
> eventually for her mate) is wisdom. . . . Wisdom, in this case, means hav-
> ing the ability to accept the human condition—namely, sexuality and
> death—being realistic, opting for the species immortality instead of an
> impossible individual mode of immortality. (Pardes, 30)

This celebration of the woman's act echoes Trible's characterization of the
woman as acting courageously, driven by an (ostensibly laudable) interest in
wisdom (Pardes, 24; Trible 1992, 79).

In fact, Meyers argues that Genesis 3 belongs to the genre of Hebrew
wisdom literature which, as exemplified by the books of Job, Ecclesiastes, and
some Psalms, "deals with the meaning of the paradoxes and harsh facts of
life" (91). In particular,

> The prominent role of the female rather than the male in the wisdom
> aspects of the Eden tale is a little-noticed feature of the narrative. It is the
> woman, and not the man, who perceives the desirability of procuring
> wisdom. The woman, again not the man, is the articulate member of the
> first pair who engages in dialogue even before the benefits of the wisdom
> tree have been procured. (91)

The association here between the female and wisdom emerges for a number of readers (including Trible, as Meyers notes) as an echo of a wisdom
goddess (91). While such an association is problematic,[12] where Wisdom is
personified in Proverbs (and in the Apocryphal works) as a woman, "The
Genesis text serves as preparation for what is to come in the portrayal of
Woman Wisdom, of various wise women, and of women acting wisely" (91).

In this light, the "poetic oracles" which constitute God's judgments on
the serpent, the woman (3:16), and the man emerge as explanations of the
difficult conditions of life imposed upon men and women who undertake an
agrarian-based existence in the arid highlands of Palestine (91–94). That is, as
we are about to see, the husband's apparent dominance over his wife in 3:16
is the *exception* to the rule of gender equality—an equality suggested by the
prominence of the woman in the narrative (read as ring structure), in her *priority* in the creation of man (Bal), and her apparent role as the wisdom figure
who acquires important knowledge regarding the human condition.

(4A) WOMAN'S DESIRE FOR MAN (3:16) IS GOD'S WAY OF KEEPING HER
FAITHFUL AND SUBMISSIVE TO HER HUSBAND. (4B) GOD GIVES MAN THE RIGHT TO
RULE OVER WOMAN (3:16). Meyers devotes an entire chapter to a close read-
ing of the four-line oracle delivered to the woman at Gen. 3:16. She notes
that the history of translation of this text in the West, beginning with the
Septuagint (the oldest translation of the Hebrew Bible) and Jerome's
Vulgate, and concluding with several contemporary translations, appears to
incorporate at least one element of the now-suspect reading of the Genesis

story—namely, the subordination of the woman to the man (95). Turning to the text itself, she observes that the four lines break into two two-line units; in each unit, the parallelism between each line reflects and amplifies the meaning of the other (98–99). After careful consideration of each word and its possible meanings and usages, she proposes the following translation:

> I will greatly increase your toil and your pregnancies (105).
> (Along) with travail shall you beget children (108).
> For to your man is your desire,
> And he shall predominate over you (118).

Briefly, Meyers understands the first two lines as a wisdom teaching, from which the audience—the man and woman—are not told simply

> that women work and have children. Rather, they are learning that the work is unremitting and is not mitigated by the procreative demands placed on female existence. Moreover, they are learning . . . that the fulfillment of God's charge does not automatically entitle one to bliss and joy, that anguish is inevitably an accompaniment to the carrying out of life's tasks. (108)

In this way, the first two lines "depict an intensification of two main aspects of female existence: an increase of work load and of procreative responsibilities" (111)—an intensification which matches the requirements for social survival in the relatively harsh environment of the Palestinian highlands, including, according to archaeology, a high infant mortality rate (111–13). For Meyers, the text further implies a reluctance on the part of the woman to assume such an intensification of her labor and responsibilities (110). Yet, as the third line announces, she nonetheless experiences "desire" (*tesuqa*) for the man. Meyers considers the use of *tesuqa* in both Genesis 4 and the Song of Songs, and takes it to mean "A strong urge of one being for another. . . an emotional and/or physical attraction that transcends thought and rationality." As such, it appropriately designates what she sees as "the sexual nature of the mutual attraction of a female and a male" (111).[13]

Following the lead of Medieval Jewish commentators, Meyers then sees the man's "rule" in line 4 to be restricted precisely "within the context of the female's 'desire' for the male. As such, those words do *not* constitute a general assertion of male dominion" (114). In short:

> . . . lines 3 and 4 together should be understood as responses to the situation established by lines 1 and 2. Women have to work hard and have many children, as lines 1 and 2 proclaim; their reluctance to conform, which is not explicitly stated but can be reconstructed by looking at the biological and socioeconomic realities of ancient Palestine, had to be overcome. Lines 3 and 4 tell us how: female reluctance is overcome by the passion they feel toward their men, and that allows them to accede to the male's sexual advances even though they realize that undesired pregnancies (with the accompanying risks) might be the consequence. (117)

More generally, this oracle to the woman parallels that addressed to the man, who must also work hard to eat (Gen. 3:17–19). Indeed, given that the poetic oracles (including the one addressed to the serpent) are textually distinct elements, it is possible to read them as earlier elements which are only later incorporated in the prose framework. On this reading, however, the oracles themselves are not "punishments" but simply etiologies or explanations of human existence which indeed fits the social conditions and inhospitable soils of ancient Palestine (118). (Indeed, the prose framework concludes with its own punishment, namely the expulsion from the Garden. This means that the poetic oracles, as textually distinct from the prose framework, are further not required to express some string of "punishments," because that task has already been accomplished by the prose material. Hence, to read them as punishments is to project upon them an alien meaning—one belonging properly only to the prose framework.)

In this way, Gen. 3:16 emerges for Meyers as clearly *not* a text which originally establishes a mythic archetype of the woman as uniquely responsible for sin, nor as "punished" for disobedience by being placed in a patriarchal relationship of male dominance and female submission. Rather, the text indeed operates as a foundational myth, one defining the female role and the value of that role: simply, it articulates a cultural value which encourages increased conceptions in a context where population growth is indeed mandated for survival; at the same time, the oracles delivered to both the woman and the man establish "complementary life roles for the archetypal couple . . ." (119), a complementarity which Meyers later argues as the likely social structure of early Israel (see esp. 168–88).

(5) Man names woman (2:23) and thus has power over her. Pardes begins her analysis with the observation that whatever differences may be found among various feminist commentators on the creation of woman, their readings are largely confined to Genesis 1–3. She rightly points out that Genesis 1–3 are part of a larger "primeval history," one which ends at Genesis 11. Pardes attributes the relatively arbitrary focus on Genesis 1–3 to the continuing influence of the Christian (as we have seen, Augustinian) reading of Genesis 3 as a Fall which concludes Creation. As we have also seen, however, Genesis does not immediately support the Augustinian reading. Rather, as Pardes puts it:

> There is, however, no concept of an Original Fall in Genesis. Primeval characters fall time and again in a variety of ways. The first fall is not singled out. Fratricide, sleeping with the Sons of God, incest, and the building of the Tower of Babel are transgressions as exemplary as the eating of the forbidden fruit. Similarly, creation is an ongoing process. The world is wholly destroyed and recreated in the story of the Flood; and on a less cosmic level, this is true of most stories in this unit. (39–40)

In particular, Eve does not disappear after Genesis 3; rather she rises and falls "once again" in Genesis 4 (Pardes, 40). Pardes develops her reading of Genesis 2–3 in light of the larger context established by further examining

Genesis 4–5. In this way, her interpretation forcefully makes the point that while feminist critics such as Stanton, Millett, Mary Daly, Trible, and Bal have sharply attacked patriarchal, especially Christian readings of the Genesis stories—so as to "provocatively turn the story of man's Fall through woman (as in Paul's reading) into the story of woman's Fall through man. . . ." (40)—these critiques, by remaining within the largely arbitrary boundary of Genesis 3, remain within the larger framework of Christian (especially Augustinian) readings.

Central to Pardes' reading is the observation that in Gen. 4:1, "Eve, who previously was an object of naming, becomes a subject of naming." Pardes takes up Cassuto's translation of Eve's naming-speech, "I have created a man [equally/together] with the Lord" (Cassuto, 198, in Pardes, 40). Pardes thus corrects, for example, Mary Daly (1973) who takes naming as exclusively the power of Adam, and goes on to point out that in fact, in the Hebrew Bible there are many more cases of maternal naming-speeches (eighteen) than paternal naming-speeches (eight: see 41; 163 n. 2). Contra Bal (and others) who see Adam's naming of Eve as the Fall of woman which further seals her sexual and social role (defined in Gen. 3:16), Pardes thus argues that "Eve's impressive comeback as a name-giver in Genesis 4—and not the emergence of the proper name 'Eve'—is the final stroke in the formation of the first female character" (41).

A naming-speech, moreover, "usually reveals more about the character of the name-giver than the recipient" (41)—a claim which allows Pardes to exploit Eve's naming-speech to more fully develop the character of Eve, especially "as it offers a glimpse of her own perception of motherhood and (pro)creation" (42). Briefly, Pardes follows Cassuto's reading of the text:

> The first woman, in her joy at giving birth to her son, boasts of her generative power, which approximates in her estimation to the Divine creative power. The Lord formed the first *man* (ii 7), and I have formed the second *man . . . I stand together (i.e., equally)* WITH HIM *in the rank of creators.*" (201, in Pardes, 44)

Cassuto supports his translation in part by observing that the verb *qnh* in 4:1 is used elsewhere in the Hebrew Bible both to refer to God's creation of the world (Gen. 14:22) and "divine parental procreation" (Ps. 139:13, Prov. 8:22: Pardes 44–45). Cassuto further notes "a Ugaritic parallel in which the same root (*qny* or *qnw*) appears in the title of Ashera, the Ugaritic mother goddess. . . ." (Pardes, 45) This and other findings (Skinner, 102; Kikawada) for Pardes

> reinforce the notion that Eve is endowed with traits which in pagan works characterized the creatress. . . . Eve's naming-speech may be perceived as a trace from an earlier mythological phase in which mother goddesses were very much involved in the process of creation, even if in a secondary position, under the auspices of the supreme male deity. (45)

To claim that a Goddess tradition is echoed here, as we have seen, is problematic. But for Pardes this insight is crucial as it suggests Eve's hubris:

> A speech of this sort cannot but be a bold provocation in a monotheistic context. If a mother goddess—be it Ashera, Aruru, or Miami—had delivered a similar speech, it could have been construed as "factual" or even as a token of modesty, but when the primordial biblical mother, who is a mere human being, claims to have generative powers which are not unlike God's, she is as far from modesty as one can get. (45–46)

For Pardes, Eve's hubris here is consistent with the earlier hubris apparent in her violating God's prohibition, so as to become like gods, knowing good and evil. Indeed, Pardes sees a connection between the two acts:

> If in Genesis 3 she sought to acquire a potential, in Genesis 4 the primordial mother explores the ways in which the knowledge she illegally acquired in the Garden of Eden may be realized. Her hubris is transferred to the realm of creativity. By defining herself as a creatress, she now calls into question the preliminary biblical tenet with respect to (pro)creation—God's position as the one and only Creator. (46)

Eve as a hubristic character, more broadly, places her among the many hubristic figures in the Genesis primeval history. Pardes points out Enoch and Noah, the Daughters of Adam who sleep with the Sons of God, and the people of Babel as instances of primeval characters who "exceed human limits in one way or another" (46). Eve nonetheless stands apart from these figures in that

> . . . her speech is a critique not only of monotheistic principles but also of the underlying patriarchal presuppositions of monotheism. Unlike the inhabitants of Babel . . . the first woman challenges *both* the divine restrictions on human creativity and the exclusion of the feminine from the representation of creation. (47)

In this way, Eve emerges as an instance which illustrates that ". . . while the dominant thrust of the Bible is clearly patriarchal, patriarchy is continuously challenged by antithetical trends" (51). In particular, she sees Eve's naming-speech as "a response to his [Adam's] naming of woman; it is a response to his almost dreamlike reversal of the order of things, to his indirect claim to have created woman out of his body, to his celebration of the generative capacity of his flesh and bones" (47–48). Indeed, Pardes sees in this response a challenge to Adam's "reversal" of sexual roles in Genesis 2 where, especially from a psychoanalytic view as represented in Rank, Freud, Roheim, Fromm, and Horney, the man exclusively "owns" the powers of generation, as he births the woman as his daughter (Pardes, 48–50; cf. Thistlethwaite 1989a, 311). Pardes points out that Adam's naming of woman is in fact

> the only time in the Bible where a man names a newly born female and delivers a speech to celebrate the occasion! Adam's naming of woman,

which has been taken to be representative of male dominion in language, thus turns out to be the exception to the rule. (49)

Given the larger context Pardes stakes out for her reading of Genesis 2–3, she can now turn back to criticize especially Bal's claim that Adam's naming the woman "Eve" thus imprisons her in motherhood. Rather,

> What is most striking about Genesis 2–3 is the extent to which woman is *denied* her role as mother, as creatress, by both God and Adam. She is called the "mother of all living" only at the very end, after all things already have been created by God and the first man. (49)

Rather than an Eve who acquiesces to a prison of motherhood imposed upon her by male powers, the Eve who emerges in Pardes' consideration of Genesis 2–4 celebrates her procreative powers as the basis for challenging both Adam and God:

> In quest of what is lacking in him, Adam seeks to appropriate the (m)other. But Eve doesn't acquiesce in this appropriation. She is not the perfect Other, nor is she a (m)other devoid of subjecthood. First in the Garden of Eden, and then in her naming-speech, the primordial mother challenges the attempts of both God and Adam to be the sole subjects of procreation. (51)

Finally, Pardes considers Eve's second naming-speech in Gen. 4:25, where Eve names her third son "Seth" in a pun referring to God as the sole creator, as the one who grants (*shat*) a seed. Of course, this speech follows Cain's murder of Abel and Cain's banishment—what Pardes sees as a "fall" consequent upon Eve's first and hubristic naming-speech. This circumstance and other features of this speech suggest for Pardes a change in Eve—from her originally hubristic celebration of her creative powers in 4:1 to an acknowledgement of God, no longer as cocreator, but as *the* Creator. Following Cassuto again, Pardes sees here that "Her [Eve's] words now convey respect for the boundaries between the human and divine realms" (52).

Given this reading of Genesis 4, Pardes suggests that this story of a fall between the first and second naming-speeches thus locates the story in "the long list of Yahwistic stories of pride/crime and punishment in primeval history." (53) Pardes is careful, however, to indicate that this reading does not in the end simply replicate the Augustinian notion of a Fall which is squarely the fault of the woman:

> . . . the tragedy which befalls Eve's sons is meant, among other things, as a retributive deflation of her hubris. The son who was the object of her (pro)creative pride turns out to be the destroyer of her creation. This by no means implies that the killing of Abel and the banishment of Cain are Eve's fault; rather it is an indication of the complex interweaving of these two Yahwistic texts. Interestingly, not unlike other stories which pertain to this list (the Garden of Eden, Cain and Abel, and the Flood, for example), destruction is followed by re-creation. The punishment is

followed by a certain reconciliation between God and the "sinner": the first woman receives another son and renders unto God what is His. (53)

This reconciliation, moreover, by no means implies Eve's acquiescence to patriarchal rule and ownership of the powers of procreation:

> Eve's acknowledgement of God's power, however, does not entail an acceptance of Adam's rule. The primordial mother still treats procreation as if it were an outcome of a transaction between God and her alone. Such transactions are a common topic in maternal naming-speeches (see Gen. 30:24; I Sam. 1:20). In a sense they serve as a female counterpart to the long conversations men have with God concerning seed and stars. (53)

Indeed, Pardes argues that Eve's naming-speeches, as her insistence upon her own generative powers, are thus (contra Bal) attempts to dissociate motherhood from the subordination required of her by the "official" hierarchy of patriarchy (God // Adam // Eve): indeed, "By taking pleasure in her creativity she attempts to undo God's punishment in Gen. 3:16, to misread God's linking of female procreation with sorrow and with subjugation to man" (54). This means, interestingly enough, that "the first feminist reader of the creation story is none other than Eve herself" (54).

Conclusion

By developing Thistlethwaite's insight and lead, we have seen that the Genesis 2–3 narrative may in fact be understood as a foundational myth of patriarchy, one which legitimates both the subordination of the female and male violence against her as a chaos agent who threatens the hierarchy of male dominance. This reading, as it depends especially on locating the narrative within the framework of Near Eastern myth, thus reflects and reinforces the reading familiar from Christian orthodoxy—namely, the Augustinian view which again subordinates the woman to the man as it associates her with body and sexuality, and as it accuses her of primary responsibility for introducing sin and death into the world.

This image of woman as chaos agent, we have seen, continues to inhabit modern myth, whether in the form of Ursula the Seawitch, or in the ongoing belief that the woman of Genesis 2–3 is the cause of sin and death in the world, who must be controlled through violence if she seeks to evade male dominance. But this image of the female cannot be grounded in the Genesis story itself. Beyond Phyllis Trible's ground-breaking refutation of the Augustinian interpretation, Carol Meyers, Tikva Frymer-Kensky, and Ilana Pardes seek to establish a reading of the text more carefully defined by both the mythic *and* social contexts of the ancient Near East. Meyers uncovers the poetic couplets of Gen. 3:16—read for millennia as "punishments" which justify, among other things, male dominance over the woman as erotically charged chaos agent—as wisdom oracles independent of the larger narrative framework of disobedience and punishment. These oracles do not articulate divine sanction for patriarchy; rather, they serve as explanations for why *both* woman and man must labor so hard—an explanation befitting the social requirements of life in the hostile environment of ancient Palestine. This reading is reinforced, indeed, radicalized, by Bledstein, who sees the couplets addressed to the woman as a dire warning against the possible domination and violence she may face as the consequence of her desirability.

Pardes likewise helps us break free of the Augustinian reading, as she extends our attention to include Genesis 4. By holding together the Eve of Genesis 2–3 with the Eve of Genesis 4, we see a character emerge whose original hubris—her effort to become like the gods, first through acquiring wisdom and second through creation in the form of reproduction—is overturned by expulsion from the Garden and the death and banishment of her sons. Eve is by no means the only character in the Genesis narrative who learns through hard experience the limits of humanity vis-à-vis the divine. Rather, just as Meyers sees in Eve the beginnings of a "Woman Wisdom" theme in the Hebrew Bible, so Pardes sees in Eve's story the first of a series of "fall" stories in the Hebrew Bible, stories which illustrate precisely the common Middle-Eastern motif of disaster as the natural consequence of hubris, of human beings forgetting their own limits. In this way, the woman is indeed an archetype—but she is an archetype for all humanity, both male and female. In this sense, she is indeed Eve, the Mother of All Living.

In light of these readings, Eve is neither the inferior, erotically-charged chaos agent who stands as the legitimized victim of male violence, nor is she simply "the first feminist" (Pardes) who struggles to maintain an original equality and complementarity against male efforts to subordinate and control her. Rather, as an archetype for the human pursuit of wisdom and our tendency towards hubris, Eve emerges as fully coequal with the man: both are created and contained within the 'earthling,' the earth creature whom Yahweh splits to make into female and male. As partner with her mate in the arduous labor of agrarian society, she glories and sorrows in her additional power—and burden—of reproduction. And perhaps we can see her warned against the further dangers of male dominance and violence, precisely because males will find her "desirable."

Such an Eve clearly escapes the outlines of the narratives presented by Augustine and suggested by Thistlethwaite, narratives which provide the mythic foundations for patriarchy and male violence against women. Such an Eve provides no justification whatever for male violence: she is neither inferior nor any more threatening to the order of things than her male counterpart or her descendants. On the contrary, the narrative as read by Trible, Meyers, Pardes, Frymer-Kensky, and Bledstein, emphasizes her equality with the male. If anything, the explanation as to why she is controlled by the male, but *only* in the domain of reproduction (Meyers), as possibly a warning against the danger of such domination as aroused by her desirability (Bledstein), implies that male dominance and violence are distortions of an intended equality. Indeed, as the explanation only grudgingly admits of male control in the context of a particular need for a population in a given environment, and as an apparent exception in an otherwise egalitarian and complementary relationship between male and female, we may draw the conclusion that such dominance in the domain of reproduction is no longer justified when the social conditions calling it into existence in the first place no longer hold. Especially given this last nuance, the story of the man and the woman in Genesis 2–4 condemns those readings which endorse patriarchy and male violence: such readings are both unsupported by the text and contradicted by its sense.

❧

Notes

I would like to thank Kathleen Clark and Stephen Clark (University of Liverpool, United Kingdom) for help in understanding Augustine; Rev. Peter Sawtell for research assistance; and my colleagues Rev. Dr. Peter Browning (Drury College), Dr. Karen Taylor (Drury College), Dr. Kathy Pulley (Southwest Missouri State University), and Rabbi Rita Sherwin (United Hebrew Congregations, Springfield, Mo.), whose suggestions and careful reading contributed significantly to the scope and clarity of this paper.

1. Battering is purposeful behavior on the part of batterers which serves to establish power and control over their victims. Some batterers may employ the mythology which arises from the Genesis story of Eve (which is reinforced by attitudes and beliefs in the dominant culture) as a rationalization of their behavior. This same rationalization may also be utilized by a victim, family member or outside observer to excuse the batterer's conduct.

2. This philosophical approach to myth, developed in Jung, Levi-Strauss, Mircea Eliade, Joseph Campbell, Alan Watts, and others, is only one among many. For an overview of myth along these lines, see Hall et al, 43–45; Schmidt, chap. 7, "Sacred Stories" (181–206). For a critical discussion of this and other views of myth, see Strenski.

3. Thistlethwaite relates her experience with a battered woman, whose husband justified his violence against her by paraphrasing the Genesis text:

   > This at last is bone of my bones
   >   and flesh of my flesh;
   > she shall be called Woman (*ishshah*)
   > because she was taken out of Man (*ish*).
   > (2:23, RSV)

   The woman's husband took this text to mean that "your bones are my bones," justifying his ownership of his wife's body, and thus justifying his right to abuse her. As this instance suggests, the story of Eve thus works as a fundamental myth, one which suggests that male superiority—in the form of male ownership and control of women's bodies—is "built in" to the nature of things. Understood this way, the story suggests that male ownership and control reflects some divine plan, and in this way, using Thistlethwaite's phrase, the story divinizes male superiority. In doing so, it reinforces "patterns of dominance and submission that legitimate violence against women. . . ." (1989a, 311–12).

At the same time, however, the poetic comment of 2:23 is followed by a second, the explanation that "Therefore a man leaves his father and his mother and cleaves to his wife, and they become one flesh" (2:24). Gerhard von Rad, in his classic commentary on Genesis, observes here that "Curiously, the statement about forsaking father and mother does not quite correspond to the patriarchal family customs of ancient Israel, for after the marriage the wife breaks loose from her family much more than the man does from his. Does this tendentious statement perhaps preserve something from a time of matriarchal culture?" (83) The notion of an earlier matriarchy, understood as a *political* system of female dominance, is flatly refuted by Kinnear (19). Nonetheless, reading here the trace of a *matrilineal* social system (i.e., one which defines family ancestory and descendents by way of the mother), commonly found among hunter-gatherers and preserved in Judaism's sense that a child born of a Jewish mother is Jewish, would be consistent with the situation of the primal couple as essentially gatherers in a Garden.

4. Tikva Frymer-Kensky develops a more complete account of Inanna (whose Semitic name is Ishtar) as an "anomalous" goddess in the Sumerian pantheon, one who is not constrained within more usual social roles for women.

   Further, Inanna is literally the embodiment of sexuality as a powerful force (47–48); her representative thus plays a crucial role in the ritual of sacred marriage, in which sexual intercourse with the king (who represents the vegetation God Dumuzi) creates the union of male (fertility) and female thought to be necessary for agricultural fertility (50–57). At the same time, Inanna thereby serves as the bridge between the human and the divine; indeed, as goddess of love *and* war, Inanna often awards power to the beloved/king in the form of military conquest (58–63).

   Finally, Frymer-Kensky observes that the association of war and ferocity with Inanna as a goddess of sexuality is due in part to her functioning as what I have characterized as a chaos agent: as erotically charged, and unrestrained by "normal" female roles, she represents a threat to male control—on both social/political and personal/psychological levels. This is especially true in a culture in which "Sex is frequently about control and dominance. . . . The goddess who personifies sexual attraction must personify the power of one human to attract another, a power which is inherently threatening as long as we perceive of sex as power" (68).

5. Stordeur and Stille, 46, with reference to Gondolf; cf. 27, with reference to Straus. See also 35 and 45 for a summary of recent clinical studies demonstrating "the batterer's need to control and dominate." Compare as well their summary of studies which indicate societal approval of a husband's violence towards his spouse (21).

   In addition, this reading of the story (i.e., as a myth legitimating male violence against women) is consistent with both personal experience and research demonstrating *higher* rates of domestic violence in conservative Christian communities (namely, just those communities which stress this reading of the story, as it becomes the Orthodox Christian reading: Patton).

6. Meyers incorporates and recommends both Trible and J. Higgins, whose readings assault especially the Christian/Augustinian view of Eve as

temptress and source of sin (79). To do so, she begins by identifying the literary genre of the Genesis story as a creation myth, one which incorporates elements of wisdom parables (79, 91–92). To say that the narrative is myth, she is careful to point out, is *not* to say that the story is either false or somehow antiquated. Rather, as a story about *origins*, "it is a story meant to help human beings come to grips with the nature and meaning of their own purpose" (79). More specifically, the story is an etiology—that is, a narrative which works to *explain* how things have come to be, why things are the way they are (80). In sum, Meyers reiterates in this way the sense of the story as myth which defines this essay.

7. It must be stressed that sexuality—beginning precisely with the affirmation of humanity as the creation of God in the Genesis narratives—is seen in Jewish traditions in largely positive terms, as the celebration of sexuality in the Song of Songs makes clear (see Plaut, 22, 877–80). As Plaut points out, sexuality becomes negatively valued in the ancient world only in the context of Greek Cynicism and Stoicism, as these develop a dualism between mind and body which tends to affirm the control of reason and the correlative suspicion of passion (878). Especially as it grew in the Hellenistic world, Christianity appropriated these attitudes, though in complex ways. See Peter Brown for the involved history of Christian attitudes toward sexuality in the first four centuries of the Church.

8. Cf. Ralph, 154. Augustine's (mis)reading of Genesis through the lens of 1 Timothy, in fact, may rest on a misreading of 1 Timothy as well. Sharon Hodgin Gritz carefully examines the 1 Timothy passage, along with others in the Christian Scriptures which take the Genesis story to endorse woman's subordination to man (1 Cor. 11:2–16, 1 Cor. 14:34–36, and Eph. 5:22–33). Gritz argues that these passages rather commend a relationship of mutual submission, in harmony with what she sees as the consistent affirmation of women in Jesus' ministry, the early Christian communities, and the original relationship of "cooperation and complementariness" between woman and man in Genesis 1–2 (54–59, 158).

9. Markus points out that Augustine explicitly rejected "classical" models which used analogies of God/World, mind/body, and parent/child to justify the political authority of rulers over their subjects or masters over their slaves (92–93). Nonetheless, Augustine's justification of the state rests on a strong sense of the "precariousness" of social order in the face of human sinfulness (176–77)—precisely the sinfulness he sees as now embedded in human nature. Again, political authority is legitimated as "blessed and commissioned by God, for keeping chaos and disintegration in check" (178)—i.e., the chaos and disintegration caused by naturally sinful human beings. In this way, Augustine remains an example of what Schüssler-Fiorenza describes as "love patriarchalism"—i.e., the endorsement of hierarchical and patriarchal modes of authority, in which the sting of submission is to be diluted by authority exercised with care and compassion (Carmody, 167).

10. Trible 1978, 73. Trible lists these in the sequence defined by the verses constituting the story. I use a different order, one reflecting the sequence in which I will treat these elements in what follows.

11. Frymer-Kensky observes most modern commentators have followed this reading since Trible first established this translation in her

"Depatriarchalizing in Biblical Interpretation" (1973). See Frymer-Kensky, 108, and 250, n. 5.

12. Even among feminist scholars, opinion regarding a goddess religion—argued to have existed prior to the rise of patriarchy and the hierarchically organized city-states of ancient Sumer—is divided. Rosemary Radford Ruether, for example, suggests that Eve, like Pandora, may represent "debased" goddess figures (1975, 15)—but in turn, she rejects the feminist reconstruction of a goddess tradition as such, first of all as unhistorical, and, indeed, as itself framed by the Christian notion of a Fall as it presumes an Edenic matriarchy out of which we have fallen into repressive patriarchy (Ruether, 1975, 4).

   Meyers' association of Eve with an earlier goddess can certainly find support, for example, in the work of Buffie Johnson, who sees in Eve "a Mistress of Vegetation and lady of the Beasts" (Johnson, 186), a view developed with still greater care by Miriam Robbins Dexter (46; cf. Patai). Over against such views, however, stand the work of Ruether, Dawne McCance (critiquing Phyllis Trible, Letty Russell, Carol Christ, Naomi Goldenberg, Starhawk, Ruether, Rita Gross, Diana Paul, and others), Joan Townsend (critiquing Maria Gimbutas, Evelyn Reed, Starhawk, and Merlin Stone), and Tikva Frymer-Kensky.

   In particular, given the scholarly controversies surrounding the goddess tradition, to assume "the death of the Goddess" at the hands of the writers and redactors of the Hebrew Bible may implicate anti-Semitism. As Phillips points out, in modern characterizations of the Goddess, "fascination with blood and soil seems reactionary to anyone who recalls twentieth-century German history" (176). The anti-Semitic dimension of "the death of the Goddess" theme is explored more fully by Marie-Theres Wacker (1991), with reference to the work of Jewish feminist Judith Plaskow and Katharina von Kellenbach.

13. Bledstein further argues that the word *tesuqa* can be understood to mean "desirable." On her reading, YHWH's statement is better translated as "You are *attractive* to your man; yet he can rule over you." Especially in the contexts of other J stories (Bledstein refers to Joseph and Potiphar's wife, Tamar, the beautiful daughters of men desired by "the sons of God" [Gen. 6:2], Dinah, Bilhah, Bathsheba, Uriah's wife, and Abishag), to be desirable is dangerous. Bledstein observes that "These examples suggest that J [the author of the Yahwist story of Genesis 2–4] does not envision woman flinging herself in abject desire at a man but rather is concerned with men's arrogant abuse of power with regard to exploiting another person sexually" (45). In the more general context of Middle-Eastern story, to become desirable or alluring, as a second dimension of becoming "like the gods"—in the woman's case, like a goddess—is likewise dangerous, "a negative consequence of becoming like divine beings" (44), as exemplified in the Gilgamesh epic, as Gilgamesh's attractiveness to the goddess Ishtar, followed by Gilgamesh's rebuff, results in the death of Enkidu, Gilgamesh's best friend (Bledstein, 45: see Kovacs, 51–56).

   On this reading, then, YHWH's statement emerges not as a curse, but a warning, one which makes clear the danger of sexual attractiveness she has achieved through her becoming like a god(dess). To warn about the danger, however, suggests that the violence it may bring on against the woman is by no means intended by God as a "punishment," nor can such violence be seen as justified or legitimated by her alleged sin. Rather, the parallel uses of *tesuqa* Bledstein argues for imply just the opposite: just as sin in 4:7, despite its powerful attractiveness, can be successfully resisted and controlled—so Eve's sexual attractiveness, however powerfully it works on the male, can also be resisted and controlled, precisely in order to avoid falling (!) into the male temptation of responding to the woman's sexual attractiveness by attempting to dominate and rule over her.

Bledstein's analysis thus radically undermines a central element in the patriarchal reading of the story—namely, that it is the woman who is erotically driven, and thus requires the authority and control of her ostensibly less passionate man.

Works Cited

Bal, Mieke. 1987. *Lethal Love: Feminist Literary Interpretations of Biblical Love.* Bloomington: Indiana University Press.

Beauvoir, Simone de. 1952 (1949). *The Second Sex.* Trans. H. M. Parshley. New York: Vintage Books.

Bograd, M. 1984. "Family Systems Approaches to Wife Battering: A Feminist Critique." *American Journal of Orthopsychiatry* 54: 548–68.

Brown, Peter. 1988. *The Body and Society: Men, Women and Sexual Renunciation in Early Christianity.* New York: Columbia University Press.

Carmody, Denise. 1989. *Women and World Religions,* 2d ed. Englewood Cliffs, N.J.: Prentice Hall.

Cassuto, Umberto. 1961 (1944). *Commentary on Genesis I: From Adam to Noah.* Trans. Israel Abrahams. Jerusalem: Magnes Press.

Christ, Carol. 1987. *Laughter of Aphrodite: Reflections on a Journey to the Goddess.* San Francisco: Harper & Row.

Clark, Elizabeth A. 1986. *Ascetic Piety and Women's Faith: Essays on Late Ancient Christianity.* Lewiston: Edwin Mellen Press.

The Epic of Gilgamesh. 1985. Trans. Maureen Gallery Kovacs. Stanford, Calif: Stanford University Press.

Frymer-Kensky, Tikva. 1992. *In the Wake of the Goddesses: Women, Culture, and the Biblical Transformation of Pagan Myth.* New York: The Free Press.

Fuchs, Esther. 1985. "Who is Hiding the Truth? Deceptive Women and Biblical Androcentrism," in *Feminist Perspectives on Biblical Scholarship,* ed. Adela Yarbro Collins. Chico, Calif: Scholars Press. 37–144.

Gimbutas, Maria. 1982. *The Goddesses and Gods of Old Europe, 6500–3400 B.C.: Myths and Cult Images.* Berkeley/Los Angeles: University of California Press.

Gondolf, E. W. 1984. "Fighting for Control: A Clinical Assessment of Men Who Batter." *Social Casework* 66/1: 48–54.

___. 1985. *Men Who Batter: An Integrated Approach for Stopping Wife Abuse.* Holmes Beach, FL: Learning Publications.

Gritz, Sharon Hodgin. 1991. *Paul, Women Teachers, and The Mother Goddess at Ephesus: A Study of 1 Timothy 2:9–15 in Light of the Religious and Cultural Milieu of The First Century*. New York: University Press of America.

Hall, T. W., Richard B. Pilgrim, and Ronald R. Cavanagh. 1985. *Religion: An Introduction*. San Francisco: Harper & Row.

Higgins, J. 1976. "The Myth of Eve the Temptress." *Journal of the American Academy of Religion* 44: 639–47.

Homer. 1963. *The Odyssey*. Trans. Robert Fitzgerald. New York: Anchor Books.

Keller, Catherine. 1986. *From a Broken Web: Separation, Sexism, and Self*. Boston: Beacon Press.

Kikawada, Isaac M. 1972. "Two Notes on Eve." *Journal for Biblical Literature* 91: 33–37.

Kinnear, Mary. 1982. *Daughters of Time: Women in the Western Tradition*. Ann Arbor: University of Michigan Press.

The Little Mermaid. 1989. Directed by Glen Keane and Duncan Marjoribanks. Walt Disney.

Markus, R. A. 1970. *Saeculum: History and Society in the Theology of St. Augustine*. Cambridge: Cambridge University Press.

McCance, Dawne. 1990. "Understandings of 'the Goddess' in Contemporary Feminist Scholarship," in *Goddesses in Religions and Modern Debate*, ed. Larry Hurtado (Vol. 1, *University of Manitoba Studies in Religion*). Atlanta, Ga: Scholars Press. 165–78.

Meyers, Carol. 1988. *Discovering Eve: Ancient Israelite Women in Context*. New York: Oxford University Press.

Millett, Kate. 1969. *Sexual Politics*. New York: Ballantine.

Pagels, Elaine. 1988. *Adam, Eve, and the Serpent*. New York: Random House.

Pardes, Ilana. 1992. *Countertraditions in the Bible: A Feminist Approach*. Cambridge, Mass.: Harvard University Press.

Patton, Sandra (Director, Family Violence Center, Springfield, Mo., and domestic violence survivor). 1993. Personal interview with the author.

Phillips, John A. 1984. *Eve: The History of an Idea*. San Francisco: Harper & Row.

Plaut, Gunther W. 1981. *The Torah: A Modern Commentary*. New York: Union of American Hebrew Congregations.

Ralph, Margaret Nutting. 1989. *Plain Words about Biblical Images: Growing in our Faith Through the Scriptures*. New York: Paulist Press.

Reed, Evelyn. 1975. *Women's Evolution: From Matriarchal Clan to Patriarchal Family*. New York: Pathfinder Press.

Ruether, Rosemary Radford. 1974. "Misogynism and Virginal Feminism in the Fathers of the Church," in *Religion and Sexism: Images of Woman in the Jewish and Christian Traditions*, ed. Rosemary Radford Ruether. New York: Simon and Schuster. 150–83.

____. 1975. *New Woman, New Earth: Sexist Ideologies and Human Liberation*. New York: Crossroad.

———. 1989. "The Western Religious Tradition and Violence Against Women in the Home," in *Christianity, Patriarchy, and Abuse: A Feminist Critique*, ed. Joanne Carlson Brown and Carole R. Bohn. New York: Pilgrim Press.

Schüssler Fiorenza, Elisabeth. 1983. *In Memory of Her*. New York: Crossroad.

Shaw, Brent D. 1987. "The Family in Late Antiquity: the Experience of Augustine." *Past and Present*, 155 (May): 3–51.

Skinner, John. 1910. *Genesis: The International Critical Commentary*. Edinburgh: T. & T. Clark.

Stanton, Elizabeth Cady. 1985 (1895, 1898). *The Woman's Bible: The Original Feminist Attack on the Bible*. Edinburgh: Polygon Books.

Starhawk [Miriam Semos]. 1979. *The Spiral Dance: A Rebirth of the Ancient Religion of the Great Goddess*. San Francisco: Harper & Row.

Stone, Merlin. 1976. *When God was a Woman*. New York: Dial Press.

Stordeur, Richard A., and Richard Stille. 1989. *Ending Men's Violence against their Partners: One Road to Peace*. Newbury Park: Sage Publications.

Strenski, Ivan. 1987. *Four Theories of Myth in Twentieth-Century History: Cassirer, Eliade, Levi-Strauss and Malinowski*. Iowa City: University of Iowa Press.

Straus, M. 1976. "Sexual Inequality, Cultural Norms, and Wife Beating." *Victimology: An International Journal* 1:54–76.

Thistlethwaite, Susan Brooks. 1989a. "Every Two Minutes: Battered Women and Feminist Interpretation," in *Weaving the Visions: New Patterns in Feminist Spirituality*, ed. Judith Plaskow and Carol P. Christ. San Francisco: Harper & Row. 302–13.

———. 1989b. *Sex, Race, and God: Christian Feminism in Black and White*. New York: Crossroad.

Townsend, Joan B. 1990. "The Goddess: Fact, Fallacy and Revitalization Movement," in *Goddesses in Religions and Modern Debate*, ed. Larry Hurtado (Vol. 1, *University of Manitoba Studies in Religion*). Atlanta, Ga: Scholars Press. 180–203.

Trible, Phyllis. 1976. "Depatriarchalizing in Biblical Interpretation," in *The Jewish Woman: New Perspectives*, ed. Elizabeth Koltun. New York: Schocken Books. 217–40.

———. 1992 (1973). "Eve and Adam: Genesis 2–3 Reread," in *Womanspirit Rising: A Feminist Reader in Religion*. ed. Carol P. Christ and Judith Plaskow. New York: Harper & Row, 1992. 2d ed. Reprinted from *Andover Newton Quarterly* 13 (March, 1973).

———. 1978. *God and the Rhetoric of Sexuality*. Philadelphia: Fortress Press.

von Rad, Gerhard. 1961. *Genesis: A Commentary*, trans. John H. Marks. Philadelphia: Westminster Press.

Wacker, Marie-Theres. 1991. "Feminist Theology and Anti-Judaism: The Status of the Discussion and the Context of the Problem in the Federal Republic of Germany." *Journal of Feminist Studies in Religion* 7/2 (Fall, 1991): 109-16.

Structures of Forgiveness
in the New Testament

FREDERICK W. KEENE

The relationship of forgiveness and repentance is among the most difficult concepts in Christian theology. The argument usually is carried out
along the lines of whether repentance is required for forgiveness to be
granted, or whether forgiveness is (or should be) granted unconditionally,
with repentance required in order to recognize and accept the unconditional
forgiveness. The first position usually is regarded as one taken by more "conservative" Christians and, biblically, is based on such texts as Mark 1:4 (paralleled in Luke 3:3 [we will indicate such parallelism here by using //]:

> John the baptizer appeared in the wilderness, proclaiming a baptism of
> repentance (*metanoia*) for the forgiveness (*aphesis*) of sins.

The second position usually is regarded as more "liberal," and finds its biblical roots in passages such as Mark 2:1–12 (// Matt. 9:2–8; // Luke 5:17–26),
especially Mark 2:5:

> When Jesus saw their faith, he said to the paralytic, "Son, your sins are
> forgiven (*aphiēmi*)."

This is a somewhat more nuanced position than is the first. It finds much of
its basis in Paul's explicit assertion of unconditional grace, with a classic
expression in Paul Tillich's famous sermon, "You Are Accepted"(Tillich
1948, 153–63).

With respect to forgiveness in human interactions, the model of forgiveness usually is taken to be that of divine forgiveness. This again raises the
question as to whether repentance is required for forgiveness, the answer usually depending on the answer accepted with respect to divine forgiveness.
Biblically, of course, this can be traced back to such passages as the Lord's
Prayer in the Sermon on the Mount, Matt. 6:12 (// Luke 11:4),

> And forgive (*aphiēmi*) us our debts,
>   as we also have forgiven (*aphiēmi*) our debtors,

where human beings are to model their forgiveness on the divine forgiveness,
and possibly find their access to divine forgiveness contingent upon their forgiving others. Snaith, for example, puts forward a version of the "conservative"

stance by claiming that the "moral" of the parable of the Unforgiving Servant (Matt. 18:23–35) is that the person "who does not forgive can not repent"(Snaith 1972, 86). The more "liberal" position, which posits unconditional divine forgiveness, runs into trouble here. It wants human forgiveness to be unconditional, too, reading Matt. 6:12 as a description of how the petitioner is to emulate divine forgiveness, not as an expression of the contingency of that forgiveness. Unfortunately, though, the liberal also tends to believe in justice. But if forgiveness is always to be available, would a requirement that the oppressed and the abused must forgive their oppressors and abusers be just, or even possible? In human interactions, does unconditional forgiveness conflict with a cry for justice—or, to reverse the question, does an insistence on justice deny a requirement that the abused must forgive the abuser? These are hard questions, even if they often are raised by those who would support and protect oppressors and abusers, and who would never dream of claiming *divine* forgiveness is unconditional.

An alternative model to the "repentance required" versus "unconditional" models of forgiveness with respect to human interactions can be found by looking at the structure of the way the New Testament treats forgiveness. The development of this model looks briefly at the cultural anthropology of the New Testament world, but primarily examines the words for and ideas about forgiveness that occur in the texts themselves. Once this alternative model is set up, it becomes possible to reexamine justice and abuse issues.

The concept of forgiveness would have been difficult, and sometimes even dangerous, in the agonistic society of the first century Mediterranean world. One person forgiving another would have been seen as laudable only if the forgiver were in a higher socio-economic position than the forgiven, and hence in a position to act as a patron. Even then, the receiver of forgiveness would have been expected to seek the forgiveness—that is, the receiver would need to offer to become a client, unless already born into clientship. This is because in an agonistic society an offer of forgiveness is a challenge to the honor of the person being forgiven, at least in the case of a male recipient (Malina 1981, 30–33, 79–82; Malina and Neyrey 1991, 49–52); it may have been a positive challenge, but a challenge nevertheless. Such a challenge from an inferior would be an insult, but from a superior or an equal could be accepted. It would depend on how it were proffered. Thus in the first century Mediterranean world, the problem with forgiveness would not be with whether repentance was required, either before it was offered or in order to accept it. The problem with forgiveness would lie in the context in which it was offered or available: who forgave, who was forgiven, and what was the nature of the relationship between them that caused the question of forgiveness to arise in the first place.

This cultural-anthropological picture points to a model of forgiveness, and possibly of repentance, that can be examined in terms of the words and the structures of the New Testament. The model would posit that, from the point of view of the New Testament, interpersonal forgiveness is possible only when, within the context of the interaction in which the question of forgiveness arises, the putative forgiver is more powerful than, or at least an equal of, the person being forgiven. In particular, it is not possible from the point of view of the New Testament for one person to forgive another person of greater power. This would mean that if a tenant has a grievance against a landlord as part of their landlord/tenant relationship, the tenant not only is not called upon to forgive, but in fact can not forgive the landlord so long as that relationship exists—and this is independent of whether or not the landlord "makes restitution." It would also mean that if a man beats his wife, the battered woman not only is not required to forgive her husband, but in fact *should not* forgive him so long as the hierarchical power relationship exists within the marriage. The tenant can forgive a financial wrong only of a financial equal (or inferior). A wife can forgive a marital wrong only as a marital equal. Within the Christian context, a landlord might be expected to forgive the debts of his tenants, but he can not and should not expect to be forgiven for any wrongs he has committed—unless, possibly, he ceases to be a landlord.

From a linguistic perspective, how does this model fit the New Testament? There are only three Greek words used for the verb "to forgive" in the New Testament: *aphiēmi* (αφιημι) with its associated noun *aphesis* (αφεσις); *charizomai* (χαριζομαι); and *apoluō* (απολυω). *Apoluō* occurs in the sense of "to forgive" only in Luke 6:37c (twice). It usually means to dismiss or to divorce; it is used in Matt. 5:32 (// Luke 16:18; // Mark 10:11–12) in the pronouncements on divorce. Divorce in the New Testament context being a hierarchical process controlled by the husband, Luke 6:37c would carry a connotation of the forgiveness coming from the more powerful person.

The predominant verbs of forgiveness are *aphiēmi* and *charizomai*. The words *aphiēmi* and *aphesis* occur with this meaning almost exclusively in the Synoptic Gospels and in Acts, while *charizomai* is almost exclusively Pauline. *Aphiēmi* and *aphesis* have two basic meanings which can be related. The first is an essentially juridical meaning of "to leave" or "to release." This can be seen in Luke 4:18, "He has sent me to proclaim release (*aphiēmi*) to the captives." This can be extended to many cases where someone or something is leaving, for example the earliest disciples leaving their livelihood to follow Jesus in Mark 1:18 (// Matt. 4:20),

And immediately they left (*aphiēmi*) their nets and followed him,

and in Mark 1:20(// Matt. 4:22),

. . . and they left (*aphiēmi*) their father Zebedee in the boat with the hired men, and followed him.

The other meaning is essentially commercial, to remit or forgive, especially a debt. This carries over from both common Greek usage and from the LXX, and can be seen in Matt. 6:12 (// Luke 11:4),

And forgive (*aphiēmi*) us our debts,
    As we also have forgiven (*aphiēmi*) our debtors,

and in the parable of the Unforgiving Servant, Matt. 18:27 and 32,

... and forgave (*aphiēmi*) him the debt. ... I forgave (*aphiēmi*) you all that debt.

The two meanings can be seen to be related by the use of the noun *aphesis* to mean release from debt or obligation or penalty (TDNT 1985, 48; Ringe 1985, 65–66). The use in LXX shows a shift from Hebrew words for forgiveness that connote a cultic removal and expiation of sin to Greek words that have juridical and commercial meanings of release or remission. This in turn gives a religious connotation to the secular words (Ringe 1985, 65–66, 112–13). What should be noticed, however, is that the words for forgiving and forgiveness now have an implication of a more powerful being, whether God or a person, releasing another from a debt or an obligation or a penalty. The term *aphesis ton hamartia*, forgiveness of sins, takes on an implication of a release from sin (or from the penalty of sinning) or a release from debt; it does not have an implication of a religious or a cultic cleansing.

Paul "prefers the verb χαρίζομαι [*charizomai*], 'to be generous,' perhaps because it stresses the generous and personal character of God's action and avoids the juridical associations of αφιημι [*aphiēmi*]" (Quanbeck 1962, 319). *Charizomai*, to give freely, is from the same root as *charis*, which is the word usually translated as "grace" in the Pauline literature (TDNT 1985, 1298). In the New Testament, it occurs only in Luke, Paul, and the deutero-Pauline literature. In secular Greek, it usually meant "to show pleasure" or "to show oneself to be pleasant" (TDNT 1985, 1301). In Luke, it usually refers to favors granted to someone (TDNT 1985, 1304); in Acts 4:14, for example, it is said that Barabbas was released as a favor to the people:

> But you rejected the Holy and Righteous One and asked to have a murderer given (*charizomai*) to you.

In fact, Luke uses *charizomai* in the sense of forgiving debts in the story of Jesus' anointing by a woman, Luke 7:42–43:

> "... When they could not pay, he canceled [RSV: forgave] (*charizomai*) the debts of both of them. Now which of them would love him more?" Simon answered, "I suppose the one for whom he canceled [RSV: forgave] (*charizomai*) the greater debt."

We note, however, a few verses later, that when Jesus forgave the woman's sins in Luke 7:47–48 he used *aphiēmi* rather than *charizomai*. For Paul, though, it is the giving freely part of *charizomai* that tends to be emphasized, as in Rom. 8:32:

> He who did not withhold his own Son, but gave [or delivered] him up for all of us, will he not with him also give (*charizomai*) us everything else?

This giving freely is almost always by God, and very rarely in the sense of "forgiving" anything, whether sins or debts.[1]

For a concept that has achieved such prominence in Christian theology and piety, there are relatively few references to forgiveness in the New

Testament. The large majority of these have to do with God's forgiveness of sins, with Jesus' forgiving of another's sins, or, especially after the Resurrection, a blending of these two categories in which God's forgiveness is mediated in some way by Jesus. All of these references are of necessity hierarchical: within the context of the New Testament, God and Jesus are always in a (or the) position of power with regard to sin. Furthermore, the words used are almost always *aphiēmi* or *aphesis*, giving this forgiveness of sin juridical or commercial overtones. When it comes to people forgiving other people, there are not very many references. When Synoptic parallels are taken together, there are seven such references in the gospels, and four in the epistolary literature.

One of the major themes in the treatment of forgiveness by human beings is its relationship to forgiveness by God. This can be seen in the forgiveness petition of the Lord's Prayer, Matt. 6:12 (// Luke 11:4),

And forgive us our debts,	And forgive us our sins,
as we also have forgiven our	for we ourselves forgive
debtors.	everyone indebted to us.

This relationship can be expressed in several ways, depending on the bias of the speaker. Thus one can say that humans must forgive one another in order to be forgiven by God, or one can say that humans must forgive each other in order to be able to accept the forgiveness of God. The petitions, of course, ask God to forgive human beings *because* they forgive others, leaving open the question of whether God would forgive humans if they did not forgive others. But the petitions do more than that: they set up a hierarchy. In Matt. 6:12, the petition says that since "we" have forgiven (*aphiēmi*) our debtors (*opheilētes*), then God should forgive (*aphiēmi*) our debts (*opheilē*). These all have a primary reference to commercial or financial terms, although they can be extended to cover spiritual usage (TDNT 1985, 746–48). Luke does in 11:4 by asking God to forgive (*aphiēmi*) "our" sins (*hamartia*) as "we" forgive (*aphiēmi*) everyone who is indebted (*opheilē*) to us. To be indebted in a commercial transaction is to be in the inferior position; the creditor is in the position of power. Thus the hierarchy is that we forgive those over whom we have power; therefore we can ask God, who has infinite power, to forgive us. Nothing is said about those who have power over us and against whom we might have a grievance. In this situation, forgiveness flows down, from the more powerful to the less powerful.

Forgiveness continues to flow down from the more powerful to the less powerful in the discussion in Matt. 6:14–15 of the forgiveness petition from the Lord's Prayer, and in the similar discussion in Mark 11:25. (Mark 11:26, which carries the discussion forward along the lines pursued by Matthew, is not admitted into most modern translations.) Here, instead of debts (*opheilē*) or sin (*hamartia*), it is trespasses (*paraptomata*) that are to be forgiven (*aphiēmi*), but again in the line of the Father forgiving the person, who then forgives the trespasses of others.

This trend also is found in the unique saying in Luke 6:37–38a in the Sermon on the Plain:

> Do not judge, and you will not be judged;
>> do not condemn, and you will not be condemned.
> Forgive (*apoluō*), and you will be forgiven (*apoluō*);
>> give, and it will be given to you.

(Luke 6:37a parallels Matt. 7:11.) In each of these commands, the clause in the passive voice is in the "divine passive" used to avoid a direct reference to God. This would point to a replication of the power-driven hierarchy already seen, except that the word for forgive/forgiven used here is *apoluō*, not *aphiēmi*. In fact, this is the only place in the New Testament where *apoluō* is used to indicate forgiveness. It usually means "to divorce" or dismiss, and is the verb used in the divorce discourses in Matt. 5:31 and 19:7 and in Mark 10:4. Divorce was a purely hierarchical act in biblical times, of course, a fact pointed out in the divorce narratives. The man, who had all the power, could divorce his wife, but she did not have the power to give him "a bill of divorcement." While a case can be made that Jesus allowed divorce if mutually agreed upon,[2] the meaning of *apoluō* contains no hint of mutuality; it was strictly a hierarchical concept where the one with power is the one who performs the action of the verb.

The gospels also treat the concept of forgiveness in two narrative complexes, Luke 7:36–50 and Matt. 18:21–35. Both contain parables or illustrative stories that, while capable of other interpretations, are used to carry on the discussion of forgiveness in the received redactions. The Lukan passage is Luke's treatment of what in the other three gospels is presented as the anointing at Bethany. A complete discussion of this passage is beyond the scope of this study; Ringe (1983, 66–71) studies the Lukan passage, while Schüssler Fiorenza[3] has an excellent presentation of the Synoptic parallels. The Lukan presentation differs substantially from the others. It not only is removed in time—from the week before the Crucifixion to early in Jesus' ministry—and place—from Bethany to Galilee—but also its entire emphasis is different. While the other three presentations emphasize the anointing, and the Synoptics play with the idea that the anointing of the head is both the anointing of the messiah/king and an anointing for burial, the anointing in Luke seems to be secondary. In Luke, the primary emphasis is on forgiveness: forgiveness of the woman, who in stark contrast to the other three gospels is described as "'a woman of the city who was a sinner,'" but also, in an illustrative story, the forgiveness of debtors.[4] The story is in Luke 7:41–43:

> "A certain creditor had two debtors; one owed five hundred denarii, and the other fifty. When they could not pay, he canceled [RSV: forgave] (*charizomai*) the debts for both of them. Now which of them will love him more." Simon answered, "I suppose the one for whom he canceled [RSV: forgave] (*charizomai*) the greater debt." And Jesus said to him, "You have judged rightly."

The use of *charizomai* for debt cancellation is particularly noticeable here; it emphasizes the "free gift" part of the forgiveness, but does not disguise that

Jesus is talking about creditors and debtors, and hence a hierarchy of power. Later in the narrative, when the discussion turns to the forgiveness of the woman's sins, Jesus ties it to the debt language by switching from *charizomai* to *aphiēmi* in vv. 47–48,

> "Therefore, I tell you, her sins, which were many, have been forgiven (*aphiēmi*); hence she has shown great love. But the one to whom little is forgiven (*aphiēmi*), loves little." Then he said to her, "Your sins are forgiven (*aphiēmi*)."

This illustrates the hierarchical nature of forgiveness even when Jesus forgives sins: a "woman of the city who was a sinner" was near the bottom of any power hierarchy of the time, and Jesus, as a Teacher who was a guest (albeit mistreated) of a Pharisee, was well above her.

The other narrative complex, Matt. 18:21–35, includes the parable of the Unforgiving Servant (vv. 23–34), framed by a passage (vv. 21–22 and 35) paralleled by Luke 17:3–4,

Then Peter came and said to him, "Lord, if another member of the church [RSV, NRSV margin: my brother] sins against me, how often should I forgive (*aphiēmi*) him? As many as seven times?" Jesus said to him, "Not seven times, but, I tell you, seventy-seven [RSV, NRSV margin: seventy times seven] times."	"Be on your guard! If another disciple sins, you must rebuke the offender, and if there is repentance, you must forgive (*aphiēmi*). And if the same person sins against you seven times a day, and turns back to you seven times and says 'I repent,' you must forgive (*aphiēmi*)."

In Matt. 18:21, the NRSV, presumably reacting to this passage coming at the end of chapter 18, much of which is devoted to `"church" discipline, reads "member of the church"; the RSV (and the NRSV margin), reflecting the actual Greek, reads "brother." (For consistency, the NRSV should read "a brother or a sister.") This parallels "another disciple" in Luke 17:3. Here is one of the few cases where an absolute hierarchy is not set up; a "brother" or "another disciple" or "a member of the church" is neither above nor below the person offended, but is an equal. While forgiveness is neither expected nor required when the offender is higher in the power hierarchy—indeed, it probably is neither possible nor desirable—it is expected when the person is an equal in the power structure. This frame in Matthew is concluded at verse 35:

> So my heavenly Father will also do to every one of you, if you do not forgive (*aphiēmi*) your brother or sister from your heart.

Here the NRSV goes back to its inclusive language convention, and continues to reinforce the idea of equality—but not of forgiving the more powerful. The rest of the verse is an effort within the context of the Matthean redaction to present a particular interpretation of the parable of the Unforgiving Servant.

Within the Matthean redaction, the parable of the Unforgiving Servant is a parable on the necessity of forgiving others.[5] A lord (*kyrios*) forgives a slave with a large debt, but this slave refuses to forgive one of his debtors. This causes the lord to revoke the original forgiveness and turn the unforgiving slave over to the torturers. The verb "to forgive" is *aphiēmi* throughout, emphasizing the financial aspects. The story itself could hardly be more hierarchical, and the way Matthew presents it makes it an almost paradigmatic form of the forgiveness petition in the Lord's Prayer.[6] Yet again, forgiveness comes down from the most powerful to the least powerful—and if the progression is broken at one place it is broken everywhere. As Ringe puts it:

> . . . if one opts to live with the pattern of forgiveness, that choice must govern those situations from which one benefits as well as those where one's own debt is insurmountable. (Ringe 1985, 95)

But the progression of forgiveness can be broken only by a more powerful person refusing forgiveness to a less powerful person. The progression of forgiveness does not move up the structure of power, only down.

The final example of humans forgiving humans within the gospels is also the only example that presents the question of one with less power forgiving those with relatively more power. It is Luke 23:34, one of the Last Words on the Cross[7]:

> Then Jesus said, "Father, forgive (*aphiēmi*) them, for they do not know what they are doing."

This is a situation where Jesus has no power; he is speaking from a cross about those who have crucified him. What is noticeable is that he does not forgive them. Instead, he asks his Father, he asks God, to forgive them. Having no power within the situation, he can not forgive. About the only way the structures of power can be invoked for forgiveness is the way Jesus chose: to ask God, who remains all-powerful, to forgive. This is the one place where, if Jesus wanted the weak to forgive the strong, he could have indicated it. He did not. He asked the strongest to forgive, and, being the less powerful, did not offer the forgiveness himself. The relative positioning within the power structures remain the same: only the more powerful can be expected to forgive. The less powerful are not expected to forgive, and, in the case of Jesus on the cross, do not forgive the more powerful.

Outside the gospels, there are only three references in the New Testament to interpersonal forgiveness; a fourth, 2 Cor. 12:13, is a bit of sarcasm by Paul. All four of them are in Pauline or deutero-Pauline literature, and, as would be expected, all four use *charizomai* for the verb "to forgive." The two deutero-Pauline occurrences are in the context of advice about church life. Eph. 4:32,

> . . . and be kind to one another, tenderhearted, forgiving one another, as God in Christ has forgiven you.

comes at the end of a section beginning at verse 25 with "for we are members of one another." This is a setting of equality, as in Matt. 18:21–22, although the hierarchical emphasis, with the human forgiveness stemming from the divine forgiveness, is there too. Similarly, the other deutero-Pauline reference, Col. 3:13, also refers to the life of the church, as can be seen by beginning at verse 12,

> As God's chosen ones, holy and beloved, clothe yourselves with compassion, kindness, humility, meekness, and patience. Bear with one another and, if anyone has a complaint against another, forgive each other; just as the Lord has forgiven you, so you also must forgive.

This is virtually the same as Eph. 4:32: the equality due to church membership is there, but the hierarchy of power that governs forgiveness is also there. Any hint that the less powerful might be called upon to forgive the more powerful most emphatically is not there.

The remaining passage is the only place in the New Testament where Paul writes about forgiveness by humans, 2 Cor. 2:5–11. Here he is addressing a specific incident that seems to have occurred during the period of contention between him and the Corinthian church documented in his Corinthian correspondence. This passage comes in a section of that correspondence that dates from the end of the period of contention, after Paul has brought the church back to his way of thinking. During the dispute, one of the members of the church seems to have affronted Paul in a manner sufficiently unpleasant to have caused the church to exact punishment (vv. 5–6). The nature of the punishment is not specified; traditionally, it is held to have been some form of excommunication or "shunning" of the offender. Paul, magnanimous in victory, writes in this section that the congregation should now "forgive and console [the offender], so that he may not be overwhelmed by excessive sorrow" (v. 7). Paul continues along this line, a few sentences later saying in verse 10,

> Anyone whom you forgive, I also forgive. What I have forgiven, if I have forgiven anything, has been for your sake in the presence of Christ.

Paul, now being firmly in the leadership position and wielding the power in the relationship, can and does encourage forgiveness. He nowhere indicates that anyone should forgive the more powerful, and, when in the weaker position in the course of the Corinthian dispute, never indicated that he was going to forgive those more powerful than he who had been so offensive to him. In this case, the only one from Paul's writings, the trend in the New Testament continues. Forgiveness is desired between equals in a relationship; when the relationship is unequal, only the more powerful are to forgive. If an offence is committed against the weaker by the more powerful, the weaker are not expected to be forgiving.

This model, based on the structure of forgiveness in the New Testament, is one where forgiveness occurs only when the parties involved possess equal power in the relationship where forgiveness is applicable, or else when the person with the grievance has the greater power within that relationship. Even Jesus in the one case where he was in the weaker position did not forgive those who both were more powerful and had harmed him. Instead, while on the Cross, he asked God—the most powerful—to forgive them. The fact that Jesus himself did not opt for forgiveness in this situation points to a further possibility, that forgiveness is not even possible when it is to go up the power structure. Surely the idea of a forgiving Christ would tell us that if he could he would forgive. But he did not, and thus no one should be asked or expected to forgive those who retain the power in a relationship where forgiveness might be applicable.

This model of forgiveness provides a tool for addressing several problems in contemporary and biblical theology. In particular, it provides a way of reconciling the apparent dichotomy between the supposed New Testament emphasis on forgiveness (and mercy) and the supposed Hebrew Bible emphasis on justice. In contemporary theology, this dichotomy is nowhere more apparent than in liberation theologies. As Ringe has put it:

> . . . theologians of liberation . . . seem not to be drawn to the theological motif of forgiveness, and for very good reason. . . . it is heard as a word that would whitewash past abuses whose present consequences continue to be felt. (1985, 95)

This, of course, is a point of view not unique to liberation theologies; any theology "from the underside" which takes seriously the condition of the abused, the hurt, those in pain, will look with much suspicion on almost all treatments of forgiveness. The model of forgiveness explored here would, for example, put the lie to the male clergy who counsel and preach to abused women that they "must forgive." In the social and political arena, forgiveness would be "far from becoming an easy or cheap route of escape for the privileged" (Ringe 1985, 95) as opposed to the way it is commonly preached in American churches.

This model would allow theologians of liberation to address the idea of forgiveness with some specificity within the context of justice. To receive forgiveness, to be forgiven, the powerful would have to do more than "make restitution"; they would have to give up their power. From a Christological point of view, of course, the relinquishing of power at the Cross is the basic requirement of salvation, but it goes beyond the Cross. To return to the Sermon on the Mount, forgiveness by others as well as by God is a prerequisite for worship, and hence for any true relationship with God:

> So when you are offering your gift at the altar, if you remember that your brother or sister has something against you, leave your gift there before the altar and go; first be reconciled to your brother or sister, and then come and offer your gift. Come to terms quickly with your accuser while you are on the way to court with him, or your accuser may hand you over to the judge, and the judge to the guard, and you will be thrown in prison. (Matt. 5:23–25)

This reconciliation, which in this case requires forgiveness, must be sought out—first from equals, but then from anyone with a grievance. This forgiveness can be hoped for, and even expected, except from those further down the power scale. To receive forgiveness from them, power must be relinquished. If this relinquishing of power is to be given a name, it is the *metanoia*, the repentance, spoken of in the New Testament, or the "turning," the *shub*, spoken of by the prophets.

This relinquishing of power, this *metanoia*, this *shub*, is what the theologians of liberation are talking about when they demand justice. It is the giving up of power that ties together forgiveness and justice. In this sense, the demands of forgiveness—whether *aphiēmi* or *charizomai*—are the demands for *metanoia*, and for justice, the *mishpat* demanded by the covenant through the prophets, and brought about by a "turning," *shub*, back to God. The requirement for forgiveness and the requirement for justice become aspects of the same drive toward fundamental, radical change in the power relationships among people, a drive that can not help but be revolutionary in a real, material sense. The theologians of liberation have recognized this as part of the demand for justice. They also have recognized that

> to move too quickly to "forgiveness" . . . without addressing the way the patterns of oppression have become institutionalized, risks simply perpetuating the status quo. Before "forgiveness" can find its way back into the lexicon of liberation, it must be linked to justice. (Ringe 1985, 94)

In the requirement that power be relinquished for forgiveness to occur, the link between forgiveness and justice can be established.

Use of this model of forgiveness can be made more focused and given greater specificity and individuality by looking at a specific issue, the recovery of those who have been sexually abused as children. This is an area where the question of relative power is at its starkest, and where the church commonly sides with the abuser and bludgeons the survivor with a doctrine of premature forgiveness. The worst cases of the church siding with the abuser, of course, come in cases of clergy sexual abuse. In these cases the common reaction is for the laity to make excuses for the clergy, often acting as if the survivor were the perpetrator—or just treating the survivor as a liar. The church as an institution tries to protect the clergy by reassigning them to other parishes, as the Roman Catholic dioceses of Chicago and of Santa Fe have done in recent years, or by devoting its pastoral resources to caring for them at the expense of the victims and survivors. After treating the survivor as though she were at fault, the church then compounds the damage by telling her that she should forgive her abuser. This last is an actual act of abuse by the church itself.

If the church feels that the survivor should forgive her abuser, then, in cases of clergy sexual abuse, it has but one choice. No matter what the ecclesiastical tradition, no matter what official or traditional doctrine of ordination a church as an institution may hold, the reality of the relationship between clergy and laity is one of relative power, with the clergy holding the power of priest and/or pastor.[8] So long as the clergy/laity relationship exists, the power relationship also exists, and forgiveness of a clergy sexual abuser by the survivor can not, and should not, occur. If the church counsels forgiveness, then the church has but one choice: strip the abuser of his ordination. It should be emphasized that this is not intended as a *punishment* for the clergy. It is a requirement that allows the survivors to forgive, and hence allows the clergy to receive that forgiveness. An implication of the New Testament structure of forgiveness is that sexually abusive clergy should be stripped of their status as ordained members of the church.

The power relationships between abuser and abused can be seen in the common example of father/daughter incest. The forgiveness of the father by the daughter typically can not occur until the relative power relationship has been reversed, when the daughter has reached adulthood and the father has reached old age. This may or may not be a psychological requirement, but the New Testament model of forgiveness explored here would indicate that it definitely is a theological and biblical requirement. Only when the patterns of power are reversed can the act of forgiveness be considered.

This requirement that the patterns of power be reversed is the kind of change, of turning around, of *metanoia* or of *shub*, that is meant by repentance. It would then be what Jesus is getting at in Mark 10:21 when he tells the rich man[9] to "sell what you own, and give the money to the poor, and . . . follow me," and later notes (v. 25) that "it is easier for a camel to go through the eye of a needle than for someone who is rich to enter the kingdom of God." In this sense, repentance is required for forgiveness to occur, at least between people. But repentance is not required of everyone; it is required only of those with power,[10] any power.

Notes

1. Rudolf Bultmann, who also wrote an article on *aphiēmi/aphesis* in the *Theological Dictionary of the New Testament*, noted in 1941 that Paul never uses the phrase *aphesis ton hamartia*, forgiveness of sins, "though it reappears in the deutero-Pauline literature; see, e.g. Col. 1:14; Eph 1:7" (Bultmann 1961, 32 n. 1), Paul does use something similar in Rom. 4:7–8:

   > Blessed are those whose iniquities are forgiven (*aphiēmi*),
   >   and whose sins are covered;
   > blessed is the one against whom the Lord will not reckon sin.

   This is in a quotation from Ps. 32:1, 2 (LXX). Knox and Reumann suggest that Paul is reminded of this because the commercial term "reckoned," *logizomai*, in Rom. 4:5 reminds Paul of these two verses (Knox and Reumann 1991, 213 NT). They pick up on this from v. 8 (Ps. 32:2), but could also pick up on it from *aphiēmi* in v. 7 (Ps. 32:1).

   The poetry of the Hebrew Bible works by placing ideas in parallel; a line of poetry which carries on a pair of parallel ideas or images is called a *bicolon*. The bicolon in v. 7 puts "forgiven" in parallel with "covered," but there is a larger parallelism between vv. 7 and 8 that carries the idea forward (this literary device is discussed both by Miller 1986, 33–47, and by Alter 1985, 10–26) by making it more pointed. "Blessed are those" is refined down to "Blessed is the one" and "iniquities are forgiven" and "sins are covered," both in the divine passive, are treated more pointedly by "against whom the Lord will not reckon sin." If "reckon" is a commercial term, it makes the meaning of the commercial term "forgiven" (*aphiēmi*) more pointed.

2. Countryman presents arguments that, when carried to their conclusion, would imply this. See Countryman 1988, 180.

3. Schüssler Fiorenza 1983, 128–30; the Synoptic parallels are Mark 14:3–9 and Matt. 26:6–13. John's version is in John 12:1–8.

4. A careful reading of the four anointing complexes gives the strong feeling that there are two events in Jesus' ministry reflected here. One is along the lines of Luke's story, where a woman, probably a prostitute, seeks forgiveness, wetting Jesus' feet with tears and wiping them with her unbound hair. The other event is the anointing at Bethany story, along the lines of Mark and Matthew. Luke (or his tradition) seems to have conflated the anointing into his story. John seems to have taken these two versions and changed the woman to Mary of Bethany, keeping the detail of unbinding her hair and wiping Jesus' feet. The idea that a respectable woman like Mary of Bethany would unbind her hair under these circumstances is incredible, and using her hair to wipe away the expensive nard makes little sense; see Brown 1966, 447–54. Fitzmyer takes a different approach, suggesting that the anointing of the feet is more likely to be original because it makes so little sense, and hence was probably changed, possibly in the oral traditions, to the more reasonable anointing of the head; see Fitzmyer 1981, 683–92.

5. Some, such as Snaith, would go farther and read the parable as showing the necessity of repentance; he puts it that "there can never be forgiveness without repentance" while the parable shows that one "who does not forgive can not repent"; see Snaith 1952, 86. This raises the question of the nature of repentance as well as its necessity.

6. Matthew's interpretation of this parable is basically unsatisfactory, although it does reinforce the point of this study. Matthew identifies the lord (*kyrios*) of this story with God, always a dubious practice when interpreting parables. He then is forced into a reading where God reneges on forgiveness at the first mistake the servant makes in not extending forgiveness himself. This is hardly the action of a faithful God.

   An alternate reading can be constructed by looking at the phenomenal size of the first slave's debt; ten thousand talents can be put in perspective by noting that the annual revenue of Herod the Great, with all of his famous building programs, never exceeded 900 talents. A king who could forgive such a debt can not be just an earthly king, but can only be messianic. But even this messianic king can not be relied upon to remain faithful. Thus the parable would be a warning against the expectation of a messianic king. (I would like to thank William R. Herzog II of Colgate Rochester Divinity School for introducing me to this reading.)

7. The NRSV margin indicates that this verse may not belong in the Gospel of Luke.

8. This is discussed in detail in Fortune 1989, 99. See especially chap. 6, "Doing Justice and Mercy," 108–29.

9. The parallels are Matt. 19:21 and Luke 18:22. Note that this is a rich man in Mark, a rich young man in Matthew, and a rich ruler in Luke. He is nowhere a "rich young ruler." The variation in his description seems to point to the evangelists' struggle to define the nature of repentance. Mark and Matthew see him as rich; Luke adds the idea of direct power by making him a ruler.

10. I write this in Southern California as the Rodney King riots of 1992, the most destructive and bloody urban violence in contemporary American history, are winding down. I find myself drawn to the writings of Hosea, Amos, and Jeremiah to witness to an entire society in need of forgiveness, forgiveness it can not receive because it is unable and unwilling to reverse the patterns of power. The relinquishing of power can be a corporate as well as an individual requirement.

Works Cited

Alter, Robert. 1985. *The Art of Biblical Poetry*. New York: Basic Books.

Brown, Raymond. 1966. *The Gospel of John, I–XII*. Anchor Bible, Garden City: Doubleday.

Bultmann, Rudolf. 1953. Revised Translation 1961. "New Testament and Mythology." In *Kerygma and Myth*, ed. Hans Werner Bartsch, rev. ed. of trans. and trans. preface by Reginald H. Fuller. New York: Harper & Row.

Countryman, L. William. 1988. *Dirt, Greed, and Sex: Sexual Ethics in the New Testament and Their Implications for Today*. Philadelphia: Fortress Press.

Fitzmyer, Joseph A. 1981. *The Gospel According to Luke, I–IX*. Anchor Bible, Garden City: Doubleday.

Fortune, Marie. 1989. *Is Nothing Sacred? When Sex Invades the Pastoral Relationship*. San Francisco: Harper & Row.

Kittel, Gerhard, and Gerhard Friedrich, eds. 1985. *Theological Dictionary of the New Testament*. Translated and abridged by Geoffrey W. Bromley. Grand Rapids: Eerdmans, and Exeter, U.K.: Paternoster Press.

Knox, John, and John Reumann. 1991. "Romans." In *The New Oxford Annotated Bible*, ed. Bruce Metzger and Roland Murphy. Oxford: Oxford University Press.

Malina, Bruce J. 1981. *The New Testament World: Insights from Cultural Anthropology*. Atlanta: John Knox Press, 1981.

Malina, Bruce J., and Jerome H. Neyrey. 1991. "Honor and Shame in Luke-Acts: Pivotal Values of the Mediterranean World." In *The Social World of Luke-Acts: Models for Interpretation*, ed. Jerome H. Neyrey. Peabody, Mass.: Hendrickson.

Miller, Patrick D., Jr. 1986. *Interpreting the Psalms*. Philadelphia: Fortress Press.

Quanbeck, Warren A. 1962. "Forgiveness." In *Interpreters Dictionary of the Bible, II*, ed. George Arthur Buttrick. Nashville: Abingdon Press.

Ringe, Sharon H. 1985. *Jesus, Liberation, and the Biblical Jubilee*. Philadelphia: Fortress Press.

Schüssler Fiorenza, Elisabeth. 1983. *In Memory of Her*. New York: Crossroad.

Snaith, Norman A. 1950 (1972). "Forgive, Forgiveness." In *A Theological Wordbook of the Bible*, ed. Alan Richardson. New York: Macmillan.

Tillich, Paul. 1948. *The Shaking of the Foundations*. New York: Charles Scribner's Sons.

Let's Look Again at the Biblical Concept of Submission

CATHERINE CLARK KROEGER

M any feminist scholars repudiate the authority and inspiration of Scripture as inconsistent with justice for women. Others of us maintain that a great many texts have been misread and misinterpreted when it comes to a perspective on women. We insist that the problem lies in the matter of interpretation, and we ask for a more careful evaluation of the text, the historical and literary context, and the language of the difficult materials.

This is particularly important to women who view the Bible as their only infallible guide in matters of faith and practice. Rather than regarding the Bible as uninspired because it has been used oppressively against women, women and men of faith wish to return to the drawing board, to deal with matters of interpretation. We believe that the Scriptures free rather than enslave, heal rather than wound, empower rather than destroy. It is our contention that the fault lies with the readers and wife-abusers rather than with the text itself.

The Bible has been cruelly misused in the hands of those who seek justification for the abuse of women. Wife-abusers frequently insist that women are to "submit," but they give little regard to the actual meaning of the word in the New Testament. They argue for the validity of male headship but do not ask what the concept meant to the original authors. We must be careful not to handle the text dishonestly. One can prove almost anything from the Bible, including the notion that there is no God. The entire thought of the Psalmist, however, maintains, "The fool says in his heart 'there is no god'" (Ps. 14:1). How easy it is to misread if we do not seek to deal with the entire text!

The Bible is a book of human liberation, of deliverance from oppression, and a handbook of justice. The prophet Malachi declared on God's behalf, "I hate a man's covering his wife with violence as well as with his garment" (Mal. 2:16. NIV alternate translation). Isaiah wrote to a supposedly pious people who interspersed their religious observation with violence:

> Your fasting ends in quarreling and strife, and in striking each other with wicked fists. You cannot fast as you do today and expect your voice to be heard on high. (Is. 58:4. NIV)

The New Testament writers were also of the opinion that God would not heed the prayers of wife-abusers.

> Husbands, in the same way be considerate as you live with your wives, and treat them with respect as the weaker partner and as heirs with you of the gracious gift of life, so that nothing will hinder your prayers. (I Pet. 3:7)

Indeed, battering is specifically mentioned as a disqualifying factor for leadership in the church (I Tim. 3:3; Titus 1:7). This disqualification is concealed from the average lay leader because the Greek word for batterer (*plektes*) is usually translated in English versions as brawler, violent, or "striker." As with certain other terminology, the reader is at the mercy of the translator's mindset.

Translators sometimes adopt a very hard line, not recognizing that the very same words are sometimes translated differently in New Testament occurences that do not apply directly to women. At critical points they may fail to note how these terms are used in other Christian, Jewish and pagan texts from approximately the same time period. Let us remember that writers of the New Testament employed the common language which was widely used in the Mediterranean world. The New Testament language should be understood as that which was a common vehicle of expression; and the semantic values—especially when the lives and welfare of so many women and children are affected—needs to be assessed with meticulous care. For this reason, the importance of the semantic value of the actual Greek vocabulary is critical.

As a classicist, my task is to reconstruct the culture and attitudes of the ancients; and my particular work focuses on the world of the early church. Classicists work with literary texts, business and legal documents, coins, inscriptions, and many other kinds of data from the ancient world. Above all, the classicist is concerned with the use of the Greek and Latin languages—the richness of expression, the variety of nuances of meaning contained in the writings of the ancients. It is precisely this concern with language which has led me to a closer examination of certain vocuabulary terms which are sometimes applied oppressively to women in present day churches. Chief among these is the Greek word commonly rendered by biblical translators "submit".[1]

Meanings of *Hupotasso*

Let us then turn to the cluster of words commonly understood to be related to "submission" in the Greek New Testament: *hupotasso* (verb—to submit but also to behave responsibly toward another, to align oneself with, to relate to another in a meaningful way), *hupotaktes* (adjective—submissive, but more commonly, behaving in an orderly or proper fashion), *anupotaktos* (adjective opposite to *hupotaktes*—disorderly, irresponsible, confused, lacking meaning) and *hupotage* (noun—submission, attachment or copy). In early Greek writers, the original primary sense of *hupotasso* appears to have been a military one, as in drawing up soldiers into a combat unit under the command of a leader. The implication of loyalty to the leader is often present; for even in military situations, the commitment of troops to their commander is the ultimate essential. As a passive participle, the term was applied not necessarily to those under the leader's command, but rather to those who were allies, affiliates or adherents of a king or chief. The emphasis is more upon association rather than upon dominance. *Hupotasso* does not necessarily convey the notion of subordination, and most certainly does not mean putting up with any abuse which may be inflicted upon oneself.

The same words may be used in several different senses by the various writers of the New Testament, so it is not surprising that we shall find various connotations. For instance, in Rom. 8:20 we are told that the world was "subjected" unto vanity. Now this is a concept in direct opposition to the notion that God controls the world and will ultimately bring good out of the evil which we mortals seem bent on creating. Again and again the Psalmists speak of God's power and control over the universe. How then are we to understand the world being subject to foolishness? One very conservative dictionary suggests that the meaning of *hupotasso* here should be understood as "brought under the influence of."[2] Then the verse would read, "The world was brought under the influence of human folly." With this most of us would agree, for man's foolishness and stupidity have surely exerted a negative influence on the world which God gave us. Better yet, we might translate this passage, "The world *became associated with* human folly."

In 1 Corinthians 14, the term is used twice—once of prophets (v. 32) and once of women (v. 32). The passage stipulates that each worshiper should have a chance to participate and that individuals should be ready to hold themselves in check in order to give someone else a turn. Appparently great enthusiasm but little order or respect for others was being displayed. Some translators have adopted phraseology to show that the application to prophets means that they can exercise self control in their prophesying and behave responsibly toward the worshipping community.[3] The same translators have been less quick to see that the same sense may be applied to women. Since their praying and prophesying aloud has already been approved (1 Cor. 11:5), we can best understand the passage by noting that women too should behave responsibly and avoid disruptive or irrelevant conversation during services of worship.[4]

Another interesting use occurs in 2 Cor. 9:13 when Paul writes to the Corinthians that their "submission" (*hupotage*) to their confession of the Gospel has gone out to all the world. First he voices appreciation for the gift which they have made to relieve the sufferings of others.

> The ministry of this service not only provides for the needs of the saints but abounds through the thanksgiving of many unto God. You glorify God by the evidence of this ministry in your *consistency* ("submission"—*hupotage*) with your confession of the Gospel of Christ and the sincerity of your generosity.

One may obey the dictates of one's faith but how does one submit to a *confession*? On the other hand, one can align one's actions with one's previous confession of faith, making one's life consistent with the profession. I suggest that the word here is best translated "identification" or "consistency" or "conformity" with their confession. The Corinthians were willing to share their funds as well as their faith.

In Rom. 8:7 Paul discusses the mind of unregenerate humanity as it is prone to sinfulness and alienation from God. Then he declares "the mind of the flesh is not subject to the law of God. Neither can it be." The saying becomes more comprehensible if we understand the phrase as "the unregenerate mind *is not aligned, associated, or in conformity with* the law of God."

To be sure, the active form of the verb could imply subordinating or subduing someone and the passive form submitting or being subject. But its meaning does not always convey the notion of dominance or subjection. Christians are told to be subject to their rulers and to their ordinances (Rom. 13:1–7; Titus 3:1–2; 1 Pet. 2:13–17). They are to be constructive, law-abiding, and responsible members of their society, but by no means to knuckle under to what is wrong. One need only think of the Christians' refusal to offer incense to the emperor to understand that they did *not* construe this as an injunction to blind obedience. Many laid down their lives rather than to conform at this point. St. Peter firmly declared that "we ought to obey God rather than man" (Acts 5:29; 4:19). The directives to "submission" are rather calls to live responsibly and to discharge all the obligations of citizenship.

What Does "Submission" Entail for Women?

It is worth noting that while the New Testament bids servants and children to obey (*hupakouo*), wives are told to be associates or adherents of their husbands (*hupotasso*). Let us ask some questions of this verb as it occurs in passages pertaining to women. First we must note that it is used in the middle voice. The Greek language possesses not only an active and passive voice as does English but also a middle voice—usually employed when one performs an action on oneself. For instance, "I drag," (active) "I am dragged" (passive) or "I drag myself." We call this last use reflexive, but in Greek this would be in the middle voice.

Persons who have not studied Greek are frequently surprised to learn that a verb in the middle voice may have a meaning quite different from that which it usually has in the active or passive. For instance, *peitho* in the active and passive voice means "to persuade" and "to be persuaded," while in the middle the meaning is "to obey." Similarly *archo* in the active or passive means "to rule" or "to be ruled," but in the middle "to begin something." Now *hupotasso*, the verb translated "submit", occurs uniformly in the middle voice when it is applied to women or wives in the New Testament. This should make us all the more alert for alternative meanings.

Polybius, a second century B.C.E. historian, uses *hupotassso* when he explains how to relate different entities to one another in a meaningful way. Being of the impression that the earth is flat, he says that the world should be differentiated into north, south, east, and west. Then the various parts of Earth should be identified with or related (*hupotasso*) to these divisions.[5] Otherwise, the mind will have nothing with which to associate the concept. He did not want his account to be dissociated (*anupotasso*) from something recognizable in the minds of those who are ignorant of the localities.[6] His word for "not associated with" is *anupotasso,* the opposite of *hupotasso.* A concept becomes meaningless if it is not possible to make an identification of the unknown from the known, he says, while meaningful relationship with the known provides an understanding of the unknown.

In another instance, Polybius uses *hupotasso* when he says that it is justifiable to gather together under the name of traitor all who betray their native land or city.[7] In order to make such people easy to identify, he places them together in (*hupotasso*) a significant group, i.e., traitors. Thus he uses the word in the sense of making a mental association or of establishing a meaningful relationship. Ptolemy, an ancient scientist, used the antonym *anupotaktos* to mean a person who is independent, detached from others, not integrated into a group.[8] Others applied the term to individuals displaying irresponsibility or lack of accountability (1 Tim. 1:9; Titus 1:6,10).

A consideration of these positive and negative meanings can give us a better understanding of the boy Jesus' relationship with his parents after he failed to accompany them on the homeward journey to Nazareth. He was found in the temple, insisting that he must be about the things of his Father. Then he changed his attitude and went back to Nazareth with them and "was accountable to them" or "associated himself with them" (*hupotasso*) (Luke 2: 51). Here there is also the sense of his identification with the everyday world of the carpenter shop at Nazareth rather than the brilliant world of theological debate in the temple courtyards. That it was not primarily a matter of obedience is demonstrated by Jesus' continuing efforts to redirect his mother's concerns (Matt. 12:46–45; Mark 3:21, 31–35; Luke 8:19–21; John 2:4).

Hupotasso also contains the idea of mutual support and responsibility, as in Eph. 5:21. Here believers are told to be "subject unto one another." Since they are to exercise this activity in relationship with one another, the meaning cannot be one of authoritarian dominance and subservience. Clearly it indicates mutuality and sharing.

Next follows verse 22, the text most often quoted to women, "Wives be subject (*hupotasso*) to your own husbands." Non-Greek readers need to understand that this is not what the text says. There is no verb at all in verse 22. Instead, one must continue the sense of the verb found in verse 21, "being subject to one another—wives to your own husbands." Whatever "submit" or "be subject" means in verse 21 must also be its sense in verse 22—and in 21 it clearly implies mutuality. The text goes on at considerable length about Christ's self-sacrifice on behalf of the church and to challenge husbands to the same kind of treatment of their wives. Eph. 5:27–28 bespeaks Christ's concern that the church should be developed to its full potential, and just so the husband needs to help a wife grow in every respect—including that of making decisions.

This call to mutuality and commitment was not necessarily the stuff that marriages were made of in the Roman Empire of the first century C.E. Girls between the ages of twelve and fourteen were married off to older men whom they did not know, often under a "without hand" proviso which left the young woman still legally, financially and religiously part of her father's family rather than that of her husband. Husband, children, and slaves belonged to the "familia," and only she was an interloper. A skillful woman could play off the two families against one another, while her father retained the right to remove her from the marriage whenever it might suit his convenience. By the first century C.E. ancient social observers were well aware that these forces contributed to the instability of marriages throughout the Roman Empire.

If we are to judge from literary sources, frequently mother, sons, and clever slaves joined together to outwit the father of the family and gain their own advantage. By contrast, the New Testament calls for families to pull together, in mutual respect and harmony, with the wife as an integral part of the unit. A wife could by her own volitional action take legal and practical steps which would constitute her as united in every respect with her husband, rather than with her family of birth.

Commitment, responsible behavior, and meaningful relationships with other members of the family were all enjoined upon wives. Slavish servitude can only weaken the bond of marriage and create untold misery and depression. Women can be truly submissive when they take their lives into their own hands and build strong, healthy marriages based upon mutual respect and affection. The biblical call to "submission" is a call not to oppression and loss of self, but to meaningful bonding and accountability within a committed relationship.

Notes

1. For a treatment of head/headship, see my article in *Dictionary of Paul and His Letters* (Downers Grove, Ill: 1993). See also my "The Classical Concept of 'Head' as 'Source'," in Gretchen Gaebelein Hull, *Equal to Serve* (Revell, 1987).

2. See, for example *The Analytical Greek Lexicon* (Grand Rapids, Mich.: Zondervan 1970).

3. In particular, check the rendering in *The Living Bible*.

4. See R. and C. Kroeger, "Pandemonium and Silence at Corinth," *Reformed Journal* (June 1978). Reprints available from CBE, Box 7155, St Paul, Minn., 55107

5. Polybius, *Histories* III.36.6–7.

6. Polybius, *Histories* III.38.4.

7. Polybius, *Histories* XVIII.15.4.

8. Ptolemy, *Tetrabiblios* 61

The Gerasene Demoniac
and the Sexually Violated

PETER HORSFIELD[1]

The account of the "Gerasene Demoniac" as presented in Mark 5:1–20 is one of the most dramatic exorcisms and encounters by Jesus described in the Gospels. Mark's account is more direct than either Matthew's or Luke's and incorporates descriptions of the man's strength and frightfulness into the body of the story rather than as parenthesis. Indeed, were the Gospel of Mark a contemporary writing, the presence and style of the story of the Gerasene Demoniac would surely prompt scholarly speculation that Stephen King was involved in authorship of the Gospel in some way.

A number of critical questions have been raised about the nature and meaning of the story in its contemporary setting.[2] In this article I explore the close parallels between the mythology and dynamics of the demoniac narrative and the mythology and dynamics of the contemporary experience of sexual violence as experienced predominantly by women. In doing so, I think the story of the demoniac gives us some valuable and necessary insights into how we may be called to respond to those many women and children today for whom the "invasion" or "possession" of sexual assault is a reality. In turn, because the mythologic and dynamic parallels are so close, doing so may also prompt reflection and speculation on aspects of the original story.

The reason given for the demoniac's wild and uncontrollable behavior is that he was "with an unclean spirit," though there is a constant and subtle play within the story between the one unclean spirit being many, of having many forms.[3] As the story unfolds, we see details of particular (and popular) beliefs about spiritual inhabitation and spirit exorcism, such as:

- unclean spirits or demons preferred to live in unclean places, hence "a man out of the tombs with an unclean spirit" (v. 2);

- the demons would recognize the Messiah, hence "what have you to do with me, Jesus, Son of the Most High God?" (v. 7);

- knowing the demon's name gave the exorcist power, hence Jesus asks the demon's name and the demon refuses, saying only "we are many" (v. 9);

- demons were identified with a particular region and were terrified of leaving that location, hence "he begged him earnestly not to send them out of the country" (v. 10);

- demons were terrified of being without a dwelling place, hence their request to Jesus to "send us into the swine" (v. 12).

F. C. Grant suggests there is even a touch of humor in the story. Sending unclean spirits into a herd (?) of unclean pigs would seem a fair destination to a Jewish audience. There are inconsistencies in the spirit mythology also. Where did the spirits go when the pigs drowned, for example?

The mythology of the story per se would have raised few problems for its contemporary hearers. However, it raises significant hermeneutical questions for most readers today living in western societies, certainly for those educated in the behavioral sciences and the humanities. (This is not necessarily the case for that significant proportion of today's youth population whose cosmology has been shaped not only by scientific thought but also by the equally influential corpus of horror movies and science fiction.)

Behavioral science today would tend to view such "demoniacal" behavior in psychopathological terms. If presented with such a "case," probable physical or psychological causes would be identified and treated either chemically or psychodynamically—certainly not by spirit exorcism. This modern "psychologising" of events and encounters would tend to avoid or deal skeptically with the non-empirical elements and dimensions within biblical narratives, rendering them as curious archaisms rather than phenomena of contemporary relevance.

I consider it is this sense of loss of regard for the integrity of the text in modern practice that frequently motivates many Christian groups to hold fast to a literal interpretation of such events. Many see in the story of the demoniac, for example, a justification for contemporary spirit exorcism. Restricting an understanding of the story to such a literal view, however, fails to take sufficiently seriously the significant difference that now exists between the cultural mythology of the New Testament and the mythology of contemporary Western culture. A naïve literal approach to the text also provides no real basis for an engagement of the two different mythologies.

An alternative approach that takes seriously both the biblical and the modern scientific world view is one that acknowledges that both world views utilize constructed mythologies and then explores those mythologies for their strengths and weaknesses, their insights and their oversights.

The modern "scientific" view, for example, has certainly opened up whole new areas of insight and has contributed significantly to overcoming the destructiveness of many of the superstitions which have surrounded mental illness in the past. What is frequently lost in this modern mechanistic view, however—and this is encouraged by the increased specialization of the scientific disciplines—is that sickness has dimensions other than the mere disruption of "natural" physiological processes. Sickness has an impact on our lives far beyond the actual physical process of "getting sick." The "experience" of "sickness" has not only practical physiological characteristics, but also symbolic ones. At its root the experience of sickness, or violation of the integrity of our person, introduces into our lives a dimension of something beyond ourselves coming to affect us, something over which we have had no control. This experience not only affects us individually, but threatens the very foundations of secularity, viz., human instrumentation and autonomy.

Understanding this "spiritual" dimension of sickness or personal violation provides one way of understanding the contemporary significance of the "spirits" in the story of the demoniac. The demoniac was a person "possessed"—literally "owned" and "used"—by something beyond himself which ignored or refused to respect his sense of personal boundary and worth and which used him for its own purposes—in this case, as a place to live and as a personal gymnasium.

That sense of being used or taken over beyond one's ability to control, which is mythologized in the Markan story by the occupation of the demon(s), is central to understanding the existential truth of the story for us today. There are or will be times in all human lives when we are faced with situations or drives which ignore our autonomy and gifted self-worth, invade our space, one way or the other, and use us.

This dimension becomes most obtrusive in pastoral situations of violation or sickness: an active, competitive businessman who has just had a heart attack; someone faced with the prospect of losing a limb; a woman about to undergo a mastectomy; an independent elderly person who has become hospitalized and is wondering if this is the sickness that will make it impossible for them to continue to live in their own home; a person who has just been told they have cancer; or a woman who has just been beaten by her husband or raped. One cannot encounter closely people dealing with such experiences without realizing that there is more than just a physical process going on—the person becomes engaged also in a struggle with the spiritual dimension of everyday life.

Another close parallel to the biblical mythology is that when we deal with major crises (and even minor ones) such as these, we frequently conceive of them in terms of having been invaded by something outside ourselves. We ask questions like: "Will I be able to beat *this thing*?" and "Why has this *happened* to me?" It is not unusual also to find that within the experience of sickness or being violated, the unified concept of the self, the sense of well being, is broken up.

While our mythologizing (naming) of such situations may be quite different from the mythology being used in the biblical accounts, the impact and the reality being addressed is little different.

It is within this hermeneutical context that the narrative of the demoniac bears a remarkably close parallel to the dynamics found in the experience of those people (mainly women and girls) who have been victims of childhood sexual abuse or who have suffered sexual violence at the hands of men they have trusted.

The experience of sexual violence is a more common experience than is generally recognized. While precise data are difficult to establish, Australian and international research indicates that sexual assault is a major social phenomenon. One out of ten women will be raped in their lifetime.[4] Rape of women occurs in 7 percent to 12 percent of all marriages.[5] Thirty-eight percent of girls (9 percent of boys) will be sexually assaulted in some way by the time they are eighteen years of age.[6] Incest takes place in one out of ten homes.[7] Ninety-three percent of victims of sexual assault are female.[8] Ninety-eight percent of offenders are male.[9] There is no "typical" female victim: women victims come from all ages, classes, cultures, races, and creeds. Likewise there is no "typical" male attacker: male attackers commonly look and act like ordinary men and come from all social classes, income levels, races, and age groups.

Several particular characteristics of sexual violence compound the effects of such "invasion" and increase the victim/survivor's vulnerability. One is prior relationship to the assaulter. Eighty percent of women victims and 76 percent of female child victims know the man who assaulted them.[10] A child sexual offender in the overwhelming majority of instances is the father, stepfather, mother's de facto partner, brother, uncle or grandfather of the child victim.[11]

A second is that most sexual assaults are not random incidents against which a woman or child can take precautionary action, or avoid if she were only more careful. Most sexual assaults are calculated exploitations of trust relationships. They are generally premeditated and well planned and in many cases are carried out by men whom the woman or girl and society have looked on and trusted as a protector. This compounds the effect of the violence by undermining the woman's sense of confidence in trust relationships, in social institutions, and in her own judgment. It also undermines her sense of security and safety even in familiar environments. When the woman or girl is assaulted by a clergyman or male church leader, which is not infrequent, it has even more profound implications, frequently affecting deeply her sense of spiritual trust, her spiritual sense of self, and leaving her with the feeling of having been ravaged or abandoned by God.[12]

The experience of assault, which is literally an invasion of a woman or girl's bodily boundaries, confuses those boundaries and violates the sense of one's own person. It is traumatizing, confusing and shattering, with deep and long-lasting effects. When this occurs at a young age, in many cases the trauma is so great that the memory of the experience is frequently involuntarily suppressed.

> The main way I coped with the incest was deciding not to remember it until it was safe. The main thing that made it safe was finally being in a relationship where I felt I could really count on my partner. We were in couples therapy when I had my first flashback. I remembered the sensation of being molested, and I got a very clear image of the room.[13]

Even though the event(s) may not be remembered, the consequences of it generally continue to effect the girl's or the woman's attitude, perception, and actions. Because the original event(s) causing these reactions is either not generally known or forgotten, these actions appear as seemingly irrational, disruptive, disorienting, or personally destructive behavior that doesn't seem to fit. The mythology of understanding such behavior as an invasion of something separate from one's own being is a very relevant and powerful one. Women survivors of sexual assault speak frequently of the experience of being sexually assaulted in terms of being invaded, possessed and used.

> It felt like my body was inhabited by this thing that happened in my child-hood, that there wasn't a cell in my body that wasn't involved in it. The memories felt like they were invading me, in the same way my uncle had invaded my body. I spent a lot of time feeling like I was going to throw up.[14]

Because there is no readily apparent, identifiable, or socially acceptable reason for this behavior, the woman or child survivor generally suffers further. Rather than being praised for the strength involved in surviving a major, uninvited personal trauma, she is frequently blamed and feels personally guilty for being of unstable temperament. The biblical mythology that emerges in Mark's story of the demoniac should not be taken too lightly, even today, that demons live among the tombs of what is dead and stinking. This is well illustrated in the story of Jennierose Lavender, a forty-seven-year-old survivor of child sexual abuse:

> People have said to me, "Why are you dragging this up now?" Why? WHY? Because it has controlled every facet of my life. It has damaged me in every possible way. It has destroyed everything in my life that has been of value. It has prevented me from living a comfortable emotional life. It's prevented me from being able to love clearly. It took my children away from me. I haven't been able to succeed in the world. If I had a comfortable childhood, I could be anything today. I know that every-thing I don't deal with now is one more burden I have to carry for the rest of my life. I don't care if it happened 500 years ago! It's influenced me all that time, and it does matter. It matters very much.[15]

Not only can it tear apart the woman's sense of herself, but it undermines the capacity to trust and love anyone, particularly men. The integrated self is fre-quently divided into several characters (known as "splitting"), literally mak-ing the one person, many—the very words used to describe the character of the demoniac. Bass and Davis indicate that virtually everyone who is diag-nosed with multiple personality disorder has been found to be severely abused—sexually, physically, or psychologically—as a young child, a view supported by others.[16] The story of Diane illustrates this process:

> From the time I was a very young child, I had experiences which were so traumatic they split my personality wide open. There was no way for my young mind to cope with the brutality and random acts of sadism that I experienced. Instead, I completely forgot the incidents and created a totally new personality. . . . Each of these personalities began without the old scars, without the old terror, without the anger.[17]

The story of Gizelle, a forty-two-year-old survivor of childhood incestu-ous rape, also illustrates how this process of division was essential for personal survival in a totally uncontrollable assaultive situation:

I split my father into two different people, because there was no other way to sit across the breakfast table from him. The man who came down and sat at the kitchen table was my father. The man who came in the middle of the night and molested me was a shadow . . . and as I split him into two, I split myself into two. There was the little girl whose father taught her to ride a bike, who got A's and became a perfectionist. And then there was the little girl who played in the attic, felt that she was dying, wanted to commit suicide, had nightmares. But I could never speak of her. Her voice had been taken away. I felt caught, trapped in my body. That's continued into adulthood.[18]

These new insights into multiple personality offer new perspectives on the Gerasene multiple personality. Do we have here in the biblical account of Jesus in Gerasa, a description of Jesus' literal encounter with, and healing of, a survivor of severe physical or sexual abuse?

It is common for onlookers to become afraid. When a child tries to tell what has happened; when the trauma of betrayal and violation produces erratic, uncontrollable or obsessive behavior; when a woman begins to remember earlier experiences and tries to speak about them; those who see this behavior or hear these stories generally become afraid of what they are hearing and the implications they have. Onlookers deal with the fear created within themselves in different ways. It is not unusual for people simply not to hear or not believe what the woman or child is saying—to change the subject or pass over it as if nothing significant has been said.

Another common response is to try and suppress the truth or horror of what is being expressed. In terms of the biblical narrative, this is equal to trying control the demon by chaining the person. This is illustrated graphically in Gizelle's story, recounting the incident in which she was awoken when she was three years old by being raped orally and then vaginally by her father:

Within seconds he was gone, and I was alone and the room was empty. And then within seconds after that, my mother came into the room and put on the light. She found me lying in bed covered with blood and vomit all over the sheets. . . . She started screaming at me, "Bad, evil, wicked child." Even at that point, I still had my knowledge that I hadn't done this. . . . And so I screamed back to my mother, "Mommy, I didn't do it. It was Daddy." Then my mother was hitting me, over and over again. "Don't you ever say that again. You lying, evil, dirty, filthy child." She just kept hitting me and hitting me.[19]

Various devices have been used historically to suppress or isolate the impact of women's stories of assault, including physical isolation. Another common device used is to chain the woman through social or psychological labelling—with terms such as crazy, hysterical, exaggerating, lying, permissive, "that time of the month," or accusing her of behaving like a victim. The intention of such labelling is to contain or neutralize the social impact of what is being reported.[20] While this may minimize the fear, anguish, and implications for those who hear, it simply perpetuates the injustice and trauma of the assault. It complicates the agony of confusion created by the assault and its effects; compounds the damage by shifting blame for the assault and responsibility for managing its effects onto the woman; and frequently results in self-abuse by the victim/survivor. Yet this defensive behavior on the part of onlookers is common, even within the church. This is particularly the case when the assaulter is a clergyman, priest or male leader, with reactions such as—"Do you think you're overreacting or misunderstanding his intentions? It sounds a bit hysterical to me," or "You're allowing this one little experience to dominate your life"—being common.[21]

It is testimony to the persistent love of God and the power of the female spirit, that women so severely bound both personally and socially can still, like the demoniac in Gerasa, persist in breaking those chains and seeking out someone who has the courage not to run away.

According to the Markan narrative, when the demoniac saw Jesus from afar, he ran towards Jesus and met him as Jesus stepped out of the boat. I have occasionally envisaged myself in the same situation and considered my likely response. If I had just stepped out of a boat in a "pagan" territory, when, from a cave in a cemetery in the distance, these wild, filthy, naked people came running towards me, covered with dirt and dried blood from uncleaned cuts and bruises, possibly dragging bits of broken chains on their wrists and ankles, running wildly and screaming at the top of their voice as they ran—how would I respond? I expect I would jump back into the boat and get a safe distance as quickly as possible.

According to the narrative, Jesus didn't. Jesus apparently stood his ground (a quite understated act of courage, given the context). In terms of the spirit mythology of the story, the two people met, the demon was named and banished, recognizing the superior authority of the spirit of Jesus, with the effect that those who came out to see what was going on were surprised to see the former demoniac "sitting there, clothed and in his right mind, the very man who had the legion" (v. 15—again, a quite understated description).

It is difficult to know, in more contemporary mythological terms, what passed between Jesus and the demoniac when they met on the beach. What non-verbal communication occurred between the two? Was the one with the demon struck by the fact that here was someone who didn't run away, who could face him as he was? Was there the perception that here was someone whose integration was stronger than his disintegration? Was there a sense of spiritual presence in Jesus that commanded authority? Whatever it was, it was apparently communicated in such a way, with such compassion and confidence, that the one with the demons was restored to wholeness—the deep divisions, conflicts and wildness were removed.

That same possibility and reality is spoken of frequently by victim/survivors when they encounter someone who embodies those qualities that appear to have been embodied by Jesus.

It was (Frank's) belief in my strength that kept me moving forward. He'd say, "Look at what you've done. You're an incredibly strong woman." Time and time again when I lost belief in my healing, Frank would say: "Trust your process, allow it to lead you. Trust yourself, listen to yourself." The greatest gift Frank gave me was his unwavering faith in the wisdom and power of my own healing spirit.[22]

Judith was like this barnacle. She just hung on through all my acting out, all my fear, all my resistance. First I thought I was crazy. Then I thought they were crazy. My fears and doubts just got flushed right out of me. . . . I burst into tears, and I hung onto her, and I started weeping, and I said, "I'm not crazy anymore." I realized at that moment how far I had come. I felt the integration happening right then. And Judith burst into tears, and she rocked me. And at that point, for the first time, I knew that I had a future.[23]

Christians would identify that wisdom and redemptive power within the human spirit and between human spirits as the wisdom and power of God incarnate in human life, signalled and embodied in Jesus Christ. In relation to victim/survivors of sexual abuse, that embodiment of the spirit of Christ is found in someone having the caring and courage to hear the horror of abuse, to face the personal threat and challenge it poses to their perception of particular people or institutions, and to deal with it by naming the personal and social demons of sexual abuse rather than chaining the woman or running away.

One would expect that people who came out of the town would be glad to see the man who was once possessed by demons sitting peacefully and composed with a totally different self-understanding. But they weren't. The biblical narrative says they were afraid and begged Jesus to leave the neighborhood. This fearful and angry reaction is frequently condemned in pulpits whenever the text is preached on. But it is a reaction that is well known to those who work in women's refuges and sexual assault centers, and it is a reaction that frequently comes from the church. Breaking the silence around sexual violence and challenging the abusive treatment of women calls into question entrenched social attitudes and advantages, institutional self-interest, and comfortable social illusions. We do not always celebrate when a woman who was once thought to be crazy regains "her right mind" and then says the reason she was crazy was because she was assaulted by a man we generally hold in high regard.[24] The talk, behavior and challenges of a "crazy" person can be pitied, ignored, and rationalized; a right mind cannot so easily be dismissed.

Every society appears to accept that there will be a few human sacrifices in the maintenance of social order. We are, after all, as individuals and as a society, not perfect. There is even the expectation that those unfortunate enough to receive unfair measure because of the way our society is structured should remain quiet for the sake of the broader social good. It is okay if women who have been violated deal with the demonic effects personally—in their own groups or even in the privacy of therapy. But if all the women who have experienced sexual violence at the hands of men in trust relationships start naming the demon publicly, they could disrupt the very structures of our social institutions and the good those institutions achieve. For the good of the whole, it is better that those who are dealing with the demons of violence fight those demons in the cemetery on their own and not disrupt the rest of us. Someone should have told Jesus that!

🌺

Notes

1. The author acknowledges the significant contribution made by the women in SHIVERS to the ideas and understanding presented in this article.

2. See, for example, F. C. Grant in *The Interpreter's Bible*, Vol. VII (New York: Abingdon Press, 1951), 712; C. S. Mann, *Mark: A New Translation with Introduction and Commentary (The Anchor Bible)* (Garden City: Doubleday, 1986), 278; E. Schweizer, *The Good News According to Mark: A Commentary on the Gospel* (London: S.P.C.K., 1970), 113; Ched Myers, *Binding the Strong Man: A Political Reading of Mark's Story of Jesus* (Maryknoll, N.Y.: Orbis Books, 1988).

3. Mann departs from the more common contemporary psychological under-standing of this in noting that the word "legion" was often used as a term to describe a large number (279). Myers sees it as being used specifically to describe a division of Roman soldiers (191). The T.E.V. graphically uses a term more familiar to Australians, the term "mob."

4. C. Offir, "Don't Take It Lying Down," *Psychology Today* (January 1975); H. Haines, *The Extensiveness of Sexual Abuse: A Brief Literature Review* (Mental Health Foundation, U.S.A., 1985), quoted in *Breaking the Silence: A Guide to Supporting Victims/Survivors of Sexual Assault* (Melbourne: The Centre Against Sexual Assault, Royal Women's Hospital, 1989), 5.

5. D. Finkelhor and K. Yllo, *License to Rape: Sexual Abuse of Wives* (New York: Holt Rinehart, 1985), and D. Russell, *Rape in Marriage* (New York: Macmillan, 1982), quoted in *Breaking the Silence*, 5.

6. D. Finkelhor, *Sexually Victimized Children* (New York: Free Press, 1979); D. Russell, "The Incidence and Prevalence of Intrafamilial Sexual Abuse of Female Children," in *Child Abuse and Neglect* 7 (1983); and R. Goldman, Study Presented to the Congress on Child Abuse, Sydney, 1986; quoted in *Breaking the Silence*, 5. Studies by the Australian Bureau of Statistics indi-cate that in Australia fewer than one in ten sexual assault victims report the assault to the police. See E. Klimkiewicz et al. *Care for Victims of Sexual Assault: A Manual*. Law Foundation of New South Wales, 1984; and Haines, 1985 quoted in *Breaking the Silence*, 5.

7. National Coalition against Sexual Assault Conference, 1987 quoted in *Breaking the Silence*, 5.

8. Finkelhor, 1979, quoted in *Breaking the Silence*, 5.

9. *Project Anna: CASA House with the Churches Against Violence to Women* (Melbourne: CASA House, Royal Women's Hospital, 1990).

10. M. Amir, *Patterns in Forcible Rape* (Chicago: University of Chicago Press, 1971); R. Hall, *Ask Any Woman: A London Inquiry into Rape and Sexual*

Assault (London: Falling Wall Press, 1985), quoted in *Breaking the Silence*, 5. One Australian study found that in more than 20 percent of cases of incest, the assault took place while the girl was in her own bed or sleeping. See *Breaking the Silence: A Report Based upon the Findings of the Women Against Incest Phone-in Survey* (Haberfield NSW: Dympna House, 1987), 32.

11. Finkelhor, 1979, quoted in *Breaking the Silence*, 5.

12. See Ann-Janine Morey, "Blaming Women for the Sexually Abusive Male Pastor," *The Christian Century* (October 5, 1988): 866–69; Pamela Cooper-White, "Soul Stealing: Power Relations in Pastoral Sexual Abuse," *The Christian Century* (February 20, 1991): 196–99; Marie Fortune, *Is Nothing Sacred? When Sex Invades the Pastoral Relationship* (San Francisco: Harper & Row, 1989); *A Pastoral Report to the Churches on Sexual Violence against Women and Children of the Church Community* (CASA House, Royal Women's Hospital, 1990).

13. Quoted in Ellen Bass and Laura Davis, *The Courage to Heal: A Guide for Women Survivors of Child Sexual Abuse* (New York: Harper & Row, 1988), 411.

14. Ibid.

15. Ibid., 33.

16. Ibid., 423. See also, for example, psychiatrist Robert Phillips Jr. in his introduction to The Troops for Trudi Chase, *When Rabbit Howls* (London: Pan Books, 1987): "The majority of reported cases of multiple personality occur in men and women who have experienced severe and repeated sexual and physical abuse over a significant period of time" (xi).

17. Ibid., 422.

18. Ibid., 448.

19. Ibid.

20. Marilyn Born provides an extensive description of this labelling in relation to complaints by women of sexual harassment and assault by clergy in "Sexual Harassment in the Church: The Kiss of Betrayal" *Compass* 25 (1991): 29–32.

21. Ibid.

22. Giselle in Bass and Davis, *The Courage to Heal*, 451. That the same sort of experience can be mythologized quite differently is suggested in one of the verses of the missionary hymn, "Rescue the perishing," which says:

> Deep in the human heart, crushed by the tempter,
> Feelings lie buried which grace can restore.
> Touched by a loving hand, wakened by kindness,
> Chords that were broken will vibrate once more.

23. Quoted in Bass and Davis, *The Courage to Heal*, 428–29.

24. D. Rowan found that in a South Australia refuge, 80 percent of the men who beat their wives were reported as being charming to everyone else. The result was that the women tended not to be believed when reporting the violence done to them. ("Syndrome of Battered Women," Unpublished paper, National Conference on Domestic Violence, November, 1985, 3.)

Part III
Ethical Appraisals

Bringing Justice Home:
The Challenge of the Battered Women's
Movement for Christian Social Ethics

SARAH BENTLEY

Awareness of the extent and nature of violence in the family has been
dramatically increased due to the efforts of the battered women's
movement, a grass-roots effort which has resulted in the establishment of
over 1200 shelters, safe homes, crisis centers, counseling programs, and state
and local coalitions in response to the widespread existence of violence
against women in their own homes. The movement began during the early
1970s in Great Britain and the United States as a direct outgrowth of feminist
organizing around a variety of issues, including rape.[1]

For the past several years, I have worked as an educator, advocate, and
counselor in the context of the battered women's movement. Early on, I
observed that activists in this movement—those who daily confront the needs
of battered women for protection, legal and economic aid, and emotional support—are constantly engaged in a process of *education*. Whether answering
crisis calls, helping a woman get into a shelter, or calming a frightened child,
they are implicitly learning and teaching about the dominant *values, norms,
and institutions* of American society. Across the broadest scope of the movement's activities, which include legal advocacy, attempts to reform the criminal
justice system, and lobbying for legislative changes, significant questions are

being asked—and answered—about women's rights, about society's responsibilities to its citizens, about the nature of justice itself.

These observations stand in contrast to my experience outside the context of the movement. In or out of the religious community, most persons seem unaware of the movement's struggle to address these essentially ethical questions. Those who know about battering often deny its character as a social problem, arguing instead that violence in the home is a "family matter," primarily psychological in nature.[2]

Still another group of interactions reveals individuals who dispute this general view. Unlike the proverbial "person on the street," or even many of my religious colleagues, battered women themselves show a generalized intuition of the injustice of their situation. Hiding from violent partners, confronting hostile or indifferent judges, desperately struggling to feed and clothe their children and to recover a sense of personal power and self-respect, they consistently contend: "It's so *unfair* that we are treated this way. After all, we haven't done anything wrong."

The battered women's movement does indeed challenge the value assumptions of American culture. It does this by making clear moral judgments—about violence, about the right of women and children to be safe in their homes, and about the unjust character of laws and institutional practices which do not protect them and, indeed, often render them powerless and vulnerable to abuse. Through the movement's ongoing efforts—and the resultant awareness of the larger society—the situation of battered women has emerged as a preeminently ethical issue.[3]

However, the significance of the movement goes beyond the fact that it has identified a hitherto-ignored ethical problem. In the course of addressing the situation of battered women, the movement has introduced a new set of moral obligations which challenge dominant cultural assumptions about women and family life.[4] These can be identified through what I call core ethical themes in the movement's ongoing work. Although they are only outlined here, each of these themes deserves to be explored in terms of its broader significance for Christian social ethics. Together with other critical issues which are being lifted up by feminist ethicists, these themes form an important guide for contemporary discussions of family life and the construction of an ethic which is responsive to battering and other forms of family violence.

Ethical Themes in the Movement's Work

Behind Closed Doors: Male Violence and Women's Rights

The primary thrust of the battered women's movement is to bring the harsh reality of woman-battering into public awareness and to effect structural and cultural reforms which will not only make battering less acceptable, but will also begin a long-term process of resocialization which in turn will make such violence against women less likely in the future. A key aspect of this struggle is to lift women from social and economic *invisibility* as the property of men, particularly their husbands.

There are several components to this task: Since battered women have typically experienced blame for their situation, the movement seeks to identify *the batterer's violence* as the critical problem and to transform cultural and institutional responses which have consistently minimized the violence women experience in their homes. However, a supportive response to battered women must include the accompanying statement to batterers that their conduct is not acceptable according to community norms and, more importantly, that there will be *consequences* if their violence continues. In other words, batterers need to hear a loud and effective "no" from the *authoritative institutions* of society (especially the criminal justice system), a judgment which is backed up by the concrete possibility of retribution.

The invisibility of battered women is directly linked to the overall *privatization of the nuclear family* in Western society. Viewed as a separate sphere of activity from the public arena of work and politics, the "personal" world of the home becomes the battered woman's prison. Involvement by the public institutions of society, therefore, constitutes the needed recognition that the plight of countless individual battered women is a *communal concern*. Ending the hidden violence in homes thereby becomes a *public* responsibility.

Safety: Making Victims' Needs A Priority

The core concern to provide shelter for battered women and their children has raised some elemental questions about women's needs and the constraints of family life in a male-dominated society. For instance, the movement has continually argued that in the case of violent families, the *victim's* needs must take priority. Against the power differential which usually operates in a family, according respect, privilege, and socio-economic resources to the father/husband, the movement operates on the principles that the needs of those who are *most vulnerable* must come first. Children and women with no or scant financial resources, no way to make a living, no place to hide are accorded the prior response of compassion and aid. The needs of the overall family unit, dominated as it has been by the man's perceptions and behavior, can be considered later.

The offer of shelter to battered women rests again on the premise that society has a responsibility to protect and provide for its vulnerable members, particularly through the fundamental respite of *safety*. Thus the historic principle of sanctuary is extended to a new domain: whether an individual seeks refuge from an oppressive government, a hostile community, or an abusive family member, the same right to safety should pertain.[5]

Redefining Responsibility: The Battered Woman As Moral Agent

By offering alternatives to a life of violence, the battered women's movement is calling on victims to become not merely survivors, but *choice-makers* in their own right. Indeed, the underlying premise of all movement strategy is to provide the opportunities by which battered women may become the subjects of their own lives. The creation of safe space for battered women is thus symbolic of a deeper reality: a woman's right to have a *separate identity* from that of her husband. Over against the obligations of being a good wife and mother, through counseling and other supportive services, she is presented with a different moral claim: the *responsibility to support her own life*, to be loyal to herself. This self-authorizing existence stands in distinct contrast to her usually extensive dependence on her husband and her reliance on external authorities such as family, church, or social mores.

"We're All At Risk:" The Social Context of Battering

Against all interpretations that battered women stay in abusive relationships for psychologically pathological reasons, the movement's perspective insists that *any* woman is "one step away" from battering. Whether through economic or social dependence on a man, she may find herself paralyzed if suddenly confronted with abuse. Even if not literally trapped by financial limitations, her *perceived* options and resources may indeed be few. As a result, she is *constrained to stay* through the ever-escalating cycles of abuse until she finds a way out.

The claim that battered women are, in effect, like any other women, rests on the assumption that economic dependence is not a circumstantial factor in some women's lives, but a fundamental element of oppression for *all* women. Indeed, as individual battered women struggle to find the necessary resources to end the violence in their lives, they become increasingly aware of the socioeconomic context which limits their efforts. Thus the conviction remains strong that violence against women and children in the home can end only as the overall system which encourages and supports such violence is changed.

Theological and Ethical Responses to Battering

Feminist responses to the plight of battered women and the efforts of the movement on their behalf have brought a variety of perspectives to bear on these ethical themes. For instance, movement activists have argued that the Church is not merely silent, but actually contributes to the cultural attitudes which support and reinforce battering. Noting the authoritative role of the Church and biblical teaching in the lives of many battered women, theologian Susan Thistlethwaite proposes the use of a feminist interpretation of Scripture which begins explicitly with battered women's experience, thus breaking the specific silence of the Church's denial about woman-abuse and according authority to women's own lived experience.[6]

Not only biblical teaching but also church teaching and theology have promoted the subordinate position of woman in the family and articulated a theology of suffering which keeps battered women from seeking help.[7] The central and problematic character of a such a "theology of the cross" is the main theme in Joy Bussert's work, *Battered Women: From a Theology of Suffering to an Ethic of Empowerment*.[8] Significantly, Bussert links violence against women (and its minimization) to the Church's historically negative attitudes toward the body and sexuality. A corrective perspective must necessarily include awareness that the impact of physical violence is *total*, encompassing the woman's spiritual as well as her mental, emotional, and physical sense of self.

Seen in this light, abuse is an "ontological violation," according to Mary Pellauer, a profaning of the individual's very woman-beingness.[9] Put another way, abuse radically "de-selfs" the victim by destroying the freedom which is foundational to human identity and development. The battered woman, notes Lois Livezey, is "disenfranchised" from participation as an equal participant in family life and, by extension, in society as a whole.[10]

Feminist Ethical Concerns

In addition to these specific responses to battering, feminist ethicists have consistently concerned themselves with issues which clearly have relevance to battered women. Most obviously, feminist methodology itself finds a central resource in women's lived experience, thus affirming that this is the necessary starting point for any theo-ethical perspective which would counter the chronic powerlessness which characterizes battered women's lives.[11]

Feminist ethicists also argue for a holistic viewpoint which refutes the Christian tradition's ambivalence toward embodied existence and the overwhelming tendency to dualism of mind and body. For instance, Beverly Harrison identifies the loss of contact with the body as the cause of dis-connection within the self and between persons.[12] Such a perception is central to the construction of an ethic in response to battering because it points to the development of a moral perspective which begins with the fundamental right to bodily integrity. Without norms to affirm the constitutive claim of "body-right," there are no grounds for the judgment that battering is unjust and a crime.[13]

These two central commitments—to give a priori value to women's experience and to embrace a holistic view of personhood and relationship—interweave in feminist ethical approaches to the question of suffering.[14] They are also implicit in what may be one of the most central feminist ethical concerns: the development of an ethic of mutuality which balances autonomy with accountability, nurture, and support.[15] This effort is of particular significance because it implies an understanding of relationship which can overcome the tendency of women to lose one's very self in intimate partnerships. Of even greater importance are the efforts of feminist theologians and ethicists to reinterpret the relationship between mutual love and self-sacrifice, for herein lies one of the central dilemmas for battered women.

When Love Becomes Justice

Feminists have consistently criticized the notion of "self-less" love as being problematic for women and even distorting of the nature of loving, be it human or divine.[16] Taken to an extreme, such an ideal denotes the most characteristically Christian love as precisely that which is *least* concerned with reciprocity in relationship. Many a battered woman will persist in returning to increasingly dangerous relationships, citing this very model of Christian love as "turning the other cheek" or "following Jesus' example." Yet there is repeated evidence that far from improving the situation, her refusal to protect herself has the opposite effect on her partner, encouraging continued and often more serious abuse.

The notion of self-less love as particularly virtuous in such a situation is a morally bankrupt proposition on two accounts. First, it subverts the value of the woman's life to an abstract ideal which is in no way borne out in her experience. Second, it reinforces the illusion that love practiced by one party to a relationship has the power to overcome the other's lack of commitment to the same relationship.[17] Self-sacrifice could be of value if it were able to create or enhance mutual love.[18] But for the battered woman, increased submission tends to reinforce the batterer's claim that he is in the right when he assumes the position of domination and control. So, in reality, the woman's negation of self cannot be said to be morally good, i.e., life-giving, because it contributes neither to her own well-being nor to the development of greater mutuality within her relationship. On the contrary, it *increases* the likelihood that she and her children will face more severe violence and that her partner will only be reinforced in behavior which can arguably be described as destructive to them both.

In this sense, battered women's experience supports feminist ethicists' rejection of self-giving love as an exclusive norm for relationship. The more adequate model must be one of mutuality which presupposes a balance between other- and self-regard, with neither party habitually opting for (or being forced to choose) the other's interest over their own. But again, no battered woman is truly at liberty to make such decisions as long as she faces the continuing threat of abuse. Instead, she is usually paralyzed by the chronic fear and powerlessness which characterize her relationship. The additional factors of economic dependence and the responsibility for children also inhibit her freedom.

Taking into account the potential for violence in intimate relationships, it seems then that the true norm of mutual *love* must actually be *justice*. Margaret Farley describes such a "just love" as fundamentally expressing *the equal worth* of those loved. As such, it becomes an important element in an ethic which would respond to the key themes raised by the battered women's movement:

> ... (I)n a strict sense, justice requires that we affirm for persons, both women and men, what they reasonably need in order to live out their lives as full human persons, and within the Christian community, what they need in order to grow in their faith. It is therefore clear that to refuse to persons, on the basis of their sex, their rightful claim to life, bodily security, health, freedom of self-determination, religious worship, education, etc. is to violate the norms of a just love. Any pattern of relationship in home, church, or civil society, which does not respect persons in these needs and claims is thereby an unjust pattern of relationship.[19]

Behind Closed Doors: Social Ethics and Family Life

Implicit then in the feminist ethical search for an adequate ethic of relationship is this challenge: to recast the relationship between love and justice in order that both norms may be appropriated by social ethicists in such a way as to unite the formerly separate arenas of private and public life. Despite the many-faceted nature of theo-ethical responses to the battered women's movement's concerns, there has been little discussion specifically about the link between the Church's minimal response to battering and the culturally-reinforced privatization of family life in general. This is a significant area to explore because it concerns the question of how to locate women's rights *within* the family as well as in the larger society.

The battered women's movement has made it clear that the Church, like other cultural institutions, has participated in the false division of private and public life, encouraging the implicit view that family relations are "off limits" for any but the most minimal intervention. So if social ethicists are to address the problem of battering, it is imperative to overcome this bias toward defining family life as a separate world in contradistinction to the values and norms of public life. Instead, this fundamental realm of everyday life must be seen as part of the overall moral order which governs all social (i.e., human) life, and, as such, reflective of the patterns of domination and subordination present at every level of society.[20]

For, while it is true that battering has been ignored because of sexist attitudes across the range of theological disciplines and within the Church as a whole, there is this other aspect of the problem. By definition, battering is abuse which takes place between two persons in *intimate* relationship, typically in the confines of their home life. However, with the exception of issues of sexual behavior, this same "private" sphere has not been the subject of substantive moral reflection in Christian social ethics. In fact, until recently there has been a striking lack of attention to the question of ethical norms for relationships within the family. Battered women are thus doubly invisible, both as female victims and as members of a community (the family) whose moral values and behavior have been only minimally explored.

Restoring the Importance of Family Life

In order to overcome the traditional separation between family and public life, ethicists must fundamentally reconsider the importance of the family as a crucial area of moral life. This is both obvious and necessary because the family is the foremost locus of *social* identity: "the first community in which human sociality is developed and nurtured," "the social context in which the individual becomes a person, a social being."[21] Thus the foundations of one's identity, and, by extension, one's values and norms, are laid in the context of family relationships.

However, despite their obvious centrality, family relationships have alternatively been ignored or idealized by Christian social ethics. The result is an absence of specific ethical norms, or "action-guides" for persons in their family lives. In response to this crucial omission, Farley has called for a twofold approach on the part of the Church: to reassess the place of family in overall Christian life, and to address the specific problems confronting families "by examining the family itself as a place of justice."[22]

Significantly, Farley judges the true context for such ethical reflection to be the "life and death" problems of abuse and family violence. The real situation of families thus necessitates critically evaluating the significance of Christian teachings with regard to:

... *power in* family relationships, tolerance of physical and psychological *violence* as long as it is contained within the family, manner of *conflict resolution* in intimate relations, *rights of persons to reciprocity of care* as dependency roles change through a lifetime, limits to burdens that can reasonably be borne by persons of varying ages and capacities.[23]

Family violence is not then a special case, but the *paradigm* of the sort of injustice which pervades family life. So ethicists must take seriously the economic, political, and social systems upon which the family is dependent and which play a crucial role in its formation. The Church has erred in this regard in two important ways: by not adequately addressing the cultural shift of the nineteenth century which separated family life from productive work and significant public activity; and by further sacramentalizing a domestic role of motherhood and childbearing for women, while simultaneously reinforcing men to abandon family life in favor of the workplace.[24]

In the Church's view, the family became primarily the sphere of women, "historically and in principle subordinate to men's sphere, to the public worlds of church and society." Clearly, the importance of the family cannot be restored until it is once more seen as an arena of moral action: "the place where both women and men are called to labor and to struggle with the fundamental challenges of human love and the making of human history." Indeed, in this respect, the true significance of family relationships will not be discerned until they have "neither subordinate importance for men nor predominate importance for women," but become a mutual task, "the concern of the whole church."[25]

The Social Character of Family Relationships

The failure of the Christian community to adopt a critical view of cultural norms about women and family is no surprise to feminists. Throughout her work Beverly Harrison has addressed the tendency of Christian social ethics to baptize existing patterns of relationship which in fact derive their form and character from the socio-economic conditions of the wider society.[26] For instance, arguing that previous normative assessments of marriage and families actually regarded marriage as a *social status* (albeit legitimized by theological and religious meanings). Harrison and psychologist James Harrison suggest that the relationship itself is best construed in another manner:

> We propose a normative definition of marriage as a *moral relation* involving the binding of two persons, freely and in good faith, in the intention to live together, support each other, and grow in the capacity for caring, (not merely caring for each other, but caring) through their mutual life time.[27]

In this view, the marriage relationship is clearly and originally based in *choice,* involves a commitment to enhance the life of each partner, and includes the moral development of each, that is, their growth as persons capable of responsive relation to others. At one and the same time, the marriage relationship is thus defined as an area of concern to social ethicists and criteria are provided for making moral judgments about any specific partnerships which fall in this category. Rather than ignore or dismiss questions of moral judgment within marriage, this view opens up the possibility of positively identifying what "performative failures" violate that relationship.[28] The importance of this claim is obvious in the context of the search for an ethic of family which responds constructively to issues of violence and abuse.

In the feminist view then, marriage cannot be considered in isolation from the wider network of social relationships of which it is necessarily a part. In fact, failure to connect the kinds of dilemmas experienced by marital partners with issues of justice and empowerment in the wider society is a mistake in analytical judgment which social ethics too often shares with psychoanalytic theory. The result is a diminished appreciation for the social roots of so-called personal problems as well as a compromised ability to identify those larger issues which are affecting the moral quality of family life.

Locating marriage inextricably in the social context and identifying those aspects which constitute its moral character reveals the mistaken ethical thrust in simply upholding that institution apart from the quality of life with which it is associated in a wider social context. The existing ethical tradition is thus at fault for ignoring the actual experience of persons in marriage relationships and, especially, for failing to protest the existence of truly destructive patterns in their lives as partners. In this light it is a mistake to equate moral failure in marriage only with divorce, a particularly egregious judgment in the face of evermounting data describing "the widespread substrate of brutality, violence, and psychic cruelty which characterizes marital relations in all socio-economic groups across this society."[29]

In such a context, social ethics must more seriously consider the future consequences of continuing to ignore the significance of family relationships. Preoccupation with the well-being of the persons in families must replace insistence on maintaining a marriage relationship. This in turn means a reassessment of what is best for children. Since, "distortions in the moral relations of marriage work themselves out in the crises of intergenerational intimacy,"[30] another whole set of human beings face the prospect of seriously impaired identity and capacity for caring.

Equality and Dignity in the Family

So the stakes are indeed high in redefining the nature of marriage and, by extension, the ensuing family relationships. In fact, in order even to approach the subject, ethicists first must arrive at a definition of the family which actually reflects current social scientific data. For instance, the traditional norm of the nuclear family, consisting of two parents (male and female) and their offspring (1.8 children to be exact), is simply no longer a fact. By the 1980s, less than one-fifth or American families could accurately be described in this way.[31] The radically changing character of the family is an even stronger reason for

Christian social ethics to recognize the reality of the family as socially grounded and to make an integral connection between the structural pressures (such as unemployment, racism, sexism) exerted on families in contemporary society and any consideration of those norms and values ("domestic virtues") which have previously pertained to family relationships.

With other feminists, John Wilcox calls on ethicists critically to appraise male-female roles in the family, specifically in terms of the lack of dignity accorded to women in the traditional nuclear family. This deep and basic inequity is the central problem which families currently face:

> The enduring and constant ethical issue in family life across the varia-
> tions in form is the need for a nonexclusionary and dynamic *respect* of
> the person. The impetus to overcome the traditional family's patriarchal
> structure and its concomitant abuse of power derives from this respect.[32]

The normative criteria of "individual dignity rights and social justice demands" thus can be placed at the heart of social ethics and in turn must provide the appropriate window through which to look at contemporary family relationships.

Making Justice A Priority

Overall, the feminist ethical perspective on family life shares three common features: (1) an insistence on understanding family relationships as essentially moral in nature; (2) a recognition that family relationships are inseparable from other areas of social life; and (3) a conviction that social justice is the fundamental norm to be considered in evolving a more adequate ethic of family relationships. The ethical themes lifted up by the battered women's movement are obviously in accord with this emerging feminist perspective, particularly the absolute necessity of incorporating a concept of justice in any normative view of family relationship.

This shared assumption affects at least three crucial areas of a joint conversation between the two groups: how to define a family; which dynamics of family life have been traditionally neglected; and what basic norms should pertain in family relationships. In each case, there are a host of relevant questions which can only be touched upon here.

Definitions of Family

Obviously, the starting point for an ethic of justice in family relationships will be an adequate definition of family. Should the definition of family explicitly describe the relationship between family members and the larger society? Recently, this intrinsic connection has been lifted up by feminist ethicists and has significant import in the area of family violence, where questions of appropriate intervention arise. For instance, suppose a married couple is childless and the woman suffers violence at the hands of her male partner. If she were a minor abused by a parent, the state could intervene, regardless of whether criminal charges had been pressed. Similarly, if there were children present who were being abused by her husband, some kind of intervention would also be likely to occur.

But typically, marriages without children are more consistently regarded as "off limits" by friends and community institutions alike. Despite changes in criminal codes, as well as police and judicial attitudes, troubles between adult partners, no matter how serious, are popularly judged to be their "private" concern. A definition of family which overcomes this distorted perception would obviously clarify some of the difficulties which the battered women's movement has faced in arguing for community sanctions against battering.

Many have argued that a more adequate definition of the family will move in the direction of inclusivity:

> Whether state-sanctioned or ritualized by private commitments, whether heterosexual or homosexual, behind the bedroom door, whether related by blood or consanguinity of spirit, all kinds of families who love and support their members should on that basis alone be welcomed into the family of families.[33]

Thus, expanding rather than limiting the possible configurations of relationship which constitute family should be the ultimate goal.

But recalling the central feminist concern for the moral character of marriage, the question remains of whether and how to define the *normative* character of family life, no matter who its members are. For instance, James Nelson sees love as "the central meaning" of marital and family relationship.[34] However, like Harrison and Harrison, he also characterizes such relationship by commitment to "the otherness of the other," to "the other's uniqueness and growth," and "an unwillingness to absorb and possess."[35] Would an abusive relationship be disqualified as a "family" by this criteria?

Neglected Dynamics of Family Life

Just as an adequate definition must reflect the reality of contemporary family relationships, so the ensuing dialogue about the nature of family life must give credence to previously neglected dynamics of those relationships. One specific goal must be to understand how power is differentially distributed among family members and, as a result, what kinds of patterns of authority pertain among them.

Of concern here would be the effects of women's social, economic, and political inequality and the related question of differential access to resources. Similarly, the effects of sex-role socialization on attitudes toward power and control are another important area of exploration. Some social ethicists, like Nelson and Wilson Yates, for instance, may acknowledge family life as the locus of intimacy and emotional expression, affirm the family as central to the development of fundamental values, and evoke the family's potential as an agent of social transformation.[36] But such an analysis is distorted if it does not also consider the destructive, dehumanizing aspects of the socialization which takes place in the family. Indeed, it is questionable ethics to celebrate the benefits to the wider society of the family's role in forming the religious, economic, and political attitudes and behaviors of individuals, and not also give attention to the parallel detrimental effects of training persons in sex-role inequality, abuse, violence, and neglect.

Until recently such questions were notably absent in discussions of inter-personal relationships by Christian social ethicists. Yet only by identifying and understanding the dynamics of power and authority can criteria be estab-lished for just relations among family members.[37]

Finding Adequate Norms: The Language of Rights

In the end, it remains a necessity to establish foundational norms for family life. One option is to consider what *rights* should apply in family relationships as a whole. There are several reasons why I favor this area of exploration.

The experience of the battered women's movement indicates that the question of rights is critical to developing an effective response to woman-abuse. Since a battered woman's rights have traditionally been obscured in sexist legal and criminal justice systems, the movement has focused a great deal of energy on the task of expounding a woman's right to safety and to protection by criminal and legal authorities. These efforts would be enhanced by an ethical perspective which clearly articulates an understanding of how rights apply *within* the family as well.

In its focus on rights, the battered women's movement is characteristic of modern movements, including the larger women's movement, which seek redress for those who have been dispossessed by the norms of the dominant society.[38] As we have seen, the same concern for justice informs feminist dis-cussions of rights in family life as well. For instance, Margaret Farley notes that the new order of equality and full mutuality which is replacing hierarchi-cal patterns of relationship is specifically based on a view of women "as claimants of *the rights which belong to all persons*."[39] Both she and Wilcox point to the specific use of rights language as a concrete means of giving expression to this notion of individual worth within the family.

But there are other reasons why this focus on rights has particular signifi-cance for battered women. A concern for justice leads women to a character-istic suspicion of "anything going by the name of love which wills less than genuine equality of personhood, *concretely expressed*.[40] Thus, the deep urge for justice in family relationships, particularly in its embodiment in concrete rights, is directly related to the distinctly problematic notions of love which feminists have already begun to critique.[41]

Social critic Andrea Dworkin makes an even more direct link between these two concerns when she argues that the very nature of male violence against women is such that it is *disguised as love*:

> When a man tyrannizes a people, he is hostile to their rights and freedom; when a man tyrannizes a woman, he is well within the bounds of his role as husband or lover. . . . Confining a group, restricting them, depriving them of rights because they were born into one class and not another are

hostile acts, unless women are being confined, restricted, and deprived of rights by the men who love them so that they will be what men can love.[42]

In the context of sexist culture then, the definition of love is taught with such *injustice* that is cannot serve as an adequate starting point for relationships between women and men. The fact that the relationship is of an intimate character does not change this basic fact:

> There is hostility in the world, which one recognizes as historical and social cruelty; and then there is the love of man for woman. . . . The torturer is just *a real obsessed lover* when the victim is a woman whom he knows intimately. . . . Beat up a man for speaking his mind and there is a human-rights violation—hunt him or capture him or terrorize him and his human rights have been violated; do the same to a woman and the violation is sexy. *Nothing that falls within the purview of the love of man for woman qualifies as a violation of human rights*; instead violation becomes a synonym for sex, part of the vocabulary of love. . . . When men love women, every hostile act demonstrates that love, every brutality is a sign of it; and every complaint that a woman makes against the hostility of male *dominance* is taken to be a complaint against love. . . .[43]

Being Concrete: The Importance of Everyday Freedoms

So in a feminist ethical perspective a discussion of rights within the family becomes virtually imperative. For as Dworkin suggests, at the heart of feminism is the absolute commitment to "a single standard of human dignity."[44] This same value is reflected in the fact that virtually all feminist ethicists suggest the central importance of honoring the "personhood" of each individual in a relationship. The consistency of this emphasis suggests a consensus for establishing as a foundational norm in family relationships the *right to respect* of one's integrity, one's unique identity as a human being, a "child of God."[45]

Obviously there is a connection between respect for persons and recognizing their rights. Also, the use of rights language may promote a deeper sense of *self*-respect, a key issue for battered women.[46] On the other hand, merely talking about rights will not suffice to establish the criteria for norms that are useful in an ethical response to battering. For instance, in *Loving Relationships*, Robert Shelton claims that ethicists "are coming to see that justice does belong in the private realm, through respect and mutuality," but in a discussion of power and dignity he is hard-pressed to articulate this understanding beyond the "rights" to "grow," to "be free," and to become "the person one is destined to be."[47]

The experience of battered women suggests that generalized notions of respect or vague commitments to well-being are of little use if concomitant *specific* rights are not also enumerated. Thus an ethic of justice in family life must be intentionally grounded in the concrete realities of embodied existence. The stories of battered women provide the first criteria for such an ethic, for theirs has been a struggle explicitly for the right to *exist*. Given this starting point, additional rights include: the right to *physical safety*; the right to *live free of physical violation*; and the right to *a fair share of those family resources* which provide for the physical necessities of food and shelter.

If such minimal freedoms seem self-evident as personal rights, it must be remembered that the privatized quality of family life often obscures the fact that they apply within the home as well as without. For, as the experience of the battered women's movement so clearly demonstrates, far from being regarded as an a priori condition of family living, the right to physical safety, for instance, is fundamentally at stake in abusive relationships. Then too, even if no physical violence takes place, it is still the batterer who determines the woman's right to be safe from physical harm, so any right of hers *to live free of fear* is completely abrogated.

Another basic area of concern is the individual's right to *freedom of association* with friends and other members of one's extended family network. A great deal of a batterer's power is exerted by limiting the woman's mobility and her access to material and financial resources. Control over her social contacts effectively completes the circle of emotional and spiritual oppression because these are very often a literal life-line for the battered woman and their curtailment contributes greatly to her physical and emotional vulnerability.[48]

A Broader Context

The task of delineating specific rights to be included in an ethic of relationship based on justice requires serious reflection on the many and varied issues raised in a socio-historical analysis of woman-battering. It must also be done in light of the Radical Right's profoundly disturbing efforts to develop another, very different, set of rights for families and indeed for the American public as a whole.[49] Indeed, the international context may be brought into play as well, because an adequate ethic must at least see that those same human-rights criteria which have increasingly gained acceptance among a broad range of nation-states are applied to the world of the home as well.

Meeting Our Obligations

Clearly there is a great deal of work to be done in constructing a view of family life which *delegitimates* violence and abuse. Using the norm of just love and delineating individual rights within family relationships is an appropriate beginning, in part because language about "love" is not only inadequate, but indeed is finally inappropriate for this task.

There are other reasons why this direction holds promise as well. The battered women's movement has stipulated that a woman has the right to safety within as well as outside her home and has placed that right squarely within the framework of the community's *obligation* to protect her. So an ethical perspective which focuses on rights within the family will have to address the means by which to guarantee such rights. Thomas Ogletree has characterized this type of approach as "obligation-dominant," that is, a style of moral reasoning which focuses concern on "the primacy of the obligation to protect *basic human rights*." Significantly, Ogletree asserts that the obligation-dominant position places prior importance on such rights and "permits us to turn to the larger possibilities of life enrichment only after due provision has clearly been made for these basic matters."[50]

An "obligation-dominant" approach is thus in keeping with the predominant bias inherent in the moral claims of the movement. By contrast, feminists have contended that the dominant perspective in twentieth-century Christian social ethics has tended to idealize family life, raising the question whether this tradition can even usefully be appropriated to address the dilemmas which contemporary families face. Obviously, a full review of relevant ethical works in this regard is impossible here. But my own sampling of Barth and Brunner does suggest that they share a tendency, albeit for different reasons, to dehistorize marriage and family life. When coupled with Reinhold Niebuhr's general disinclination to reflect on personal relationships, the resulting twentieth-century ethical legacy has indeed been problematic.[51]

As a result of the biases in this tradition, the real need for adequate norms in the area of family life is ignored: on the one hand, justice cannot apply to family relationships, while on the other, these relationships are simply not a significant area of concern for social ethics. This leaves love as the only appropriate standard in an ethic of family life, and the discipline of social ethics is rendered incapable of speaking effectively to critical issues such as family violence. Where inequality or abuse produce depersonalization and even danger, appropriate categories of judgment or even criminalization cannot apply: there is never social oppression or injustice in family life, only "failure to love."

In this respect it is possible that much scholarly as well as popular thinking about Christian family life relies on what Ogletree describes as a "virtue-dominant" style of moral reasoning, which implicitly assumes that "the intuitive insight of morally discerning persons" can be relied on to resolve difficult family problems.[52] The qualifying criteria for a loving relationship—and the ability of persons to act lovingly—are, quite simply, assumed. Such an approach is particularly problematic when, as is the historical case, it is developed in the context of the moral blindness of male-dominated social ethics. As a result, it is simply unlikely to bring sufficient attention to the questions of equality and abuse within the family.

Some may argue that much of twentieth-century ethics, including some contemporary views as well, is better described as a "value-dominant" style of moral reasoning, one which is concerned with "maximizing the total well-being of persons." In this view, "values essentially concern the full functioning of human persons within a community of fulfilled persons" and actions are judged according to the anticipated good which arises from them.[53] Thus attention focuses on the consequences of human choices for "the gratification of basic human needs or in the realization of human aspirations." Again, it seems unlikely that such language will serve to clarify and address the thorny issues related to abuse. What constitutes "needs" and "aspirations" may certainly be subject to debate—and those with more socioeconomic power are likely to define the terms in light of their own perceptions and interests.

So neither the virtue-dominant nor the value-dominant style of moral argument seem appropriate and in fact may prove downright dangerous as a means of dealing with the life-and-death problem of family violence. Instead, we must follow more closely the lead of the battered women's movement in urging the primacy of the obligation to protect basic human rights. For only the language of rights will ultimately suffice to *protect* the victim and *judge* the crime.

But Is Justice Fair?

The question of judgment may lead some to call for discussion of the various dimensions of justice (e.g., distributive, commutative, and so on) in relation to family life.[54] However, with specific reference to battering and other forms of abuse, it is important to keep in mind that the question of *retribution* is particularly pressing. This is not to suggest that a kind of one-sided vindictive justice will become the norm. Rather, an ethic of family relationships based on the foundation of human rights may provide the means for Christian social ethics to understand and respond to the family, not only as an important center of mutuality and commitment, but also as, equally and fundamentally, an arena of *social conflict*.

Prior to present feminist discussions, most ethicists have virtually ignored this important aspect of family life as inherently conflictual. Lacking such an orientation, the discipline is prevented from lending insight, motivation, and, most importantly, empowerment to families beset by the pressures of changing sex roles, economic displacement, and conflicting moral obligations, as well as the trauma of emotional or physical abuse.[55] The language of rights can remedy this limitation because it explores, in Daniel Maguire's words, the tension between "what is owed to the common good and what an individual can insist on as his [sic] right. . . ." Thus, rights language will also enhance consideration of the important relationship between the need for individual sacrifice and the demands of the common good.[56]

Seen in this light, concern for individual rights does not, however, reflect some sort of "fixation" on justice which can even become, as Maguire fears, "countersocial." Rather, where family life is concerned, the attention to rights represents an accurate perception that women are only now emerging from a state of having *no rights* at all or, alternatively, from an understanding of themselves in which the claims of the family community *superseded* their rights at every turn.

Nor does the language of rights reflect a reactive, punitive view of justice—a concern which may derive from what Maguire describes as a preeminently American perspective on justice which is characterized by defensiveness and a stubborn commitment to protect individual freedom at *all costs*.[57] Such a view bears no relation to the biblical imperative of justice as *shalom*, the communal response of striving toward wholeness in response to God's grace. Nevertheless, such uneasiness is understandable because the *anger* generated in the struggle to end battering is frighteningly deep, and the desire for retribution can at times seem uppermost. However, it must be remembered that, far from being preoccupied with reciprocal punishment, the perspective espoused here is driven by the motive to establish a single standard—not of violence and abuse, but of human *dignity*. Ours is a commitment to a justice which is, ultimately, the most complete form of empowerment and healing—*for all persons*.

This correlation of mercy and justice in the ideal of *shalom* most aptly describes the vision which must fashion an ethic in response to battering. As I continue to learn alongside battered women, as we mourn their losses and celebrate their successes, I marvel at their continued capacity for strength and healing. Listening to their stories only confirms that we must begin the constructive ethical task with justice, with the fundamental cherishing of one another and the passionate protecting of each one's right to be. With this commitment, Christian social ethics will no longer be silently complicit in the struggle to end battering, but will become, as it should be, a force for hope and transformation.

❧

Notes

1. The best single history of the battered women's movement is Susan Schechter, *Women and Male Violence* (Boston: South End Press, 1982). For a more anecdotal account of the early work to establish shelters, see Erin Pizzey, *Scream Quietly or the Neighbors Will Hear* (Hillside, N.J.: Enslow, 1977).

2. In considering the moral problem of battering, the judgments which the battered women's movement makes about it, and the adequacy of a constructive ethical response, I am referring primarily to repeated acts of physical aggression against a woman by her intimate partner which establish the latter's control and maintain the woman's subordination. The broad range of such acts includes beatings, forced sex, assault with a weapon, and homicide. It is widely agreed that such physical violence is always accompanied by some kind of psychological abuse which serves to sustain the victim's sense of low self-esteem, powerlessness, and fear.

3. Gerard Fourez has asserted that the evolution of an ethical issue is invariably due to "a new awareness of some oppression or conflict." It is "concrete historical struggles" which account for the gradual development of "the discipline called 'ethics.'" *Liberation Ethics* (Philadelphia: Temple University Press, 1982), 93.

4. In addition, the working methodology of the battered women's movement can be said to offer an alternative model for doing normative ethics. For discussion of this aspect of the movement, see Sarah R. Bentley, "For Better or Worse: The Challenge of the Battered Women's Movement to Christian Social Ethics," Ph.D. dissertation, Union Theological Seminary, 1989.

5. For an overview of theological and biblical perspectives on sanctuary, see Gary MacEoin, ed., *Sanctuary* (San Francisco: Harper & Row, 1985). The sanctuary movement is compared with the abolitionist movement in Renney Golden and Michael McConnell, *Sanctuary: The New Underground Railroad* (Maryknoll, N.Y.: Orbis, 1985).

6. See Susan Brooks Thistlethwaite, "Battered Women and the Bible: From Subjection to Liberation," *Christianity and Crisis* 41/17 (November 16, 1981) and "Every Two Minutes: Battered Women and Feminist Interpretation," in Carol Findon Bingham, *Doorway to Response: The Role of Clergy in Ministry with Battered Women* (Illinois Conference of Churches, 1986).

7. Pioneer educator Marie Fortune has identified suffering as a central religious issue for battered women and has addressed the important distinction between voluntary and involuntary suffering in her book, *Keeping the Faith: Questions and Answers for Battered Women* (San Francisco: Harper & Row, 1987). See also, "A Commentary on Religious Issues in Family Violence," in Bingham, ed. *Doorway*, 53–61.

8. Joy M.K. Bussert, *Battered Women: From A Theology of Suffering to an Ethic of Empowerment* (New York: Division for Mission in North America/Lutheran Church in America, 1986).

9. Mary Pellauer, "Violence Against Women: The Theological Dimension," *Christianity and Crisis* (May 30, 1983): 211.

10. Lois Gehr Livezey, "Sexual and Family Violence: A Growing Issue for the Churches," *Christian Century* (October 28, 1987): 941–42.

11. For a basic discussion of feminist methodology, see Carol S. Robb, "A Framework for Feminist Ethics," in Andolsen et. al., eds., *Women's Consciousness*, 211–34.

12. See Beverly Harrison, "The Power of Anger in the Work of Love: Christian Ethics for Women and Other Strangers," in *Making the Connections: Essays in Feminist Ethics* (Boston: Beacon Press, 1985), 3–21.

13. For a succinct statement of this important point, see Beverly Harrison, "Theology and Morality of Procreative Choice," in *Connections*, 129–30. See also, Linda Gordon, *Woman's Body, Woman's Right: A Social History of Birth Control in America* (New York: Grossman, 1972).

14. See Dorothee Soelle, *Suffering* (Philadelphia: Fortress, 1975) and "Life Without Suffering—A Utopia?" in *The Strength of the Weak: Toward a Christian Feminist Identity* (Philadelphia: Westminster, 1984).

15. Catherine Keller delineates the issues at stake in "Feminism and the Ethic of Inseparability," in Andolsen, et al., *Women's Consciousness*, 251–64. See also Isabel Carter Heyward, *The Redemption of God* (Washington, D.C.: University Press of America, 1982). The importance of mutual relationship is at the heart of Heyward's theological work.

16. The best exposition of this view is in Barbara Hilkert Andolsen, "Agape in Feminist Ethics," *Journal of Religious Ethics* 9/1 (Spring 1981): 69–83.

17. Paula Cooey makes this important point in "The Word Become Flesh: Women's Body, Language and Value," in Paula M. Cooey, Sharon A. Farmer, and Mary Ellen Ross, eds., *Embodied Love: Sensuality and Relationship as Feminist Values* (San Franciso: Harper & Row, 1987), 17–33.

18. This is Christine Gudorf's argument in "Parenting, Mutual Love, and Sacrifice," in Andolsen, et al., *Women's Consciousness*, 175–92.

19. Margaret Farley, "New Patterns of Relationship: Beginnings of a Moral

Revolution," in Walter Burkhardt, ed. *Woman* (New York: Paulist Press, 1977), 67–68.

20. Some feminist ethicists have specifically sought to counter the historical tendency of the discipline to define the stuff of everyday life as secondary to the "real" world which occupies men's attention. For instance, see Barbara Hilkert Andolsen, "A Women's Work Is Never Done: Unpaid Household Labor as a Social Justice Issue" in Andolsen, et al., *Women's Consciousness*, 3–18.

21. Jane Cary Peck, *Self and Family* (Philadelphia: Westminster, 1984), 57.

22. Margaret Farley, "The Church and the Family: An Ethical Task," *Horizons* 10/1 (1983): 51.

23. Ibid., 65–66. My emphasis.

24. Ibid., 55–56.

25. Ibid., 63.

26. For example, see Beverly Harrison, "Toward A Just Social Order," *Journal of Current Social Issues* 15/1 (Spring 1978): 63–70; and "Sexuality and Social Policy," *Connections*, 83–114.

27. Beverly Harrison and James Harrison, "Some Problems for Normative Christian Family Ethics," in *American Society of Christian Ethics Annual* (1977): 74. Emphasis added.

28. Ibid.

29. Ibid., 78–79. In a similar vein, Merle Longwood suggests that precisely because the marriage relationship is fundamentally moral in nature, divorce itself can in fact contribute an important means of "personal reorganization and development," providing an impetus for "understanding and refining an individual's own development of moral character." See his thoughtful essay, "Divorce and Moral Reconstruction," in *American Society of Christian Ethics Annual* (1977): 229–49.

30. Ibid., 82.

31. John R. Wilcox, "Conflict Over Sexuality: The Family," in Beverly W. Harrison, Robert L. Stivers, Ronald H. Stone, eds. *The Public Vocation of Christian Ethics* (New York: Pilgrim Press, 1988), 263. In fact, Dolores Curran suggests that the ratio is even lower, that a mere 15 percent of American families are now composed of a working father and a mother and children at home. Dolores Curran, *Traits of A Healthy Family* (Minneapolis: Winston Press, 1983), 15.

32. Ibid., 267. Emphasis added.

33. Letty Cottin Pogrebin, *Family Politics* (New York: McGraw Hill, 1983), 28. Pogrebin's work is a good basic survey of the important questions involving contemporary family life from a feminist's perspective.

34. James B. Nelson, "The Family: Some Theses for Discussion," in *Between Two Gardens: Reflections on Sexuality and Religious Experience* (New York: Pilgrim Press, 1983), 128.

35. Ibid., 135–36.

36. Ibid., See also Wilson Yates, "The Family and Power: Towards An Ethic of

Family Social Responsibility," *American Society of Christian Ethics Annual* (1981): 121–51.

37. Resources for this discussion abound. For example, see Pogrebin, *Family Politics*. See also Dana Y. Hiller and R. Sheets, eds., *Women and Men: The Consequences of Power* (Cincinnati: Office of Women's Studies, University of Cincinnati, 1977); Elizabeth Janeway, *Powers of the Weak* (New York: Alfred A. Knopf, 1980); and Ronald Sampson, *The Psychology of Power* (New York: Vintage, 1968). Interestingly, the sociologist who first contributed the notion of coercive power to discussions of family relationships, has more recently argued that male attitudes toward personal power are in fact the major impediment to making changes in family life. See William J. Goode, "Why Men Resist," in Barrie Thorne, ed., *Rethinking the Family: Some Feminist Questions* (New York: Longman, 1982): 131–50.

38. See Beverly Wildung Harrison, "The New Consciousness of Women: A Socio-Political Resource," *Cross Currents* 24/4 (Winter 1975): 446. On the complexities of rights language and its relation to social change, see Jon Gunneman, "Human Rights and Modernity: The Truth of the Fiction of Individual Rights," *Journal of Religious Ethics* 16/1 (Spring 1988): 160–89. Gunneman's basic stance seems to confirm the applicability of rights language to the dilemma of battering, because he argues that such language is appropriate to the discourse of "morality out-of-place," that is, to situations of moral dispute. It "appears when there is a moral failure or some other moral difficulty, when the community breaks down, or when people try to found new moral community" (171). Thus the *growth* of rights language is inherently connected to the increasingly pressing task of discerning how communities may be "based on power relations that distort the application and interpretation of morality" (172).

39. Farley, "New Patterns," 54. Emphasis added.

40. Harrison, "New Consciousness," 450. Emphasis added.

41. For a helpful discussion of the relation between rights and Christian notions of other-love, see Joseph L. Allen, "A Theological Approach to Moral Rights," *Journal of Religious Ethics* 2/1 (1974): 119–41.

42. Andrea Dworkin, *Right-Wing Women* (New York: Perigee Books, 1983), 211.

43. Ibid., 210–11. Emphasis added.

44. Ibid., 220.

45. Daniel Maguire makes respect one of the "indispensable prerequisites of human life," along with hope. See "The Primacy of Justice in Moral Theology," *Horizons* 10/1 (1983): 82.

46. Karen LeBacqz links rights and respect as "the justice of regard" in *Justice in an Unjust World* (Minneapolis, Minn.: Augsburg, 1987), 104–5.

47. Robert Shelton, *Loving Relationships* (Elgin, Ill.: Brethren Press, 1987), 100, 137–38. By focusing primarily on psychology as a resource for interpersonal ethics, Shelton's work lacks a truly social base. This may explain why he maintains a view of the family as "private" and why he misses the necessary sociopolitical grounding in his understanding of rights. For a discussion of the lack of critical perspective in Shelton's work, see Mary E. Hunt, "Struggling to Love Well," *Christianity and Crisis* (January 11, 1988): 466–67.

48. Margaret Farley has affirmed the importance of "relationships that are as essential to persons as is their freedom or autonomy." See *Personal Commitments* (San Francisco: Harper & Row, 1986), 83. Her work is a useful resource for considering the general characteristics of "just love." However, while earlier essays suggested sensitivity to socio-economic factors and the concrete questions of abuse, these same concerns seem oddly lacking in this more fully developed statement of her work.

49. For a good introduction, see Daniel C. Maguire, *The New Subversives: Anti-Americanism of the Religious Right* (New York: Continuum, 1982), especially chap. 5, "Blueprint for A Fascist Family."

50. Thomas W. Ogletree's categories are developed in "Values, Obligations, and Virtues: Approaches to Biomedical Ethics," *Journal of Religious Ethics* 4/1(1978): 105–30.

51. For example, Karl Barth, *Church Dogmatics* II, 4 (Edinburgh: T. and T. Clark): 3–47; 116–323. See also Emil Brunner, *The Divine Imperative* (Philadelphia: Westminster, 1947), 291–383 and *Man in Revolt* (Philadelphia: Westminster, 1947), 278–300; 345–61. Also see Reinhold Niebuhr, "Love and Law in Protestantism and Catholicism," *The Essential Reinhold Niebuhr*, ed. Robert McAfee Brown (New Haven: Yale University Press, 1986), 142–59; *Man's Nature and His Communities* (New York Charles Scribners' Sons, 1965); and *Moral Man and Immoral Society* (New York: Charles Scribners' Sons, 1932).

52. Ogletree, "Values," 106.

53. Ibid., 107.

54. See Daniel C. Maguire, *A New American Justice* (Garden City, N.Y.: Doubleday, 1980), 194 n. 5. Maguire's work is an excellent introduction to the thorny issues of justice. However, I also think Maguire is right that the "befuddling multiplication" of terms for different forms of justice contributes to confusion and for this reason I have stayed with the more or less straightforward category of human rights. No matter what the categories, there remains the difficult task of bringing together private and public spheres of relationships. For instance, criminalization of battering as violence within the context of the home becomes an issue of social justice as the individual batterer pays a "debt" to the *common* good, thus acknowledging his responsibility for the welfare of others, including all women and especially his abused partner. Another helpful resource in the task of deciding what notions of justice are most appropriate in this overall discussion is Karen Lebacqz, *Six Theories of Justice* (Minneapolis: Augsburg, 1988).

55. James Gustafson gives some attention to the possibility of using justice as a norm for family life in *Ethics From A Theocentric Perspective*. However, his approach is more successful in relating the concerns of family life to the wider society than when dealing with individual rights within the family. See *Ethics From A Theocentric Perspective*, vol. 2 (Chicago: University of Chicago Press, 1984).

56. Maguire, *American Justice*, 96.

57. Maguire, *American Justice*, 72. See also "Primacy of Justice," 76.

Moral Agency of Women
in a Battered Women's Shelter

ALLISON MAUEL MOORE

What does an analysis of the lives of some women in a battered women's shelter contribute to an understanding of moral agency? My training in ethics led me to see a woman's decision to leave an abusive relationship as a moral decision. However, many battered women do not recognize that leaving an abusive relationship is an option. If they do, they do not believe they are capable of leaving. A minimum level of self-respect (the ability to believe in one's own intrinsic worth) and self-assertion (the ability to trust one's own abilities enough to identify and ask for what one needs) are essential aspects of moral agency. Abuse erodes women's sense of self so that they may not feel worthy enough or capable enough to act on their own behalf; hence, their moral agency is diminished. The racist, sexist, and economically exploitative social institutions that further reinforce women's image of themselves as unworthy and ineffectual also undermine moral agency. On the other hand, counselors in shelters systematically encourage women to respect themselves and develop their abilities by providing affirmation and access to material resources such as housing and income.

Attention to the factors that erode and factors that nurture self-respect and self-assertion expands understanding of moral agency in several important ways. First, examination of the experiences of some women on the margins of American society provides an expanded understanding of the social constitution of selves. Then, it reveals the psychological and the material constituents of women's lives, as women who have become one sort of self in relations with their abusers become different selves in the presence of people who encourage their well-being. Finally, it demonstrates that the development of self-respect and self-assertion are the responsibility both of individual women and of the social, economic, and political institutions in which women live. My analysis is based on experiences in counseling sessions, staff meetings, support groups, and informal conversations at Sanctuary for Families, a battered women's shelter in Manhattan.[1]

The Social Constitution of Some Battered Women's Selves

Selves are constituted by the patterns of interactions they have with other people and institutions from birth on. To say that selves are socially constituted is to say that there is no aspect of a person that is separable from her or his inter-actions with other people and institutions. Some kinds of interactions encour-age women to develop self-respect and self-assertion, while others lead women to believe that they are worthless or unable to act effectively in the world. The ability to note stages of abuse and recovery from abuse makes battering a use-ful illustration of the social constitution of the self.

In the past fifteen years many people have documented the effects of vio-lence against women on battered women's sense of self-esteem, capabilities, and self-respect.[2] They have identified patterns of behavior for both abusive men and battered women.[3] Any woman can be battered. A relationship that begins with expectations of some degree of mutuality and support may quickly become a fairly systematic experience of domination and control of women by the men they love.

Abusive relationships have several identifiable characteristics. First, the man characteristically lacks respect for the woman and her needs. Abusers communicate this through insults and constant criticism, refusal to acknowl-edge the woman's emotional or material needs, isolation, verbal threats, and various forms of violence and threats of violence. Violence and fear become a constant part of the woman's experience. Most abuse increases in severity and frequency over time and can result in the woman's death.

Second, both people center their attention, consciously and uncon-sciously, on the abuser's perceived needs, wants, and moods. Battered women learn to pay attention to partners' needs instead of their own in hopes of pleasing their abusers and reducing the violence. Many battered women per-ceive themselves to be primarily dependent on their abusers for physical, emo-tional, and financial support, even when this may not be true. This sense of dependency and powerlessness is increased when women are isolated from family and friends who might provide other sources of self-esteem or remind them of skills they exercise daily.

Third, abused women begin to distrust their own judgment and sense of themselves. Significantly, they come to distrust their judgment in the moral domain as well as in other areas. They come to accept some of the belittling, critical, and fearful things they are told repeatedly by their abuser. Many women come to distrust their initial sense that it must be wrong for men to act this way. This pattern is exacerbated when family, friends, and social institutions disbelieve or blame or trivialize battered women's experiences and do not respond to their appeals for help.

What is most important for ethicists to note in this cycle is that women do not recognize many of the options open to them because their ability to evaluate their situations, to feel capable of taking steps to direct their lives, and actually to take those steps is significantly eroded by their interactions with their abusers. For instance, a battered woman who always turns her paycheck over to her partner, out of fear of his retaliation or out of desire to prove her love to him, may not believe that she could (and perhaps *should*) choose not to do so. Women's moral agency is limited by abuse and by their internalization of the effects of that abuse.

Escaping Abuse:
The Reconstitution of Battered Women's Selves

Time in shelter illustrates dramatically the tensions between that part of a woman's self which has been defined by the battering and that part of herself which seeks healing and growth. Drawing on my experiences at Sanctuary, I want to describe some of the ways women come to believe in themselves despite systemic obstacles and personal struggles—how they reconstitute their moral identity in life-affirming ways.

There is a profound disparity between the rhetoric of our cultural institutions and the realities that women in abusive situations face. For instance, it seems obvious that abuse is morally wrong, yet battered women's shelters exist because at present it is almost impossible to make abusive men stop battering or to hold abusers accountable for their actions. The language and images available in patriarchal culture to describe women's lives systematically distort the actual abilities, contribution, or material conditions of women whether or not they are battered. The conflicts and confusions experienced by battered women are directly traceable to the inconsistency between a social rhetoric which piously pronounces violence to be wrong and a social reality which (1) makes it difficult for most women to meet their material and emotional needs in patriarchal and racist political and economic structures, (2) systematically treats women as the offenders rather than the victims in situations of abuse, and (3) provides little or no help (or protection) to women seeking to escape from abuse.

Social Expectations of Women

> This is what happened. If you're not trained to do something, and you're married to a man, and you have small children and you're all of a sudden stuck, that's when the abuse starts. I hear that two or three times a night from other women. What they say is that once they're pregnant or have a child that's when everything goes downhill very quickly. . . . What I think is once you're dependent on a man then he can do anything.[4]

Patriarchal society defines women's roles and behaviors in some very specific ways, although each woman also has her own particular cultural and personal history of messages about what it is be female. These social expectations are relayed by family members, teachers, clergy and religious traditions, and the media. They are embodied in the organizations of social, economic, and political institutions, and they are supported by ideas of "women's nature."

Patriarchal family structures require that women subordinate their needs to the needs of men and children.[5] The divorce laws in most states still reflect an implicit contract where men provide economic support for the family while women take care of husbands, children, and the home.[6] Girls are consistently socialized to assume responsibility for nurturing relationships. Violence is a socially accepted way of addressing conflicts, especially for men and boys. The use of violence to enforce control is intrinsic to patriarchal culture.[7] Is it any wonder, then, that many women attribute their partners' violence to some real or imagined failure on their part to provide adequate care? Over and over again women ask what they could have done differently to control their partner's behavior: "Should I have been more attentive?" "He had a terrible childhood, he can't help it if he hits me." "I am not smart enough (or intuitive enough) to anticipate his needs." Some women want to cure their husbands of drug or alcohol addiction, physical illness, or psychological problems because they find satisfaction in and derive their identity from catering roles. The woman's family, clergy, and friends may support her in this and judge her by her ability to maintain the relationship. Very few women or men ever hold the man accountable for his violence.

Social roles for all women are based on the norm of women who remain in the private sphere caring for a family. This has two important consequences, one economic and one relational. Paid work violates some social expectations that "good women" stay home and raise children for no salary. Some women say that their partners would not let them work outside of the home because their working made the men feel that they would be seen as inadequate providers. The net effect of such subtle messages is that women who try to satisfy social and moral expectations tend to become economically dependent on abusers. In addition, this identification of women's identity with familial relationships creates moral and emotional bonds that shackle women in destructive marriages. Often women fear the stigma of being single or divorced, or they worry that if they disrupt their current relationship, they will never be in an intimate relationship with a man again. Judgments about single parents vary considerably in different ethnic groups. Some women say they stay with an abuser because their children need a father; they consider that need to be more important than their own need for safety.

Legal Help

> Tina, an African-American woman with an administrative job had a valid order of protection. She called the police when her husband started throwing furniture. Her husband ripped one phone out of the jack before she could finish the call, so she called again, hysterical. Four officers came twenty minutes later, after her husband started to beat her. Tina pleaded with the officers to arrest her husband, pointing to broken furniture, her blackened eye, and her order of protection. Her husband, very charming now, told the police that they were just having a little argument, and that she had scratched his face, too. The officers said that if anyone were to be arrested it would have to be both of them since both appeared to be hurt. They escorted her husband out of the apartment and left. Her husband came back later and waited outside her door, threatening to kill her when she came out.[8]

Women often need police or court intervention to get away from and to be protected from a violent man. Until 1874 it was legal in the United States for husbands to beat their wives. Between 1874 and the early 1970s women had few legal means to stop husbands because the courts refused to "interfere" with the private world of the family.[9] With the establishment of the battered women's movement, protective legislation was enacted in many states, making it easier for women to get orders of protection, although criminal prosecution of batterers is still very difficult. Many people question the usefulness of going through the process of getting an order of protection. In Manhattan Family Court the procedure requires at least two days, one to request the order and another to have a judge hear the woman's plea and her partner's response. Since the woman must either serve the summons herself or find someone who will do so, many women are justifiably afraid to pursue this action. However, the order of protection makes it more likely that police officers will honor the woman's request for help in the case of another attack; it also makes it easier for them to arrest the man. Yet women still have to call the police and wait for them to arrive.

Women's perception of legal protection is likely to come from police actions. Until recently most police department procedures recommended that officers responding to domestic violence calls try to establish peace rather than arrest the attacker. The underlying assumptions were that domestic violence is not serious and that police ought not to interfere with "domestic squabbles."[10] Women's reports of police intervention show that responses vary widely depending on the procedures of the precinct and on how credible the woman can appear. Unfortunately, the officers' assessment of a woman's credibility seems to have a lot to do with her ethnicity (for instance, Euro-American women seem to be taken more seriously by officers of all ethnic groups) and with her abuser's ability to manipulate the sympathy and fellow-feeling of the officers.[11] Arrests are extremely infrequent, and even if an arrest is made the man is usually freed within twenty-four hours.

There is a tension between a battered woman's belief that she does not deserve to be hurt or that abuse is not acceptable and her experience of abuse as a normal part of her daily life. Women are better able to believe that they have the right to stay away from an abusive partner if court actions show women that their need for safety is respected, and if police actions show women that they have the law behind their attempts to maintain that safety. The knowledge that the law protects her can help a woman argue with her husband, family, pastor, or whoever tells her that it is her duty or her lot in life to endure abuse.

Source of Income

Lena, an African-American woman with no children, had been working at a fast food restaurant when she left her boyfriend. Before he had moved in with her, she had been a switchboard operator, a job she had liked, but he made her quit and work for one of his friends at the restaurant. Once she moved into shelter she applied for emergency welfare benefits, but found a new job as a receptionist within three weeks. Lena said she was amazed that her supervisor appreciated her skill. "I'm making twice as much money as at (the restaurant). . . . I'm beginning to feel like a person again!"[12]

Paid employment, public assistance, or friends and relatives are the usual sources of income for women. Many women are accustomed to receiving some or all of their income from their partners, since salaries for women are often inadequate to meet living expenses. Women who work outside the home have many fewer job choices than men, and they receive lower salaries than men. Latin and African-American women have even fewer choices than Euro-American women.[13]

It is also difficult for some women to keep their jobs once they come into shelter. Because abusers often threaten women at work and may follow them back to the shelter from work, many working women have to find new jobs. Women are frequently dismissed or asked to take an unpaid leave when injuries, court proceedings, or apartment hunting require them to take time away from work. Undocumented women are especially likely to be exploited in work places because employers can always threaten women with the possibility of job loss or deportation. Sanctions against hiring undocumented workers make it more difficult for undocumented women to find new jobs.

Despite these hazards, employment can be an important source of self-assertion. A regular paycheck enables women to meet some of their basic needs. Co-workers and supervisors sometimes affirm women's abilities, whereas in abusive relationships, women's financial contributions and decisions are most often ignored but can also provoke unexpected and inconsistent consequences. The ability to meet basic needs and decide how money is spent helps women believe that they can influence the directions their lives take.

Public assistance is often the only way women can get enough money and time during the day to arrange day care, pay for medical care, find new jobs, look for apartments, or go to court. It enables mothers to remain at home with children and obtain minimum material necessities when fathers do not provide economic support. The process of applying for public assistance creates a costly trade-off between a battered woman's emotional and psychological need for affirmation and support and her material needs for money, housing, and medical care. In public assistance offices women must explain that they have been battered in order to receive emergency benefits. They often have to fight for benefits from workers who assume that women do not deserve what they receive, in a society that condemns "free handouts." After all of that, they still may not receive enough money to meet basic needs. This process tells women that they are not worthy or able to make decisions for themselves about the course of their lives.

Housing

Elizabeth, an African-American private duty nurse with one child, sought to obtain a court order of exclusion. The judge told Elizabeth that although she wanted to exclude Elizabeth's boyfriend from the apartment because of the severity of his abuse she could not "in good conscience" make the man homeless.[14]

Many women derive their identity from their ability to maintain a clean, comfortable home. When battered women leave partners who have good

salaries, their economic class and hence their social status and their ability to
provide for themselves and their children usually decrease radically. Court
orders of exclusion which mandate that the abuser leave the residence and
refrain from harassing the woman are rarely granted; if granted, they are difficult to enforce. It is appalling that a woman has to leave the residence she has
worked hard to maintain because her partner is threatening her life. The incident
related at the beginning of this section provides an especially telling example of a
judge's response to a woman's request for an order of protection. Elizabeth and
her child had to leave the home! Social sanctions of this fundamental injustice
cause women to wonder whether they really do have the right to live in safety.

It is usually safer for a woman to find a new apartment and keep the
address confidential so that her partner does not know where she lives. Yet the
difficulties of finding affordable permanent housing in the city make some
women think seriously about returning to their abusers. Affordable apartments are usually in high-crime, poor neighborhoods with poor schools and
public services. It is often impossible for women in low-paying jobs to provide
adequate living conditions for themselves and their children without apartment
shares or financial help from friends or relatives. The option of moving to a
drug-infested apartment building does little to encourage a woman's sense that
she can act in ways that promote her well-being or that of her children.

Because of racial and ethnic tensions, some neighborhoods that are safe for
women of one ethnic background are unsafe for women of different ethnic
backgrounds. For instance, many Euro-American women dread the thought of
living in Harlem, while many African-American women fear harassment in predominantly Euro-American neighborhoods. Poorly lit and poorly patrolled
streets exacerbate the fears and possibility of rape or mugging that plague all
women. Leaving a known neighborhood forces some women to choose
between loyalty to their friends and family and loyalty to themselves. In New
York this may also mean leaving the only part of town where women can buy
certain ethnic foods or find other vital cultural supports. This adds another level
of anxiety about isolation and abandonment when women may already feel
lonely. Fears about living alone exacerbate some women's concerns about
whether it is really all right to break a commitment to someone they have loved.

Despite these hardships, finding an apartment is perhaps the most tangi-
ble sign that a woman can really make it on her own. A lease in hand ends
fears of having to live in shelters indefinitely or return to the abuser in defeat.
Women simultaneously build a new home and a new sense of self in the
process of finding schools, grocery stores, child-care facilities, even furniture
and decorations for "their own place." These concrete actions reinforce both
self-respect and self-assertion.

Child Care

Nida, a Puerto Rican woman, chose not to transfer her two boys from
their school even in the face of severe threats to her life from her ex-
husband, because the boys had been in two different schools already that
year. Her nine-year-old finally had a teacher he liked and was reading

for the first time. She spent ninety minutes twice a day delivering the boys and picking them up after school for the three months she was in shelter. She had to call her sister-in-law each time before she left to make sure that her ex-husband was at work and unable to meet her.[15]

Women raising children alone do not have access to the resources that would enable them to care for their children as they did with their partner's presence and income. Women with children cannot work outside the home until they have a safe place for their children to stay. When women leave their homes, they also must usually remove their children from familiar schools, day-care sites, or baby-sitters; they do this to prevent their abusers from harassing them at the child-care site or from kidnapping the children. Affordable child-care placements are scarce, and arrangements for transfers usually take at least a week. Before deciding to leave their abuser, mothers also consider how much their children will suffer if they have to move from private to public schools or change schools twice within a few months.

Providing adequate care for children is one of the primary sources of identity for most women in patriarchal cultures. Women come to value themselves in terms of how well their children's needs are met. Counselors in shelter often find that women who are reluctant to take steps to secure their own survival or well-being can be convinced to do so by the argument that their survival is important to their children. Counselors can then help women move from feeling that they should live "for the sake of the children" to feeling that they should live because their lives have intrinsic value.

The lives of women who have sole responsibility for their children are shaped by their children's needs and desires as well as their own. This implies that any agency which intends to serve single mothers has to provide resources for child care and has to help women address children's needs as well as their own. Mothers' choices are defined by how various options accommodate children, yet courts, public assistance offices, employers, therapists, and most other agencies rarely make provisions for children. The daily lives of mothers are shaped by school and child-care schedules and locations, not to mention the requirements of dressing, feeding, teaching, disciplining, and otherwise caring for one or more growing human beings. The lines between self and other which are usually assumed in ethical theory are very blurry for mothers and children.

Finally, mothers are held accountable when their children do not have adequate material or emotional necessities, even though batterers and uncooperative social institutions often make it difficult for women to acquire these necessities. Women blame themselves and often interpret their inability to meet their children's needs as a sign of incompetence, while fathers are usually absolved of responsibilities for daily care because they have been violent.

Implications for Feminist Understandings of Moral Agency

The social, political, and economic structures which determine access to housing, legal protections, income, and child care create obvious concrete difficulties for women who are trying to establish safe lives. More importantly, women can internalize the dangerous hidden messages about the roles of Caucasian, African-American, and Latina women which the institutions pervasively convey. For women in shelter, the question is whether these messages and obstacles will overpower their commitment to their own well-being demonstrated by their leaving home in the first place. Some women leave their abusers and then return to them several times before they are convinced that the abuse will not stop and that they deserve to live in safety. Understandings of moral agency have to include the ways women interpret their lives and the ways women's lives are structured by social, political, and economic institutions.

Self-Respect and Self-Assertion: The Heart of Moral Agency

Self-respect and self-assertion are themes that emerge again and again in reflection on the goals of counselors in the shelter and on the experiences of women living in the shelter. Self-respect includes a will to live which is social as well as biological.[16] The will to live is a motivating factor seen in women's desires to develop their abilities, to care themselves, and to keep struggling against those people and events that are dangerous to their well-being. It is often what leads a woman to flee from her abuser and what enables her to respond to actions of affirmation and support. Self-respect also includes acknowledgment of the particular characteristics which make each person unique.

Self-assertion depends on self-respect but is not reducible to it. I include in self-assertion a basic sense of competence, practical and moral, which is exactly what abusers undermine in the women they abuse. It is the ability to identity one's own needs and to seek ways to meet those needs. It includes the ability to make plans and carry them out, to envision new possibilities for one's own life, and to begin to realize some of them. Self-assertion entails learning to ask for help when necessary, a skill that contradicts most of what women have been taught about ignoring their own needs and caring for others. But this basic sense of competence is also specifically a sense of *moral* competence. As such, it includes an ability to develop clear moral expectations and to bring those expectations to bear in complicated personal situations; it also includes a willingness to trust one's own sense of what constitutes right and wrong behavior in the face of indifference, opposition, or ridicule from intimate partners, family members, and representatives of public agencies.

Both self-respect and self-assertion are present in any woman's life as long as she holds out any hope of living. There is a range of activities that exemplifies self-respect and self-assertion, from basic concern for survival to active pursuit of the many things needed for a woman to develop her talents fully. It is not easy to call a hotline or shelter and ask for help. It is not easy to pack bags, gather children, and leave home unobtrusively. Yet some women are unable to give themselves credit for the resourceful things they have done or for their commitment to their own survival. Their conversations focus instead on what they have left undone or how helpless and weak they feel.

Counselors in shelter commend any spark of self-assertion or self-respect that women demonstrate until women can recognize their strengths and believe in themselves. Shelters provide a space where women can re-interpret the self-negating messages they have heard from abusers and oppressive institutions and where they can develop patterns of action which affirm their own well-being. The reconstitution of women's lives ultimately depends both on the presence of supportive others and on their own choice to nurture self-respect and self-assertion in their own lives. This is a choice women have to make for themselves again and again in their lives, as they make their way within social structures which often impede their well-being.

The ability to nurture self-respect and self-assertion is at the heart of moral agency, because it preserves a role for personal choice while acknowledging the social dimensions of that choice. The actions and decisions of women in the shelter are more diverse and more concrete than the actions analyzed in much current ethical theory. I list several examples of moral agency here as a step towards expanding theoretical understandings of moral agency.

Moral agency includes the actions women take to respect and care for themselves. Women in shelter are engaged in a process of emotional and psychological healing in which they learn to shift attention from their batterers' needs to their own needs, talents, and desires. For example, counselors sometimes recommend that women do at least one activity a day purely for their own pleasure. This helps women remember what makes them happy rather than what pleases their partner, and the action affirms self-care as a virtue. It is rare for ethical theory to recommend that people ask for things for themselves from other people or institutions. Yet it is in *asking* that battered women discover options, begin to trust their own abilities to secure the material necessities of life, and acknowledge their own independent identities.

Moral agency means that women take actions to shape their own lives rather than expecting other people or situations to shape their lives for them without their participation or assent. Courage and perseverance are moral qualities strengthened in and through daily battles with agencies, people, and institutions which often do not have women's well-being at heart. In those battles women learn that unless they act they will not have access to material necessities, they are capable of accomplishing plans, and that even recalcitrant officials and programs can eventually help them get what they need.

Moral agency also means challenging the definition of "the good woman" expressed in prevailing social norms. I frequently hear women using moral language, "Do I have the right to do this?" or "What someone did to me was not fair," but the standards of morality women use to evaluate whether they have the right to "abandon" their partner or seek safety are usually the social norms which govern family life. They believe that morally good women are those who fulfill well familial roles such as "the good mother," "the caretaker," or "the dutiful wife," regardless of the negative consequences these roles have for women's own self-respect or well-being. In formal support groups or in informal conversations in the shelter, women can remind each other that patriarchal social roles are inherently unfair and that they do have a right and responsibility to take care of themselves.

Moral agency includes assuming appropriate responsibility for themselves or others while letting go of their determination to change or manipulate the behavior of others. When women blame themselves for their partner's abuse, for instance, they are often trying to change their partner's behavior by taking better care of him. The result is that the abuser is not held accountable for his actions and no one takes care of the woman. Women have been trained to try to meet their own needs under the guise of caring for others; they need to learn, instead, to meet their own needs directly and discern when to let others care for themselves.

Directions for Further Research

Beverly Harrison, Ruth Smith, and bell hooks are feminist ethicists and social theorists whose work on moral agency has significantly informed my approach to the study of women in shelter.[17] My analysis suggests ways to expand their understanding of the socially constituted self and to highlight the elements of personal responsibility that shape women's moral agency. If ethicists consider both material and psychological needs, we may discover definitions of responsibility that are more compatible with socially constituted selves and less dependent on assumptions of individual autonomy. My analysis underscores the importance of responsibility to oneself, but ethicists should also consider questions of institutional responsibility. If a certain quality of relationship is essential to the development of self-respect or self-assertion, how can a society establish and preserve the conditions which sustain empowering relations?

Considering self-respect and self-assertion as constitutive of moral agency raises many questions about how to distinguish "moral" from "non-moral" agency. Many of the tasks that women undertake in shelter are not moral tasks per se. Yet in performing everyday tasks, battered women can recover the confidence in themselves and their abilities that is the essential prerequisite to making informed moral decisions such as whether to have an abortion, or lie to a welfare worker, or return to an abusive relationship. The situation of battered women is an extreme situation, but the insights gained from close observation of their behavior and development have broad implications. Study of the situation of battered women throws into high relief the systemic patterns of domination which color the lives of all women. In addition, sustained examination of the patterns of thought and behavior of women trying to escape abuse reveals the moral dimensions of actions that seem objective at first glance. Conversation about specifically moral agency must begin with much more careful attention to agency in and of itself.

In addition, analysis of the lives of women trying to escape abuse makes visible moral dilemmas that many ethical theories completely ignore. For instance, women should not have to decide between their well-being and that of their children. Yet that is precisely the dilemma that confronts a woman when leaving a violent spouse also means leaving good schools and a home where children have private rooms and a backyard. The lack of options for battered women, especially when they are poor, is morally intolerable. Yet the dilemmas faced by women in such situations remain strangely invisible, receiving virtually no attention when moral agency, moral conflicts, and social injustices are discussed in ethics textbooks, in classes in ethics, in professional journals in the field of ethics, and at meetings of ethicists.

Abuse erodes the concrete options women have to shape their lives, women's ability to identify and attend to their own needs, and women's sense that they are able to understand their situation and act effectively. More often than not, the very institutions to which women must look for help function to obstruct their development, reinforce their moral confusion, and support the designs of their abusers. Yet many women are still able to escape abuse, challenge the social expectations that would keep them in abusive relationships, and build a new life for themselves. Ethicists need to celebrate these moral achievements and incorporate them into understandings of moral agency. We also need to differentiate among the moral tasks required of battered women, their advocates (who may work to bring about institutional reform but cannot wait patiently until oppressive institutions change to get the resources they need for the clients today), and the theorists (feminists and others) whose reflective analysis should clarify and enrich our understanding and guide our work. It is the task of women trying to escape abuse to find resources and a community which will help them develop self-respect and self-assertion. The task of people responsible for social institutions is to make changes that reflect women's needs, that will encourage rather than defeat the development of responsible action in individual agents, and that will alleviate oppression. The task of feminist ethicists is to listen carefully to the accounts of battered women and of the people who work with battered women in order to develop a theory more adequate to these experiences and a prescriptive strategy for desperately needed social change.

✿

Notes

The author is indebted to Anne Gilson, Nancy Malone, and Mary Morgan who offered constructive suggestions through several drafts of this paper.

1. Sanctuary for Families offers shelter, crisis counseling, support groups, legal advocacy, and help in locating housing, child-care, or other necessities. It serves women of all ethnic groups, religions, and economic classes, although the women with fewer economic resources are more likely to have to live in a shelter.

2. See Lenore Walker, *The Battered Woman* (New York: Harper & Row, 1979); Del Martin, *Battered Wives* (New York: Simon and Schuster, 1983); Ginny NiCarthy, *Getting Free* (Seattle: Seal Press, 1985); and Ginny NiCarthy, *The Ones Who Got Away* (Seattle: Seal Press, 1987).

3. Some men are battered, and some women are battered by other women; this analysis focuses on heterosexual battering. Recent statistics gathered by the National Coalition against Domestic Violence show that approximately 95 percent of adult battering is by men against women.

4. Susan, a Euro-American homemaker with two children. Interview with author, November 1987.

5. Cf. Carl Degler, *At Odds: Women and the Family in America from the Revolution to the Present* (New York: Oxford University Press, 1980).

6. R. Emerson Dobash and Russell Dobash, *Violence against Wives: A Case against the Patriarchy* (New York: Free Press, 1979), 23.

7. Lenore Weitzman, *The Marriage Contract: Spouses, Lovers, and the Law* (New York: Free Press, 1981), 2.

8. Tina, counseling session, February 1988.

9. Del Martin, *Battered Wives*, 32–33.

10. Ibid., 95.

11. I base these statements on conversations in support group and on accounts given by women during intake interviews when I asked about a history of police intervention.

12. Lena, conversation with author, March 1988.

13. Source: Table 658, "Employed Civilians by Occupational Group, Sex, Race, and Educational Attainment: 1986," *U.S. Bureau of the Census, Statistical Abstracts of the United States: 1987, 107th ed.* (Washington D.C.: U.S. Government Printing Office), 387.

14. Elizabeth, support group, December 1988.

15. Nida, conversation with author, March 1988.

16. Psychological perspectives on the social constitution of the will to live in infants can be found in the work of object-relations theorists such as D. W. Winnicott, John Bowlby, Margaret Mahler, or Luise Eichenbaum and Susie Ohrbach, or in experimental research such as D. M. Bullard, H. H. Glaser, M. C. Heagarty, and E. C. Pivchek, "The Failure to Thrive in the Neglected Child," *American Journal of Orthopsychiatry* 37 (1967): 680–90.

17. Cf. Beverly Harrison, *Our Right to Choose* (Boston: Beacon Press, 1982) and Beverly Harrison, *Making the Connections*, ed. Carol Robb (Boston: Beacon Press, 1985); bell hooks, *Feminist Theory from Margin to Center* (Boston: South End Press, 1982); Ruth Smith, "Feminism and the Moral Subject," in *Women's Consciousness, Women's Conscience*, ed. Barbara Andolsen, Christine Gudorf, and Mary Pellauer (Minneapolis: Winston Press, 1985); and Ruth Smith, "Morality and Perceptions of Society: The Limits of Self-Interest," *Journal for the Scientific Study of Religion* 26 (1987).

"Swing Low, Sweet Chariot!": A Womanist Ethical Response to Sexual Violence and Abuse

TOINETTE M. EUGENE

Prolegomena to an Ethic of Care

. . . *journal of a girl missing*: Day 12 I sleep with a baseball bat beside my bed. I think I always will. I swear I'll use it if I have to . . . I swear I'll kill him . . . Day 15 Saw a girl in the swimming pool with welts on her legs. I asked her who did it. She said her daddy beat her last night. Nobody would look at her in the locker room. I didn't know white people beat there [*sic*] kids like that I'm glad mine don't show. Day 23 I have not written for a while. Talked to Trina last night. Told her about my bat and she told me to keep it and use it. She said daddy raped her three years ago. That is why he had to leave for a while. I'm glad. She said hit to kill and don't stop till he stops moving. Day 29 I am afraid. I had a dream. I was trying to run away and daddy was chasing me. I wonder if I'll ever be able to leave here.[1]

This brief vignette of a Black girl's story embedded in her journal provides the compass for my effort toward responding to sexual abuse in the lives of African-American women. Here the realities of sexual abuse, race, and gender converge. Here the legendary prophetic chariot of the Black spiritual seemingly fails to rescue a suffering soul within an abused and badly brutalized woman's body. "Swing Low, Sweet Chariot" fails to come and carry safely home a Black woman who has been severely victimized by a member of her own race and family.

It is clear to me that sexual abuse in the lives of African-American women should be a concern for the African-American Church, as well as the civic community and wider society. The intergenerational nature of sexual abuse in my family led me, some time ago, to consider the ramifications of sexual abuse for the functioning of the African-American family and community, and the wider society. The prevalence of sexual abuse in the lives of African-American women confirms that my experience of sexual abuse is not an anomaly. Instead, experiences such as mine concur with research indicating

that the threat and reality of sexual abuse is a prevailing element in the socialization of the majority of African-American women.[2]

Overview of Abuse, Violence, and African-American Women

My struggle has been embedded in the question of living with integrity and commitment in the Church, and particularly the Catholic Church. Its history of violation of trust and body, and lack of liberating response reveals its culpability in
the continued oppression of women and children. As a seminary professor, my
struggle to make sense of God in the midst of violence and chaos is a struggle I
hear from an inordinate number of the women whom I have known as students
and as colleagues. This lack of response to sexualized violence is not unusual.[3]

Pastoral psychotherapy with African-American sexually abused, homeless,
and runaway youth, adolescent mothers, or chemically dependent women and
their families over the last ten years, has also confirmed the wider impact of
the sexual abuse of African-American women.[4] As a theologian and social
ethicist teaching seminary courses on pastoral care with African-American
families, I have witnessed the dynamics of secrecy and denial with regard to
sexual abuse. More often than not, participants in my classes are initially resistant to addressing experiences of sexual abuse. Pastoral ministry with African
Americans in counseling, parishes, and educational situations has helped me
clarify the social science and theological questions that must be raised in order
to fully understand sexual abuse in the lives of African-American women.

Central to my effort is distinguishing what is the relationship between
race, gender, and sexual abuse? What are the historical and contemporary
factors that must be examined? How does healing and transformation occur?
Who is God in light of women sexually violated? What is the impact of sexual abuse on the individual's and community's psyches? These questions, and
my familiarity with violence and terror in my own life, and in the experiences
of women who have exposed their wounds to me, compel me to respond.

My effort has a threefold premise: (1) sexual abuse is a prevalent factor
in the lives of many African-American women, and this has negative implications for these women and the African-American community. (2) Responses
to sexualized violence in the lives of African-American women has not been
adequately addressed from the perspectives of theology, psychology, or sexual
abuse theorists. (3) A womanist approach is necessary because a) it articulates
an analysis which examines the dynamics between race, gender, and sexual
abuse, b) it examines the historical and contemporary factors effecting the
lives of African-American women, c) it constructs a response which asserts a
perspective on healing that retains the link between healing, liberation, and
transformation of the whole African-American community.

A Womanist Definition of Sexual Abuse

A womanist-informed definition of sexual abuse is constructed in terms of the
experiences of African-American women within a historical context, and in

terms of the ethical, religious, and psychological issues regarding sexual violation. Therefore, the elements of sexual abuse are the violation of one's bodily
integrity by force and/or threat of physical violence. It is the violation of the
ethic of mutuality and care in relationships of domination. It is a violation of
one's psycho-spiritual-sexual integrity by using sexual abuse to control and
express violence. Sexual abuse is the violation of the Spirit of God incarnate
in each of us.

The traditional response of the Black community to violence committed
against its most vulnerable members—women and children—has been
silence. This silence does not stem from acceptance of violence as a Black cultural norm (a view that the media perpetuates and many whites believe), but
rather from shame, fear, and an understandable, but nonetheless detrimental
sense of racial loyalty. Beth Richie-Bush, co-chair of the National Coalition
Against Domestic Violence Women of Color Task Force writes:

> I gradually realized that some strong, culturally identified families
> were dangerous places for women to live. . . As I began to look
> closely, the incidence of battering, rape, and sexual harassment
> became obvious. . . Fear of being cast out by the community silenced
> me in the beginning. Loyalty and devotion are enormous barriers to
> overcome. Black women be forewarned: there is already so much neg-
> ative information about our families that a need to protect ourselves
> keeps us quiet. It is a painful, unsettling task to call attention to vio-
> lence in our community.[5]

A pernicious combination of internal and external forces have prevented the
Black community from addressing the multiple issues of violence as they are
manifested through rape, incest, and domestic violence. Dangerous and culturally threatening though it appears to be, it is critical that this silence be
broken. For it is impossible to build productive communities or strong, loving
families if Black women and children continue to be the physical and psychological targets of the Black man's rage. This problem need not be approached
(as perhaps many Blacks fear) with finger pointing, cruel accusations, lame
excuses, or feelings of betrayal. It can begin, as self-love and liberation have
historically for Black people, with hazardous but ultimately healing procla-
mations of truth.

The truth is, of course, that both Black men and women are weak, vulnerable, and because of racism, extremely damaged individuals. We are in the
complex, often paralyzing position of being enlightened enough to know that
we cannot depend on the police, social workers, or the criminal justice system
to protect us from abuse or intervene on our behalf. They have in fact, been
some of the worst offenders in perpetuating and blatantly ignoring the violence in Black communities. And yet, when we turn to each other to stop the
violence in our lives, we are confronted with a myriad of cultural myths,
internalized self-hatred, and a benign trust in the Lord. We need to put our
faith into action and make the commitment to stop hurting and begin trusting
and respecting ourselves.

Womanist Ethical and Theological Reflections
on Sexual Violence and Abuse

By definition a womanist is a Black woman or woman of color who has appropriated Alice Walker's term "womanist" to "describe the liberative efforts of Black women." Walker's definition emerges out of the language, experiences, and ways of African-American communities.[6] Womanist ethicists and theologians recognize that African-American women are oppressed by a minimum of a tridimensional reality of racism, sexism, and classism. Womanist scholars conclude that there are inextricable links between these oppressions, and from this juncture ethics and theology are constructed. A framework for womanist ethics and theology includes attention to sources, methodology, and content that clarifies as well as codifies the experiences of violence and abuse.

Sources

EXPERIENCE: The role of experience is a primary source for womanist ethics and theology. Doing ethics and theology with the experiences of African-American women at the heart of the liberative effort means that racism, sexism, classism and heterosexism converge in our analysis, and inform our understanding of oppressive experience as socially constructed. This includes oppression in the broader culture, the Black community, the Church, love and family relationships, and the internalization of oppressive ideology. Experience also includes the liberating praxis Black women employ to reduce and eradicate oppression in their lives and the community. Experience also must include those occasions where Black women have engaged in violating others.

LITERATURE: Womanist ethicists and theologians draw on the African-American literary canon as a source for searching out truth. African-American women's literature is appropriated because it points toward the truth of African-American women's lives. Mary Helen Washington says:

> Their writing is about women; it takes the trouble to record the thoughts, words, feelings, and deeds of black women, experiences that make the realities of being black in America look very different from what men have written. In this tradition, women talk to women. Their relationships with women are vital to their growth and well being.[7]

Here, the real concern for the personal lives of their characters with the sociopolitical reality of being Black in a racist society, and woman in a sexist community, is combined. In African-American women's literature, we encounter the language and communication style—call and response, oral tradition, the listener's active engagement and response—that is of the African-American community, to render a vivid analysis of the impact of African Americans' experience.[8] This literary canon is a source for exploring the metaphors that shape African-American women's lives.

BIBLICAL MOTIFS: Womanist theology shares the exodus and liberation biblical motifs with Black liberation theology. These are a part of the community's historical use of the Bible whereby hope and resistance reign during times that were bad. Womanists, however, are shifting the focus in its examination and appropriation of biblical texts toward motifs specifically relevant to African-American women's experiences. Womanist theologians recognize the importance of an interested stance of the African-American woman reader.[9] Womanist theologians recognize parallel relationships with those the Israelites oppressed, enslaved, and sexually violated.[10] Womanists appropriate the Bible as inspired of God while recognizing that not every text has the same authority in the community. A reading by African-American women and other oppressed women restores and embodies the voice of the oppressed in the biblical text.

Methodology

CONTEXTUAL: This work emerges from a contextual methodology—that is, a methodology characterized by doing ethics and theology contextually, communally, and concretely.[11] This is ethics and theology of a particular context, and works toward the articulation of the inseparable link between theory and praxis—it is concrete. The convergence of racism, sexism, classism, and heterosexism is the contextual reality of African-American women's lives. Womanists do not limit the discourse on their oppression to one aspect such as race, gender, or class. Womanists also examine the relationships that exist between white women and Black women because of white women's use of their "connections to [white] male institutions and relation of submission to [white] men"[12] against women of color as well as relationships with Black men.

HISTORICAL: Womanists have determined that race history is significant for an analysis of factors affecting African-American women's lives. The dynamics that emerged during slavery, and immediately following, have continued to impact relations between African Americans and the white dominant culture as well as the relationships that exist within the African-American community. It is also important to continue including race history because history portrayed not of African-American perspective often distorts this experience. As I have noted in another essay:

> The treatment of African-Americans forced them to contend with systemic distortions of African-Americans' values and life. It is impossible for many white Americans reared on this pathological mythology to think, speak, or write with historical accuracy or ethical understanding about the integrity of black love relationships.[13]

Toni Morrison, Gloria Naylor, and Alice Walker join others who make the experiences of the oppressed their starting place for a rereading of history.

DIALOGICAL: Womanists engage in dialogue with other theologians, social scientists, and religious communities who also advocate on behalf of those oppressed. However, this dialogical approach does not divert womanists' attention from the oppression of the African-American community.[14] This dialogical intent facilitates the engagement around the issue of difference and class analysis among feminists and womanists. It also keeps womanists engaged in dialogue with the African-American community and Church. This ensures that the construction of womanist theology remains rooted in the African-American religious journey as experienced by African-American women.[15]

CLASS AND ECONOMIC INJUSTICE ANALYSIS: In the lives of African-American women classism and economic injustice must be components of the contextual analysis. An analysis of the difference that class and economic status make in the experience of oppression (between white and Black women as well as the class and economic differences between Black women) is crucial. The economic exploitation of African Americans was endemic to the institution of slavery, and created the ideological framework for the continued exploitation of the African-American community.[16]

PSYCHOLOGICAL: Womanists are concerned with the impact of oppression on the psyches of the African-American community. Womanists are aware that violence done to African Americans is linked with the violence we commit against one another.[17] The psychological perspective we articulate must equate healing with liberation of the African-American community.

Content

ETHICAL NORMS AND MORAL AGENCY: Black women's love of women and community has been lifted up in the work of womanists who are now drawing on the ethical principals lived out by African-American women not previously sought out as examples of moral agency. In the *Journal of Feminist Studies in Religion*'s roundtable discussion "Christian Ethics and Theology in Womanist Perspective," one very salient focus of the discussion appears regarding the appropriation of "womanist" for ethical construction. Issues related to heterosexism, homophobia, Black family life, and ethical norms for the expression of sexuality provided the focus.[18] These issues must be grappled with by womanist ethicists and theologians if we are to articulate a theology and praxis of liberation. Raising the issue of homophobia in a critical and visible context, has furthered ". . . the theoretical analyses of the links between sexuality and power"[19] and focused attention on heterosexism and homophobia, the context where African-American women realize the potential to oppress, and where "there are few pure oppressors or victims."[20]

The liberation and transformation of the Black family is part and parcel of the liberation of Black women. Delores Williams notes that at the end of *The Color Purple*, Celie and the family experience liberation.[21] Family in womanist theology is understood to be extended and diverse in its models. Mary Helen Washington in her collection helps us see family as "living mystery, constantly changing, constantly providing us clues about who we are, and demanding that we recognize the new and challenging shapes it takes."[22]

Emerging womanist perspectives on the African-American family, themes that arise out of the Black experience, i.e., bloodmothers, community othermothers, and women-centered networks of activism, are necessary for understanding the contemporary expression of Black family.[23] We must heed a previous caution offered to examine to what degree our pastoral practice with Black families has been influenced by studies which were undertaken from a pathological framework.[24] Womanists note that many studies on the Black family have insisted on confining family to patriarchal assumptions related to "head of the family," "heterosexism" and "male privilege." The impact of economic deprivation is phenomenal, and generational. Marian Wright Edelman's work with Black children and families is a crucial resource.[25]

Womanist ethicists and theologians suggest relational principles that are nonoppressive and emerge out of relationships based on "mutuality, community-seeking, and other-directed."[26] Relationships must be held together by commitments to the transformation and liberation of society. Womanism calls us to a relational praxis emerging out of a "system of Black moral value indicators . . . based on justice and love, [and] to express in word and deed an alternative way of living in the world."[27]

WOMANIST SPIRITUALITY: Womanist spirituality is a dimension of womanist ethics and theology, and in Alice Walker's construction, "God is inside of you and inside everybody else. You come into the world with God,"[28] it is understood as a feature of Black femaleness. It is the pulse that permeates the relational principles of womanism, and is a praxis of spirituality [that is] a conscious response to the call of discipleship by Jesus . . . [it] includes every dimension of Black life.[29] In womanist theology, it is an embodied, incarnational and holistic spirituality immanent in its union with the womanist challenge to injustice, and is inextricably linked with a liberating and healing praxis.

CHRISTOLOGY, IMAGO DEI, REVELATION, INCARNATION: Womanist construction of Christology approaches the task from several important positions: that Black women are fully human, fully *imago Dei*, that Christ "can be incarnate wherever there is movement to sustain and liberate oppressed people,"[30] and that Christological constructions must attend to issues of oppression and Jesus' relationship to structures that perpetuate oppression, and must unite the struggle for liberation and healing with the experiences of Black women. Jacquelyn Grant contends that it is not Jesus' maleness that is so significant, but his humanness. The realities of Jesus' life—birth, life of ministry, crucifixion, and the resurrection—are the events most relevant:

> The significance . . . in one sense, is that in them the absolute becomes concrete. God becomes concrete not only in the man Jesus, for he was crucified, but in the lives . . . of those who will accept the challenge of the risen Savior. . . . Therefore, Christ discovered in the experience of black women, is a black woman.[31]

A Womanist Context for Examining Sexual Abuse

Experience and Literature

As noted previously, experience and literature are primary sources for womanist ethics and theology. Doing ethics and theology with the experiences of African-American women at the heart of the liberative effort means that the socially constructed nature of experience that converges in racism, sexism, classism and heterosexism converge is integral to our analysis. The girl in the opening vignette of this essay slept with a baseball bat. She is abused and terrified. She provides a glimpse into the realities that are shaping her life. Her childhood has been ruptured by violence and terror. Like her sister, she is terrified that she may be raped by her father. Her only protection is to sleep with a bat.

Terrorized that someone will see her bruises, she is relieved that hers do not show. And, terrorized by the violence taking root within her, she embodies the struggle to retain a sense of her humanity in an oppressive situation. Yet, she is prepared to beat her father and "not stop until he stops moving." From her, we learn the choice of non-violence in a violent situation is neither simple nor easy.

We know little of the community in which she lives except that she is astounded that white people beat their children. We know that her father has sexually violated her sister. Her nightmares threaten her day. In despair she wonders if she will ever be able to leave home. We know she has run away. She is not alone.

I recall Toni Morrison's *The Bluest Eye*,[32] and Alice Walker's *The Color Purple*.[33] These stories contextualized the sexual abuse of Black female children. Each gave testimony to the reality of sexual violation in the lives of Black female children and, with integrity, gave this experience voice and form for Celie and Pecola. Pecola is poor and Black, and is raped by her father. Her deepest desire is for blue eyes. Celie is poor and Black and is raped by her stepfather. Both suffered sexual and physical violence in their homes, and both are further victimized by the realities of racism and poverty as well as by their community's response.

We are witnesses to Pecola's fragmented self that is born out of the dynamics of abuse in the family and community. Each embodies the internalization of a racist and sexist culture that attacks Blackness on every front. The missing girl believes that only Black people violate one another. Pecola's deepest desire for blue eyes, and Celie's God are the legacy of a racist culture that set the prototype for feminine beauty, and divinity—and has the power to institutionalize these images. Pecola Breedlove utilized fantasy (of obtaining blue eyes) as a means of warding off more trauma to herself. Celie survives by journaling, and by expecting little from her environment. Neither is able to experience a sense of genuine entitlement to agency and subjectivity.

In Celie's case, she only knows how to survive. Pecola's disturbance is so severe that she becomes convinced that her desire for blue eyes has been granted after fervent prayer. Their lives are permeated with Black bodily scapegoating. Perhaps most disturbing is the fact that Celie, Pecola, and the missing girl call us to consider how the impact of racism and sexism permeate the psyches of an oppressed people. This is the embodiment of "the way cultural . . . and social practices regulate . . . and transform the human psyche . . . "[34] Pecola Breedlove goes insane. Celie, after years of sexual and physical violation is loved into healing and wholeness. In the process, the community who is her family is transformed.

Race History Context

Womanists recognize the important legacy of dualistic thinking in terms of its significance in the justification of the slavery, contemporary attitudes toward the rape and mistreatment of African-American women, and its expression in the African-American community. As a result of the enslavement of Africans in the Western hemisphere, the widespread sexual assault of African women and children became the norm. African women were dragged from their home, raped, beaten, separated from family and culture, and impregnated for the financial benefit of slave owners.

Darlene Clark Hine's work on African-American women and rape reminds us that almost all narratives of female slaves speak to the prevalence of rape. The links between Black women and illicit sexuality consolidated during the antebellum years had powerful ideological consequences for the next hundred and fifty years. Hine addresses the psychological impact of living with the threat of rape as a constant concern.[35]

The resistance of African Americans to enslavement handed down in the accounts of runaways, suicide, and rituals recognizing love and marriage witnessed by slave communities—even though such events were illegal—is an expression of embodied moral agency. The resistance among African-American women was sustained by an enduring perspective among Black women about the meaning of oppression and the actions that Black women can and should take to resist it.[36]

The emergence of the Black Church experience was integral to responses of resistance.[37] The Black Church has been one of the places where African-American women exercised power and influence in the Black community. However, there was and is a level of ambivalence in the Black Church regarding the exercise of leadership by women. This is one expression of dualistic ideology that is operative in the Black community and wider society.[38] Consequently, the Black Church has been, for many Black women, a place of resistance as well as sustenance. It is the capacity of the Black Church to embody the essence of Black struggle for wholeness, and the enduring presence of Black women in the Church who embody the struggle within and outside the Church, that makes the Black Church a potentially liberating agent for African-American women sexually abused.

The Black Family

Black family life must be understood within the multiple context in which it has developed. While examining its strengths we also must note that in spite of those working for a liberated African-American community, we regularly observe that the realities of oppression have taken a toll on African-American families. This is evident in the interpersonal and intrapsychic functioning of African Americans. We see that violence, based on subjugation of the least powerful, is most often targeted against women and children.

Consider the impact of poverty on Pecola's life in Morrison's novel. Her mother is a domestic worker in a white home. The nurturing she has to give goes to the little blond girl. When she is frustrated and angry, Pecola is the victim of her rage. When poverty is an additional feature of oppression, women and children are most often trapped. Black women's liberation must mean the liberation of the Black family, and the social structures affecting Black families.[39]

Womanist models challenge the Eurocentric perspective on family relationships, including the measure or components of who constitutes family. Single mothers and children make up a family in authentic Afrocentric family systems. Gay and lesbian couples and their children make up a genuine family; "play" brothers and sisters (non-sanguininally related, or informally adopted children) add to extended family systems; age-dominant figures (usually grandmothers) often serve as mothers in Afrocentric households. Many of the rationales used for informal adoptions by Black families resemble those of traditional West African families. Martin and Martin describe families who gave their children up to kin who needed companionship after the death of a spouse. The sense that children belong to the community is evident in the authors' description of family members who, without permission, simply took children, whom they felt were neglected by their [male] parents. Other families who needed financial relief sent their children to live with a favorite aunt.[40]

Theological Reflection: Ethical Norms For Relationship

These women's lives reveal the means whereby African-American women's lives are personally, socially, and spiritually oppressed and transformed. Consider in Walker's novel, Mr._____'s view of Celie, a young woman given to him, along with a cow, in marriage by her stepfather—a stepfather who had raped her throughout her childhood: "Who you think you is? he say. You can't curse nobody. Look at you. You Black, you pore, you ugly, you a woman. Goddam, he say, you nothing at all."[41]

Alice Walker succinctly expresses one legacy of the treatment of Black women and Black children in the immediate historical era after slavery. Celie's oppression emerges out of an earlier context in which the option to abuse Black females was considered tolerable. As far as Mr._____ is concerned, Celie, by virtue of the fact that she is Black, poor, and a woman is nothing. Not a far leap from Black and animal. Certainly not a person. The values implied here undergird the belief that Black liberation means that Black men will have equal capacity to control and dominate Black women and Black families.[42] The conclusion is that relationships of care and mutuality are a struggle, are *the* struggle. In understanding African-American relationships we must understand that an aspect of racism and sexism is to define not only who we are and can be, but who we are *to be with one another*.

In contradiction to the racist and sexist models for relationship, womanists reveal that a love of self and community is a necessary element for creating relationships of healing and liberation. This love grounded the liberating responses that empowered African slaves to respond to racism in struggle, resistance and survival. African Americans risked loving one another in spite of the effects of enslavement, and loved their children even though they would later be separated from them. Celie barely saw her children before they were taken, yet she harbored a love that lasted a lifetime.

Celie's transformation occurs in stages. First, she cares for the very sick Shug Avery. As Shug recovers and begins to witness the oppression of Celie's life, she helps Celie see herself. Celie, who knew little about her body, takes a mirror, and with Shug's tutelage, claims her Black vagina and her Black breasts—her Black body—and takes an elementary step toward loving herself, regardless. Celie's healing grew out of a relationship that embodied the convergence of race, gender, and Black sexuality. This convergence was a union of sexuality and spirituality. Recall that her healing involved a transformation of the oppressive and distant God to one not confined by gender designation. This God was the immanent Spirit who permeates the world. Spirituality is the pulse that permeates the principles of womanism—and Black life.

This developing love of the Spirit is central to religious expression and experience in the African-American community, and results in movement from isolation to connection. Celie comes to address her journal to "Dear God. Dear stars, dear trees, dear sky, dear peoples. Dear everything. Dear God. Thank you . . . "[43] Healing brings with it gratitude. Celie's transformation was also an economic transformation. She acquired the means to be financially independent.[44] Celie's healing also involved the transformation of Mr. Albert, Sophia, Harpo, their children, and Squeak's capacity to define herself and the relationships that existed among this family.

Where domination and sexual violence is transformed into life-giving choices, liberation of the community emerges. This conscious and intentional response of creating relationships grounded in mutuality and struggle, love of Black women, Black children and Black men—the community—and the Spirit, is one that promises a just future. Our response to the sexual abuse in the lives of African-American women must be grounded in the experiences of African-American women today in light of our communal history and our religious and ethical principles for relating, and the task must be transformation and healing. We must determine how we are to live with one another. The following principles unite the liberating pulse of the Black community and church with the task of liberation and transformation of African-American women's lives.

(1) It is in the context of Black relationships embodying a common vision of a transformed society, that runs counter to the culture of domination, where we find the convergence of race, gender and sexuality that is liberating. The African-American community of faith emerged during the experience of slavery, and in the context of oppression, in order to challenge, transform, and liberate our faith, society and Church.

(2) It is in the context of Black relationships of deep commitment and attachment to one another and the dream of a world made whole, that runs counter to the culture of alienation, that we find the convergence of race, gender, and sexuality that is healing.

Concurrent with this understanding of the African-American community's praxis, is a Black interpretation of Jesus' relationship with those marginalized and oppressed and his relationship with the dominant religion/culture as paradigmatic for the community of faith.

(3) It is in the context of Black relationships formed and affirmed in the Black family, the Black community, and the Black Church, that runs counter

to the culture of despair, where we find the convergence of race, gender, and sexuality that guides us to our past and calls us into a future of justice and sustained hope.

When the Black Church is faithful to the liberating example of Jesus, we embody African-American ethical principles that realize our struggle to create relationships grounded in mutuality and love—of Black women, Black children, and Black men—our community, and our future. When the Black Church and the Black community are faithful to the tradition of a salvific and ever-vigilant God who is present to save, then indeed the chariot of the favored Black spiritual does offer a redemptive metaphor for realized eschatology made manifest in our experience.

We are weak and strong—a truly creative, resilient, caring, and faithful people. But this is impossible to remember when we live in silence and fear. To eliminate the violence that is crushing the vibrant spirit of our families, and communities Black men and women must talk, cry, and as we've always done, sing to each other. "Swing Low, Sweet Chariot, comin' for to carry me home!"[45]

Notes

1. This vignette is from the diary of a girl who stayed, for a brief period, at a shelter for homeless and runaway youth. She threw it away when she was leaving. I received a rewritten copy as an exercise for a course in which she later participated as a seminarian. I begin with her because I recognize the convergence of stories—race, gender, and the threat of sexual abuse. I also slept with "protection" at one time in my life, just in case. Her experiences and feelings also represent the cherished stories of many other women that I have heard during my teaching career.

2. Gail E. Wyatt, "The Sociocultural Context of African American and White American Women's Rape," *The Journal of Social Issues* 48 (Spring 1992): 77–91; "Kinsey Revisited: Comparisons of the Sexual Socialization of and Sexual Behavior of Black Women over 33 Years," *Archives of Sexual Behavior* 17 (August 1988): 289–332; "Reexamining Factors Predicting Afro-American and White American Women's Age at First Coitus," *Archives of Sexual Behavior* 18 (August 1989): 271–98; "Differential Effects of Women's Child Sexual Abuse and Subsequent Sexual Revictimization," *Journal of Consulting and Clinical Psychology* 60 (April 1992): 167–73; "Internal and External Mediators of Women's Rape Experiences," *Psychology of Women Quarterly* 14 (June 1990): 153–76; Darlene Clark Hine, "Rape and the Inner Lives of Black Women in the Middle West: Preliminary Thoughts on the Culture of Dissemblance," *Signs: Journal of Women in Culture and Society*, 14/4 (1989): 912–20. Eleanor Johnson, "Reflections on Black Feminist Therapy" in *Home Girls: A Black Feminist Anthology*, ed. Barbara Smith (New York: Kitchen Table: Women of Color Press, 1983), 320–24.

3. See: Gail Wyatt, "The Sexual Abuse of Afro-American and White American Women in Childhood," *Child Abuse and Neglect*, (1985): 507–19; Linda

Hollies, "A Daughter Survives Incest: A Retrospective Analysis" in *Double Stitch: Black Women Write about Mothers and Daughters*, ed. Patricia Bell-Scott, Beverly Guy-Sheftall, Jacqueline Jones Royster, et al. (Boston: Beacon Press, 1991), 152–63; Andrea R. Canann, "I Call Up Names: Facing Childhood Sexual Abuse," in *Black Women's Health Book: Speaking for Ourselves*, ed. Evelyn C. White (Seattle: Seal Press, 1990).

4. See the following works linking childhood sexual abuse and chemical dependency, teenage runaways, and teen pregnancies: Judith S. Musick, "Child Sexual Abuse: Findings from a Statewide Survey of Teenage Mothers in Illinois," *Report of the Executive Director of Ounce of Prevention Fund*, Chicago, Ill. 1991; Judith Kovach, "Incest, Chemical Dependency and Women: Theory and Practice," Paper presented at the Western Michigan Psychological Association Spring Conference (May 1986); Jane Powers and Barbara Weiss Jaklitsch, *Understanding Survivors of Abuse* (Lexington, Mass.: Lexington Books, 1989); Jeffrey J. Haugaard, N. Dickon Reppucci, *The Sexual Abuse of Children* (San Francisco: Jossey-Bass, 1988).

5. Beth Richie-Bush, "Facing Contradictions: Challenge for Black Feminists," in *Aegis* Magazine, as quoted in Evelyn C. White, "Life is a Song Worth Singing: Ending Violence in the Black Family," *Working Together to Prevent Sexual and Domestic Violence* 5/2 (November/December 1984).

6. Alice Walker, *In Search of Our Mothers' Gardens: Womanist Prose*. (New York: Harcourt Brace Jovanovich, 1983), xi. While Walker's definition includes women of color, the development of Mujerista theology, and Asian women's theological work has meant that womanist is appropriated primarily by African-American women. See Ada Maria Isasi-Diaz and Yolanda Tarongo, *Hispanic Women: Prophetic Voice in The Church* (San Francisco: Harper & Row, 1988; Letty M. Russell, Kwok Pui-lan, Ada Maria Isasi-Diaz, Katie Geneva Cannon, *Inheriting Our Mother's Gardens: Feminist Theology in Third World Perspective* (Philadelphia: Westminster Press, 1988); Elena Olazagasti-Segovia, "Mujeristas," *Journal of Feminist Studies in Religion*, 8 (Spring 1992): 109–12. For a dissenting Black feminist perspective on the use and appropriation of the term "womanist," see Cheryl J. Sanders, "Christian Ethics and Theology in Womanist Perspective," *Journal of Feminist Studies in Religion* 5/2, (1989): 83–112. See also Jacquelyn Grant, *White Women's Christ and Black Women's Jesus: Feminist Christology and Womanist Response* (Atlanta: Scholars Press, 1989); Toinette M. Eugene, "To Be of Use," Special Section on Appropriation and Reciprocity in Womanist/Mujerista/Feminist Work, *Journal of Feminist Studies in Religion* 8/2 (Fall, 1992): 141–49.

7. Mary Helen Washington, "Introduction," *Invented Lives: Narratives of Black Women, 1860–1960* (New York: Anchor Press, 1987), xxi.

8. Maggie Sale, "Call and Response As Critical Method: African-American Oral Traditions and 'Beloved,'" *African American Review* 26/1 (1992): 41–50.

9. Renita J. Weems, "Reading Her Way through the Struggle: African-American Women and the Bible," *Stony the Road We Trod*, ed. Cain Hope Felder (Minneapolis: Augsburg Fortress Press, 1991): 57–77.

10. Delores S. Williams, *Sisters in the Wilderness: The Challenge of Womanist God Talk* (Maryknoll: Orbis, 1993).

11. Susan Brooks Thistlethwaite, Mary Potter Engel, "Introduction: Making the Connections among Liberation Theologies around the World," in *Lift Every Voice: Constructing Christian Theologies from the Underside*, ed. Susan Brooks Thistlethwaite and Mary Potter Engel (San Francisco: HarperSanFrancisco, 1990), 3.

12. Rita Nakashima Brock, "The Feminist Redemption of Christ,"in *Christian Feminism*, ed. Judith L. Weidman (San Francisco: Harper & Row, 1984), 56. Quoted in A. Roy Eckart, "Women and Jesus," *Bridges*, 3 (January /February): 33–40.

13. Toinette M. Eugene, "While Love Is Unfashionable: Ethical Implications for Black Spirituality and Sexuality," in *Women's Consciousness, Women's Conscience: A Reader in Feminist Ethics* ed. Barbara Andolsen, Christine Gudorf, and Mary Pellauer (Minneapolis: Winston Press, 1985), 121–41.

14. Delores S. Williams, "Black Women's Literature and the Task of Feminist Theology," in *Immaculate and Powerful: The Female in Sacred Image and Social Reality*, ed. Clarissa W. Atkinson, Constance Buchanan, and Margaret R. Miles (Boston: Beacon Press, 1985), 88–109.

15. Ibid.

16. Audre Lorde, "Age, Race, Class, and Sex: Women Redefining Difference," in *Sister Outsider: Essays and Speeches by Audre Lorde* (Trumansburg, New York: 1984): 114–23; Julianne Malveaux, "Gender Difference and Beyond: An Economic Perspective on Diversity and Commonality among Women," in *Theoretical Perspective on Sexual Difference*, ed. Deborah L. Rhode (New Haven: Yale University Press, 1990), 226–38.

17. Toinette M. Eugene, "While Love . . ."; Darlene Clarke Hine, "Rape and The Inner Lives"; Audre Lorde, "Age, Race, Class."

18. Cheryl J. Sanders, "Christian Ethics and Theology in Womanist Perspective."

19. Patricia Hill Collins, *Black Feminist Thought: Knowledge, Consciousness, and the Politics of Empowerment* (New York: Routledge, 1992), 192.

20. Ibid. See also Jewelle L. Gomez, "A Cultural Legacy Denied and Discovered: Black Lesbians in Fiction by Women," and Cheryl Clarke, "The Failure To Transform: Homophobia in the Black Community," in *Home Girls: A Feminist Anthology* (New York: Kitchen Table: Women of Color Press, 1983).

21. Delores S. Williams, "Black Women's Liberation and the Task of Feminist Theology," 88–111; Alice Walker, *The Color Purple* (New York: Washington Square Press, 1982)

22. Mary Helen Washington, "Introduction," *All Our Kin: Stories about Family by Black Writers* (New York: Anchor Books, Doubleday, 1991), 1–2.

23. Patricia Hill Collins, "The Meaning of Motherhood in Black Culture and Black Mother-Daughter Relationships," in *Double Stitch: Black Women Write about Mothers and Daughters*, ed. Patricia Bell-Scott, Beverly Guy-Sheftall, Jacquelyne Jones Royster, et al. (Boston: Beacon Press, 1991).

24. Toinette M. Eugene, "The Black Family That Is Church," in *Families: Black and Catholic, Catholic and Black*, ed. Sr. Thea Bowman, FSPA, Ph.D.

Commission on Marriage and Family Life, Department of Education, United States Catholic Conference (1985), 55.

25. Marian Wright Edelman, *Families in Peril: An Agenda for Social Change* (Cambridge: Harvard University Press, 1987), 7–10.

26. Toinette M. Eugene, "While Love . . . ," 138–39.

27. Toinette M. Eugene, "Moral Values and Black Womanists," *Journal of Religious Thought* 44/2 (Winter-Spring, 1988): 23–44.

28. Alice Walker, *The Color Purple*, 178.

29. Toinette M. Eugene, "While Love . . . ," 121–41.

30. Kelly Brown in James Evans, *We Have Been Believers* (Minneapolis: Fortune Press, 1992), 94.

31. Jaquelyn Grant, "Womanist Theology: Black Women's Experience as a Source for Doing Theology, with Special Reference to Christology," *African American Religious Studies*, ed. Gayraud S. Wilmore (Durham: Duke University Press, 1989), 208–27.

32. Toni Morrison, *The Bluest Eye* (New York: Washington Square Press, 1970).

33. Alice Walker, *The Color Purple* (New York: Washington Square Press, 1982).

34. Richard Schweder, "Cultural Psychology: What Is It?," in *Thinking through Cultures*, ed. Richard Schweder (Cambridge: Harvard University Press, 1991), 73.

35. Darlene Clark Hine, "Rape and the Inner Lives of Black Women in the Middle West."

36. Patricia Hill Collins, "The Social Construction of Black Feminist Thought," *Signs: Journal of Women in Culture and Society* 14/4 (Summer 1989): 875–84.

37. See C. Eric Lincoln and Lawrence H. Mamiya, *The Black Church in the African-American Experience* (Durham: Duke University Press, 1990); and Albert Raboteau, *Slave Religion: The "Invisible Institution" in the Antebellum South* (New York: Oxford University Press, 1978).

38. See Cheryl Townsend Gilkes, "The Roles of Church and Community Mothers: Ambivalent American Sexism or Fragmented African Family-hood?," *Journal of Feminist Studies in Religion* 2 (Spring 1986): 41–59; and "Together and in Harness: Women's Traditions in the Sanctified Church," *Signs: Journal of Women and Culture and Society*, 5/4 (1985): 678–99; Teressa Hoover, "Black Women and the Churches: Triple Jeopardy," in *Black Theology: A Documentary History*, ed. Gayraud Wilmore and James Cone (New York: Orbis Books, 1979): 377–88; Delores S. Williams, "James Cone's Liberation: Twenty Years Later," in *A Black Theology of Liberation: Twentieth Anniversary Edition*, (New York: Orbis, 1990): 189–95; and Toinette M. Eugene, "While Love . . . ."

39. Toni Morrison, *The Bluest Eye*, 86–87. Delores S. Williams, "Black Women's Liberation and the Task of Feminist Theology," 103.

40. Robert Staples and Leanor Boulin Johnson, *Black Families at The Crossroads: Challenges and Prospects* (San Francisco: Jossey-Bass, 1993), 203, quoting E. P. Martin and J. M. Martin, *The Black Extended Family* (Chicago: University of Chicago Press, 1978).

41. Alice Walker, *The Color Purple*, 187.

42. bell hooks, "Radical Black Subjectivity," *Yearning: race, gender, and cultural politics* (Boston: South End Press, 1990), 16.

43. Alice Walker, *The Color Purple*, 249.

44. Ibid., 192–93.

45. With profound appreciation to Judith S. Lichtenstein, M.D., James N. Poling, Ph.D., and Phillis I. Sheppard, M.A. for their invaluable assistance and support in the development of this essay.

Forgiveness: The Last Step

MARIE M. FORTUNE

Forgiveness is a pastoral resource available to those who have been victimized by other's actions; it is a means of restoration to wholeness. It should be viewed from the experience of the victim and understood as only one aspect of the healing process.

Because of the obligation to forgive which is taught in Christian formation, persons who are the victims of family violence often feel that they must forgive their offender immediately. This obligation is communicated through pastors, family, and friends. For the victim, however, there is beyond the obligation a desire to forgive that is related to the hope that forgiveness will being healing and resolution to the pain of the experience.

To Forgive and Forget

For many victims or survivors of family violence, the longing or obligation to forgive is superseded by the subjective sense of not feeling forgiving. The guidance they are receiving from family members, friends, their pastor, and their church points in the direction of "forgive and forget." Even though they may speak the words of forgiveness, they cannot forget; they know very well that popular piety and platitudes are not enough; they know that nothing has changed for them.

Forgiveness is the last step in a process of healing from the brokenness of family violence. Prior steps are necessary in order for a victim of violence and abuse to be *freed to forgive*. In Luke's Gospel, Jesus describes part of the process very concretely:

> Take heed to yourselves; if your brother sins, rebuke him, and if he repents, forgive him; and if he sins against you several times in the day, and turns to you seven times, and says, "I repent," you must forgive him. (Luke 17: 3– 4, RSV)

The scripture clearly points to the need for preliminaries to be accomplished before forgiveness is considered. These prerequisites are best described as elements of justice. Once justice has been accomplished, even in a limited way, forgiveness becomes a viable opportunity. Prior to justice, forgiveness is an empty exercise.

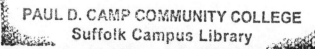

From the offender's perspective, forgiveness is often viewed as an immediate way to be relieved of guilt for wrongful actions. An offender may approach a pastor seeking forgiveness or may ask the victim to forgive. Usually these requests are accompanied by genuine remorse and promises of changed behavior: "I'm sorry, honey; I'll never hit you again." Or the offender may bargain with the victim: "If you forgive me and take me back, then I'll go into treatment." But forgiveness by the victim or by the church is inappropriate and premature in these situations. Forgiveness before justice is "cheap grace" and cannot contribute to authentic healing and restoration to wholeness for the victim or for the offender. It cuts the healing process short and may well perpetuate the cycle of abuse. It also undercuts the redemption of abusers by preventing them from being accountable for their abusive behavior.

Justice as Precondition

Making justice begins with acknowledgment that harm has been done to one person by another. In Luke's gospel, this is referred to as "rebuking," or confronting, the offender. Pastorally, the offender's act of confession is the beginning of acknowledgment. To be confronted (whether by family member, pastor, or district attorney) is to be called to accountability for unjust acts. To confess is to acknowledge responsibility for harm done.

Second, repentance is needed. Remorse may be easily forthcoming, but repentance is harder; repentance is derived from *metanoia*, or fundamental change. The prophet Ezekiel called for repentance:

> Repent and turn from all your transgressions . . . and get yourselves a
> new heart and a new spirit! . . . so turn, and live! (Ezek. 18: 30–32, RSV)

But change from a pattern of abuse in the family is not accomplished through good intentions; it requires time, hard work, and therapy. Involvement in a treatment process may be the most useful penance that could be prescribed for an abuser.

Another aspect of "justice-making" is restitution. It is the responsibility of the abuser to provide materially for the restoration of those harmed. Thus, paying expenses such as medical treatment, housing, and therapy that a victim incurs as a result of the abuse is a very concrete and symbolic act of justice. Some adult incest survivors have sought and won restitution from their offenders in civil court. Restitution acknowledges the real cost to the victim and represents an effort to make right what was broken.

Each step is dependent on the willingness of the offender to participate in the healing process, but often the offender is unwilling or unavailable.

Providing Elements for Justice and Forgiveness

Justice, forgiveness, and healing for the victim cannot be dependent on the offender. These steps then become the responsibility of the wider community. The church, the legal system, and family and friends can also make justice for victims. It is the task of helping professionals to provide the elements necessary for justice. These include the following:

1. *Truth-telling/acknowledgment of the harm done to the victim.* In expressing this acknowledgment to the victim, belief and outrage are fully communicated.

2. *Deprivatization/breaking the silence.* Dealing with the offense openly breaks down the secrecy that has sustained the abuse for so long. The silence only protects offenders from the consequences of their acts; it does not protect the victim or future victims. (But care should be taken to respect the privacy of the victims and their choices as to public discussion of the experience.)

3. *Deminimization/hearing the whole story.* Many people tend to minimize the seriousness of family violence. It is one way of dealing with the horror of its truth. Deminimizing—being willing to hear and believe the experiences of victims—is a means of standing with the victim.

4. *Protection of the vulnerable.* Regardless of what action is taken by the courts or by the offender, the responsibility remains to protect any others who might be at risk.

Thus, when an incest offender is not remorseful or repentant, the survivor needs justice from other sources. Victims need to have their experience acknowledged by others within some wider context, and they need to know that others will help keep the children away from the offender. If a victim chooses to bring civil suit for damages, the choice should be supported and not discouraged.

When a batterer is not remorseful or repentant, the victim needs support for her decision to leave that relationship and try to make it on her own. If she chooses to file criminal charges, she needs support, not someone trying to talk her out of this action. She needs safe shelter rather than someone trying to get her to return to the abuser.

What Is Forgiveness?

For the victim, forgiveness is letting go of the immediacy of the trauma, the memory of which continues to terrorize the victim and limit possibilities. The memory is the lens through which the world is viewed. Forgiving involves putting that lens aside but keeping it close at hand. It is the choice to no longer allow the memory of the abuse to continue to abuse. But this step of healing must be carried out according to the victim's timetable. For the incest survivor who is now thirty to forty years old, but is just now remembering the incestuous abuse, the traumatic events may be long past but the memory fresh and painful. Healing will take time.

Forgiveness is not forgetting. Victims never forget experiences of abuse in families. Consciously or unconsciously, the memory remains. Trying to forget is a waste of valuable energy. Putting the memory into perspective so that it no longer dominates one's life is more useful.

Forgiving does not necessarily mean automatically trusting or returning to the offender. Trust that has been so savagely broken can be regained only over time, if at all. The return to a relationship is entirely dependent on trust: can the survivor genuinely trust this person not to abuse her again? The choice to forgive should not be tied to these decisions.

Pastoral Encounters and Treatment Suggestions

From a pastoral perspective, the temptation to skew the justice and forgiveness process is great because the road to healing and restoration is long and arduous. But shortcuts never serve the victim, the offender, or the wider community.

The first pastoral encounter with a situation of family violence may well be with the offender who is arrested or who comes to the pastor expressing remorse and asking for forgiveness. One incest offender approached his pastor and told him that he had been molesting his daughter for two years: Could God forgive him and could the pastor forgive him? The pastor assured him that God forgives those who repent of their sin, and then he offered to pray with him. He also said that as soon as they were finished praying, he (the pastor) wanted the father to call the Child Protection Service and report himself. The man was surprised; but he did as he was instructed. Then the pastor explained to the man that he would eventually be placed in a treatment program for incest offenders and the pastor wanted him to attend that program once a week. He also wanted to see him once a week for Bible study and prayer, and he wanted him in church every Sunday.

The pastor could easily have said a prayer over this man and sent him home. The offender would have felt absolved of any responsibility and, although genuinely desiring at that moment not to repeat the offense, would be highly likely to do so. Instead, the minister used the authority of his pastoral office to give guidance and direction to the offender, which he knew would be in the offender's best interest in the long run. (Reporting any suspicion of any form of child abuse is required of most helping professionals in every state. In some states, clergy are exempt from this requirement.)

Conversion

Another fairly common circumstance a pastor will encounter is the offender's religious conversion. This is particularly common when arrest has already taken place. A pastor would be well advised to approach this situation with caution.

An experience of religious conversion may well be genuine, but should not then be used as a reason to avoid the consequences of the offense: "Judge, I've found Jesus Christ; I'm a new man, and I promise you this will never happen again." If it is a genuine experience, this conversion becomes an invaluable resource to the offender who faces incarceration and possibly months of treatment. The pastor's task is to help guide and direct this religious resource in order to support the offender's process of repentance. If it is not a genuine experience, the pastor is virtually the only person who has the authority to call the offender's bluff. It is the pastor's responsibility not to allow the offender to manipulate and distort the process in order to avoid negative consequences.

Mediation

Another temptation for the pastor is the resource of mediation. Mediation is the process now widely available (often through church channels) for conflict resolution. It is sometimes recommended as a resource to families dealing with violence and abuse. Mediation is not an appropriate resource with which to address a situation of violence for the following three reasons:

1. Mediation seeks to resolve a conflict between two parties as a way of stopping the abuse. Since the abuse is not the result of a conflict or disagreement, but is a chronic pattern of abusive behavior by the offender, mediation is not appropriate.

2. Mediation is used primarily as an alternative to the criminal justice system. Avoidance of the criminal justice system is usually unwise in addressing family violence. There may be some legitimate reasons why a victim or offender would seek to avoid this system, such as the unequal treatment often given to people of racial or social differences. But it is more likely to be white, middle-class families that seek to avoid this system. It is important that the criminal justice system be used if at all possible because it unequivocally communicates that the offender is held accountable for the abuse and it has the best chance of directing the offender to treatment.

3. Mediation presupposes that two equal parties come to the table to resolve a conflict. Victims of abuse in families can never come to that situation and feel safe from, much less equal to, their abuser.

Mediation may be a valuable resource to call upon *after* the violence and abuse have stopped and family members need to resolve division of property, custody, and other such problems. But it should not be used as an intervention to stop the violence.

Conclusion

For the Christian, it is finally the power of the Holy Spirit that enables the healing process to take place. This spiritual power gives the victim the strength to forgive, to let go. It gives the victimizer the strength to repent, to change. It gives the church the strength to help both persons in the justice-making process. But the power of the Holy Spirit is released only when justice is made manifest for the victim and offender. Whenever there is an attempt to cut the process short and jump to premature reconciliation, the possibility of authentic healing is lost.

A group of incest offenders in a treatment program made a powerful plea: "Don't forgive so easily." All were Christians and had gone to their pastors as soon as they were arrested, asking to be forgiven. Each had been prayed over, forgiven, and sent home. They said that this pastoral response had been the least helpful to them because it enabled them to continue to avoid accountability for their offenses. Withholding forgiveness and absolution from an offender until certain conditions have been met may be the best way to facilitate a permanent change. Waiting patiently with the victims until they are ready to forgive may be the most charitable and compassionate act the church can offer. In these ways, we take seriously the power of forgiveness to bring people to healing.

Part IV
Historical Revisioning

❧

Augustine on Rape:
One Chapter in the Theological Tradition[1]

MARY PELLAUER

In the last twenty-five years, questions have blossomed about the theological significance of sexual victimization. How did the theologians of the centuries before us view rape? This essay will look at Augustine's remarks in *The City of God*. His comments were short (14 of 867 pages in translation) and have been little remarked. Nonetheless, these few sections are of great potential interest today. I will provide a close reading of them, lingering with the details, to explore as fully as possible the treatment of rape by a giant of the tradition.

Augustine's major claim in these sections was simple and clear: Consecrated virgins raped in the sack of Rome did not need to commit suicide; indeed, he forbad them to do so. The distinctiveness of this point needs clarifying. Both Roman ethics and early Christian ethics favored suicide in the face of rape. Jerome, for instance, explicitly made rape the exception to all his strictures against suicide:

> It is not man's prerogative to lay violent hands upon himself, but rather to freely receive death from others. In persecutions it is not lawful to commit suicide *except when one's chastity is jeopardized.*[2]

Comments like these persisted down the ages into our time, plus the examples of those who did commit suicide either after rape or before a threat of rape. This is why we used to say that rape was "a fate worse than death."

In what follows, I will be critical of Augustine's argument—how he made it, nuances in it, what he did not say as much as what he did say, incoherences with other arguments, plain mistakes, and ways we cannot help but disagree even with his best points. I emphasize that I am in no wise defending the ancient practice of suicide in the event of rape. Readers might wish to remember that even today, some victims of sexual offenses do become suicidal. Those who have been sexually abused as children may be most at risk, but one study (Warshaw 1988, 66) found that 30 percent of the women who experienced date rape became suicidal.

As I provide a close reading of Augustine's comments, I will note likely reactions of people today who have worked closely with rape victims. Some may consider this anachronistic or heavily ideological, and perhaps it is. But activists today will compare these ideas to what we know about rape. That may mean deep pain and anger. It is better to get these reactions out into the open so that we can assess them.

I will argue that Augustine was redefining rape, much as we are today, but that the terms by which Rome understood rape largely vitiate his arguments. The Latin language of his time was as much a part of his problem as is twentieth-century English to us today. So were Augustine's own theological understandings. As a result, these arguments become part of our problem. The concluding sections aim to assess the meaning of Augustine's reflections. I will point out both Augustine's mistakes and the buried elements in his treatment that we can use more creatively.

The Context of Augustine's Case

The City of God was a product of the mature Augustine. When he began writing this work in 413, he had been eighteen years the Bishop of Hippo, struggling with the Donatist heretics of northern Africa; finished in 425, the book had become a major theological treatise. He began it because refugees from the fall of Rome were arriving in North Africa. Present day readers ought not exaggerate the violence involved. The symbolic importance of an enemy army entering the city outweighed the actual damage done in three short days in the autumn of 410 (Villari 1902). The city was not levelled as it had been centuries earlier; the number of deaths was small. The government had already been removed to Ravenna. Some burning and looting occurred. But the Visigoths were more interested in extorting money and position from the Empire than in wrecking the city or any military gains (Bury 1923).

Some Christian refugees may have experienced what they described; others brought second- or third-hand reports. I consider it highly unlikely that Augustine heard directly from any rape victims. Shame was so highly intertwined with rape that it seems improbable that he would have heard a first-hand account.

Unhappily, we have only fragments of a history of rape in the west (Tomaselli 1986). This is a serious obstacle to any theology taking sexual violence seriously. Rape is not eternal, though rape mythologies would have us believe so. Some societies are more prone to rape than others (Sanday 1981); so are some historical periods. One historian thinks rape increased in the early middle ages (Rouche 1987, 469–71); another claims that rape increased in times of instability and unrest, though he may be thinking more of stranger rape than other kinds (Porter 1986).

The definition of what counts as rape in a specific society or epoch has serious consequences for the experiences of victims/survivors. In much of the ancient world, indeed in much of western history and perhaps in our own time, rape was an offense whose severity and meaning were determined by the social status of the people involved, whether victims or assailants. It mattered whether they were members of another society or one's own; free or slave; highborn or lowborn; married or not married. Some groups of women were defined as outside any protection. One historian notes that "indulgent Roman morality" turned a blind eye to gang rape of prostitutes by adolescents (Veyne 1988, 108).

Rape was taken for granted in wartime in the ancient societies around the Mediterranean (Brownmiller 1975), so much so that Augustine noted an occasion when a Roman general made an exception (I:5 and 6). For a woman, "The worst disaster in being a prisoner of war is to be prey to a stranger's lust," said Jerome in *Against Jovinian*.

However, we should not conclude that all these ancient societies viewed rape in the same way. Greek, Roman and Israelite forms of patriarchy were not identical (Hallett 1989; Fantham et al. 1994); there were also different understandings of rape. One scholar points out that the precise distinctions of Deuteronomy 22:22–28 about the status of the victims mean that Israel viewed rape as a means of bride-capture (Biale 1984). Another notes that in ancient Greece, seduction was more heinous than rape because the seducer gained the trust of the one seduced (Pomeroy 1975).

Rape seems especially salient in ancient Rome. The Rape of the Sabine Women was one of its founding stories, the tale of the capture of brides for the first (male) immigrants. It was recalled annually in several rites (Scheid 1992). Similarly, the founding of the Republic, that period of freedom and honor so cherished by Romans, was initiated by the Rape of Lucretia and the subsequent overthrow of the rule of kings. (Augustine took up Lucretia's story, so I'll look at this below.) A late revision of Rome's legal codes instituted laws about rape that were eerily reminiscent of some provisions of the Deuteronomic laws. The absence of a clear picture, even an outline, of rape in any of the differing periods of ancient Rome makes it risky to assess Augustine's comments.

An Argument in "a Strait between Modesty and Logic"

The comments about rape have a peculiar place in the whole structure of *The City of God*. They seem self-contained, like a little essay in themselves, with little consequence in the rest of the text. While there were passing comments about rape elsewhere in this book,[3] rape did not become systematically important to the vision of the whole work. Perhaps it is the sense that they were an aside, a parenthesis, that accounts for the fact that so few scholars comment on them.

The first half of the whole text, including Book I, was a polemic refuting the attacks of pagans who "lay at Christ's door the miseries which the city [Rome] suffered." He wanted not merely to refute this claim but to prove a series of points: Rome's proliferation of gods was absurd; the pantheon did not protect Rome in any case; the one true Christian God was the real reason Rome flourished when it did; and most especially, alongside the earthly cities, down through history there was one eternal city, both co-existing with the temporal cities and awaiting believers at the end of time. Its glories and virtues would outshine any glories Rome knew.

So Book I began by attacking pagans who were "insolently and shamelessly insulting the servants of Christ." This led to considering "all the slaughter, plundering, burning and misery" (I:7). These afflictions fell equally upon the unjust and the just, the pagans and the believers, due to God's mercy. Christians suffered robbery and torture (I:10), slaughter (I:11-12), captivity (I:14), and rape.

The comments on rape in parts 16 to 29 began like this:

> They fancy they bring a conclusive charge against Christianity when they aggravate the horror of captivity by adding that not only wives and unmarried maidens, but even consecrated virgins, were violated (I:16).[4]

Notice those three categories of victims: matrons, maidens and those who had taken vows of chastity. Yet the maidens and matrons disappeared altogether from Augustine's treatment. In all the sections that follow he focused solely on the consecrated virgins.

No sooner had Augustine announced the topic than there was a deflection in the argument. The very next sentence said,

> We find ourselves forced by certain difficulties into a strait between modesty and logic, not that our faith or religion or the virtue called chastity is itself in any strait, but rather the course of our argument. Nor are we here concerned so much to deliver a reply to those not of our kind as to bring comfort to our own people themselves.

Both logic and comfort reappear in the final sections, indeed, intertwined with each other. In the end he believed he had given the church "its proper message of comfort, free from fallacy" (I:29).

So let's look a bit at the structure of the argument. The headings of the sections sketch this deflection in the case, or perhaps more than one. Sections 16, 18, 19, 25, 26, 28, and 29 were the heart of his consideration of rape:

16: Whether the violation of captured virgins, even those consecrated, defiled their virtuous character, though their will did not consent.
17: On suicide caused by fear of punishment or disgrace.
18: Violence from others and sexual pleasure experienced by an unwilling mind in the subjected body.
19: On Lucretia, who commited suicide because she was violated.

20: That there is no authority that allows Christians in any case the right to die of their own will.

21: What cases of homicide are excepted from the charge of murder?

22: Whether suicide is ever a sign of greatness of mind.

23: What are we to think of the precedent set by Cato, who, unable to bear Caesar's victory, slew himself?

24: The virtue for which Regulus was more distinguished than Cato, reaches much greater heights in the Christians.

25: That a sin should not be avoided by a sin.

26: What explanation we should adopt to account for the saints' doing certain things they are known to have done which it is not lawful to do.

27: Whether one should commit suicide to avoid sinning.

28: By what judgment of God the enemy was permitted to sin against the bodies of the continent.

29: What the servants of Christ should say to infidels, when they cast the reproach that Christ did not free them from the enemy's rage.

Section 17 (and then sections 21 to 24) moved from rape to suicide, because suicide was the expected response to dishonor in ancient Rome. Alongside the pastoral motive (comfort), the apologetic motive was also maintained, to prove Christianity right. This apologetic motive produced asides within the aside, as it were. The male examples in parts 23 and 24 may look especially odd to a woman in the late twentieth century in an argument about rape; they were present as illustrious examples of suicide. After these extended digressions, sections 26, 28, and 29 return to the topic of rape. Section 27 on preventive suicide has a small aside implying rape, as we shall see.

Readers should notice that what started his concern was that "they" charged that Christian virgins were violated. As in the heading to section 29, Augustine often cast his reflections in terms of what Christians should answer back, as if in a rhetorical debate. This rhetorical flavor was essential, though it appears alien to us today.[5] It meant that he often struggled with the ordinary use of the language. Throughout *The City of God*, many of his arguments turned on the proper use of verbal expressions, customary usage of words, common idiom, how terms applied and what words signified (IV:8–9). Even in these sections about rape, he said we "should not misapply words" (I:18).

Thus, typical Roman understandings of rape were involved in Augustine's arguments. He set himself to argue with his society's viewpoint, to provide an alternative understanding of rape—just as activists do today. What other people believed, thought, feared was therefore central to the case.

Modesty and the Latin Language

Let's look more closely, then, at the Latin language, for it was part of the problem—and so is its rendering into English. In the English titles for sections 16 and 19 above, the words violation and violated were euphemisms. The Latin does not use *violare* (from which we get violate). Nor does it use *raptus*,[6] from which we get the word rape. *Raptus* meant tearing off, rending away; seizing, abduction, also rape; plunder. Hence a "raptor" was not primarily a rapist in our sense, but a robber, a plunderer; but it could also mean a rapist in our sense. (This was what made the capture of the Sabine women "rape" in Rome.) Disentangling abduction from sexual offenses was centuries long in the making (Brundage); even today some rapists abduct their victims. So the captivity of the women was more relevant to the topic than we might ordinarily think.

Instead of these words, the text says *stuprum*, a unique Latin word which apparently has no descendent in English.[7] It originally meant "disgrace in general" but

> came to be specialized of a sexual disgrace, i.e., an illicit sexual act, whether an adulterous liaison or a forcible violation. . . . The word is not necessarily used of a violation perpetrated against the will of the victim. . . . [I]t implies disapproval on the part of the user. But often it denotes a forcible violation. . . . The range of sexual acts which might be described thus was unlimited (Adams 1982, 200–1.)

With this range of application, *stuprum* sounds like our English "f-word."[8] Later in the text we shall see *adulteria*. (Yes, it's just what you think).

A similar ambiguity was present in the range of other expressions he used. In fact, three fields of language come together in this treatment: violence, sexuality and shame. (See the box on the opposite page for details.) Augustine used four clear expressions for violence, seven terms for sex, and no less than fifteen expressions for shame/modesty. Shame and modesty were intertwined so much that a range of related words are translated either as shame or modesty depending on the context. The Sanskrit root *pu* was the common foundation for both pure (*purus*) and shameful (*pudor*), as in the first seven terms for shame. The presence of so many words linking sexual violence and shame may set off alarm bells in our heads today.

So that accounts for the modesty. What about the logic?

"In the First Place . . ."

The very next paragraph of I:16 asserted the logical grounds for the later argument:

> Let this, therefore, in the first place, be laid down as an unassailable position, that the virtue which makes the life good has its throne in the soul, and thence rules the members of the body, which becomes holy in virtue of the holiness of the will; and that while the will remains firm and unshaken, nothing that another person does with the body, or upon the body, is any fault of the person who suffers it, so long as he cannot escape it without sin.

Augustine's Language for Rape

Language Expressing Violence:

Comprimo: compress, press or squeeze together; press tightly, hence, embrace; suppress, hold back.

Opprimo: press upon, press down; weigh down, burden, crush, suppress; from it is derived our English "oppress." These first two were polite but clear language for sexual assault.

Opprimens concumbere: by force to lie with or have intercourse.

Violentia libidinis alienae: the violence of the lust for another.

Language Expressing Sexuality:

Cupiditas: eager desire, passionate longing; it could be used for many objects but certainly for sex; hence, Cupid, the god of love.

Concupiscentia: from a root meaning to desire eagerly, to covet, to aim at, to endeavor after; we too say "concupiscence."

Concumbere: to lie with, to sleep with; hence, "concubine."

Libido: violent desire, appetite, longing; related to *libet*—"it pleases"; hence often translated as lust, though Augustine said in XIV:15 that *libido* was the general term for desire.

Voluptas: delight, enjoyment, pleasure, usually sensual or sexual pleasure, from which we get "voluptuous."

Carnis voluptas: pleasure of flesh.

Concupiscentia inoboedientia: disobedient concupiscence.

Language Expressing Modesty and Shame:

Pudere: to be ashamed or to cause shame.

Pudens: modest or shamefaced.

Pudicus: modest, chaste, virtuous.

Pudor: shame, bashfulness, modesty, decency, honor.

Pudicitia: modesty, virtue, virginity. (But it could also be used of married women.)

Impudicitia: impurity, lewdness, unchastity.

Pudenda: the sexual organs, literally "that which is shameful or disgraceful." This word appeared in Book XIV, the well-known section on the Fall, with precisely this definition.

Turpitudinis alienae: disgraceful, shameful, base [deeds] of others, related to our "turpitude."

Foedus: foul, filthy, horrible, abominable, cruel—from which we get words like "foetor" and "foetid," of rotting things.

Corruptus: corrupt.

Maculare: to spot, to stain, morally, to pollute, defile; thus, our word "immaculate" comes from roots meaning unstained.

Scelere: to pollute, defile, profane with guilt; hence derivatives in Latin meaning impious, wicked, profane.

Inquinatus: dirty, foul, polluted, sordid, from a root (*caene*) that meant mud.

Immundiatia: uncleanness, impurity, dirty, foulness.

Pollutio: pollution; its roots were *pro* plus *lutum* (mud).

At first glance, this may look unobjectionable. Or is it? Scrutinize it. See what happens for you. For me, problems emerge. Feminist/womanist theologians will no doubt notice the soul-body dualism immediately. What Augustine thought "unassailable" is vulnerable today. This is not only because of feminist/womanist cases, but because our whole modern understanding of the person as a whole makes this perspective untenable.

The longer I look at these claims, the more complex, intriguing, and difficult they become. Why was Augustine worried about bodies "becoming holy"? This seems a bit odd. But Augustine did believe that believers could grow into greater holiness. Believers could advance toward the divine, with the help of divine grace. The gradual rising or soaring toward God, Augustine's Christian Platonism, was the theme especially of Books IX–XII. Movement toward God was especially associated with chastity.

In other words, it was no accident that Augustine was talking about consecrated virgins, not about women in general. It may be that the omission of the other victims (so striking to us today) was built into the logic of the case. Virgins had not only given up all sexual activity but were to have repressed all sexual feelings. Or more accurately, in his own terms, since finally one could not extinguish all sexual feelings (XXII:23), one was not to *consent* to them. (*Consentire* meant to share in feeling; to agree, to assent, to be unanimous about; to harmonize.)

So, the will was central. A whole anthropology was implicated in these brief words. Though we continue to talk about the will and willpower, I am not certain I really understand what Augustine meant by it, partly because we do not any longer live out of his psychology—called "faculty psychology" because the soul was believed to have certain distinct faculties: the passions, reason, and the will. Both reason and will were governing faculties, they were to order and guide; body and passions were to obey. How these governing faculties related to each other was less important than that they ruled while the body and the passions obeyed. Sometimes he listed them in tandem: ". . . the spirit which commands and the body which obeys . . . the rational soul which rules and the irrational desire which is ruled . . . the contemplative virtue which is supreme and the active which is subject" (XIV:22).

He used two images to illustrate the governing faculties. Reason was "posted as it were in a kind of citadel, to give rule to these other parts [passions, body], so that while it rules and they serve, man's righteousness is preserved without a breach" (XIV:19). Another image, the bridle, indicated guiding the passions as a rider guided a horse; it did not mean merely putting down the passions or the body, but directing them rightly. Like the body, the soul made "motions," turning toward or away from things. Indeed, these motions were will itself (XIV:6). Consenting was a matter of the will turning toward the object of one's passion.[9] "The right will is . . . well-directed love, and the wrong will is ill-directed love" (XIV:7).

Readers today may have many different perspectives on such ideas about the human person. For me, there are contradictions. For Augustine, conflict in the self, like conflict in the city, was a sign of sin. It is curious and difficult to understand, then, how the non-consent of the soul could be saintly rather than sinful, since to me it seems it would produce and even increase disharmony. For Augustine, this was not a contradiction, for he asserted a hierarchy of goods. Bodily goods (strength, beauty, youth, health) were less good than the goods of the soul. (To the classic virtues—temperance, fortitude, justice, prudence—he added chastity, which was not a classical virtue.) The right ordering of the goods and virtues (or the loves) was a prime task of the will; right ordering did not precisely stop such conflict in the self but it arranged the conflict hierarchically. Strictly speaking, there was another contradiction here, for in Augustine's theology, domination, too, was a sign and consequence of sin (XIX:15; see below). Conflict in the soul/self would not cease until we rest in God, as in the famous opening words of The Confessions, "our hearts are restless until we rest in Thee."

Stare at those words at the head of this section a little longer. Think about other parts of Augustine's theology. Think about The Confessions for instance, which more people are likely to read today than The City of God. In The Confessions Augustine convicted himself of original sin because of the theft of a pear in his youth, probing his soul for traces of culpability in such a small act. We often think of him as intellectual kin with existentialism (Outler; Miles). These words up the existential ante, so to speak. "While the will remains firm and unshaken"—did this imply that if the will trembled, however slightly, fault did enter into the victim? One may legitimately wonder about what it meant to say that there was no fault on her part so long as she "cannot escape it without sin." Did that imply that fighting back against a rapist was a sin? Augustine did not say.

We need to keep these concerns in mind as we look at the arguments that follow. More than one logical problem arises as we pay close attention to his case.

"The Most Enticing Pleasure"

To work out the implications of this logical premise was the task of the sections immediately following. They make a first cluster of related arguments focused on the status of sexual pleasure in rape. I cannot tell whether Augustine himself was deeply concerned with whether these women enjoyed the rape, or whether he was concerned that *others* might believe they enjoyed it:

> But as not only pain may be inflicted, but lust gratified on the body of another, whenever anything of this latter kind takes place, shame invades even a thoroughly pure spirit from which modesty has not departed—shame, lest that act which could not (*non potuit*) be suffered without some sensual pleasure, [perhaps] should be believed to have been committed also with some assent of the will. (I:16)

Notice that Augustine mentioned pain. This reference, however, is the only one in these fourteen pages. Considering whether the victims experienced lust/pleasure in the act of assault was the major concern.

Worst was the statement that rape *could not* be suffered without some pleasure. This was thoroughly odd and completely wrongheaded. That this was really Augustine and not the suspicions of others was clear from the language. (*Non potuit* quite literally means "could not").

The terms in which he posed his compassionate exhortations against suicide were all sexual; they were preoccupied with the possible sin of the victim, and that sin was *sexual* in nature:

> There is ground to fear that, when the body is subjected to the enemy's lust, the insidious pleasure of sense (*inlecebrosissima voluptate*) may entice the soul to consent to the sin, and steps must be taken to prevent so disastrous a result. (I:25)

The Latin, once again, was fascinating. *Inleceber* meant attractive, enticing, alluring; the ending was the superlative. Hence, *inlecebrosissima voluptate* reads, "most attractive, most enticing, most alluring" sensual or sexual pleasure. (Who do you suppose feared this?)

This is not to say that Augustine did not notice violence and coercion in rape. He did. But in these sections, the sexuality is so intermingled with the violence that they cannot be disentangled from each other. Even the most positive aim of this work—exonerating victims from blame, sparing them suicide—is vitiated by the persistent intertwinement of sex in the argument.

Most victims of rape do not experience sexual pleasure, even in civilian cases. Most are frightened and hurt, fearing that they will be killed in the course of the assault (though this may depend on how much other violence is used). When the subject is virgins raped in the sack of a city, it is even less plausible to us today that pleasure is the most important theme to consider. However, it should be acknowledged that some do experience some pleasure, and often guilt and confusion as a result. Advocates today are likely to explain these sensations as resulting from the sheer mechanics and physiology of the nervous system being manipulated. Furthermore, Augustine's focus on lust/desire may distort the experiences of rapists as much as of victims. Rapists do not rape primarily for sexual motives, and they do not always experience pleasure in their assaults either (Groth 1979).

While these comments reflected a problem with the language of rape in his time, they also reflected Augustine's larger theological framework. Augustine had extremely peculiar ideas about sex (Ruether 1974). Book XIV was the special occasion for him to explore them in reflecting on the Fall of Adam and Eve. These blessed first parents "were agitated by no mental perturbations and annoyed by no bodily discomforts" (XIV:11). But they sinned. Therefore, desire/lust (*libido*) was "the penal consequence of sin" (XIV:12). Readers today may wish to pause to think about this: sexual desire itself was punishment for sin.

So was shame. Shame was especially appropriate to sex, because in desire the body parts moved by themselves without the will—or sometimes did not move when one willed them to. This was disobedience in the flesh, both a witness to disobedience and a punishment for it (XIV:17). Thus, the involuntary movement of the genitals was the cause of shame (XIV:19). We might want to pause here also. For a female like me, it is hard not to think this was very male-centered. This was about the penis, not the vulva. Were I to characterize desire in my female body, genital *movement* is not what I would select.

So long as the will did not consent, "bodily sanctity" was preserved:

> If, on the other hand, it [purity] belongs to the soul, then not even when the body is violated is it lost. Nay more, the virtue of holy continence, when it resists the uncleanness of carnal lust, sanctifies even the body, and therefore when this continence remains unsubdued, even the sanctity of the body is preserved, because the will to use it holily remains and, so far as lies in the body itself, the power also. (I:18)

Those affirmations were strong. But so were the suspicions that this was very difficult. That it was not impossible for a consecrated virgin allowed Augustine to conclude that such a woman ought not commit suicide. The conclusion was that

> When a woman is violated while her soul admits no consent to the iniquity, but remains inviolably chaste, the sin is not hers, but his who violates her. (I:18)

Dods's translation may intensify the contradictions here: How can one be inviolate while being violated? Perhaps, however, it is in keeping with Augustine's passion for redefining terms. For instance, in *On Marriage and Concupiscence*, he asserted that when husband and wife engaged in sex for the purpose of pleasure, they were *not really* husband and wife but adulterers.

These complications should not prevent us from affirming that the principle was and is important. It laid the responsibility for the assault squarely on the assailant rather than the victim. We can only affirm this, even while questioning the way the case was made.

In a context where rape was a matter of lust and sexual pleasure, the existentialist tendencies up the ante for rape victims, for they imply that women must consider the shame/guilt of rape as sexual. Did they "really" enjoy it, all appearances to the contrary? Did they "really" want it? These qualifications invite victims to search their own consciences to discover whether they participated in the sin of rape.

Women today still suffer the consequences. Rape victims often say that they do not know if they "can call it rape" because they let him buy her a drink, let him come up to her apartment, talked to him, told him he did not need to tie her up, etc. These are all qualifications that indicate that others might believe the women consented. Such women today bear the existential burdens of the qualifications inherent in Augustine's principles as they were argued. The rest of us might indeed believe it "really" is not rape. Thus, we have judges in recent cases saying it is NOT rape when (1) the victim asked the assailant to wear a condom to protect her from the risk of AIDS, or (2) both she and the assailant agree that she repeatedly said "NO," but did not fight.

Readers may have noticed above that Augustine insisted that the pure one was to resist the "uncleanness of carnal lust." Sex was unclean, defiling by its very nature. It is a strong element in Augustine that he faces pollution squarely.

An Aside about Pollution

Section I:18 began, "there is a fear that even another's lust may pollute." Ancient notions of pollution and purity may be difficult for people today to understand. They were most often operative without being thematized (Fink). That is, people took them for granted and used them rather than defining or reflecting systematically about them. We have begun to notice and reflect upon it, largely due to anthropologist Mary Douglas and philosopher Paul Ricouer. William Countryman has applied these notions to the sexual ethics of the New Testament. Oddly, Peter Brown does not mention pollution in his whole exposition of *The City of God*, nor do other expositors.

"There is a fear—" I cannot help but ask: Whose fear was this? It may be important not to leap too easily to the conclusion that it was primarily Augustine's; considering the objections of others was part of the rhetorical technique *praemonitio*, forewarning (Kennedy 1972). Nonetheless, insight into the objections of others may indeed involve listening to one's own heart and one's own fears. According to recent social historians (Dupont 1992), Romans had to be quite sensitive to the opinions of those around them and were seriously governed by them. This is why I waver between seeing the problem as Augustine's own and seeing it as that of his society.

Again Augustine responded with a bare assertion: "It [lust] does not pollute if it is another's; if it pollutes, it is not another's." This claim was integral to the attempt to rescue the raped virgins from suicide. It was an *extraordinary* claim in the Roman tradition.

Perhaps Augustine was aware that his claim would not be readily granted by his readers, for he embarked upon a series of "logical" moves to prove that purity was a virtue not of the body but of the soul:

> But since purity is a virtue of the soul, and has for its companion virtue the fortitude which will rather endure all evils than consent to evil; and since no one, however magnanimous and pure, has always the disposal of his own body, but can control only the consent and refusal of his will, what sane man can suppose that, if his body be seized and forcibly made use of to satisfy the lust of another, he thereby loses his purity? (I:18)

But this was *precisely* what "sane men" supposed about rape in the ancient world, that rape victims lost their purity. He asserted that "not even when the body is violated is it lost" *provided* that the soul remained "unsubdued." It was "firmness of purpose" which kept "bodily sanctity" intact.

Saying "since" purity was of the soul made a premise of what was supposed to be his conclusion. The rest of this section asked rhetorical questions and made assertions designed to "prove" that purity was a good of the soul. If it were nothing better than a good of the body, "why should the body be perilled that it may be preserved?" A good question, the reader today may think; note that Augustine assumed that purity was more important than the safety of the body.

On the one hand, purity could not reside in the body, he asserted, because surgeons and midwives performed operations on the body. No one supposed that if a midwife destroyed some girl's virginity that she had thereby "lost anything even of her bodily sanctity."

On the other hand, consider this case: If a virgin went out to meet someone with the intention of sex,

> shall we say that as she goes she is possessed even of bodily sanctity, when already she has lost and destroyed that sanctity of soul which sanctifies the body? Far be it from us to so misapply words. (I:18)

One may doubt whether this logic was going to convince anybody who did not already agree.

A reader today may suspect that experiences of pollution are not just capable of being reasoned away. Some victims of rape and other sexual abuses experience compulsive needs to wash; these can profitably be understood as experiences of pollution (Pellauer 1987). They cast doubt on the assertion that defilement is "a moment of consciousness that we have left behind" or which has been "abolished by the progress of moral consciousness itself" (Ricouer 1967, 26, 30).

This discussion was a bridge to the case of Lucretia in the next section. Augustine was also redefining pollution in order to redefine the honorable Lucretia as dishonorable.

That Well-Known Lucretia . . .

"All know how loudly they extol the purity of Lucretia," said section I:19. Lucretia's story was a classic of Roman ethics. We are not so familiar with her as were Augustine's ancient readers. Her story[10] went like this:

The earliest Romans (before 367 B.C.E.) were ruled by kings. One night around a fire after a battle, King Tarquin's son and several members of his clan were amusing themselves—talking about their wives back home. They made bets about what those wives were doing. Riding back to verify their bets, they found only Lucretia in virtuous industry. Tarquin, seeing her, was inflamed. The next night, he rode back alone, intruded into the house, and blackmailed or coerced Lucretia: unless she had sex with him, he would kill both her and a male slave and then tell her family he found them having sex. (For women, death was the penalty for adultery.) So she had sex with him. The next day when her menfolk returned, she told them the whole story, made them promise to avenge her, and stabbed herself to death. Her male relatives, led by Brutus, overthrew Tarquin and established the Republic, the memory of which enshrined glory and virtue to later generations. So this was a story of origins, a myth in the strong sense of an account of sacred beginnings.

As a result, there was a saying: "Here was a marvel: there were two, and only one committed adultery." By it Romans affirmed Lucretia's honor.

Indeed, by it they interlaced women's private honor and men's public honor, both the foundation of the Republic. Thus Seneca said, "to Brutus we owe our freedom—to Brutus and Lucretia." Augustine subjected this story and this saying to a searing scrutiny. To spear the contradictions of this traditional Roman ethic, he made it into a dilemma.

On the one hand: If she was guiltless, why did she slay herself? "How is it that she who was no partner to the crime bears the heavier penalty of the two?" (Tarquin was banished—what was to become the typical penalty for sexual crimes in later imperial Rome.) Her suicide could not be just. A murder at least was committed by her, her own; therefore she was not innocent. "Why do you extol with such unmeasured laudation her who slew an innocent and chaste woman?"

On the other hand: maybe she was not just guilty of self-murder, but of something else. The sexuality in the story was also caught up in his attack. He performed a thought-experiment, asking "What if . . . ?" *What if* she slew herself "conscious of guilt, not of innocence?" Worse, much worse, he insinuated sexual pleasure: "What if—but she alone could know—she was betrayed by the pleasure (*libidine*) of the act and gave some consent . . . ?" In this case, of course, "she did not kill an innocent woman." Thus, the Roman ethic was untenable. "There is no way out of the dilemma, when one asks, If she was adulterous, why praise her? If chaste, why slay her?"

To construe this scene as a dilemma was not enough. That proved only that the Roman ethic was not defensible, not that the Christian ethic was superior. This was what Augustine was really after. "For those unable to comprehend true sanctity and therefore insult our outraged Christian women," he advanced two more steps by introducing *two more sins* into Lucretia's case.

He convicted Lucretia of a weakness of shame/modesty: *pudoris infirmitas*. Dods translated this "the overwhelming burden of her shame," McCracken as "irresolute shame." Even though he had only insinuated pleasure by asking "what if?," here he asserted that it *was obvious* (*quo ergo se ipsam*, lit., what therefore [follows] from itself) that she killed herself not from the love of chastity but from the infirmity/weakness of shame.

Shame was intertwined in the language, some of his strongest, sometimes for the assailant, sometimes for her. For instance, he was covering the assailant in shame and defending Lucretia's honor when he pointed out that the traditional saying noticed

> the utterly foul passion (*inquinatissimam cupiditatem*, lit., dirtiest lust) on one side and the utterly chaste will (*castissimam voluntatem*, lit., chastest will) on the other. (I:19)

But something else was going on when he said:

> Then sick at heart and unable to bear (*aegra atque inpatiens*) the shame (*foedi*) put upon her, she took her life.

He was projecting back onto this very old story, many centuries before him, something that was not in the received versions, namely, her state of mind (*aegra atque inpatiens*). And by the premise about pollution he laid down in section 18, if Lucretia was polluted (*foedi*), then that pollution was hers and not just her assailant's.

The language of weakness was important for more than one reason. It also came up in relation to those males in sections 20–25 who were special examples of virtue (and will return in section 28–29). Cato was thought to be strong precisely because of his suicide after Caesar's army defeated him. But Augustine attributed *infirmitas* to him, precisely because he chose not to bear adversity. Also, strength and weakness were gender-marked in ancient Rome. Men were to be strong and hard, women to be weak and soft. This gender marking may be built into the word *infirmitas*, for its root *firmus* meant firm, strong, stout, healthy; lasting, valid, constant; morally strong. The virtues had "solidity and firmness" (V:20). So it was perhaps not surprising that Lucretia was accused of weakness.

As if this were not enough, she was guilty of something even more serious in his overall case in *The City of God*: greed for praise (*laudis avida*), or "the Roman love of glory." Praise, glory, honor—these were central in Augustine's attack on the basic principles of Roman life. The earliest Romans, according to him, were greedy of praise: "Every other desire was repressed by the strength of their passion for that one thing" (V:12); they suppressed many other vices for this one vice, though it also got mixed with the lust of domination (V:13). The love of praise was virtually synonymous with pride (*superbia*) as "the craving for undue exaltation" (XIV:13); pride was the most fundamental sin of all. This was the root of all the accomplishments of Rome the earthly city. So, convicting Lucretia of the love of praise connected her case to the fundamental vice of Roman society. And indeed, to all unbelieving life, since virtue without faith was not virtue (XIX:25).

Virgins, on the other hand, were not to be interested in the love of praise, which was hostile to pious faith (V:14). Human honor was "smoke which has no weight" (V:17). Many times in *The City of God* Augustine returned to reiterate these points against glory and praise. Christians were to despise glory (V:19). The desire for glory was even a "defilement" (*immunditia*, lit., uncleanness, the same word used for the uncleanness of lust above). "The purer one is from this defilement, the liker is he to God" (V:19).

The virgin-victims were to be concerned with conscience alone and *not* to be distressed over the suspicions or thoughts of others.

> Within their own souls, in the witness of their own conscience, they enjoy the glory of chastity. In the sight of God, too, they are esteemed pure, and this contents them; they ask no more; it suffices them to have opportunity of doing good, and they decline to evade the distress of human suspicion, lest they thereby deviate from the divine law. (I:19)

Once again, this was extraordinary, since glory and praise were firmly inter-twined in this ancient world. "Glory" here became something that one had all alone; it did not consist in the praise of others. God's esteem alone was enough. Indeed, this focus on the women's own estimate of their chastity/ virtue, his detaching them from the opinions of others, may be one reason that we today see compassion in Augustine's comments. (I don't believe we need to choose between compassion and distortion here.)

Lucretia's story was handled with serious venom by Augustine. While Peter Brown suggests that no section of *The City of God* was more vitupera-tive than the later Book XIX on pagan virtue, I do not agree. (He calls this sec-tion on Lucretia "a flamboyant 'set-piece,'" [Brown 1967, 309].) Lucretia was an *exemplum* of moral virtue for women, a strong, clear representative of that pagan ethic. The virtue of women and the virtue of men were two halves of one whole, inextricably intertwined in one social ethic (Fantham et al. 1994, 294–327). In other words, the vituperation was directed at the same end and for the same reasons: to smear pagan virtue in favor of Christian virtue.

Perhaps this attack on eagerness for praise was especially apt to the age in which Augustine lived. The desire for good standing in the eyes of others may have been integral to the earlier Republic, when citizens voted each other into office or shamed each other out of office (Dupont 1992). But the reign of emperors, beginning with Caesar Augustus in 37 B.C.E., stopped this ethic as a practical matter in daily political life. It did not disappear, but it became impotent. In the bloody and chancey arbitrariness of emperor rule, when obe-dience was far more important than honor, it is entirely convincing to me that human honor was merely so much smoke.

Classically, however, women were not to love praise. On the contrary. Praise meant being talked about by others—public notice and public regard. Ancient honorable women were not to be talked about at all. The clearest statement of this perspective was Pericles's admonition to women "not to be talked about for good or for evil." Romans were not so emphatic about this, perhaps because they did not sequester women as the Greeks did (Hallett 1989). Nonetheless, privacy was women's realm and fame in the public more a matter for censure than praise. In Rome only those who fought in war were eligible for public life. Because women did not fight, they had no rights, could not defend themselves or bring suit; and legal battles provided a good deal of Roman public life (Tellegen-Couperus 1993). I worry, at times, whether Augustine's distress about Lucretia was related to the fact that by her death, she ensured that her version of her experiences, her story, was the one that was told.

Augustine's reasoning ought not be taken for granted. While I have no particular brief for the ancient Roman ethic, my reaction to Lucretia's story is different. It just makes me weep. I cannot condemn her, because I am too busy mourning. As he said elsewhere, those who cannot weep when a subject requires weeping are less than human (XIX:7)—an argument against the Stoic virtue of *apatheia*. We understand suicide very differently today, at least in part because of Augustine's attacks on it. That is, we do not view suicide as a matter of honor, but as a response to agony, despair, or psychopathology. (For some of the problems with Augustine's attacks on it, see Droge and Tabor 1992.)

Unhappily for a reader today, destroying Lucretia's reputation has a rebound effect on the very rape victims Augustine was trying to rescue. It casts doubt on whether anybody was able to escape the dirty foulness, the filth cast about by rape. For why not ask "what if?" about the consecrated virgins also? Especially those who committed suicide just like Lucretia?

Augustine had an answer for that.

Special Pleading for the Saints

The heading of section 26 was an extended euphemism: "What explanation we should adopt to account for the saints' doing certain things that they are known to have done which it is not lawful to do." It might well read, "what explanation we should adopt for those saints who did commit suicide after rape," for this was its subject. To stress the parallel with Cato, it might have said, "What are we to think of the precedent set by the saints, who, unable to bear rape, slew themselves?" Or it might have read, "On the saints who committed suicide because they were violated," stressing the parallel with Lucretia. But these parallels were precisely what he wanted to avoid; hence, the vagueness of his language.

Just as Romans revered Cato and Lucretia, Christians also revered virgins who committed suicide. Another set of "what ifs?" arose here, some of Augustine's weakest. "I dare not give any rash judgement," he said, for "I do not know" whether God commanded the church to venerate them. And why don't those Christian suicides, virgin-victims, come in for the same slashing attacks Lucretia got? Instead of attacking, he conjectured: *What if* God commanded them to commit suicide? Just as a soldier obeying the commands of his general in war was not guilty of murder, so these suicide victims were not even guilty of self-murder. (Unlike Lucretia.) "Who can accuse religious deference?" he asked. Because, you see, obedience "is the mother and guardian of all virtues" (XIV:12). Those who thought God commanded them to suicide, however, must be very, very sure that there was no doubt about it.

Augustine was redefining more than his society's terms about rape. He was also struggling to redefine the church's terms about rape. His arguments were in grim contrast to the comment of Jerome (cited above). Indeed, I suspect that because Augustine had just redefined women's glory to be the property of a relationship only between her and God, he had to take this on, however weakly. Not even the opinions of the church counted. This too we might wish to affirm.

"Why Did God Let This Happen?"

There was a second cluster of arguments in sections 28 and 29. The terms changed considerably. The topic here was why God allowed barbarians to rape Christian virgins. This discussion is virtually a model for theological questions still arising today among Christian women victimized by rape. "When God exposes me to adversity, God is either testing my merits or chastising my sins" (I:29). These responses to suffering, including that of rape victims, are virtually unchanged today (Fortune).

First, Augustine's answer was that strictly speaking we do not know:

> It is a deep providence of the Creator and Governor (*rector*) of the World; and "unsearchable are His judgments and His ways past finding out." (I:28)

Nonetheless, we can speculate or conjecture; and Augustine did here just as much as earlier.

He asked those "what if" questions again. "Interrogate your hearts," Dods' translation said, or "faithfully question your souls" in another. *What if* the raped virgins were *proud* of their chastity? *What if* they too were taking pleasure in human praise? Oddly enough here—unlike in Lucretia's case— Augustine went out of his way to say, "I do not accuse, where I do not know and I do not hear what answer your hearts make when questioned" (I:28). But *if* the answer was yes, then

> do not marvel that you have lost that by which you can win men's praise, and retain that which cannot be exhibited to men. If you did not consent to sin, it was because God added His aid to His grace that it might not be lost, and because shame before men succeeded to human glory that it might not be loved. (I: 28)

Notice this reference to grace, the only one in these pages.

There was a good reason for rape, it seemed. This correction of sin by God was fully intended by Augustine to be a comfort and consolation:

> In both respects even the fainthearted among you have a consolation (*In utroque consolamini, pusillanimes*), approved by the one experience, chastened by the other; justified by the one, corrected by the other. (I:28)

Perhaps McCracken is a little clearer in rendering this, "In respect to both, faint-hearted ones, take comfort." But it is hard not to hear a deeper reproach in the Latin "*pusillanimes*"—tiny-hearted ones, usually used in contrast to *magnanima*, big-hearted or large-souled.

On the other hand, maybe there were some "whose hearts when questioned answered that they have never been proud of their chastity," who never let their hearts get inflated. This did not stop Augustine's endless need to conjecture:

> Moreover, it is possible that those Christian women, who are unconscious of any undue pride on account of their virtuous chastity, whereby they sinlessly suffered the violence of their captors, had yet some lurking infirmity (*latentis infirmitas*) which might have betrayed them into a proud and contemptuous bearing (*superbia*), had they not been subjected to the humiliation that befell them in the taking of the city. (I:28)

In case anyone did not get the point: the first group, the proud ones, were treated for "a tumor already swollen," the second, the not-yet-proud ones, for a tumor that was going to swell.

In other words, in both cases, rape was for their own good. This is so upsetting that I can hardly speak. My rage and distress jumble together to silence me.

When I calm down, I can notice other complications. Both languages, English and Latin, are implicated in the problems. Both words in *latentis infirmitas* create these. We have already seen issues about gender related to *infirmitas*. *Latentis* meant merely concealed, hidden. It was sometimes used for God's purposes. "Lurking" was a comment of the translator.

Pride, that "lurking infirmity" of women, has often been the occasion in the tradition to condemn women *even if we are humble*, even if our pride is so deeply buried as to be *unconscious*. Even if they hadn't sinned yet, they *might* sin one day; rape was a prophylatic punishment, so to speak, preventing them from the potential sin.

Augustine was bitterly sarcastic at the notion that anyone ought to commit suicide today to prevent falling into sin tomorrow: If that were so, why not suicide right after baptism (I:26)? He did not apply such a train of thought to God, but we might. If we are to attribute such evils as rape to God (by no means a given), why not say it is wrong of God to do an evil (like rape) to a woman today to prevent her from another evil (like pride) tomorrow? Of course, it is unthinkable, even blasphemous, in most of the tradition to say that God is wrong about anything. If we agree with this premise, the only way out is to refuse God's causality of rape. But unhitching the moral sovereignty of God from the causality of God for anything that happens is a very long and arduous spiritual task. (It certainly involves considering more than Augustine.)

These arguments were directed to insuring that these rape victims accepted that rape was part of God's government, for God here was named not only as Creator but also Governor. (*Rector* meant king, rule-giver, right-maker.) It happened; therefore, it was God's will. It was God who exposed human persons to adversity, not some other less ultimate agent. This perspective is widespread in Christian theology down through the tradition, though more often implicit than clearly stated. It is the *theology of the status quo*. It does not encourage, affirm, or advance the struggle against wicked and unjust conditions. That "whatever is, is right," the classic comment of Alexander Pope from much later, is for a feminist, the lurking infirmity of much theology.

This was the objective side, so to speak, of the case. There was a second, more existential side. There was a lesson, or more than one, to be learned.

First, a philosophical one in tune with his larger thought. These virgins may have been mistaken about whether bodily goods were better than the goods of the soul. "From this error they are probably now delivered" (I:28).

Furthermore, these good Christian women "will not refuse the discipline of this temporal life, in which they are schooled for life eternal; nor will they lament their experience of it"(I:29). Rape was a "discipline," a schooling. (Striking and punishing students was part of the ancient model for learning.) It was not just for their own good, it was for their *eternal* good. They should not even weep about it, wail or complain. Job was his favorite example of the way good Christians bear suffering (I:24); he did not seem to notice that Job complained and lamented aplenty.

God will punish the rapists in the last judgment (I:28). This might have been comforting to many rape victims down through the ages. It is not a comfort to me or to many of us any more.

The Status Quo—and Slavery

Readers may fear at this point that I am making too much of a few nuances in Augustine's language. But these claims were fundamentally entwined with Augustine's larger theological categories. Elsewhere in *The City of God*, he was quite explicit that whatever human beings suffer must be traced back to God.

> Therefore, whatsoever a man suffers contrary to his own will, he ought not to attribute to the will of men, or of angels, or of any created spirit, but rather to His will who gives power to wills. (V:10)

God as both creator of the natural order and governor of all that happened made some people rulers and others slaves (XIX:15). While God did not intend that people should have domination over each other but only over the rest of creation, still "it is with justice, we believe, that the condition of slavery is the result of sin." Like death, desire, and shame, domination too was punishment for sin (XIX:15). Slavery was the result of conquest in war; wars were won or lost because God made it so; God "humbles the vanquished either for the sake of removing or punishing their sin" (XIX:15). God alone gave kingdoms and empires to those who have them (V:21). Sinful as it may be, this order was still God's order, and was not to be rebelled against:

> This servitude is penal and is appointed by that law which enjoins the preservation of the natural order and forbids its disturbance. (XIX:15)

He repeated the Pauline comments about slaves; indeed, he added that slaves were to serve their masters "heartily and with good will" and even with "faithful love" (XIX:15). To our eyes today, this also looks curious when we recall the importance of not consenting to sin when *sex* was the subject. We might see here what Margaret Miles called "the totalitarian scope of his anxiety" (1992, 8).

These arguments about slavery were heinous in any case; I cannot help but see them as even more detestable when we think about rape. To me they raise the almost unbearable thought of slaves raped by their masters. And it may have also occured to Augustine. In section I:17 arguing against suicide for the purpose of preventing one from committing a sin, he claimed that it was not just foolish but mad to say to someone, "Kill yourself, lest to your small sins you add a heinous sin, while you live under an unchaste master, whose conduct is that of a barbarian."

Romans availed themselves sexually of their slaves (and did not consider it barbarian to do so). Christian masters might have refrained from sexual exploitation of their human property, but all Christian slaves were not owned by Christian masters. Every indication is that slaves were completely at the sexual disposal of their masters in antiquity as in the nineteenth-century United States.

> Women [slaves] were always employable for sexual purposes, either in addition to their other domestic responsibilities, or as a primary occupa-tion. The master had access to all his slave women. . . . Slave women were also available for sexual relations with the male slaves in the house, with the master's permission. (Pomeroy 1975, 192)

While Rome certainly took many thousands of slaves in conquest, it also bred slaves (Bradley 1987), largely because of the sexual accessibility of this class of people who were property.

Think of the heartrending contradictions for a slave (woman or man), told on the one hand never to consent to unchastity, and on the other to serve one's master "heartily and with good will" (XIX:15). This dilemma might have been even worse than the one Augustine created in Lucretia's story, for the sexual depradations of slavery were chronic, repeated, and long-lasting.

But he did not outline such a dilemma. Possibly he could not, not only because he was talking primarily about consecrated virgins, but also because *status* was all-encompassing in ancient ethics. Three status cate-gories took up Augustine's Christian concern, as he exhorted believers "either to virginal chastity, to widowly continence or matrimonial fidelity" (I:26). Virgins, widows, and the married took up the major portion of ancient Christian sexual ethics. Though some Christians were slaves in the ancient world, slaves were not on the list at all, any more than they were for Aristotle. It is hard to see how they could have been, given the accep-tance of the status quo.

So What?

Taking stock of what went on in Augustine's discussion of rape is complicated. It involves us in several overlapping enterprises at once. Assessing this compli-cated, rich, and mistaken perspective invites us to be no less complicated and rich than was Augustine. That's the only way to correct his mistakes.

Both clusters of Augustine's comments can only arouse the anger, sad-ness, and irritation of anyone who works with rape victims today. And they should. They are deeply mistaken. They are a prime example of the *system-atic distortion* of women's experience by the patriarchal theological tradition.

In what follows I want to point in several different directions. I want to make some Augustinian comments about Augustine's view of rape. That is, if we take some of this theologian's other arguments seriously, they cast doubt on the ways he argued about the rape of women in the sack of Rome. I will also point to some themes that take us beyond Augustine and finally, describe an experience of my own.

What We Got from Augustine

Even readers as exasperated as I am with this material may wish to pause to think about some of the positive elements in it. Considering both the positive and the negative together may make for more balanced judgement, of course. Balance appeals to many feminists as well as to many Aristotelians looking for the path of virtue between two extremes. But to me it is important in order to understand ourselves fully as historical beings—that is, embedded fully in a contingent, messy pathway of collective life. I am concerned especially that anti-rape activists find something here to affirm. If we do not, we may be erasing our own history, leaving ourselves (in Adrienne Rich's phrase), "orphaned of our own past." These judgments will of course reflect our own wider theological options, our differences in points of view. I invite readers explicitly to consider what they may find affirmable in Augustine's comments.

I am glad that Augustine attacked the notion that the most appropriate way to face rape was to commit suicide. We may have quite different reasons, today, from Augustine's belief that this would be to double the sin. But lowering the ante on the suffering faced by rape victims is surely one good result of this trend in the argument.

It heartens me that rape came up in Augustine's theology because of some actual experiences of believers in his time. So much of the theology of the ancient church seems to me to center on topics of an extraordinarily abstract nature (like the doctrine of the trinity) that I am relieved to find a topic that was concrete, even a bleak one. The lives of the saints are an important occasion for beginning a theological journey; in the case of *The City of God*, a whole magnificent visionary enterprise, begun because of a concern for what believers went through in the sack of Rome. I am also encouraged that Augustine combined a pastoral motive—consolation for the virgin-victims—with his more apologetic and logical points. Those of us today who do theological reflection about rape share this pastoral aim.

Indeed, rape was so often ignored—by theologians in our time as well as those in early centuries—that I am pleased to have even these few pages. We can see so clearly from them how thoroughly a theological view of rape is intertwined with both one's society's views of rape and with the full sweep of a theological system. (This is one way that a critique of rape in *The City of God* leads one to other theological critiques.) Augustine's theological premises helped him to be critical of both his society and his church. Indeed, we may take heart that he was countering the perspectives of both society and church in his era. Surely feminist/womanist theologians today who think seriously about rape find themselves, like Augustine, needing to replace mistaken elements in both.

What Augustine Left out Were His Best Points

I noticed above that Augustine mentioned pain, once. That single reference disappeared as the possibility of pleasure overwhelmed his terms. There were no theological, moral, or existential terms spelling out the meaning of pain.

No language was supplied to bring forward nuances of meaning in the experiences of pain. This, of course, is tragic. Pain is prominent in the experiences of many victims.

Even more puzzling is that Augustine never mentioned *fear* or its variants: terror, nightmares, startle reactions, shaking, phobias. These are even more prominent in the experiences of victims than pain, and there is not much reason to believe things were different in the ancient world. When Romans discussed war, they were clear about the fears of women and children. Terror was a serious element of mythological depictions of the rape of mortal women by the gods, at least in some versions (Curran 1978). Not even to mention fear in the discussion of the sack of Rome is at least odd.

This absence was not just an oversight. For Augustine asserted and reiterated the steadfastness and unshakeability of the will in arguing against the rape victim's culpability. Shakiness of body might have suggested shakiness of will and was therefore to be avoided. To introduce any notes of fear, trembling, terror into this discussion might have cast doubt upon the steadfastness of will so necessary to his account of the rape victim's innocence. Given that fear was will itself, not just a feeling (as it would be to us), we can see more clearly why Augustine could not mention it.

But that insistence on the unshakeability of the will becomes even more peculiar when we look beyond *The City of God*. The very next chapter in Augustine's struggles involved his controversies with the Pelagians—the part of his story which we may know best and for which we revere him most. Casting an eye on these kinds of arguments sheds quite a different light on what he said about the consecrated virgins. Because, you see, these were the arguments *against* the steadfastness, clarity, and univocity of the will.

Augustine's anti-Pelagian arguments were directed to showing the incapacity of the will to do what it wills, and therefore its perpetual need for grace. The will may will something, but this ability did not guarantee the ability to do what is willed, for the will was thoroughly vitiated by sin. The human self was not in natural goodness; it was *dislocated*, out of true, skewed. The self was a dark abyss; humans did not know what was going on inside ourselves. This was why Augustine rejected what he saw as Pelagian perfectionism. It made his view of the human person more complex, nuanced, and congenial to us in the post-Freudian and post-existentialist setting of theology in the twentieth century (Battenhouse 1956; Miles 1992).

And these reflections point up that what Augustine left out of this account was *grace*. Why on earth did Augustine start "in the first place" by saying that it was the virtue of the soul that hallowed the body? Why didn't he say grace? Grace was mentioned in section 28—in other words, very late, and no more prominent than pain.

Indeed, why didn't he say *healing*? Probably because he didn't say grace, since for Augustine grace and healing were fundamentally intertwined with each other. For us today, healing after rape and other sexual abuses may be the most important theological topic of all. When contemporary feminist/womanist theologians take up the healing process after rape (Pellauer and Thistlethwaite 1990), we are pursuing an Augustinian path, one that Augustine himself did not follow.

Augustine made no reference whatsoever to any biblical texts on rape. Although the rest of *The City of God* was saturated with biblical quotations, often used as the capstone of the logic of arguments, this neglect of the Bible about rape was probably not an oversight. Once again I suspect it was because he was focused on consecrated virgins. While the laws in Deuteronomy 22:22–28 are too complicated to go into here, notice that in the case of an unbetrothed virgin, verse 28 prescribed marriage between the victim and the rapist. This would have been impractical when the rapist was in the enemy army and unthinkable for women who had made vows of chastity. For us today, however, it is essential to consider the Deuteronomy texts and the many other rape stories of the Old Testament.[11] He also took no notice of Old Testament stories of suicide (Droge and Tabor 1992) except for Samson, who he claimed had "secret instructions" from God.

Five other themes in *The City of God* strike me as intriguing when we think about rape today.

The first of these was the longing for domination. Feminist/womanist theologians are passionately interested in opposing domination and hierarchy. That might be enriched by considering Augustine's explicit statement that God did not intend people to dominate each other and in exploring his denunciations of the lust of domination, often subtle.

Second, central to the notion of the eternal city was the sense that it came alive in people's hoping for it. Peter Brown translates this as pining, yearning, sighing for what ought to be. Activists in the movement against violence against women will recognize this. We pine for a day when there will be no more rape. Our yearnings for that day have led us to create rape crisis centers and to work to prevent rape. Nowhere in the lyrical descriptions of the eternal city did he say that women would be safe from rape; he may well have assumed this, but he did not say it. He sometimes used "true peace" or "safety" to characterize the true city, a theme that has returned when we think about sexual victimization. Healing requires safe places, and preventing sexual offenses also leads us to think about safety. I thirst and pine for a rich theological treatment of this theme.

Related is a third point: those speculations and conjectures and endless "what if?" questions. It is tragic that Augustine used them to speculate whether Lucretia enjoyed being raped and whether virgins were raped because they might have been proud or might have become proud some day. This use may make us so sick at heart that we might not notice that Augustine's theology was drenched in the *imagination*. We can turn this human capacity, this method, to better use. Imagination is one of the central gifts we need to struggle against rape in our society; and it is one of the central gifts we need to do good theology.

If there is anything in the notion of the dislocated self, it needs to come to terms with patriarchy, racism, and classism. Indeed, they are among the ways that we specify the distortions and dislocations of the self in our time. But we may also wish to spare attention for the inadequacy of the faculty psychology with which Augustine worked and with which many of us still work without knowing it. We need more than "the will" (or its contemporary version, commitment) to understand human action, moral being, sin, sexuality, coercion and choice, the involuntary and the voluntary, etc. And perhaps we need quite different views of reason as well.

Bodily sanctity is the last item in Augustine's account that strikes me as intriguingly filled with potential. We are all awaiting an account of this from Christian theologians. It remains to be seen what might be done with such a theme in the hands of someone who is not a Platonist.

Forgiveness and Grieving

Today when I listen to victims, I notice how important it is for many (in the church especially) to hear a representative of the church say, "I am so sorry that this happened to you." Augustine did not say this. This simple statement may be more consoling than any logical arguments about souls and bodies. *Certainly* it is much more consoling than the idea that rape was God's will, or that rape was a punishment for sin or a test of faith. Augustine possibly *could not* say he was sorry *because* he thought it was God's will. We need to say that we do not believe any of this.

We need to say we're sorry. It is very sad that Augustine misunderstood like this. We need to say that straightforwardly and not merely pass it over in silence or as though we all assumed it.

When forgiveness comes up in the context of rape, it is usually about whether the victim needs forgiveness—just as it was with Augustine. (Sometimes it is about whether the victim needs to forgive her assailant, a question ignored by Augustine.) But this may be very seriously mistaken. It may be the rest of us who need forgiveness—that we misunderstand rape, that we tolerate rape, that we are blind to rape and the experiences of rape victims.

We need to grieve for the mistakes Augustine and the church around him made about rape. Surely we need to be sad. Many of us will also be very, very angry, as I am. Today we may believe that grieving is essential to healing rape and indeed to many other elements of moral action.

Even more, if we are truly sorry, we repent. The church has always said that repentance means turning around to go in the opposite direction. So we struggle to stop rape, to heal rape, and to prevent rape. This involves us in a *serious* theological reconstruction—one that involves both practical efforts to change our institutions and working out the implications of our insights into full theological statements.

If we are not to be just as mistaken as he was, there are some things we need to do very differently. While I cannot fully explore these here, several topics need to be indicated.

Theologies of the status quo can never be adequate for rape. Just anything that happens is not God's will. Liberation theologies open clearer ways for us to think about this than any theologies that stress order. It remains to be seen whether they will also be able to explore rape in ways that enrich the struggle against it.

Pollution is an important theme for theology; it is intertwined with shame. Shame is returning to public view and public consideration, so much so that there is a whole literature now. For Augustine, shame was inevitably involved with *what other people thought or said* about the victim. It is so sad that more than a millenium after Augustine, what people may say or think about rape victims has barely changed.

What other people think was intimately tied up with Augustine's under-standing of sin. The word for pride in the hearts of rape victims was *superbia*. In *The City of God*, *superbia* was especially *the desire for praise by others*. Today we may think quite differently about this than Augustine did. We may distinguish between "mirroring validation" of one's experiences and a desire for "good feedback." Both are different from a compulsive need for praise (which we are likely to consider narcissist). We may also think that a sense of competence is created and maintained by praise. All this alters our perspective on whether a desire for praise from others is sin or not.

Feminist/womanist theologians may wish to ask whether our English word "pride" covers more variety than we usually think. Recent commenta-tors on Greek materials suggest that we need to see the note of violence in *hybris* (Sissa 1990). This has a different flavor from desire for praise from others. Other periods too may have meant different things by pride. For instance, Luther's late medieval view seemed to mean trying to get above one's social station. Today by pride we are more likely to mean self-esteem, self-respect, and an appreciation of one's basic rights.

Redefining Rape Today as in Augustine's Time

Augustine was redefining his society's terms and his church's terms for rape. This is what we are doing too, as we talk about rape as a crime of violence and not one of sex. Augustine was redefining rape to mean acts in which no trace of sexual pleasure was experienced by victims.

He could not take up "real sex" because he was discussing virgins. To do that we have to look beyond those consecrated virgins. It is up to us to take up real sex, and to distinguish it from rape. We need to explore female sexuality with a seriousness and a subtlety that matches Augustine's. I believe we would find themes vastly different from his—a different relation-ship to the involuntary, for instance. Nobody today thinks that sexual desire itself is a punishment for or sign of sin, but male-centered perspectives on sexuality still thrive.

Today we have listened to rape victims. In the last twenty years we have learned more about their experiences than in the previous twenty centuries. Rape Trauma Syndrome is based on the perception of victims that their lives are threatened (Burgess and Holmstrom, 1974), making it a variety of Post-Traumatic Stress Syndrome. This is essential to a theological perspective on rape (Pellauer 1987). Unhappily, Augustine's thought does not appear to help with thinking theologically about lifethreatening experiences. The way we confront death did not matter (I:11).

Looking beyond the consecrated virgins is important for another reason. We cannot be concerned about the safety or healing of only one privileged set of survivors. Today we must listen to the experiences of those young maidens and matrons—and also the whores. We have to listen to the women in the Christian churches, yes, but also the post-Christians, the unbelievers, atheists, agnostics, Jews, Buddhists, Hindus, Muslims. We have to listen to women who are liberal, conservative, radical, middle-of-the-road. We have to listen to heterosexual, bisexual, and lesbian women. We have to listen to females especially but also to males; to the wartime rapes, the date rapes, the marital rapes, the family rapes, the gang rapes, and yes, the stranger rapes too. To the victims who are poor, middle-class, and also rich. To women who are Caucasian, African-American, Hispanic, Native American, Asian—not to mention the women on all the other continents.

Listening to the stories: For us, this is the grounds of doing feminist/womanist theology. In the modern world, women have been telling our stories, whether about rape or about theology. So it may be especially fitting that I end with a story of my own.

Reenacting Augustine

Frankly, finding and poring over these comments about rape in *The City of God* gave me a crisis of faith. While I have had several crises of faith over my adult life, this one is particularly longlasting. I found this text in early 1986. Indeed, I wrote much of the body of this manuscript that spring. It upset me very deeply. I wept; I screamed at the office walls; I got depressed and saddened. How could I believe anything in Christianity if this giant of the tradition got so much wrong about a basic experience of women like me?

It happened that one of the following weeks I went to Sunday worship. It happened to be Pentecost Sunday. It happened that when I heard the invocation, opening worship "in the name of the Father, Son, and Holy Spirit," something snapped in me. By the end of the Gloria, I had to leave. I cried all the way home. Nothing in my previous sixteen years of struggle about sexist language had prepared me for the rage and pain I felt at hearing that language while thinking about Augustine on rape.

In the days that followed, into June, I decided that I owed both my pastor and myself an account of this experience. He was a friend; I needed help. It is very hard to be alone with Augustine on rape. I went to him. "I am having a spiritual crisis," I said, and told him the whole story about Augustine on rape and what happened when I heard the invocation.

He exploded. "You can't do that!" he said, and proceeded to lecture me for what felt like quite a long time. First, he told me that he was very well-informed about, and tired of, feminist reactions to God-language. (He didn't seem to notice my distress about the rape language.) "Maybe you don't realize that some people *like* Father language for God," he said. (This floored me more than a little, since I had been hearing that since 1968.) He was caught in the whiplash between feminists on the one extreme and the patriarchalists on the other, and to be in the middle in this conflict was tiring. Second, he was tired in general. He worked long and hard, and was committed, seriously committed, to justice and its requirements in the mission of the local congregation. This was true. The church ran a lively set of programs in relation to its ghetto neighborhood, as well as a ministry with gay and lesbian people. He took flak for both of those, and he was steadfast in persisting. I supported all that. I had spent time listening and expressing my concern for his fatigue.

Perhaps it was this memory that made me notice the structure of this conversation. Because now, you see, I'd turned to him for support. He was my pastor, after all—and to us Lutherans, "pastor" means something pretty serious. Somehow, I gathered together enough lucidity to notice this and to say, "Pay attention to the dynamics of what happened here. From my point of view, the story goes like this: I came to you in a spiritual crisis. You have first of all, forbidden me to have such a crisis, and second, taken up most of our time by asking me to help you with yours. This may be connected to the fact that I'm a woman and you're a man, that I'm lay and you're clergy. Think about it."

It was only when I walked out the door of the office toward my car, blind with tears, that it occured to me that he had done to me *precisely what Augustine had done* to the consecrated virgins: *he hadn't listened*. This afflicted me with terrible rage, for now it seemed to me that Augustine was alive and well and repeating himself, many centuries later.

So I turned to a woman pastor. I went to her with my tears and rages and told her all this story. I sat there, recounting each chapter, weeping uncontrollably. She sympathized. She understood how painful and confusing Augustine's comments were. She resonated with the problems of the invocation. She said things like, "oh, how sad," and she had tears in her own eyes when I told her about my pastor's reaction. She was a living lesson in empathy.

Oddly enough, all this made me more tense and nervous. This was weird, because I'd turned to her for exactly these responses. Finally I realized how strange this was. I blurted out, "Aren't you going to shame and blame me for my responses—either to Augustine or to my pastor?" She looked surprised and sad all at once. "No, I'm not going to shame and blame you," she said.

I cried all the more, in a new and different way. Because you see—and we explored this—I really expected her role as an ordained minister to obliterate her gender and everything I knew about her. I expected her to do to me what he did and what Augustine did. Or at least for her ordained status to recombine with her gender so that she would exhort me to renewed patience with the church in its patriarchy. And she didn't do that, either.

That she did none of those explains why I am still related to Christianity in any form. For she reenacted the Gospel for me instead of reenacting Augustine. She provided the understanding and empathy that are fundamental to love and nurture (as have other ordained and lay women). Her responses changed my tears from helpless victimization to transformative grief. She was not just "right." She re-presented the Gospel to me. Not so much with her words (which were unremarkable) but with her actions in the whole context of my/our narratives.

Or perhaps it is more accurate to say that our whole dialogue re-presented the Gospel to me. If I hadn't said I expected her to shame and blame me, she could not have responded. My response constituted part of what made the Gospel occur here. After decades of *kerygma* theology, proclaiming the Word as a one-way communication, we rarely think of the Gospel as a dialogue, a relationship, in which the responses of the needy have a constituent part. But this is what always happens as we try to translate good news into terms that communicate with our own time and our own situations. In other words, this is one way to fulfill Augustine's apologetic motive.

This is one small experience with the aftermath of Augustine; I've had others (such as being shouted at for criticizing him), and so have other people. It is only a small part of what makes it so serious for us to explore the terms in which earlier ages made sense of rape.

We Need More of This History

I can hardly help wondering how many rape victims throughout the centuries had suffering heaped upon suffering by these misbegotten theological ideas. Does no one ever listen to us? At present there is no way to know whether Augustine's comments about rape influenced anyone, and especially anyone in the congregations. We do not know, for instance, whether any of those consecrated virgins read Augustine's text. We can hope that they did not.

We do know that women did not stop committing suicide. A recent social historian of Frankish society of the early middle ages tells us that suicide and rape continued to be associated:

> Those unfortunate enough to be raped blamed their assaults on demons, and it was not unusual for women who had been defiled to kill themselves. We know that some accused of adultery committed suicide rather than stand trial. (Wemple 1981, 41)

It has been suggested that suicide by rape victims was a major factor in the condemnation of suicide in 1184 at the Council of Nimes (Stengel 1964, 60). These two examples may suggest that Augustine's comments were not very influential. Of course, the later fate of rape victims was the result of more than Augustine. The Franks, Germans and the people in the British Isles had their own laws about rape and their own understandings of women (Rouche 1987). Canon law was more influenced by Roman law than by Augustine (Brundage 1982, 1987).

On the other hand, Augustine's views on sexuality did influence the penitential manuals of the medieval church. Medieval manuals divided sexual sins into natural and unnatural ones by virtue of their procreative end. The result was that rape and incest were classified among the natural sins, while masturbation and sex with a "wrong" organ or orifice or position were classified among the more severe unnatural sins (Tentler 1977, 140). This understanding, once again, is extremely difficult for those who work with rape victims.

In the end we will need to know much more than just Augustine. We will need to know about the Middle Ages and rape—about canon law and secular law, about Aquinas and Bonaventure and other medieval theologies, about sexual torture in the witch trials. We'll need to know a lot more about Christian saints who were rape victims, from Pelagia in the ancient church to Maria Goretti in our own century. We'll need to know about rape in the Renaissance and Reformation—about Luther's comments on rape, Calvin and Geneva, the Anabaptist wing of the Reformation, legal changes in Reformation cities, and the ways that Protestants brought these heritages forward. We'll need to know about changing rates of rape and the church's responses, other experiences of violence and other evaluations of sex, changing senses of defilement, the changes in healing for victims/survivors. We'll need to know a lot more about the church's understandings of power and domination. And grace. These will take awhile.

We will find many other woundings. We will need to grieve, in all the complexity we understand in grieving—combining denial, anger, bargaining, sadness. We may also find other intriguing resources that the tradition did not use to their full advantage. It is a confusing and messy legacy. It is up to us today to do something different with all this than has been done before.

Notes

1. Special thanks to those who have helped me struggle with this material over the years, especially the Reverend Diane Vezmar-Bailey, Dorothy Fisker and Nancy Biele. Susan Thistlethwaite gave me an initial chance to explore this topic (Pellauer and Thistlethwaite 1990). Anne Carr, Rosemary Ruether, Randy Nelson and Carol Adams provided helpful comments on an early draft.

2. Emphasis mine. See Schulenberg for this and other evidence from the early church before she explores self-mutilation to avoid rape into the medieval period. (She argues that the origins of the saying, "to cut off one's nose to spite one's face," were to be found here.)

3. These were of four kinds: rape in ancient war (I:5 and 6); the Rape of the Sabine Women (II:17, III:13); the unchastity of pagan divinities, that is, the rape of mortal women by male gods (though Augustine did not call it that) (III:3–5, IV:25); and a fascinating concern on Augustine's part that the example of the pagan gods raping women led men to rape women too, for which he had found evidence in Terence (II:7, 13).

4. I have primarily used Marcus Dods's translation (Augustine 1950). When I refer to the Latin, I use the Loeb classical library edition (Augustine 1964); volume 1 was translated by George E. McCracken.

5. Rhetoric was the center of ancient Roman education; on Augustine's education and his years as a teacher of rhetoric (see Brown 1967); on Augustine's specific rhetoric, and especially the Biblical influences on it (see Kennedy 1980).

6. Augustine used *raptus* only on two occasions. In I:26 he described the virgins who suicided by throwing themselves into rivers. Though Dods rendered this as "ravished" by rivers, it might better say, "violently carried away" by rivers. The second is in I:28, with the same meaning, carried off or snatched away: "Just as some people were carried off by death (*rapti sunt*) so that evils did not change their understanding, so some women's [chastity] was ripped away from them by violence (*ab istis vi raptum*) so that good fortune did not change their modesty."

7. Unless it be in "stupid" and "stupefied," which I have seen related to *stuprum* by some authors. These come from the root *stupeo*, which meant stunned, struck senseless; astounded, amazed. One expert on the Latin sexual vocabulary remarks that the largest field of metaphors for the sex act in the language were variants of beating, hitting, striking (Adams 1982, 145–70). Metaphors for the male genitals abounded in military terms (Adams 1982, 19–22). Augustine used neither of these fields of metaphors.

8. Lewis Thomas has suggested that "fuck," from northern European languages, originally meant, "evil, hostile, fated, to die, feud" or "die before your time!" (Thomas 1975, 160–61). Hughes (1991, 27) emphasizes striking/beating in the early centuries of its use. These are the elements in "fuck" which make it a synonym for "hurt, degrade, debase."

9. Therefore, feelings were described in terms of the will's relationship to them. It seems peculiar to a twentieth century reader like me that Augustine considered sadness, sorrow, fear, and joy to be acts of the will; *none* of these "motions of the soul" was "anything else but will" (XIV:6).

10. See Donaldson (1982) for a thorough but disturbing treatment of versions of Lucretia's story down through western history; disturbing because he suggests that in the Renaissance and Reformation era, Lucretia's story became a joke.

11. Lot's offering his daughters to be raped by the men of Sodom (Genesis 19); paralleled possibly by Abraham's offering Sarah to the ruler (Gen. 12:10–16; Genesis 20) as well as the rape/dismemberment of the concubine in Judges 19 (note the subsequent abduction of the daughters of Shiloh by the men of Benjamin, Judg. 21:15–25); the story of Dinah (Genesis 34); the rape of Tamar by her brother (2 Samuel 13).

Works Cited

Adams, J. N. 1982. *The Latin Sexual Vocabulary*. Baltimore: Johns Hopkins Press.

Augustine. 1950. *The City of God*. Trans. Marcus Dods. New York: Modern Library.

———. 1964. *The City of God against the Pagans*. 7 vols. Vol. I trans. George E. McCracken. Loeb Classical Library. Cambridge: Harvard University Press.

Babcock, William S., ed. 1991. *The Ethics of St. Augustine*. Atlanta: Scholars Press.

Balsdon, J. P. V. D. 1962. *Roman Women: Their History and Habits*. Westport, Conn.: Greenwood Press.

Battenhouse, Roy W., ed. 1956. *A Companion to the Study of St. Augustine*. New York: Oxford University Press.

VIOLENCE AGAINST WOMEN AND CHILDREN

Biale, Rachel. 1984. *Women and Jewish Law: An Exploration of Women's Issues in Halakhic Sources*. New York: Schocken Books.

Bradley, Keith R. 1987. "On the Roman Slave Supply and Slavebreeding." In M. I. Finley, ed., *Classical Slavery*, 42–64. London: Frank Cass.

———. 1991. *Discovering the Roman Family: Studies in Roman Social History*. New York: Oxford University Press.

Brown, Peter. 1967. *Augustine of Hippo: A Biography*. Berkeley: University of California Press.

———. 1978. *The Making of Late Antiquity*. Cambridge: Harvard University Press.

———. 1988. *The Body and Society: Men, Women and Sexual Renunciation in Early Christianity*. New York: Columbia University Press.

Brownmiller, Susan. 1975. *Against Our Will: Men, Women and Rape*. New York: Bantam Books.

Brundage, James A. 1982. "Rape and Seduction in Medieval Canon Law." In *Sexual Practices and the Medieval Church*, ed. Vern L. Bullough and James Brundage. Buffalo: Prometheus Books.

———. 1987. *Law, Sex and Christian Society in Medieval Europe*. Chicago: University of Chicago Press.

Burgess, Ann Wolbert, with Lynda Lytle Holmstrom. 1974. *Rape: Victims of Crisis*. Bowie, Md.: Robert J. Brady.

Bury, J. B. 1923. *History of the Later Roman Empire*. 2 vols. London: Macmillan and Co.

Cameron, Averil and Amelie Kuhrt, eds. 1983. *Images of Women in Antiquity*. Detroit: Wayne State University Press.

Carcopino, Jerome. 1940. *Daily Life in Ancient Rome: The People and the City at the Height of the Empire*. Trans. E.O. Lorimer. New Haven: Yale University Press.

Countryman, L. William. 1988. *Dirt, Greed and Sex: Sexual Ethics in the New Testament and Their Implications for Today*. Philadelphia: Fortress Press.

Curran, Leo. 1978. "Rape and Rape Victims in the Metamorphoses." *Arethusa* 11: 213–41.

Deane, Herbert A. 1963. *The Political and Social Ideas of St. Augustine*. New York: Columbia University Press.

Donaldson, Ian. 1982. *The Rapes of Lucretia: A Myth and Its Transformations*. Oxford: Clarendon Press.

Douglas, Mary. 1966. *Purity and Danger: An Analysis of Concepts of Pollution and Taboo*. London: Routledge and Kegan Paul.

Droge, Arthur J. and James D. Tabor. 1992. *A Noble Death: Suicide and Martyrdom among Christians and Jews in Antiquity*. San Francisco: HarperSanFrancisco.

Dupont, Florence. 1992. *Daily Life in Ancient Rome*. Trans. Christopher Woodall. Oxford: Blackwell.

Evans, John K. 1991. *War, Women and Children in Ancient Rome*. London and New York: Routledge.

Fantham, Elaine, Helene Peet Foley, Natalie Boymel Kampen, Sarah B. Pomeroy and H. Alan Shapiro. 1994. *Women in the Classical World*. New York: Oxford University Press.

Fink, Eugen. 1959. "Les Concepts Operatoires dans la phenomenologie de Husserl," in *Husserl, Cahiers de Royaumont*, Philosophie no. 3. Paris: Les Editions de Minuit, 214–30.

Finley, M. I. 1980. *Ancient Slavery and Modern Ideology*. New York: Viking Press.

———. 1987. *Classical Slavery*. Totowa, N.J.: Frank Cass & Co.

Fortune, Marie Marshall. 1983. *Sexual Violence, The Unmentionable Sin: An Ethical and Pastoral Perspective*. New York: Pilgrim Press.

Gardner, Jane F. 1991. *Women in Roman Law and Society*. Bloomington: Indiana University Press.

Groth, A. Nicholas, with H. Jean Birnbaum. 1979. *Men Who Rape: The Psychology of the Offender*. New York: Plenum Press.

Hallett, Judith P. 1989. "Women as Same and Other in Classical Roman Elite." *Helios* 16/1, 59–78.

Higgins, Lynn A. and Brenda R. Silver, eds. 1991. *Rape and Representation*. New York: Columbia University Press.

Hughes, Geoffrey. 1991. *Swearing: A Social History of Foul Language, Oaths and Profanity in English*. Cambridge, Mass.: Blackwells.

Kennedy, George. 1972. *The Art of Rhetoric in the Roman World, 300 B.C.–A.D. 300*. Princeton: Princeton University Press.

———. 1980. *Classical Rhetoric and Its Christian and Secular Tradition from Ancient to Modern Times*. Chapel Hill: University of North Carolina Press.

Lefkowitz, M. R. and M. B. Fant, eds. 1982. *Women's Life in Greece and Rome*. London/Baltimore: Johns Hopkins University Press.

Malherbe, Abraham J. 1986. *Moral Exhortation: A Greco-Roman Source Book*. Philadelphia: Westminster.

Markus, R. A., ed. 1972. *Augustine: A Collection of Critical Essays*. Garden City: Doubleday.

McLeod, Glenda. 1991. *Virtue and Venom: Catalogs of Women from Antiquity to the Renaissance*. Ann Arbor: University of Michigan Press.

Meeks, Wayne A. 1986 *The Moral World of the First Christians*. Philadelphia: Westminster.

Miles, Margaret. 1992. *Desire and Delight: A New Reading of Augustine's Confessions*. New York: Crossroad.

———. 1979. *Augustine on the Body*. Missoula, Mont.: Scholars Press.

Neuhaus, Richard John, ed. 1993. *Augustine Today*. Grand Rapids, Mich.: Eerdmans.

O'Daly, Gerard. 1987. *Augustine's Philosophy of Mind*. Berkeley: University of California Press.

Pellauer, Mary. 1987. "A Theological Perspective on Sexual Assault." In *Sexual Assault and Abuse: A Handbook for Clergy and Religious Professionals*, ed. Mary D. Pellauer, Barbara Chester and Jane Boyajian. San Francisco: HarperCollins.

Pellauer, Mary with Susan Thistlethwaite. 1990. "A Conversation on Healing and Grace." In *Lift Every Voice: Reconstructing Christian Theology from the Underside*, ed. Mary Potter-Engel and Susan Thistlethwaite. San Francisco: HarperCollins.

Phipps, William E. 1985. "Christian Perspectives on Suicide." *The Christian Century* (October 30, 1985): 970–73.

Pomeroy, Sarah B. 1975. *Goddesses, Whores, Wives and Slaves: Women in Classical Antiquity*. New York: Schocken Books.

———. 1991. *Women's History and Ancient History*. Chapel Hill: University of North Carolina Press.

Porter, Roy. 1986. "Rape—Does It Have a Historical Meaning?" In *Rape: An Historical and Social Enquiry*, ed. Tomaselli and Porter. 216–36.

Rawson, Beryl, ed. 1986. *The Family in Ancient Rome: New Perspectives*. Ithaca: Cornell University Press.

Ricoeur, Paul. 1967. *The Symbolism of Evil*. New York: Harper & Row.

Rouche, Michel. 1987. "The Early Middle Ages in the West," In *A History of Private Life*, vol. I. *From Pagan Rome to Byzantium*, ed. Paul Veyne. Trans. Arthur Goldhammer, 411–550. Cambridge, Mass.: Harvard University Press.

Rousselle, Aline. 1989. "Personal Status and Sexual Practice in the Roman Empire." In *Fragments for a History of the Human Body*, ed. Michel Feher, with Romona Haddaff and Nadia Tazi. Vol. 3. New York: Zone Books. 300–333.

Ruether, Rosemary Radford. 1974. "Misogyny and Virginal Feminism in the Fathers of the Church," in *Religion and Sexism: Images of Women in the Jewish and Christian Traditions*, ed. Rosemary Ruether New York: Simon and Schuster. 150-83.

Ruggiero, Guido. 1975. "Sexual Criminality in the Early Renaissance: Venice, 1338–1358." *The Journal of Social History* 8 (Summer 1975), 18–37.

———. 1980. *Violence in Early Renaissance Venice*. New Brunswick: Rutgers University Press.

Russell, Diana E. H. 1984. *Sexual Exploitation: Rape, Child Sexual Abuse and Workplace Harassment*. Beverly Hills, Calif.: Sage Press.

Sanday, Peggy Reeves. 1981. *Female Power and Male Dominance: On the Origins of Sexual Inequality*. New York: Cambridge University Press.

Scheid, John. 1992. "The Religious Roles of Roman Women." In *A History of Women: Vol. I. From Ancient Goddesses to Christian Saints*, ed. Georges Duby and Michelle Perrot. Cambridge: Harvard University Press. 337–408.

Schulenberg, Jane Tibbetts. 1986. "The Heroics of Virginity: Brides of Christ and Sacrificial Mutilation." In *Women in the Middle Ages and Renaissance: Literary and Historical Explorations*, ed. Mary Beth Rose. Syracuse: Syracuse University Press.

Sissa, Giula. 1990. *Greek Virginity*. Trans. Arthur Goldhammer. Cambridge: Harvard University Press.

Stehle, Eva and Adele Scafuro, eds. 1989. "Studies on Roman Women," special issues of *Helios: A Journal Devoted to Critical and Methodological Studies of Classical Culture, Literature and Society*, Part I, Spring (16: 1); Part 2, Autumn (16: 2).

Stengel, Erwin. 1964. *Suicide and Attempted Suicide*. London: Harmondworth.

Tellegen-Couperus, Olga. 1993. *A Short History of Roman Law*. London: Routledge.

Tentler, Thomas N. 1977. *Sin and Confession on the Eve of the Reformation*. Princeton: Princeton University Press.

Thomas, Lewis. 1975. *Lives of a Cell: Notes of a Biology Watcher*. New York: Bantam Books.

Tomaselli, Sylvia, and Roy Porter, eds. 1986. *Rape: An Historical and Social Enquiry*. Oxford: Basil Blackwell.

Treggiari, Susan. 1991. *Roman Marriage: Iusti Coniunges from the Time of Cicero to the Time of Ulpian*. Oxford: Clarendon Press.

Trible, Phyllis. 1984. *Texts of Terror: Literary-Feminist Readings of Biblical Narratives*. Philadelphia: Fortress Press.

Veyne, Paul. 1988. *Roman Erotic Elegy: Love, Poetry and the West*. Trans. by David Pellauer. Chicago: University of Chicago Press.

Villari, Pasquale. 1902. *The Barbarian Invasions of Italy*. Trans. Linda Villari. London: T. Fisher Unwin.

Warshaw, Robin. 1988. *I Never Called It Rape*. New York: Harper & Row.

Wemple, Suzanne Fonay. 1981. *Women in Frankish Society: Marriage and the Cloister, 500–900*. Philadelphia: University of Pennsylvania Press.

Wolff, Hans Julius. 1951. *Roman Law: An Historical Introduction*. Norman: University of Oklahoma Press.

Historical Theology and Violence against Women: Unearthing a Popular Tradition of Just Battery

MARY POTTER ENGEL

Authentic liberation of women from the oppressive attitudes, structures, and practices of a patriarchal society entails the transformation of women from the "appropriate victims" of sexual terrorism to free and responsible persons who cooperate with equals to build a just and caring society for all.[1] Historical theologians can contribute to this radical transformation by exposing and analyzing the ways in which women have been oppressed in the past; recovering the challenges and alternatives to women's oppression buried in the past; and using both of these to reconstruct the view of history that informs our lives today.

Historical theologians are beginning to respond to this feminist challenge. In-depth examinations of the theory and practice of the subordination of women and recoveries of long-buried spiritual traditions of women are appearing more frequently. None of this work, however, has been incorporated in general church history or history of theology textbooks. Jaroslav Pelikan's five-volume history of doctrine, *The Christian Tradition*, though critical of histories of theology that ignore the ecclesial context of doctrinal development, does not include women as part of the church.[2] Williston Walker et al.'s *A History of the Christian Church*, one of the classic church histories still widely used today, contains only a few mentions of women.[3] At least three factors contribute to this silence. The first and most obvious is the androcentrism of those who recorded the histories and those who interpret them today. The world of the conquered is not known or recorded by the conquerors and therefore is not heard by later interpreters. The second factor is the focus in history of theology on intellectual history. If one considers only the development of ideas important, the reality of most women's lives will not come to light. The third factor is the focus in church history on the organization and development of the church as institution. If one considers only the public life of the community significant and not the private lives of ordinary Christians, the reality of most women's lives will not come to light; for they were often restricted to the domestic realm.

In the last few decades social historians have criticized histories of theology and church histories as histories of the elite who influenced public life. These social historians have argued that for a more representative or comprehensive history, sources other than published treatises or official church documents must be consulted. In order to gain access to the lives of ordinary men and women, they have turned to court, convent, and consistory records, household inventories, private letters, pamphlets, woodcuts, and other visual art.

The turn to social history is necessary but not sufficient for exposing violence against women, as the few histories that adopt a more social-historical approach and take gender distinction seriously show. Justo L. González's excellent two-volume work, *The Story of Christianity*, which begins to move beyond "the history of the conquerors" model in so many ways, ignores violence against women.[4] Barbara J. MacHaffie's *Her Story: Women in Christian Tradition*, though it focuses on women's lives as they intersect and parallel official church history, is also silent on this issue.[5] And Margaret R. Miles's *Image as Insight* and *Practicing Christianity*, both attempts to tell the history of Christianity from a feminist social-historical point of view, do not contain any references to violence against women.[6]

This silence about violence against women is notable not only in general histories of Christianity but in studies of marriage in Christianity and histories of the family as well. Martin Ingram's *Church Courts, Sex and Marriage in England, 1570–1640*, while concerned with divorce practices, does not mention violence.[7] James Casey's *The History of the Family*—which analyzes the politics of the family, considers marriage contracts, and situates the family in society—does not mention domestic violence.[8] Clearly the turns to a feminist perspective and social history are not enough to bring to light the violence women have suffered.

We are left with the conclusion that violence against women, a key factor in society's oppression of women, has received "selective inattention" in historical theology.[9] At best this neglect suggests to students of historical theology that the violent reality of women's lives is of no significance for our understanding of the history of theology and spirituality. At worst it is a sign of the tradition's continuing complicity in the practice of violence against women.

Breaking the Silence

This silence about Christianity's role in the cultural practice of violence against women is beginning to be broken. More often than not, however, those breaking it come out of the broader feminist movement or the movement to end violence against women. Two early historical overviews of sexism have been instrumental in focusing attention on the link between the Christian tradition and the violence of wifebeating. *Not in God's Image*, a collection of legal, philosophical, theological, and popular sayings against women from antiquity to the present in European culture, contains a wide variety of statements of the inequality of women and several quotations that explicitly recommended wifebeating.[10] Elizabeth Gould Davis's *The First Sex* also contains references to physical cruelty against wives.[11] Both these works are frequently quoted and cited by researchers in domestic violence who want to set a historical context for this issue. For example, many of the primary source quotations in Del Martin's *Battered Wives*,[12] Dobash and Dobash's *Violence against Wives*, and Nancy Hutchings's *The Violent Family* come from these two sources.[13] *Not in God's Image* and *The First Sex* have played an important role in uncovering the history of violence against women by breaking open the question of the relation of Christianity to this violence. They will not prove of much help in the future, however, for they (1) do not provide an analysis of the individual quotations in the contexts; (2) suggest rather than demonstrate that a connection between an ideology of inequality and recommendations to batter exists; and (3) do not focus on wifebeating.

Two pieces by Terry Davidson, the essay "Wifebeating: A Recurring Phenomenon throughout History" and the historical chapter of her book *Conjugal Crime*, do focus on wifebeating and the Christian tradition.[14] Pulling together legal, religious, and historical data drawn from *Not in God's Image*, Davidson sketches in large and bold strokes the complicity of Christianity—from its earliest days to the present—in the crime of wifebeating. Both pieces are notable because they are the first to focus on the relation between Christianity and wifebeating and the first to acknowledge a connection between the church's teachings on inequality and its practice of contempt for women, its legitimation of women as objects of antagonism and its explicit violence against women.

Although Davidson's works have played a critical role in furthering the discussion, they will not be of much help in future investigations because they: (1) assume rather than explore or argue for the connection between inequality and violence; (2) do not use primary sources; and (3) do not provide an analysis of the quotations used. They end up telescoping a wide variety of materials culled from the works of others into an overly generalized condemnation of the church that allows little room for distinctions in the kind or degree of sexism from person to person, culture to culture, or period to period. "The Christian church," Davidson concludes, "from Constantine on, has had a record of practicing and recommending physical abuse to women."[15]

Two other works connecting Christianity and wifebeating, Rosemary Radford Ruether's "The Western Religious Tradition and Violence against Women in the Home" and Joy Bussert's brief historical discussion in her book *Battered Women*, are welcome continuations of Davidson's research. Both are built on the recognition that wifebeating is rooted in the "basic patriarchal assumptions about women's subordinate status."[16] Both claim that there is a connection between the inferiority of women in a dualistic system and the justification of violence against them. Both call for radical reform. But these works, too, are of limited value. Neither analyzes the connection between the ideology of gender inequality and the practice of violence against women. Both single out dramatic quotations for effect, raising the question of whether such statements are exceptional or normative. And both run far too quickly over twenty centuries.

The fact that Davidson, Ruether, and Bussert have kept this issue before us and the directness and clarity of their claims are to be commended. But if the investigation of Christianity's roles in tightening the knot of gender inequality and the practice of violence against women is to proceed, their work must be complemented by more circumspect (though not necessarily less radical) conclusions supported by detailed historical analyses of primary sources. As scholars begin to research specific aspects of this issue, they will pay attention to distinctions between periods, geographical areas, cultures, and personalities. They will base their generalized conclusions on analyses of sources that utilize the categories of gender, the intersection of gender, class, and race, and the intersection of gender and local culture. For example, it has been argued that sexism increased in the late Middle Ages and Reformation periods with the arrival of a preindustrial capitalist economy.[17] It has also been argued that local contexts need to be considered more carefully when one generalizes, because life in medieval Paris was not equivalent to life in Basel, Heidelberg, or Canterbury.[18] These survey essays, then, serve best as invitations to further studies that will supplement and critique them.

Detailed analyses of primary sources mentioning violence against wives have begun to appear. Much has been done by social historians, for example, to further our understanding of wifebeating in France and England from the fifteenth to the nineteenth centuries.[19] Much of this work, however, has not paid attention to the way in which the Christian tradition has informed or contributed to this practice. Two books do contribute detailed historical research into the issue of violence against women specifically within the context of Christianity—Edward J. Bayer's *Rape within Marriage* and Steven Ozment's *When Fathers Ruled*.[20] Bayer's study is an exercise in constructive church history, concentrating on canon law discussions of marital rape from 1600 to 1749 and their implications for current Roman Catholic ecclesiastical decisions. Ozment's book is an exercise in the social history of the Protestant ideas of marriage and the family. Drawing on an impressively wide variety of popular materials, including "housefather" books, woodcuts, and vernacular pamphlets, Ozment focuses on Swiss and German family life during the Reformation. Both authors make significant contributions to the study of Christianity's role in the history of violence against women. Neither, however, focuses on wifebeating. And neither stresses the connection between gender inequality and the practice of violence against women. In fact, Ozment's argument seems to obscure this relation. His choice to highlight exceptions to the rule of male dominance rather than the rule itself, his stress on occasional references to restraint of wifebeating, and his recurrent qualifications of the patriarchal structure of the Reformation family appear to be evidence of his reluctance to consider violence against women as an established pattern in the Christian tradition.[21]

Recently, occasional references to wifebeating have appeared in social-historical articles on marriage and divorce in the Reformation. For example, William Monter's study of Geneva based on the consistory records of 1559–64 notes that several men were excommunicated for beating their wives.[22] While it is encouraging to see scholars paying attention to these kinds of details, there is still insufficient information available to draw significant conclusions from such data. Thomas Safley's caution about the difficulty of drawing conclusions from studies of litigation that are hampered by narrow chronological limits is pertinent here.[23]

Furthermore, even when we do have sufficient data, we will still need to analyze the meaning of these statistics in their social and historical contexts. Safley's work on the actions of the Basel marital court between 1529 and 1554 points to the need for this. He reports that out of 148 divorces granted in Basel in this period, nineteen were granted on grounds of "deadly abuse."[24] Three things are important to note here as we consider how to interpret such information. First, although deadly abuse is the third leading cause for divorces granted, it is not a well-recognized cause. Second, these statistics do not by themselves enable us to conclude how common wifebeating was, for as Safley himself notes, often divorces were granted on other grounds, such as adultery or impoverishment, even when abuse was part of the claim. Third, the court was reluctant to grant divorces on the grounds of abuse alone, except in cases of the most extreme abuse. In other words, it was not physical abuse but "deadly abuse"—that which caused premature births, insanity of the wife, or the maiming or death of the wife—that could be claimed as a grounds for divorce in the Basel court.[25] Such a qualification is critical for understanding the excommunications and other disciplinary actions recorded in legal and ecclesiastical records. Rather than assuming that the excommunication of several men for beating their wives indicated the Basel court's rejection of all battery as anti-Christian, we need to ask if it is not rather the case that it indicated the acceptance of wifebeating, as long as it took place within prescribed limits of moderation. In other words, these men may have been punished not for beating their wives, but for beating them without just cause or immoderately.[26]

Grethe Jacobsen's article "Women, Marriage, and Magisterial Reformation" raises similar cautions about interpreting court statistics. Jacobsen notes that the marital court records of Malmø, Denmark, contain explicit directives to the wife to be "humble and obedient" and to the husband to discipline her physically, "within reason," if she is not.[27] Thus, while women were able to make use of the courts, and the courts *sometimes* ruled in their favor on the grounds of deadly abuse, one cannot conclude that the courts were in women's favor, supported egalitarian marriages, or condemned all physical abuse.

What can he learned from these recent social-historical studies that include some mention of wifebeating is that we need to move beyond extrapolations from limited data to more detailed analyses of gender relations if we are to understand the complex ideology controlling the oppression of women in any given period or local culture. While it is encouraging to see wifebeating recognized, the conclusions of many of these studies remind us of the importance of a feminist perspective for interpreting the findings. In particular, if one does not see a connection between ideologies of inequality and the practice of violence, one may too quickly interpret a move toward companionate marriage as a critique of wifebeating. And if one does not allow for the possibility that the rule may be one of justified violence against wives, one may too quickly interpret the existence of calls for moderation or greater restraint of wifebeating as indications of a shift to greater justice for women.

These studies also point to the fact that sources have been and will continue to be a problem for historical theologians investigating violence against women. Today we know that a very small percentage of marital violence is reported and the official records of intimate relationships are not always easy to interpret. These problems are compounded for the historical theologian. What we can do is continue to investigate records of divorce proceedings and other legal documents to determine the incidence and meaning of wifebeating. And we can turn our attention to more popular sources—such as accounts of public shamings, sermons, and so on—that will help us uncover community attitudes toward and practices of violence against women.

Finally, these studies raise the question of the periodization of history. Once we include gender relations and violence against women in the mix of factors that determine how we identify significant shifts in history and divide it into periods, we may end up with a different picture of the past. Ozment's argument for an advance for women in the Reformation over the Middle Ages, for example, is based on the assumption that the medieval church's exaltation of celibacy and virginity led to a gross denigration of marriage and women, which the Protestant Reformation successfully countered with its notion of companionate marriage. Thus, for Ozment, the Protestant Reformation represents a significant advance for women and retains its status as a major period.[28] But if, as I will soon argue, the Reformation did not challenge the ideology of inequality and continued to accept wifebeating, within limits, as the rule, it can by no means be said to represent an unqualified advance for women. If we count Christianity's teaching and practice of violence against women in our assessment, we cannot say a reformation has occurred for women.

In order to complete a comprehensive history of Christianity's relation to women that includes attention to violence against women and in order to reconstruct a genuinely common and liberating history of Christianity that includes both women's and men's experiences, we need more studies in historical theology that:

1. recognize that violence against women has occurred and does occur and that it is an urgent problem;
2. focus on different kinds of violence against women, including rape and wifebeating, instead of lumping these with other instances of sexism;
3. operate from a feminist perspective—that is, analyze rather than ignore, simply acknowledge, or explain away the connection between ideologies of inequality and the practice of violence;
4. are interdisciplinary, paying attention to a wide variety of texts and especially to the interplay of the Christian religion with other dimensions of culture;
5. take a social-historical approach, paying attention to (a) the private lives of ordinary women as they are recorded in private letters and in court, consistory, convent, and church records; and (b) the cultural

attitudes toward violence against women that are suggested in visual images, pamphlets, sermons, and so on;

6. engage in detailed analyses of limited time periods and locales rather than remain at the survey level;

7. move beyond argument by means of exceptional statements (either positive ones as in Ozment's argument or negative ones as in Ruether's and Bussert's arguments) and probe for complex patterns that normalize violence against women and that can be used to interpret individual statements of or decisions about violence against women;

8. recognize that new discoveries will have implications for our understanding of the "development" and periodization of the Christian tradition.

Wifebeating in Popular French Literature from 1150 to 1565

As a way of pointing in this direction of future research in historical theology and violence against women, I will summarize here my recent study of wifebeating in popular French tales and sermons from 1150 to 1565. The *fabliaux*—ribald, rhymed tales of the follies of family life recounted for public entertainment—were widespread from the early thirteenth through fourteenth centuries. A variation on the ancient genre of fables, they use men and women rather than animals to teach moral lessons. These tales, recited in public by traveling storytellers (*jongleurs*), passed into written culture when anonymous editors collected them for publication. They finally gave way to prose versions treating the same subject matter with an equally irreverent and bawdy approach. The *nouvelles* or *contes* were extremely popular until the sixteenth century.

Collections of *exempla*, brief concrete illustrations of vice and virtue used by uneducated priests to teach their illiterate congregations religious or moral doctrines, began to appear in the eleventh and twelfth centuries. Maurice de Sully (d. 1196), Alain de Lille (d. 1202), and Jacques de Vitry (d. 1240) were early apologists for the use of *exempla* in preaching, arguing that sermons should not only edify but entertain, the better to hold the interest of mass audiences. Their use of *exempla* in their folk sermons in the vernacular and their compilation of sets of popular *exempla* as sermon starters for local priests to use reflect the renaissance in preaching that occurred during this period. Early collections, such as Eudes de Cheriton's *Parables*, contained mainly ancient fables, illustrations from nature, or lives of saints. Later collections expanded to include descriptions of actual situations, and eventually *fabliaux* and *nouvelles*, and gained great popularity in the fourteenth and fifteenth centuries. This practical, eclectic style of preaching that drew on secular as well as religious stories became so abused that the use of stories or fables was prohibited at the Council of Milan in 1565.

I chose these genres for several reasons. First, each was a well-used form of mass oral communication that depended on the common human desire to be entertained rather than on the education of speaker or audience. Second, each was an effective medium for training the majority for social life. In illustrating the working vices, the *fabliaux* and *nouvelles* handed down social expectations to and circumscribed the behavior of the non-nobility—peasants, farmers, and the growing bourgeoisie. Likewise, sermons in the vernacular taught lay people the Rule of the Order of Marriage. Third, in keeping with their pedagogical intent, each of these genres was constructed with actors who were stereotypes rather than characters. Fourth, each focused on the everyday lives of men and women, highlighting sex, sexuality, and gender.

Fifth, although two genres (the *fabliaux* and the *nouvelles*) are secular and the other (the *exempla*) is religious, each form of popular communication conveys a remarkably similar message concerning wifebeating. In fact, each genre influenced the other. The *fabliaux* writers were well-acquainted with the *exempla* of the church. In turn, the secular stories influenced by the early sermon manuals found their way into later preaching manuals. The dynamic interplay of the secular and religious worlds evident in these literary forms suggests that mono-dimensional or mono-causal theories of women's oppression are inadequate.

Finally, together the collections of *fabliaux* and *nouvelles* and the sermon manuals provide a rich resource for understanding gender relations in this period that can supplement the information provided by canon law, secular law, and statistics. As Michel Foucault states, "Methods that are employed at all levels and go beyond the state and its apparatus" contribute a great deal to ensuring certain power relations.[29] The normalization and control of gender relations one finds in this popular literature make these genres perhaps more potent supports for and indicators of the complex relationship between the ideology of subordination and the practice of violence than ecclesiastical and secular laws. At the very least, they provide us with new ways to interpret marital statistics.

I approached these sources with the feminist conviction that ideologies of inequality and the practice of violence are inextricably linked. I also approached them with the suspicion that those studies pointing to the abatement of wifebeating in the Protestant Reformation had highlighted evidence of limitations to wifebeating and minimized the larger social patterns that insured women's subordination and accepted violence against them. These assumptions did not prepare me for the shock of discovering in this literature a popular tradition of justifying violence against wives. As I read the sermons and tales, I slowly began to see the outlines of a pattern of gender relations in which the practice of violence against wives was justified by means of an ideology of gender inequality and served to maintain such an ideology. I describe the pattern I found as follows: All women are created to be subordinate to men. All wives, therefore, are subordinate to their husbands. Because the health of society depends on this ordered relationship, if a wife is insubordinate in any way, not only domestic peace but the entire social fabric is threatened. The husband, then, has not only a right but a duty to discipline her. This social responsibility may be called the "office of chastisement."[30]

The right to exercise this legitimate office of chastisement is not absolute. As with all divinely ordained offices, the duties of the office of chastisement must be executed within limits set by society. I discovered the limits to this office specified in six conditions. First, the wife must be the aggressor, that is, initiate the conflict by stepping outside the boundaries of behavior set for Good Wives. This is the *condition of just cause*, based on the assumption of female subordination. Second and third, the discipline must be administered after other corrections have failed and in moderation, that is, so as to correct effectively (i.e., not maim or kill). These are the *conditions of last resort and just means*. Fourth and fifth, the wife must be disciplined not out of rage or revenge but out of love, with an aim to preserve the peace of the household and the right order of society. These are the *conditions of right intention and just end*, which are based on the distinction between punishment and correction. Sixth, it must be the husband as head of the family who administers the blows. This is the *condition of right authority*, based on the assumption of male dominance. Violence against wives is acceptable moral and social behavior when some or all of these conditions are met.

Given that these conditions had not been uncovered before, my first task was to name them, as the above paragraph shows. To the entire interlocking set of conditions for justifying violence against wives, I gave the name "just battery of wives."

All six conditions for justifying wifebeating are implicit in the tales and sermons. The condition of just cause is associated with the use of female stereotypes. Five stereotypes, Gateway to Ruin, Temptress, Adulteress, Deceiver, and Shrew, together form the antitype to the Good Wife (*preude fame et sage*), who is wise in conserving and administering her husband's goods, solicitous of his welfare, understanding of his failings, submissive to his sexual desires alone, honest, and willingly deferential and obedient at all times. The type of the Good Wife and the antitype of the Bad Wife contribute to a theory of just battery by providing specific material for the just cause rule. If a wife does not adequately fill the role expected of her, to be a good wife wisely administering the household and her body (the two commodities entrusted to her care though owned by her husband), she *deserves* to be disciplined.

The *fabliaux* and *exempla* clearly connect the use of these stereotypes with the condition of just cause. They often portray wives being beaten because they have caused economic ruin by squandering money to satisfy their covetousness, wasted their husband's reputation by satisfying their lust in adultery, or broken the peace of the household by giving in to their proud and defiant natures in acts of subordination. Thus, the use of stereotypes undergirds the condition of just cause by specifying just causes for violence against women in particular circumstances. The use of these stereotypes also undergirds the condition of just cause in another, equally powerful and more insidious way: by implying that all women eventually behave in these ways. Therefore, even when one's wife is not acting wrongly, she is perceived as being on the verge of revealing her true nature as Gateway to Ruin,

Temptress, Adulteress, Deceiver, or Shrew. In other words, the use of these stereotypes implies that all women inevitably act out their evil nature and therefore are always deserving of whatever chastisement they receive. The *fabliaux* contain several examples of husbands beating their wives because they *feared* their wives would commit adultery or squander their resources in other ways. Although some of the tales warn against acting on suspicion alone, the pervasive use of these stereotypes engenders a fear and hatred not easily controlled by instructions to beat wives only when they have *actually* committed a fault or exhortations to treat wives with mercy and understanding.

The conditions of last resort and just means are evident in one of the most arresting *fabliaux*, "Sir Hate and Lady Hateful." The tale begins with the claim to have

> Proved by logic
> That whoever has a cantankerous wife
> Is furnished with a wicked beast.[31]

The story opens with examples of Lady Hateful's constant quarrelsomeness and creative unwillingness to "serve him the way he wanted." Sir Hate tries to coddle and soothe her, but to no avail. When she throws the fish he has brought for dinner in the dirt, and he is shamed before his neighbors by her lack of respect for him, he finally becomes angry and challenges her to a contest for the right to rule the household. She agrees, and he takes off his pants and puts them in the yard, telling her that whoever can get to them first wins. Before witnesses they battle it out, each one promising to inflict the worst possible. Before they begin a character named Simon warns Sir Hate to use restraint and

> Be careful not to strike
> With anything which will do
> Harm to your wife, except your hands.

Sir Hate gives her a "Persian blue" eye. She almost knocks him over. He knocks her in the teeth, causing her blood to flow freely and him to exclaim triumphantly, "I've painted you two colors!" She recovers enough to hit him on the ear, and he responds by threatening to kill her. When he almost breaks one of her ribs, she draws back and calls for peace from the witnesses. Simon's wife, Peacewell, comes to her aid, but Simon threatens to beat her if she interferes again, and she "keeps quiet because she feared him." The fight continues.

When Lady Hateful is upended in a basket and Sir Hate, having put on the pants, returns to finish by giving her "penance," Simon intervenes. He sends Sir Hate away with the warning, "Don't do any killing!" and asks Lady Hateful if her pride has finally been beaten down. She equivocates and Simon refuses to help her until he extracts this promise from her:

> That you will be under the control
> Of Sir Hate forevermore,
> And that you will never do

Anything that he forbids. . . .
For you will serve your lord
Just as a decent wife ought to do.[32]

Freed from her prison, she proves very willing to serve her husband, "since she feared his blows," and Sir Hate lived happily thereafter.

The moral of this story is clear: wives are to be subordinate to their husbands; insubordination *should* be corrected by the husband; this correction is to be peaceful and verbal first; if and when this does not work, threats of violence may be used (as when Simon corrects Peacewell); when this, too, does not work, correction may take the form of blows; and these blows, given with the hand, should harm the wife enough to correct her but not maim or kill her. It is clear here that insubordination provides just cause for battery, and that battery should be done in moderation. It is not as clear that battery is always the last resort, as the *fabliau*'s concluding moral shows:

If your wives lord it proudly
Over you at any time in any evil way,
You should not be so lazy
As to endure it long,
But do exactly as
Hate did with his wife,
Who would not respect him before,
Except in the smallest way she could,
Until the time that he
Had beaten her on her bones and back.[33]

A particularly violent *conte*, "The Woman Whose Balls Were Cut Off," ends with a similar message: "Blessed be those who chastise their bad wives and shamed be those who submit to their wives; a curse on wives who defy their husbands."[34]

There are similar tales in the *exempla*. One man, for instance, tricks his disobedient wife into violently piercing her finger with a nail, whereupon she learns to obey him.[35] Alan of Lille, in his instructions on how to preach to the estate of married persons, refers to the knot of inequality, insubordination, and the office of chastisement by noting that "the flesh, like a woman, may obey the spirit, and the spirit, like a man, may rule his flesh as if it were a woman."[36] The implication is clear: if the woman offends you, it is your Christian duty to subdue her.

The *exempla* do not teach as clearly the conditions of last resort and just means. They do not warn against "deadly abuse" as many fabliaux do, and, in fact, suggest that it may be acceptable. Jacques de Vitry tells of a man whose wife was so contrary that he tricked her into drowning herself and then turned it into a community joke.[37] He also includes a tale of a contrary woman who continued in her defiance even after her husband had cut out her tongue.[38] Further, the *exempla* go beyond promoting the husband's office of chastisement and add to it the wife's office of suffering. Etienne de Bourbon has an entire section entitled "The Gift of Force," and Bozon expounds at great length on Prov. 27:6: "To be hit by one's friend is better than to be kissed by one's enemy."[39] This justification is not as apparent in the secular tales, though one can find occasional references there to women's "crown of thorns."

The conditions of right intention and just end are not as clearly present as the other four conditions in any of the genres, but there is enough evidence to suggest that they do operate as part of a pattern of gender relations for justifying violence against wives. Some of the tales and sermons move toward a distinction between punishment (harm done out of anger or meanness) and correction (harm done with the loving intention of persuading the woman to assume her rightful place in the household). Almost all assume the condition of just end—that is, that the harm is to be administered toward the end of reestablishing peace in the household and right order in society. The right order, as the following shows, is a patriarchal one.

Finally, the condition of right authority—that is, the assumption that the husband is the rightful "master" of the house whose duty is to maintain order by controlling those "under" him—pervades the tales. It lies behind the construction of the stereotypes. It serves as the foundation for the condition of just cause, as is especially evident in the tales concerning the specific just cause of insubordination. It provides the basis for the conditions of right intention and moderation with its use of hierarchical monism to set the spirit/male as director over the flesh/female. The development of the notion of the office of chastisement exercised under the other conditions makes it clear that it is the husband's duty to beat his wife when necessary and his shame when he fails to do this. In addition to promoting these themes, many of the tales depend for their humor on the technique of reversal of expectations. Scenes of wives beating their husbands are funny precisely because it is assumed that right authority for this behavior can belong only to the male.[40] A condition of right authority, therefore, is also embedded in the tales.

Exceptions and the Rule

This set of conditions for justifying wifebeating found throughout the *fabliaux*, *nouvelles*, and *exempla* suggest that a continuing, popular tradition of just battery existed during this time in French history. On the basis of my research I was not able to conclude that this tradition took exactly the same form in each of the five centuries and in each of the three genres. I was able to conclude, on the basis of the remarkable similarity among conditions or rules for husbands' treatment of wives in these different genres across these centuries, that it is likely than an ongoing popular tradition justifying wifebeating existed.

This provisional conclusion calls into question those social-historical interpretations of the Reformation that stress the improvement of domestic conditions for women in comparison to conditions in the Middle Ages. Specifically, it challenges those studies that support this interpretation by arguing that (1) the instances of violence against wives in the popular literature of this period are exceptions to a new rule of restraint of wifebeating, and (2) the instances of exhortation to moderation in this literature constitute a prohibition against all battery. In light of the existence of an ongoing popular tradition of just battery, these interpretations appear to be overly optimistic assessments of gender relations; for they obscure the rule of the subordination of women, justified violence against them, and the connection between these two.

One can find instances of both extreme violence against wives and explicit rejections of wifebeating during the medieval, Renaissance, and Reformation periods. The question is: How does one interpret this contradictory evidence? What is the rule, the normative pattern for gender relations, against which other evidence is to be interpreted as "exceptions"? Is the rule that of increasing justice toward wives, and the exceptions those instances of physical cruelty that remain? Or is the rule that of an ongoing tradition of just battery, and the exceptions those instances in which wifebeating is rejected? My investigation of popular sources leads me to adopt provisionally the latter as a more accurate interpretation of these centuries.

The stories I highlighted are not exceptions to a rule of equality, mutuality, and conciliation, but rather extraordinary cases that illuminate ordinary circumstances. There are *fabliaux* and at least one *exemplum* that warn husbands of the dangers of irrational jealousy, false accusations of adultery, unreasonable expectations for the completion of wifely chores, and immoderate hitting. The point of these stories, however, is that *unjust* punishment leads to no good and is therefore unacceptable, not that any or all correction or chastisement is unacceptable. None of the stories I read challenges the just battery theory I have described: that correction of wives by violent means is justifiable on the conditions of just cause, last resort, moderation, right intention, just end, and right authority.

Take, for example, two tales that appear to condemn wifebeating. "The Doctor in Spite of Himself" is the story of the cure of an alternately rageful and repentant husband. Three of the king's men hear the wife's graphic tale of unmerciful beatings *for nothing* and decide to bring the husband to the court as a doctor. When he is unable to cure the king's daughter, he is beaten. So he learns the injustice of his behavior toward his wife and returns home never to beat her again but to love and cherish her.[41] In the *fabliau*, "The Braids," a man who is outrageously jealous of his wife violently beats her on account of his suspicions. Finally she can stand it no longer and commits adultery. The *jongleur* concludes:

> He does not do well
> Who harms his wife *too much*;
> If she commits folly with her body
> When away from home,
> She has good reason
> To bring shame upon her husband.[42]

Both tales criticize wifebeating only because it is done *for no reason*. Because both assume that there can be just cause for wifebeating, they do not call into question the theory of just battery but confirm it.

Likewise, stories that teach moderation, such as "Sir Hate and Lady Hateful," do not reject but confirm the theory of just battery. One of the woodcuts Ozment uses to support his theory of greater justice for wives in the Reformation, *The Nine Lives of a Bad Wife*, has an accompanying text that ends thus:

> So punish your wife modestly,
> And if there is any honor in her,
> She will become an obedient wife. . . .
> But if she remains self-willed,
> And refuses what is fair and reasonable,
> And opposes you in all you request,
> Ever disobedient and rebellious,
> On those occasions when she spurns your cooperation,
> You may punish her with blows—
> Yet do still with reason and modestly,
> So that no harm is done to either of you.
> Use both a carrot and a stick
> To bring about companionship.[43]

The call for moderation one reads in this moral is not indicative of a self-critical moment within a society moving toward greater justice for women in the domestic sphere, but confirmation of the existence of an ongoing tradition of just battery.

The Ideology of Gender Inequality and Just Battery

In addition to questioning the exception/rule argument as support for interpreting the Renaissance/Reformation period as one of greater justice toward women, this argument for the existence of an ongoing popular tradition of just battery of wives raises the question of how to assess the work of advocates of women during this period. For example, Christine de Pisan (d. 1429) and Margaret of Navarre (d. 1549) are two women often studied and cited by scholars as examples of women who, if not feminist, did indeed make significant contributions to understanding and improving women's lives by crying out against injustices done to them. By raising objections to insults and slurs against women, both women challenged the popular misogynism conveyed through stereotypes. Both condemned physical violence against women. In *The Heptameron*, her own set of *nouvelles* creatively combining the traditions of the *fabliaux* and *exempla*, Margaret of Navarre criticizes battery, saying, "For with beating there is an end to love."[44]

Their criticisms of female stereotypes and the use of violence against wives are important steps toward rejecting the popular just battery tradition and are historically significant as such. I do not believe, however, that these criticisms constitute a clear countertradition defending wives' unqualified right to freedom from being beaten by their husbands. Both Christine de Pisan and Margaret of Navarre continue to accept the subordination of

women to men and the principle that insubordination is just cause for battery. In her popular manual of advice for women of all classes, *The Treasure
of the City of Ladies*, Christine de Pisan counsels wifely submission and lauds
the virtue of obedience.[45] In her *Book of the City of Ladies*, after crying out,
"How many harsh beatings—without cause and without reason—how many
injuries . . . have so many upright women suffered?" she immediately goes on
to teach that "men are masters over their wives" and not the reverse.[46] Even
though she makes it clear that the husband's authority is not to be misused,
her assumption of the conditions of right authority and just cause suggests
that she continues the tradition of just battery. Margaret of Navarre appears
to reject battery outright. But she accepts the subordination of women, saying, "It is reasonable that the man should rule us, but it is not reasonable that
he should forsake and ill use us."[47] The question here is how she would differentiate proper from ill use. Is all physical violence against wives ill use? Or
only that which does not fulfill the condition of just cause? On the basis of
my reading of the popular tradition of just battery, I would guess that the second is more likely.

Much more work needs to be done on the criticisms of and challenges to
wifebeating in this period. By raising questions about the work of two of the
most outspoken advocates of women during this time, I want to suggest that
it is likely that in spite of calls for moderation and criticisms of wifebeating
during this period, the popular tradition of just battery of wives was not
interrupted. Such an interruption cannot occur until the linchpin of the tradition, the subordination of women to men, is removed. In assuming the subordination of women to men and accepting the conditions of right authority
and just cause, Christine de Pisan and Margaret of Navarre may have unwittingly perpetuated the tradition of just battery even as they argued against
wifebeating. The ideology of gender inequality, which serves as the basis for
the conditions justifying violence against wives, is inseparable from the practice of violence against them. As long as female subordination is accepted,
therefore, the tradition of just battery will continue.[48]

A Popular Tradition of Just Battery and the Just War Tradition

Secular and religious popular French literature from 1150 to 1565 provides
evidence for the existence of a continuing, identifiable tradition of just battery
of wives. The six conditions for justifying violence against wives found in
these tales and sermons constitute a pattern for connecting an ideology of
inequality with the practice of violence against women in such a way that
wifebeating is justified. This popular tradition of just battery provided a powerful, informal determinant of the rule for the normal and acceptable treatment of wives and reveals the pattern of gender relations operative in France
during this time. Evidence for criticism or moderation of this rule may be
read as confirmation of it rather than as an indication of a trend toward
greater justice toward wives. Evidence of women's domestic lives from legal
and ecclesiastical records, in order to be adequately interpreted, should be set

against the background of this evidence for a dominant social rule of just battery of wives.

How far such a tradition of just battery of wives extends culturally and historically has yet to be determined. I deliberately chose the terminology of just battery not only because it accurately reflects the pattern of gender relations I discovered, but also to call attention to the analogy between this tradition and the just war tradition. While the just war tradition varies over the centuries (as the popular tradition of just battery may), it exists as a clearly identifiable tradition with a set of criteria that forms its nucleus: right authority, right intention, just cause, right means, last resort, and just end.

By referring to the popular tradition I unearthed as one of just battery, I do not intend to suggest that the criteria developed for justifying violence in the public realm can be imposed upon the domestic sphere. Although the conditions I have identified as constituting the just battery tradition resemble the just war criteria, they emerged from the stories and sermons themselves. I also do not intend to suggest that the two traditions functioned in exactly the same way. In fact, there are important differences. One is that the moral tradition of the just war acknowledged the tragedy in the use of all violence, while this does not seem to be the case in the just battery tradition. Another is that the just war criteria were announced, defended, and debated in public, whereas those of the just battery tradition were tacit assumptions. A third is that the just war tradition is still accepted as a moral guideline by the majority in Western culture. By contrast, the just battery tradition, though not without proponents, has been challenged to such an extent that most persons now believe that violence against wives can never be morally justified.

By referring to this popular tradition connecting gender inequality and violence against wives as just battery, I do intend to suggest the *possibility* that a moral tradition of justifying violence may exist in the domestic sphere in Western Christian culture that is comparable in extent, longevity, influence on behavior and attitudes, and significance for the study of morality and history to the moral tradition of justifying violence in the public sphere. This possibility must be investigated. And, if it turns out that such a domestic counterpart to the just war tradition does indeed exist, we must be prepared to alter dramatically the way we tell the story of our past, the way we identify its high and low points, the way we label its significant advances and "dark ages."

Conclusion

If historical theologians do not probe new sources with questions about power relations between men and women and do not investigate the connections between ideology of gender inequality and the practice of violence against women, we will unwittingly perpetuate a tradition of silence that is complicity. Whatever historical and theological judgments we make on the basis of our research, we must continue to investigate these issues.

As historical theologians committed to ending violence against women, we must be willing to allow out present commitments to influence what we look for and what we see in the past. And we must be ready to alter dramatically our constructions of the past on the basis of what we find. The possible existence of an ongoing popular tradition of just battery of wives certainly challenged us in these ways.

As persons who are committed to ending violence against women and who are also historical theologians, we must be willing to admit that our study of the past can transform our lives and our time as well. For example, we need to open ourselves to the possibility that discoveries of the interconnection of the ideology of gender inequality and the practice of violence against women in the Middle Ages, Renaissance, and Reformation may inform our understanding of patriarchy and our practice toward women in the present. Specifically, such an analysis of a popular tradition of just battery of wives may teach us today that if contemporary Christianity and society are to counter the practice of justifying violence against wives, they must move beyond teaching the complementary offices of chastisement and suffering to a mutual covenant of love between equals built on integrity, trust, and responsibility.

For this to happen, three steps are essential: condemnation of any and all violence against women; eradication of stereotypes of women; and rejection of all theories of inequality. As long as we do not root out the contemporary versions of the stereotypes of women as Gateway to Ruin, Temptress, Adulteress, Deceiver, and Shrew, we will not break with the just battery tradition. And as long as we do not unequivocally reject the ideologies of gender inequality, we will perpetuate that tradition, for there will always be at least one just cause for battery of wives: insubordination. Only when we have accomplished all three steps will we have completely interrupted the popular tradition of just battery and moved to a gender "arrangement based not on force and deception but on consensual reciprocal dependence."[49] Only when women are free and responsible selves rather than appropriate victims will we be able to speak of justice for women. Only when all women are able to live at home and abroad free of the fear of violence by men will be able to speak of a Renaissance or Reformation *for women*.

❧

Notes

1. Rebecca E. Dobash and Russell P. Dobash have popularized the phrase "appropriate victim" in their *Violence against Wives* (New York: Free Press, 1979), 32. Carole J. Sheffield defines "sexual terrorism" as the use of ideology, propaganda, and indiscriminateness to perpetrate violence and the threat of violence against women in order to control through fear and maintain the patriarchal definition of women's place. See "Sexual Terrorism," in *Women: A Feminist Perspective*, ed. Jo Freeman (Palo Alto, Calif: Mayfield Publishing Co., 1979), 3–19.

2. Jaroslav Pelikan, *The Christian Tradition*, 5 vols. (Chicago: University of Chicago Press, 1971–89).

3. Williston Walker et al., *A History of the Christian Church*, 4th ed. (New York: Charles Scribner's Sons, 1985).

4. Justo L. González, *The Story of Christianity*, 2 vols. (San Francisco: Harper & Row, 1984).

5. Barbara J. MacHaffie, *Her Story: Women in Christian Tradition* (Philadelphia: Fortress Press, 1986).

6. Margaret R. Miles, *Image as Insight: Visual Understanding in Western Christianity and Secular Culture* (Boston: Beacon Press, 1985); idem, *Practicing Christianity: Critical Perspectives for an Embodied Spirituality* (New York: Crossroad, 1988).

7. Martin Ingram, *Church Courts, Sex and Marriage in England, 1570–1640* (New York: Cambridge University Press, 1987).

8. James Casey, *The History of the Family* (Oxford: Basil Blackwell, 1989).

9. Richard J. Gelles, *The Violent Home: A Study of Physical Aggression between Husbands and Wives* (Beverly Hills, Calif.: Sage Publications, 1974), 13.

10. Julia O'Faolain and Lauro Martines, eds., *Not in God's Image: A History of Women in Europe from the Greeks to the Nineteenth Century* (New York: Harper & Row, 1973), 145, 152, 168–69, 175, 202.

11. Elizabeth Gould Davis, *The First Sex* (New York: Putnam, 1971), 254–55.

12. Del Martin, *Battered Wives*, rev. ed. (San Francisco: Volcano Press, 1981).

13. Nancy Hutchings, *The Violent Family: Victimization of Women, Children, and Elders* (New York: Human Sciences Press, 1988).

14. Terry Davidson, "Wifebeating: A Recurring Phenomenon throughout History," in *Battered Women: A Psychosociological Study of Domestic Violence*, ed. Maria Roy (New York: Van Nostrand Reinhold, 1977), 2–23; idem, *Conjugal Crime: Understanding and Changing the Wifebeating Pattern* (New York: Hawthorne Books, 1978), chap. 5.

15. Davidson, "Wifebeating," 7.

16. Rosemary Radford Ruether, "The Western Religious Tradition and Violence against Women in the Home," in *Christianity, Patriarchy, and Abuse: A Feminist Critique*, ed. Joanne Carlson Brown and Carole R. Bohn (New York: Pilgrim Press, 1989), 31; Joy Bussert, *Battered Women: From a Theology of Suffering to an Ethic of Empowerment* (New York: Lutheran Church in America, 1986).

17. Roberta Hamilton, *The Liberation of Women: A Study of Patriarchy and Capitalism* (London: George Allen and Unwin, 1978).

18. H. C. Erik Midelfort, "Toward a Social History of Ideas in the Reformation," in *Pietas et Societas: New Trends in Reformation Social History*, ed. Kyle C. Sessions and Phillip N. Bebb (Ann Arbor, Mich.: Edwards Brothers, 1986), 11–22.

19. Carol Bauer and Lawrence Ritt, "A Husband Is a Beating Animal: Francis Power Cobbe Confronts the Wife-Abuse Problem in Victorian England," *International Journal of Women's Studies* 6 (1983): 99–118; Leonore Davidoff, "Mastered for Life: Servant and Wife in Victorian and Edwardian England,"

Journal of Social History 7 (1969): 406–28; R. Emerson Dobash and Russell Dobash, "Community Response to Violence against Wives: Charivari, Abstract Justice and Patriarchy," *Social Problems* 28 (1981): 563–81; Margaret May, "Violence in the Family: An Historical Perspective," in *Violence and the Family*, ed. J. P. Martin (Chichester: John Wiley and Sons, 1978), 135–67; Roderick Phillips, "Women and Family Breakdown in Eighteenth-Century France: Rouen 1780–1800," *Social History* 1 (1976): 202–18.

20. Edward J. Bayer, *Rape within Marriage: A Moral Analysis Delayed* (Lanham, Md.: University Press of America, 1985); Steven Ozment, *When Fathers Ruled: Family Life in Reformation Europe* (Cambridge: Harvard University Press, 1983).

21. For example, he comments that there was not a "total subjection of the wife" because "authority was shared by husband and wife" (*When Fathers Ruled*, 11); and "despite male rule an ordered equality existed between husbands and wives" (ibid., 99). He also consistently places the terms *sexist* and *patriarchal* in quotation marks (ibid., 12, 99).

22. William Monter, "The Consistory of Geneva, 1559–64," in *Renaissance, Reformation, Resurgence*, ed. Peter De Klerk (Grand Rapids, Mich.: Calvin Theological Seminary, 1976), 81 n. 34, 82 n. 36.

23. Thomas Safley, "Protestantism, Divorce, and the Breaking of the Modern Family," in *Pietas et Societas*, 44.

24. Ibid., 45–46.

25. Ibid., 46–47.

26. Safley's claim that "abuse" served as a grounds for divorce in Basel, therefore, must be qualified ("Protestantism," 49), as must Ozment's report of a colleague's conclusion: "Wife-beaters in Protestant towns and territories were haled before the marriage court or consistory, and nowhere more speedily than in Geneva, which by century's end had gained the reputation of 'the woman's Paradise'" (*When Fathers Ruled*, 208 n. 79).

27. Grethe Jacobsen, "Women, Marriage, and Magisterial Reformation: The Case of Malmø, Denmark," in *Pietas et Societas*, 71.

28. Ozment, *When Fathers Ruled*, 9.

29. Michel Foucault, *The History of Sexuality*, trans. Robert Hurley (New York: Random House, 1980), 1: 89.

30. Phrase taken from A. Salmon, ed., *Coutumes de Beauvaisis* (Paris, 1899), par. 335.

31. James Wilhelm and Lowry Nelson, Jr., eds., *The French "Fabliaux,"* 2 vols. (New York: Garland, 1984–85), 1: 45.

32. Ibid., 1: 57–59.

33. Ibid., 1: 61.

34. Nora Scott, ed., *Fabliaux des XIIIe et XIVe siècles: Contes pour rire?* (Paris: Union Générale, 1977), 204.

35. Thomas Frederick Crane, ed., *The "Exempla" or Illustrative Stories for the "Sermones Vulgares" of Jacques de Vitry* (London: Folklore Society, 1890), 226.

36. Alan de Lille, *The Art of Preaching*, trans. Gillian R. Evans (Kalamazoo, Mich.: Cistercian Publications, 1981), 164.

37. Crane, *Exempla*, 225.

38. Ibid., 223.

39. Etienne de Bourbon, *Anecdotes historiques, légendes et apologues*, ed. A. Le Coy de la March (Paris: Renouard, 1877), 202–335; Nicholas Bozon, *Les contes moralisés de Nicole Bozon, Frère Minuer*, ed. Lucy Toulmin Smith and Paul Meyer (Paris: Firmin Didot, 1889), 49–55, 61.

40. This is supported by Dobash and Dobash's study of *charivari* (ritualized ridicule for unacceptable domestic behavior). Men thought to be dominated by their wives were shamed in public because such behavior was "an extraordinary threat to the patriarchal order" ("Community Response," 566).

41. Phillipe Menard, ed., *Fabliaux français au moyen âge* (Geneva: Droz, 1979), 1: 83–94. See Bozon's version of this story, which begins, "A man was contrary to his wife and often beat her *without reason*" (*Les contes moralisés*, 62; emphasis added).

42. T. B. W. Reid, ed., *Twelve "Fabliaux"* (Manchester: University of Manchester Press, 1977), 3; translation mine; emphasis added.

43. Ozment, *When Fathers Ruled*, 77.

44. Margaret of Navarre, *The Heptameron of the Tales of Margaret, the Queen of Navarre* (1558; reprint, Paris: D. Trenor, 1902), 403. See also "Tale 46," 397–405, which focuses on preaching and wifebeating.

45. Christine de Pisan, *The Treasure of the City of Ladies or the Book of the Three Virtues*, trans. Sarah Lawson, (New York: Penguin, 1985), 62–65, 138–41.

46. Christine de Pisan, *The Book of the City of Ladies*, trans. Earl Jeffrey Richards (New York: Persea Books, 1982), 119–20.

47. Margaret of Navarre, *Heptameron*, 355.

48. Murray A. Straus has said, "Full sexual equality is essential for the prevention of wifebeating" ("A Sociological Perspective on the Prevention and Treatment of Wifebeating," in Roy, *Battered Women*, 233). Other scholars, not necessarily agreeing with Straus's implied theory of social causation, have also connected sexual inequality and male violence against women. See Peggy Reeves Sanday, *Female Power and Male Dominance: On the Origins of Sexual Inequality* (Cambridge: Cambridge University Press, 1984); Dobash and Dobash, *Violence against Wives*, 33–34; Frances Power Cobbe, *Wife Torture in England* (London: Contemporary Review, 1878).

49. Albert Memmi, *Dependence: A Sketch of the Portrait of the Dependent* (Boston: Beacon Press, 1985), 155.

The Power to See and the Power to Name: American Church History and the Problem of Domestic Violence

ANN TAVES

For the most part, American church history simply has not dealt with the issue of domestic violence. In the past, church historians tended to focus on the history of theology, the church as institution or movement, and the history of denominations. With the rise of religious studies departments in secular colleges and universities, many scholars have begun thinking of themselves as historians of Christianity or historians of religion in America. However we label ourselves or the field, it has undergone substantial changes in the last two decades.

The most striking development is the new appreciation of religious pluralism signaled by Sydney Ahlstrom's attempt at inclusivity in *A Religious History of the American People* (1972) and in the various editions of Winthrop Hudson's *Religion in America* (1965, 1992). It has been manifest most fully in Catherine Albanese's *America: Religions and Religion* (1981, 1992), Peter Williams' *America's Religions* (1990), and Edwin Gaustad's *Documentary History of Religion in America* (1982–83, 1993). While Hudson and Gaustad made some attempt to include the experience of women in their texts, the feminist scholarship of the eighties, including what little historical work has been done on domestic violence, has yet to have a serious impact on textbooks in American religion. In general, when textbooks have moved beyond more narrow denominational or institutional concerns, they have focused on the role of religion in the public life of the United States. Women have received attention in so far as they entered the public realm. Recent studies of the role of religion in the "private" realm and the impact of the public/private distinction on women and religion in the United States have yet to reshape the basic way that introductory textbooks are written.[1]

While time certainly plays a part in this, it is clear that the way in which the history of Christianity is conceived will ultimately determine the extent to which research on domestic violence, that is violence within the "private" sphere, can be integrated into textbooks and introductory courses. If the call to take the problem of domestic violence seriously is construed as a demand that we add yet another special topic to a syllabus already bulging at the seams, few are likely to rise to the challenge. Both theoretically and pedagogically, I believe that we have reached a dead end with the "add-on" approach. New theoretical frameworks, building perhaps on the Albanese's pioneering efforts, are needed to organize introductory courses in American religion or American church history. I would like to suggest that violence, whether violence directed toward women and children or Native Americans, African Americans, immigrants, or Roman Catholics, can provide a conceptual tool for rethinking a traditional course in American church history or American religion.

Violence is a slippery concept. What has counted as violence has differed both synchronically and diachronically. To define something as violence, that is as "an unjust or unwarranted exertion of force or power," (*Random House Dictionary of the English Language*, 1987) is to make a statement about what is just or ethically warranted. Religious traditions have been and are still deeply invested in defining what is just or unjust. The issue of violence thus takes us directly into the heart of the process whereby religious traditions shape and are shaped by social relationships ranging from relationships between peoples (ethnic or national) to relationships within families.

Because the Euro-American Christian tradition in its dominant forms has legitimated, indeed tended to sanctify, social relationships which are simultaneously patriarchal, Eurocentric and heterosexist, violence has traditionally been defined rather narrowly within mainstream Christianity. Thus, any attempt to focus on issues of violence within American history must attend carefully to definitions of violence. Attention must be paid not only to violence which is recognized and visible in a particular time period or cultural context, but also to the violence which remained invisible and unseen (given their definitions). Discussions of violence, whether historically-grounded or not, are political discussions carrying within them normative understandings of social relations, human nature, and the sacred.

To focus on domestic violence requires a further level of definitional awareness both with respect to the present and the past. I think that the term domestic violence may be more useful (at least historically) than the term family violence. Domestic violence is violence that occurs in "private" within the confines of the "household" rather than in "public." The idea of a domestic sphere has its roots in the Greek distinction between the *polis* (city) and *oikos* (household) which emerged with the creation of the democratic Greek city-state. Traditionally in the West, the social construction of the *oikos* (household) or domestic sphere, involved notions of gender, property, and rule, such that for the Greek city-state and much of American history, freeborn, male property owners held the right to participate in the public sphere while women, children, servants, and slaves were legally dependent on (if not literally or metaphorically the property of) such males and relegated to the domestic sphere (Torjesen 1989, 4–12).

Conceptually, domestic violence is, in other words, a potentially more inclusive term, especially in historical time periods when the "household" and the "family" were not necessarily coextensive. Thus, to take the most pertinent example, while servants or slaves in the United States may or may not have thought of themselves or been thought of by others as part of their master's family, they were clearly a part of the master's household. A focus on domestic violence allows us to examine the patterns of violence that occurred across racial lines within slaveowning households where kinship, if present, was often denied.

To illustrate the political character of definitions and the interplay of definitions of violence with what is seen and not seen, I will examine the discourse around violence in the domestic realm in three contexts: Puritan New England, the antebellum South, and Victorian Protestantism.

Puritan New England

As Elizabeth Pleck points out, the New England Puritans had an extremely good track record on many of the issues we today associate with domestic violence. The Massachusetts *Body of Liberties* passed in 1641 included laws prohibiting wifebeating (soon amended to include husband beating) and "unnatural severitie" toward children, servants, and domestic animals. Children who were treated severely were allowed to "complain to Authorities for redresse" and servants who were treated abusively were allowed to flee without penalty. While most of these laws were adapted from biblical law or English custom, the law against wifebeating was new and, according to Pleck, originated with the English Puritans (Pleck 1987, 21–22).

Early New England law, however imperfectly implemented, attempted to prevent domestic violence by setting clear limits on what was permissible in relations of dependence. In company with most other Europeans of their day, New England Puritans defined appropriate relations of dependence broadly. Specifically, the Puritans took relationships of dependence for granted not only between children and parents, but also between servant and master, wife and husband, people and magistrate, humans and God. Puritans differed from other Europeans in their understanding of these unequal relationships as covenant relationships. This meant that although one partner was clearly subordinate to the other, each partner had certain rights and responsibilities. While the relationships remained hierarchical in character, the duty of the subordinate partner to obey or submit was conditional on the superior partner's fulfillment of the covenant (Taves 1989, 11).

The covenantal understanding of marriage resulted in more liberal divorce laws in New England than in England or the other colonies. Thus, it was possible, at least in theory, to obtain a divorce on the grounds of adultery, incest, extreme cruelty, or desertion. Studies of the way the law was applied in Massachusetts suggest that the Puritan's emphasis on preserving the family whenever possible made it difficult to obtain a divorce on the grounds of cruelty (i.e., wifebeating) alone. More often, in practice, cruelty was cited as grounds for divorce only in conjunction with other charges (Pleck 1987, 17–24, 31–33).

Moreover, although Pleck implies that incest as we think of it today (i.e., as a breach of sexual boundaries between non-peers within a family) was grounds for divorce in Puritan New England, that was not precisely the case. The bill against incest passed by the Massachusetts deputies in 1695 was primarily intended to prevent incestuous marriages between an extended set of relatives.[2] Incest outside of the marital relationship, while punishable under Puritan law, was often subsumed, when it came to divorce, under the heading of adultery. The view that incest outside the marital relationship (e.g., father-daughter incest) could logically be subsumed under the general heading of adultery followed from the assumption, made by the Christian tradition more generally, that adultery and incest (along with homosexuality and rape) were "unnatural acts." They were considered "unnatural" first because they occurred outside marriage and second because their "intention" was not procreation. Thus, father-daughter incest was categorized as a form of adultery rather than child abuse and was seen primarily as a threat to the wife, the marriage, and the social order. In this view, the wife rather than the child was seen as the primary victim of father-daughter incest (Taves 1989, 26; Fortune 1983, 61–64).

The Memoirs of Mrs. Abigail Bailey, the first autobiographical account of domestic violence published in the United States, illustrates a number of these points. Mrs. Bailey, an eighteenth-century New England woman of Puritan sensibilities, was the mother of an incest victim. Her memoir focuses on her struggle, first, to interpret what has happened to *her* in light of her religious beliefs and second, to extricate herself from her marriage. She spends little time examining the effect of her husband's actions on her daughter. Moreover, although there are intimations of her husband's physical and emotional violence in the memoir, Bailey's primary concern, and the reason she ultimately sought a divorce, was the incest. Because in her context incest between persons who were not married to one another was understood as a form of adultery and physical or emotional violence as a form of cruelty, Bailey did not make connections between them, beyond seeing them both as manifestations of her husband's sinfulness and failure to fulfill his covenant responsibilities (Taves 1989, 24–25).

While Bailey viewed her husband's sexual relations with their daughter as such a serious violation of his covenant that she could not remain married to him, her interpretation of her husband's emotional and physical assaults on herself and their children is more ambivalent. While she clearly fears and dislikes such behavior on her husband's part and while she clearly views herself and her children as, in general, not deserving of such treatment, she does not state in an unequivocal way that her husband's behavior, apart from the adultery, is unjust or unwarranted.

In fact, in the wake of the incest, Bailey summarized her feelings about her marriage as follows:

Just as we see the feeble vine, that needs
Support, intwining with the pricking thorn.
She feels the smart; her need she also feels,
Both of support, and healing for the wound.
Nor will her hold let go, till forced and torn. (Taves 1989, 91)

In the poem she clearly conveyed her feelings of love and dependence ("the feeble vine") on a husband who hurt her ("the pricking thorn"). She wanted the one who inflicted the wound ("the pricking thorn") to heal it as well, and she would not "let go" of her husband until he was "forced and torn" from her. It was the incest that tore him from her, not his "prickly" nature. She would have been content, it appears, to have spent the rest of her life "with the pricking thorn" had he not been "faithless" (Taves 1989, 31–32).

Abigail Bailey, in keeping with her culture, viewed her dependence on her "prickly" husband as appropriate until he so flagrantly violated their marriage covenant that she felt she would dishonor God by staying in the marriage. During the period in which she disentangled herself physically and emotionally from her marriage, Bailey depended both on God and her relatives and friends at church, all of whom encouraged her in her efforts (Taves 1989, 19–24). The memoir, following Puritan tradition, was written to "honor God" and published to illustrate the virtues of total dependence on God in the midst of affliction. The fact that in this theological context Bailey and everyone else believed that it was God who brought this affliction upon her aroused no doubts, since it was assumed that depraved humans deserved whatever they got, by definition. Afflictions, although "caused" by God, and thus manifestations of God's power, were not by theological definition unjust or unwarranted and thus were not, again by definition, acts of violence.

The irony, from a modern point of view, lies in the parallels between her description of her relationship with her husband before the incest and her relationship to God in the wake of the incest. At a critical point in the process of separating from her husband, she claimed that God brought the Isaac Watts hymn, "The Darkness of Providence," to her attention in order to sustain her. The hymn reads:

> Lord, we adore thy vast designs,
> Th' obscure abyss of providence!
> Too deep to sound with mortal lines,
> Too dark to view with feeble sense.
>
> Now thou array'st thine awful face
> In angry frowns, without a smile:
> We through the cloud, believe thy grace,
> Secure of thy compassion still. . . .
>
> Dear Father, if thy lifted rod
> Resolve to scourge us here below;
> Still let us lean upon our God,
> Thine arm shall bear us safely through. (Taves 1989, 154)

As with her husband, it is the one who lifts his rod to scourge her and her children that she wants to lean on to bear her safely through.

Although she did not enjoy being "wounded" by Asa or "scourged" by God, she clung to both (at different points) hoping initially that Asa would "heal" the "wounds" he inflicted and then later that God would allow her to "lean" on him while he "scourged" her. The paradigm in both instances was that of a dependent loving (and being comforted by) an authority figure who afflicts. This understanding of love was neither idiosyncratic nor culturally problematic; indeed, it lay at the core of the Calvinist understanding of how people *ought* to understand God. To name this as violence, Bailey would have had to have viewed these as unjust or unwarranted exertions of force or power. Although her writings suggest that she had doubts about the justice of her husband's acts, only in extreme moments of despair did she allow herself to question the justness of God.

The dilemma she faced was structurally similar to that of the abused child as portrayed in contemporary literature on domestic violence. As Linda Gordon points out, in both sexual and nonsexual child abuse, "the child is treated badly, injuriously, by one who is supposed to be a caretaker. The dilemma for the child . . . is that her molester is one on whom she must depend for love and sustenance" (Gordon 1988, 214). According to psycho-analyst Alice Miller, abusive family systems are usually maintained through the idealization of abusive parents and the fiction that the abuse is "good" for or deserved by the child (Miller 1983; 1984, 79–103).

Given that in colonial New England relationships of dependence were legally maintained between husband and wife, as well as parent and child, and that the ideal relationship with God was also one of total dependence, it becomes clear that issues of power (and the abuse of power) in relationships of dependence extended far beyond the parent-child relationship. In such a context it is not surprising that Abigail Bailey, again like many abused children, idealized those upon whom she was dependent. Although she gradually came to view her husband more realistically, she maintained an idealized view of God throughout the memoir. In order to do so, she, like many abused children, defined herself as deserving of the "afflictions" visited upon her by God. She did so in a theologically orthodox fashion either by linking the "affliction" with something she believed she had done wrong or more often, given her generally exemplary behavior, with her "depraved nature."

The parallels, however, are not exact. Bailey was not physically dependent on God in the same way that a child is physically dependent on its parents. Moreover, while she *was* emotionally dependent on God, the ramifications of doubt went beyond the psychological to the theological and political. To question God's justice and name God's actions as violent was to fly in the face of a theological tradition which insistently defended God's goodness and omnipotence. Theodicies, or attempts to explain how a God who is simultaneously good and omnipotent can allow evil to occur, typically defend God by blaming evil on those who suffer (sometimes directly and sometimes indirectly through the doctrine of original sin) (Hick 1966, 121–50, 178–84). Such theodicies uphold an idealized understanding of God at the expense of human beings. A theology which idealizes the powerful and denigrates those who are in positions of dependence can not help but carry political overtones as well. To question God's justice in such a context is to call into question the entire patriarchal social order.

The Antebellum South

In the South, slavery was an integral part of the domestic sphere. According to Elizabeth Fox-Genovese, "throughout much of the South, the empirically self-evident unit of the contiguous farm or plantation was coterminous with the boundaries of the household." Defining households "as units that pooled income and resources," she argues that "slaves can more appropriately be regarded as members of the household of their master—defined as plantation or farm—than as members of distinct slave households" (Fox-Genovese 1988, 93–95).[3] Thus, any survey of domestic violence in American history must contend with the issue of violence within slave-owning households. Moreover, the sharply defined differences between the views of slaveowners and abolitionists (both slave and free) around issues of religion, violence, and slavery highlight both the political nature of discussions of violence and the role of religion in defining what is or is not considered violent.

For those who viewed slavery as legitimate, physical punishment of slaves by masters or overseers was taken for granted and viewed as a necessary and proper means of disciplining the disobedient slave. For those who viewed slavery as illegitimate, physical punishment of slaves was viewed as violence. Orlando Patterson and others have argued that violence or "naked force" was essential to the creation and maintenance of a slave system. Patterson explores the relationship between violence and dishonor, arguing that slaves were persons who had been dishonored because they were "without power except through another". Psychologically, "what was universal in the master-slave relationship was the strong sense of honor the experience of mastership generated, and conversely, the dishonoring of the slave condition." What slavery "really meant," Patterson concludes, was "direct and insidious violence, . . . namelessness and invisibility, . . . endless personal violation, and . . . chronic inalienable dishonor" (Patterson 1982, 3–4, 10–12).

The dishonoring of slaves, especially female slaves, often included sexual as well as physical violence. Within the southern slaveowning household, sexual relations between masters and slaves were tacitly accepted. They were not defined in the eyes of the law as either adultery (abuse of the wife) or rape (abuse of the slave). The tacit acceptance of such relations had an indirect impact on divorce law. In contrast to New England, the southern states for the most part refused to sanction divorce and remarriage, while at the same time granting women an unusually high degree of economic independence within marriage.[4] Citing the case of South Carolina, Marylynn Salmon states that

> the tragic sexual dynamics of slaveholding South Carolina families made it extremely difficult for lawmakers to sanction divorce and remarriage. They could not grant women absolute divorces for the sexual misconduct of their husbands. Because this was the charge that most often resulted in a divorce decree in the early United States—in New York, for example, divorces could be obtained only on a charge of adultery— South Carolinians could not grant absolute divorces at all. . . . In

exchange for the law's acceptance of male sexual privileges, South Carolina jurists gave women the right to financial autonomy within marriage. (Salmon 1986, 79–80)

Salmon, in other words, suggests that in general southern law granted white women greater financial autonomy within marriage in exchange for granting their husbands sexual privileges with their (female) slaves.

Harriet Jacobs' autobiography, *Incidents in the Life of a Slave Girl*, first published in 1861, describes both the physical and the sexual violence that was typical of slaveowning households. Writing under the pseudonym of Linda Brent, Jacobs portrays her life as a teenager in the home of James Norcum ("Dr. Flint"), a physician in Edenton, North Carolina. Norcum, the father of at least ten children by his first and second wives and at least eleven children by his female slaves, attempted to force her into a sexual relationship with him (Jacobs 1987, 35, 266). Speaking as Linda Brent, she writes:

> My master met me at every turn, reminding me that I belonged to him, and swearing by heaven and earth that he would compel me to submit to him. . . . The light heart which nature had given me became heavy with sad forebodings. The other slaves in my master's house noticed the change. Many of them pitied me; but none dared ask the cause. They had no need to inquire. They knew too well the guilty practices under that roof; and they were aware that to speak of them was an offense that never went unpunished. (Jacobs 1987, 28)

Dr. Flint demanded that she keep silent about his sexual overtures under threat of death. Mrs. Flint's growing awareness that something was going on between Jacobs and her husband, however, led to "repeated quarrels between the doctor and his wife" and angry outbursts directed at Jacobs. When Mrs. Flint finally ordered Jacobs to tell her what was happening, Mrs. Flint cried, claiming that "her marriage vows were desecrated, her dignity insulted" (Ibid., 33).

Like Abigail Bailey, Mrs. Flint focused on the implications of her husband's actions for her marriage, rather than on the harm which had been done to the sixteen-year-old Jacobs. Unlike Bailey, however, Mrs. Flint did not have the option of seeking a divorce, given the legal situation in the South. White men having sex with slave women was so much a matter of course that as Jacobs noted, "If a pastor has offspring by a woman not his wife, the church dismiss him, if she is a white woman; but if she is colored, it does not hinder his continuing to be their good shepherd" (Jacobs 1987, 74).

White Southern Christianity of the late antebellum period developed a proslavery ideology that owed much to the conservative Congregationalism of the New England Federalists. Inspired by the Federalists' ability to blend a hierarchical conception of social order with Republican values, proslavery "evangelicals substituted a theory defining slavery as part of a social hierarchy which reflected the reality of human inequality, and which was maintained by a feeling of mutual obligation between superiors and inferiors" (Mathews 1977, 168). According to Donald Mathews:

The appropriate attitude of people at all levels of society was submission to the authority of persons in ranks superior to their own, so the only legitimate motive force for social change was not the confrontational demand for justice from the bottom rung of society upward, but benevolent instruction and guidance proceeding in the opposite direction. (1977, 168)

Within such a framework, obedience was presented as the primary obligation of the Christianized slave. When Dr. Flint joined the church and encouraged Linda Brent to do the same, she replied that she would if she were "allowed to live like a Christian," that is, as a self-determining moral agent. To which Flint replied, "You can do as I require; and if you are faithful to me, you will be as virtuous as my wife." In his response, Flint shifted the precondition for virtue from self-determination to acceptance of enslavement and the content of virtue from sexual purity (bodily integrity) to obedience. When she disagreed with him, citing scripture, he responded, "What right have you, who are my negro, to talk to me about what you would like, and what you wouldn't like? I am your master, and you shall obey me" (Jacobs 1987, 75).

While slaves were encouraged to adopt a form of Christianity which legitimated their dependence and fostered their compliance, few embraced their master's version of Christianity with the thoroughness evidenced by Abigail Bailey. Baptized as a child, Jacobs appropriated Christianity critically. After the Nat Turner revolt led slaveowners to intensify their missionary efforts "to keep [the slaves] from murdering their masters"(Jacobs 1987, 68), Jacobs was invited as a literate light-skinned house slave to participate in a segregated, but still elitist, Episcopal service. She reports that she and the others in attendance were amused by the priest's sermons on the duty of servants to obey their masters. Although she apparently attended Methodist class meetings on occasion, she describes the enthusiastic style of worship (the "shouting and singing") of her fellow slaves in a detached, yet sympathetic way. She shows no signs of having had an evangelical conversion experience and her critical comments about southern white church life and her refusal to join a white church suggest her ambivalent feelings toward Christianity (Taves 1987, 60).

Jacobs' own understanding of Christianity, as portrayed through the character of Linda Brent, reflected a female-oriented tradition that linked purity, freedom, and justice. This countervailing tradition, passed on to Jacobs by her mother, her grandmother, and her first mistress, seems to reflect the resistance of both slave and free women to the sexual promiscuity of many slaveowners. Jacobs makes clear that purity refers to sexual purity or bodily integrity, and that the power to say no to sexual overtures outside marriage and the legal sanction of sex within marriage were integral to maintaining one's purity. For slaves, she points out, both were impossible.

In an attempt to preserve some semblance of honor in the face of her master's harassment, Jacobs chose to enter into a sexual relationship with an unmarried slaveowner ("Mr. Sands"). She felt that it was "less degrading to give one's self, than to submit to compulsion" and she hoped that such an action might provoke her master into selling her. Looking back on her choice, Jacobs states that "the painful and humiliating memory [would] haunt [her] to her dying day" (Jacobs 1987, 55–56). The shame that she continued to feel with respect to this choice suggests that despite her conscious belief that "slave women ought not to be judged by the same standards as others," she still felt dishonored and humiliated by the choices she was forced to make while a slave. The link that she makes between purity and true piety suggests that this dishonoring was not simply physical and emotional, but also spiritual.

Because she resisted the violence inherent in the master-slave relationship, her relationship with God was more complex and more ambivalent than was Abigail Bailey's. During the years she was hidden in her grandmother's attic prior to her escape to the north, she writes that "dark thoughts passed through my mind as I lay there day after day. . . . Sometimes I thought God was a compassionate Father, who would forgive my sins for the sake of my sufferings. At other times, it seemed to me there was not justice or mercy in the divine government. I asked why the curse of slavery was permitted to exist and why I had been so persecuted and wronged from youth upward." Similar thoughts continued to plague her after her escape. As she wrote to a friend just prior to the Civil War, "When I see the evil that is spreading throughout the whole land my whole soul sickens. Oh my dear friend this poor heart that has bled in slavery is often wrung most bitterly to behold the injustice, the wrongs, the oppression, the cruel outrages inflicted on my race. Sometimes I am almost ready to exclaim—where dwells that just Father whom I love—and in whom must be might—and Strength—Liberty—and Death" (Taves 1987, 71–72).

While Jacobs' feelings of shame led her at times to doubt that God would forgive her, her clear sense that slavery was wrong and that she had been oppressed allowed her in most cases to direct her feelings of outrage and disillusionment outward toward God rather than inward onto herself. Jacobs' social position and social context led her to interpret a wider range of actions as violence than people in more privileged positions in the social order. She rejected the dominant white southern understanding of Christianity because it legitimated the physical and sexual violence necessary to maintain the slave system. A just God in her view would oppose slavery. In periods of discouragement, she was even able to entertain doubts that such a just God existed, without in turn blaming herself for her doubts.

Victorian Protestantism

During the latter part of the nineteenth century, issues of domestic violence simmered close to the surface of public discourse within (predominantly) middle-class white Protestant women's organizations, such as the Woman's Christian Temperance Union and the women's home and foreign missionary societies. Within these circles, the drunken husband was the preeminent symbol of male violence (Gordon 1988, 254).[5] These groups gained a fairly respectful hearing because, as Elizabeth Pleck has argued, their efforts were "perceived as helping to strengthen the family." In assessing these more moderate reformers, Pleck writes:

> As long as male dominance was confronted indirectly, women temperance reformers could succeed. But their remedies, while useful, failed to recognize that for many abused women, the best hope was separation or divorce and child custody. . . . Any efforts that came close to making separation, divorce, child custody for women, and court-ordered support more available went down to defeat. The public . . . believed instead that women had to reshape the traditional family and make men more responsible. (Pleck 1987, 106–7)

Temperance literature thus routinely contrasted the ideal temperance home with the alcoholic home. Frances Willard, the second president of the WCTU, described how a "steel engraving" depicting this contrast "hung on the dining-room wall of [her parents'] house . . . from [her] earliest recollection." In her words, "the little picture represented a bright, happy temperance home with a sweet woman at the center, and over against it a dismal, squalid house with a drunken man staggering in, bottle in hand" (Willard 1889, 331).

The contrast between the bright, happy, woman-centered temperance home and the dark, dismal, squalid man-centered alcoholic home carried latent overtones with respect to race, class, religion, and nationality. As Willard candidly admitted, WCTU members were not for the most part wives or mothers of alcoholics. In fact, she states that "ninety per cent. of our workers never knew the drink-curse [in their own homes]" (Willard 1883, 237). In calling upon women "born in the church and nurtured at [temperance] Crusade altars" to oppose "a horde of ignorant voters committed to the rum-power," she was mobilizing women who were, for the most part, white, middle-class and Protestant to offset the votes of men who were predominantly foreign-born, working-class, and Catholic (Willard 1889, 370–71). The homes that needed protection were not white middle-class Protestant homes; in fact, white middle-class Protestant homes were the model; the violence such women feared generally lurked elsewhere.

In addition to the homes of the Catholic working class, violence also seemed to lurk for these women in the homes of "degraded heathens" overseas. Speaking at the Woman's Congress of Missions in 1894, Ellen Parsons claimed that "what . . . roused the women to united systematic, concentrated action . . . was a *human cry*. . . . It sounded out from black heathenism, ages old, lost, vast, awful—the heartbreak of motherhood, the stifled cry of distorted childhood; *this* was what happy women heard in their happy, protected homes" (quoted in Hill 1985, 60). Here the "happy, protected homes" of Protestant Americans were contrasted with the "heartbreak" and "distortions" experienced by women and children raised in "heathen" darkness.

The tendency to associate domestic violence with non-Christians is illustrated and commented upon by Rev. Huie Kin, a Chinese-born Presbyterian minister, who describes the reaction to a talk given by a female missionary at a church in New York City upon her return from China.

The address was well received by the audience until the speaker, in her desire to bring out the contrast between Christian and heathen civilization, overdid herself in painting a black picture of Chinese homes without a ray of redeeming love, little children crushed under inhuman cruelty, women denied an education and treated as the plaything of the predatory male, etc. The storm broke when she generalized that all Chinese men beat their wives without cause. One Chu vehemently remonstrated in his broken English against this obvious exaggeration: "Fourteen year in China, no Christian, no beat wife one time." I also stood up to say that in my own village I had never seen a man beating his wife. (Huie 1932, 53–54)

Rebecca Latimer Felton, a member of the WCTU and the Women's Home Missionary Society of the Methodist Episcopal Church South, criticized the emphasis which was being placed on foreign mission work in the late nineteenth century, claiming that there was much work to be done among the "heathen" in the South in order to ensure that white women were protected from being raped. Viewing black men as a threat, Felton sanctioned lynching in a speech to the Agricultural Society of Tybee, Georgia in the early 1890s:

It is positively unsafe to allow young white women to walk along on the highways, or to be left at home without male protectors. The brutal lust of these half-civilized gorillas seems to be inflamed to madness—for five lynchings took place in Georgia for the crime of week preceding my address at Tybee. . . . When there is not enough religion in the pulpit to organize a crusade against sin; nor justice in the court house to promptly punish crime, nor manhood enough in the nation to put a sheltering arm about innocence and virtue—if it needs lynching to protect woman's dearest possession from the ravening human beast—then I say lynch, a thousand times a week if necessary. (Felton n.d.)

In each of these images, the white Protestant home is idealized, and violence is for the most part thought to be lurking elsewhere. The white Protestant Christian home is depicted as pure and non-violent, while men of the working class, men of color, and foreign men are depicted as violent. Violence is associated with male perpetrators, but the perpetrators are not for the most part middle class white males. The tendency to deny problematic aspects of white middle class domestic life, and especially to absolve white males of responsibility, is illustrated by the Beecher-Tilton scandal.

In 1872 feminist Victoria Woodhull accused Henry Ward Beecher, the most prominent minister of the period, of sexual involvement with Elizabeth Tilton, a member of his congregation and wife of his best friend. Although the evidence was overwhelming and Beecher admitted the truth of the charges in private, he was unwilling to make a public confession and was acquitted in court (Fortune 1989, xi–xii; Waller 1982, 18–37). While Beecher's parishioners accepted "his self-exoneration and thus unwittingly encouraged his lack of responsibility, Elizabeth had to face more severe consequences."

Elizabeth Tilton continued to believe that Beecher was a "good man" and blamed herself for having "invited" the affair through "her unwitting use of her sexuality to tempt Beecher"! (Waller 1982, 127–28; emphasis added). A similar pattern appears in the relationships between clergy and female congregants in the fiction of the era.

In a study of "parsonage romances," Ann-Janine Morey argues that the popular romance novels written by nineteenth and twentieth century women about the ministry "represent an enactment of religio-sexual dynamics that serve to reinforce patriarchal structures of religion and culture" (Morey 1990, 87). She concludes by suggesting that there are parallels between the romantic hero and heroine of the popular love story and the clerical hero of the parsonage romance and his inevitable romantically sexualized involvement with a female parishioner.

> The relationship between the romantic hero and heroine, and the minister and his congregant are both built upon the same model—the relationship of God to the sinner. God is not really cruel or unjust; rather the sinner misunderstands the Word, or the sinner is simply unworthy. The hero is not really cruel and rapacious, rather, the heroine misinterprets his actions, or she is unworthy of his love. The minister is not really a lecher, rather, the heroine has failed to understand and support him, or the heroine is finally a whore. Nothing really happened. *A woman under patriarchal religion must learn that there are distances and cruelties that are the product of her own unworthiness.* . . . What she thinks she knows about him and his religion proves to be entirely wrong, just as the persistent rumors of maladjusted and misfired clergy sexuality prove to be entirely the opposite. (Morey 1990, 102–3; emphasis added)[6]

As in the case of Abigail Bailey, the bottom line is that women are unworthy and that God and, in this case, the clergy, are neither abusive nor unjust. Which is simply to say that historically the violence of those in power and their deity has not been discussed, because those in positions of power have not, for the most part, viewed their actions or the actions of their God as unjust or unwarranted and thus were able to rest assured that their actions were not, by definition, violent.

Those who were not in positions of power, like Harriet Jacobs, frequently commented on the inability of those in power to see what they found to be rather obvious. Speaking at the World Columbian Exposition in 1893, Fannie Williams, an African-American woman, stated:

> "I regret the necessity of speaking of the moral question of our women . . . [but] the morality of our home life has been commented on so disparagingly and meanly that we are placed in the unfortunate position of being defenders of our name." . . . [According to Paula Giddings,] Williams went on to tell the group that the onus of sexual morality did not rest on Black women but on the White men who continued to harass them. While

many women in the audience were fantasizing about Black rapists, she implied, Black women were actually suffering at the hands of White ones. (Giddings 1984, 86)

In a similar fashion, when Huie Kin indicated that he had never seen a man beating his wife in his home village in China, the missionary responded by asking "how many wives [his] father had." Huie Kin replied

> that he had only one wife, my mother; and as a return thrust, I added that it seemed that even preachers in Christian America sometimes could not avoid difficulty with their wives. This aroused ripples of laughter in the audience, for just at that time the newspapers were featuring the domestic troubles of a prominent minister in the city." (Huie 1932, 53–54)

Conclusion

The critical questions for the historian interested in the problem of domestic violence, thus, have to do with issues of power and authority. First, who, in any given historical situation, has the power to define what is just or unjust and thus what is violent? Second, how have the actions of those with this power been perceived by those who do not have it? Third, what allows some to adopt a critical stance relative to those in power, while others simply internalize it?

The examples discussed here suggest that one of the powers of a dominant class is the power to define what is just or unjust and thus what is violent. For much of American history this has meant primarily educated white men of northern European descent. It is also clear that those such as Harriet Jacobs, Fannie Williams, or Huie Kin, who either did not have access to the dominant class or chose to reject it, often defined what is just or unjust rather differently and defined violence more radically. Finally, it is clear that many white women, such as Abigail Bailey, "Mrs. Flint," the women of the WCTU, and Elizabeth Tilton were in a peculiar position of seeing and not seeing. While these women could bemoan and attempt to change the actions of particular men, they did not feel they could afford to challenge the structures of male dominance (patriarchy) directly. These women appropriated the religion of the dominant class and attempted to turn it to their own purposes, with rather mixed results. Unlike those located further from cultural centers of power, these women believed it to be in their best interest not to alienate those in power. As a result their definitions of violence tended to be more moderate.

Postscript

This essay, originally written in the late eighties, emphasizes the historically constructed nature of definitions of violence and points to the role of social location and social power in the definitional process. It was written with a mind to challenging the status quo and illuminating the difficulties of doing so at a time when issues of domestic violence and sexual harassment were still of concern primarily to feminists. Since that time these issues have received widespread media attention in conjunction with the Clarence Thomas hearings and O. J. Simpson trial. The feminist movement, and many feminists within academia, have garnered a sufficient degree of institutional clout to warrant the examination of a new series of questions.

In contrast to this essay's comparison of the "status quo" in three different eras, further historical explorations might focus on the role of redefinitions of violence in generating movements for social change. Thus, for example, future studies might examine the abolitionist movement's use of images of physical violence and sexual degradation or the social purity movement's use of images of sexual abuse as rhetorical strategies that, by redefining popular conceptions of violence and/or abuse, were able to mobilize both social movements and public opinion and in the process generate political power.

While the present essay tacitly assumes that the power to name lies at the political "center," an emphasis on movements and social change would highlight the ability of those on the "margins" to mobilize the power to challenge the status quo by redefining the meanings of violence and abuse. While the role of religion, either traditional or emergent, in providing warrants for such redefinitions of violence could remain a central concern, historical research alert to the various sources of social power and the rhetorical strategies mobilized to gain and maintain such power will help to heighten our self-awareness as we work our way through the controversies of the present day.

Notes

1. Of the recently published textbooks, Peter Williams is the only one who begins to move in this direction. See, in particular, his chapter on "Victorian Evangelicals."

2. It was specifically aimed at preventing marriages between a man and his wife's sister. See M. Halsey Thomas, ed., *Diary of Samuel Sewell*, 2 vols. (New York: Farrar, Straus, and Giroux, 1973), I:333.

3. Fox-Genovese acknowledges that slaves did in most cases have their own living quarters and thus, in a certain sense, their own "households," but she argues that these are more accurately viewed as "sub-households" since slaves had no legal right to their own quarters and they maintained them only at the sufferance of their master (1988, 93–95).

4. According to Salmon, in the case of South Carolina, "Matrons enjoyed rules allowing them significant property rights after marriage. Marriage settlements creating separate estates for women were fully recognized, as were postnuptual separation agreements created for the purpose of dividing property. In addition South Carolina had a strong commitment to feme sole trader rights" (Salmon 1986, 79).

5. The only reference I have found to domestic violence in an introductory textbook in American religion is a reference to the fact that the Woman's Christian Temperance Union condemned alcohol, "not simply because it

inebriated, but because it left women and children destitute, broke up homes, and engendered domestic violence." This portion of the text was illustrated by a nineteenth-century temperance poster which included a scene in which a mother is cringing in the corner of a room while a drunken father beats his cowering daughter (Noll 1983, 304–5).

6. With respect to the "persistent rumors of maladjusted and misfired clergy sexuality," see M. E. Billings, *Crimes of Preachers in the United States and Canada from May 1876 to May 1883* (New York: The Truth Seeker Publishing Co., 1884). The author of this freethought publication compiled and analyzed clerical crimes based on accounts published in newspapers for the years cited. Of the 917 crimes allegedly committed, 206 fell under the heading of "adultery" and 103 under the heading of "seduction generally." Overall, Billings states "456 have been against women in a sexual way, and 81 against women in others ways, or 544 against women especially" (Ibid., 67–68).

Works Cited

Ahlstrom, Sidney. 1972. *A Religious History of the American People*. New Haven: Yale University Press.

Albanese, Catherine. 1992. *America: Religions and Religion*. 2d ed. Belmont, Calif: Wadsworth.

Felton, Rebecca Latimer. N.d. Newspaper clipping. Felton Papers. Hargrett Rare Book and Manuscript Library/University of Georgia Libraries.

Fortune, Marie. 1989. *Is Nothing Sacred?: When Sex Invades the Pastoral Relationship*. New York: Harper & Row.

———. 1983. *Sexual Violence: The Unmentionable Sin*. New York: Pilgrim Press.

Fox-Genovese, Elizabeth. 1988. *Within the Plantation Household: Black and White Women of the Old South*. Chapel Hill and London: University of North Carolina Press.

Gaustad, Edwin S. 1982–83/1993. *A Documentary History of the American People*. 2d ed. 2 vols. Grand Rapids: Eerdmans.

Giddings, Paula. 1985. *When and Where I Enter: The Impact of Black Women on Race and Sex in America*. New York: Bantam Books.

Gordon, Linda. 1988. *Heroes of Their Own Lives: The Politics and History of Family Violence*. New York: Viking.

Griffin, Susan. 1981. *Pornography and Silence: Culture's Revenge Against Nature*. New York: Harper & Row.

Hick, John. 1966. *Evil and the God of Love*. New York: Harper & Row.

Hill, Patricia R. 1985. *The World Their Household: The American Woman's Foreign Mission Movement and Cultural Transformation, 1870–1920*. Ann Arbor: University of Michigan Press.

Hudson, Winthrop S., and John Corrigan. 1992. *Religion in America*. 5th ed. New York: Macmillan.

Huie, Kin. 1932. *Reminiscences*. Peiping, China: San Yu Press.

Jacobs, Harriet A. 1987. *Incidents in the Life of a Slave Girl, Written by Herself* ed. Jean Fagan Yellin. Cambridge: Harvard University Press.

Mathews, Donald. 1977. *Religion in the Old South*. Chicago: University of Chicago Press.

Miller, Alice. 1983. *For Your Own Good: Hidden Cruelty in Child Rearing and the Roots of Violence*. Trans. Hildegard E. and Hunter Hannum. New York: Farrar, Straus, Giroux, 1983.

———. 1984. *Thou Shalt Not Be Aware: Society's Betrayal of the Child*. Trans. Hildegard E. and Hunter Hannum. New York: Farrar, Straus, Giroux.

Morey, Ann-Janine. 1990. "The Reverend Idol and Other Parsonage Secrets: Women Write Romances about Ministers, 1880–1950." *Journal of Feminist Studies in Religion* 6/1 (Spring 1990): 87–103.

Noll, Mark A., et al. 1983. *Eerdmans' Handbook to Christianity in America*. Grand Rapids, Mich.: Eerdmans.

Pleck, Elizabeth. 1987. *Domestic Tyranny: The Making of American Social Policy Against Family Violence from Colonial Times to the Present*. New York: Oxford University Press.

Salmon, Marylynn. 1986. *Women and the Law of Property in Early America*. Chapel Hill and London: University of North Carolina Press.

Random House Dictionary of the English Language. 1987. 2d ed. Unabridged. New York: Random House.

Taves, Ann, ed. 1989. *Religion and Domestic Violence in Early New England: The Memoirs of Abigail Abbot Bailey*. Bloomington: Indiana University Press.

Taves, Ann. 1987. "Spiritual Purity and Sexual Shame: Religious Themes in the Writings of Harriet Jacobs." *Church History* 56/1 (1987): 59–72.

Torjesen, Karen J. 1989. "Excavations in the Deep-Structure of the Theological Tradition: The Social Origins of Theology." *Occasional Papers of the Institute for Antiquity and Christianity*, 14. Claremont, Calif.: Institute for Antiquity and Christianity.

Waller, Altina. 1982. *Reverend Beecher and Mrs. Tilton: Sex and Class in Victorian America*. Amherst: University of Massachusetts Press.

Willard, Frances. 1889. *Glimpses of Fifty Years*. Chicago: Women's Temperance Publication Association.

———. 1883. *Women and Temperance: Or, The Work and Workers of the Woman's Christian Temperance Union*. Hartford, Conn.: Park Publishing Co.

Williams, Peter W. 1990. *America's Religions: Traditions and Cultures*. New York: Macmillan.

The Imperishable
Virginity of Saint Maria Goretti

KATHLEEN ZUANICH YOUNG

W ithin Roman Catholicism, many female saints have been virgin martyrs whose lives exemplify a feminine Christian ideal.[1] Young
women who "gave" their lives because of a spiritual commitment to the
preservation of the hymen are held up as role models. Virginity is viewed as a
spiritual commitment more important than the young Catholic woman's life.

The physical fact of virginity indicates spiritual valor. A preserved hymen
may not guarantee entrance into heaven but the inappropriate loss of the
hymen diminishes the chances for eternal salvation. For the young Catholic
virgin, sexual history and spiritual identity are difficult to separate, and when
the Catholic woman "loses" her virginity because of rape, her spiritual life is
damaged or diminished. Virgin rape is as devastating as incest in trespassing
the boundary between the personal and spiritual self. The suffering that follows rape, especially virgin rape, is not just physical but also metaphysical
and spiritual. The spiritual importance placed upon virginity makes Roman
Catholic women especially vulnerable following rape or incest.

This paper examines the legend of the modern virgin martyr, Maria
Goretti, whose sainthood and idealization are used to regulate Catholic
women's lives and condone violence against them. The institutionalization of
violence (and male dominance) in the Catholic Church is accomplished
through the handing on of stories of virgin martyrs as one facet of the social
control of women, their sexuality and their bodies. Maria Goretti is a modern
mythic figure, with many levels of meaning to the myth.

The Rape of Maria Goretti

In July 1902, Maria Goretti, a twelve-year-old Italian girl, was stabbed in a
sexual assault and died. Although details of the story have been influenced
over the years by constant retelling and adaptation, the basic facts are as follows: Maria Goretti was from a poor rural family. Home one day alone,
Maria was attacked by a young man, Alessandro Serenelli. He threatened to
kill her if she did not have sex with him. Maria refused, and he stabbed her
repeatedly with a knife. She died twenty-four hours after the attack. Serenelli
was caught and tried for murder. He was sentenced to thirty years in prison.

When he was released, Serenelli went to live with an order of monks. Reportedly, Maria appeared to him in a vision during his imprisonment. She forgave him, and he repented of his sin. When she was canonized by the Roman Catholic Church in 1950, Serenelli was present, along with Maria's mother and her family.

There are discrepancies in almost every account of Maria Goretti. Marina Warner describes her as an eleven-year-old murdered "by a young man from her village, whom she knew" (Warner 1967, 70). However, according to other sources (Delaney 1980; MacConastair 1951), Alessandro Serenelli lived in the same house, and Maria cooked, cleaned, and waited on him. He was neither consanguineal nor affinal kin, but he was part of the "family." In these accounts, Serenelli is described as the twenty-year-old son of Maria's mother's partner in a share-cropping venture, a widower who lived with Assunta Goretti, a widow, and her six children in a barn on the estate of Count Mazzoleni. However, Serenelli is sometimes described as a nineteen-year-old neighbor (Buehrle 1976, 632) and sometimes as the son of her deceased father's partner who lived with the Goretti family (Delaney 1980, 262).

Maria Goretti died in the hospital in the town of Nettuno on the Feast of the Most Precious Blood. The religious celebration brought people from the surrounding countryside into town, and a crowd gathered at the hospital for the deathwatch. Her funeral took place two days later. According to a biography of Serenelli, "Mourning thousands from Nettuno, Anzio and even distant places came to the hospital chapel and filed tearfully past Marietta's bier. Though it was a work day, Nettuno's shops closed for the funeral" (DiDonato 1962, 73).

The immediate public acclaim for Maria Goretti was unprecedented. Why were thousands touched by her story? Why did so many go to her funeral? Why did her life and death reach mythic proportions almost immediately? She was known by many of the people of Nettuno (eight miles from her village) since she regularly stood on the street corner selling pigeon eggs. Her extraordinary beauty and obvious poverty made her memorable, according to one account (MacConastair 1951, 89). She was also different from most young women in either her innocence of sexual desire or her determination to protect her virginity. According to his biographer, Pietro DiDonato (1962), Serenelli reasoned:

> In every man lurked the possible rapist and killer. If, fearing the shame of the violation being known or to save her life, the girl acquiesces, the sensual man is then not included in the public criminal ranks. Supposing he had been a Mazzoleni or one of the wealthy ruling class? One never or rarely heard of the rich and powerful being punished for an act of passion. . . . If Marietta had submitted he would have made a habit of it. . . . Sooner or later she would have become the mother of his child—a not uncommon happening amongst the peasants and the poor. . . . [H]e would have married Marietta and perhaps developed a sentiment for her also. (107)

But Serenelli's self-portrayal as a potentially attractive lover can be questioned. Speaking for Serenelli at his trial, the lawyer, Canalintas, blamed the pornography industry for inciting Serenelli (DiDonato 1962, 91). Pornography and women's own behavior were said to be the reason for men's "uncontrollable urges" (similar to Ted Bundy's excuse for his serial murders). Maria may not have been innocent or chaste but repulsed by him.

Most biographies recount Serenelli's "attempt to seduce her" (Delaney 1980, 262) and her resistance to his "advances." According to these biographies, his seduction technique consisted of advancing upon her with a weapon while threatening to kill her. The weapon is variously described as a stiletto (Warner 1983, 71), a dagger (Buehrle 1967, 632), a brush hook (DiDonato 1962, 89), or a machete (MacConastair 1951). Serenelli said he would not have hacked her up if she had submitted to him when he confronted her with the weapon (DiDonato 1962, 94).

Nevertheless, seduction is suggested because they knew each other and because he protested that he would not have stabbed her fourteen times if she had submitted (DiDonato 1962, 51). Apparently, she did not "submit," but some sources vary as to whether he raped her while murdering her (Rivers 1973, 150). Her clothes were ripped off, and she was stabbed repeatedly, but she was not vaginally penetrated according to most accounts (Buehrle 1967; DiDonato 1962; MacConastair 1951). The prevailing myth is that she died with her virginity intact.

The Sainthood of Maria Goretti

Maria Goretti is a modern virgin martyr, canonized in 1950. The short amount of time from her death to her canonization, only forty-eight years, is extraordinary. In the modern era, only two people have been made saints in a similar amount of time: the first American citizen to be canonized (1946), the Italian immigrant-nun, "Mother" Frances Cabrini, and recently (1982), the Polish priest, Maximilian Kolbe. The canonization process has always been influenced by social and political considerations, as well as moral theology. As a model of chastity, Maria Goretti was preached to a generation of Roman Catholics in parochial schools before Vatican II. According to Debra Campbell (1988, 668), "It was impossible for a girl to attend a parochial or convent school at any time during the six decades prior to Vatican II and not learn about Maria Goretti, who constituted the core curriculum in moral theology for Catholic girls during this period."

Hagiographies often compare Maria Goretti and two saints of an earlier era, Agnes and Agatha, both tortured and killed by spurned "suitors." Saint Agnes was beheaded rather than sacrifice her virginity. Saint Agatha was subjected to various tortures, most notably tearing off her breasts. The saint's torture was typically directed to the femaleness of the victim, reflecting the elements of sadism or pornography in the legend. Hagiographies usually record the name of Agatha's attacker (Attwater 1965; Hoever 1963) just as most of the compendium biographies refer to a relationship between

Maria Goretti and her murderer, Alessandro Serenelli. In these accounts, Goretti, the innocent virgin, is the spiritual principle, and Serenelli, her murderer, the profane. She is beautiful, innocent, and good. He is evil and guilty.

In the hagiography of female virgin martyrs, the symbolic dualism of the male-female dyad establishes them as a couple reflecting the dichotomy between matter and spirit. It is impossible to imagine any sort of gender role reversal. There are no popular heroes or male saints who went to their death rather than surrender their virginity. Older women are rarely portrayed as life-threatening rapists or potentially murderous, unless it is within the supernatural realm of witches.

At the canonization of Saint Maria Goretti, Pope Pius XII read a homily which said Serenelli was a "vicious stranger burst upon her" (Second Vatican Ecumenical Council 1975, 1525). But the Pope must have known that Serenelli was no stranger. A life-threatening rape is described as "an attractive pleasure" by Pius XII: "From Maria's story carefree children and young people with their zest for life can learn not to be led astray by attractive pleasures which are not only ephemeral and empty but also sinful" (1526). The Pope, a male celibate with the power to define and construct appropriate sexuality, compared the attempted sexual assault to the sexual seduction of a passive young female.

The legends and myths of virgin martyrs reinforce passivity and the victimization of Catholic girls and women. In these accounts, the passive female exhibits a potential that is activated by the male. Women are potentially dangerous in themselves for what they might incite men to do. When a man murders a virgin in the course of a sexual assault, he facilitates for her the eternal reward of heaven that is promised to virgin martyrs. But women are responsible for men's actions. When women don't incite, but resist, they help men to be good. Thus, the virgin martyr is an ideal woman—for men.

The Symbolism of Maria Goretti

Serenelli's trial placed blame on Maria for struggling and on the Church for inspiring her struggle. A twelve-year-old facing a menacing weapon was expected to be reasonable, to submit. The assumption was that by struggling, she precipitated, even if unwittingly, her own victimization. But from the Church's perspective, her struggle is what made her a martyr and a saint. July 6 is the feast day of Saint Maria Goretti. The liturgy of her feast day mass includes the following prayer:

> O God, who among the other miracles of your power, have given even to the weaker sex the victory of martyrdom, grant, we beseech You, that we, who are celebrating the heavenly birthday of Blessed Maria, Your Virgin and Martyr, may, by her example draw nearer to You. (Hoever 1963, 261)

These cultural paradigms of virginity and martyrdom have implications for the construction of sexuality, codes of reproduction, gender identity, and life experience for Catholic women.

Anthropologists have often noted the cross-cultural concern for female chastity. Among others, Pitt-Rivers (1954) and Peristany (1966) have discussed the values of honor and shame, particularly in the Mediterranean. According to Jane Collier (1986):

> A man's honor was a function of his mother's, sisters', and wife's sexual chastity. A family's reputation depended on the sexual shame of its women and on the readiness of its men to defend with violence if need be, its women's purity. (101)

Sherry Ortner has stated that all complex agrarian societies have forms of the "virginity complex" (1978). The complex is found in societies where inheritance is associated with legitimate birth and is the basis of status inequalities. Legitimate inheritance and status or place in society is dependent upon the social perception of female chastity. The appropriate construction of female sexuality is linked to preservation of the social order and legitimate inheritance (Ortner 1978). A man's honor rests upon the control of his female relatives. The good reputation of his mother is imperative since her recognized virginity at marriage ensures publicly that he is legitimate. The public perception of his wife's "appropriate sexuality" (her good reputation) ensures that his heirs are accepted as legitimate. As Collier (1986) says:

> In such a world, women's bodies appear as gateways to all privileges. But women's bodies are gateways any man may enter. Women's penetrability is their most significant feature. The status and reputation of a family thus rest on the degree to which its women are protected from penetration—by women's own sense of sexual shame, by being locked away, and/or by the courage of family men in repelling seducers. (101)

A man's honor is contingent upon his control of others. A woman's honor is associated with her own sense of sexual shame. How others treat her affects her own personal and internal spiritual life. Sexual transgressions committed against her reflect her own lack of sexual shame even if she did not precipitate the transgression. Sexual transgressions jeopardize her place in the material and spiritual world and are the gateway to her material and spiritual disgrace and that of her family. Religious values portrayed in myths that spiritualize virginity are functional in a society based on the ownership and control of property by men.

The legends of the saints that Roman Catholic women are raised with associate female sexuality with virginity and motherhood. Personal identity and sexual identity, both associated with virginity and motherhood, are conjunctive. "Inviolate" is a synonym for virgin. The virgin has not yet been sexually violated, the mother obviously has been. Sexuality is not the gateway to autonomy for women but instead implies social and spiritual vulnerability and lack of autonomy. The cultic idealization of virginity both reflects and participates in the degradation of women, defining them as actual or potential rape victims. By being identified with the codes of procreation and patrilineal inheritance, women embody sexual shame. The lives of the females saints, primarily virgin martyrs, exemplify this construction of non-virgins and non-mothers as the embodiment of sexual shame and pollution.

In 1950, as traditional social mores were shaken in the aftermath of the horrors of World War II, the Catholic Church apparently perceived a need for an exemplar like Maria Goretti. According to DiDonato, "The military occupation by enemies and allies alike, tended to profane family life and shamefully deprave the moral fiber of the young. As never before, the spirit of Maria Goretti was needed as a virtuous hope and inspiration towards purity for girls in Italy and all lands" (1962, 157).

Maria Goretti not only exemplified the glorification of chastity and the duty of women to uphold family purity, but she had an additional use—to forgive men their sins. Maria Goretti forgave her attacker before she died. Because Maria forgave him, her mother forgave him. Because Maria and her mother could forgive him, Alessandro Serenelli could forgive himself and expect society to do likewise. Thus, the rape victim, the sexually abused girl, and the battered wife are given a message by the Catholic Church to take responsibility for their abusers, to forgive them, and by forgiving them, redeem them.

A Feminist Reading of Maria Goretti

In the Western cultural tradition, women's sexuality makes them physically and spiritually vulnerable. Their vulnerability is a necessary cultural production. A sexually autonomous woman undermines patrilineality and the legitimacy of children. Christendom and patriarchy, by turning women into the protectors of chastity, dialectically strengthened and encouraged their sexual suffering:

> It is possible that the woman in the pornographic movie . . . is a tired secular relic of this Western tradition of Christendom which links female sexuality with pain and humiliation. The alliance of pain and punishment with women and sex is clearly in line with the sexual disgust that informed Christian emotion. Men have been taught in our culture to take pleasure in the sight of a woman suffering; suffering is seen as a female virtue and it is also, obscurely, seen as sexy. (Armstrong 1986, 210)

Christianity, and Catholicism in particular, emphasizes suffering as redemptive. For women, that suffering has been rooted in sexual shame. Simply by being alive and having a body all people will suffer, but women will especially suffer because of sex. Men may contribute to, but they are not the cause of, women's shame. Women's embodiment of suffering not only affects them but also their family relationships. For example, before she died, Maria Goretti reportedly apologized to her mother for upsetting her by being murdered (DiDonato 1962). Apparently, she felt guilty for "causing" her mother pain. Her body suffered physically, and her mind suffered mental anguish.

If Maria Goretti had "preferred" to be raped rather than stabbed to death, she wouldn't be a saint today. According to the legend, she preferred to die rather than commit such an "ugly sin" (MacConastair 1951). The legend emphasizes her choice. Did she prefer death, or was she given no choice? If she did have a choice, what are the implications for Catholicism today? By today's secular standards, the twelve-year-old would not be perceived as sinful if she "chose" to be raped and live. But rape is traumatic for a female of any age or religion, and is a compounded trauma if the survivor is a virgin, since it robs her of control over the transition into adult sexuality. For Catholic women, there is the additional element of spiritual victimization portrayed in the Maria Goretti myth. Any sex outside of marriage, including rape, is associated with a female's "moral disgrace," and myths of virgin martyrs, like Maria Goretti, are used as a kind of sexual terrorism.

A motif of suffering is feminized in a virginity fetish exemplified by Maria Goretti. The cultural fetishization of female virginity reduces the female's identity to sexuality. The result is the objectification of part of the body separate from the self. Maria Goretti died in order to preserve her hymen; her physical intactness was the only metaphor for her value to her family, her church, her community, and her culture. Any other contribution she might have made didn't count.

It would be easy to dismiss virgin martyrs and the valorization of female sexual suffering as a reflection of the masculinist tradition of the Catholic Church. That dismissal ignores the societal, historical, and spiritual function of these myths. When Maria Goretti was made a saint in 1950, World War II had been over for only five years and the process of healing and forgiving and rebuilding Western civilization was still incipient. Women's roles were changing in response to spreading urbanization and increased industrialization. Maria Goretti, as a virgin martyr, became a useful reactionary symbol of patriarchal, religious, and family values.

Notes

1. The author wishes to thank Robert C. Marshall who commented on an earlier draft of this article.

Works Cited

Armstrong, Karen. 1986. *The Gospel According to Woman*. Garden City, N.Y.: Anchor Press.

Attwater, Donald. 1965. *The Avenel Dictionary of Saints*. New York: Avenel Books.

Buehrle, Maria Cecilla. 1967. *New Catholic Encyclopedia*. New York: McGraw Hill.

Campbell, Debra. 1988. "Dorothy Dohen's Reclamation of Virginity." *The Christian Century* 7/20: 667–70.

Collier, Jane F. 1986. "From Mary to Modern Woman: the Material Basis of Marianismo and its Transformation in a Spanish Village." *American Ethnologist* 13: 100–7.

Delaney, John L. 1980. *Dictionary of Saints*. Garden City, N.Y.: Doubleday.

DiDonato, Pietro. 1962. *The Penitent*. New York: Hawthorn Books.

Hoever, Hugo. 1963. *Lives of the Saints*. New York: Catholic Book Publishing.

MacConastair, Alfred. 1951. *Lily of the Marshes*. New York: Macmillan.

Ortner, Sherry. 1978. "The Virgin and the State." *Feminist Studies* 4 (1978): 19–37.

Peristany, J.G., ed. 1966. *Honour and Shame: The Values of Mediterranean Society*. London: Weidenfield & Nicholson.

Pitt-Rivers, Julian. 1954. *The People of the Sierra*. Chicago: University of Chicago Press.

Rivers, Caryl. 1973. *Aphrodite at Mid-Century*. Garden City, N.Y.: Doubleday.

Second Vatican Ecumenical Council. 1975. *The Liturgy of the Hours*. New York: Catholic Book Publishing.

Warner, Marina. 1983. *Alone of All Her Sex*. New York: Vintage.

Prophetic or Followers?
The United Church of Canada, Gender, Sexuality, and Violence against Women

TRACY TROTHEN

Violence against women and children is not a new phenomenon. It is only recently, however, that this type of violence has been clearly named a problem or issue by the churches or in wider society. Now that the issue is on the agenda, it is important to ask how the problem is being defined and how institutions such as churches are responding. As Gillian Walker points out, different institutions have defined the issue of violence against women in different ways (Walker 1990, 101). These definitions have determined, and often limited, the way in which institutions have responded. For example, when the problem is defined as a legal issue, the means employed to address it are often reduced to court actions or other judicial procedures. The danger is that the phenomenon of violence against women gets abstracted from the everyday lives of women, men, and children and cut off from the full range of reforms of the women's movement. As Marilyn Legge contends, "in order to honor women's different and specific experiences, we must ask if women's experiences of concrete suffering and sources of hope in everyday life have been adequately addressed" (Legge 1992, 5). By exploring the ways in which the issue of violence against women came to be recognized by the United Church of Canada (UCC), I hope to clarify the strengths and limitations of how the problem is currently being defined and how the reality of violence is being addressed.

Formed in 1925 by the amalgamation of the Methodist, Presbyterian, and Congregationalist Churches, the United Church of Canada has a long-standing commitment to addressing social issues and seeking justice. Church union occurred in the context of, and at least partially as the result of, the Social Gospel movement (Allen 1971, 250). Consequently, changes in theology and sociocultural analysis and awareness have occurred. Based on a conciliar model, the UCC was designed to be accountable to the various concerns and interests of its three founding churches. Often, highly contentious issues have first emerged on the UCC agenda because members at the grass roots decided that the issue should be addressed and that the UCC needed to make its position clear.[1] Since the mid eighties, "family violence" and violence against women have emerged as issues on the agenda of the UCC, partially as a result of concerns raised at the grass roots level.[2] As will become evident throughout this essay, the UCC continues to address these issues. As the official statement of United Church policy and General Council debate, the records of proceedings (*ROPs*) provide an excellent documentary record of the church's thinking over the years. Generally, every two years, since the formation of the UCC in 1925, the United Church General Council gathers to receive studies and reports, and to discuss, debate, and sometimes vote upon these submissions and other areas of concern. The General Council is composed of representatives—ordered and lay—from all pastoral charges, presbyteries, and conferences.[3] Based largely on the *ROPs*, since 1925, I will offer a brief summary of formative shifts that have occurred throughout the history of the UCC. These shifts are changes in thinking, theology, and the sociocultural context that are manifested in the *ROPs*. Furthermore, I am interested in naming these changes since I believe that they will serve to indicate some foundational reasons why the issue of violence against women first appeared as an issue on the agenda of the UCC. To complete this essay, I will situate the UCC in the broader contemporary Canadian context in terms of responses to the issue of male violence against women. This will better enable me to evaluate the importance of ongoing change in the areas that I have identified. For most of its history, violence/abuse against women and/or children was not named as an issue. Two questions must be asked: why was this violence previously not understood as an issue of violence and deep concern, and why did it emerge as an issue?

I will identify and discuss three shifts in the approach of the UCC to gender and sexuality-related issues since 1925. These changes did not occur consecutively or in chronological order. Rather, these changes were overlapping and parallel to each other, occurring gradually over time. These shifts concern the following: the understanding of sin and sexuality, the dismantling of traditional gender stereotypes, together with the erosion of the traditional understanding of family, and a developing self-critical awareness within the church. Of particular importance to these three shifts is an emerging understanding of women as moral agents. These changes are still very much in process and, I hope, will continue. As Clifford Geertz points out, symbol systems such as religions tend to be tenacious and pervasive (Geertz 1965, 1–46). For example, the symbols of sex, as representative of sin, and of the traditional patriarchal family, as representative of morality and eschatological hope, have persisted over time and have only recently begun to be challenged and alternatives offered. As will become evident, these symbols have not yet been entirely dismissed and, in some arenas, remain dominant. Furthermore, as Legge states, "historical structures are *not* objectively 'out there' but alive and well and forming the *ongoing* dynamics of the present" (Legge 1992, 26). However, a dominant desire to maintain traditional order has been increasingly challenged by a growing recognition of the oppressive nature of many of these enduring symbols. The resulting dialectical relationship between this recognition and the desire of many to hold on to tradition and order has created space for alternative, more inclusive symbols to begin to be developed. This process is necessary in order for the roots of violence to be addressed and lasting change wrought. A self-conscious awareness of our story is necessary if we are to continue this process of struggle and hope. Without a knowledge of and a familiarity with our stories and, therefore, our identities, we are in danger of reverting to previous oppressive symbol systems that serve to keep us ignorant of necessary institutional change and perpetuate the status quo.

Sin and Sexuality

The UCC's understanding of human sexuality, as reflected by the ROPs, has changed significantly since 1925; the understanding of human sexuality has been transformed from primarily an act-centered ethic to primarily a relational ethic. By this I mean that in the earlier years issues concerning sexuality were defined primarily in terms of the rightness or wrongness of certain sexual acts, whereas in later years, sexuality came to be understood primarily in terms of the quality of the relationships involved. However, it is important to note that although the quality of the relationship gained importance as a criterion for evaluating the expression of human sexuality, deontological ethical reasoning continues to play a significant role in the evaluation of sexual relationships.[4] Moreover, the understanding of human sexuality initially tended to be limited to the act of sexual intercourse but, over time, came to be understood to encompass much more.

From a moral standpoint, sexual expression was understood to be exclusive to the marital relationship, although within marriage, as the authors of the 1932 report, *The Meaning and Responsibilities of Christian Marriage* contended, sexual activity was not believed to be limited to purely procreative purposes (*ROP 1932, 279–81*). The 1936 General Council confirmed this view and supported the availability and use of contraceptives after concluding that "there is no religious obligation to have intercourse only when no precaution is taken against resulting conception" (*ROP 1936, 326*). Thus, although the primary purpose of sex within marriage was procreation, the UCC acknowledged that sexual interaction purely for pleasure and bonding, free from the concern of a possible pregnancy, could benefit the marital relationship and, most importantly, help to strengthen family life (*ROP 1936, 326–27*).

A belief in women's moral agency does not seem to have been the motivating factor behind the UCC's support of contraception, as the protracted controversy that followed this decision indicates. The decision to support the availability of contraceptives was a long-standing source of anxiety for many UCC members: would this move serve to promote extramarital sex and therefore lead to national moral disaster? (*ROP 1936, 328; ROP 1946, 134*[5] and *ROP 1948, 132 and 362*) Were women able to be sexually responsible without the fear of an unwanted pregnancy to control their behavior?

The decreasing age and increasing number of girls admitted to "redemptive homes" because they "break the moral code" is cited as further evidence of this increasing danger (*ROP 1958, 411*).[6] The mission of the superintendents of these homes was, in large part, to "save . . . ['young girls'] from moral disaster" (*ROP 1925*, 127). Significantly, the authors of these reports refer to girls in these homes as "inmates" (*ROP 1930*, 109). These unwed girls and young women were placed in these homes primarily because of pregnancy, prostitution or delinquency. Clearly, the nature of most of their sins centered around sex; their crime being deviation from the female's sexual moral code.[7] Since morality and sexuality were typically equated, and females were seen as the primary caretakers of the sexual moral code, then through the redemption of those girls and young women who threaten the sexual codes, the country could approach salvation (*ROP 1932*, 109 and *ROP 1946*, 112–13).

The 1960s witnessed the emergence of greater concern for the relational quality of sexual acts within marriage.[8] For instance, the authors of the 1960 report on *Christian Marriage and Family—Toward a Christian Understanding of Sex, Love, Marriage* raised the issue of "mutual consent":

> Mutual consent is an important element of that sexual union which fulfils the intent of creation and satisfies the needs of both partners. Where consent is not mutual the personal integrity of both partners is desecrated. Harm is done to both victim and violator. Moreover, in order to be completely in accord with the intent of creation, the mutual consent must be consent to marriage and not just consent to a particular act of sexual intercourse. (*ROP 1960*, 157)

This concern for "mutual consent" within the marital relationship is significant although it is also important to note the authors' contention that "harm is done to *both* the victim and violator"[9] and that this issue is not defined in gender-specific terms.

By the mid seventies, concern was clearly directed more towards the quality of the relationship within which sexual acts were engaged than towards the sexual acts per se. For instance, in 1977 the General Council noted that pornography was sinful, not because it dealt with sex, but because it served to objectify God's people and communicate hatred and abuse of women and children (*ROP 1977*, 154). Previously, since the early forties, the time of World War II, the church had expressed its concern regarding the moral "challenge" to the family and the nation posed by "printed and photographic material and movies of the baser sort" (*ROP 1942*, 312), whereas recognition of the abuse of women and children in pornography is quite new.

This awakening concern with the quality of the relationship was heightened during the eighties. The highly controversial 1980 study document—*In God's Image . . . Male & Female*—contended as a central thesis, that in and of itself, sexuality is neither divine nor demonic (UCC 1980, 27). Importantly, the term sexuality took on a much broader meaning and pertained to us all as embodied beings, as opposed to meaning only the act of sexual intercourse. The critical factor was the quality of the relationship within which sexual intimacy was expressed. Sin was defined not in act-centered terms but as the violation of right relationship (UCC 1980, 84). Council approved a subsequent document—*Gift, Dilemma and Promise—A Report and Affirmations on Human Sexuality*—in 1984. Although quite different from the 1980 document in terms of its conclusions, this report affirmed the same central beliefs as those expressed above. One particular issue that resulted in much heated debate, in these two reports, was sexual orientation. Over much controversy, the 1988 General Council declared that one's sexual orientation is neither good nor bad in and of itself. The quality of relationship was the important factor (UCC 1988; *ROP* 1990, 198–202).

Although the quality of relationship is named the critical factor in determining the ethical nature of the expression of human sexuality, the authors of this document did not yet recognize the reality and impact of the systemic gender power imbalance in our yet patriarchal culture. For instance, the authors claimed that the exclusivity of the marital relationship can lead to extreme "possessiveness and jealousy" or to deep-seated "resentment for the loss of his or her independent lifestyle." They argue that the resulting anger sometimes leads to abusive episodes: "the stored anger may become expressed in harassment and put-downs, or explode into acts of physical and sexual violence" (UCC 1984, 26). This theory is non-gender specific and implies that this violence is the manifestation of internalized, built-up anger that eventually becomes uncontrollable. Pathologized and individualized, this explanation fails to recognize the sociocultural gender power imbalance.

However, in 1986, the Women in Ministry Committee drafted a policy statement on sexual harassment that pointed specifically to the power imbalance between men and women as a central causal factor of sexual harassment. The exploitation of an unequal power relationship, as is the case regarding sexual harassment, is named sinful.[10] Their policy statement reflects this understanding:

> Sexual harassment is a sin. We believe that women and men are equal before God and in creation. Sexual harassment is a violation of the integrity of persons based on unequal power relationships. Sexual harassment degrades persons and does not allow their gifts of creativity and wholeness to be used in the Church. Jesus emphasizes mutuality and respect in relationships. To harass is to misuse power and to distort relationships. It leads to alienation and distrust. (*ROP* 1986, 207–8 and 221)

The quality of the relationship was understood to be the criterion for determining what constitutes ethically acceptable patterns of interaction. Within this criterion are several clearly stated norms: men and women are equal both spiritually and on earth, sexual harassment is wrong because it is wrong to degrade people, and mutuality and respect are essential to whole relationships. Moreover, at this point, a recognition of the gender power imbalance also informed the development of this policy and theological understanding.

Thus, we see a gradual shift in the understanding of human sexuality between the years 1925 and 1990. In brief, the UCC formerly understood any act of sexual intercourse outside marriage as sinful and a threat to the welfare of the entire nation. Sexual intercourse inside marriage was unquestioningly accepted, although it was expected that the marital relationship would be characterized by mutual love and respect. Beginning in the sixties, a relational understanding of sexuality provided a basis for evaluating some forms of marital sex. It was no longer assumed that all marital sex was ethically acceptable. By the early eighties the quality of the relationship was a more relevant criterion for assessing the ethics of sexual behavior than whether or not the partners were married. Monogamy continues to be upheld as normative and desirable in covenantal relationships. However, the manner in which each person treats the other (e.g., with respect, as a mutual partner and autonomous agent) is equally essential; indeed, the two are often inextricably bound together. This recognition combined with a growing understanding of the reality and implications of a systemic gender power imbalance, has served to create the *base* for a recognition that male sexual violence against women is widespread and is primarily an issue of *violence* not sex (Fortune 1983, 30–33).

Gender Stereotypes[11] and the Family

Throughout the greater part of UCC history, women have generally been expected to follow their vocation of wife and mother and to devote themselves to the care and nurture of their husband—who was understood to be responsible for the economic well-being of the family—and, particularly, their children. Women, in this designated role, were considered central to the stability of the family unit. The preservation of this family unit was a constant concern for the UCC particularly throughout the thirties, forties and fifties. The well-being of the family was believed to have been inextricably linked to the well-being of "the nation and her citizens overseas and at home" (*ROP* 1942, 83).[12] The onset and duration of World War II amplified this concern. Moreover, as with sexuality, there was an eschatological component to this issue: the preservation of the family was believed to be essential to the coming Kingdom of God (*ROP* 1940, 89). Further to this, one could speculate that the war brought the coming of the "Kingdom" to the forefront of many minds.

The Social Gospel movement propounded a radical commitment to mutual love and solidarity with the oppressed (Scott and Vlastos 1989). In accordance with these values, the UCC sought to support what it perceived to be the humanity and agency of women. For instance, the authors of the 1932 report entitled *The Meaning and Responsibilities of Christian Marriage* expressed appreciation for the changing status of women:

> the Church would view with the most serious misgiving any practices which menace the slowly acquired gain of centuries in enhanced respect for womanhood, especially in the emancipation of womanhood either within or outside marriage. (*ROP* 1932, 282)

The "emancipation of womanhood" was supported as long as this emancipation did not threaten the basic social order and, in particular, the order of the family. To this end, the authors of this report contended that the primary function of marriage was "the rearing of children and the protection of the mother during their period of infancy" (*ROP* 1932, 277). The bearing and rearing of children by women was thought to be the highest and best example of the then-lauded virtue of sacrificial love.[13] The Christian family, as defined by this report, consisted of two parents—a woman and a man—and their children. Ideally, there was mutual care and love between all family members (*ROP* 1932, 280). This understanding of the nature of the Christian family was reiterated through to the sixties (*ROP* 1946, 118 and *ROP* 1960, 174).

When the role of the woman as wife, mother, and self-sacrificing caregiver began to be challenged, confusion, fear, and struggle resulted. In the thirties and forties, UCC reports indicated that the "new freedoms" gained by women were to be celebrated but were also viewed with suspicion, particularly concerning how they would affect the family as traditionally understood. For instance, Lydia Gruchy persisted for ten years before she became the first ordained woman in 1936. Notably, even at Gruchy's ordination service, a speaker felt compelled to assert the power and control of men over women:

> We have come tonight to mark a step in our church's history—a development which we owe, not to the intransigent demand and agitation of women, but in the first instance, perhaps to our revered and affectionately esteemed Dr. E. H. Oliver. His knightly and chivalrous attitude and advocacy have finally prevailed. (*The New Outlook* November 18, 1936).

Following this momentous decision, there were many gender-specific restrictions placed on women in order to be considered eligible for ordination. These restrictions were in accordance with traditional gender role expectations: women who were raising children or who were married (or planning to be married) and were of childbearing age, or who did not pass a test that indicated their "emotional stability," (*ROP* 1948, 123–25) were not considered to be eligible for ordination.[14] Moreover, in the fifties ordained women were expected to pursue different ministries from ordained men. Specifically, they were to focus more on children and youth as this was understood to be women's natural role (*ROP* 1954, 174).

Further examples of this tension between the recognition of women's autonomy and agency and the desire to maintain traditional gender roles can be seen in the aforementioned debate surrounding the council's acceptance of birth control and in the controversy regarding the increasing availability of paid employment for women which occurred mostly as a result of the war (*ROP* 1944, 307–8). For instance, reports from the redemptive homes indicated great concern regarding the increase in the number of working single mothers:

> The fact that unmarried mothers can quickly find work, has resulted in their stay in our redemptive homes being made all too short, with the result that not a few newly born babies do not receive the love and attention that they should have from their own mothers. (*ROP* 1944, 269)[15]

These women were not fulfilling their roles as full-time family caregivers. Women's place was still believed to be the domestic sphere while men's was the public sphere. Later, the Council reiterated this claim declaring that "family life" depends "upon the spiritual resources of the parents and particularly of the mother" and that "there is no substitute for a mother's care for young children" (*ROP* 1954, 232). However, in the sixties a watershed report by the Commission on the Gainful Employment of Married Women concluded that there was no harm done to the families of working wives and mothers and, furthermore, these women needed the support of the church (*ROP* 1962, 262–77). Interestingly, there was still some tension in this area as evidenced by the continued restrictions on women's eligibility for ordained ministry (*ROP* 1962, 393–96). Challenges to and defenses of the traditional gender roles were occurring within the church as well as in "secular" society.

However, challenging traditional family gender roles has been a slow journey. The 1960 report of the Commission on Christian Marriage and Divorce, *Toward a Christian Understanding of Sex, Love, Marriage*, reaffirmed traditional gender roles within the marital relationship: "Men are expected to play the roles of lover, husband, and father. Women are expected to accept men as lovers, to be their wives, to conceive, bear, feed, and cherish their children" (*ROP* 1960, 174). Men's role was active whereas women's role continued to be relatively passive and nurturing.

At the same time that women were strongly encouraged to remain at home caring for their husband and children, the traditional Christian family was protected further by teachings against divorce. The 1946 report regarding *Christian Marriage and the Christian Home* named divorce sinful and called for "every means of reconciliation [to] be employed for the salvation of the home" (*ROP* 1946, 147).[16] The war had just ended and the need to return to some sense of order and stability was very strong at this time. At least partially as a result of this context, the preservation of the home and family took precedence over virtually any other need or ethical cause. In 1956, this view of divorce as sinful was repeated (*ROP* 1956, 90).[17] In the fifties, the Marriage Guidance Council was created with the mandate to save marriages (*ROP* 1956, 267 and *ROP* 1958, 265). It was simply assumed that the well-being of *all* family members was best served by preserving the family unit itself—it was not then recognized that the family itself often involves an unjust distribution of power and privilege.

In 1962, the UCC began to recognize that in some families, divorce is a necessity in order to protect the physical safety of some family members. The 1962 report of the Commission on Christian Marriage and Divorce—*Marriage Breakdown, Divorce, Remarriage: A Christian Understanding*—argued this point:

> In some cases divorce may be sought solely to achieve personal protection by the legal separation it enforces. A woman who has separated from her husband because of cruelty, drunkenness or mental instability may not have adequate protection under the law so long as she is married to him. (*ROP* 1962, 142)[18]

Regarding marital separation, the authors of the report contend that "it is better for some married partners to separate rather than continue to abuse each other grievously, to harm their children, or to demoralize their neighborhood" (*ROP* 1962, 154). Thus, the emergence of a more pronounced tension between the recognition that some marriages are damaging and potentially dangerous, and the desire to preserve marriage and the traditional family can be observed. The needs of family members were beginning to challenge the absolute priority of the preservation of the family as traditionally understood. As important as this move is, it must be recognized that the church maintains the powerful message that sustaining the family unit is one of the most important Christian duties, particularly for women. Given this, it would likely have been (and often continues to be) more popularly admirable, as well as more personally acceptable, for an abused woman to present the appearance of "family bliss" (Bussert 1986) and to be the long-suffering sacrificial victim for the sake of preserving the family (Shapiro and Turner 1988, 123–24; and NiCarthy 1988, 120).

In 1974 Council approved a report affirming the "Permanence of Christian Marriage" (*ROP* 1974, 284), stressing that couples must enter the marriage relationship with the *intention* of permanence, but recognizing that in spite of all intentions there can arise reasons that necessitate separation or divorce. This recogition underscores the realization that the continuation of a marriage is not desirable at any cost. Shortly thereafter, the UCC Task Force on Women and Partnership Between Men and Women in Church and Society, and the subsequent Working Group, began to note the damaging role of gender stereotyping on family members. The 1977 General Council identified exclusive language as a painful issue for many women (*ROP* 1977, 270–80). The authors of this report acknowledged that this was a newly named issue and, as such, would require much time and work before root change, manifested in both words and actions, occurred (*ROP* 1977, 281). In 1980, the authors of the study document *In God's Image . . . Male and Female* affirmed the belief that gender stereotyping is sinful since it serves to alienate and limit people. A desire to preserve the family as understood in a traditional sense was being tempered by the emergence of a critical eye.

The eighties were groundbreaking regarding the perception of the family. The Task Force on the Changing Roles of Women and Men in Church and Society, in 1982, identified the root of the problem of family gender stereotyping as a power imbalance between men and women (*ROP* 1982, 403–4). These task force members considered themselves a task force on sexism, understanding 'sexism' to mean "any attitude, action or structure which discriminates against people on the basis of gender" (*ROP* 1982, 403).[19] Thus, in the early eighties, the issues of gender stereotyping and exclusive language became identified, at least by part of the UCC, as manifestations of the greater issue of sexism. Building on this insight, in 1984, the Task Force on Pornography drew direct links between gender stereotyping and the violent, destructive nature of pornography. Stereotypes prescribe certain roles for both men and women that lend themselves to the violence of pornography:

society encourages men to express anger and aggression through sexual violence. Pornography sets up women as scapegoats for male anger with its obsession with rape, bondage, snuff films, mutilation, dissection of female anatomy; its fascination with humiliating, conquering, penetrating, sodomizing and objectifying women. . . . Pornography lies about men in that it says they can only be violent, angry and hateful. Pornography also promotes the lie that women get sexual pleasure from pain. (*ROP* 1984, 315)

The authors of this report argued that stereotyping is the primary cause of male sexual violence against women.[20]

By the mid eighties, the UCC specifically named violence against women and children, particularly in the context of "family violence," as important issues for the church. The UCC's response to these issues can be divided into three categories: policy and protocol, education, and ecumenical and networking efforts. Initially, most of the work was reactive and focused on the development of policy and procedure. In 1988 the working group on family violence wrote a protocol on wife abuse for church staff (Winnipeg Presbytery 1988). The authors designed this protocol as a "step-by-step guide for responding to cases of family violence." Based on other protocols already developed by other helping professions, this protocol is an important step in the UCC, if slow in coming. Three "general principles" cited by the authors are the insurance of the physical "safety of the woman and her children", and the importance of "believing" and "affirming" the woman (Winnipeg Presbytery 1988, 2). The protocol begins with a confession of the collusion of the church, historically and currently, in the abuse of women, a brief discussion of some relevant theological issues, and a call for breaking the silence in the church, and for transformation and healing (Winnipeg Presbytery 1988, 3–6). The guidelines are clear and helpful both for emergencies and ongoing pastoral involvement. This document is an educational tool for church staff as well as a protocol on wife abuse.

More recently, in 1993 the Council received and approved, for official use, a report produced by the Division of Ministry Personnel and Education (MP&E) entitled *Sexual Abuse (Sexual Harassment, Sexual Exploitation, Pastoral Sexual Misconduct, Sexual Assault) and Child Abuse*. Developed by the Women in Ministry Committee, which "has been engaged in education, advocacy, and policy development regarding sexual abuse" since 1984, this extensive report contains a theological statement, a policy statement, definitions and in-depth procedural guidelines. The authors of this report make the deontological claim that God intends that all people have the right to "enjoy a full life free from abuse and injustice." "Sexual and physical harassment, abuse and exploitation" are defined as sinful since they violate "persons" and the norm of mutuality. These violations "arise from unequal power relationships, usually based on age, gender, and/or position of authority." Moreover, the "church has a particular responsibility for the protection of the vulnerable, the weak, and those with limited voice," if we as a community desire to model ourselves after the example of the historical Jesus. The authors substantiate these claims with scriptural passages (UCC 1993, 3).

Throughout this document, the authors focus on the root of abuse which they claim to be the exploitation of unequal power relationships. As a result of this recognition and the above theological claims, the stated purpose of the procedures for addressing "cases of sexual abuse: harassment, exploitation, misconduct, assault and child abuse is to protect the vulnerable, stop the abuse, and to promote restoration/healing" (UCC 1993, 6). A significant part of healing for the abused involves accountability of the offender: some kind of restoration to the victim, acknowledgement, apology, genuine remorse and repentance. Moreover, the authors clearly state that even if all of this occurs on the part of the offender, forgiveness by the abused person is not expected and it "does not mean forgetting the experience." Forgiveness, meaning a "letting go" of the power of the experience over one's life, may come after repentance, but only after repentance and time (UCC 1993, 22, 27–29).

In recognition of the systemic imbalance of power between the genders, the authors of the report concluded that at least two-thirds of the members of the conference coordinating committees are to be women: "Because women can more easily speak to the reality of women's experience than men can, and because the vast majority of those experiencing sexual abuse: harassment, exploitation, misconduct, assault are women, it is important that the make-up of the co-ordinating committee reflect those realities." (UCC 1993, 9). For similar reasons, pastoral relations come under particular scrutiny in this document. The quality of relationship, rather than the morality of sexual acts, per se, is the focus of much concern regarding sexual relations between a minister and someone under his/her pastoral care. This document names the sexualization of any such relationship as "unethical because: it is a violation of role; it is a misuse of power and authority; it takes advantage of vulnerability; it reduces the possibility of meaningful consent" (UCC 1993, 25–27).

The authors of this document place the physical safety and spiritual, psychological, and emotional well-being of the victim as primary concerns. They designed the procedures giving these concerns priority, but there is also care taken to hear the accused's story in the "rare" event that the complainant is not telling the truth (UCC 1993, 24). The authors clearly state that this is indeed rare and that all persons involved in the proceedings as committee members, etc., will be educated regarding the dynamics of such abuse.

In 1993 the working group on family violence developed a protocol for child abuse. The goal is the same as that named in 1988: "Our goal is that this protocol may help all of us working in the church to hear the cries of those in our midst, and to have ways to respond once we recognize the cry." (Winnipeg Presbytery 1993, 2). Child abuse is broken down into three types of abuse: physical, emotional, and sexual. Definitions and indicators—physical and behavioral—are outlined for each type of abuse. Clearly stated responses to child abuse of all types are listed, beginning with the need to listen, to believe and reassure the child. Referral agencies are listed; the importance of making referrals to "specially trained counsellors or agencies," unless you have specific training in sexual abuse counselling, is stressed. Helpful suggestions for communicating with children are included.

Importantly, included in this protocol is a training and education section for church workers and volunteers. Beginning with the ethical claims that we are all made in God's image, that "all abuse is a violation of God's will," and that we are all called as Christians "to oppose the abuse, to say clearly that it must end, to comfort the victims and bring healing, to challenge the victimizers and bring judgement," the authors proceed to an analysis and deconstruction of scripture that has been used to justify child abuse (Winnipeg Presbytery 1993, 12–13). The authors conclude that, based on Jesus' ministry, "there is nothing inherently sacred about a family—it all depends on how we relate to each other. Are we doing what God wants?" (Winnipeg Presbytery 1993, 13–15). The quality of relationship is given decisive precedence over the maintenance of the appearance of a traditional family unit.

Equally importantly, under a section entitled "Paths to Healing and Some Roadblocks on the Way," relevant and controversial theological issues are addressed. For example, the authors explore the meaning of forgiveness, concluding that forgiveness can neither be forced, nor should it be, and "There can be no forgiveness without justice." Also, the church's historical glorification of suffering is named and critiqued in light of the incredible damage that such a theology has on victims of child abuse (or any abuse).[21] The value of expressions of anger (which women, in particular, are often told to deny in traditional Christian theology), the importance and relatedness of inclusive God-imagery (particularly where "Father" language is used), and the theology of "honoring thy parents" are all issues that are discussed (Winnipeg Presbytery 1993, 17–21). Recognition of the power that our traditional understandings of gender roles, the family, and sexuality have in maintaining the conditions for violence against women, and how our faith serves to perpetuate and/or challenge these ideologies is a necessary precursor to realizing the end of such violence.

In the realm of education, the UCC has attempted to raise this awareness. In 1985 a training event was held for church leaders on wife abuse and later, in 1987, the UCC's Division of Mission in Canada (DMC) produced a video entitled *One in Ten* which dealt with "the reality of wife abuse, community response and the role of the church" (*ROP* 1990, 502). These resources have been directed primarily at church members and leaders.[22] The DMC also published a series of pamphlets addressing various forms of violence in families.

In 1988 DMC produced a training manual entitled *Ending Violence in Families—A Training Program for Pastoral Care Workers*. The purpose of this publication is to raise consciousness "about the extent of family violence," to train church workers how to recognize possible "violence in families," and to offer practical suggestions regarding intervention. Morris argues throughout her manual that the sanctity of the patriarchal family is a root cause of the perpetuation of family violence: "the maintenance of the family unit [is placed] before the health and safety of women, children and the elderly within the family" (Morris 1988, 7). Unfortunately, the title is problematic. As both

Walker and the Canadian panel have pointed out, the term "family violence" focuses attention on the damage done to the family instead of the gendered nature of woman abuse:

> the term "family violence" was widely used in both research literature and service delivery in the 1970s and 1980s to describe what actually constitutes abuse of women—not family. We feel that the term 'family violence' masks the huge spectrum of violence that women encounter outside their intimate relationships or families. (The Canadian Panel on Violence Against Women 1993, 6–7)

The use of this term reflects the power that the sanctity of the patriarchal family continues to hold.

In more recent years, the UCC has begun to focus more on proactive responses to woman abuse. One such important response has been an increased focus on education around the family and the meaning of family. The Working Unit on Sexuality, Marriage and Family produced a revised definition of the family in 1987. It recognizes the wide variety of families without explicitly stating examples. The definition reads, in part, "By family we mean persons who are joined together by reason of mutual consent (marriage, social contract or covenant) or by birth or adoption/placement." Since then, pamphlets entitled "Blended Families" (UCC 1990) and "Spirited Families" (UCC 1992) have been distributed, both of which offer alternative symbols to the traditional understanding of family. The most specific example of who could comprise a family, in the latter pamphlet, is the sketch on the front page depicting two women, a girl and a dog. The most recent endeavour of DMC is a proposal for a congregational study guide and video series on family well-being and unhealthy families.

A draft proposal from the Sexuality Education for Children and Youth Task Group, in September 1992, expresses a felt need to further clarify and communicate our understanding of sexuality, as a faith community, to children, youth and families. The proposal acknowledges the work of the UCC, historically, in this area, and calls on the UCC community to further pursue this.

Ecumenical networking on violence against women and children continues to be an important concern. The Church Council on Justice and Corrections, on which the UCC is represented, has been and continues to be actively involved in work on violence against women and children. For example, in 1988, they published *Family Violence in a Patriarchal Culture—A Challenge to Our Way of Living*. The stated purpose of this publication "is to give expression to the hurt in Canadian families, to seek ways to make that hurt more speakable, to open us to deeper understandings of the roots and causes of violence, to help each of us attend to the pain in our communities and to begin a process of healing" (Church Council on Justice and Corrections 1988, 1). Further examples of similar organizations include the Women's Inter-Church Council, who have produced a much used resource entitled *Hands to End Violence Against Women* (Women's Inter-Church Council 1988) and a relatively new ecumenical group—the "Inter-Church

Working Group on Violence and Sexual Assault"—whose stated purpose is "to foster ecumenical reflection, understanding, networking, witness, and action concerning issues of sexual abuse and other forms of violence in families and communities" (Kennedy 1993, 1). Work needs to continue to be shared among denominations in order that a critical dialogue can be fostered and self-awareness and critique further developed.

Since its formation, the UCC has struggled with the changing role of women and, related to this, the changing understanding of the family. The issues and the UCC's responses have never been clear cut. The tension between the recognition of women as moral agents and the desire to maintain order and, therefore, traditional gender roles, is a theme throughout UCC history. Moreover, the tension between the desire to preserve the sacredness of the traditional patriarchal "Christian family" and the growing recognition that within this sacred domain, destructive and even life-threatening behavior can lurk, has gradually increased over the years. These changes must continue, for, "[U]ntil sex roles are eliminated, until the family no longer serves as that convenient arena for male violence, until wifebeating is no longer a logical extension of male domination, in other words, as long as sexism exists, the beatings [and other male violence against women] will continue" (Cole 1982, 66).

The Church and Critique

1. Internal Critique and Confession

As the family became increasingly open to critique, so too did the church family. During the early years of the Social Gospel movement, the church saw itself as part of the solution to the country's problems (Allen 1971; Scott and Vlastos 1989). In more recent years, particularly since the advent of the second wave of feminism in the early seventies, the UCC began to recognize that it could be part of the problem.

In the earlier years, the UCC, along with other churches, assumed the role of the conscience of the nation. As previously noted, the UCC saw itself as protecting the survival and salvation of the entire nation through its efforts to safeguard the family. The church took on the mission of waging war on the evils of the public realm that threatened the sanctity of the home.

Some questioning of long-held beliefs concerning marriage and divorce began in the sixties (ROP 1962, 142), but it was not until the late seventies that two noticeable changes occurred regarding the role of the UCC in areas pertaining to gender and human sexuality. First, there was the emergence of open internal debate and critique. By this I do not mean simply the debate that naturally emerges when a motion is put forward. Rather, I am referring to a broadly based and ongoing internal critique. In 1980, the Division of Mission in Canada challenged the church to become more active in issues related to the status of women (ROP 1980, 155). At least partially in response to this general concern, the Executive approved the formation of the Task Force on the Changing Roles of Women and Men in Church and Society (ROP 1982, 399).

Significant to this discussion is the ongoing critique articulated by these task forces and, more recently, by the subsequent Committee on Sexism. The work of these groups was not always readily embraced. In 1982, the task force accused the Executive and Council of attempting to coopt and silence their voice of dissent and challenge to the status quo (*ROP* 1982, 405–6). Later, the subsequent Committee on Sexism identified a similar frustration with the Executive of the UCC. The 1988 General Council resolved

> that the General Council, through the Standing Committee on Sexism, ask each church court to examine attitudes, policies, and practices to identify where sexism is operative and to develop educational programmes and systematic ways to assist in eradicating such practices. (*ROP* 1988, 113)

The committee reported in 1990 that questionnaires were sent to each conference executive secretary asking what the conferences and presbyteries were doing to address sexism. Four of the ten conferences did not respond. The responses that were received showed that sexism continues to be a problem. In order to fulfil the rest of the above mandate, the committee met with the General Council Executive in November 1989. The committee decided that they would focus on two main areas at this meeting: "gender analysis and power equity in groups" (*ROP* 1990, 251). Unfortunately, the Committee did not feel that the meeting was successful:

> Many of the items on the Executive's agenda were power equity issues and yet they were not viewed by the Executive as issues of sexism. The Committee felt devalued and marginalized. . . . Ironically, the massacre of fourteen women in Montreal happened only two weeks after the Executive Meeting. (*ROP* 1990, 252)[23]

On the one hand, it is unfortunate that this type of critique needs to be made; however, on the other hand, I find it hopeful that it *can* be made.

The second change that occurred concerning the role of the UCC in these issues is the emergence of a confessional response. The 1984 General Council as a whole confessed the "church's complicity in sexism" (*ROP* 1984, 90). Furthermore, at the same Council, the task force argued that the time had come to be critically aware of the church family:

> Many of us have been taught that the church is different from other institutions, in the way that it is structured and in the way that it functions. We believe that it is important to de-mystify and de-idealize that notion that the church as an institution is unique and therefore better and sinless. (*ROP* 1984, 499)

This critical theme continues in the UCC. However, in the 1988 records of proceedings, the report of the Committee on Sexism concluded that although changes have been made, sexism still permeates the UCC:

> We believe that significant inroads have been made . . . [but] [s]exism is evident still in our structures, throughout our theology and faith

expression, in our concept of family, in economic policies, in theological education, in our very image of ministry. It is an issue that affects us all. (*ROP* 1988, 350)

These moves are symptomatic of a more general change in the role of the church itself; from being the nation's moral conscience, the church is very gradually moving to a new identity: that of witness to justice and peace, in an effort to follow the model of Jesus Christ, even when that means seeing the sometimes painful reality of our own lives.

2. *The UCC Located in the Wider Canadian Context*

A second integral component of self-critique is the locating of oneself in the wider sociocultural context. Contextually, the DMC questioned the prophetic nature of the church's response to women's concerns—

> The church which once played a prophetic role in justice issues now lags behind the state in many of these areas. The church as a whole has taken some positive steps in relation to the justice issues as they concern women. . . . If the UCC is to give leadership in women's concerns it must continue to work on two fronts: within its own courts and inner life, and as a goad and example to society as a whole. (*ROP* 1980, 155)

Are there any parallels between the developments in the church in this area and Canadian society in general? Has the UCC taken a prophetic role in solidarity with the disadvantaged? As will become evident, the answer is twofold: in some areas the UCC has acted as a goad and prophet to society but in others, different segments of wider society, particularly women's groups,[24] have prodded the UCC to further self-examination and action.

The women's groups emerging with the second wave of feminism, beginning in the late sixties, first raised issues related to sexuality, particularly contraception and abortion (Adamson et al. 1988, 45). The sixties were brought to a close with legislation that changed section 179 (c) of the 1892 Canadian *Criminal Code* in that it "ended the ban on the advertising and selling of contraceptives" (McLaren 1986, 136). The same legislation made abortions legal when approved by a Therapeutic Abortion Committee (TAC). This was far from satisfactory for many feminists and a call for equal access to abortion for any woman who requested it resounded throughout the land in 1970 (Adamson et al. 1988, 46; Wall 1982, 19; McDonnell 1982, 32).[25]

The UCC was clearly ahead of the state regarding its positions in these areas. As previously discussed, in 1936 General Council supported the use and availability of contraceptives, albeit with motivation that was not rooted in a belief in women's moral agency. Nonetheless, at the time it was a radical move. Perhaps the most pivotal contemporary issue directly tied to women's moral agency is the abortion issue (Harrison 1983). In 1971, General Council received and approved a report on abortion and contraception which argued that abortion was an issue of "personal conscience" and "should be a private matter between a woman and her doctor" (*ROP* 1971, 157 and 160). The

1980 report on abortion affirmed this controversial position—that "abortion should be a personal matter between a woman and her doctor"—and was subsequently approved by Council (UCC 1982). Significantly, similar wording was used to express the church's stand regarding contraception in 1936; in both cases the issue is described as a "personal" and "private" matter. As feminists argue, the personal is by its very nature political. The stand taken by the UCC indicates at best an attempt to recognize women as moral agents in the context of an unresolved tension between the recognition that abortion is a serious issue that affects *all* of us in some way and the desire to maintain the less painful illusion that abortion is an issue restricted to an exceptional few. At worst, it is indicative of a dualistic split between the public and private realms in which the issue is deliberately silenced and avoided. Interestingly, on January 28, 1988, the Supreme Court of Canada took a position similar to that of the UCC when it struck down section 251 of the *Criminal Code*; TACs were no longer legislated since the court decided that abortion was a "[woman's] personal and private decision."[26]

During the seventies, women's organizations—both grass-roots and institutional—proliferated and the number of issues addressed multiplied.[27] Prodded by this wider concern with women's issues, task forces concerned with women's issues and gender issues began to emerge in the UCC in the mid seventies. In 1973, the first rape crisis center was opened in Canada, in Vancouver, British Columbia (CASAC 1986, 13). In 1975 the Canadian Association of Sexual Assault Centres (CASAC) was formed and by 1978 included twenty-one crisis centres. By 1982, the number had increased to forty-eight (Toronto Rape Crisis Centre 1985, 67). The mid to late seventies was a time when feminist groups began to pay particular attention to the widespread nature of physical and sexual violence against women and the need to respond to it collectively and on a practical level. Importantly, the UCC recognized as early as 1962 that violence did exist in marital relationships and, as a result, agreed that divorce was necessary in these instances in order to protect persons in the family and neighborhood. Although an example recorded in the ROPs, to illustrate this type of situation, depicted the husband as violent towards his wife, the official statement does not recognize spousal violence as a gender issue (*ROP* 1962, 142).

By the late seventies, pornography had become a serious concern for many feminists, particularly radical feminists, working against male violence against women (The Canadian Panel on Violence Against Women 1993, 49). Women Against Rape in British Columbia called for November 5, 1977, to be a "National Day of Protest against Violence against Women." Women marched down Yonge Street in Toronto on this day and collected in front of a pornography cinema where "the demonstration became violent and some women were arrested" (Adamson et al. 1988, 72). The link between pornography and violence against women and children has been a dominant concern and hotly debated topic in Canada ever since, drawing lines of division within the feminist movement as well as other segments of society (Bjorge 1992, 5). The current legislation regarding pornography was established in 1959 and is found in the *Criminal Code*, section 163, under the heading "Offenses Tending to Corrupt Morals." It was not until February 27, 1992 that the Supreme Court of Canada recognized a link between "hard-core pornography . . . [and] violence against women" (Bjorge 1992, 5). Similar to the UCC in the past, Canadian law was primarily concerned with the corruption of "sexual morals" rather than the abuse of women and children. Sooner than the court system, but clearly after women's groups, the ROPs show a recognition of this link between violence and pornography by 1977.

The late seventies to mid eighties witnessed a new focus on racism (Adamson et al. 1988, 61, 83, 108–10) and heterosexism both within the women's movement and as issues intertwined with sexism. From this time on, "moving beyond a white middle-class viewpoint" has been a concern and goal of the Canadian women's movement (Adamson et al. 1988, 79). Working towards this goal has involved forming alliances and networking with various organizations—both inside and outside the women's movement—which have been important in challenging and supporting the women's movement. The importance of solidarity among those working for systemic change became increasingly clear. In their 1982 report to the Council, the UCC's Task Force on the Changing Roles of Women and Men in Church and Society also recognized the necessity of addressing racism and classism when addressing sexism: "We believe that to understand and deal with sexism we need to examine the areas of racism and classism because they are all linked; they are different aspects of the same thing: power relationships" (*ROP* 1982, 404).

Government, the legal courts, and women's groups continued to wrestle with sexual assault and "family violence" in the eighties. In 1980 a Supreme Court decision in the case of *Pappajohn v. R.*, stated that the appellant could "be excused from criminal responsibility if he had honestly, albeit mistakenly, believed that the complainant was a willing partner"(*Pappajohn v. R.* 1980). The question is, who's perception/story is regarded as normative? As Ada Maria Isasi-Diaz aptly points out, "power always rests with those who define the norm" and, in this case, the court defined the male perspective as normative (Isasi-Diaz 1988, 98). In so doing, sexual assault was sanctioned. The issue of consent was officially first addressed in the UCC in 1960 but was not explicitly defined; it was recognized, albeit in an abstract and non-gender-specific way, as necessary to any sexual act in a marital relationship. However, in the legal sphere, recognition of the importance and necessity of consent was later in coming; rape within marriage was not considered a crime until 1983 (*The Canadian Panel on Violence Against Women* 1993, 17).

I will point out two further relevant changes to the law that have been made at this point. In 1991 the Supreme Court of Canada struck down the "rape-shield" law which protected women from having their past sexual lives used as evidence to discredit them as victims of sexual assault. Bill C-49, passed on August 15, 1992, was partially an attempt to compensate for the removal of the "rape-shield" law: "The legislated changes provide judges with clear guidelines for determining whether a complainant's sexual history can be admitted as evidence in sexual assault cases." But, more importantly, this bill defined "consent" as "the voluntary agreement of the complainant to engage in the sexual activity in question" (*The Canadian Panel on Violence Against Women* 1993, 236). Hence, the experience of the abused is given greater credibility; the accused's perspective is no longer considered normative by law. The question remains, have these changes in the law and government fundamentally changed women's experience of male violence?

Two years and $10 million later, in 1993, the federal government's Canadian Panel on Violence Against Women submitted its final report. The goal of the panel is zero tolerance of violence against women in Canada by the year 2000. The method delineated to achieve this goal is largely education—enforced by law where necessary. However, once again this approach assumes that violence against women can be eradicated without radical upheaval of the economic, legal or government structure. Is the issue merely being studied to death?

Although it is important that the existing structures, in particularly the government and legal system, recognize violence against women and related issues, there have been significant difficulties regarding the *ways* in which these structures define these issues. In a detailed Canadian study, Walker observes what she terms a "process of appropriation and absorption" of the issue of violence against women by these existing structures (Walker 1990, 57). That violence does occur within the family was not overtly disputed (Walker 1990, 132). The difficulties arose in determining how this issue should be defined and, therefore how it would be addressed. As the issue became aligned with both the Health and Welfare Department and the justice system, the issue was defined in certain ways and increasingly removed from women's experience of male violence. As a concern of Health and Welfare, the central concern became the family. Commitment to "'traditional family values'" as well as a tendency to medicalize this violence has resulted in a failure to recognize this issue as a "social problem" resulting from the power imbalance between men and women (Walker 1990, 1991; *The Canadian Panel on Violence Against Women* 1993, 205). As a criminal issue, the men and women involved are individualized as they are reduced to "victims and assailants or perpetrators" (Walker 1990, 153). In summary, Walker concludes that "[w]hen assault as a category was merged with family violence as a subset of deviant behavior, . . . [t]he [resulting] definition pathologized certain aspects of gender relations and made them amenable to various treatment strategies without attacking the structures that determine them" (Walker 1990, 167). Without challenging the nature of these structures, the way in which many people understand violence against women will continue to be shaped by the resulting definitions of this issue. I believe that a similar critique is true of our churches: without being open to and actively embracing critique of our fundamental underlying symbols and theology, we will continue to perpetuate such violence.

In summary, the UCC has followed the prodding of wider society, particularly feminist women's groups, in some areas and has been a goad to society in others. The UCC, as represented by the records of proceedings, historically has been prophetic in matters related to the marital relationship and sexuality but in matters related to a conscious recognition of a systemic power imbalance between the genders, it has been more responsive than prophetic. For instance, the UCC approved the use of contraceptives in 1936 and named mutual consent regarding marital sexual relations as an issue as early as 1960. Divorce was recognized as necessary in some marriages in order to protect vulnerable family members from a violent spouse/parent in 1962. Furthermore, the UCC in 1988 supported the full participation of people regardless of sexual orientation in the ordered ministry and life of the church. On an organizational level, these actions were far ahead of many of the responses of wider Canadian society.

Areas in which the UCC has clearly *followed* the call of women's groups were those that required a clear recognition of the systemic power imbalance between the genders. Shortly after the start of the proliferation of women's organizations in wider Canadian society, task forces addressing women's concerns and changing gender roles emerged in the UCC. It was largely at the urging of these groups and a growing awareness in the wider society that the UCC began to directly address this power imbalance between men and women and the resulting violence against women. Now, as indicated in the previous section, the UCC is taking a stronger leadership role, particularly in terms of our understanding of the family and human sexuality.

Clearly, dialogue, mutual critique, and challenge need to be further nurtured between the church and wider society. Unfortunately, the work in which the UCC and other churches have engaged is often ignored or dismissed by the wider "secular" society. For instance, various church leaders have rightly criticized the final report of the Canadian Panel on Violence Against Women as missing "'the extent to which the churches have been grappling with these issues over the years'" (*Observer* October 1993, 28). The lack of awareness and widespread dialogue between members of the church and "secular" society has served to perpetuate the false dualistic split between the spiritual and the political (Spretnak, 1982) and, in so doing, has helped to maintain the powerfully entrenched systems and symbols that provide a foundation for male violence against women, both inside and outside the church.

Addressing the three areas that I have cited—sexuality, gender and critique—is, I believe, a necessary precursor to any fundamental change that will lead to the end of male violence against women:

> The first step of a critical theological method is the choice of a particular locus for work, then examination of the function of faith in a particular situation, the way in which faith maintains or challenges structures of oppression. The second step is a search for alternative symbols and structures of religious life that might effectively challenge oppressive manifestations of faith (symbols, rituals, polity, doctrines) and that might meet, in less oppressive ways, some of the needs being met by problematic religious discourse. (Welch 1990, 158)

As we have seen, the symbols of sex as a source of sin, of the traditional patri-archal family with its corresponding roles for men and women, and the sym-bol of the church as the answer to problems, as opposed to the church as an institution that is very much grounded in a broken humanity, have demon-strated a tenacity and power over time, both inside and outside the church. As Geertz (1965) wrote, these symbols function in part to create "conceptions of a general order of existence." Within this particular order created in the UCC, it has been very difficult to recognize and then address the issue of vio-lence against women and children. In order for the UCC to do this, it has been necessary to do two things: firstly, to ask some critical questions of this order or "world view." For instance, as Pamela D. Young queries:

> Where do men and women, male and female symbols, concepts of mas-culine and feminine fit into this general order? Is there a hierarchy of val-ues that is gender based? Does this system too easily use its conception of 'order' to justify injustice and inequality for women? Who has the power, who has the status in this 'order' and whose interests are served by it? (Young 1990, 21)

As questions such as these began to be asked by members of the UCC, a ten-sion mounted between the desire to maintain previously accepted symbols and norms and the recognition that many of these symbols and norms are at the least limiting and, at worst, destructive and life-threatening. Secondly, alternative symbols have had to be created in order to replace symbols found to be unjust and oppressive. As Carol Christ explains, "Symbol systems can-not simply be rejected, they must be replaced. Where there is not any replace-ment, the mind will revert to familiar structures at times of crisis, bafflement, or defeat" (Christ 1982, 73).

The UCC has struggled with a growing recognition that some of its most closely held symbols can be unjust, dangerous, and not reflective of an inclusive and holistic theology. The desire to maintain the traditional order has been juxtaposed with this recognition and the resulting dialectic has helped to create a space in which new, alternative symbols can be presented and struggled with. Clearly, it was not until these traditional patriarchal symbols began to be challenged and replaced that we have witnessed the emergence of violence against women and children as an issue on the agenda of the UCC.

Notes

My sincere thanks to Dr. Roger Hutchinson for his guidance and many helpful criticisms of this essay.

1. For example, the explosive issue of sexual orientation was initially urged onto the agenda by petitions from concerned pastoral charges and/or presby-teries requesting clarification of the church's position.

2. Congregational petitions definitely contributed to the recognition of issues concerned with abuse. For instance, regarding child and youth abuse, General Council began to receive petitions in the latter part of the eighties. In 1986, the Council received a petition from Winnipeg Presbytery which requested that the report of the Badgely Commission (i.e., a nationally represented committee appointed by the Department of Justice and the Department of Health and Welfare to study and report on the sexual offenses committed against children and youth) be studied by the UCC, that the UCC urge the federal Government to implement the main recommendation, and that "the DMC [i.e., the Division of Mission in Canada] present recommendations to the 1988 General Council to guide the thinking and action of the church on the issue of child sexual victimization"(ROP 1986, 645). The thirty-second Council, in response to this petition, reported that the DMC had established a programme unit— "Children, Adults and Family Ministries"—to "coordinate work in the areas of pornography, prostitution, and family violence." More specifically, in response to this petition, this unit has corresponded with the Minister of Health and Welfare regarding "violence in the family"(ROP 1988, 513).

3. Presbyteries are formed by pastoral charges, on a geographical basis and, in turn, presbyteries form conferences. There are ten conferences in the UCC. Representatives for General Council are chosen from each of these three areas, by members of their respective areas, with the intent of being as inclusive as possible. For instance, youth delegates are mandated.

4. The UCC continues to cite certain norms as criteria for the ethical understanding of sexual relationships. For instance, monogamy within a covenantal relationship is believed to be a norm to which couples should aspire.

5. The increase in venereal disease is cited as evidence of the sinful nature of sex outside of marriage (see also ROP 1946, 379).

6. In an effort to preserve the family and, therefore, the country from moral decay, the UCC continued the "rescue and redemptive work" begun by the Methodist Church in 1910 (ROP 1925, 125). Until 1935 there were eight redemptive homes (ROP 1936, 361) supported and overseen by the UCC. They were all under the oversight of the Board of Evangelism and Social Service. These redemptive homes were all for young women and girls although the superintendents usually attempted to help misguided boys, as well, by referring them to other resources. There seems to have been limited concern for boys and young men although there was one farm for boys. The Farm Centre typically housed about twenty to twenty-five boys (ROP 1938, 307).

7. This moral code finds its roots in the Eve/Mary dichotomy which is based on a denial of women's body and sexuality. This dichotomy assumes that women either succumb to their carnal nature or rise above it. Those who succumb are sexual temptresses as, supposedly, was Eve. On the other hand, traditional notions about Mary maintain both her virginity and her nurturing nature as mother of Jesus. Thus, by this model, women can only be virtuous by denying their sexual selves and, paradoxically, by being nurturing mothers. In order to fully understand the implications of this theology, the link between this dichotomy and the male/female dualism needs to be explored. The separation of male and female into dualities in which the former is judged superior to the latter, has characterized much of Christian history.

Historically and theologically, men have been associated with the mind and spirit whereas women have been identified with the carnal, bodily side of humanity. This hierarchical dualism (Plaskow 1990, chap. 5) serves to both reflect and perpetuate negative and fearful views of the body, sexuality and women. Joy Bussert summarizes the seriousness of this issue: "projected fear and hatred at women as the fallen 'inferior' bodily half of the mind-body dichotomy, and male 'superiority' and alienation from their own bodily selves are the root causes of violence against women"(Bussert 1986, 15). As a corollary to this, it is important to realize that as long as women participate in the patriarchal myth of Mary, and refrain from breaking the sexual code that lies at the foundation of this gender stereotype, then social rewards are imminent. However, if this code is broken and Eve materializes, some form of social control is necessary in order to protect and preserve both the moral code and the patriarchal order. In the twenties through to the fifties, redemptive homes provided one such source of social control. For an in-depth analysis of violence against women as social control, see Hamner and Maynard 1987.

8. It should be noted that the 1936 report—"The Meaning and Responsibilities of Christian Marriage"—stated that women have the right not to be exploited.

9. I added the emphasis in order to underscore the fact that this violence is seen as mutually damaging; it is not more or less damaging to either the victim or perpetrator. Although harm is done to both the victim and violator (Kaufman 1993, chap. 2), I believe that it is necessary to point out the different types of harm and to underscore the fact that the abuser is the agent who inflicts harm on his victim; the abuser exercises *power over* the victim.

10. In 1984, the Women in Ministry Committee wrote a protocol and policy statement regarding "Sexual Harassment in the Church." Subsequently, it was approved in 1985 by the General Council Executive. In the 1986 *ROP*, an initial set of "principles and assumptions" are listed on 207–8.

11. Based on an in-depth study of convicted rapists and other convicted felons, Scully argues that those men who have the "most rigid demands for female virtue" based on gender stereotypes, seem to be "the best candidates for hostility because they cannot accept women as fully human. . . . These attitudes also allow men to believe that their victims were 'legitimate victims'"; they deserved to be attacked since they did not fully conform to the stereotype of a modest, demure, dependent, and nurturing female (Scully 1990, 81). Morris echoes this same view, contending that most abusers are characterized by rigid thinking which is "frequently based on traditional sexual stereotypes"(Morris 1988, 23).

12. This belief was, of course, particularly important during the war years.

13. For a helpful discussion of women, self-sacrifice and agency, see Carr 1988, 58.

14. These restrictions continued to be enforced in the sixties. In the 1962 *ROPs*, it was noted that it was important to "acknowledge the changed status of women in the modern world" but traditional gender roles continued to be desired and were reflected in the conditions under which women were eligible for ordination.

15. Furthermore, the 1946 report on *The Christian Home and Christian Marriage* related the increase in the divorce rate to the increasing freedoms, particularly paid employment outside the home, given to women (*ROP* 1944,

277; and *ROP* 1946, 108 and 110–13). This rapid increase in paid employment for women was largely due to the opening of jobs when men left to fight in the war. Moreover, with many men overseas, there was a significant rise in the number of single mothers.

16. Furthermore, regarding the increase in the divorce rate, the authors of the report surmised that "[i]f this trend is unchecked it can destroy the basis upon which our national life is founded"(*ROP* 1946, 125).

17. It is interesting to note that by this time women had been given the right to initiate divorce. This was often cited as one of the "new freedoms" that women were given that were laudable but, at the same time, potentially dangerous to the preservation of traditional order and morality.

18. This is a particularly significant claim in view of the fact that the Canadian legal system, at that time, rarely recognized any cause for divorce aside from adultery.

19. However, they were not officially named as such until November 1984 when the General Council Executive established the Standing Committee on Sexism (*ROP* 1986, 248).

20. Control and power are not directly addressed.

21. For an excellent exploration of this issue see Brown and Bohn 1989.

22. Notably, training has been strongly urged for theological students by numerous reports. (For example, see The Church Leaders' Submission to the Canadian Panel on Violence Against Women March 1992, 2). However, the results of a recent survey of twenty Canadian universities and theological colleges, carried out by the ecumenical Women's Inter-Church Council, indicate that we have a long way to go in terms of this type of education: "The issue of violence against women has been identified as a component within 35 courses given at 20 universities or theological colleges. In most instances, the subject is treated as a part of a course whose focus is marriage and family, or pastoral care. . . . In general, students—even those preparing for ministry in a congregation or parish—were not required to take courses addressing wife abuse or domestic violence" (Women's Inter-Church Council of Canada 1991, 4).

23. On December 6, 1989, Marc Lepine murdered fourteen women engineering students at the Montreal Ecole Polytechnique. Screaming that they were a "bunch of feminists," Lepine slaughtered these women in a dramatically horrifying display of violence. After the killings an Angus Reid poll reported that "65 percent of Canadian men felt Marc Lepine's murderous attack had no connection to male violence toward women in general" (Landsberg, November 30, 1991).

24. It is important to be cognizant of the multifaceted nature of the women's movement in Canada. As Adamson, Briskin, and McPhail point out, particularly since the early seventies, the women's movement has been characterized by diversity: "The women's movement has a shifting, amoeba-like character; it is and has always been, politically, ideologically, and strategically diverse. It is not, and never has been, represented by a single organizational entity; it has no head office, no single leaders, no membership cards to sign"(Adamson et al. 1988, 7).

25. Since the early seventies, any popular attention given to the abortion issue has focussed largely on the court system. Aside from this attention given to legal decisions, the issue has been relatively quiet in Canada, particularly as

compared with the United States, since then. In attempting to explain relative silence, McDonnell observes that, "[i]n contrast to the United States, where the Hyde amendment and the rise of the new right have thrown the abortion struggle into dramatic and highly visible relief, the situation in Canada is vague, much less polarized. Instead of a clearly visible threat to abortion rights, what we have is a complicated, slowly eroding situation whose impact is difficult to convey to the public"(McDonnell 1982, 33).

26. Since then, a report of the Law Reform Commission, released in 1989, rejected this position and recommended a return to criminal legislation. (*Healthsharing* [Fall 1989]: 24). Moreover, although such legislation has not been passed, as Joy Thompson, spokesperson for the British Columbia Coalition of Abortion Clinics, stated: "'access to abortion has not improved one iota since January 1988'" [(Brown 1991): 3].

27. For an in-depth explanation of the history and characteristics of these different types of feminist organizations, see Adamson et al. 1988, 62–71.

Works Cited

Adamson, Nancy, Linda Briskin and Margaret McPhail. 1988. *Feminists Organizing for Change*. Toronto: Oxford University Press.

Allen, Richard. 1971. *The Social Passion—Religion and Social Reform in Canada 1914–28*. Toronto: University of Toronto Press.

Bjorge, Corinne. 1992. "Porn, Obscenity and the Supreme Court." In *Kinesis—News About Women That's Not in the Dailies* (April).

Brown, Jackie. 1991. "Abortion Bill Defeated: Too Close for Comfort." In *Kinesis—News About Women That's Not in the Dailies* (March).

Brown, Joanne Carlson and Carole Bohn, eds. 1989. *Christianity, Patriarchy, and Abuse—A Feminist Critique*. New York: The Pilgrim Press.

Bussert, Joy M. K. 1986. *Battered Women*. Division for Mission in North America, Lutheran Church in America.

The Canadian Association of Sexual Assault Centres. 1986. "Evaluation 1979–1982, to the Department of Health and Welfare."

The Canadian Panel on Violence Against Women. 1993. *Changing the Landscape: Ending Violence, Achieving Equality—The Final Report*. Ottawa: Minister of Supply and Services Canada.

Carr, Anne E. 1988. *Transforming Grace*. San Francisco: Harper & Row.

Christ, Carol P. 1982. "Why Women Need the Goddess." In *The Politics of Women's Spirituality*, ed. C. Spretnak. New York: Anchor Books.

Church Council on Justice and Corrections. 1988. *Family Violence in a Patriarchal Culture—A Challenge to Our Way of Living*. Ottawa: The Keith Press Ltd.

The Church Leaders' Submission to the Canadian Panel on Violence Against Women. 1992. *And No One Shall Make Them Afraid (Micah 4:4)*. March 27, 1992.

Cole, Susan. 1982. "Home Sweet Home?" In *Still Ain't Satisfied—Canadian Feminism Today*, ed. M. Fitzgerald et al. Toronto: Women's Press.

Fortune, Marie Marshal. 1983. *Sexual Violence—the Unmentionable Sin*. New York: Pilgrim Press.

Geertz, Clifford. 1965. "Religion as a Cultural System." In *Anthropological Approaches to the Study of Religion*, ed. Michael Banton. London: Tavistock Publications.

Golding, Gail. 1988. *Hands to End Violence Against Women—A Resource for Theological Education*. Toronto: Women's Inter-Church Council of Canada.

Hamner, Jalna and Mary Maynard, eds. 1987. *Women, Violence and Social Control*. Atlantic Highlands, N.J.: Humanities Press International.

Harrison, Beverly. 1983. *Our Right to Choose—Toward a New Ethic of Abortion*. Boston: Beacon Press.

Hutchinson, Norah. 1988. "No New Law." In *Healthsharing—a Canadian Women's Health Quarterly*. Toronto: Women Healthsharing Inc. (Winter 1988).

Isasi-Diaz, Ada Maria. 1988. "A Hispanic Garden in a Foreign Land." In *Inheriting our Mothers' Gardens*, ed. L. M. Russell et al. Louisville: Westminster Press.

James, Barbara. 1982. "Breaking the Hold: Women Against Rape." In *Still Ain't Satisfied*, ed. M. Fitzgerald et al. Toronto: Women's Press.

Kadar, Marlene. 1982. "Sexual Harassment as a Form of Social Control." In *Still Ain't Satisfied*, ed. M. Fitzgerald et al. Toronto: Women's Press.

Kaufman, Michael. 1993. *Cracking the Armour—Power, Pain and the Lives of Men*. Toronto: Viking.

Kennedy, Joy, on behalf of The Interchurch Working Group on Violence and Sexual Abuse. 1993. "Letter to Elaine Scott, Director, Family Violence Prevention Division of Health and Welfare Canada." Ottawa, January 7, 1993.

Landsberg, Michelle. 1991. "More Men Now Taking Violence Crisis Seriously." *The Toronto Star*. November 30, 1991.

Legge, Marilyn. 1992. *The Grace of Difference—A Canadian Feminist Theological Ethic*. Georgia: Scholars Press.

McDonnell, Kathleen. 1982. "Claim No Easy Victories: The Fight For Reproductive Rights." In *Still Ain't Satisfied*, ed. M. Fitzgerald et al. Toronto: Women's Press.

McLaren, Angus and Arlene Tigar McLaren. 1986. *The Bedroom and the State*. Toronto: McClelland and Stewart Ltd.

Morris, Roberta. 1988. *Ending Violence in Families—A Training Program for Pastoral Careworkers*. Toronto: United Church of Canada.

NiCarthy, Ginny. 1988. "Building Self-Esteem: Overcoming Barriers to Recovery." In *Abuse and Religion—When Praying Isn't Enough*, ed. Anne Horton and Judith A. Williamson. U.S.A.: D. C. Heath and Company.

Pappajohn v. *R.* (1980), 111 D.L.R. (3d) 1 (S.C.C.).

Plaskow, Judith. 1990. *Standing Again At Sinai—Judaism from a Feminist Perspective*. New York: HarperCollins Publishers.

Ruether, Rosemary Radford. 1983. *Sexism and God-Talk*. Boston: Beacon Press.

Scott, R. B. Y. and Gregory Vlastos, eds. 1936/1989. *Towards the Christian Revolution*. Canada: Ronald P. Frye & Company.

Scully, Diana. 1990. *Understanding Sexual Violence—A Study of Convicted Rapists*. Massachussetts: Unwin Hyman Inc.

Shapiro, Constance H. and Susan Turner. 1988. "Helping Battered Women through the Mourning Process" In *Abuse and Religion—When Praying Isn't Enough*, ed. Anne Horton and Judith A. Williamson. Lexington, Mass.: D. C. Heath and Company.

Spretnak, Charlene, ed. 1982. *The Politics of Women's Spirituality.* New York: Anchor Books, Doubleday.

Toronto Rape Crisis Centre. 1985. *No Safe Place: Violence Against Women and Children.* Toronto: Women's Press.

United Church of Canada General Council, *Records of Proceedings* 1925–1990.

United Church of Canada. 1936. *The New Outlook.* November 18, 1936.

United Church of Canada. 1980. *In God's Image . . . Male and Female.* Toronto: UCC.

United Church of Canada. 1984. *Gift, Dilemma and Promise—A Report and Affirmations on Human Sexuality.* Toronto: UCC.

United Church of Canada. 1985. "Child Abuse." Toronto: DMC, UCC, February 1985.

United Church of Canada. 1987a. "The Family." Toronto: DMC, UCC.

United Church of Canada. 1987b."Women in Abusive Relationships." Toronto: The DMC, UCC (November 1987).

United Church of Canada. 1988. "Toward a Christian Understanding of Sexual Orientations, Lifestyles and Ministry." Toronto: UCC.

United Church of Canada. 1989. "Abuse of the Elderly." Toronto: DMC, UCC.

United Church of Canada. 1993. "Sexual Abuse (Sexual Harassment, Sexual Exploitation, Pastoral Sexual Misconduct, Sexual Assault) and Child Abuse." Toronto: Division of Ministry Personnel and Education, UCC.

Van Wagner, Vicki and B. Lee. 1989. "Legal Assault—A Feminist Analysis of the Law Reform Commission's Report on Abortion Legislation." In *Healthsharing—a Canadian Women's Health Quarterly.* Toronto: Women Healthsharing Inc. (Fall 1989).

Wall, Naomi. 1982. "The Last Ten Years: A Personal/Political View." In *Still Ain't Satisfied,* ed. M. Fitzgerald et al. Toronto: Women's Press.

Walker, Gillian. 1990. *Family Violence and the Women's Movement—The Conceptual Politics of Struggle.* Toronto: University of Toronto Press.

Welch, Sharon. 1990. *A Feminist Ethic of Risk.* Minneapolis: Fortress Press.

Winnipeg Presbytery and the UCC Conference of Manitoba and Northwestern Ontario. 1988. "No Fear In Love . . ." Winnipeg: United Church of Canada.

Winnipeg Presbytery. 1993. "Protocol on Child Abuse—As Yet Untitled—Draft." Winnipeg: United Church of Canada.

Women's Inter-Church Council of Canada. 1991. "Report on the Theological Education Project on Violence Against Women." Toronto: Women's Inter-Church Council.

Young, Pamela Dickey. 1990. "Geertz Revisited: A Model for Feminist Studies in Religion." *Perkins School of Theology Journal* (January/April 1990).

Part V
Contemporary Revisioning

When The Mountain Won't Move

LINDA H. HOLLIES

I

There has been a gigantic mountain in my life since the age of twelve or thirteen. This mountain could not be moved, and it was too overwhelming for me, a child, to attempt to climb. I didn't have the faintest idea that a mountain could be chipped away at, or even tunneled through. So, what did I do with this mountain? I tried to ignore it! I was positive that no other individual could have a mountain like this in her life. This type of mountain didn't have a name; it was never mentioned in my world. The mountain didn't have a face; it appeared in the night, simply as an ugly mess. Now, if it had no name or face, how could I describe it to anyone? If I didn't talk about it, maybe it would just go away.

My father brought this mountain into my world, for you see, I am the victim of incest. He was a very angry man. He was called "Thor, god of thunder" by his children. He yelled, screamed, and hurled insult upon insult at us. His demeanor was seldom pleasant, whether at home or away. He was a strict disciplinarian and quick to whip with the handy strap. He was emotionally, physically, and mentally abusive to me and my seven siblings; his behavior toward my mother was the same. I cannot remember one kind or encouraging remark my father ever made to me; my accomplishments were usually belittled or ignored.

The act of incest alone is enough to cause one psychological trauma and lifelong emotional damage, but when coupled with heavy theological ramifications, one is in double-trouble! My father was the assistant pastor of the small, family-type, Pentecostal church I was raised in where God's love was constantly preached; respect for parents was another favorite topic. But the most popular theme was the sinner and the sinner's abode in hell. Well, I had problems. I could not love this man who came into my bedroom and did unmentionable things to me; I could not believe that God could love me and yet allow this to continue. I surely had no respect for my father as a parent. Therefore, I was a sinner, right?

Another dynamic at play was the fact that my father found scripture to justify the liberties he took with me (the story of Lot and his two daughters, who had sex with him after they made him drunk, to perpetuate his lineage). Now, if this was a biblical injunction, sanctioned by scripture, why was I threatened and physically abused when I was told not to talk about this to anyone, and especially not my mother? Of course, my father had an answer: "Your mother has had one heart attack, and if she really doesn't understand the Bible, this might kill her"—a typical threat. I did not know that this was just another lie, but I did know that I didn't want my mother to die. What would happen to me then?

Now, when I was growing up, there were no "Just Say No" programs, no television coverage, no Oprah Winfrey show—there was no one to talk to about this mountain that I faced. I wondered what I had done to invite this invasion of my person, this assault against what I had been taught was good and decent behavior? Was I really going to hell? I could not receive any clarification or reassurance because there was no one to talk to about this ugly mess. I felt I should love my parents because "this is the first commandment with the promise of long life," and I surely wanted to live long. What was I to do? Ignore the mountain? Try to push it out of my mind? Pray about it? Have faith? Would it disappear?

As I have since learned, my rationalizations were indicative of someone raised in a dysfunctional family: Don't talk about the issue! Don't be disloyal to the family, and do not allow outsiders to know what's going on. I knew outsiders should not be brought into this mess, but why couldn't my mother see, hear, tell, and know what was going on? Couldn't she notice my anguish—intuit my grief—how could she not be aware of my pain?

My mother was a "total woman." She was always well-groomed, in a starched house dress, and she would never wear curlers or sleepwear around the house. She was a good cook and an immaculate housekeeper. She was the "perfect" wife; whatever her husband said was *law*! She related to all of us as the woman who carried out her husband's orders and commands. My siblings and I went almost everywhere she went, because my father was "too much of a man" to baby-sit! He was "too saved" to allow her to use any form of birth control, and she was "too saved" to disobey. She never made any decision without consulting him. Although we spent a great deal of time with her, she was not emotionally available to any of us; seldom did she smile or display affection toward us, except for the perfunctory good-morning, good-bye, hello and good-night kisses that my father demanded from all of us. She was repressed, afraid of conflict and rejection and never knew what "living" was all about. Her husband would not allow her to work because that might incite rebellion—against her role as wife; her function was to be mother to his children.

As I reflect on the experiences and traumas of my childhood, I am amazed and grateful that I have sanity today, but I realize that I have the natural instincts of a survivor. The atmosphere in our home was perhaps similar to a slave labor camp, with father as master and mother as general overseer. There were no loving relationships; we related to my father out of fear and to my mother out of respect. My father used the word love to justify his cruel behavior—"it's because I love you that I must whip you." I recall the one time he asked me if I loved him and I honestly replied, "No." He tried to slap the "hell" out of me. "Little saved girl, you *must* love your father and respect him as well!" I was an adult, married and pregnant with my first child, when I challenged my mother and heard her say to me, for the very first time, "I love you." And they were my primary caregivers, nurturers, protectors from the outside world? From them I was to learn trust and intimacy?

I married my childhood sweetheart immediately upon graduation from high school. He was shy and introverted and had a horrible relationship with his parents. He was just what I needed, a man who was an emotional mess, who wouldn't make too many demands upon me. We were together long enough to have two sons and to make life miserable for each other. He was a decent human being; I simply refused to be "wife." My earliest prayer was to never be like my mother, the "total woman."

The most significant incident in this lifelong struggle involved my sister, Jacqui. She was "my" baby. She was three years younger, and I looked after her. As a matter of fact, with mother's constant pregnancies, I looked after all of my siblings and my mother as well. After I moved out of the house, my father approached my sister to molest her. The same pattern and the same threats were involved, but my sister didn't accept this "strange" behavior. She called me.

I approached my husband, who was somewhat aware of my personal history. I had explained to him why I would not visit my mother, except when my father was at work, and why I would not allow my sons to stay overnight. When I told him about the situation, we went to see an attorney. His advice was to consult with my mother, have a warrant sworn out and have my father arrested. My husband even told my mother that we would move into her home and take over financial responsibility. She absolutely refused. However, she did confront my father, and the molestation of my sister ceased.

I felt relieved for Jacquie, but I became very angry with my mother as I thought about her behavior when I finally told her what was going on with me at the age of sixteen. This was after enduring three years of hell alone, not having a big sister to turn to, and not trusting that my mother would believe my word against my father's. She was wise enough to set my father up—she walked in and caught him in the very act. He cried, asked forgiveness, and of course she forgave him. When I asked to move out-of-state in order to reside with her brother, she replied, "You have to stay here. Your father loves me, nothing will happen to you again!" When the molestation and rape resumed, there was no reason to return to her. My back was against the wall. My mother was no protection for me: she could not provide the emotional nurturing I needed for growth and development.

After the break-up of my first marriage, I was a single parent, a working adult, and enjoying a measure of success, yet the mountain was still in control. My sense of worth was steadily diminishing; nothing covered my deep sense of shame. The "filth" of my secret was eating me up, and there was no one to confide in. I desired intimacy, but I was afraid to allow anyone, male or female, to come close to knowing me. I had no experience in relating in honest relationships. The demands that I placed on myself to "be perfect" did not allow for leisure, nor did I have the patience with others who wouldn't or couldn't measure up to my specifications.

I was a very unhappy woman. I remarried. This time I selected a man who was twelve years my senior. He, too, was from an unstable home, and had been in a bad marriage, and was an active alcoholic. Once again I selected a man who would need me and yet was emotionally unavailable to me. To further complicate matters, we had a daughter.

My sons did not prevent me from working long hours (my job was in the steel mills), as long as I provided the monetary benefits, but having a daughter meant to me that some major lifestyle changes were necessary. So, I went back to school to complete degree requirements, and to get a professional position so that I would have quality time to spend with my little girl. My husband's insecurities caused him to challenge this desire for additional education, and since I refused to compromise (or to be controlled), I left him, moved to a city miles away, and enrolled.

While living with a friend and her family, I began to attend church services at the United Methodist Church. Their theological stance was broadly based; their "God" was not so restrictive. And in this setting I again considered my personal relationship with God. This God loved me, just as I was; this God invited me to come and receive the abundant life. This was appealing to a survivor—I wanted to know what "authentic" living was all about. But the mountain was still there, and I was not able to talk to anyone. I *still* hated my father; I went to talk with him and apologized for hating him all those years. He did not understand my pain or my anger. Forgiveness was supposed to follow my repentance, but I never felt forgiven, for I honestly could not forgive him! Most importantly, I would not forget! But this new-found relationship with God and a new community were too delightful to turn my back on. Once again I felt that if I could just pray correctly and ignore this mountain, it would go away.

Finally, the burden of carrying this secret became too much to bear, so I went to the pastor to "confess." With much emotion, I told my story and he listened attentively, after which he advised me to "agree with him in prayer."

I was a wife, mother of three, an established career woman, who dared risk everything to seek God "fully" in order to have God help me move this mountain! As an African-American female, with the "herstory" of incest in my life, I approached seminary with some illusions, fantasies, and hopes. I believed that in this place of spiritual illumination and theological education I would be led to great insights and truths about my inner pain. From class to class, course to course, seminar to workshop, I sought diligently for someone, something to help me examine my mountain. Foolish woman that I was! Seminaries are not prepared to teach you how to map out mountains as a cartographer, nor are they equipped to teach you how to examine mountains as a geologist. Seminaries, I soon found out, are established institutions that perpetuate the silence of the status quo in regards to mountains and mountain movers.

There was not one class, not one professor who was willing to engage with me, from a biblical base, in the exploration of my mountain. I was a student, a number, one to be helped through the system, but not helped by the system with tools, methods, or principles to assist me in becoming a mountain mover. I was simply "a certain woman." And, the mountain did not move!

During my second year of searching, seeking, and struggling through seminary, I attended our chapel service in observance of Christian Unity Week. Cardinal Joseph Bernadin, the leader of Chicago Catholics, stood to deliver his message. As he stood, a group of women from the seminary community also stood. They did not stand in unity with the Cardinal, but they stood in unity for a common purpose, symbolizing the oppressive treatment of women in the Catholic Church. They remained on their feet, in the audience, in front of him and, in the choir behind him, during his entire homily on "Unity." He never gave any indication that he saw anything amiss during this service. He completed his message and took his seat. All of the women sat down. Our president came to the podium, concluded the service, making no mention of having noticed these women doing anything out of the ordinary. The services concluded, and life in the seminary went on. And so did the pain of women.

The matter did not die, the issue was not settled. Male professors approached the president and dean, seeking some sort of appropriate measures to take against these women, students, and leaders of local congregations, who were not "hospitable" to the Cardinal. Some talked of writing to their bishops, telling of their rebellious natures. Some of them even talked of expulsion. Finally, a community open forum was held to address the issue of hospitality. Not one seminary official made mention of the pain of the women. Not one approached the group to say, "I see your pain and I realize that your anguish is authentic."

This is the reality of the seminary. This is the reality of the institutional Church at large. This is the reality of our society in regards to the abuse, neglect, and pain that is continually perpetuated against women and children. This segment is not really heard, their plight is never fully addressed as individuals who are being prepared for professional ministry. Seminaries are truly "inhospitable" to those who enter with mountains in their life. They become "non-persons" within those hallowed halls.

When I left, I had two secrets: one from my childhood, and the newly found secret that my "new" relationship with God did not perform the miracle of wiping my memory clean or restoring love for my father within my heart. The fault/blame had to be mine; this was the only logical conclusion. The mountain was yet in control.

Where was the peace in my life? My other endeavors, such as working with the Christian Education Department and the young adult ministry in the local church, completing university requirements, and reuniting with my husband after two years did not bring release from the mental and emotional bondage to the mountain. The cycle continued—better jobs, more material gains, even professional positions and recognition—but the shame and humiliation which caused me to doubt my self-worth and faith remained.

The Christian experience challenged me to grow and expand my horizons. I felt "called," but I did not feel worthy, and I certainly was not ready. I decided to continue to work in the church, but I would keep my full-time, well-paid position as supervisor at General Motors. On the other hand, I was getting more and more involved in the life of the local congregation. Could God actually require more? Besides, my father was a minister, and I had no trust in him. Would I be accepted/trusted if the story of the mountain was known? For surely I had a great part in the mountain, right? If I was going to minister to others, I had to look good—to act as if I had it all together and had *most* of the answers.

At the age of forty, I met Dr. Lee M. Jones, a United Methodist pastor. He challenged me to attend seminary and to allow God full use of my time, talents, and gifts. But this man did not know my story! Unfortunately, Dr. Jones was in my life for only two months, as he and his family were transferred to the East coast for another assignment. His wife, my husband, he, and I all discussed this matter of seminary and spent time in prayer together. My husband, surprisingly, was open to this new idea and did not oppose me at all. So, in September 1984, I entered Garrett Evangelical Theological Seminary. My daughter and I moved to Evanston, Illinois, and rented an apartment; my husband remained in our home and visited on his days off. This was one of the most exciting periods of my life. New knowledge, new people, new avenues for expressing ministry!

II

The Chinese character for crisis is also the same symbol for opportunity. Life has a way, a manner, even a habit of providing victims with the opportunity to choose different avenues of exploration. Facing mid-life, I entered seminary. In the midst of a mid-life crisis I had to select new patterns of dealing with the issues in my life which continued to cause me daily pains and nightmares. I was tired of dancing around this same mountain. I wanted to face it squarely, speak to it and watch it disappear. For does not the scripture declare that with faith, the size of a mustard, I could "speak to this Mountain, 'Be moved to another place', and it shall move; and nothing will be impossible for you." (Matt. 17:20).

This incident gave me great focus and clarity as to just how much the Church and the seminary had failed me, a victim of domestic violence in both my childhood and adult life. For I realized that not only was I a victim of incest by my father, but the "hushed," secret and quiet atmosphere of the seminary made me a rape victim of the Church! As I sat in that chapel service I realized that seminary education is primarily focused on white, male, western European values. None of these categories fit my life!

The abuse in my life, which formed the mountain which controlled me even after his death, was caused by a male parent, trained in interpreting a male God who was powerful, threatening, vengeful, and the Creator of mountains! If anything, seminary reinforced this image of "the male God," with a predominately male administration, staff, and faculty. The core courses required of all students were taught, for the most part, from a male-centered focus and bias. Any course where curriculum focused on the eradication of violence against women and children was held only at the urging of female focus groups, and seldom would you find a significant number of men registering or attending.

The Church as an institution, and the seminary as its training ground, are primarily concerned with the perpetuation of the status quo, which is a white, male hierarchy. Where was the hospitality for me, an African American, female, who was "a stranger in a foreign land?"

My soul yearned for answers. I felt the mountain closing in on me. My spirit was perishing for lack of nurture, affirmation, and acceptance. My hope was diminished in this sacred place that offered me no help with my mountain climb, search, and watch! Seminary could not handle the crisis of a woman of color, who lived daily in the presence of a mountain of evil. My classes in theology did not deal with my theodicy and my personal search for answers to help me in order that I would be prepared to help others like myself.

III

In the middle of my crisis, feeling that I was living on the edge, seminary offered me the opportunity to explore Clinical Pastoral Education (CPE). I had heard of CPE, but I could find no Black students who had taken it. The school required a full battery of psychological tests as well as two counseling sessions. God, the mountain will show up! I will not pass these tests, for I am determined to be honest—well, as honest as I can be. I will talk about an abusive father, but I won't say that I was sexually abused—the white male pastoral counselor might not understand. With fear and trembling I attempted to tell "most" of the truth of my past by revealing that I was a physical abuse victim.

I passed the assessment sessions and was allowed to enter CPE where I began to investigate and acquire additional information about me and my mountain. CPE made me a mountain scout. And yet even CPE has its boundaries when it comes to mountains like mine! However, the movement that I made in CPE caused me to think that the mountain had moved!

I wanted a female supervisor because I felt she would better understand, and I applied to one center where I knew a female would supervise during the summer. I was accepted. Beth Burbank was relatively young and fairly reserved, but she was aware of mental abuse issues as her mother had a history of psychotic breaks. It was not my issue, but I decided to give it a chance and work toward moving the mountain.

My goals were to risk being vulnerable; to work on a personal statement of theodicy; to learn how to relax and have fun; and to come to terms with my own mortality. Supervision was not easy for me. I couldn't open up and be honest with Beth. She related that she had never supervised a northern Black woman before, so I wanted to "look good" to this white woman. And I wanted to impress her because I had shared that CPE just might be the vehicle for my ministry.

The group experience was so powerful for me. When I finally established a trust level with the group and the process allowed me to risk letting them know about my mountain, I did share—I told of my experience as a child and young adult, with no emotions being expressed. "It happened, I survived." The youngest woman in the group told me that she felt my pain and said that I didn't have to be strong. Then she gave me permission to cry. This was a breakthrough! This experience was the beginning of my grieving process over a lost childhood and innocence, over the rejection by both parents, and the lack of love and trust in my life.

Finally I was able to place blame where it belonged—on my father, not on myself. I was also able to experience anger freely for the first time. Because our family's church had equated anger with sin, there was never a way for my siblings or me to have an open or positive expression of anger. As children, the admission of anger had been cause for a whipping.

One day Beth was sharing "story theology" with us and read Psalm 139, which is her favorite passage. As she read verse 13, "For you have formed my inward parts; you have covered me in my mother's womb," the word "formed" seemed to swell within my head. I could actually see myself as a dot sitting on the head of a pin in my mother's womb. I began to watch the forming, shaping and becoming of "baby" Linda. God seemed to be a mockery to me at that instant as never before. Overwhelmed, I jumped up and ran from the group into the women's toilet. Beth concluded her remarks to the group and found me sitting in a stall, crying. When she inquired what was wrong, I replied, "nothing." When she questioned why I had run out of the group, I replied, "I don't know." Beth then asked, "Linda, are you angry?" I replied, "Of course not!" I could not conceive of anyone who would admit to being angry with God. Beth managed to talk me out of the stall, and that day, in the toilet, we had one of our best supervisory sessions. She taught me about anger, constructive and destructive. I realized authentic anger that day. I claimed my anger. I chipped at the mountain. The mountain moved.

After only one quarter of CPE, I learned more about myself than I had ever known. I became vulnerable, took risks, and grew because I was cared for and accepted, with my faults and limitations, by my peers and supervisor.

I entered into therapy after the quarter, for I wanted to learn more and to continue this growth. The time had now fully come that I could explore all of my issues. Beth pressed me to seek therapy.

I wanted a Black, female, feminist therapist but could not find one. I did find a white feminist pastoral counselor, working on a Ph.D. in pastoral psychology at Garrett-Northwestern. Peg Garrison and I worked well together. I continued chipping away at the mountain. But I didn't want to touch my mother and her part in my pain. I wanted to place all of the blame on my father. I wanted to go on pretending that my mother cared and that she really could not have known the horrible trauma I had undergone. The therapist suggested that we role play: "Tell your mother that she failed you. Tell her that she was a poor mother for not protecting you." My mind rebelled. The words would not come. No! My mother was not the issue!

Scaling a mountain is a tremendous task, requiring months of preparation, deliberation and determination. Peg Garrison and I worked diligently at picking, chipping and digging away at the many layers of painful shame that lay at the base of my present rage and anger. However, two years is not long enough to work through a mountain as huge as one with forty years of growth and spread. I graduated with honors from seminary, capable and prepared "they said," ready to go into the local parish and become a mountain-mover for others.

IV

Off I went to face the Conference Board of Ordination, degree in hand, willingness in head, fear in my heart, for my own mountain was yet alive, not quite as huge, but alive, nevertheless. For I have come to understand that mountains do not simply move as you name them, speak to them, and claim them as your own! But, they move as you move further away from them with growth, development, and acceptance of the past.

I was raped by the Board! My theology was attacked, my anger became an issue, and my vision for ministry as a full-time pastoral counselor was crushed. Knowing that I must proclaim and teach from my own experiences, I tried to help them see that my anger stemmed from my mountain, and the mountain would always be in my life. The examination group took on the dynamics of my family of origin. There was a violent parent who took the lead in the abuse, a silent parent who pushed back against the wall, and several non-verbal and non-rescuing siblings! As a candidate, I was both different and powerless. In that room I became a victim of the system. On that day I watched the mountain take on new dimensions in the church.

After the rape of my personhood was complete, the "family" wanted to pray for me. I was aware enough of the growing mountain, prepared enough by my days of therapy, and professional enough to refuse their prayers, and walked out of the room with my head held high! *I* was in control, not the mountain! They were shocked, surprised, and angry. But, I would not lie down and be a willing victim of violence by another system. I would not enter the duplicity of silence, and I would not perpetuate the family "lie." And, certainly, I would not be controlled through their prayers!

I do believe in prayer. Prayer is a powerful force which connects me with a God who cares, understands, guides and empowers me to act in the future. It is my understanding that when prayer ceases, living must be done. Prayer has been used against survivors of violence to keep them silent, humble, submissive, and "in their place." My God does not expect me to cry, pray, and continue to accept violence in my life. My God has given me more tools to utilize as I pray, work, and continue to speak to the mountains and to those who erect them. My God is an AWESOME God, full of power, balanced by love, who provides me strength to take a stance against anything or anyone who attempts to use mountains to block my life.

In her book, *Struggle to Be the Sun Again*, Asian theologian, Chung Hyun Kyung, writes for herself and many other women of color: "My learning did not help me to discern the activity of God in my people's everyday struggle. Instead, it was the student movement that enabled me to see the false ideology embedded in my formal theological education. Deconstruction of every aspect of theological imperialism became a main focus in my theological work. I decided that I would not waste my life solving the theological puzzles of the people who were the cause of our suffering; I wanted to spend my energy debunking their theological imperialism and studying (my) people's history and culture as I listened to my people's inner voice, in their struggle for survival and liberation . . . for 'the master's tools will never dismantle the master's house.'"[1]

The realization crept in on me that I had to do theology from my own experiences of mountains, pain, anger, shame, and guilt. For too many years I tried to hide the mountain in my life. But a mountain is part of my life story, a major force in my walk of faith. To ignore the mountain was to ignore my struggle to find God in, around, beneath, or at the foot of it! Finally, I understood that the "stuff" of the mountain could be used to help me speak to it and move it!

My new reality meant talking about my mountain to those who did not want to hear. But, in speaking out, I put a voice to millions of untold stories. My speaking led to my writing about the shame that held me bound to the mountain for too long. The writing led me to conferences, retreats, seminars and ADVANCE, where I was able to make sense out of the *non*-sense of our lives for many other survivors. The workshops meant digging into scriptures from a new perspective and then preaching and teaching with another voice!

V

My father died in 1981 and I thought that with his death the mountain would lose some of its hold on me, but I did not find that to be true. I needed my mother. I wasn't ready to *know*. All of my adult life I had attempted to "buy" my mother's love, as well as that of my brothers and sisters. I refused to confront my mother. But growth demands risk-taking. Removing mountains requires digging into everything around them. My unrealistic expectations of my perfect mother had to be faced.

June 1985 found me living in Lansing, Michigan and assigned to my first pastorate. Again, my husband was remaining behind for awhile, so I asked mother to travel with me and stay for a couple of weeks. In the middle of her second week with me, I asked the question that I needed an answer to, and her response was: "I thought it had started again, but I didn't want to know. I needed your father to love me." How sad! How pitiful!

After this confession, all of my illusions were destroyed. I knew that my mother had sacrificed me for what she hoped and wished was love. I refused to see my family for almost a year. I remained in therapy, but found a white, female psychiatrist. I worked on becoming whole. I worked on "cutting the ties" to my family so that I would never need them in the sick, dependent manner I had experienced. I worked on understanding how I was more like my parents than how I was different. On April 26, 1986, I had a dream that my mother was trying to join my father. I knew she was going to die. I had to work on saying appropriate good-byes. I never accomplished this.

On May 16, 1986, my mother had a massive brain stroke; she remained in a coma for twelve days. All the siblings agreed to stop life-support systems, and my mother died May 30. I did not grieve. I was too angry. She was only fifty-nine and had never experienced life. To wait for death is to die by slow torture. To do nothing is to rot. I saw in my mother's death the story of many Black women, wives, mothers, sisters, and daughters. They exist in an empty place, a vast interior of emptiness.

I knew that if I did not continue to chip away at the mountain, I would be in trouble. So, in May of 1986, I resigned from the church to take a rest, both mentally and physically. I also tried to immerse myself in "doing" so as to escape the inescapable grief. I realized that as long as my anger remained, the grieving could not begin.

In September 1986, I began a residency in clinical pastoral education at the Catherine McAuley Health Center in Ann Arbor, Michigan. I was very much in touch with my anger, because it would not allow others to reach me. I had shut down again because I did not want to hurt. I did not fully comprehend that I had to hurt in order to stop the hurt. My goals were centered around being open to feedback on the impact of my anger on relationships and to understand what purpose my shutting down and closing myself off to feedback served. I had much trust in the group process to see me through what I knew would be stormy times.

I have grown to understand and to accept that the mountain will always be a part of my history—there was no magic "memory eraser." I have come to accept the strength of being a survivor, as well as negative aspects, which prevent me from knowing what real living is all about. I have accepted as a gift the grace of God that allowed me to come through this situation with the determination not only to help myself, but to reach out to others with mountains in their lives they cannot name. Those things in my life that I have worked so hard to hide, tried so desperately to keep secret, have produced some of the greatest "stuff" for doing ministry. Sharing my story gives hope to others, and it also reaffirms the value of who I am.

The greatest gift I received during that year was another woman with the story of incest. One day in group, as I struggled not to break down under the weight of knowing that my primary caregivers were not capable of giving me care, this Catholic nun gently reached over and touched my hand. Who knows at what point of discouragement and despair the simplest act of love may reach a soul and turn it again to the light? This simple act of love taught me that my family of origin might never be there for me, but in the providence of God many others have been sent to reach out and touch my life with love, concern, compassion, and care.

Many truths came together for me during that intense one-year journey. I realized that my whole life had been lived in grayness. I realized that my mother had only given me birth, for she did not know how to teach me about life; for no one had been there to teach her. I have experienced "the New Birth." I'm learning ways to express my anger so that it is constructive. I have learned how to share and to be vulnerable.

I am committed to learning as much as I can about myself and how to be a mountain-mover so that I can be an example for my sister, for my "mothers," and for my daughters. I have gone through the pain of reconciling with both my parents after their deaths. I am able to say that I love both of my parents. My anger at the pain they caused me has not dissolved the love. I hate what my father did to me as a child. I hate that my mother was not willing to leave him or capable of doing so when confronted with the truth of my situation. I hate that she had a "poor me" attitude and a victim's stance in life. I hate that he was a sick man and abused me, my sister, and my mother.

My mother was a woman with hopes, dreams, and aspirations before she elected to become a wife and mother. My often unfounded expectations of her kept us at a distance for many years. I wanted her to be perfect for me, but she was human. She lived the life she chose though often she was sad, disappointed, and hurt. She wanted her own prince charming and never got him. She wanted a perfect daughter. She never got that either. She was a failure as a mother, but this was not her number one priority in life. She chose to be a wife. I am grieving for my mother. I miss her terribly, and I love her. From my father I have gained my love of knowledge and excellence; a love of good clothes and grooming habits, and an outgoing personality. Yet, I realize that I have a mean, rebellious streak that is just like him and a deep-seated anger that will feed on itself if left unchecked. My father is who and what he was. There is no changing my past. I cannot make him better or different.

I now understand that many of our actions and reactions today are based on early experiences with our parents that we continue to transfer to significant others, mates, and children as well as to work, church, and social relationships. Adult awareness gives us the power to change our mental tapes and to re-parent ourselves in a different manner. Every occasion in life is one from which we can learn. Our lives begin with loss, the loss of the security of our mother's womb. To be able to truly cut the cords that bound me to both parents has been the first step toward living my life in its fullness.

VI

I have found that as a daughter of a loving God, who is not bound to the gender of my father, I have rights and privileges. I have the right to be delivered and made whole. I have a right to be freed from the demonic spirits which kept me at the foot of that mountain, chained in pain for so many years. I searched until I discovered that the covenant decreed that Jesus was my Shalom and that I could be made whole. My digging uncovered that my shame and my pain did not have to remain in control of my life and that if the mountain didn't want to move, I could.

Clinical Pastoral Education, therapy, and my personal life of faith began to utilize the mountain as the place to begin sharing my story. Wisdom allowed me the time necessary to comprehend the fact that my hurt and my pain held the potential for the unique and beautiful within me to be released. With time for renewal, refreshing, and revival I moved away from the mountain in order to get a new view. I came to understand that God's original intent for my life was to be a blessing to the Kingdom. Even though evil had been permitted to touch my life, invade my space and erect a mountain, the original intent remained. My former fears turned into compassion. My destruction, rage, and anger were changed into a hunger and thirst for wholeness. And my perfectionist tapes were changed to new tunes of "let me tell you how to scale a mountain!" And day by day new instructions have been played, through prayer and meditation.

Climbing a mountain is never a once-and-for-all-time event. For new mountains are yet being created, and old mountains are intact. However, learning to do theology from the underside, the backside or even on the side of the mountain gives new hope and courage in the God of mountains. My God has called me to be that "virtuous woman" of Proverbs 31. Truly, this *sister-girl* was a mountain mover and shaker who did many things well. As a younger woman, I felt that this chapter spoke about a little soft-spoken, docile woman, dressed in white, whose honor came from knowing how to be submissive to her "man" who sat in the council of elders at the gate.

Searching for new tools, methods, implements, and equipment to help move my mountain, led me to understand and to experience that she was an ISCHAR CHAHIL. This Hebrew term means a woman of strong force, courage, and tenacity. Her perseverance and strength to climb over, go through, or simply walk around and away from obstacles and mountains to achieve her status, spoke to me in a new way. She fulfilled her destiny and became one of the many women in the Old Testament who refused to let mountains dictate her life and lifestyle. Today, I realize and accept the fact that I am called and compelled to be a "virtuous woman!"

On this side of the mountain, from a different vantage point, I thank God for the journey of examining my mountain. My journey has enabled me to talk about the painful effects of domestic violence to other sisters, and free them to speak of their own experiences. My journey has forced me to write about my journey and to share my points of wholeness which will encourage other sisters to keep digging and shoveling away. My journey with the mountain forced me to seek out help in order to become a helper, to search for comfort in order to become a comforter, and to become a storyteller for those who cannot yet speak.

The mountain is part of my life. The mountain is no longer in control, but it is a piece of my "herstory" which impels me, motivates me, and assists me in reaching out, speaking out, and doing ministry with other women. The mountain caused me to form a *para*-church group, *Woman to Woman Ministries, Inc.*, which provides both education and support for women of color and lets them know that mountains do exist and that you *can* choose to move!

Seminary and the church would receive a failing grade when it comes to making mountain-movers. And yet, seminary forced me to continue seeking for answers to the missing piece. Seminary taught me that faith was living, experiencing, reflecting, and acting with God, who is very real and very present, even in spite of mountains. I learned how to "do" theology in seminary, with all of its confining and limiting boundaries. For Church History especially taught me and gave me an appreciation for wrestling with truth, as we understand it. I continue to wrestle with my own truth as I learn how to make space and room for myself in the church of the Living God.

I am an ordained elder in the United Methodist Church, a product of a seminary with a fine reputation and a quality faculty, and I am a survivor of these systems of sameness, which is an idol god! God said to the wandering, chosen people of Israel long ago, and to the victims and survivors of violence today, "You have been circling this mountain too long, it's time for you to turn . . ." (Deut. 2:3) Mountains won't move easily, but, *sister-friend*, you *can* move, you *will* move and you MUST!

❧

Notes

Parts of this article appeared in *Double Stitch: Black Women Write about Mothers and Daughters*, ed. Patricia Bell-Scott et al. (Boston: Beacon Press, 1991), 152-62.

1. Chung Hyun Kyung, *Struggle to Be the Sun Again* (Maryknoll, N.Y.: Orbis Books, 1990), 3.

Seduced by Faith:
Sexual Traumas and Their Embodied Effects

JENNIFER L. MANLOWE

This essay presents a psychosocial case study and an analysis of the sexually traumatic roots of eating disorders and the faith that reproduces them. It is based on my Ph.D. dissertation in psychology and religion, in which I interviewed nine women who had three experiences in common: all of the women were sexually abused as children by a trusted family member or family friend; all had struggled with problems of body image, appetite, and weight; and all considered themselves to be (or to have been) "women of faith." I call them Melinda, Janine, Natalie, Renita, Margery, Haddock, Samantha, Stephanie, and Cherise. Because I worked without a control group, posing open-ended questions to women I knew, this research is subjective and "unscientific." But the advantage of an in-depth, qualitative method is that it allows the respondent the freedom to say as little or as much as is comfortable. Since issues of control were central to the women interviewed, I felt the advantages of this "unclean" research style outweighed the disadvantages.

I selected college-educated women of various races, ethnicities, sexual preferences, class backgrounds, and affiliations to Christian denominations. All were participants in Overeaters Anonymous, a twelve-step recovery group. Such groups bill themselves as spiritual programs (successful recovery is dependent on a Higher Power) that facilitate abstinence from a destructive substance or pattern of behaviors.

Before undertaking this study, I suspected important relationships between a woman's eating disorder and her religious and sexually traumatic past. From the work I have done since 1983 with victims of rape and physical, verbal, and emotional abuse as well as from my own experience dealing with sexual abuse and eating problems, I believe many women "wear" the struggle to regain self-respect on their bodies; and I have seen more than one woman make sense of a depriving relationship to her body—her enemy—with religious language. Christian scriptural precedents for this kind of sense-making are abundant. The following examples show how central violent suffering and deprecation of the individual will are to redemption:

> He was wounded for our transgressions, he was bruised for our iniquities; upon him was the chastisement that made us whole, and with his stripes we are healed. (Isa. 53:5)

I know that nothing good dwells in me, that is my flesh. I can will what
is right, but I cannot do it . . . sin dwells within me. (Rom. 7:18–20)

I expected to hear throughout the interviews a sense of bodily shame,
born of the incest trauma, being explained theologically or *spiritualized*. In
my early work with battered women (1985–90), I heard women reflect on
their own abuse in ways that divinized their suffering: "Like Jesus, I must suffer for my husband to come to Christianity." At other times I have heard
women with eating disorders blame themselves for their inability to resist
binging. One woman said, "I am powerless over my fleshly appetite. It's as if
I have a monster within me that cannot be satisfied." I expected to hear incest
survivors reiterate similar themes. Instead, I heard more nuanced versions of
these same issues. Jesus was rarely mentioned as a role model of self-sacrifice;
but Christian notions of *a good woman*—one who is long-suffering, selfless,
obedient, passive, and nonappetitive—emerged in every interview. Christian
discourse is deeply inscribed in female flesh, particularly through the medium
of sexual violence.[1] Incest teaches a woman that she is unworthy of respect,
that she must obey to live (or to earn affection), that she must sacrifice to preserve the family unit, and that her own needs are dangerous.

I bring together these themes throughout this essay, and I offer a critique
of paternalistic methods of empowerment found in Christian discourse and in
twelve-step groups. I believe that as long as the survivor of incest depends on
a paternalistic God who will save her if she surrenders her will to Him, her
struggle for power and meaning—masked by preoccupation with food,
appetite, and weight—will forever be a source of conflict. Her psychosocial
conflict is not about food but about a particularly-gendered identity. As a
woman, a survivor has been taught, in a multitude of ways, to hang her security upon external validation. Female redemption is to come from outside herself—from the approval of others, from a male savior, or, in twelve-step
parlance, from a Higher Power. I argue that a survivor's empowerment
process includes disentangling these internalized messages and meanings. As
long as survivors of incest rely on a paternalistic and transcendent rescue,
they are seduced into repeating the paradigm of helpless victim and powerful
parent—the paradigm of their abuse. Such a model for recovery is a model
for a permanent trance that ultimately disempowers the survivor. Her future
needs to include affirming relationships that do not depend on her surrender.

I hope readers will discern through the examples drawn from my case
studies how frequently these survivors reveal psychological and social conflicts, born from their incest trauma, in their religious discourse. Religious
language is available to give spiritual meaning to the abuse survivor's psychosocial symptoms. But faith does not mitigate the signs of past abuse in her
relationship to her body. Instead, religious discourse both shapes and is
shaped by the abusive past and, at points, reflects a double wounding.

Below, I explore some interconnected themes found in the survivors'
religious discourse: (1) that the survivor's hunger and food behaviors are
symptoms of her evil; (2) that food rituals are a source of meaning and

value; (3) that the female survivor is guilty and worthy of blame; (4) that her parent's nature is God's nature; (5) that prayer will heal her wounded self; and (6) that a survivor's suffering has a divine purpose.

Hunger Is a Symptom of Evil

Like fasting medieval saints, incest survivors experience their bodily sensations—especially hunger—as forces that could mushroom out of control. The saints who directed their hunger toward the eucharist did so partly because it was a self-limiting or self-contained food: since the communicant receives only one serving, there is no chance of a binge.[2] Like contemporary incest survivors with eating disorders, these ascetics felt desperately vulnerable before bodily needs and used food refusal to destroy them.

The survivor may express her damaged sense of self through her behavior with food. For Janine, refusing food or eating only selected kinds of food were means of self-repair and purification:

> When I was hungry, I felt like I was living right. I even felt better when I would eat only fruits and vegetables, even when hungry. Pretty soon I was able to convince my mind and my body that such feelings of purity were much better than any fattening food. I was on my way to becoming the invulnerable perfection that I really craved. To eat bad foods when hungry would so annihilate my self-esteem that it was never worth the indulgence. If I ever binged, it would be on what I called "air foods"— ones that were virtually calorieless. I believed the kind of food that went into my body had the power to absolve or disgrace me, and I would feel these feelings deeply depending on what I had ingested.

What the survivor does with food corresponds to her history of being violated. She enacts the violence against her as she binges. What was "put into her" (whether a finger, an object, a penis, or a tongue) in sexual abuse had the power to taint her and make her feel ashamed. The metaphor of food reveals and extends the defiling power that sexual abuse had on her. When she ingests the foods she calls bad, the degrading memories that she experienced while being abused again emerge. Food refusal, purging, and consumption of only "good" foods regulate these memories' entry into conscious awareness.

Food Rituals Create Meaning and Value

All of the women I interviewed grew to crave sensations that would provide comfort and relief from shame-producing memories, body-image dread, powerlessness, and a sense of doom. All nine of the survivors developed relationships to food that reveal a spiritual quest for redemptive attachment. Having no one whom they could trust, they bonded with food, animating it with cultural meanings. Whether what the survivor did or avoided doing with food produced positive or negative feelings, food, unlike the people closest to her, was a trustworthy object—it was in her control. Through her private food behavior, the survivor could evoke and numb her shame, seeking to atone for her felt character flaws—a project which becomes a self-destructive cycle.

Samantha told me that "not being able to trust a God or a Higher Power" was a direct outcome of being abused. Yet she felt that her inability to surrender to this God was the source of her current problems. She said, "I resent having to do it all alone." Her description of her pattern of coping through food reveals a process of social withdrawal. Food took the place of both God and her parents as a vehicle to transcend emotional desolation:

> The only person I could ever trust was myself—the only person who could save me was myself. My caretakers were either abusive or were not saving me, they were not rescuing me. So I could not trust anyone. I think insofar as I could not turn to any sort of benign God for comfort, I had to be able to do something that I could do for myself—you know, I mean, my parents certainly had no clue how to comfort me. So I turned to food. I had to do it; comfort wasn't one of the options in my family.

When we try to empower ourselves in isolation, we are likely to turn to a method of coping that works to mask as well as to manage the enormity of our pain. Addictive food consumption or refusal can work temporarily to displace the anxiety and depression that develop as a result of the trauma of sexual abuse. Habits and compulsions are addictive by virtue of their arousing archaic narcissistic fantasies and blissful moods that provide relief from painful emotions.[3] These anaesthetizing escapes map out—and disguise—a search for compensation for the deprivation that survivors experience in their human relationships. Food is often the most accessible escape. As Cherise said, "Food is the only legal drug available to a child."

Females Are at Fault

The biblical account of the Creation, as Christians have traditionally interpreted it, blames Eve for the advent of universal sin. Her sexualized disobedience was the cause of humanity's fall from grace, by bringing lust into the world. The message to any girl is simple: "I'm a female just like Eve, therefore I, too, bring about lust."[4] As a child, and even now, Renita wonders whether her perpetrators, who accused her of being seductive, were right. In her words,

> I did feel responsible for what had happened. . . . I start feeling like, well, maybe they were right. Maybe I shouldn't have tried to look good, or wear, you know, fashionable clothes. I was always defiant as a child. Like if they said don't wear something that showed my arms or stomach, I'd wear it. So I'd feel like, well, if I hadn't done that . . . if I had covered up my body—it wouldn't have happened . . . maybe if I were fat and unattractive, you know, nobody would touch me.

For females raised in the Roman Catholic tradition, as were Renita and Janine, the focus on asexuality, via adoration of the Virgin Mary, could begin early. Identifying with Mary as an icon of asexuality can help the child victim dissociate from her sexuality. Although neither Renita nor Janine explicitly expressed this identification, other Catholic women survivors with whom I have worked have identified with "the virgin" out of a desire to be impenetrable. But the untenable image of Mary can also work to shame the child who was sexually abused. For no one can be like Mary—a virgin mother.

Childhood sexual assault exploits the child by prematurely introducing her to her sexuality. Her body may be involuntarily aroused, and consequently she feels betrayed by and alienated from it. She incorporates these feelings into her developing perception of her body.[5] Eventually the survivor has to realize that the crime was not caused by her sexuality or by her body, but that the sexual relationship was the means through which the offender made use of the child for his own satisfaction.

Parents and God Are Alike

Freud posited that God was an exaltation of parental images; but too often, mental health professionals pay little attention to their clients' ideas of God.[6] Because one's God-image is formed in relation to early experiences with one's parents, listening to the content of a survivor's God-language and religious imagination is essential to discerning her world of wishes, fears, hopes, and dreams.

Samantha reacted very strongly to my question about her idea of God: "I refuse to use the term God; it's too loaded for me. It's the God of wrath, it's the God of judgment, it's the God of shaming, it's the God of punishment." The parental aspect of this rejected deity was very clear to Samantha. She told me directly, "As a little kid, my parents were God, always shaming and forever punishing me."

Cherise's response indicated that God and Satan were both inseparable in her mind from her father. Her church community and her father left her feeling like "a perpetual sinner." She told me:

> My grandmother took me to church and I hated it. I remember people who I'd never seen before would be telling me I was a sinner, and that I was bad and that it was because of me that Jesus died. I didn't even know who Jesus was. I thought he was the boy down the street and I wondered out loud, "Was he the one who was hit by a car?" They would respond back, "Heathen! Satan has her!" Nobody explained, and this made me more confused, because Satan I did know—he was my father. My concept of God mirrored my relationship to my father.

Because one's relationship to God grows out of relationships to parents, the survivor's conflicts concern ultimate questions about who she is and why she is here. Her sense of meaninglessness does not represent a vague philosophical angst about being mortal, but evolves out of the specific experience of incest, which teaches the survivor acutely painful lessons about the meaning of her life as a woman. The survivors I interviewed all struggled against the lessons that being objectified had taught them. None wanted to believe that the only way she could find relational meaning was through her ability to please. Each one wrestled with these issues through her body, managing conflicts over the threat of meaninglessness by ritually imbuing food with symbolic content that helped her determine her worth and identity.

At times food served as a good god, a wished-for parent. It comforted when she felt lonely, soothed her anxiety, nourished her when she felt emotionally deprived, and rewarded her for coping with a life that would crush most people. At times food served as a guide, praising the survivor's goodness when she ate the "right" amount and wasn't greedy or self-focused. Not only the larger culture's messages about proper female behavior, but also the controlling voice of the offender, may be heard in this god. At other times, the survivor's food behavior revealed a cruel god who teased her with temptation and then berated her for having indulged herself. This god too has the voice of the perpetrator, holding her accountable for all her appetites and punishing her with shame. This despotic voice also proclaimed her doomed to a failed, isolated life due to her abnormally voracious appetite, which would surely make her body repulsive.

Prayer Will Heal

When the father seduces his daughter into sexually earning his favor and the mother does not see such offenses, the survivor realizes that the human world offers her no protection. She learns that she "will not be able to get her emotional needs met nor be active in the world; she must serve the needs of others."[7] All nine of the survivors I interviewed had moments when they prayed to God to protect them, to heal their pain, to rescue them from their helpless situation, to guide them in the right way to live so that they would not have to suffer.

At age ten, Janine would pray daily from a devotional book called *My Utmost for His Highest*. She would ask God for "strength to have the discipline to serve only Him." She spoke of writing diaries full of prayers that her "selfish nature would be purged . . . so that I could better serve God." She prayed, "He must increase and I must decrease." She "would search in the Bible for psalms and prayers that affirmed celibacy and my wish to eat only vegetables." Her father fought with her over her refusal to eat meat. She told me, "It was a battle that I felt powerful enough to stand up for. I could say no to food, but I could not tell my father to leave me alone." Janine clearly uses God's "largeness" and the Bible to legitimate her righteous need for boundaries, but unfortunately boundaries around food were the only ones that, as a woman, she could assert with a biblical foundation.

Many of these survivors went through periods when they felt something was dreadfully wrong within them as a result of the sexual violation. They pleaded to God not only to protect them, but also to purify them from their essential sinfulness. Stephanie articulates how deeply she feared being tainted by her grandfather's abuse:

> I was always extremely ashamed of my body. I had frequent dreams about ugly things growing in my body. I felt my grandfather transmitted

his evil inside of me and I lived in terror most of my life waiting for those evil seeds—that evil root—to bear fruit. When I was nine or ten especially, I'd wake up at two or three in the morning and I would open a Bible and—I couldn't understand anything, but I would try to read and would think, if I set the Bible by my bed, it will protect me. And then if I die, they will say the last thing she was doing was reading the Bible.

Stephanie's prayers reveal that she believed the perpetrator's messages holding her responsible for the incest, and believed that God, like the perpetrator, blamed her. The same God had the power to absolve her and make her "good," in much the way that the parent who was not the perpetrator holds the power to affirm the child's goodness by believing her.

The survivors in this study received no reparation until, as adults, they found psychotherapeutic support. They seemed to know cognitively that the disgrace belonged to their offenders, but their affect, posture, and voice volume revealed a continuing sense of shame and self-blame. Victims of trauma often experience self-cognition which would be more appropriate to the perpetrator. A culture that blames the victim collaborates with the perpetrator in making it excruciatingly difficult for the survivor of sexual crime to overcome a feeling of being sinful, unredeemable without the favor of God.

Suffering Is God's Will

All of the nine survivors interviewed for this study went through periods of believing that the abuse was God's will. In her struggle with her abusive past and painfully compulsive present, Renita saw God as the only possible source of meaning for her life:

I'm more desperate than any normal person, in the sense that I really need to believe in God to just—just to kind of make it. If there weren't a God, that would be awful. I mean all this suffering and very hard work has to pay off. If there is a God, then maybe I'm supposed to go through this, then there's some sort of purpose to my life. . . . If there is no God, then there's no purpose . . . and my working through the pain of my past has no point. My living today has no point. Why bother if there is no reward for all this?

Janine, like Renita, related a desire for a God figure, though she was not fully able to convince herself that such a figure exists. To hold an omnipotent God in her mind would entail holding herself responsible for her past; if God (always a male pronoun) is potent, then why would "He" allow violence against a child? Because that child deserved punishment? To maintain a sense of innocence while simultaneously believing in a potent God meant to Janine that God could not be just. Yet without God, life was painfully empty. Janine wrestled with her construction of God: "I ache inside when I think that there's no one out there who cares about me. I mean, why go on if no one's there? I wish I could believe that there was some power that could help me reclaim my power." Hope depended on help from an outside source for the majority of the survivors

I interviewed. Their horizontal, human relationships had failed them, so they moved into a vertical one. As Stephanie put it, "God's the only one I can trust."

Yet, as children, all nine survivors believed that God was silent and that his silence revealed that he was ashamed of them. More mature solutions to the problem of God's silence might be to believe that God is ineffectual, or that God is a fiction made up out of our boundless wish for parental love and protection. Survivors of chronic childhood trauma face the task of grieving not only for what they lost but also for what was never theirs to lose—the early development of a foundation of trust. They must mourn the lack of belief in a good parent, a loss tantamount to abandonment by God. As they recognize that they were not responsible for their fate, they confront the despair that they could not face in childhood.[8]

Looking to secular culture for aid in finding meaning, the survivor finds that it is not just her offending male relative who experiences females as the "touchable class." Her female body is humiliating to her because the choice to make it visible and sexual is not her own. Renita is a survivor of multiple molestation by the men in her family. She does not know what it would be like to be out from under a minimalizing male gaze. She recalls times when she would analyze her eating disorder and doubt God's existence: "I start feeling sorry for myself sometimes over having this problem with food and my self-image and then I start overanalyzing everything and then I doubt God— and the meaning of God, and wonder if my life has any meaning really."

The pattern of Renita's "overanalyzing" reveals the connection between her symptoms of trauma and the core grief of loss of a source of meaning. Focusing on her helplessness around her bulimia becomes a way to distract her from "heavier" issues. Attending Overeaters Anonymous to talk about hopelessness over feeling "fat" is a common distraction from the weighty matter of incest. To diagnose oneself with an eating disorder is far more manageable than to name a parent as one's sexual violator; and kicking sweets is far easier than kicking flashbacks or the myriad feelings of depression and rage that follow remembering rape.

Spiritual or magical solutions to trauma have their appeal and may help increase enrollment in twelve-step programs. But, as Samantha illustrates, when one prays and nothing changes, it's frustrating:

> I was wondering where was God when I was being abused? I mean he totally ignored me as a child. Even today, I get the feeling that there is something wrong with me and I am a freak from outer space and all that stuff. A protestant minister at the twelve-step meeting once said, "Well, all your Higher Power wants is for you to be happy." And so on and so forth. So, why doesn't my Higher Power do something? I don't know, I guess I need more trust.

* * *

Samantha's temerity in asking, "Where was God when I was being abused?" is the very courage that she must nurture to see the trauma as more than a personal injustice. That Samantha ended up feeling she needed to surrender her skepticism to her Higher Power exemplifies the central theological issue in this project. The paternalistic discourse that weaves through both Christianity and the language of twelve-step programs keeps women stuck in cycles of shame, passivity, isolation, and the self-blaming belief that their only real problems are their addictions and their "stubborn wills." A survivor seeking a better sense of self must find a place where her will is not seen as the source of her problems. Her will, her power to act on her own behalf in the social world, is something she must recognize and nurture.

As a feminist working with survivors, I cringe when I think of a woman seeking the will of an external, masculine God. To the extent that recovery through twelve-step programs depends on reliance on a Higher Power, these programs are based on a patriarchal ideology that has no place in female liberation. Twelve-step groups have been known to save lives. But "surrendering our wills" is at the core of female oppression in patriarchy. Like other feminists in psychology and theology, I believe we need to find an inner will which is both our own voice and part of a collective liberating movement.

Asking a survivor to search within herself for strength, hope, and courage is also asking her to contend with the horrors of memories she has been trying to avoid, to manage through symptoms, or to soothe through her quest for external spiritual meaning. No survivor can empower herself without help from others. Sexual trauma profoundly affects the survivor's human relationships, which can become infused with suspicion and vulnerable to disruption. Help or friendship may be perceived as counterfeit nurturance, as insincere and unreliable. Trust in people and communities can be impaired and difficult to recover.[9] The survivor's wish for an external redeemer reveals that she has internalized the perpetrator's view of her, and that her religious community does not support her empowerment. Feelings of abandonment fester inside a survivor who has been betrayed not only by the perpetrator of abuse but by her social environment as well. Yet in order to move past destructive patterns, the survivor will need to reach out to others. She needs support in finding her own voice, her own language; and encouragement to honor her will to survive can help her begin overcoming a wish for paternal rescue.

For survivors with devout Christian backgrounds, rethinking Christian rhetoric and institutions is paramount for overcoming the valorization of female self-abnegation. As survivors question patriarchal notions of God, they move away from giving theological meaning to their abuse experience. They see that such an experience makes sense only in a culture that justifies the sexist allocation of power. For some survivors, to question paternalistic constructions of God and self can provoke feelings of a second abandonment. In facing their victimized pasts, they have had to leave the enchanted notion of home. In challenging the ways in which their religions of origin and twelve-step groups silence them into daughterly obedience to divine will, they confront the possibility of having to leave home—that which is familiar—a second time. As one survivor asks, "How many homes can a person leave?"

A survivor needs ongoing support to deconstruct the governing masculinist world view that has so deeply encoded itself upon her flesh. Natalie garnered such support by taking a women's studies course. Because of the breadth of the questions she could explore there, she was able not only to ponder the reality of oppression, but also to explore possible ways of dealing with such evil. For a just future, the absence of a patriarchal god seemed to be paramount. In Natalie's words, "After I read Mary Daly, I found myself feeling like how could God allow this to happen to women all these centuries and all these millions of women . . . generation after generation, it keeps happening. Just getting a sense of being overwhelmed with this, and the rage of it, and feeling like if there is a God—that God would either have to be completely powerless, or evil." Natalie eventually dethroned the patriarchal god who does not respond to atrocities against female humanity. She experienced the vacancy that such a dethronement allowed and filled it with her idea of a god who cares about humanity. She made clear that such a god needs allies in the world to bring about social justice.

Resisting Christian misogyny includes exposing the politics behind the burdensome religious rhetoric that portrays women as dangerously appetitive, virtuous only insofar as they are self-depriving. When external salvation achieved through appeasing a magical masculine parental rescuer is recognized as a cultural myth, we see that the psychosocial gender arrangements which that myth supports need to be radically altered. Despair underlies the Christian theology of redemption—a despair masked as hope through a miracle man. When one depends on a transcendent miracle for "redemption," one is in crisis.

The crisis that incest survivors experience is both personal and cultural. They need support in working through the facts of their history: no one was there to protect them, no one is there to heal their grief and rage, and not even the best therapy or spirituality group can totally repair the emotional, physical, and social damage that they have suffered. There is no grand cure because incest is not a disease; it is a crime that too often has the sanction of cultural myths. Only in the context of supportive and politically conscious advocacy can a survivor begin to accept the reality that recovery is always partial in a patriarchal culture. With support, one can begin to work through the aftermath of trauma, focusing on constructively resisting and preventing abuse. As survivors take small steps toward their own partial wholeness, they often find connections that lead them to work for social change.

One step that I believe is necessary in effecting broad cultural change is to expose the false theological underpinnings of "thin" myths, the messages our culture circulates about women's bodies. Both individually and socially, acknowledging the realities of our past and present circumstances forms a basis for making practical decisions as to where we want to go. Metahistorical solutions, saviors who love us so much they will die for us, paternal Gods (or any powerful others) who promise to protect and heal us if we loyally surrender our wills, are all patriarchally engendered false hopes. They may be seductive to those of us who have felt consistently hopeless, but they impede our authentic empowerment.

Notes

1. For key literature on this topic, see Joanne Carlson Brown and Carole R. Bohn, eds., *Christianity, Patriarchy, and Abuse: A Feminist Critique* (New York: The Pilgrim Press, 1989); Annie Imbens and Ineke Jonker, *Christianity and Incest* (Minneapolis: Fortress Press, 1992).

2. See Caroline Walker Bynum, *Holy Feast, Holy Fast: The Religious Significance of Food to Medieval Women* (Berkeley: University of California Press, 1987).

3. Richard Ulman and Doris Brothers, "A Self-Psychological Reevaluation of Posttraumatic Stress Disorder (PTSD) and its Treatment: Shattered Fantasies," *Journal of the American Academy of Psychoanalysis* 15/2 (1987): 175–203.

4. See Sheila S. Redmond, "Christian Virtues and Child Sexual Abuse," cited in Brown and Bohn.

5. Elaine Westerlund, *Women's Sexuality After Childhood Incest* (New York: W.W. Norton, 1992) 59–60; Carol Adams, conversation with author, March 24, 1993.

6. See Anna Maria Rizzuto, *The Birth of a Living God* (Chicago: University of Chicago Press, 1979).

7. See Kim Chernin, *The Hungry Self: Women, Eating, and Identity* (London: Virago Press, 1986).

8. Judith L. Herman, *Trauma and Recovery: The Aftermath of Violence—From Domestic Abuse to Political Terror* (New York: Basic Books, 1992), 193.

9. Robert J. Lifton and Charles B. Strozier, transcribed conversation. Center for Violence and Human Survival, New York, N.Y. Spring 1992.

Born Again, Free from Sin?
Sexual Violence in Evangelical Communities

ANDY SMITH

[When you become Born Again] You are no longer alone. The father-hood [*sic*] of God forms the true brotherhood of man [*sic*] . . . when you encounter another Christian . . . no introductions are necessary. You share the greatest bond on earth. There is no fellowship on earth to compare with it.

—Billy Graham[1]

As my father abused me, he quoted Bible verses to show how bad I was. . . . He said I was going to hell because I didn't love him. I would tell him I did love him and would do whatever he asked except that sexual stuff but he would again work it around that I was sinning. In the last days before Christ returns, there will be children with "inordinate" (not the usual) affection for their parents. I was one of this last generation's terrible sinners.

—A Survivor[2]

When I became Born Again, I believed I was in a fellowship like no other on Earth, the kind of fellowship Billy Graham describes. I knew I was certainly safe from sexual violence. Evangelical men were the only trustworthy men. When I was taking a class on the New Testament and Women, the professor discussed the problems of sexual and domestic violence in Christian communities. I immediately left the class, telling my friends that this professor obviously did not know anything about evangelicals. We certainly did not have these kind of problems. The professor recommended that we read Marie Fortune's *Sexual Violence: The Unmentionable Sin*. I refused even to look at this book, certain that the author must be crazy and nothing she would say could have anything to do with me.

My world collapsed when my Bible study leader sexually assaulted a friend of mine. At first, I thought this experience was just one horrible aberration from what I could expect from evangelical men. But as I opened my ears to the sexual violence that was becoming increasingly commonplace in my evangelical community, I realized that the church was no longer a safe place. I began to think that it was I who knew nothing about evangelicals, and I finally read Fortune's book. I began to discover that sexual/domestic violence was not an aberration, but it was intrinsic within evangelical communities. In fact, sexual abuse is *more likely* to occur in conservative religious homes.[3] How is it that evangelical theology, which promises safety and fellowship, seems to contribute to the epidemic of violence in women's and children's lives?

Evangelical theology is not monolithic.[4] However, for the sake of making some generalizations, I will use a representative sample of evangelical thought, Billy Graham's *How to Be Born Again*, to explore how some of the tenets of evangelical theology reinforce a culture of violence within evangelical communities. I will then explore how evangelical theology can be redefined so that it can be an instrument in resisting this violence.

In *How to Be Born Again*, Graham explains the necessity of becoming Born Again. He argues that when Adam and Eve disobeyed God, they committed a sin that was punishable by death. Humanity became separated from God by sin. Because God takes sin seriously, and because God could not go back on His word that if they sinned they must die, there had to be a sacrifice to atone for this death.

> He [God] had said to Adam and Eve at the very beginning when they broke His law, "You shall surely die."... Man had to die or God would have had to go back on His word, and God cannot be a liar or He would no longer be God. We can see that because man still sins, still defies authority and still acts independently of God, a great gulf exists between him and God.[5]

However, God also loves humanity; God wants to be reconciled with us. Consequently, God incarnated himself as Jesus who would pay that penalty of death. The only way to escape death is to accept Jesus Christ as our Lord and Savior and accept that Jesus paid our penalty by dying on the cross.

> God put my sin on Christ, who had no sin; He punished Him in my place.... By God's action the righteousness of Christ was put on us who believe, "that we might become the righteousness of God in Him."... When the Bible says that the person who believes in Jesus is justified as a gift by His grace, this sounds like more than a mere pardon. If I'm a criminal whom the president or the governor pardons, everyone knows I'm still guilty. I simply don't have to serve my sentence. But if I'm justified, it's *just-as-if-I'd* never sinned at all.[6]

Even though people may do good works, they still have a sinful nature that separates them from God. After they become Born Again, however, even if they commit immoral acts, they are still justified before God. Jesus' death wipes away one's sins in God's eyes.

Although Graham recognizes that Born-Again Christians may still commit immoral acts, he posits that Born-Agains can be distinguished by their moral behavior. That is, when one becomes Born-Again, one no longer wants to sin. "You are now 'born again.' You don't want to do the same old wrong things; your desires are changed."[7] Consequently, we are led to believe in evangelical communities that evangelical men will be more moral and less violent than non-evangelical Christian men. As one woman told me, "The good thing about being Born-Again is that you don't have to worry about date rape." (In fact, unbeknownst to her, her Bible study leader had sexually assaulted his girlfriend.)

The notion that evangelicals are more moral than non-evangelicals makes it difficult for evangelical women to defend themselves against potential assaults or to recognize abusive behavior. For instance, since rapists plan their crime in advance, they generally give off many warning signals. One signal is that they generally "test" the victim to see if she is vulnerable to assault. They do this by overstepping the potential victim's boundaries in some way (i.e., they may be overly friendly, touch her when she feels uncomfortable, or try to get her to drink) to see how she reacts. If she does not assert herself then, he may assume she will not say anything if he attacks her.

Because women trust evangelical men and assume that they would never think of assaulting someone, they often ignore obvious warning signs. In fact many women are so shocked by the assault, they have a difficult time fighting back at all or even yelling "NO!" In addition, evangelical women often think to themselves afterward that, since evangelical men do not assault, then what happened to them could not have been an assault. They must have asked for it in some way.

The practice of defining Born-Again Christians in terms of their expected moral behavior has also created an atmosphere of denial in evangelical communities. The pervasive attitude is that this violence cannot happen here. It is very difficult to admit that the place we thought was safe is not so safe after all. Consequently, when victims of violence speak out, evangelicals come up with explanations to dismiss their stories: it was a misunderstanding; it was no big deal; or she was leading him on. In one church, many women were complaining that their boyfriends had "the spirit of perversion," and no leader of that church thought to ask what they meant by that. It was easier to ignore their pain.

In addition, because evangelicals often see themselves as more righteous than non-Christians, they often discourage victims from seeking help in secular agencies should the church prove incapable of handling the assault. In some churches, if a woman brings a Christian man to a secular court of law for sexual assault charges, she is excommunicated. The church is supposed to be the place where all conflicts are resolved.

If a Christian victim does seek help outside the church, her problems can be compounded by the insensitivity of many secular agencies to religious concerns. In my experience, many secular feminist counselors become impatient with the religious views of evangelicals and encourage them to change their views rather than to redefine them so that they can be healing for the survivor. For instance, one woman was seeing a non-Christian counselor, and the survivor insisted that she needed to forgive her assailant. Her counselor became very frustrated with the client, trying to explain that she did not need to forgive him. She did not take into account that there is much pressure in evangelical communities to forgive and forget. Instead, it would have been more helpful to the client if she had helped her redefine forgiveness so that it could be more healing to the client.[8]

It is not only Christians but non-Christians who tend to define evangelicals in terms of their expected moral behavior. A classic example was the Jim Bakker/Jessica Hahn scandal. When this scandal became public, it was framed by the mainstream media as a sex scandal. The titles of the articles discussing the scandal included: "In God We Tryst?"[9] and "Money, Sex, and Power."[10] Virtually no one, including feminists in the anti-violence movement, framed the discussion in any other way.

This is very curious when one reads Jessica Hahn's version of what happened to her.

> Hahn told Roper [a friend of Jessica Hahn] that Bakker had pressured her into sex. Roper says, "She was overwhelmed by being in the presence of this man [Bakker], who was second to God in her mind."[11]

This is a description of a sexual assault. Bakker used his authority as a Christian minister to coerce Hahn into having sex. This would have been an excellent opportunity to highlight issues of clergy abuse and sexual violence in the church. Instead, the public, including feminists, took this as an opportunity to ridicule Born-Again Christians rather than to analyze the complexities of the situation. The message expressed was that sexual violence among Born-Again Christians is not to be taken seriously.

Why did the secular public react in this manner? They, as well as evangelicals, define evangelicals in terms of expected moral behavior. Since Born-Agains are not supposed to think about sex, non-evangelicals are eager to hear that evangelicals are all repressed sex maniacs. As Richard Neuhaus states:

> It is assumed that professional publicists of righteousness must be hiding some very juicy wickedness. . . . [Secular individuals] make no secret of their devout hope to discover that the leaders of the movement are sleeping around with loose women.[12]

This attitude prevents non-evangelical Christians from seeing Born-Again Christians as people instead of as stereotypes, and consequently, it prevents them from taking seriously the violence they face within the evangelical community. This further inhibits evangelicals from seeking help outside the church when they fear that their beliefs will not be respected.

Both evangelicals and non-evangelicals need to define Born-Again Christians in terms of their faith commitment, not in terms of their moral behavior. In other words, what distinguishes evangelicals is not that they are holy and moral, or that they will exhibit certain behavioral characteristics, but that they accept Jesus Christ as their Lord and Savior. Belief in a certain faith does not make one a better person.

Crucial to analyzing the nature of sexual violence is the issue of consent. What qualifies as consent? A popular slogan in the anti-sexual movement is "No means no." When a woman says "no" to sexual activity, then there is not consent. However, this is an insufficient description of what constitutes consent. In a situation where one person has authority over the other person, then it may be difficult or impossible to have consent.

The most obvious example is that of incest. Even if a girl agrees to sexual activity with her father, this still constitutes sexual abuse because she is in no position to say no. As Marie Fortune states, we need "a *sexual ethic which clearly and unequivocally requires consent.* Sexual contact between persons is appropriate only when both persons are fully informed and freely choose such contact" [13] (emphasis in the original).

If two individuals are in an unequal power relationship, then sexual contact between them "cannot *with any certainty* be consensual" [14] (emphasis in the original). Other examples beside incest include therapist/ patient relationships, lawyer/client relationships, etc. Within a Christian context, Fortune argues that if a minister, who has the authority of God behind him, has sex with a parishioner, this cannot be seen as consensual because of the power differential between the two. (This is why Jessica Hahn's story qualifies as sexual abuse.)

The issue of consent is further complicated in an evangelical context because of the power differential between *all* Christian men and women. Not only do ministers have the authority of God behind them, but so do all evangelical men. Although Graham does not deal specifically with the subordination of women to men, his language clearly reflects this attitude. "God could have created us as human robots who would respond mechanically to His direction . . . [however] God wanted sons, not machines." [15]

The subordination of women to men is prevalent in evangelical thought. Women must obey their husbands, women should not be ordained. As Carl F. H. Henry argues in *Christianity Today*:

> Identical yet different by creation, man and woman have by nature different physical and psychological needs and even in the realm of redemption are intended for special roles. . . . At stake is the acceptance or rejection of a divinely established order; to annul this order leads finally to rejection not only of apostolic authority but also of divine authority. . . . The woman's proper subordination to the authority of man under God is sanctified by the subordination of Jesus Christ to God.[16]

When women are taught that they must obey and follow men, it is not surprising if they are not sure they have the right to refuse sexual contact when it is forced upon them. Consequently, evangelical women often have a particularly difficult time fighting back, or even saying "no," when they are assaulted by evangelical men. If an assault takes place within a romantic relationship (which in an evangelical context is generally seen as a precursor to marriage), a woman may feel that she has no choice but to obey the man she is going to have to obey anyway when she marries. When she is married to him, she has no right at all to refuse sexual contact. If she is abused, it is because she did not obey him sufficiently.

I am not arguing that evangelical men can never have sex because of the power differential between them and all women. However, they do need to acknowledge the power they have and to be committed not to abuse it. This would require them to be very honest with women about their intentions and have lengthy discussions with women to discover what it is the women they are with really want.

This power differential also shows that it is not possible to address sexual or domestic violence within the church without addressing its patriarchal structure. Evangelical feminists have wrestled with this issue extensively. They have proposed alternative ways of interpreting the Bible such that it does not advocate female subordination. However, these attempts are often mired in controversies of whether or not their approach is sufficiently inerrant or infallible.[17] If evangelical feminism is going to be effective in questioning the oppression women face, it may need to take more indirect approaches. One such approach, that of confronting the issues of violence against women, is suggested in Susan Thistlethwaite's "Every Two Minutes: Battered Women and Feminist Interpretation."[18]

Thistlethwaite engages in pastoral counseling of battered women. She studies the Bible with these women, pointing out the liberating passages for abused women (e.g., Jesus' defense of the woman who was about to be stoned for adultery, John 7:53–8:11). As they begin to question traditional Biblical interpretations that have not addressed the abuse with which they live, they also begin to question the teachings of female subordination that have reinforced their position as victims. As Thistlethwaite explains:

> Women can learn to imagine themselves in the text . . . that does affirm women (such as women's discipleship) and on the basis of their own experience, which shows that they have been the ones to hear the Word of God and do it. This type of imagining challenges traditional interpretation . . . and moves interpretation to a new level of engagement with the contemporary life of the church.[19]

Traditionalists often justify the subordination of women by saying that women's subordination will be rewarded by the love and caring of their husbands. Although men are leaders of the household, they are supposed to be benevolent leaders. In battering relationships, men are not showing benevolence toward their wives; however, traditionalists often do not have any solutions for the problem of men who abuse their power. It is in these situations that evangelical feminists have the opportunity to minister to women in order to fill in the gap left by traditionalists. By showing abused women how the Bible does not condone the abuse they are undergoing, evangelical feminists can also indirectly encourage women to question the traditional view of male/female relationships that have contributed to their victimization.

I once attended an evangelical conference that addressed issues of sexuality. The conference presenters and participants were very conservative.[20] One presenter, a survivor of sexual abuse, conducted a workshop that stood out from the rest. She said that sexual abuse continues in the church because it is so strongly patriarchal. Women are expected to obey their husbands, children are expected to obey their parents, and parishioners are expected to obey their pastor unquestioningly. She also argued that survivors must be free to make their own choices, even if that choice is to leave the church and join the New Age movement. The only reason she said she was in the church now was because a pastor said it was okay for her to leave for nine years. I suspect that if she had made this comment in any other context, she would have been deemed heretical. However, in this context where she was talking as a survivor to an audience that had many survivors, her words were affirmed. By pointing to the reality of abuse, we can belie the notion that patriarchal relationships are healthy.

The manner in which evangelicals address issues of sexuality compounds issues of sexual violence. Evangelicals tend to look at sexuality in terms of purity (sex is pure only within marriage). As Graham states, "Chastity was the one completely new virtue which Christianity brought into the world. [One should not even look] at a man or woman with an attitude of desire or lust. To God, purity is first a matter of the heart, then of action."[21] In church we hear a lot of how we can avoid impurity by not having sex and next to nothing on how we can avoid sexual violence. We concern ourselves with the question of "the right organ in the right orifice with the right person. Little attention has been given to the context of power, consent, and choice regarding what happens to one's bodily self in a sexual relationship."[22]

Consequently, evangelicals (like everyone else) confuse sex with sexual violence. When an evangelical woman is raped, she assumes she has "sinned" by having sex because she has never been told how rape is different from sex. I have heard evangelical women say they would kill themselves if they were raped because it would mean that they were no longer "pure." Virginity needs to be redefined as something you choose to give away; it cannot be taken from you. Sexual assault does not take away your virginity.

In addition, evangelical women often assume that because they lead conservative lifestyles and dress modestly that they are invulnerable to rape. To the contrary, they are very vulnerable. Evangelical men know that women trust them and that it will be very difficult for these women to speak out. They know women would never expect an assault and will not be prepared to fight back.

In addition, evangelical churches often see the sin of the rapist as being overcome by lust, not that he perpetrated an action of violence against another person. Consequently, all he needs to do to "atone" is to pray for forgiveness from God (which is immediately granted); it is not necessary for him to seek forgiveness from the survivor, or be held accountable in a larger context, in the community and in the church.

This points to a larger problem in evangelical thought—the concept that one's relationship with God is separate from one's relationship with the community. Graham states:

> Some churches preach good works, social change, government legislation, and neglect the one thing that will help solve the problems of our world—changed men and women. Man's basic problem is first spiritual, and then social.[23]

Graham does say that if one commits a crime, one must repent and mend that broken relationship. However, his above statement suggests that it is possible to be right with God without being right with the world. While one's relationship with community is important to Graham, it is subordinate to one's relationship with God.

This thinking contributes to an atmosphere in which many evangelical men lead double lives. They are holy men in church and abusers and rapists outside of the church. Dan, a survivor, describes his "perfect Christian father":

> My father was two-faced. He appeared to be the perfect Christian, attending church on Sunday. . . . My father never used bad language and several times he even led the choir. But the rest of the time he was a different man. . . . He forced me to have sex with business partners.[24]

Because the relationship with community is subordinate to the relationship with God, survivors have little voice when evangelicals address sexual violence. Graham describes a situation in which Chaplain Gerecke talked to a Nazi general who converted to Christ. "With his Bible in his hand he said, 'I know from this book that God can love a sinner like me.' What an amazing love God exhibited for us at the cross!"[26] Nowhere in this discussion is it indicated that this general sought forgiveness from his victims or the families of the victims. Nowhere does it say that he actually did anything to fight fascism, racism, anti-Semitism, or do anything to change the world. All we know is that he read the Bible, and God forgive him of genocide. The same situation happens for rape victims when the pastor decides whether or not the perpetrator is forgiven without any input from the victims.

We need to develop an understanding that the self-in-community is not separate from self-in-God. It is not possible to be saved in Christ if one is not doing anything to make the world a better place. It is not possible to violate someone and be right with God. And it is not possible to restore one's relationship with God until one has restored one's relationship with a survivor to the satisfaction of that survivor.

Religious institutions are beginning to look at the issues of sexual violence, even evangelical institutions. However, evangelical Christians want to see instances of violence as an aberration rather than the norm. In fact, sexual violence is an integral part of the history of the church. The history of sexual abuse in Christian boarding schools which American Indian children were forced to attend is a testimony to this legacy of violence. (See Smith, this volume, pp. 377–403.) It is not sufficient for the church to deal with sexual abuse on an individual basis. We need to analyze the structure of the church and its theology and determine how they reinforce systems of violence.

Rosemary Radford Ruether discusses in *Faith and Fratricide* how the church has lost much of its ability to criticize and reform itself. She says in her discussion of the theological roots of anti-Semitism that early Christians saw themselves primarily as Jewish. Consequently the remarks they made that might seem anti-Semitic (such as railings against the Pharisees and other sectors of the Jewish community) must be seen within the context that they saw themselves as part of the same community.

> We must think ourselves back into a framework in which Christianity was within, not outside of, Judaism. The "Jews," the "leaders" who are being attacked, do not represent some "other people," but one's own people, one's own "Church" leaders, who are perceived as antithetical to authentic faith. The schism is not one that divides Christian from Jew, but one which divided Jew from Jew then and which today divides Christian from Christian.[26]

Early Christians were not maligning Judaism, but rather they were trying to reform the institutional abuses in Judaism. However, when Christianity moved outside of Judaism, these attacks against members of the Jewish community took on a whole new meaning. Then, Judaism came to represent all that was evil, and Christianity came to represent all that was good. Christianity consequently lost its prophetic and reforming message as all its own institutional abuses were projected onto Judaism and other religious traditions.

> The Church Fathers interpreted the Jewish Scriptures as though they spoke of "two peoples," a people who were sinful and condemned, the Jews, and the people of the Promise, the Church. . . .

> The meaning of the prophetic dialectic of judgment and promise is destroyed when its cohesion in a single people is pulled apart . . . the Church deprived itself of the tradition of prophetic self-criticism. The revolution of the prophets was undone by the Church. Prophetic faith was converted into self-glorification and uncritical self-sanctification. Judgment was projected upon "the Jews."

> One may also criticize any new tendency simply to project the negative side of our judgments on new "enemies" who are not ourselves or for whom we do not take responsibility. Only when prophecy is read as self-criticism can the Church recover the power of prophecy from the ideology of ecclesial triumphalism.[27]

Evangelicals continue the tradition of the Church fathers of ignoring all abuses within the church and condemning all others outside of the church. This tradition prevents these communities from looking at abuses within the church. For instance, Graham discusses the evils of non-Christian religions:

> Extreme cruelties and great injustices have been perpetrated in the name
> of religion. In China when my wife was growing up, frequently babies
> who died before cutting their teeth were thrown out to be eaten by
> pariah dogs. In India a missionary who passed the banks of the Ganges
> noticed a mother sitting on the river bank with two of her children. On
> her lap was a beautiful new baby . . . On her return home that night . . .
> the baby was gone . . . She had given her perfect baby to the god of the
> Ganges. People have made human sacrifices in the name of religion.[28]

Graham conveniently ignores the evils that have been perpetuated in the
name of Christ: the Inquisition, the Crusades, etc. As Graham's statement
indicates, the Christian practice of projecting institutional abuses onto
Judaism and other religious traditions is continuing today. This practice not
only oppresses people from non-Christian traditions, it prevents evangelicals
from critically looking at the abuses within their own communities.

When evangelicals look at the reality of sexual/domestic violence, they like
to think that it is more pronounced in other communities or that it is because
of the influence of secular/heathen cultures. However, if we are really going to
put Jesus in our context, then we must recognize that Jesus would be spending
less time ranting about the evils of other traditions and more time raging
against the evils within the Christian tradition. This is what his life was about.
The roots of sexual/domestic violence in the evangelical community are in that
community. There is no one we can scapegoat as the cause of this problem.

I think the Born-Again experience can also be redefined in such a way
that it more directly confronts the reality of institutional oppression and violence. We live in a society where racism and sexism are pervasive. All societal
institutions, the government, the media, and the church, reinforce notions of
hierarchy and domination. Since oppression is so pervasive, no one born here
can escape it. We have all internalized these messages. We can see this as part
of our "original sin."

We do not ask to be born racist or sexist, and we may have the best of
intentions, yet we receive messages before we are old enough to sort them out.
In addition, if we are white or male, we have privileges that we have, even if we
do not want them. For instance, if a woman of color is denied a job because of
her race and sex, she knows that she is the victim of racism and sexism.
However, if a white man comes in the next day and gets the job, he is completely unaware that it was his race and sex that got him the job. He assumes it
was because of his qualifications. It is the internalization of racism and sexism
and all forms of oppression that keeps us away from the God of Justice.

When we accept Christ, we accept the commitment to actively fight sexism,
racism, sexual and domestic violence, and all forms of oppression. However,
we know that despite our commitment, we will still continue to exhibit oppressive behaviors; it is a lifelong process to educate ourselves. But we commit ourselves to honesty, self-reflection, and action against the powers of oppression.
When we decide that we will no longer be loyal to the institutional systems of

violence, when we decide that we will fight injustice wherever we see it, when we educate ourselves so that we will actually be able to see injustice in all its forms—then we are truly following Christ, then we are Born Again.

❧

Notes

1. Billy Graham, *How to Be Born Again* (Waco: Word Books, 1977), 219.
2. Carolyn Holderread Heggen, *Sexual Abuse in Christian Homes and Churches* (Scottsdale: Herald Press, 1993), 46.
3. Ibid., 73.
4. I use the term "evangelical" to describe a specific grouping within conservative Christianity that split from the fundamentalist movement in the 1940s. Fundamentalism emerged as a movement within American society in the late 1800s when conservative Christians began to react to religious liberalism. However, after World War II, as fundamentalism became increasingly associated with dogmatism, anti-intellectualism, and social isolationism, a sector of the fundamentalist community attempted to break away from this label and its negative connotations and apply the name of "evangelical" to themselves. Evangelicalism did not question the basic doctrines of fundamentalism, the five fundamentals. The five fundamentals are (1) The divine inspiration (or inerrancy, depending on which fundamentalists or evangelicals you are talking to) of the Bible; (2) the deity of Christ; (3) Personal atonement through Christ's blood and the need for a personal relationship with Christ; (4) Christ's bodily resurrection; (5) Christ's second coming. Rather, it has sought to disassociate itself from society's negative image of fundamentalism by becoming more engaged in social issues and scholarly study of the Bible, by cooperating to some extent with more liberal Christians, and by showing latitude of interpretation in issues that are not encompassed in the five fundamentals (particularly in the area of eschatology).

    Since the evangelical break with fundamentalism, there have been further rifts in both groups. Evangelicals have split over the issue of biblical inerrancy. Fundamentalist groups have split with moderate fundamentalists cooperating with evangelicals or even non-Christians to advance conservative social causes and militant fundamentalists denouncing such behavior. Consequently, the distinction between moderate fundamentalists and conservative evangelicals is rather vague. I also use the term "Born-Again" interchangeably with "Evangelical" for sake of simplicity, although I realize they are not equivalent terms.

    See Ronald Nash, *Evangelicals in America* (Nashville: Abingdon, 1987); William Trollinger, "How Should Evangelicals Understand Fundamentalism?," *United Evangelical Action* 44 (September–October 1985); Edward Dobson, "Standing Together on Absolutes," *United Evangelical Action* 44 (September-October 1985); Harold J. Ockenga, "From Fundamentalism: Through New Evangelicalism to Evangelicalism," *Evangelical Roots* (Nashville: Thomas Nelson Publishing Company, 1987).
5. Graham, 36.

6. Ibid., 141–42.

7. Ibid., 143.

8. For a redefinition of forgiveness for survivors, see Marie Fortune, *Sexual Violence: The Unmentionable Sin* (New York: Pilgrim Press, 1983), 208–15. She argues that forgiveness takes time—as much time as the victims wants. Also, forgiveness cannot take place until the assailant repents. Repentance is not just a confession, but it involves a complete turning around of one's life and reparations for damages. Survivors can also see forgiveness as something that happens somewhere along their healing process when they let go of the pain so that it is no longer the biggest thing in their lives. This is not the same as pretending the abuse never happened or that they have to have any kind of relationship with the assailant.

9. "Holy Wars," *US News and World Report*, April 6, 1987, 58–67.

10. "Money, Sex, and Power," *Newsweek*, April 6, 1987, 16–22.

11. "TV's Unholy Row," *Time Magazine*, April 6, 1987, 63.

12. Richard Neuhaus, *The Naked Public Square* (Grand Rapids: Eerdmann's Publishing Co., 1984), 56–57.

13. Marie Fortune. *Sexual Violence: The Unmentionable Sin.* (New York: Pilgrim Press, 1983), 105.

14. Ibid., 110.

15. Graham, 79.

16. Carl F. H. Henry, "The Battle of the Sexes," *Christianity Today* 19/20 (July 4, 1975), 45–46.

17. See Andy Smith, "Virginia Ramey Mollenkott: An Evangelical Feminist Vision" (unpublished senior thesis, Harvard University Archives, 1988).

18. Susan Thistlethwaite, "Every Two Minutes: Battered Women and Feminist Interpretation,"in *Feminist Interpretation of the Bible*, ed. Letty Russell (Philadelphia: Westminster Press, 1985), 96–107.

19. Ibid., 104.

20. For instance, one presenter stated that you would assume all Republicans will go to heaven, but that is not true. They need to be saved first.

21. Graham, 88.

22. Fortune, 71.

23. Graham, 178.

24. Connie Brewer, *Escaping the Shadows, Seeking the Light: Christians in Recovery from Childhood Sexual Abuse* (San Francisco: Harper Collins, 1990), 31–32.

25. Graham, 147.

26. Rosemary Radford Ruether, *Faith and Fratricide* (Minneapolis: Winston Press, 1977), 231.

27. Ruether, 230–32.

28. Graham, 62–63.

Is Nothing Sacred?
The Betrayal of the Ministerial
or Teaching Relationship

Marie M. Fortune

I was asked to address the problem of sexual harassment within the academic setting. But I would like to expand the context to include the institutions in which we work: church, synagogue, seminary, and university. The problem is one of professional misconduct, that is, conduct within the professional role of minister, teacher, or administrator which betrays the trust of the professional relationship.

In the best sense of the word, we are all professionals: our profession is a calling; it requires specialized training; there are standards of conduct within the profession; we are accountable within the profession to those whom we serve and for whom we have a fiduciary responsibility. In this discussion, I will focus on ministry *and* teaching as professions because I believe that the parallel dynamics and potential for harm to those whom we serve are instructive.

Introduction

All ministers have friendships with congregants and clients; all teachers have friendships with students; all ministers have experienced sexual attraction to congregants and clients; all teachers have experienced sexual attraction to students; all ministers have experienced sexual "come ons" from congregants and clients; all teachers have experienced sexual "come ons" from students; to some extent, all ministers and teachers have probably violated the boundaries of our ministerial or teaching relationships, if not sexually, then emotionally.

These may seem like powerful indictments against the ministry and the academy. Yet to deny these assertions is to fail to comprehend that these realities are facts of life in both settings. Our professions of ministry and teaching, unlike many others, bring us into some of the most intimate, sacred, and fragile dimensions of others' lives. Paradoxically, it is because of these intimate connections that ministers and teachers face the risk of engaging in inappropriate or unethical behavior with those whom they serve or supervise. The task of the institution (whether church, synagogue, or academy) that bears responsibility for the professional conduct of its clergy or teachers is twofold: to maintain the integrity of the ministerial, teaching, or mentor relationship and to protect those persons who, due to a variety of life circumstances, are vulnerable to clergy, professors, or administrators (congregants, clients, staff members, students).

Scope of the Problem

Violation of boundaries involving sexualization of a relationship can take place in the ministerial relationship or the counseling relationship, as well as the staff supervisory, teaching, or mentor relationship. When the minister sexualizes the ministerial or counseling relationship, it is similar to the therapist's violation of the therapeutic relationship. When the teacher sexualizes the supervisory or mentor relationship with a staff member or student, it is similar to sexual harassment in the workplace and the principles of workplace harassment apply. When a child or teenager is the object of the sexual contact, the situation is one of pedophilia or child sexual abuse which is by definition not only unethical and abusive but also criminal.

Sexual contact by ministers and counselors with congregants or clients undercuts an otherwise effective ministerial relationship and violates the trust necessary in that relationship. Sexual contact by teachers or administrators with students in the academic setting undercuts an otherwise effective teacher/student or mentor relationship. It is not the sexual contact per se that is problematic but the fact that the sexual activity takes place within the ministerial or teaching relationship. The crossing of this particular boundary is significant because it changes the nature of the relationship and the potential harm that it causes is enormous.

The behaviors which occur in the sexual violation of boundaries include but are not limited to sexual comments or suggestions (jokes, innuendos, invitations, and the like), touching, fondling, seduction, kissing, intercourse, molestation, and rape. There may be only one incident or a series of incidents or an ongoing intimate relationship over time.

The Equal Employment Opportunity Commission of the United States Government defines sexual harassment in the workplace or academic setting as:

> The use of one's authority or power, either explicitly or implicitly, to
> coerce another into unwanted sexual relations or to punish another for his
> or her refusal; or the creation of an intimidating, hostile or offensive working
> environment through verbal or physical conduct of a sexual nature.

More specifically, sexual contact by ministers, counselors, or teachers in professional relationships is an instance of professional misconduct that is often minimized or ignored. It is not "just an affair" although it may involve an ongoing sexual relationship with a client, student, or congregant. It is not "merely" adultery although adultery may be a consequence if either person is in a committed relationship. It is not just a momentary lapse of judgment by the professional. Often it represents a recurring pattern of misuse of the professional role by one who neither comprehends nor cares about the damaging effects it may have on the congregant/client/student.

Actual research on the sexual involvement of clergy with congregants is sparse. A recent study, however, provides some data: 12.67 percent of clergy surveyed reported that they had had sexual intercourse with a church member. This percentage is statistically equal across denomination and theological orientation. In addition, 76.51 percent of clergy in this study reported that they knew of another minister who had had sexual intercourse with a church member.[1] But the research which is most needed to give us a clear picture of the extent of this problem is a survey of the laity themselves.

Research on sexual harassment in the workplace of the church is also limited. The United Methodist Study done in 1990 found that 77 percent of clergywomen were sexually harassed in the church. Among students responding, 54.5 percent of the women and 35.4 percent of the men reported sexual harassment. Only 8.2 percent of these students took formal action to address their situation. In 15.3 percent of these cases of harassment of students, instructors were identified as the harasser.[2] In the academy, recent research among women students finds that from 12 to 30 percent report sexual harassment.[3] Although the vast majority of offenders in reported cases are heterosexual males and the vast majority of victims are heterosexual females, it is clear that neither gender nor sexual orientation exclude anyone from the risk of offending or from the possibility of being taken advantage of in the professional relationship.

Who are the typical faculty offenders? According to Dziech and Weiner, tenured, senior faculty.[4] Who is the typical victim in the academic setting? The victim is likely to be female, a graduate student (or if undergraduate, aspiring to graduate school), has returned to school after hiatus, is divorced or separated, is a person of racial or ethnic minority, holds traditional sex role beliefs, is economically disadvantaged, appears to be a loner, or is physically attractive. In a congregation, the ministerial offender is often a very effective, charismatic leader who misuses his or her power. The victim can literally be anyone who seeks help from the clergyperson and who, in her or his vulnerability at the time, crosses the path of an unethical minister.

An Ethical Analysis

It is a violation of professional ethics for any person in a ministerial role or teaching role to engage in sexual contact or sexualized behavior with a congregant, client, employee, student (adult, teen, or child) within the professional (pastoral, teaching or supervisory) relationship. Sexual activity in this context is exploitative and abusive. Why is it wrong for a minister or teacher to be sexual with someone whom he/she serves or supervises?

1.   It is a *violation of role*. The ministerial or teaching relationship presupposes certain role expectations. The minister/teacher is expected to make available certain resources, talents, knowledge, and expertise which will serve the best interest of the congregant, client, staff member, or student. Sexual contact is not part of the professional role.

2. It is a *misuse of authority and power*. The role of minister or teacher carries with it authority and power and the attendant responsibility to use this power to benefit the people who call upon the minister or teacher for service. This power can easily be misused, as is the case when a minister or teacher (intentionally or unintentionally) uses his/her authority to initiate or pursue sexual contact with a congregant or student. Even if it is the congregant or student who sexualizes the relationship, it is still the minister's or teacher's responsibility to maintain the boundaries of the professional relationship and not pursue a sexual relationship.

3. It *takes advantage of vulnerability*. The congregant, employee, or student is by definition vulnerable to the minister or teacher: she/he has fewer resources and less power than the minister. When the minister takes advantage of this vulnerability to gain sexual access, the minister violates the mandate to protect the vulnerable from harm. The protection of the vulnerable is a practice which derives from the Jewish and Christian traditions of a hospitality code.

4. There is *no meaningful consent*. Meaningful consent to sexual activity requires a context of not only choice but also of mutuality and equality; meaningful consent requires the absence of fear or even the most subtle coercion. There is always an imbalance of power between the person in the ministerial or teaching role and those whom he/she serves or supervises. Even in the relationship between two persons who see themselves as "consenting adults," the difference in role precludes the possibility of meaningful consent.

The essence of an ethical analysis of ministers or teachers sexualizing a professional relationship is the measure of harm caused by the betrayal of trust which is inherent in each of these four factors. Important boundaries within the professional relationship are crossed, trust is betrayed. The sexual nature of this boundary violation is significant only in that the sexual context is one of great vulnerability and fragility for most people. The essential harm, however, is that of betrayal of trust.

A Dual Relationship

The sexualization of the ministerial or teacher/student relationship is an attempt to have a dual relationship, that is to be both minister and lover or teacher and lover with the same person. Sexual and emotional intimacy change the nature of the relationship and significantly diminish the effectiveness of the minister or teacher in his/her role. A sexually intimate relationship presupposes an agenda of mutual needs which often runs counter to the agenda of ministry or teaching. There is always a question of whose needs are being met and of whether it is in the interest of the congregant or student to change the relationship to an intimate, sexual one. When this occurs, the congregant or student invariably loses a minister or teacher. This loss and the subsequent complication of an intimate relationship can have devastating consequences.

Power is always a factor in a ministerial or teaching relationship. Regardless of the good intentions of the minister or teacher, there is always a difference of power between minister and congregant or between teacher and student. The particular power difference between the two is determined by a variety of factors (gender, race, age, life experience, circumstance) but the difference in role is the most significant factor.

For students, the consequences are significant, and coping strategies, while necessary, undermine the efficacy of the learning environment. Students may experience some of the following consequences:

- General depression, disruption of sleep, eating, activity
- Dissatisfaction with studies
- Sense of helplessness
- Loss of self-confidence and decline in academic performance
- Isolation from other students
- Changes in attitudes regarding sexual relationships
- Irritability
- Fear and anxiety
- Lack of concentration
- Alcohol and drug abuse[5]

When the harassment is experienced as trauma, the student may experience post-traumatic stress disorder.[6]

The stakes are high and the potential loss enormous:

Though sexual harassment in any situation is reprehensible, it must be a matter of particularly deep concern to an academic community in which students and faculty are related by strong bonds of intellectual dependence and trust. Further, the vulnerability of undergraduates to such harassment is particularly great and the potential impact upon them is particularly severe. Not only does sexual harassment betray the special bond between teacher and student, but it also exploits unfairly the power inherent in an instructor's relationship to his or her student. Through grades, recommendations, research appointments, or job referrals an instructor can have a decisive influence on a student's academic success and future career. If this influence should be used overtly or implicitly in an attempt to exact sexual favors, a situation is created that may have devastating implications for individual students and for the academic community as a whole. Through fear of academic reprisal, a student may be forced to comply with sexual demands at the price of a debilitating personal anguish, or to withdraw from a course, a major, or even a career, and thus is forced to change plans for a life's work.[7]

A Progress Report

Since 1983, the Center for the Prevention of Sexual and Domestic Violence has been addressing the issue of professional ethics and sexual abuse by clergy. That was the year we received our first call for help from a survivor of clergy sexual abuse. Between 1983 and 1995, we have had some contact with well over 2,000 cases in the United States and Canada. We have served as advocate, minister, or consultant with victims, survivors, offenders, judicatory and seminary administrators, and lawyers.

In 1986, the first United States conference on abuse in helping relationships was held in Minneapolis. There we shared questions and strategies across professional disciplines. The title of the conference was significant: "It's Never O.K." By the end of the conference, we wanted to add a subtitle: "And It's Always Our Responsibility." This is the bottom line—and it's never simple.

In 1989, my book *Is Nothing Sacred?: When Sex Invades the Ministerial Relationship* was published.[8] This book was the first critical appraisal of the violation of the ministerial relationship which named it an issue of professional ethics and sexual abuse. The discussion of the problem has expanded; disclosures by victims/survivors have increased; lawsuits against churches and denominations have multiplied. Our religious institutions now face serious challenges. A number of denominations at the national and regional levels are moving to develop policy and procedures and they are being faced with an increasing number of complaints. More research projects are underway. Some denominations are beginning to focus attention at the seminary level of theological education, preparing ministers in order to reduce the risk that they will violate the integrity of the ministerial relationship.

The good news is that *some* denominational and academic leaders are moving swiftly and carefully to name the problem and to remove offending ministers and teachers in order to protect our institutions from further harm and erosion of credibility. They also are moving effectively to bring healing to victims, survivors, and congregations. Their leadership is significant and substantial. Careful, thoughtful, committed leadership is beginning to build a firm foundation for our religious institutions to fulfill their responsibilities. In many quarters, however, there is strong resistance to policies which state clear standards of professional conduct and to procedures which intervene to stop unprofessional conduct.

In the academy, for example, the resistance is being framed as a concern for academic freedom and free speech. In a recent forum at Duke University, the argument went like this: "One early draft of the Duke policy prohibited 'verbal conduct of a sexual nature' that interfered with performance or created an offensive environment. . . . However after concerns were raised by some Duke faculty that the prohibition would place Duke in opposition to freedom of speech, the policy was modified."[9]

Our efforts are played out against a backdrop of case after case being disclosed and adjudicated, often involving high-profile religious leaders. For example, in the recent past:

- John Howard Yoder's ministerial credentials have been suspended following complaints brought by eight women alleging improper sexual behavior and unsuitable use of overt sexual language. Yoder has accepted the church's action and recommendation that he seek therapy. He is a theologian and ethicist and member of the faculty at the University of Notre Dame.

- John Finch, a Christian psychologist who founded the School of Psychology at Fuller Theological Seminary in Pasadena, lost his license to practice psychology in Washington State after the state examining board found that he had engaged in "repeated acts of immorality and misconduct" with his clients over a span of twenty years. Fuller Seminary had named a building and lectureship after Finch and his portrait was prominently displayed there. After the state psychology board's action, the seminary undertook an internal investigation which resulted in severing all ties with Finch.

- Notre Dame Provost James Tunstead Burtchaell, a Holy Cross Father and prominent theologian, resigned his tenured position after an investigation into charges of sexual contact with male students whom he was counseling.

Although these cases and hundreds more like them are a painful reminder of the betrayal of trust by our leaders and teachers and of the unfinished business of rectifying these situations, they are also a witness to the fact that the church, synagogue, and academy are beginning to deal with this problem of professional misconduct. Although every case brings us pain and confusion, every case also brings an opportunity to make justice as a means to healing the brokenness. But even in these efforts to address complaints, the results are mixed. Some judicatory and academic administrators, although now informed and prepared with policy and procedures, are still not acting to stop offending ministers or teachers. In these situations, it would appear that the prevailing agenda is to protect the perpetrator from the consequences of his/her behavior; to keep the abusive behavior a secret; and to preserve the facade of pleasantry and normalcy in the institution.

When a victim of clergy professional misconduct or academic sexual harassment finally sues the church, synagogue, or university for damages, we have frequently seen the institution, at the urging of its lawyers, seek to settle out of court for significant sums of money *if* the victim agrees to silence, that is, not to discuss the particulars of her or his experience ever again. Many institutions have appeared more interested in secrecy than justice and are willing to pay people off in order to preserve their public image.

The result of this practice is never healing but rather *de-evangelization*: people are leaving or being driven out of the congregation, university or seminary not only because of the professional misconduct of *some* of our clergy or teachers but also by the lack of response to their complaints. For these people, trust in the clergy and the teacher is forever shattered. The credibility of these institutions is on the line.

Why in some quarters is there so little action? Why does it seem to be so difficult for judicatories or university administrations to act swiftly and unequivocally on behalf of those harmed by offending clergy or teachers? I used to think that the primary reason for the lack of action was ignorance: leaders lacked information, analysis, and tools with which to act. I assumed that education and training would provide the information, analysis, and tools and then, having girded their loins with truth and having put on the breastplate of righteousness, these leaders would walk into the breach, name, and confront the violations of professional ethics they encountered, and remove offending ministers and teachers from positions of trust. My assumption that leaders, when informed and prepared, would be eager to act has not been borne out. In fact some judicatory administrators who know better continue to circumvent the process or are stymied when an offending minister or teacher flatly denies the charges even in the face of multiple complaints. I have concluded that the primary reason for inaction is that for some, there is little will and less courage.

There certainly are some judicatory administrators, local leaders, and administrators with strong commitment and great courage who have acted effectively to put policy in place and to use it. It is clear that education and preparation have empowered them. But they remain few in number. And they run the risk of being marginalized for their actions.

The lack of will has to do primarily with an unwillingness to challenge the privilege of sexual access to congregants, staff, and students which seems all too commonplace within a patriarchal institution. The lack of courage has emerged in the face of legal anxieties: offending ministers may threaten to sue the church for slander, libel, or the loss of livelihood. These threats have in many cases halted disciplinary proceedings. Yet an offending minister has no basis on which to win such a suit and has not yet succeeded in doing so.

Ironically, it is another legal threat which may eventually embolden these institutions to act. In the absence of any effective action from their church, synagogue, or university, many victims/survivors are turning to the courts for redress, for justice. People do not want to sue these institutions, but they will if they find themselves not only mistreated but stonewalled in their attempts to find justice.

Legally, the cost is high. The Roman Catholic Church in the United States expects to spend $1 billion by the year 2000 in settlements for cases of professional misconduct by clergy.[10] Recent United States case law is unequivocal: the institution is responsible for the hiring and supervision of its personnel. If we credential our representatives, we must also be accountable for their actions. Development and consistent implementation of prevention and intervention strategies are fundamental steps toward maintaining the integrity of ministerial or teaching relationships. In short, the church, synagogue, or academy has the right and responsibility to remove ministers or teachers who are a danger to the well-being of members or students and the institution as a whole. The cost of *not* acting is enormous—morally, spiritually, and legally.

There are signs of hope and possibility. In a lawsuit against a local congregation of a nondenominational church for the sexual abuse by one of its staff members, a jury found in favor of the survivor and against the church. In a second case involving another survivor and the same perpetrator, the church's lawyers urged the church not to settle but to go back to court. The church council recommended this strategy to the congregation but the congregation overrode the decision and said that they now understood that their minister had harmed several of their members and so felt they should pay for the counseling and resulting expenses. They did the right thing and, ironically, it probably cost them less than if they had gone back to court and lost again. But ultimately William White, author of *Incest in the Organizational Family*,[11] is correct when he observes that establishing policy and procedures is not going to solve this problem. It provides the mechanism, yes; but there must be a commitment to a much broader and deeper change in our religious institutions. It will require a commitment to challenge the patriarchal core of our collective religious and academic life.

Conclusion

In the face of the continuing revelations of pedophilia by Roman Catholic priests in the United States and Canada, the resignation of bishops and other prominent clergy from judicatories or local congregations after being faced with charges of ministerial misconduct involving sexual abuse of congregants, an increasing number of complaints brought against faculty, and numerous complaints in every denomination, many ending in law suits, there can be no question that our religious and academic institutions are in crisis. A secret long hidden has been disclosed, and we face the challenge to respond in ways which can restore the integrity of the ministerial or teaching relationship. If we fail in this challenge, our witness to a hurting world will be sorely compromised, and our institutions may never recover from this crisis. We have the capacity to maintain institutional environments where persons who seek the resources of these institutions can expect to find help without being taken advantage of. This is the only way that we can provide a setting in which an individual's faith and/or intellectual gifts may flourish. We can do no less.

Notes

1. Richard Allen Blackmon, "The Hazards of Ministry" (Ph.D. diss., Fuller Theological Seminary, 1984).

2. "Sexual Harassment in the United Methodist Church" (Dayton, Ohio: The Office of Research, General Council on Ministries, The United Methodist Church, 1990), 3, 7, 8.

3. Michele Paludi et al., "Myths and Realities: Sexual Harassment on Campus," in *Ivory Power*, ed. Michele Paludi (Albany: SUNY Press, 1990), 3.

4. Cited in Vita C. Rabinowitz, "Coping with Sexual Harassment," *Ivory Power*, 113.

5. Ibid.

6. Ibid.

7. Paludi et al., "Myths and Realities," 5.

8. Marie Fortune, *Is Nothing Sacred?: When Sex Invades the Ministerial Relationship* (San Francisco: HarperSan Francisco, 1989).

9. Geoffrey Mock, "Harassment Policy Proposed," Duke *Dialogue* 7/20 (November 6, 1992): 12.

10. Kathe A. Stark, "Child Sexual Abuse in the Catholic Church," in *Psychotherapists' Sexual Involvement with Clients*, ed. Gary Schoener et al. (Minneapolis: Walk-In Counseling Center, 1989).

11. William White, *Incest in the Organizational Family* (Bloomington, Ill.: Lighthouse Training Institute, 1986).

Taking Sides against Ourselves

ROSEMARY L. BRAY

The Anita Hill–Clarence Thomas hearings are over; Judge Thomas is Justice Thomas now. Yet the memories linger on and on. Like witnesses to a bad accident, many of us who watched the three days of Senate hearings continue to replay the especially horrible moments. We compare our memories of cool accusation and heated denial; we weigh again in our minds the hours of testimony, vacuous and vindictive by turn. In the end, even those of us who thought we were beyond surprise had underestimated the trauma.

"I have not be so wrenched since Dr. King was shot," says Jewell Jackson McCabe, the founder of the National Coalition of 100 Black Women, an advocacy group with chapters in twenty-one states and the District of Columbia. "I cannot begin to tell you; this thing has been unbelievable."

The near-mythic proportions that the event has already assumed in the minds of Americans are due, in part, to the twin wounds of race and gender that the hearings exposed. If gender is a troubling problem in American life and race is still a national crisis, the synergy of the two embodied in the life and trials of Anita Hill left most of America dumbstruck. Even Black people who did not support Clarence Thomas's politics felt that Hill's charges, made public at the eleventh hour, smacked of treachery. Feminist leaders embraced with enthusiasm a woman whose conservative political consciousness might have given them chills only a month earlier.

Even before the hearings began, the nomination of Clarence Thomas had taken on, for me, the quality of a nightmare. The particular dread I felt was one of betrayal—not a betrayal by President Bush, from whom I expected nothing—but by Thomas himself, who not only was no Thurgood Marshall but also gradually revealed himself to be a man who rejoiced in burning the bridges that brought him over.

I felt the kind of heartbreak that comes only to those of us still willing to call ourselves race women and race men in the old and honorable sense, people who feel that African Americans should live and work and succeed not only for ourselves but also for our people.

The heated debates about gender and race in America have occurred, for the most part, in separate spheres; the separation makes for neater infighting.

But Black women can never skirt these questions; we are their living expression. The parallel pursuits of equality for African Americans and for women have trapped Black women between often conflicting agendas for more than a century. We are asked in a thousand ways, large and small, to take sides against ourselves, postponing a confrontation in one arena to address an equally urgent task in another. Black men and white women have often made claims to our loyalty and our solidarity in the service of their respective struggles for recognition and autonomy, understanding only dimly that what may seem like liberty to each is for us only a kind of parole. Despite the bind, more often than not we choose loyalty to the race rather than the uncertain allegiance of gender.

Ours is the complicity of guilty survivors. A Black man's presence is often feared; a Black woman's presence is at least tolerated. Because until recently so much of the work that Black women were paid to do was work that white men and women would not do—cleaning, serving, tending, teaching, nursing, maintaining, caring—we seem forever linked to the needs of human life that are at once minor and urgent.

As difficult as the lives of Black women are, we know we are mobile in ways Black men are not—and Black men know that we know. They know that we are nearly as angered as they about their inability to protect us in the traditional and patriarchal way, even as many of us have moved beyond the need for such protection. And some Black men know ways to use our anger, our sorrow, our guilt, against us.

In our efforts to make a place for ourselves and our families in America, we have created a paradigm of sacrifice. And in living out such lives, we have convinced even ourselves that no sacrifice is too great to insure what we view in a larger sense as the survival of the race.

That sacrifice has been an unspoken promise to our people; it has made us partners with Black men in a way white women and men cannot know. Yet not all of us view this partnership with respect. There are those who would use Black women's commitment to the race as a way to control Black women. There are those who believe the price of solidarity is silence. It was that commitment that trapped Anita Hill. And it is a commitment we may come to rue.

As I watched Hill being questioned that Friday by white men, by turn either timid or incredulous, I grieved for her. The anguish in her eyes was recognizable to me. Not only did she dare to speak about events more than one woman would regard as unspeakable, she did so publicly. Not only did she make public accusations best investigated in private, she made them against a man who was Black and conservative, as she was—a man who in other ways had earned her respect.

"Here is a woman who went to Sunday school and took it seriously," says Cornel West, director of the African-American Studies department at Princeton University and a social critic who felt mesmerized by what he called "the travesty and tragedy" of hearings. "She clearly is a product of the social conservatism of a rural Black Baptist community." For Black women historically, such probity, hard-won and tenaciously held, was social salvation. For white onlookers, it suggested an eerie primness out of sync with contemporary culture.

In the quiet and resolute spirit she might very well have learned from Sunday school, Hill confronted and ultimately breached a series of taboos in the Black community that have survived both slavery and the post-segregation life she and Clarence Thomas share. Anita Hill put her private business in the street, and she downgraded a Black man to a room filled with white men who might alter his fate—surely a large enough betrayal for her to be read out of the race.

By Sunday evening, Anita Hill's testimony lay buried under an avalanche of insinuation and innuendo. Before the eyes of a nation, a tenured law professor beloved by her students was transformed into an evil, opportunistic harpy; a deeply religious Baptist was turned into a sick and delusional woman possessed by Satan and in need of exorcism; this youngest of thirteen children from a loving family became a frustrated spinster longing for the attentions of her fast-track superior, bent on exacting a cruel revenge for his rejection.

These skillful transformations of Anita Hill's character by some members of the Senate were effective because they were familiar, manageable images of African-American womanhood. What undergirds these images is the common terror of Black women out of control. We are the grasping and materialistic Sapphire in an "Amos 'n' Andy" episode; the embodiment of a shadowy, insane sexuality; the raging, furious, rejected woman. In their extremity, these are images far more accessible and understandable than the polished and gracious dignity, the cool intelligence that Anita Hill displayed in the lion's den of the Senate chamber. However she found herself reconstituted, the result was the same. She was, on all levels, simply unbelievable.

Anita Hill fell on the double-edged sword of African-American womanhood. Her privacy, her reputation, her integrity—all were casualties of an ignorance that left her unseen by and unknown to most of those who meant either to champion or abuse her. As credible, as inspiring, as impressive as she was, most people who saw her had no context in which to judge her. The signs and symbols that might have helped to place Hill were long ago appropriated by officials of authentic (male) Blackness, or by representatives of authentic (white) womanhood. Quite simply, a woman like Anita Hill couldn't possibly exist. And in that sense, she is in fine historical company.

More than a century earlier, Black women routinely found themselves beyond belief, and thus beyond help, solace, and protection. In 1861, the most famous of the few slave narratives written by a Black woman, *Incidents in the Life of a Slave Girl*, was published. (The book was regarded as fiction for more than 100 years, until in 1987 Jean Fagin Yellin of Pace University completed six years of painstaking research substantiating the existence of its author, Harriet Jacobs, and her harrowing story.) Writing under the pseudonym "Linda Brent," Jacobs outlined for the genteel white woman of the nineteenth century the horrors, both sexual and otherwise, that awaited the female slave. Jacobs spent close to seven years hiding from her master ensconced in a garret, with food smuggled in by her recently freed grandmother.

In the story of Harriet Jacobs, the powerful man she fears is white. In the story of Anita Hill, the powerful man she fears is Black. But the vulnerability of each woman is a palpable presence in the stories they tell. Jacobs' tale is enlivened by the dramatic structure of the nineteenth-century sentimental novel, Hill's accounts are magnified through the image of her presence on television. Indeed, Jacobs' first lines are a plea to her audience to be taken seriously. "Reader, be assured this narrative is no fiction. I am aware that some of my adventures may seem incredible; but they are, nevertheless, strictly true."

Later she recounts the beginning of her owner's pursuit of her, the year she turned fifteen: "My master began to whisper foul words in my ear. Young as I was, I could not remain ignorant of their import. I tried to treat them with indifference or contempt. . . . The other slaves . . . knew too well the guilty practices under that roof; and they were aware that to speak of them was an offense that never went unpunished. . . . I longed for someone to confide in. I would have given the world to have laid my head on my grandmother's faithful bosom, and told her all my troubles. . . . I dreaded the consequences of a violent outbreak; and both pride and fear kept me silent."

Harriet Jacobs had good reason to fear; even free African-American women of the nineteenth century possessed no rights that anyone was bound to respect. Regarded as immoral and loose, Black women spent an inordinate amount of time in the years after slavery in attempts to establish themselves as virtuous women, as a rebuke to the rash of hypersexual images that flooded contemporary consciousness in those days, images that rationalized the routine sexual abuse of Black women—both slave and free—by white men.

It was a stereotype that had consequences for Black men as well: "Historically, the stereotype of the sexually potent Black male was largely based on that of the promiscuous Black female," explained Paula Giddings, in *When and Where I Enter*, her history of Black women in America. "He would have to be potent, the thinking went, to satisfy such hot-natured women."

Such myths of sexual potency and promiscuity, written and disseminated by trained nineteenth-century historians, fueled the widespread fears of Black men as rapists of white women—and provided the engine for a campaign of terrorism against newly freed Black people that included a rash of lynchings. Thus, it was especially troubling that Clarence Thomas should refer to the second round of hearings as "a high-tech lynching."

Thomas evoked one of the most emotional images in African-American consciousness, flinging himself across history like Little Eva clinging to an ice floe and, at the same time, blaming a Black woman for his troubles. A century earlier, it was the courageous and single-minded investigative reporting of a Black female journalist, Ida B. Wells, that finally galvanized a recalcitrant United States into taking lynching seriously.

Incidents in the Life of a Slave Girl would have made far more instructive reading for the Senate Judiciary Committee than *The Exorcist*. It was, after all, the Senate's appalling lack of familiarity with what it feels like to be powerless, vulnerable, and afraid that rendered Anita Hill and her behavior incomprehensible to most of them. In her preface, Jacobs writes that she has "concealed the names of places and given persons fictitious names. I had no motive for secrecy on my own account, but I deemed it kind and considerate toward others to pursue this course." It is likely that she is more fearful than she lets on.

But it is just as likely that Jacobs evokes a way of seeing the world that transcends nineteenth-century female gentility, that Jacobs is acting out of Christian charity to those who have persecuted her. And it is just as likely that she held on to her fragile dreams of connection, however slight, to home and friends, however frightening the context in which she enjoyed them.

Studying this connected way of seeing the world has been the work of Carol Gilligan's professional life. The author of *In a Different Voice: Psychological Theory and Women's Development*, she has written extensively on women's psychological development and the issues of justice and care that characterize the relationships of many women, both personal and professional. Thus she did not find it implausible that Anita Hill might have experienced the events she described, yet continued to work with Judge Thomas.

"It amazed me that no one understood the underlying logic of what she did," Gilligan says. "Her basic assumption was that you live in connection with others, in relationship with others. Now, her experience of that relationship was one of violation; it was offensive to her. But she was making the attempt to work it through in the relationship; trying to resolve conflict without breaking connection." The possibility that such an ethic might have motivated Anita Hill in her choices is rarely voiced in discussions about her.

It may be that this low-key approach does not fit the image of the Black woman who stands ready to challenge and confront offensive behavior. The surly Black wife with a frying pan in her hand is the flip side of the nurturing mammy, and it is abundantly clear to millions by now that Anita Hill is neither.

Thus her profound self-possession, particularly in the face of the behavior she ascribed to Thomas, seemed impossible to observers—in large part because her response was not the conditioned one for Black women. Hill showed no signs of the Harriet Tubman Syndrome, the fierce insistence on freedom or death that made Tubman an abolitionist legend. Anita Hill grabbed no blunt objects with which to threaten her superior, she did not thunder into his office in righteous anger or invoke the power to bring suit. She was not funny, or feisty, or furious in response to the behavior she described. She was disgusted, embarrassed, and ambivalent. Therefore, it must have been a dream.

"It was quite fitting that the bulk of the hearings took place on the weekend that Redd Foxx died," says Stanley Crouch, a cultural critic and author of *Notes of a Hanging Judge: Essays and Reviews 1979–1989*. "A bunch of the material sounded like stuff from a Redd Foxx–Richard Pryor–Eddie Murphy routine."

But few people were laughing. That week in October, my phone rang nonstop. Friends called to talk about their stories of sexual harassment, their memories of vengeful, jealous women who lie, their theories of self-loathing

Black men who act out their hostility toward Black women while lusting after white women. My sister, Linda, called from Chicago the night before the vote, then used her conference call feature to add her good friend to the line, with whom she had been arguing for an hour already. "I already know you believe her," Linda announced to me. "I just want to hear you tell me why."

The buses and trains and elevators were filled with debates and theories of conspiracy. Hill set up Thomas to bring a Black man down. Thomas was a man; what man didn't talk about his prowess? In a Harlem restaurant where I sat with a cup of tea and the papers that Saturday, the entire kitchen staff was in an uproar. The cook, an African woman, wanted to know why Hill waited ten years to bring it up. The waitress, an African-American woman, said she couldn't tell what to think.

A young Black man in his twenties announced he had a theory. "Clarence got jungle fever, and she got mad," he said with a laugh. Jungle fever is the code term, taken from the Spike Lee film of the same name, for a Black man's desire to sleep with a white woman. Clarence Thomas's second wife is white, therefore Anita Hill was overcome with jealous rage and hungry for revenge.

"We all know that the animosity of Black women toward Black men who marry white women is on the level of the recent fire in Oakland," Stanley Crouch said. "That's a major fact. They might be as racist about that as white people used to be."

Then again, some Black women might not care at all—a reasonable assumption, given the statistics indicating that interracial relationships between Black women and white men have more than tripled in the last twenty years.

Some Black women may feel rejected or betrayed by Black men lured by a white standard of beauty few of them could emulate. Some may just hate white women. But there is no real evidence to suggest that any of these scenarios apply to Anita Hill and her galvanizing testimony. Most people with an opinion about why she stepped forward regard it as a matter of ideology, not, as some people still want to think, romance.

Yet the issues of race and sex illuminated by the hearings remain. So, too, do the myriad ways in which race and gender combine to confuse us. But for the first time in decades, the country has been turned, for a time, into a mobile social laboratory. A level of discussion between previously unaligned groups may have begun with new vigor and candor.

Segments of the feminist movement have been under attack for their selective wooing of Black women. Yet many of these same women rallied to Hill with impressive speed. Some Black women who had never considered sexism as an issue serious enough to merit collective concern have begun to organize, including a group of Black female academics known as African American Women in Defense of Ourselves. And even in brusque New York, people on opposite sides of this issue, still traumatized by the televised spectacle, seem eager to listen, to be civil, to talk things over.

"I am so pleased people are starting to ask questions, not only about race and gender, but about the America that has frustrated and disappointed them," says Jewell Jackson McCabe. "People who had become cynical, people who have not talked about issues in their lives are talking now. I think the experience was so bad, it was so raw. I don't know a woman who watched those hearings whose life hasn't been changed."

"It was an international drama," says Michael Eric Dayson, assistant professor of ethics, philosophy, and cultural criticism at Chicago Theological Seminary. "Anita Hill has put these issues on the American social agenda. She has allowed Black men and women to talk freely for the first time about a pain that has been at the heart of our relationships since slavery. Black wives are beginning to tell their husbands about the kind of sexism they have faced not at the hands of white men, but Black men."

What was most striking about the hearings, in the end, was the sense of destiny that surrounded them. There was something rewarding about seeing what began as a humiliating event become gradually transformed only in its aftermath. Two African Americans took center stage in what became a national referendum on many of our most cherished values. In the midst of their shattering appearances, Anita Hill and Clarence Thomas each made us ask questions that most of us had lost the heart to ask.

They are exactly the kinds of questions that could lead us out of the morass of cynicism and anger in which we've all been stuck. That is an immensely satisfying measurement of the Hill-Thomas hearings. It would not be the first time that African Americans have used tragedy and contradiction as catalysts to make America remember its rightful legacy.

The Difference Race Makes:
Sexual Harassment and the Law
in the Thomas–Hill Hearings

Karen Baker-Fletcher

In October 1991, Black and white Americans sat captivated before their television sets to listen to the Clarence Thomas–Anita Hill hearings before a Senate committee composed entirely of white men. American businessmen and administrators, stunned into awareness of what might be considered sexual harassment, began to ponder rules for behavior toward women in the workplace. Some women identified with Hill on the issue of gender discrimination and rallied around Hill to demand attention to the problem of sexual harassment in the workplace. Many Black men and women identified strongly with Thomas's angry assertion that he was the victim of a "high-tech lynching." Other Black women and men called attention to Anita Hill's double jeopardy of racial and gender discrimination.

The public was given little concrete or accurate information about sexual harassment issues in relation to the law. The hearings were not a legal proceeding, nor could Hill press legal charges some ten years after Thomas's alleged sexually inappropriate behavior. No one seemed to be too clear as to what the point of the hearings was. Was the purpose to raise questions about Thomas's fitness to serve on the Supreme Court of the United States? Or was the purpose to discredit the reports solicited from Professor Hill? Was legality a genuine concern? Or were the deliberations simply a contest in which the point was for one of the parties to win?

Toni Morrison writes that because of racial perceptions in America, Black people are rarely individualized. Morrison argues that to go beyond the superficial questions about what took place, to move to the deeper questions of what happened in the hearings, it is necessary to understand the social-historical context in which the hearings took place. And the context is the context of a historically "racialized and race-conscious society" where standards are changed based on skin color.[1]

To carefully analyze the hearings, Morrison proposes, requires that we consider the signification of racial representations in American culture and history. African Americans, she explains, are used as an unindividuated group "to signify the polar opposites of love and repulsion." They signify "benevolence, harmless and servile guardianship, and endless love" on the one hand and "insanity, illicit sexuality, and chaos" on the other hand. Morrison argues that in the confirmation hearings these two racial fictions were "at war and on display." Thomas, Morrison argues, was "cloaked in the garments of loyalty, guardianship, and limitless love"; Hill in the "oppositional garments of madness, anarchic sexuality, and explosive verbal violence."[2]

Morrison suggests that the hearings took on the form of a contest, in which the goal was to see which racial fiction would prove the winner. In Morrison's view, Hill's testimony did not produce a search for the truth but an exchange of racial tropes in which the purpose was to establish (1) which one was lying, and (2) which one was benevolent and which one insane. Morrison carefully illustrates the racial presuppositions of the Senate Judiciary Committee about Hill. They would not investigate her accusations seriously because "she was a mixture heretofore not recognized in the glossary of racial tropes: an *intellectual* daughter of black *farmers*; a *black female* taking *offense*; a black *lady* repeating *dirty words*."[3] Morrison, Hazel Carby, and Barbara Andolsen have all explored the ways in which Black women in America have been excluded from prevailing white American ideals of womanhood. In the Black Women's Club Movement of the 1890s, Black women proclaimed their humanity and their womanhood in protest against stereotypes of Black women as morally and sexually wanton.[4] One century later, Black women still must fight negative stereotypes. Hill, as a Black woman intellectual, was particularly anomalous for the Senate Judiciary Committee.

As for the issue of sexual harassment and the law, it seems the only place the law came into play in any concrete way, was that a Black man, Clarence Thomas, was being considered as a replacement for another Black man, Thurgood Marshall, for a seat on the highest court of the nation. The hearings were not about law per se, but were ostensibily about moral character. But the concern regarding moral character was not grounded in moral consciousness of the reprehensible nature of sexual harassment. Rather, it was deeply rooted in racial curiosity mixed with political interests.

The hearings were racial and political in nature, more than legal *or* moral. Rhetoric regarding the moral character of Thomas as a candidate for a seat on the United States Supreme Court functioned as a thin veneer for racial and political obsessions. As Morrison observes, "under the pressure of voyeuristic desire, fueled by mythologies that render Blacks publicly serviceable instruments of dread and longing, extraordinary behavior on the part of the state could take place. . . . the chairman of the committee could apply criminal court procedure to a confirmation hearing."[5] The procedure the chairman employed, then, gave the confirmation hearings the *appearance* of a courtroom session.

Viewers never really learned much about sexual harassment from a legal perspective. We did learn that Hill's time to press formal charges had long run out. Viewers also began to reflect on attitudes and behaviors in their own workplaces and seriously began to ask what the law has to say about sexual harrassment. Perhaps the most positive outcome of the Clarence

Thomas–Anita Hill hearings is that the nation began to question sexual attitudes toward women in the workplace in an unprecedented way.

This outcome of the hearings is more positive than anything that actually happened during the hearings themselves. Questioning sexual attitudes of employers toward employees and between co-workers in the workplace is at heart an ethical issue. To take sexual harassment seriously requires that Americans consider legal concerns in concert with the larger ethical issues of sexual behavior in the workplace. In short, a genuine ethical concern for the dignity of women and men ought to be the motivating force behind all of our inquiry regarding sexual harassment and the law.

The hearings, and particularly feminist response to those hearings, have motivated American institutions, run predominantly by white men, to take seriously the damage sexual harassment can do in the workplace. At best the hearings raised consciousness regarding the abusive language and behavior many women experience in the workplace from male superiors and colleagues. It sent an alarm to many men that their behavior could be legally questioned and prompted a self-interested concern among many men to protect themselves and their institutions from expensive law suits. At worst, since Thomas was confirmed in the final vote, it sent a signal that men's solidarity with one another overrides women's justice issues, especially those of Black women.

In sum, all, male and female, have been required to consider what may be at stake for them in terms of gender relations in the workplace. Moreover, all have been required to consider that behavior that had once been accepted as normal in places of employment and education, may now be legally questioned. America is now required to participate in a transformation of behavior and values. The problem, as Toni Morrison points out, is that as is so often the case, "these issues have been worked out and inscribed in the canvas/flesh of black people."[6] Such language accurately depicts the ways in which African Americans in the modern era have been used as means for working out ethical questions regarding human rights in American culture, with little genuine regard to their actual personhood.

Looking at the Thomas–Hill hearings from another angle, it is also true that for many women Hill has emerged as a heroic figure and courageous role model, because she dared to speak out. That Hill withstood the hearings with dignity is testimony to her courage. White feminists, but also womanists, find meaning in Hill's act of speaking out on the problem of sexual harassment. And yet, it is important to probe once again America's racial understanding of Black womanhood to uncover and debunk the racial myths that inform our impressions of Hill's heroism.

Even praise of Hill as a role model is suspect because we must question the ways in which much of America has objectified Hill, rather than treated her as an individual subject. It is important not to assign the *myth of the Black superwoman* to Hill. Patrica Morton has carefully delineated the plethora of stereotypes regarding Black women: "Mammy," "Matriarch," "Superwoman," "Mean and Evil Bitches," and "Castrators."[7] The "superwoman" image is yet another stereotype that fails to recognize Black women as fully human and fully women. To conceive Black women as being above womanhood is as problematic as conceiving Black women as beneath womanhood.

From a womanist perspective, what makes Hill extraordinary is her ordinariness—that she, until recently a relatively *anonymous* Black middle-class woman, risked assault to her dignity and came forward with an ordinary story that is familiar to ordinary women. She reminds us that we all face the rather ordinary challenge of garnering such courage in our everyday lives. In her failure to do so for ten years and in her decision to do so *after* she was a tenured law professor—a class privilege that few women share in America— Hill reminds us of our ordinary fears and our tendency toward caution and reserve in the face of danger. And, in her references to her Baptist faith, extended family, and Black Southern heritage, Hill reminds us of the spiritual power in Black American religion and culture that sustains Black women's moral decision-making.

Given the significance of Hill's courage for many women, why have so many African Americans looked on the hearings as a dehumanizing process for Hill, Thomas, and Black America? Martin Luther King, Jr. warned that it is easier to change laws than hearts. It is easier to change laws than moral values and behavior toward women, particularly women of color. Moreover, it is easier to change laws than racial-sexual attitudes regarding Black women and men. The editors of *Court of Appeal* contend that the final court for the Thomas–Hill case is the Black community. They present views from diverse Black writers, scholars, and leaders, male and female, on the Thomas–Hill hearings. W. H. McLendon writes that:

> the judiciary committee's actions in dealing with Ms. Hill's presence were demonstrations of excessive malicious adversarial disdain, discourtesy and disrespect. Had she been a less secure person her life could have been made irreparably unstable. Racism and gender bias expressed in the Senators' admonitions, opinions and questions, along with their self-targeted compliments, filled every crevice.[8]

And, in relation to both Hill and Thomas, McLendon further criticized the Senate hearings arguing that:

> In acting to preserve a psycho-social history of keeping Blacks in their place, the Senate risked trashing the United States Supreme Court. . . . The extreme racism and chauvinism manifested by Senators during the hearings shook the sensitivities of the nation.[9]

McLendon questions the ethical character of the Senate hearings. He argues that from a Black perspective the hearings were racist *and* sexist. They assaulted the dignity of Anita Hill, Clarence Thomas, and Black Americans generally. Maulana Karenga argues for serious attention to gender issues, but "not at the expense of Black men." He writes that "the process and claims of the Thomas-Hill spectacle were, in fact, deceptive . . ." In Karenga's view the hearings created and masked the "difficulties of a complex and protracted struggle for gender and justice."[10] Barbara Smith discusses her fury "at how

Anita Hill was treated by the Senate, by the media, and by the majority of the U.S. populace." As a Black feminist, socialist, and lesbian, she contends that the opinions of women seem not to count in a white-male ruling-class culture. Thus, she did not "expect justice from either the Rupublicans or the Democrats . . ." or from "the mainstream women's movement's singular solution to run as many women for office as possible."[11]

David Lionel Smith argues that "though this episode convulsed the Black community, it has little bearing on us. After all, it was primarily an exchange between two lily-white enclaves, the White House and the Senate, who cynically used Anita Hill and Clarence Thomas to stage rhetorical gestures toward the public."[12] He views Hill and Thomas as victims of extraordinary humiliation. For Rebecca Walker, daughter of Alice Walker, "the hearings were not about determining whether or not Clarence Thomas did in fact harass Anita Hill. They were about checking and redefining the extent of women's credibility and power."[13]

Maya Angelou sees Machiavellian principles at work regarding human weakness in the political strategies involved in the Clarence Thomas hearings. She, like so many Black folk, including one of my grandfathers, warns that Black Americans must be conscious of "divide-and-conquer" tactics in racist and imperialist cultures: "Divide the masses that you may conquer them, separate them and you can rule them."[14]

The point I want to make here is that a diversity of Black writers—male, female, conservative, radical, socialist, liberal, Afrocentric, feminist, womanist—point to America's political system as a common nemesis to the social justice concerns of Black women and men. So, in discussing sexual harassment and the law, a discussion profoundly impacted by the Clarence Thomas/Anita Hill case, the larger issue that emerges is whether Black women and men can expect gender and racial justice in our current legal, economic, and political systems.

Is the law all we have? Clearly not. There must be a transformation of consciousness on the part of those who are in political power. Until racist and sexist stereotypes about Black women and men are self-consciously faced and questioned by white America, there can be no justice for Black women and men in America. This leaves many Black folk wondering if the Black community is indeed the final court of appeal?

Is the Black community the final court of appeal? Historically, Black leaders like Maria Stewart, Frederick Douglass, Sojourner Truth, Alexander Crummell, Anna Julia Cooper, and Martin Luther King, Jr. have appealed to the ethical and religious sensibilities of white Americans and embraced as scriptures the Declaration of Independence and the Constitution. Others, like Nat Turner, Gabriel Prosser, and Denmark Vesey have engaged in military revolt. Still others like Marcus Garvey, Elijah Muhammed, Malcolm X, and Louis Farrakhan have advocated a Black nationalism.

Today, regardless of the diversity of Black perspectives on justice in America and regardless of where those perspectives may fall in relation to historical and contemporary public figures, there is a profound questioning as to whether we can appeal to white conscience, ethics, and religious principles as we move into the twenty-first century. To name a collection of essays on the racial and sexual politics of Thomas vs. Hill from across the political spectrum, *Court of Appeal*, is in a sense a last appeal to white American ethical consciousness. But that is not the only aim of the book. If the authors share any common ground it is that they identify a common enemy which they criticize in solidarity. That common enemy is the prevailing political and legal system. America must take seriously the racial and sexual discrimination Anita Hill faced during the hearings. Further it is important to recognize the ways in which both Hill and Thomas were made into objects of sexual fantasy, manipulated to fulfill white racist mythologies regarding Black sexuality.

Morrison and the contributors to her book *Race-ing Power, En-gendering Justice* offer the most compelling argument regarding the ways in which America, Black and white, is mystified by racial tropes. Morrison argues that had Hill and Thomas been white, the mere question of improper sexual conduct on Thomas' part would have disqualified him. No other strategies were entertained, she argues, because of the predominantly white male judiciary committee's voyeuristic desire. She describes the hearings as an "unprecedented opportunity to hover over and to cluck at, to meditate and ponder the limits and excesses of black bodies." Given such an opportunity, no other strategies would be entertained:

> There would be no recommendation of withdrawal . . . No request for or insistence that the executive branch propose another name . . . No. The participants were black, so what could it matter? . . . Under the pressure of voyeuristic desire, fueled by mythologies that render Blacks publicly serviceable instruments of private dread and longing, extraordinary behavior on the part of the state could take place.[15]

Morrison contends that if the candidate accused of sexual harrassment and his accuser had been white, the hearings would never have taken place. Never have white nominees to the Supreme Court and their accusers been placed on display as objects of sexual inquiry in the way that Thomas and Hill were. The accusation of sexual misconduct alone would probably have disqualified a white candidate, no proof required. The mere possibility that the accusation was publicly verifiable, Morrison argues, would have "nullified the candidacy."[16] Another candidate would have been proposed.

Morrison finds it further disturbing that President Bush invited Thomas into his bedroom to finalize his nomination. She argues that this is an inappropriate setting in which to discuss a nomination and that it reveals America's deep sexual obsession for Black skin. Morrison argues that "to begin to comprehend exactly what happened, it is important to distinguish between the veneer of interrogatory discourse and its substance. . . . To know what took place, summary is enough," she suggests. But "to learn what happened requires multiple points of address and analysis."[17] Morrison, like many other African-American writers who have participated in the conversation about Hill and Thomas, urges us all to demythologize the content of the hearings and to ask why they were put on display. Womanist ethicist Joan Martin has commented that Thomas and Hill were displayed like slaves on an auction block. Paula Giddings, pursuing a similar line of thought, demonstrates how eighteenth- and nineteenth-century white racial constructs of Black sexuality persist today.[18]

A close analysis of the hearings and Black America's response to the hearings reveals two allegations of sexual harrassment. One was brought by Anita Hill against Clarence Thomas. Her allegation has effectively been followed by a second informal allegation of sexual harassment, and also of race discrimination, by segments of the African-American public. This second allegation is against the American political system for effectively sexually harassing both Hill and Thomas. Anita Hill was harassed at least twice—first by Thomas when working as his employee; second by members of a white male Senate panel who participated in a voyeuristic line of questioning based on racial fictions of Black female sexuality and morality. Thomas was harassed at least once, by the white male senators who probed his sexual character more than his moral character in the name of moral interests.

America must debunk its myths of the sexual prowess of Black men and the moral laxity of Black women before its justice and legislative systems can engage Black women and men in a fair hearing. Victims of harassment are often members of racial or ethnic minorities. Black women are disproportionately represented in the statistics. Until white America divests itself of its investment in racist and sexist attitudes as a means for maintaining an imbalance of power, until it grapples with a higher moral law regarding attitudes toward women and people of color, there is no justice for Black Americans, female or male, on the issue of sexuality and the law.

But is the Black community a final court of appeal? As Beverly Guy-Sheftal notes, Black women "too often become suspect and discredited in our communities when we raise issues of sexism . . . or when we speak openly and honestly about what we have experienced as women under patriarchy," patriarchy which exists both in the larger society and in the Black community.[19] Certainly, these are the kinds of criticisms that have been made against Hill for speaking out on Thomas's sexual misconduct; against Alice Walker for writing *The Third Life of Grange Copeland* and *The Color Purple*; Ntozake Shange for publishing and producing her choreopoem, *for colored girls who have considered suicide when the rainbow is enuf*; Desiree Washington for bringing rape charges against Mike Tyson; and Michelle Wallace in publishing *Black Macho and the Myth of Superwoman*.

The Black community must recognize sexual harassment as both a larger social problem and an internal community problem before it can function adequately as a final court of appeal. As Cornel West puts it so succinctly, we must replace "racial reasoning with moral reasoning,"[20] freed from the racial guilt of standing in opposition to Black men who are Black in pigment but fail to adequately represent the moral values of Black culture.

Sexual harrassment is an ongoing problem in America. Women are increasingly reporting cases at educational institutions. We must consider the responsibility of colleges, universities, and seminaries in dealing with this problem. Moreover, an adequate assessment requires consideration of the ways in which racial attitudes complicate sexual harassment cases for minority and ethnic groups.

❧

Notes

1. See Toni Morrison, ed., "Introduction," *Race-ing Justice, En-gendering Power: Essays on Anita Hill, Clarence Thomas, and the Construction of Social Reality* (New York: Pantheon Books, 1992), xvii.
2. Ibid., xv–xvi.
3. Ibid., xvi (italics in the original).
4. See Morrison, *Race-ing Justice, En-gender-ing Power*; Hazel Carby, *Reconstructing Womanhood: The Emergence of the Afro-American Woman Novelist* (New York and London: Oxford University Press, 1987); and Barbara Andolsen, *Daughters of Jefferson, Daughters of Bootstraps* (Macon, Ga.: Mercer University Press, 1986). See also chapter 5 of my dissertation, *A Singing Something: The Literature of Anna Julia Cooper as a Resource for a Theological Anthropology of Voice* (Ann Arbor, Mich.: UMI, 1991).
5. Morrison, xvii–xviii.
6. Ibid., xix–xx.
7. Patricia Morton, *Disfigured Images: The Historical Assault on Afro-American Women* (New York: Praeger, 1991), xi–xiii. Morton furthers the work of Black women writers like Michelle Wallace, Alice Walker, Mary Helen Washington, and bell hooks.
8. W. H. McLendon, "From Dismal to Abysmal," in *Court of Appeal*, ed. Robert Chrisman and Robert L. Allen (New York: Ballantine, 1992), 152.
9. Ibid., 153.
10. Maulana Karenga, "Under the Camouflage of Color and Gender: The Dread and Drama of Thomas–Hill," *Court of Appeal*, 134.
11. Barbara Smith, "Ain't Gonna Let Nobody Turn Me Around," *Court of Appeal*, 185–86.
12. David Lionel Smith, "The Thomas Spectacle," *Court of Appeal*, 192.
13. Rebecca Walker, "Becoming the Third Wave," *Court of Appeal*, 211–13.
14. Maya Angelou, "I Dare to Hope," *Court of Appeal*, 33.
15. Morrison, xvii–xviii.
16. Ibid., xxvii.
17. Ibid., xi–xii.

18. Joan Martin, comment in the response to this paper, AAR Annual Meeting, November 23, 1992. Paula Giddings pursues Morrison's criticism of voyeuristic desire by exploring Europe's fascination with Sara Bartman whose body was displayed in Paris and England in 1810. After her death in 1817, Bartman's autopsy involved study of her genitalia and her sexual organs were given to the Musee de l'Homme in Paris where they remain on display. See Giddings, "The Last Taboo," in *Race-ing Justice, En-gender-ing Power*, 444–45.

19. Beverly Guy-Sheftal, "Breaking the Silence: A Black Feminist Response to the Thomas/Hill Hearings (for Audre Lorde)," *Court of Appeal*, 75.

20. Cornel West, "Black Leadership and the Pitfalls of Racial Reasoning," in *Race-ing Justice, En-gender-ing Power*, 390–401.

Christian Conquest and the Sexual Colonization of Native Women

ANDY SMITH

Feminist theologians have analyzed the ways in which Christian theology has served to oppress women and to contribute to their sexual victimization. Their analyses have seldom addressed the experiences of Native women inasmuch as they do not incorporate an anticolonial perspective. Similarly, Native and non-Native scholars have also addressed the manner in which Christian imperialism has oppressed Native peoples without addressing the specific impact of imperialism on Native women. This essay will attempt to build on the work of Native women activists who have been analyzing the intersections between Christian conquest and violence against Native women in their efforts to heal Native societies. While the relationships between Christian conquest and sexual victimization are complex, this essay will look at five paradigms prevalent in mainstream Christian theology and their impact on Native peoples—in particular, on Native women.

Wives, Be Subject to Your Husbands

"Where are your women?" The speaker is Attakullakulla, a Cherokee chief renowned for his shrewd and effective diplomacy. He has come to negotiate a treaty with the whites. Among his delegation are women "as famous in war, as powerful in the council." Their presence also has ceremonial significance: it is meant to show honor to the other delegation. But that delegation is composed of males only; to them the absence of women is irrelevant, a trivial consideration.

To the Cherokee, however, reverence for women/mother Earth/life spirit is interconnected. Implicit in their chief's question, "Where are your women?" the Cherokee hear, "Where is your balance? What is your intent?" They see the balance is absent and are wary of the white men's motives. They intuit the power of destruction.[1] (Marilou Awiakta—Cherokee)

Wives, be subject to your husbands as you are to the Lord. For the husband is the head of the wife just as Christ is the head of the church, the body of which he is the Savior. Just as the church is subject to Christ, so also wives ought to be, in everything, to their husbands. (Eph. 5:22–24)

While stereotypes persist that Native women were beasts of burden for their men, pre-colonial Indian societies were, for the most part, not male-dominated. Women served as spiritual, political, and military leaders. Many societies were matrilineal and matrilocal. Violence against women and children was infrequent, unheard of in many tribes.[2] Native peoples did not use corporal punishment against their children. Although there existed a division of labor between women and men, women's and men's labor was accorded similar status.[3] As Winona LaDuke (Anishinaabe) states:

> Traditionally, American Indian women were never subordinate to men. Or vice versa, for that matter. What native societies have always been about is achieving balance in all things, gender relations no less than any other. Nobody needs to tell us how to do it. We've had that all worked out for thousands for years. And, left to our own devices, that's exactly how we'd be living right now.[4]

As women and men lived in balance, Native societies were consequently much less authoritarian than their European counterparts. Paul LeJeune, a Jesuit priest, remarked in the 1600s:

> [Native peoples] imagine that they ought by right of birth, to enjoy the liberty of wild ass colts, rendering no homage to anyone whomsoever, except when they like. . . . All the authority of their chief is in his tongue's end, for he is powerful insofar as he is eloquent; and even if he kills himself talking and haranguing, he will not be obeyed unless he pleases the savages.[5]

Seventy percent of tribes did not practice war at all.[6] When societies did practice war, the intent was not to annihilate the enemy, but to accrue honor through bravery. One accrued more honor by getting close enough to an enemy to touch him and leaving him alive than by killing him. Tom Holm states:

> Traditional Indian warfare had much more in common with Euroamerican contact sports, like football, boxing, and hockey, than with wars fought in the European manner. This, of course, is not to say that nobody was ever killed. . . . They were—just as they are in modern contact sports—but the point of the exercise was not as a rule purposefully lethal.[7]

Paula Gunn Allen argues that Christian colonizers realized that in order to subjugate indigenous nations, they would have to subjugate women within these nations. Native peoples needed to learn the value of hierarchy, the role of physical abuse in maintaining that hierarchy, and the importance of women remaining submissive to their men. They had to convince "both men and women that a woman's proper place was under the authority of her husband and that a man's proper place was under the authority of the priests."[8]

These goals were accomplished through the boarding school system, which had their beginnings in the 1600s under Jesuit priests along the St. Lawrence River. The system reached its height in 1870 when Congress set aside funds to erect school facilities to be run by churches and missionary societies.[9]

Attendance was mandatory, and children were forcibly taken from their homes for the majority of the year. They were forced to worship as Christians and speak English (native traditions and languages were prohibited).[10]

In these schools, Indian women learned useful skills such as ironing, sewing, washing, serving raw oysters at cocktail parties, and making attractive flower arrangements in order to transform them into middle-class housewives.[11] As K. Tsianina Lomawaima points out, very few Native women were ever in a position to use these skills or become housewives. She states:

> An economic rationale of placing Indian women in domestic employment does not account for the centrality of domesticity training in their education. An ideological rationale more fully accounts for domesticity training: it was training in dispossession under the guise of domesticity, developing a habitus shaped by the messages of subservience and one's proper place."[12]

Children were subjected to constant physical and sexual abuse. Irene Mack Pyawasit, a former boarding school resident from the Menominee reservation testifies to her experience which is typical of many students' experiences:

> The government employees that they put into the schools had families but still there were an awful lot of Indian girls turning up pregnant. Because the employees were having a lot of fun, and they would force a girl into a situation, and the girl wouldn't always be believed. Then, because she came up pregnant, she would be sent home in disgrace. Some boy would be blamed for it, never the government employee. He was always scot-free. And no matter what the girl said, she was never believed.[13]

Survivors speaking out on their experiences often find that the Church is unwilling to be accountable for this abuse. When Tim Giago of Rosebud, South Dakota wrote a book of poetry that addressed his nine-year history of abuse in Red Cloud Indian School, the priests expunged his records from the school and denied that he had attended the institution for more than six months. They completely expunged the records of another student who had been there twelve years, denying he had ever attended that institution.[14]

Even when teachers were charged with abuse, boarding schools refused to investigate. In the case of just one teacher, John Boone at the Hopi school, FBI investigations in 1987 found that he had sexually abused over 142 boys, but that the principal of that school had not investigated any allegations of abuse.[15] Despite the epidemic of sexual abuse in boarding schools, the Bureau of Indian affairs did not issue a policy on reporting sexual abuse until 1987, and did not issue a policy to strengthen the background checks of potential teachers until 1989.[16]

While not all Native people viewed their boarding school experiences as negative, it appears to be the case that, after the onset of boarding schools in Native communities, abuse becomes epidemic within Indian families. Randy Fred (Tseshaht), a former boarding school student, says that children in his school began to mimic the abuse they were experiencing.[17] After Father

Harold McIntee from St. Joseph's residential school on the Alkali Lake reserve was convicted of sexual abuse in 1989, two of his victims were later convicted of sexual abuse charges.[18]

Thus, through a regimented, hierarchal boarding school system reinforced by abuse, Church boarding schools began to transform Native children "into the great body of English-speaking, home-loving, industrious, and pure-minded Americans" who adhered to "obedience to Christian principles of morality."[19] Through the subjugation of Native women and children, colonizers left Native nations with a legacy of abuse and dysfunctionality.

Not only was the subjugation of Native women necessary to subjugate Native societies, it was necessary to maintain the subjugation of white women. Karen Warren argues that patriarchal society is a dysfunctional system that mirrors the dysfunctional nuclear family. That is, when there is severe abuse in the family, the abuse continues because the family members regard it as "normal." Only when a victim of abuse has contact with less abusive families[20] may she come to see that her abuse is not "normal." She may then run into major conflict with the rest of her family members, who perceive her as challenging the very basis of that family structure. Kyos Featherdancing describes her history of abuse:

> When I was three years old, I first remember him [my father] actually putting his prick into my vagina . . . He made me believe that every father did that with their daughter. So I believed that. And I became that. And I loved it too. My parents didn't let me go to other people's houses very much. I know now my father didn't want them knowing what he was doing. But when I was nine, I went to stay with a friend, and when it was time to go to bed, her father and mother tucked us in and give us a kiss on the forehead . . . I thought that was real strange. I kept wondering if anything else was going to happen. And finally I nudged my friend and said, "Hey, does your father come in and give you nookie?" And she was like, "What? What are you talking about?". . .That was the first time I realized not everybody had a father like that.[21]

Similarly, Warren argues, patriarchal society is a dysfunctional system based on domination and violence.[22] "Dysfunctional systems are often maintained through systematic denial, a failure or inability to see the reality of a situation. This denial need not be conscious, intentional, or malicious; it only needs to be pervasive to be effective."[23]

Europe at the time of Columbus's misadventures was just such a completely dysfunctional system racked with violence, mass poverty, disease, and war. Hundreds of thousands of Jews were killed in the Inquisition with their confiscated property used to fund Columbus's voyages. David Stannard states:

> Violence, of course, was everywhere . . . in Milan in 1476 a man was torn to pieces by an enraged mob and his dismembered limbs were eaten by his tormenters. In Paris and Lyon, Huguenots were killed and butchered, and their various body parts were sold openly in the streets.

Other eruptions of bizarre torture, murder, and ritual cannibalism were not uncommon.[24]

European societies were thoroughly misogynistic. Europe's hatred for women was most fully manifest in the witchhunts. In many English towns, as many as a third of the population were accused of witchcraft.[25] As many as nine million people, with ratios of women to men as victims falling between 20:1 to 100:1, were killed.[26] The women targeted for destruction were those most independent from patriarchal authority: single women, widows, and women healers.[27]

It was impossible for these societies transplanted to the Americas to continue to exist side-by-side with non-patriarchal Native societies. Native societies would call into question the premise that abuse, violence, social hierarchy, and male domination are inevitable and "normal."[28]

In fact, the more peaceful and egalitarian nature of Native societies did not escape the notice of the colonizers. According to David Stannard, it was a scandal in the colonies that a number of white people chose to live among Indian people while virtually no Indians voluntarily chose to live among the colonists. J. Hector St. John de Crevecoeur exclaimed: "Thousands of Europeans are Indians, and we have no example of even one of these Aborigines having from choice become Europeans!"[29] Colonial leaders' response to those whites who chose to live among Indians was to hunt them down, torture them, and execute them.[30]

The egalitarian nature of Native societies was threatening the legitimacy of the abusive nature of European societies; it was imperative that Native societies be exterminated and demonized in order to legitimize the European social structure. To illustrate this demonization process, Archibald Loudon argued in 1808 that certain French philosophers are incorrect in thinking native societies are peaceful. He stated that two such philosophers attempted to befriend the so-called peaceful Native people, only to be scalped by them.[31]

The high status of women in Native societies did not escape the notice of white women either. In 1899, Mrs. Teall wrote an editorial in the Syracuse Herald-Journal discussing the status of women in Iroquois society.

They had one custom the white men are not ready, even yet, to accept. The women of the Iroquois had a public and influential position. They had a council of their own . . . which had the initiative in the discussion; subjects presented by them being settled in the councils of the chiefs and elders; in this latter council the women had an orator of their own (often of their own sex) to present and speak for them. There are sometimes female chiefs. . . . The wife owned all the property. . . . The family was hers; descent was counted through mother.[32]

In response to her editorial, a man who signs himself as "Student" replies:

Women among the Iroquois, Mrs. Teall says . . . had a council of their own, and orators and chiefs. Why does she not add what follows in explanation of why such deference was paid to women, that "in the torture of prisoners women were thought more skilful and subtle than the men" and the men of the inquisition were outdone in the refinement of cruelty practiced upon their victims by these savages. It is true also that succession was through women, not the men, in Iroquois tribes, but the explanation is that it was generally a difficult guess to tell the fatherhood of children. . . . The Indian maiden never learned to blush. . . . The Indians, about whom so much rhetoric has been wasted, were a savage, merciless lot who would never have developed themselves nearer to civilization than they were found by missionaries and traders. . . . Their love was to butcher and burn, to roast their victims and eat them, to lie and rob, to live in filth, men, women, children, dogs and fleas crowded together.[33]

The fact of women's high status in Native societies had to be demonized in order to prevent European women from leaving their society en masse. Between 1675 and 1763, almost 40 percent of women who were taken captive by Native people in New England chose to remain with their captors.[34] And these are women who had been told repeatedly about the savage nature of Indian people.

Because of the Christian patriarchal need to demonize Indian societies that might be attractive to women, the captivity narrative became a popular genre in the United States.[35] These narratives were supposedly first-person narratives of women who were abducted by "savages" and forced to undergo untold savagery. Their tales, however, were usually written by men who had their own agenda in publishing these women's stories. For instance, James Seaver in 1823 interviewed Mrs. Mary Jemison, who was taken as captive by the Seneca, but who chose to remain among them even when she was offered her freedom. He is convinced that she is protecting the Indian people by not describing their full savagery. "The vices of the Indians, she appeared disposed not to aggravate, and seemed to take pride in extolling their virtues. A kind of family pride induced her to withhold whatever would blot the character of her descendants, and perhaps induced her to keep back many things that would have been interesting."[36] Consequently, he supplements her narrative with material "from authentic sources" and Mary's cousin, Mr. George Jemison.[37] Seaver, nevertheless, attributes these supplements to her voice in this supposed first-person narrative.

Women who read these supposedly true accounts and later became captives of Indian people were shocked to find that they often went unmolested. Mary Rowlandson said of her experience: "I have been in the midst of roaring Lions, and Savage Bears, that feared neither God, nor Man, nor the Devil . . . and yet not one of them ever offered the least abuse of unchastity to me in word or action."[38] As William Apess (Pequot) once stated in the 1800s: "Where, in the records of Indian barbarity, can we point to a violated female?"[39] Brigadier General James Clinton of the Continental Army said to his soldiers as they were sent off to destroy the Iroquois nation in 1779: "Bad as the savages are, they never violate the chastity of any women, their prisoners."[40] The same could not be said of white men. But the constant depiction of Native men as savages prevented white women from seeing that the real enemy was not Native peoples, it was the patriarchy of their culture. Richard Hill argues that the non-patriarchal nature of Native society "fueled some men's hatred towards Indians. After all, they now had to worry about their prized possession being happier with savage Indians than with them."[41] Allen concurs:

> It was to the advantage of white men to mislead white women, and themselves, into believing that their treatment of women was superior to the treatment by the men of the group which they considered savage. Had white women discovered that all women were not mistreated, they might have been intolerant of their men's abusiveness.[42]

> Of course, as Jace Weaver (Cherokee), points out, while white men's fear of white women running off with Indian men is widely reflected in popular culture, there is no similar fear that white men will marry Indian women. White men assume they have unquestioned sexual access to Indian women. Weaver states: "It is a mark of patriarchy that miscegentation fears run only to White women."[43]

The Crucified Ones: The Pornography of the Cross

> Nathan Slaughter was the very model of the other-cheek ethic. . . . Little did they know that hidden under his pious pacifism was the butchering Jibbenainosay . . . the "Spirit that walks" through the district killing all Indians unlucky enough to get his way, scalping them, hacking their skulls open, and slashing his fearful mark into their breasts—a brace of deep knife cuts in the shape of a cross, Forrester learned, was the way he marked "all the meat of his killing."[44] (Description of Robert Montgomery's novel, *Nick in the Woods*, 1853.)

Joanne Carlson Brown and Rebecca Parker have critiqued the symbol of the cross because it encourages women, particularly women in abusive situations, to identify with Christ as those who should suffer. "The imitator of Christ, which every faithful person is exhorted to be, can find herself choosing to endure suffering. . . . This glorification of suffering as salvific, held before us daily in the image of Jesus hanging from the cross, encourages women who are being abused to be more concerned about their victimizer than about themselves."[45]

If those who suffer from oppression in society are encouraged to identify with the suffering Christ,[46] then with whom do those who have power identify?

In the symbol of the crucifixion, there is what Carol Adams terms an "absent referent." Adams explains this term by noting that the phrase "battered woman" ontologizes women as victims of battering. The person who is battering her is absent from this phrase.[47] Similarly, in the symbol of Christ, Jesus is ontologized as one who is crucified. The individuals who put him on the cross are erased as the perpetrators and never depicted in pictoral representations of the cross.

Andrea Dworkin argues that in a patriarchal system, "Men are distinguished from women by their commitment to do violence rather than to be victimized by it."[48] Thus, when men look to the cross, they do not identify with the individual on the cross. They identify with those who put him on the cross. As Dworkin states: "In adoring violence—from the crucifixion of Christ to the cinematic portrayal of General Patton—men seek to adore themselves."[49] But because those responsible for Jesus' death are the absent referent in the crucifix, their responsibility for the crucifixion is erased. Those in power can thus glorify the ability to crucify others without culpability. It is simply the nature of Christ, and those who share his powerless role in society, to be crucified.

It is not a surprise, then, that European colonizers have historically "crucified" those with less power than they. As discussed previously, those killed in the witch hunts and the Inquisition, which were events concurrent with the colonization of the Americas, met with torturous deaths. Similarly, Spanish priest, Las Casas, records in 1552 the brutal deaths of indigenous peoples in the hands of their colonizers in Hispanola:

> And the Christians . . . attacked the towns and spared neither the children nor the aged nor pregnant women nor women in childbed, not only stabbing them and dismembering them but cutting them to pieces as if dealing with sheep in the slaughter house. They laid bets as to who, with one stroke of the sword, could split a man in two.[50]

The connection between Native peoples as those symbolically crucified by Christian colonizers is most clear in Las Casas's description of how "they made some low wide gallows on which the hanged victims's feet almost touched the ground, stringing up their victims in lots of thirteen, in memory of Our Redeemer and His twelve apostles."[51] Similarly, Nathan Slaughter, the hero of Montgomery's *Nick in the Woods*, is driven to carve crosses into Native people's breasts as cited above.

The symbol of the cross allows those in power, and who cannot identify with weakness, to celebrate their ability to kill those who are not in power, without claiming responsibility for doing so. Similarly, in the captivity narratives of white women brutalized by savages, white men symbolically kill white women while blaming Native men for their death.

As June Namias points out, the captivity narratives and portraits are pornographic in nature.[52] They graphically (for that era) depict the brutalization and torture of white women at the hands of Native peoples. John Vanderlyn's portrait, *The Death of Jane McCrea*, for example, depicts a white woman, with her breasts half exposed. She is on her knees between two Indian men who are pulling her hair. Their axe is poised to scalp her. A white solider in the distance is attempting to rush to her rescue.

Namias argues that the point of these depictions is to instil in white women the notion that they need white men to protect them from savages.[53] While Namias is correct, Jane Caputi also suggests that in depictions of killings of women, the killer plays the alter ego to the male reader or viewer of the killing. "This convention allows the identifying viewer to gratifyingly fantasize himself in the two mutually reinforcing male roles at once. He is both . . . the protector and the menace.[54] In the case of Jane McCrea, the white man both symbolically kills her through the Indians which mirror his desires, and rushes to her rescue. In other narratives, the white male is absent. Yet, he is the one who has created the image in which the white man is the absent referent. He glorifies his ability to brutalize white women through the Indian savage while denying his culpability.

Meanwhile, Native women are completely absent from this picture, and consequently, their actual sexual brutalization at the hands of white men escapes notice. The white man literally brutalizes her while symbolically brutalizing the white woman. Native men are scapegoated for his actions such that white women see them as the enemy, and white men remain unaccountable.

America's Canaanites

The Israelites took the women of Midian and their little ones captive; and they took all their cattle, their flocks, and all their goods as booty. Moses said to them, "Have you allowed all the women to live? These women here, on Balaam's advice, made the Israelites act treacherously against the Lord in the affair of Peor, so that the plague came among the congregation of the Lord. Now there, kill every male among the little ones, and kill every woman who has known a man by sleeping with him. But all the young girls who have not known a man by sleeping with him, keep alive for yourselves. (Num. 31:9, 15–18)

We are warranted by this direction of Joshua to destroy wilful and convicted idolaters rather than to let them live, if by no other means they can be reclaimed . . . [we] may make a conquest of them . . . to reclaim and reduce those savages from their barbarous kinds of life and from their brutish manners to humanity, piety and honesty.[55] (John Gray, Puritan minister, 1609)

Robert Allen Warrior argues that the Exodus story as a Christian motif for liberation of oppressed people is of questionable value in light of the Israelite annihilation of the Canaanites in the biblical narrative.[56] Albert Cave, H.C. Porter, and others have demonstrated that Christian colonizers[57] often envisioned Native peoples as Canaanites, worthy of mass destruction.[58] As an example, George Henry Lokei wrote in 1794,

The human behavior of the governor at Pittsburgh greatly incensed those people, who according to the account given in the former Part of this history, represented the Indians as Canaanites, who without mercy ought to be destroyed from the face of the earth, and considered America as the land of promise given to the Christians.[59]

What makes Canaanites supposedly worthy of destruction in the biblical narrative and Indian peoples supposedly worthy of destruction in the eyes of their colonizers is that they both personify sexual sin. In the Bible, Canaanites commit acts of sexual perversion in Sodom (Gen. 19:1–29), are the descendants of the unsavory relations between Lot and his daughters (Gen. 19:30–38), are the descendants of the sexually perverse Ham (Gen. 9:22–27), and prostitute themselves in service of their gods (Gen. 28:21–22; Deut. 28:18; 1 Kings 14:24; 2 Kings 23:7; Hos. 4:13; Amos 2:7).

Similarly, Native peoples, in the eyes of the colonizers, are marked by their sexual perversity.[60] Alexander Whitaker, a minister in Virginia wrote in 1613: "They live naked in bodie, as if their shame of their sinne deserved no covering: Their names are as naked as their bodie: They esteem it a virtue to lie, deceive and steale as their master the divell teacheth them."[61] Furthermore, according to Bernardino de Minaya: "Their [the Indians] marriages are not a sacrament but a sacrilege. They are idolatrous, libidinous, and commit sodomy. Their chief desire is to eat, drink, worship heathen idols, and commit bestial obscenities."[62]

When Puritan missionary John Elliot encouraged a number of Native converts to make confessions of faith in 1654, they confessed primarily sexual sins. "I greatly sinned, I prayed to many gods, and used pauwauing, adultery, lust, lying and al [sic] other sins."[63] George Tinker points out that these confessions are Elliot's English translations of Native people's confessions. Thus, these confessions more likely reflect the Puritan view of Indian society rather than Native understandings of themselves.[64]

Because Native peoples personify sexual sin, their bodies are inherently "dirty." The following 1885 Proctor & Gamble ad for Ivory Soap illustrates this equation between Indian bodies and dirt.

> We were once factious, fierce and wild,
> In peaceful arts unreconciled
> Our blankets smeared with grease and stains
> From buffalo meat and settlers' veins.
> Through summer's dust and heat content
> From moon to moon unwashed we went,
> But Ivory Soap came like a ray
> Of light across our darkened way
> And now we're civil, kind and good
> And keep the laws as people should,
> We wear our linen, lawn and lace
> As well as folks with paler face
> And now I take, where'er we go
> This cake of Ivory Soap to show
> What civilized my squaw and me
> And made us clean and fair to see.[65]

Colonial literature, such as the above, link Indian peoples' sexuality with physical uncleanliness. Indians' bodies personify sexual sin. Because Indian bodies are "dirt," they are "rapable." That is, in patriarchal thinking, only a body that is "pure" can be violated. The rape of bodies that are considered inherently sexually sinful simply does not count. For instance, prostitutes have almost an impossible time being believed if they are raped because the dominant society considers the prostitute's body undeserving of integrity and violable at all times. Similarly, the history of mutilation of Indian bodies, both living and dead,, makes it clear to Indian people that they are not entitled to bodily integrity, as these examples suggest:.

> I saw the body of White Antelope with the privates cut off, and I heard a soldier say he was going to make a tobacco-pouch out of them.[66]

> At night Dr. Rufus Choate, [and] Lieutenant Wentz C. Miller . . . went up the ravine, decapitated the dead Qua-ha-das, and placing the heads in some gunny sacks, brought them back to be boiled out for future scientific knowledge.[67]

> Each of the braves was shot down and scalped by the wild volunteers, who out with their knives and cutting two parallel gashes down their backs, would strip the skin from the quivering flesh to make razor straps of.[68]

> Dr. Tuner, of Lexington, Iowa, visited this solitary grave [of Black Hawk] and robbed it of its tenant, . . . and sent the body to Alton, Ill., where the skeleton was wired together. [It was later returned] but here it remained but a short time ere vandal hands again carried it away and placed in the Burlington, Iowa Geographical and Historical Society, where it was consumed by fire in 1855.[69]

> One more dexterous than the rest, proceeded to flay the chief's [Tecumseh's] body; then, cutting the skin in narrow strips . . . at once, a supply of razor-straps for the more "ferocious" of his brethren.[70]

> Andrew Jackson . . . supervised the mutilation of 800 or so Creek Indian corpses—the bodies of men, women and children that he and his men massacred—cutting off their noses to count and preserve a record of the dead, slicing long strips of flesh from their bodies to tan and turn into bridle reins.[71]

> A few nights after this, some soldiers dug Mangus' body out again and took his head and boiled it during the night, and prepared the skull to send to the museum in New York.[72]

Through this colonization and abuse of their bodies as typified in the above examples, Indian people learn to internalize self-hatred. Body image is integrally related to self-esteem. When one's body is not respected, one begins to hate oneself.[73] Anne, a Native boarding school student, reflects on this process:

> You better not touch yourself. . . . If I looked at somebody . . . lust, sex, and I got scared of those sexual feelings. And I did not know how to handle them. . . . What really confused me was if intercourse was sin, why are people born? . . . It took me a really long time to get over the fact that . . . I've sinned: I had a child.[74]

The high rates of alcoholism and suicide in Indian communities can, in large part, be traced to the brutalization and degradation of Indian people's bodies through boarding schools and other forms of colonization.[75] Thus, Native people internalize the genocidal project through self-destruction. As Chrystos, Menominee poet, says in her poem, "We Cut Off Our Hair":

> Breathing this colonized air they take poison
> into their hearts listening for the message
> of genocide so much easier when we do it to ourselves
> & save whites the trouble[76]

While Canaanites, as sexual sin, are expendable in the biblical narrative, it is Canaanite women who are targeted for abuse. It is the women in particular who cause the downfall of Israelite men by leading them to worship other gods. "The Lord had said to the Israelites, `You shall not enter into marriage with [foreign women], neither shall they with you; for they will surely incline your heart to follow their gods'" (1 Kings 11:2).

While Israelites are commanded not to intermarry with Canaanite women, they are given license to rape them en masse. This is particularly illustrated in the story of the Rape of Dinah (Genesis 34). After the Canaanites have raped Jacob's daughter, Jacob's sons destroy their city, kill the men "and their wives . . . they captured and made their prey" (v. 29). While the Israelite woman's bodily integrity is to be defended in the narrative (even if it is because she is the property of Jacob), Canaanite women, who had no role in her rape, are deserving of rape.

Like Canaanite women, Native women are perceived as sexually loose. As such, they become "the sexual fantasy" of white men.[77] Amerigo Vespucci said of Native women:

> The Women as I have said go about naked and are very libidinous; yet they have bodies which are tolerably beautiful and cleanly . . . It was to us a matter of astonishment that none was to be seen among them who had a flabby breast.[78]

The fascination with women's sexual practices compels one Franciscan priest in the Santa Cruz mission to force an Indian couple to have sex in front of him.[79] Often the English as well captured Native men and women, expecting them to engage in wild sex. "Much to the surprise of the inquiring English, however, the captive Indians maintained their sexual distance."[80] Colonizers also used any excuse to strip-search Native women. An Aztec chronicler recalls: "The Christians searched all the refugees. They even opened the women's skirts and blouses and felt everywhere: their ears, their breasts, their hair."[81]

While Native women are the sexual fantasy of white men, they are also dangerous to the world order because they are women untamed by patriarchal control. As seen in previous citations, colonizers express constant outrage that Native women are not tied to monogamous marriages and "hold the marriage ceremony in utter disregard,"[82] are free to express their sexuality and "have no respect for . . . virginity,"[83] and love themselves. They do not see themselves as "fallen" women as they should. Their sexual power was threatening to white men; consequently, they sought to control it.

David Stannard points out that control over women's reproductive abilities and destruction of women and children are essential in destroying a people. According to Stannard, despite the mass destruction of Hiroshima and Nagasaki, the population of Japan actually increased by 14 percent between 1940 and 1950. This is because a disproportionate number of men were killed. If the women of a nation are not disproportionately killed, then that nation's population will not be severely affected. He says that Native women and children were targeted for wholesale killing in order to destroy the Indian nations.[84] This is why colonizers such as Andrew Jackson recommended that troops systematically kill Indian women and children after massacres in order to complete extermination. Similarly, Methodist minister Colonel John Chivington's policy was to "kill and scalp all little and big" because "nits make lice."[85] Says Stannard, "No population can survive if its women and children are destroyed. . . . This slaughter of innocents [is not] anything but intentional in design."[86]

Inez Hernandez-Avila (Nez Perce) concurs that Native women have been targeted for abuse because of their capacity to give birth. "It is because of a Native American woman's sex that she is hunted down and slaughtered, in fact, singled out, because she has the potential through childbirth to assure the continuance of the people."[87] Through the abduction of Indian children into boarding schools, colonizers have tried to prevent Native women from transmitting their culture to their children. Through rape and sexual mutilation, they have attempted to control and annihilate the sexual and reproductive power of Native women.

> When I was in the boat I captured a beautiful Carib woman . . . I conceived desire to take pleasure. . . . I took a rope and thrashed her well, for which she raised such unheard screams that you would not have believed your ears. Finally we came to an agreement in such a manner that I can tell you that she seemed to have been brought up in a school of harlots.[88]

> Two of the best looking of the squaws were lying in such a position, and from the appearance of the genital organs and of their wounds, there can be no doubt that they were first ravished and then shot dead. Nearly all of the dead were mutilated.[89]

> One woman, big with child, rushed into the church, clasping the alter and crying for mercy for herself and unborn babe. She was followed, and fell pierced with a dozen lances . . . the child was torn alive from the yet palpitating body of its mother, first plunged into the holy water to be baptized, and immediately its brains were dashed out against a wall.[90]

> The Christians attacked them with buffets and beatings. . . . Then they behaved with such temerity and shamelessness that the most powerful ruler of the island had to see his own wife raped by a Christian officer.[91]

I heard one man say that he had cut a woman's private parts out, and had them for exhibition on a stick. I heard another man say that he had cut the fingers off of an Indian, to get the rings off his hand. I also heard of numerous instances in which men had cut out the private parts of females, and stretched them over their saddle-bows and some of them over their hats.[92]

American Horse said of the massacre at Wounded Knee:

The fact of the killing of the women, and more especially the killing of the young boys and girls who are to go to make up the future strength of the Indian people is the saddest part of the whole affair and we feel it very sorely.[93]

While the era of Indian massacres in their more explicit form is over, the colonizers desire to control Native women's sexuality and power to reproduce continues. In the eyes of the colonizers, Native women's bodies are still rapable. In 1982, Stuart Kasten marketed a new video, "Custer's Revenge," in which players get points each time they, in the form of Custer, rape an Indian woman. The slogan of the game is "When you score, you score." He describes the game as "a fun sequence where the woman is enjoying a sexual act willingly."[94]

The disrespect of women's bodily integrity is also manifest in the sterilization abuse of the 1970s. In 1972, an Indian woman entered the office of Dr. Connie Uri, a Cherokee/Choctaw doctor, and asked to have a womb implant. Dr. Uri discovered that the woman had been given a hysterectomy for sterilization purposes and had been told that the surgery was reversible. Dr. Uri began to investigate Indian Health Services sterilization policies. Her work prompted Senator James Abourezk to request a study on IHS sterilization policies. The General Accounting Office released a study in November, 1976, indicating that Native women were being sterilized without informed consent. These investigations led Dr. Uri to estimate that 25 percent of all Native women of childbearing age had been sterilized without their informed consent, with sterilization rates as high as 80 percent on some reservations.[95]

While sterilization abuse has curbed somewhat with the institution of informed consent policies, it has reappeared in the form of Norplant and Depo-Provera. These are both extremely risky forms of long-acting hormonal contraceptives that have been pushed on Indian women.[96] Depo-Provera, a known carcinogen which has been condemned as an inappropriate form of birth control by several national women's health organizations,[97] was routinely used on Indian women through Indian Health Services (IHS) before it was approved by the FDA in 1992.[98] There are no studies on the long-term effects of Norplant, and the side-effects (constant bleeding, sometimes for over ninety days, tumors, kidney problems, strokes, heart attacks, sterility) are so extreme that approximately 30 percent of women on Norplant want it taken out in the first year,[99] with the majority requesting to have it taken out within two years, even though it is supposed to remain implanted in a woman's arm for five years. To date, over 2,300 women who are suffering from 125 side effects relating to Norplant have joined a class action suit against the company.[100] The Native American Women's Health Education Resource Center conducted a survey of Norplant and Depo-Provera policies of IHS and found that Native women were not given adequate counseling regarding the side-effects and contraindications.[101] In my experience working on Native women's reproductive health issues with Women of All Red Nations, all the Native women I know who have sought contraception counseling were advised to get either Norplant or Depo-Provera (many are not told other forms of contraception exist). Colonizers evidently recognize the wisdom of the Cheyenne saying, "A Nation is not conquered until the hearts of the women [and their bodies as well] are on the ground."

Subdue the Earth

God blessed them, and God said to them, Be fruitful and multiply, and fill the earth and subdue it; and have dominion over the fish of the sea and over the birds of the air and over every living thing that moves upon the earth. (Gen. 1:28)

Ecofeminist theorists have argued that there is a connection among patriarchy's disregard for nature, for women, and for indigenous peoples. It is the same colonial/patriarchal mind that seeks to control the sexuality of women and indigenous peoples that also seeks to control nature. Jane Caputi states:

Violence against women remains protected by custom, indifference, glamorization, and denial. Concomitantly, the culture, language, traditions, myths, social organizations, and members of gynocentric cultures, such as those of North American Indians, have been slashed and trashed. Moreover, as I will demonstrate, the basic myths, motivations, and methods behind geocide—the wasting of the organic and elemental worlds and the attempted annihilation of the planet—are rooted in gynocidal and misogynist paradigms.[102]

One major complaint colonizers had of Native peoples was that they did not properly control or subdue nature. For instance, governor John Winthrop of Massachusetts Bay declared that "America fell under the legal rubric of *vacuum domicilium* because the Indians had not 'subdued' it and therefore had only a 'natural' and not a 'civil' right to it."[103] George E. Ellis (1880) echoed: "the Indians simply wasted everything within their reach. . . . They required enormous spaces of wilderness for their mode of existence."[104] Walter Prescott Webb reasoned that free land was "land free to be taken."[105] This reasoning became the colonizer's legal basis for appropriating land from Native peoples.

Unfortunately for the colonizers, nature is not so easy to subdue and control. As we find ourselves in the midst of environmental disaster, it is clear that no one can escape the repercussions of environmental damage. Colonizers attempt to deny this reality by forcing the expendable people, the Canaanites of this country, to face the most immediate consequences of environmental destruction.

Their technique mirrors the biblical narratives in which Israelites attempt to explain the disasters they face as the result of the Canaanites. Hardships the Israelites faced are generally blamed on their being too friendly with Canaanites, especially with Canaanite women. The Israelites then attempt to divert "Yahweh's anger" to the Canaanites through mass destruction, so that they will not have to face it themselves.

It is not an accident that 100 percent of uranium production takes place on or near Indian land.[106] Nor is it a coincidence that Native reservations are often targeted for toxic waste dumps. To date, over fifty reservations have been targeted for waste dumps.[107] In addition, military and nuclear testing also takes place almost exclusively on Native lands. For instance, there have already been at least 650 nuclear explosions on Western Shoshone land at the Nevada test site. Fifty percent of these underground tests have leaked radiation into the atmosphere.[108] Native peoples, the expendable ones, are situated to suffer the brunt of environmental destruction so that colonizers can continue to be in denial about the fact that they will also eventually be affected.

As a case in point, Jessie DeerInWater (Cherokee) of Native Americans for Clean Environment was one of the organizers of the campaign to stop the Kerr-McGee Sequoyah Fules Facility (a uranium conversion facility) in Oklahoma. Kerr-McGee was eventually closed down, although it has not cleaned up its nuclear waste from the plant. In her campaign, she discovered that Kerr-McGee was using radioactive wastes to make fertilizer. The Nuclear Regulatory Commission has allowed Kerr-McGee to use this fertilizer on 15,000 acres of hay fields in Oklahoma, where cattle are grazed and then sold on the open market. The only health study conducted on the cattle revealed that ten percent of them had resulting cancerous growths. This was deemed "normal." There have been no studies on the long-term effects of this fertilizer on either the hay or the cattle. The cattle can be sold without notifying consumers that they have been fed on hay fertilized with nuclear wastes. In addition, bales of hay usually sell for $25 to $30 per bale, while Kerr-McGee bales sell for $5, thus undercutting the market on hay bales. One of Kerr-McGee's customers is Brahm's Ice Cream, an ice cream franchise in Oklahoma. Kerr-McGee has also donated the hay to the Larry Jones Ministries to their Save the Children Program. It has been delivered to drought-ridden areas all over the country so that Kerr-McGee can take a tax write off. Thus, it is not only Native peoples who are affected by radiation poisoning.[109]

Another example is the current plan to relocate all nuclear wastes into a permanent high-level nuclear waste repository in Yucca mountain on Shoshone land, for a cost of $3.25 billion. Yucca Mountain is located on an active volcanic zone where kiloton bombs are exploded nearby, thus increasing the risks of radioactive leakage.[110] In addition, if this plan is approved, the proposed repository on Yucca mountain would receive nuclear wastes from throughout the United States. Only five states would not be affected by the transportation of high-level radioactive wastes. With up to 4,000 shipments of radioactive waste crossing the United States annually, trucking industry statistics reveal that up to fifty accidents per year could occur during the thirty year period that nuclear waste would stream to Yucca Mountain.[111]

Katsi Cook, Mohawk midwife, argues that this attack upon nature is yet another attack on Native women's bodies because the effects of toxic and radiation poisoning are most apparent in their effect on women's reproductive systems.[112] In the areas where there is uranium mining, such as in Four Corners and the Black Hills, Indian people face skyrocketing rates of cancer, miscarriages, and birth defects. Children growing up in Four Corners are developing ovarian and testicular cancers at fifteen times the national average.[113] Meanwhile, Indian women on Pine Ridge experience a miscarriage rate six times higher than the national average.[114]

After the Prairie Island nuclear generating plant was opened near Prairie Island reservation, breast cancer deaths increased 43 percent in that area (compared to 1 percent for the rest of the state). A study through the Pittsburgh School of Medicine concluded that "Only 18 percent of all U.S. women live in those counties [near nuclear plants], but they account for 55 percent of all breast cancer." Because of location, a disproportionate number of these women will be indigenous.[115]

On the Akwesasne Mohawk reserve, one of the most polluted areas in the country, the PCBs, DDT, Mirex and HCBs that are dumped into their waters eventually become stored in women's breast milk.[116] Thus, through the rape of Earth, Native women's bodies are raped once again.

Looking for Paradise

> I have come down to deliver them from the power of the Egyptians, and to bring them up from that land to a good and spacious land, to a land flowing with milk and honey. (Exod. 3:8)

Both Stannard and Kirkpatrick Sale argue that colonizers, in attempting to escape the horrors of their violent society, expected to find "Eden" in the Americas, "a place of simplicity, innocence, harmony, love, and happiness, where the climate is balmy and fruits of nature's bounty are found on the trees year round."[117] Many of the early colonial narratives describe the Americas as an idyllic paradise. However, as Sales argues, colonizers approached "paradise" through their colonial and patriarchal lens. Consequently, they viewed the land and indigenous peoples as something to be used for their own purposes; they could not respect their integrity.

> The resulting tensions, then could be resolved . . . only by being played out against . . . the natural world and natural peoples . . . the only way the people of Christian Europe ultimately could live with the reality of the Noble Savage in the Golden World was to transform it progressively in to the Savage Beast in the Hideous Wilderness.[118]

Thus the healing they sought from their brutal culture was parasitic on Native peoples, ultimately replicating the brutality from which they sought to escape.

Completing the destruction of a people involves the destruction of the integrity of their culture which forms the matrix of their resistance. Colonizers not only brutalize Native peoples, but they attempt to destroy the process by which they may heal from this brutalization. The Bureau of Indian Affairs contributed to this process in the late 1800s by loaning reservation Indians to Wild West Shows, circuses, and the like. Indians at these shows displayed mockeries of their "culture" by replicating war dances. The psychological impact on Native peoples who took part in these practices was devastating. The Indian agent at Pine Ridge Agency in South Dakota reported in 1899 that "The agency physician states that nearly all of the unnameable diseases now occurring on this reservation are traceable to those Indians who have returned from shows and expositions."[119]

Hanauni-Kay Trask, Native Hawaiian activist, argues that colonizers destroy the cultural base from which indigenous people resist colonization by commodifying it to meet western consumerist needs. She terms the phenomenon "cultural prostitution":

> "Prostitution" in this context refers to the entire institution which defines a woman (and by extension the "female") as an object of degraded and victimized sexual value for use and exchange through the medium of money. . . . My purpose is not to exact detail or fashion a model but to convey the utter degradation of our culture and our people under corporate tourism by employing "prostitution" as an analytical category. . . .

> The point, of course, is that everything in Hawai'i can be yours, that is, you the tourist, the non-native, the visitor. The place, the people, the culture, even our identity as a "Native" people is for sale. Thus, Hawai'i, like a lovely woman, is there for the taking.[120]

Trask's model of prostitution as a way of analyzing the exploitation of Hawaiian culture can be applied to the 1993 Re-Imagining conference sponsored by the National Council of Churches. In this conference designed for women to re-imagine a non-patriarchal Christianity, Native women were invited to dance in traditional costumes as befitting the stereotypes of Native women. They were, as Trask articulates, "transformed to [be] complicitous in their own commodification."[121] They were not invited to speak on any struggles at any time during the conference. They were to be voiceless objects of consumption, "there for the taking." Native women had offered medicine bundles, which are to be treated with great respect, but which the primarily white audience unceremoniously threw on the floor. Native culture was something that white women could "try on" for the session, but then dispense with afterwards. Thus, the empowerment of white women took place through the disempowerment of Native women. White women still do not honor the right of Native women to heal from the rape of colonization by respecting the integrity of their culture.

    Native counselors generally agree that a strong cultural identity is essential if Native people are to heal from abuse. This is because Native women's healing entails healing, not only from any personal abuse she has suffered, but also from the patterned history of abuse against her family, her nation, and the environment in which she lives.[122] When white women appropriate Indian spirituality for their own benefit for whatever reason, they continue this pattern of abuse against Indian peoples' cultures. While I have dicussed the issue of Indian spiritual exploitation in more detail elsewhere,[123] here I want to argue that this exploitation has a specific negative impact on Native peoples' ability to heal from abuse. Shelley McIntyre of the Minneapolis Indian Women's Resource Center complains that Native women who are trying to heal from abuse have difficulty finding their rootedness in Native culture because all they can find is Lynn Andrews or other such "plastic medicine wo/men" who masquerade as Indians for profit. It is unfortunate that as many white women attempt to heal themselves from the damage brought on by Christian patriarchy, they are unable to do so in a way that is not parasitic on Native women. They continue the practice of their colonial fathers who sought paradise in Native lands without regard for the peoples of these lands.

Conclusion

The rape of Native women is the story of the destruction of their bodily integrity and their role in child rearing, the destruction of cultural and national sovereignty, and the destruction of the earth. It is through their victimization that colonizers have attempted to destroy Native nations. The restoration of Native sovereignty cannot occur while Native women and children continue to be sexually victimized. Issues of violence against women and children cannot remain secondary to issues of sovereignty because it is through violence against women and children that colonizers have sought to destroy Native sovereignty. Violence against women is a sovereignty issue. As Hernandez-Avila states: "I have no use for a political peace, for a false show of unity while our women and our children are being violated, battered, and abused or while our communities continue to suffer the effects of conquest."[124]
    At the same time, healing from both personal and historic abuse requires much more than a visit to a rape crisis center. It involves a deconstruction of Christian imperialism and how it manifests itself in myriad ways to destroy Native peoples. Native people's healing from sexual abuse must take place within the context of restoration of Native sovereignty and the destruction of Christian colonialism. Sovereignty, then, is a feminist issue. Hernandez-Avila articulates this holistic vision of healing for Native women:

> We must imagine a world without rape. But I cannot imagine a world without rape, a world without misogyny, without imagining a world without racism, classism, sexism, homophobia, ageism, historical amnesia and other forms and manifestations of violence directed against those communities that are seen to be "asking for it." Even the Earth is presumably "asking for it". . . . What do I imagine then? From my own Native

American perspective, I see a world where sovereign indigenous peoples continue to plunge our memories to come back to our originality, to live in dignity and carry on our resuscitated and ever-transforming cultures and traditions with liberty. . . . I see a world where native women find strength and continuance in the remembrance of who we really were and are . . . a world where more and more native men find the courage to recognize and honor—that they and the women of their families and communities have the capacity to be profoundly vital and creative human beings.[125]

While Native women have been challenging Christian colonialism and violence and have been analyzing the impact of Christian imperialistic violence on Native communities for centuries, the dominant society has not heard their voices. In order to eradicate violence in this society, the perspectives of Native women must become central to this struggle.

Notes

Special thanks to Justine Smith, Chrystos, Shelley McIntyre, Sharon Todd, Jace Weaver, George Tinker, and Tom Reisz.

1. Marilou Awiakta, *Selu* (Golden, Colo.: Fulcrum Publishing, 1993), 92.
2. See, for example, *A Sharing: Traditional Lakota Thought & Philosophy Regarding Domestic Violence* (Sacred Shawl Women's Society, South Dakota n.d.); *Sexual Assault Is Not an Indian Tradition* (Division of Indian Work Sexual Assault Project, Minneapolis n.d.); and Paula Gunn Allen, "Violence and the American Indian Woman," *The Speaking Profits Us* (Center for the Prevention of Sexual and Domestic Violence, Seattle, 1986), 5–7.
3. See M. Annette Jaimes and Theresa Halsey, "American Indian Women: At the Center of Indigenous Resistance in North America," in *State of Native America,* ed. Annette Jaimes (Boston: South End Press, 1992), 311–44, and Paula Gunn Allen, *The Sacred Hoop* (Boston: Beacon Press), 1986.
4. Winona LaDuke, quoted in *State of Native America,* 319.
5. Paul LeJeune, quoted in Allen, 40.
6. Jaimes and Halsey, 315.
7. Tom Holm, "Patriots and Pawns," in *State of Native America,* 355.
8. Allen, 38.
9. Jorge Noriega, "American Indian Education in the United States: Indoctrination for Subordination to Colonialism," in *State of Native America,* 380.
10. U.S. Bureau of Indian Affairs, "Rules for Indian Schools," *Annual Report of the Commissioner of Indian Affairs,* Washington DC, 1890, cxlvi, cl–clii; cited in Frederick Binder and David M. Reimers, eds., *The Way We Lived* (Lexington, Mass.: D. C. Heath and Company, 1982), 59.
11. Robert A. Trennert, "Educating Indian Girls at Nonreservation Boarding Schools, 1878–1920," *The Way We Lived,* 54.

12. See K. Tsianina Lomawaima, *They Called It Prairie Light* (Lincoln: University of Nebraska Press, 1994), 86.

13. Fran Leeper Buss, comp., *Dignity: Lower Income Women Tell of Their Lives and Struggles* (Ann Arbor: University of Michigan Press, 1985), 156. For further accounts of the widespread nature of sexual and other abuse in boarding schools, see Native Horizons Treatment Centre, *Sexual Abuse Handbook*, Hagersville Ontario, n.d., 61–68; "The End of The Silence," *Maclean's* 105/37 (September 14, 1992): 14, 16; Jim DeNomie, "American Indian Boarding Schools: Elders Remember," *Aging News* (Winter 1990–91): 2–6; U.S. Congress, Senate, Committee on Indian Affairs, *Survey of the Conditions of the Indians in the United States*, Hearings, before a Subcommittee of the Committee on Indian Affairs, Senate, on SR 79, 70th Cong., 2d session, 1929, 428–29, 1021–23, and 2833–35; cited in *Who's the Savage*, ed. David Wrone and Russell Nelson (Malabar, Fla.: Robert Krieger, 1982), 152–54.

14. Tim Giago, "Catholic Church Can't Erase Sins of the Past," *Indian Country Today* (December 15, 1994): A4.

15. "Goodbye BIA, Hello New Federalism," *American Eagle* 2/6 (December 1994): 19. Incidentally, after the allegations of abuse became public, the BIA merely provided a counselor for the abused children, who then used his sessions with them to write a book.

16. "Child Sexual Abuse in Federal Schools," *The Ojibwe News* (January 17, 1990), 8.

17. In Celia Haig-Brown, *Resistance and Renewal* (Vancouver: Tilacum, 1988), 14–15.

18. *The Province*, July 19, 1989 and *Vancouver Sun*, March 17, 1990; quoted in *Sexual Abuse Handbook*, 66.

19. U.S. Department of Interior, "Board of Indian Commissioner's Reports," in *Annual Reports* (June 30, 1905), H. Doc. 20: 59th Cong., 1st Sess., 17–18, in *The Way We Lived*, 62.

20. I think it is important not to suggest that there are healthy and unhealthy families as it is probably not possible to have a completely healthy family in a patriarchal society as all families have internalized patriarchal values of violence and domination to some degree.

21. In Ellen Bass and Laura Davis, *The Courage to Heal* (New York: Harper & Row, 1988), 394–99.

22. Warren is not arguing, however, that dysfunctional societies are based on personal problems, or that there is one definition of what a heathy society would be.

23. Karen J. Warren, "A Feminist Philosophical Perspective on Ecofeminist Spiritualities," in *Ecofeminism and the Sacred*, ed. Carol J. Adams (New York: Continuum, 1993), 125.

24. David Stannard, *American Holocaust* (Oxford: Oxford University Press, 1992), 61. See also Kirpatrick Sale, *The Conquest of Paradise* (New York: Plume, 1990), 28–37.

25. Stannard, 60.

26. Andrea Dworkin, *Woman Hating* (New York: E.P. Dutton, 1974), 130. Anne Barstow argues that Dworkin's numbers are unrealistic and thinks that about 200,000 were accused of witchcraft and 100,000 were put to death. She adds that these numbers do not include those who were accused but never made it into court records and those who may have been lynched by mobs. Despite these lower figures, Barstow states that "a statistically based figure, though lower, still makes the same point: that this was an organized mass murder of women that cannot be dismissed by historians." See Anne Barstow, *Witchcraze* (New York: Harper, 1994), 21.

27. See Mary Daly, *Gyn/Ecology* (Boston: Beacon Press, 1978), 178–222; Barbara Ehrenreich and Deirdre English, *For Her Own Good* (Garden City: Anchor, 1979), 35–39; Dworkin, 118–50.

28. I'm not arguing that all Native societies were perfect, but that for the most part they were considerably less violent than European societies.

29. Quoted in Stannard, *American Holocaust*, 104.

30. Stannard, 103.

31. Archibald Loudon, *Selection of the Most Interesting Narratives, Outrages Committed by the Indians in Their Wars with the White People* (Carlise A. Loudon: 1808), vii. Early American Imprints, 1801–1819.

32. "Onondoga's Early History," *The Syracuse Herald-Journal*, February 5, 1899; reprinted in Andre Lopez *Pagans in Our Midst* (Mohawk Nation: Akwesasne Notes), 101.

33. "Like Other Cannibals," *Syracuse Herald*, February 8, 1899, Lopez, 103.

34. June Namias, *White Captives* (Chapel Hill: University of North Carolina Press, 1993), 25. I am not arguing that the non-patriarchal nature of Native societies is the only reason white women may have chosen to live with their captors, but that it is a possible explanation for why many chose to stay.

35. It is difficult to ascertain the true nature of Indian captivity of white people based on these narratives because of their anti-Indian bias. For instance, *A Narrative of the Horrid Massacre by the Indians of the Wife and Children of the Christian Hermit* (St. Louis: Leander W. Whiteney and Co., 1833), 9, 24, sets out to prove that Indians are so biologically cruel that there is nothing else for whites to do than exterminate them. However, even the narrator admits that Indians killed his family because he "destroyed their village." He further states that Natives "are kind and hospitable, but those who *intentionally* [italics mine] offend them, the western savage [sic] is implacable." June Namias suggests that captivity of white people became more brutal as the conquest put Native people to the point of desperation. She also says that since captivity narratives by Jesuits seem to be the most graphic in nature, it is possible that they embellished their stories to enhance their status as martyrs and encourage greater funding for their missions. See *White Captives*, 50, 89. Francis Jennings argues also that there was some practice of torture among the Iroquois, though not other northeastern tribes, and that it became more pronounced as the conquest against them became more brutal. He states, however, that Native people never molested women or girls. See *The Invasion of the Americas: Indians,*

Colonialism and the Cant of Conquest (New York: Norton, 1975), 160–70. Richard Drinnon believes that most male captives were killed, except that some might be adopted into the tribe to replace those that had been killed in battle. Women and children were not killed. See *Facing West* (New York: Shocken, 1980), 151–52. All of these discussions are based on Native practices after colonization and the infusion of violence into their societies.

36. James E. Seaver, *A Narrative of the Life of Mrs. Mary Jemison* (New York: Corinth Books, 1975), xxii.

37. Ibid., xii, xxii.

38. Mary Rowlandson, *A Narrative of the Captivity and Removes of Mrs. Mary Rowlandson* (1682; reprint, Temecula, Calif.: Reprint Services Corp., 1974), 108–9.

39. William Apess, "Son of the Forest," in *On Our Own Ground: The Complete Writings of William Apess, A Pequot*, ed. Barry O'Connell (Amherst: University of Massachusetts Press, 1992), 64.

40. Quoted in *Who's the Savage*, 17.

41. Richard Hill, "Sex, Lies and Stereotypes," *Turtle Quarterly*, 19.

42. Allen, "Violence and the American Indian Woman," 5.

43. Jace Weaver, "Ethnic Cleansing: Homestyle," *Wicazo Sa Review* 10/1 (Spring 1994): 30.

44. Drinnon, 153.

45. Joanne Carlson Brown and Rebecca Parker, "For God So Loved the World," in this volume, 36–59.

46. I am not suggesting that the symbol of the cross has had no positive value for oppressed communities and that these communities have not been able to transform it into a symbol of liberation. However, this symbol has also operated in ways that can be oppressive to various communities, and consequently, it is important to deconstruct the varying meanings of the cross.

47. Carol Adams, *Neither Man nor Beast* (New York: Continuum, 1994), 101.

48. Andrea Dworkin, *Pornography* (New York: Perigree, 1981), 53.

49. Ibid.

50. Bartolome De Las Casas, *The Devestation of the Indies*, trans. Herma Briffault (Baltimore: Johns Hopkins University Press, 1992), 33.

51. Ibid., 33.

52. Namias, 94.

53. Ibid., 66–67.

54. Jane Caputi, *Age of Sex Crime* (Bowling Green, Ohio: Popular Press, 1987), 87.

55. John Gray, *A Good Speed to Virginia*, London, 1609; quoted in H.C. Porter, *The Inconstant Savage* (London: Gerald Duckworth & Co., 1979), 354.

56. Robert Allen Warrior, "Canaanites, Cowboys, and Indians," *Anthology of HONOR*, 21–26, formerly in *Christianity and Crisis* (September 11, 1989).

57. I shall not discuss how Jewish traditions have interpreted the Canaanite narratives, nor whether there even was a wholesale conquest of the Canaanites, which many scholars doubt. I am describing how the Christian appropriation of Canaanite narratives has impacted Native people; I make no claims either for or against Jewish colonialism.

58. Albert Cave, "Canaanites in a Promised Land," *American Indian Quarterly* (Fall 1988): 277–97; Porter, 91–115; Ronald Sanders, *Lost Tribes and Promised Lands* (Boston: Little, Brown and Company, 1978), 46, 181 and 292; Djelal Kadir, *Columbus and the Ends of the Earth* (Berkeley: University of California Press, 1992), 129.

59. *Who's the Savage*, 68.

60. See Hill, 14–23.

61. Quoted in Robert Berkoher, *The White Man's Indian* (New York: Vintage, 1978), 19.

62. Quoted in Stannard, 211.

63. Quoted in George Tinker, *Missionary Conquest* (Minneapolis: Augsburg, 1993), 38.

64. Ibid.

65. Quoted in Lopez, 119. It should be noted, as Allen points out, that Native people in fact bathed much more frequently than did Europeans, see *Sacred Hoop*, 217.

66. U.S. Congress. Senate, Special Committee Appointed under Joint Resolution of March 3, 1865. *Condition of the Indian Tribes*, S. Rept. 156, 39th Cong., 2d sess., 1867, 95–96; quoted in *Who's The Savage?*, 113.

67. R. G. Carter, *On the Border with MacKenize Or Winning West Texas from the Comanche* (Washington: Eynon Company, 1935), 199, 201; quoted in *Who's The Savage?*, 124.

68. John H. Fonda, "Early Wisconsin," *Collections of the State Historical Society of Wisconsin* (Madison: Published by the Society, 1907), 263, quoted in *Who's the Savage?*, 90.

69. Perry A. Armstrong, *The Sauks and the Black Hawk War* (Springfield: H.W. Rokker, 1887), 539–40; quoted in *Who's the Savage?*, 91.

70. William James, *A Full and Correct Account of the Military Occurrences of the Late War between Great Britain and the United States of America*, 2 vols. (London: printed by the author, 1818), 1: 293–96; quoted in *Who's the Savage?*, 82.

71. Stannard, 121.

72. Daniel Ellis Conner, *Joseph Reddeford Walker and the Arizona Adventure*, ed. Donald J. Berthronng and Odessa Davenport (Norman: University of Oklahoma Press, 1956), 37–41; quoted in *Who's the Savage?*, 106.

73. For further discussion on relationship between bodily abuse and self-esteem, see *Courage to Heal*, 207–22 and Bonnie Burstow, *Radical Feminist Therapy* (London: Sage, 1992), 187–234.

74. Quoted in Haig-Brown, 108.

75. See *Sexual Abuse Handbook*. The story of Alkali Lake reserve illustrates this process. Over 70 percent of natives in that area were victims of sexual abuse. In reaction to the abuse faced by the community, alcohol abuse became prevalent such that at one time there was a 100 percent alcoholism rate. Through a community-led program on alcohol, the community became over 90 percent sober. However, recovery from abuse forced the community to deal with the underlying problems of sexual abuse. The band has developed the "Alkali Lake Community Response to Sexual Assault," 66.

76. Chrystos, "We Cut Off Our Hair," *Dream On* (Vancouver: Press Gang, 1991), 103

77. Hill, 19.

78. Quoted in Berkhofer, 9.

79. Stannard, 140.

80. Ibid., 100.

81. Quoted in Stannard, 80.

82. Quoted in *Cattaraugus Republican*, February 11, 1897; in Lopez, 9.

83. Dominican monk, Thomas Ortiz; quoted in Sale, 201.

84. Stannard, 121.

85. Quoted in Stannard, 131.

86. Stannard, 119.

87. Inez Hernandez-Avila, "In Praise of Insubordination, or What Makes a Good Woman Go Bad?," in *Transforming a Rape Culture*, ed. Emilie Buchwald, Pamela R. Fletcher, and Martha Roth (Minneapolis: Milkweed, 1993), 386.

88. From Cuneo, an Italian nobleman; quoted in Sale, 140.

89. U.S. Commissioner of Indian Affairs, *Annual Report for 1871*, (Washington: Government Printing Office, 1871), 487–88; cited in *Who's the Savage?*, 123.

90. LeRoy R. Haven, ed., *Ruxton of the Rockiers* (Norman: University of Oklahoma Press, 1950), 46–149; cited in *Who's the Savage?*, 97.

91. Las Casas, 33.

92. Lieutenant James D. Cannon quoted in "Report of the Secretary of War," 39th Congress, 2d Sess., Senate Executive Document 26, Washington DC, 1867; printed in *The Sand Creek Massacre: A Documentary History* (New York: Sol Lewis, 1973), 129–30.

93. James Mooney, "The Ghost Dance Religion and the Sioux Outbreak of 1890," in *Fourteenth Annual Report of the United States Bureau of Ethnology* (Washington DC: U.S. Government Printing Office, 1896), 885; quoted in Stannard, 127.

94. "Up Front," *Perspectives: The Civil Rights Quarterly* 14/3 (Fall 1982).

95. See "The Threat of Life," *WARN Report*, 13–16 (available through WARN, 4511 N. Hermitage, Chicago, Ill. 60640); Brint Dillingham, "Indian Women and IHS Sterilization Practices," *American Indian*

Journal (January 1977): 27–28; Brint Dillingham, "Sterilization of Native Americans," *American Indian Journal* (July 1977): 16–19; Pat Bellanger, "Native American Women, Forced Sterilization, and the Family," in *Every Woman Has a Story*, ed. Gaya Wadnizak Ellis (Minneapolis: Midwest Villages & Voices, 1982), 30–35; "Oklahoma: Sterilization of Native Women Charged to I.H.S.," *Akwesasne Notes* (Mid Winter 1989), 30.

96. For a description of the hazards of Depo-Provera, see Stephen Minkin, "Depo-Provera: A Critical Analysis," Institute for Food and Development Policy, San Francisco. He concludes that "the continued use of Depo-Provera for birth control is unjustified and unethical." For more information on the effects of Norplant, see *Womanist Health Newsletter*, Issue on Norplant, available through Women's Health Education Project, 3435 N. Sheffield, #205, Chicago, Ill. 60660.

97. For a statement on Depo-Provera from the National Black Women's Health Project, National Latina Health Organization, the Native American Women's Health Education Resource Center, the National Women's Health Network, and Women's Economic Agenda Project, contact NAWHERC, P.O. Box 572, Lake Andes, South Dakota 57356-0572.

98. "Taking the Shot," series of articles from *Arizona Republic*, November 1986.

99. Debra Hanania-Freeman, "Norplant: Freedom of Choice or a Plan for Genocide?," *EIR* (May 14, 1993): 20.

100. Kathleen Plant, "Mandatory Norplant is Not the Answer," *Chicago Sun-Times*, November 2, 1994, 46.

101. "A Study of the Use of Depo-Provera and Norplant by the Indian Health Services" from Native American Women's Health Education Resource Center, South Dakota, 1993.

102. Jane Caputi, *Gossips, Gorgons and Crones* (Santa Fe: Bear Publishing, 1993), 13.

103. Jennings, 82.

104. Ibid., 84.

105. Ibid.

106. Winona LaDuke, "A Society Based on Conquest Cannot Be Sustained," in *Toxic Struggles*, ed. Richard Hofricher (Philadelphia: New Society Publishers, 1993), 99.

107. Conger Beasely, "Dances with Garbage," *E Magazine* (November/December 1991): 40.

108. Valerie Tallman, "Tribes Speak Out on Toxic Assault," *Lakota Times*, December 18, 1991.

109. Jessie DeerInWater, "The War Against Nuclear Waste Disposal," *Sojourner* (July 1992): 15.

110. Valerie Tallman, "Tribes Speak Out On Toxic Assault," *Lakota Times*, December 18, 1991.

111. Ibid.

112. Lecture at Indigenous Women's Network conference at White Earth reservation, September 17, 1994.

113. Valerie Tallman, "The Toxic Waste of Indian Lives," *Covert Action* 17, (Spring 1992): 17.

114. Lakota Harden, *Black Hills PAHA SAPA Report* (August-September 1980): 15.

115. "Expert Says Cancer Deaths Rise 43 percent Near Nuclear Plant," *St. Paul Pioneer Press*, June 2, 1994, 3C.

116. "Contaminated Milk in Mohawk Women," *Sojourner* (April 1994): 11.

117. Stannard, 166.

118. Sale, 203.

119. U.S. Commissioner of Indian Affairs, *Annual Report of 1899* (Washington: Government Printing Office, 1899), 41–43; quoted in *Who's the Savage?*, 141.

120. Haunani-Kay Trask, *From a Native Daughter: Colonialism & Sovereignty in Hawai'i* (Maine: Common Courage Press, 1993), 185–94.

121. Trask, 191.

122. Justine Smith (Cherokee), personal conversation, February 17, 1994.

123. See Andy Smith, "For All Those Who Were Indian in a Former Life," in *Ecofeminism and the Sacred*, 168–71.

124. Hernandez-Avila, 378.

125. Ibid., 388–89.

Healing in Communities Following an Experience of Mission as Oppression

Stan McKay

And so it is that Christianity came to the Americas. After much raping of the Earth, the mission to the Indians began. In Canada, Indians were useful as allies in the early conflicts that were brought from Europe. As allies, aboriginal peoples were valued, were courted, and were encouraged to be a part of various causes. This was especially true in the War of 1812, when the aboriginal peoples had a place in deciding how the boundary between the United States and Canada was to be drawn.

In a strange way, there was a sense of worth on the part of some aboriginal nations on various sides of the conflicts that occurred. Until about the turn of the century, we had continued to be of some worth in our own minds and the minds of society. We were involved in the fur trade, we supplied food and offered some cheap labor to the newcomers. We were not seen as "dependable" enough for menial tasks. But we were still of some worth for a period of time in the development of the nations that we have on Turtle Island.

Land negotiations were yet another area of contact. Sometimes there were not many negotiations; things were settled quite quickly. In Canada, at least, we try to talk at some length about the treaty-making process. In the decades following the 1860s, as settlers arrived in Western Canada, treaties between nations were made. During that time, missionaries became crucial partners of the colonial process. In the time of treaty making, there are many examples of how the churches were co-opted, sometimes with the idea of assisting aboriginal or First Nations peoples. Churches usually functioned as keepers of the peace, bringing some solution—which was really no solution at all, their intent was to take the land. The churches were the pacifiers who spoke to a people who had experienced great oppression already.

The untold story of North America—of the Americas generally, but especially of North America—is the great dying. Any aboriginal peoples who are alive today are survivors of the great dying. From millions we became tens of thousands on this land. It is not surprising that our spiritual vision was somehow clouded as a result of that experience. We wondered why our relationship to the Creator could have come to such a space, when the Creator no longer answered our prayers and whole villages of people, sometimes whole nations, died from epidemics and disease to which we were not accustomed. A spiritual relationship seemed to have been broken. The loss of confidence in our spiritual rootedness, the intrusion of aggressive peoples with infected blankets, made it difficult for us to continue.

And so it was that residential schools were established in Canada among a people of broken spirits. There has been some international coverage of the attempts of many young children to commit suicide in Davis Inlet, a small village in Northern Labrador on the east coast of Canada. Some of the children were as young as ten years of age. This desperate action happens in the context of an ongoing struggle. The average suicide rate in aboriginal territory is at least four times the national Canadian average. We have a whole generation of people within our society who are contemplating suicide. An entire generation is experiencing despair. Although the situation at Davis Inlet needs to be publicized, many other communities are undergoing the same kind of "broken-spiritedness."

The church-managed residential schools have some blame for the legacy that brings us to this point: the loss of social relationships in residential schools, the loss of parenting skills, the loss of vision. From the captivity of residential schools, "empty shells" have been turned loose on the world.

Anyone with some experience in visiting prisons hears of people who are doing "good time." "Good time" is the passing of days without any noticeable scars. It is a counting of the the sunrises and the sundowns. Five years of my life were like that. In between there was some trauma, but a lot of it was just the marking of days—the lines on the wall and the lines through the lines. It was a denial of human-beingness, of any kind of creative being as a people, or as individuals, in the context of that captivity.

This is a major topic within the Canadian society at the moment, and this involves all the historic missioning churches. In Canada, there is a royal commission established by the federal government to look into indigenous people's issues. That commission, in much of its work, has been captivated by the issue of residential schools and the genocidal results of that whole process. It is not only about cultural genocide, but it is a tremendous destructive force which continues to impede the development of indigenous peoples.

My father tells a story of taking my two eldest sisters, who were about six or seven years older than I was (I do not remember them going), to the end of our reservation where they were met by a cattle truck. In about 1949, they, with other children, were put in the back of that open cattle truck to ride for 300 miles, mostly on dusty roads, to a residential school where they were to suffer under malnutrition, terror, and captivity in the name of education; where the churches and governments were functioning in a cooperative manner to "improve" the life of pagan peoples.

The taking away of children was a very significant development. I visited four or five of the residential schools in Manitoba, in addition to the one I attended. They were usually three-story buildings, dining facilities on the lower level, class rooms on the second level, and dormitories on the third level. But everything was divided in half, because there was the boys' side and the girls' side. I had a sister in residential school when I was there, but we were not allowed to spend time with each other because boys and girls were separated. The whole family connection was broken.

It was not uncommon to be standing in line, waiting for a meal, and have the principal walk up to you and grab you by the genitals and say, "How are you?" That was the kind of locker room behavior that happened. I know there were other kinds of sexual abuse, and I do not wish now to draw images of the kinds of things that happened, but we were made to stand at the beatings of people who ran away from the school—physical beatings with a strap until they bled, because they ran away.

Punishment and degredation of this kind continued for three and four generations in some families. I was a survivor largely because I did not go away to school until I was about thirteen. There were children who were five when they went to those schools and spent twelve years in the midst of that kind of environment. This story is just now being told, and I tell you a little bit about it because I have a friend and she is, after fifty years, breaking the silence. Only this past year has she told publicly of her rape, within the residential school, when she was in the dormitory, ill, and attacked by a staff person. That legacy is now being unraveled in Canada, and it is just part of a very tremendous, traumatic experience, which is still affecting the people with whom I live and work.

How is the church a part of this, as I experienced it? After I left residential school, I became a schoolteacher. I went to teach in a northern school which also had a residential division. I remember hearing one morning that during the night, a Bombardier (a large machine capable of traveling over the snow) had left from this isolated village with one of the staff people, who was a pedophile and had been discovered in the boy's dormitory abusing the boys. This was an aboriginal community, but we never, as a community, had a chance to talk about it. It was kept quiet. The school administrator and the church officials swept him out of the community and he disappeared.

And so the scars and the pain of that may not yet be told by those who suffered. The reason I talk about this is that I think we are in a tremendous captivity. I do not know what it is like in the United States of America, but I would hazard that many of the jails in this country have an over-representation of aboriginal women and men. And the reason that I talk about residential schools in Canada is that I am concerned that at the moment our institutions have adapted so that the residential schools are almost all closed. Basically, they are closed. But we have replaced them with juvenile detention centers, foster homes, jails, and hospitals.

In all these institutions, we are over-represented. And the authorities, in many cases, perpetuate the same model of denying any opportunity for reflection and healing within our community. The scarring and the pain goes on.

The loss of self-esteem which is a part of this movement continues. Being the "unlovable" is maintained within much of the society and is especially scarring aboriginal women.

We have truly learned to hate ourselves, to distrust our own abilities, to live with lies that are taught to our children in the name of education. From the beginning of settlement in Canada, a tremendous political battle has been on-going, about two founding nations. Yet, neither of the two founding nations are aboriginal. But there are "two founding nations" in Canada. And the whole mythology that those two nations are owners of the whole history of the land is a tremendous disservice and untruth to the people who live there.

We live with racism in Canada just as people do in the United States of America. We even get broadcasts on our television in Canada of Jane Fonda and her tomahawk chop. It is sad because I know that at the opening of the baseball season in Atlanta, there was a protest by a small group of First Nations people. But where are the churches? People can be humiliated, dehumanized, objectified by this kind of action because it has not been named racism. In areas where we have named that behavior "racism" this would not be tolerated, but in the area where it has not been named, where people are still not recognized as people, it is seen as light humor, something that can be deflected and treated offhandedly.

For us, the missionaries were never naïve, nor were they innocent. Some of them were motivated by love, but we are not sure they were ever motivated by any love for the objects of their mission. We live with that heritage in Canada, and I am sure we live with it in all areas where indigenous peoples populate the face of the Earth. There has been controlling and subjugating until we hold in our hands a lifeless skull.

A friend of mine once showed me a poem about a man and woman in relationship where the man could not come to grips with the difference of the woman in this relationship. And so he held in his hand, in what he thought was love, her face, attempting to reshape it, until it was a skull. I think for a First Nations people in this land, in the Americas, that is the kind of history that we have lived out. My deepest grief, in terms of church and Christian life, is this new wave of evangelism, the new wave for Christ, where people are coming into First Nations' territories that have already been evangelized.

In 1957, a census survey in western Canada informed us that 97 percent of all aboriginal peoples had been baptized by some church or other. Not washed, baptized. A difference. And then, the churches that were historically involved in mission have been withdrawing their commitment. It is no longer romantic or exciting. The thing is falling apart. But, what is happening is a new wave of evangelism. They are coming in to Christianize, in their minds, the communities. In places where the lodges of our people are being re-established there are instances where they have been burning the lodges to the ground because they do not understand the historic aboriginal involvement in finding ourselves and a way of healing. But they believe this is the work of God to destroy them.

And so it is that judgment continues to be pronounced on aboriginal peoples. In the midst of all of this, of course, among victims there are the victimizers, and in our own villages we are self-destructive. Our women and our children suffer greatly in our villages, many of them in isolation from any kind of outside community. There are instances where women cannot leave the village because the only way out is by aircraft, and a woman who has been beaten within her own home often cannot leave the confines of that village wihout being stopped at the airstrip by her husband or someone else in the community who will not allow her to leave. That kind of captivity is horrendous; and women and children throughout our area are suffering, and we have not found a way to talk about healing. Again I say there is a tremendous responsibility for this within the whole society.

Despite that horrible reality, creative things are happening. Among aboriginal teachers, there is some hope in the whole process. But it is caught up in the idea that we are connected to the Earth, that there is some mystery of God at work, the Creator is about the healing of the Earth. We have to come at this whole process with some humility and some sense of mystery. We are objective; we do our analysis; we name the problem; we do break the silence. But having done that, we respond in a healing way to the process that is initiated by the healing spirit of God in which we are a partner. That attitude is sometimes lacking because the prophecy of the Four Winds of the elders of our people say that all the peoples must come together so that the Earth might be healed and that we too might be healed.

We need to reclaim the whole process of ecological development as a part of our healing process. It is not a scientific issue; in my mind it is a spiritual issue. Our hatred of the Earth, in our language, "our hatred of our mother, the Earth," is acted out in our hatred of all forms of feminine in the society. Unless we come to right relations with the Earth and with each other, the healing cannot happen.

I know there are many theological warnings about pantheism, there are many concerns about connectedness to the historic spiritualities of the Earth and its regions, its geography, but I would call upon the churches at least to examine in new ways how we are people of the Earth and how spirituality has a geographic context.

European theology was problematic in North America for many reasons, but in my mind the ongoing reason that it is problematic is at least in part connected to the fact that aboriginal understandings about our connectedness to creation have not yet been included in European theology and in much of the thought around North American theology. There is a tremendous problem historically of hatred for the Earth which breeds other kinds of devastation. The missing tenet is our connectedness to the Earth. There is always a spirituality of the land, a sacred mountain. There are sacred places in this land. Many sacred places. We have to identify them. That also will be a part of the healing that we seek in this time.

Another learning from aboriginal peoples that I gained was at a gathering of Anglican aboriginal peoples who were talking about the residential schools in their denomination. As they talked about it, this is what they said: "We want to have a program that involves primarily non-aboriginal people in their own healing." They said: "In talking about residential schools, we in the aboriginal community will develop our circles of healing, but unless the wider church, the wider society, begins its healing, ours will be in vain. The society with all its power, the churches with their sense of sacredness apart from the struggles of the Earth, must be involved in the healing that is necessary—

especially for those who worked in the schools and their offspring. Unless there is healing in that cycle, that oppression also will continue in the minds of many." Here is a creative model.

Here, also, is a window of opportunity. Despite all the struggles I live with I am a hopeful person. I learned in Ontario on one of my trips that the word used in Ontario for planting crops is "window of opportunity." They have got to get the crop into the ground, especially the corn, in a certain week in April. Otherwise, the crop is going to lose its ability to mature. They also have to get it off on a certain week at the end of August or they are going to miss the window of opportunity.

Well, on the prairies we have discovered a way, not a very scientific way, but we have found a way to get hold of this window of opportunity for us. What we do is, sometime about the middle of April, we go out in the field and sweep aside the stubble and the top soil. After we have cleared the ground, we pull down our pants and sit on that spot. If it is comfortable, then it is planting time.

I think the church should take this window of opportunity and be a little more realistic about who we are and what we do to people in some of our attempts to be healers and helpers. We have to get some perspective. And I do think we have windows of opportunity. I really believe that the Creator, despite all that we do and are, offers us opportunities to be about healing. And that can happen because we now have abilities to be discerning. I have talked to many members of the United Church of Canada about moving from judgment to discernment.

Why do Christians always want to be judgmental? Or persons of any religion who believe they have truth? Why do they have to deny people their truth? In a talk that I heard about fifteen years ago, Amala Rock, an aboriginal woman from Manitoba, said "My truth does not deny your truth." She has been a healing presence in my spirit ever since. I think we are so dogmatic, and we are so separated as people of faith from one another on the basis of some understanding of truth that we carry, that we miss many of the opportunities before us. There is a need for us to look at how we can make significant changes in Christian community.

I think we need to move to more interfaith contexts. I feel very good about ecumenicity that talks about healing of the whole community. But, what we call educational democracy is very problematic to the process that I'm talking about. Education teaches competitiveness, aggressive behavior, and adversarial styles. It teaches that individuality and individual accomplishment is more important than any concept of community or any relationship. That is what we call education. We put the young people, young children, through this process all the time, calling it education. We allow them to continue in it until their mid-thirties and then we ask them to go out into the world and be balanced human beings.

We are body, mind, and spirit, the elders say. And if we do not care for the spirit, the elders say, we lose it. We can remember it, but if we do not care for it, it is an inactive part of our being.

Education has to be looked at. If there is anything I would promote—as an aboriginal person, from communities of people who do not often succeed easily in academic models—it is that experiential learning is probably more important than those models we idolize in the name of academia. Modeling a gentle, patient manner is the way of the elders of my people. For me, it has meant having to deal with my anger and the adversarial style given to me in university and theological school, sometimes called debate, usually some form of attack on another person to make your point. In Canada, when I watch parliamentary discussion, I am very sad about democracy. Very sad about people who scream at one another when they are talking about serious problems within the society, who yell each other down and talk about civilization and caring for the human community.

So, in Canada, we are not blessed by democracy, not as it is practiced in our land. Let us pretend that we are going to begin again. Let us pretend that we can reshape some of the institutions, the very fundamental ones that are shaping people with lies and myths of what it is we are doing here. We are widening the gap between the powerful and the powerless and many poeple are being victimized, especially women and children, but there are also many men who are caught in this turmoil of being torn apart because we have no concept of a just society. We are aggressively materialistic, we are caught up in the idolatry of individual salvation. And I believe we are in a time, when as peoples of the earth, the four winds will blow.

I am living in a community whose people are modeling what it is to be aboriginal and Christian. I work in a small theological school where women and men come, and we call our main building "The Place of Healing," because all aboriginal peoples in this land are survivors of one sort or another. Some of us surviving in different ways than others. It is my hope and the hope of many aboriginal peoples that the next 500 years will be better than the first 500. But 1993 did not indicate that it is going to be greatly different than 1992. In fact, 1993 was supposed to be the Year of Indigenous Peoples at the United Nations. But that was a real flop; much like the Ecumenical Decade, it did not really have any basis in the life of the society or the churches.

As an object of mission most of my life, I want to say that I think the era of mission is over and that the era of listening humbly to one another must begin. Any concept of aboriginal people being involved in a process of aggressive sharing of spiritual truth over against other truths to us is a contrary process. It is self-defeating and it is soul-destroying. I would ask you to consider the end of the era of mission, of imperialistic, colonialistic, aggressive styles of presenting the Good News. I would say that we have come to an end. And aboriginal peoples are not prepared to be part of churches that are of that ilk.

The elders say the seventh fire has been lit, and the six fires of oppression for our people are over. I am hopeful that we will hear those kinds of prophecies and that women and men will stand together and be about new understandings and imagination. Without a dream, the people die. And for six generations of my people, our dreams have been denied. But now we dream, even for those unborn.

When we come into the lodge for prayer, we sing a song to the drum. It is a call to worship, it is inviting the Creator into the lodge, inviting all the people of the world into the lodge for prayer. In humility on the Earth, our mother, in the sweat lodge, which symbolizes the womb of the Earth, our mother, we call on the Creator to bring us new realization. The elder told me that when I come out of the lodge, I must remember to say "all my relations." And the elder says this includes the wood tick and the ants that are waiting there for us and the fish and the trees and everything that is created and all of you, my sisters and brothers.

I am asking you to move through the cycles of life in natural ways from dependence to independence to interdependence to independence to dependence. Those are the cycles of aging and passing through life, a circle. And I think if we allow ourselves to share life in natural and creative ways, acknowledging everyone's gifts, the Earth will be healed, and we too will be healed.

Part VI

The Contemporary Church—
Pastoral Ministry,
Liturgical Issues, and
Theological Education

Church Response to Domestic Violence

JOHN M. JOHNSON

D omestic violence partisans have set many agendas during the last twenty-five years. They have achieved success on many fronts. We have witnessed a revolution in how we perceive and deal with violence among intimates, including that which takes place within the family. For hundreds of years in families of Western societies, violence and other problems among intimates were not considered the appropriate concern of other social institutions. The phrase "a man's home is his castle" originated in medieval times, and became a taken-for-granted assumption for hundreds of years. On those rare occasions when corporeal punishment or violence became "unreasonable," church officials were seen as the appropriate ones to intervene. This understanding was institutionalized in English common law, which asserted "If one beats a child until it bleeds, then it will remember the words of its master. But if one beats it to death, then the law applies."

Child battering, child abuse, and child neglect are relatively new terms, even though injuries and fatalities involving children are old as recorded history.

The first evidence of infanticide dates from 7000 B.C. in Jerico (Johnson 1985). The first medical documentation of systematic childhood injury was published by Dr. S. West in 1888. Subsequent medical research by Caffey in 1946 and Wooley and Evans in 1955 show that important information concerning nonaccidental childhood trauma was at least known to many in the medical profession long before it emerged as a social and political issue in the early 1960s (Johnson 1986). The research team headed by Dr. C. Henry Kempe and Dr. Ray Helfer published their now famous article on "The Child Battering Syndrome" in 1962 in the *Journal of the American Medical Association*. The first state laws specifically formulated for child abuse intervention were passed in 1963, and between 1963 and 1975, forty-seven of the fifty states passed some form of child abuse and/or neglect legislation. The American Humane Association and several professional social work organizations played active roles in advocating legislative initiative, and provided expert testimony for that purpose. Various occupational and medical groups also played a key role in these developments. These developments have significantly increased the number of officially recognized and classified child abuse cases. In a 1962 study sponsored by the American Humane Association, barely 622 cases of nonaccidental trauma to children were documented for the entire United States. But, by 1980, nearly 700,000 cases achieved official recognition and status by the National Center for the Prevention and Treatment of Child Abuse and Neglect (1980). For the most part, we have seen a profound social change occur within a relatively brief period of time (Johnson 1985; Nelson 1984).

Similarly dramatic changes can be found in the area of wife battering and abuse. The first shelters for battered women in the United States date to the early 1970s, but by June 1980, about 175 shelters were located in one national survey of shelters for battered women (Johnson 1981, 827–42). And today, barely ten years later, national officials estimate that there are over 1200 shelters to aid battered and abused women throughout the United States. More importantly, many community, civic, and professional groups have acknowledged a recognition of wife battering as a social problem.

Throughout these revolutionary changes in our society, the church has remained relatively quiescent. To understand more about the nature of the church response, and how much church officials perceive the problems of domestic violence in today's society, this study was undertaken.

Nature of the Study

This study began in the fall of 1981 in a senior-level seminar on domestic violence, where questions were raised about the church response to domestic violence. It was decided that each member of the seminar would conduct, individually or with one other person, a minimum of three to five interviews with local church ministers or officials concerning their perceptions of domestic violence. These interviews were seen as important for constructing a questionnaire that would have meaningful validity. About thirty interviews were conducted with church officials during 1981–82, involving an exploratory and open-ended format. During the fall semester of 1982, a questionnaire was constructed. The questionnaire consisted of about twenty items, or about three pages in length. In addition to some demographic information, the questionnaire sought to discover how many cases of domestic violence were encountered by individual ministers within the past year, how or whether the church officials were prepared or trained to deal with such cases, the church policy concerning such cases, and what was done in them. Questions were asked about the minister's perspectives about using physical or corporeal punishment, the circumstances under which this might be appropriate, and the situations when ministers would or would not report a case to state authorities. The questionnaire utilized a version of the Conflict Tactic Scale (Straus 1979) to assess the minister's perspectives towards violence used against children and spouses. Other questions asked ministers to express their opinion about various modes of intervention, including discussions with family members, making referrals to local secular agencies, calling family members or friends for conference help, seeking legal action, separation, divorce, and the use of battered women's shelters. The questionnaire was pretested in 1982.

During 1982–83, about 1,200 questionnaires were sent to all churches listed in the Yellow Pages for the greater Maricopa County area, the county that surrounds Phoenix, Arizona. One unexpected finding of this research is that the Yellow Pages list many entities as churches which are not, in fact, religious in nature. Some are retirement communities and similar operations. In all, 281 questionnaires were returned, 198 from seven major denominations and 83 from 25 different nondenominational churches. This represents a response rate of about 25 percent, and a discussion about this informs the final section of the paper. Table 1 presents the denominational affiliations of the seven major denominational responses to the questionnaire.

Table 1 reveals that larger numbers of Baptist, Lutheran, and Mormon ministers responded to the questionnaire. The questionnaire responses show that Lutheran and Presbyterian ministers responded to the questionnaire in slightly greater numbers than their representation in the population, whereas

TABLE 1. Denominational Affiliation of Sample

Denomination	N	Percent
Baptist	53	18
Lutheran	48	17
Mormon	41	15
Methodist	22	8
Presbyterian	16	6
Catholic	10	4
Episcopal	9	3
Other Denominations (25)	83	30
Total	281	100

Note: All percentages are rounded off.

Catholic priests responded much less so. With these exceptions, the responses are relatively representative of the Maricopa County area population.

Formal Church Policy on Domestic Violence

One question we sought to answer was whether or not specific churches or denominations had policies concerning domestic violence. Table 2 shows the responses to this question.

Table 2 shows that fully two-thirds of those who responded to the questionnaire indicated that their church or denomination had no specific policy concerning child abuse, spousal battering or abuse, or other instances of violence within the family. The notable exception to this was the Church of Jesus Christ of the Latter Day Saints, or Mormon church, as it is commonly known, where thirty-six to forty-one respondents indicated that the church had an explicit policy concerning domestic violence. Even this response is not unproblematic, however, because our interviews and discussions with Mormon church officials indicated that many of them interpreted this question as asking whether biblical scripture provided guidance in cases of domestic violence. Our interviews with church officials from the other denominations indicated that some of them answered similarly, meaning that the results in Table 2 cannot be interpreted in an unproblematic manner. One straightforward inference that can be made from Table 2 is that, whether or not a church or denomination has an explicit policy concerning domestic violence, the knowledge of that policy is problematic even to the church officials themselves.

Our questionnaire sought to answer questions about whether ministers or other church officials actually counseled church members with problems of domestic violence. We asked the ministers whether they regularly counseled church members, and whether or not they had received any formal training to do such counseling. In addition, we asked whether or not they had received specific training concerning child abuse or wife battering. The results of these questions are presented in Table 3.

TABLE 2. CHURCH POLICY REGARDING FAMILY VIOLENCE

Denomination	Yes	No
Baptist	6	47
Lutheran	12	34
Mormon	36	5
Methodist	5	17
Presbyterian	3	13
Catholic	5	5
Episcopal	2	6
Total	69	127
Percent	35%	65%

TABLE 3. CHURCH COUNSELING ACTIVITIES

Denomination	Do you regularly counsel church members?		Did you receive formal training for counseling?		Did you receive specific training regarding child abuse or wife battering?	
	Yes	No	Yes	No	Yes	No
Baptist	49	4	44	9	15	37
Lutheran	47	1	40	8	5	43
Mormon	40	1	38	2	30	11
Methodist	19	2	20	2	4	18
Presbyterian	15	1	14	2	2	14
Catholic	9	1	8	2	1	9
Episcopal	8	1	8	1	2	7
Total	187	11	172	26	59	139
Percent	94%	6%	87%	13%	30%	70%

Table 3 reveals that the ministers and other church officials of the seven major denominations regularly and routinely counsel their membership on problems related to domestic violence. Overall, 94 percent of the ministers of these denominations indicated that they counseled their parishioners with these problems. There were no major differences among the denominations. Furthermore, about 90 percent of the ministers had received some training for this counseling, although again, out interviews revealed that many of the ministers interpreted this answer as "spiritual counseling." Of the seven major denominations, only Baptists and the Lutherans indicated relatively high proportions of church officials as lacking generalized counseling training. On the issue of specific training for dealing with problems of domestic violence, the results are much more mixed. In general, for the seven major denominations, fully 70 percent of the ministers indicated that they had received no specific domestic violence training. Again, for some of those who answered "yes" about the question on specific domestic violence training, our follow-up interviews indicated that some interpreted this to mean "spiritual counseling." The final section of this paper discusses spiritual counseling in more detail.

Church Response to Actual Cases

The questionnaire asked the ministers to report how many cases of child abuse, child neglect, emotional neglect, incest, wife battering, and other forms of domestic violence had been encountered during the most recent year. Table 4 represents the results of this question.

Table 4 reveals that, for the 198 ministers from the seven major denominations who responded to our questionnaire, they indicated a total of 1,200 cases of domestic violence which were known to them during the most recent year. Of these, there were 177 cases of child abuse, 290 cases of child neglect,

TABLE 4. NUMBER OF CASES OF ABUSE
ENCOUNTERED DURING MOST RECENT YEAR

Denomination	Child Abuse	Child Neglect	Emotional Neglect	Incest	Wife Batttering	Other*	Total
Baptist	53	98	117	31	68	20	386
Lutheran	41	95	114	18	54	7	329
Mormon	23	28	30	8	36	0	125
Methodist	16	12	30	6	21	0	85
Presbyterian	7	13	21	1	10	1	55
Catholic	23	26	60	18	24	7	158
Episcopal	15	18	12	2	12	3	62
Total	177	290	384	85	225	39	1200

Note:* Other includes husband battering, child beating parents, elder abuse, and marital rape.

384 cases of emotional neglect, 85 cases of incest, 225 cases of wife battering, and 39 other instances of domestic violence. The questionnaire additionally asked whether or not the church officials would report to state authorities those cases which seem to require it. Ninety percent of the church officials indicated that they would, in fact, report cases to authorities. Ten percent indicated they would not, even though Arizona State Law requires ministers and other church officials to do so (the traditional minister-parishioner confidentiality is inapplicable for cases involving child abuse and neglect in Arizona). We also asked church officials for the numbers of cases they had actually reported to state authorities during the most recent year. Table 5 summarizes the results obtained by these questions.

TABLE 5. NUMBER OF CASES OF ABUSE REPORTED

Denomination	Would Report to Authorities	Would Not Report to Authorities	Number of Cases Actually Reporterd to Authorities During Most Recent Year
Baptist	48	5	7
Lutheran	40	6	17
Morman	36	4	13
Methodist	19	2	1
Presbyterian	16	0	1
Catholic	7	2	0
Episcopal	9	0	0
Total	175	19	39*
Percent	90%	10%	

Note: * This represents 3.2 percent of the 1,200 cases reported to ministers.

The results of Table 5 are very interesting. They indicate that, whereas 90 percent of the ministers indicate that they would report cases of domestic violence to state authorities, only about three percent of the 1,200 actual cases known to ministers and other church officials were in fact reported to state authorities. The following seems to be a fair and reasonable inference: whereas church officials honor the state reporting requirements in the abstract, independently of applying them in specific situations, the questionnaire results show that they do not report cases of domestic violence in over 97 percent of the cases. We explore some of the reasons for this later in the paper.

The results seen in Tables 2, 3, 4, and 5 present the following picture about the church response to problems of domestic violence. Specific church policies concerning these problems are rare, and even whey they exist, knowledge about them is not unproblematic. Church officials, in their daily lives and interactions with their parishioners, do encounter relatively large numbers of domestic violence problems, for which very few of them are trained. Yet, even though they are inadequately trained, for the most part, they do not call state or official agencies for assistance with these problems. Nor do they consult with other outside agencies of a secular nature. So, even though they lack any specific training or knowledge of community resources, church officials generally do not seek assistance outside of the confines of their own denomination. This conclusion gains additional support from the Reverend Marie M. Fortune of the Seattle Center for the Prevention of Sexual and Domestic Violence, one of the few church officials to be active in this area. The Reverend Fortune (1984, 18–19) says, "The circle of silence about domestic violence remains tightly closed in the churches." When asked to elaborate on why this should be so, she stated further:

> Ministers are often avoided by individuals or families trying to cope with domestic violence. Many clergy say they have never had a parishioner involved in domestic violence come to them for assistance, so they conclude that no one in their church is either a victim or an offender. There are several reasons why victims of domestic violence avoid going to their clergy with domestic violence problems. Generally, any experience of sexual or physical abuse of children, or violence directed against spouses, are stigmatizing the victim. They fear the disbelief, judgment and ostracism that so often characterizes church officials responses to such problems. The silence of the church reinforces the stigmatization. Many victims also perceive that ministers, rabbis, or priests lack knowledge, sensitivity, or experience in dealing with these sorts of problems. The victim or offender fears the minister will not understand or know what to do and may be so surprised or shocked that the victim ends up having to help the minister with his reaction to the revelation. Also, female victims are reluctant to go to their minister because their minister is usually a man. The long and painful history of the patriarchal oppression of women in the church has contributed to the denial of domestic violence as a problem. The victims of sexual violence in the home are

primarily women and girl children. This victimization has been lost in silence, and the silence has helped maintain the status quo of oppression and violence. (1984, 19–20)

Clerical Theories about Domestic Violence

The study sought to discover what church officials thought to be the cause of domestic violence problems. We asked the respondents to rank in order what they saw as being the major influence for domestic problems in general. Table 6 presents the most frequent answers.

Table 6 shows that, for ministers and other church officials, alcoholism is seen as the major determinant of domestic violence problems. What one learned in one's home of origin and the inability to control anger and hostility were ranked as the next two most frequent causes of domestic violence. Stress was ranked as the fourth most frequently mentioned cause. All in all, it seems fair to say that ministers attribute problems of domestic violence almost exclusively as being the responsibility of individuals. For the most part, they do not see society or other social networks as sharing in the causal responsibility for the acts. While they are aware of the stressful impact of alcoholism, divorce, unemployment, and other stressful social situations, as a generalization, they still feel that it is up to the individual to control the impact of these factors. The questionnaire asked, in addition, about the major source of information on domestic violence problems. Over 80 percent of the ministers indicated that the mass media represented the major source of information concerning domestic violence. Other studies of mass media reporting of domestic violence problems has shown that the individualization of responsibility to be one of the major formatting characteristics (Johnson 1989).

TABLE 6. CLERICAL THEORIES ABOUT DOMESTIC VIOLENCE PROBLEMS

Denomination	Alcoholism	That's the Way They Were Raised	Something Wrong With Them As an Individual	Can't Control Temper	Stress
Baptist	17	10	4	8	1
Lutheran	19	7	2	8	3
Mormon	4	9	2	14	7
Methodist	2	7	0	4	5
Presbyterian	7	3	0	1	3
Catholic	4	1	3	1	0
Episcopal	0	5	1	2	1
Total	53	42	12	38	20

Conclusion

In-depth interviews preceded the construction of this relatively brief question-naire, which was pretested in 1982 and administered during 1982–83. The response rate (25 percent) was low, but higher than reported in other studies (see Alsdurf 1985; Bondurant 1989). Analysis of the data fails to establish any statistically significant correlations between religious denominations, in their responses to family violence. Responses from all denominations echo a common refrain: (1) formal church policies and pastoral knowledge of this is problematic, (2) specific training for family violence problems and counseling is for the most part absent from denominational training curricula, (3) pastors say they would report cases brought to their attention to state authorities, as mandated by state law, but only 3 percent of the 1,200 actual known cases were reported, (4) pas-toral use of community resources is minimal, (5) ministers and pastors believe family violence problems to result from alcoholism and individualistic factors.

While those with inside knowledge and membership of church policies toward domestic violence say individuals largely avoid ministers, because of the anticipated fear of stigma (see Fortune 1984, 1986), many persons do first go to a church official for help or assistance for family violence, as about 15 percent of Lee Bowker's sample did (see Bowker 1982). Many victims report that church officials lack knowledge or sensitivity or experience about these problems (see Fortune 1986). It is clear that churches can no longer greet family violence problems with silence, and should move expeditiously to clar-ify and update their policies and training. While some small measure of progress on this front is evident, surveys taken subsequent to the one reported here indicate that not much has changed about the church responses to domestic violence throughout the 1980s (see Bondurant 1989).

Acknowledgments

I am indebted to Martha Raby for the original inspiration for this research, and to the students in my Domestic Violence seminars during 1982–1983 for their assistance in planning, collecting data, and discussing this project.

❦

Works Cited

Alsdurf, J.M. 1985. "Wife Abuse and the Church: The Response of Pastors." *Response to the Victimization of Women and Children* 8/1:9–11.

Bondurant D.M. 1989. *Family Violence and the Church Response*. Master's Thesis, School of Justice Studies, Arizona State University.

Bowker, L.H. 1982. "Battered Women and the Clergy." *Journal of Pastoral Care* 36: 226–34.

Fortune, M.M. 1984. "The Church and Domestic Violence." *TSF Bulletin* 4 (November-December): 17–20.

———. 1986. "Confidentiality and Mandatory Reporting: A False Dilemma?" *The Christian Century* 18/25: 582–83.

Horton, A.C., and J.A. Williamson, eds. 1988. *Abuse and Religion.* Lexington, Mass.: Lexington Books.

Johnson, J.M. 1981. "Program Enterprise and Official Co-optation in the Battered Women's Shelter Movement." *American Behavioral Scientist* 24/6: 827–42.

———. 1985. "Symbolic Salvation: The Meanings of the Child Maltreatment Movement." *Studies in Symbolic Interaction* 6: 289–305.

———. 1986. "The Changing Concept of Child Abuse." In *The American Family and the State*, ed. J.R. Peden and F. Glahe. (San Francisco: Pacific Institute for Public Policy), 257–75.

———. 1989. "Horror Stories and the Construction of Child Abuse." In *Images and Issues*, ed. J. Best. (Chicago: Aldine), 1–33.

Nelson, B. 1984. *Making An Issue of Child Abuse.* Chicago: University of Chicago Press.

Straus, M. 1979. "Measuring Interfamily Conflict and Violence: The Conflict Tactics Scales." *Journal of Marriage and the Family* (February): 75–85.

Revisiting the 1982 Church Response Survey

JOHN M. JOHNSON AND DENISE M. BONDURANT

During 1989 we replicated the survey sent to clerical officials during 1982–83 by John M. Johnson and his students, to assess the clerical opinion and response to domestic violence problems, reported in the preceding article. Questions concerning demographics, education, specialized family violence training, acceptable behaviors between parent and child and husband and wife, knowledge of local referral sources, and perceived causes of family violence were identical to the prior survey. In addition, the 1989 restudy included responses to several domestic violence "scenarios," several open-ended questions about governmental policies and the issues of confidentiality, and some more general queries about the appropriate role of the church in these matters.

The questionnaire was sent to 657 clerics in the Maricopa County (metropolitan Phoenix) area. Even after two mailed follow-ups and phone follow-ups, only 105 clerics responded to the survey. This 16 percent response rate is very low by any current survey standard. It is 50 percent lower than that obtained for the same population by Johnson eight years earlier, which was obtained with less strenuous follow-up effort, but it is 300 percent higher than some other attempts to survey clerical officials about these kinds of sensitive matters (see Bondurant 1989). On an informal basis, we questioned perhaps three dozen ministers and priests about the low response rate, and what we could do to improve it. Several points emerged from these informal discussions with our many clerical friends and colleagues, many of whom we worked with over many months to plan a statewide conference and training workshop series about these issues. First, not one clerical person expressed surprise about our difficulties in doing a study of church officials about these matters. All of them gave literal or verbal "nods" when we told them of our dilemmas, and most directly expressed their lack of surprise. Second, virtually all indicated that the low response rate was "no accident," and linked the low rate to either the church's chagrin about their embarrassing policies or practices about domestic violence problems.

Findings

The basic demographic information on the 1989 survey was essentially the same as the 1982 survey. The range in age was twenty-nine to seventy-two, with a median age of forty-seven. There were four female respondents among the 105 who returned the questionnaire. Of those who responded, only 3 percent had no college, and nearly two-thirds held master's degrees. Three-fourths (76 percent) have completed coursework in family counseling, and about one-fifth (22 percent) indicated that some portion of their training had included some specific material on domestic or family violence, a slight increase over the earlier survey. Fully one-half (50 percent) of the respondents have attended some form of family violence workshop, seminar, or training session beyond their collegiate level preparation, and these were consistently described as very educational, informative, and helpful for the practicing cleric.

Formal Church Policy

Clerics were asked if their church has a formal policy on family or domestic violence. While most denominations do not have a specific policy, the answers indicated considerable confusion within denominations about whether there is or is not such a policy. For example, six Methodist ministers said there is no policy, but four said that there was. Nine Catholic priests said their church had no specific policy, but five answered affirmatively. For the entire sample, 76 percent reported that their church had no policy concerning the response to family violence, up from 65 percent who reported thusly in the 1982 survey.

The confusion about the existence of a formal policy centers on the word "policy," with some respondents clearly interpreting this to refer to some formal guideline or rule promulgated by higher denominational authority, while to others the question clearly refers to whether there is scriptural guidance to be found in the Bible. One affirmative respondent penciled in the margin: "Sure, Biblical criteria such as Eph. 5 and Col. 3."

Family Violence Cases Encountered

As with the initial 1982 survey, the 1989 study indicated that clerics commonly encounter instances and reports of domestic violence in their practice. The 105 respondents to the 1989 questionnaire reported that they had encountered a total of 885 cases within the prior year, an average of over eight per minister or priest. The 885 cases included 96 cases of physical child battery, 335 for emotional abuse or neglect of children, 134 for incest or other sexual offenses against children, 96 for child neglect, 137 for wife battering, and 87 other reports (including elder abuse, marital rape, beating of husbands, and so on).

The 292 respondents to the 1982 questionnaire reported awareness of 1,200 actual cases of family violence discovered or brought to their attention during the prior year. While the large majority indicated, in the abstract, that they would report such cases to the proper authorities if actually brought to their attention, in accordance with Arizona state law which mandates such a response in certain cases (as in child abuse or neglect), the clerics further indicated that only 39 of the 1,200 actual cases were in fact reported to official authorities as required by law. This is less than 3 percent. For the 1989 survey, we did not duplicate this question to the clerics, but we checked with the

Arizona Department of Economic Security (D.E.S.) and learned that only 42 (out of nearly 30,000) initial reports on child abuse came from identified clerical sources. So both surveys seem very consistent on the facts that clerical officials encounter relatively significant numbers of actual cases during a given year, are not well trained or prepared to deal with them, and do not report the appropriate ones to state official agencies as required by law. Of course the "failure" of clerical officials to report often involves the complicated and conflicting ethical dilemmas about maintaining the confidentiality of a client or penitent, and whether state laws can or should subordinate these more traditional canons, established over hundreds of years. We discuss these complexities below.

Perceptions of the Causes of Family Violence

Both surveys used a version of the Conflict Tactics Scale developed by Murray Straus (1979), which ". . . is designed to measure the use of reasoning, verbal aggression and violence within the family." (Straus 1979, 75). This was used to determine how clerics perceive which acts are acceptable for a parent to use with a child, and for wives and husbands. We should note Straus's (1979, 77) observations that the less severe forms of violence to children (pushing, grabbing, shoving, hitting with object) are very common among other respondents to the CTS. This perception of acceptability was common throughout these two studies of ministers and other clerical officials.

Concerning clerical CTS responses about children, 90 percent indicated that it would be appropriate to physically grab or restrain a child, and 68 percent of the 105 respondents said it was acceptable for children to be "hit with hand," and 24 percent said it was okay to "hit with object." Interestingly, 3 percent indicated the acceptability of biting a child, all saying this was a way to teach them to cease biting others. Concerning clerical CTS responses about spouses, there was not one positive response to any of the ten violence items on the CTS scale, this clearly reflecting an opinion that physical violence between spouses is inappropriate, at least for these respondents.

Survey respondents were asked to rank in order the factors they felt to be the main "causes" of domestic violence, and the 1989 restudy duplicated the rank-order revealed in the 1982 survey, namely, (1) alcohol/substance abuse was ranked at the top most frequently, followed by (2) "That's the way they were raised," (3) temporary stress within the family, and (4) failure to control anger or temper. Clerics generally see domestic violence as caused by a combination of individualist and situational factors, while nevertheless stressing the individual's responsibility to control one's behavior regardless of the facts of the situation. Again, there were no denomination differences in these responses.

Responses to the Mandated Reporting Requirement

The 1989 study included four domestic violence scenarios or vignettes, descriptions of situations that ministers or clerics might encounter, to assess their possible responses to the mandatory reporting requirement for child abuse. Three of these were designed to detect responses to Arizona's reporting mandate for cases of suspected child abuse and neglect, the fourth with battering of wives, which is not included in the reporting mandate. The first scenario referred to a man who tells a minister that he has frequently engaged in sexual activity (including intercourse) with his eleven-year-old daughter. The second refers to a physical education teacher in the church-sponsored school who tells the minister about a nine-year-old boy who comes to school covered with bruises for the second time in the last month. The third involves an eleven-year-old girl who tells the minister that her father has frequently engaged in sexual activity with her, including intercourse. Arizona law requires a minister or other cleric to report in all three of these cases. The scenarios sought to discover whether the ministers knew about the mandated reporting requirement, and if they said (in these abstracted situations) they would follow it.

The response to these hypothetical situations show 75 percent of the clerics expressing a willingness to report the boy who was physically beaten, 71 percent who said they would report the incestuous man who came to them, and 62 percent said they would report the eleven-year-old female incest victim who came to them for help. These responses open up a series of interesting questions for speculation, and one can only wonder if the church's long patriarchial tradition leads pastors to believe that incest is less serious than a physical beating.

The fourth scenario involved a woman who tells a minister that she has been frequently beaten by a violent spouse, and has received numerous injuries during her nine-year marriage. By and large the responses to this item coincide with the research literature regarding the advice battered wives receive from clerics (Bowker 1982; Pagelow and Johnson 1988). Jim Alsdurf (1985, 10) states that one-third of the respondents to his study:

> felt that abuse would have to be severe in order to justify a Christian wife leaving her husband, while 21 percent felt that no amount of abuse would justify a separation. . . . Twenty-six percent of the pastors agreed that a wife should submit to her husband and trust that God would honor her action by either stopping the abuse or giving her the strength to endure it. However, a majority of the respondents disagreed with this view.

For the Phoenix-area clerical officials, 77 percent expressed the opinion that there are some circumstances that warrant a dissolution of the marriage. About 5 percent of those who responded to the fourth scenario about wife battering indicated that they would report the case to the Arizona D.E.S., the agency authorized to take child abuse and neglect reports, thus adding further support to the earlier observations about the confusions and misunderstandings over applicable statutes and requirements.

The Clerical Conundrum on Confidentiality

Laws and governmental policies are problematic for many church officials. Mandatory reporting laws are often perceived as destructive to the traditional pastor/member relationship, and agencies responsible for family violence intervention may be seen as too intrusive, or not intrusive enough. About one-third of our respondents thought the local official agencies were too intrusive into private family life, and another third believed official agencies were not intrusive enough. Those who expressed negative attitudes about official agencies felt they were too powerful, were able to separate families too easily, and interfered with the confidentiality between clerics and church members.

Respondents tot he 1989 survey were generally much more aware of the actual or potential conflicts about the confidentiality issue. Church tradition holds statements between clergy and members as "privileged" or confidential but modern state laws on child abuse have usurped this ancient tradition. Knowledge about this and its potential ramifications is not widespread among the clergy. Today still a minority of the clergy know they are subject to criminal and civil sanctions for failing to report a suspected case of abuse or neglect. But increasing numbers are becoming aware of the nuances and complexities that are involved in actual real-world cases.

Clerical voices split on the confidentiality issue. Jeffery Warren Scott (1986) asserts that reporting cases to officials destroys the traditional cleric/member relationship, but this position is refuted by Marie Fortune (1984, 1986), Sissela Bok (1983), and Michael Garanzini (1988) who argue that clerics are primarily responsible for the spiritual needs of their members, and should cooperate with state officials if or when they become aware that crimes have been committed. Fortune (1986) stresses that confidentiality is intended to help people, not shield them from the consequences of their actions. She also asserts that rarely does an abuser or penitent "confess" to a cleric; rather, it is invariably the victim who seeks help from the church. Bok (1983, 31) insists on the distinction between privacy or confidentiality and secrecy, holding that it is the latter that undermines and contradicts ". . . the very respect for persons and for human bonds that confidentiality was meant to protect." This study and our many informal conversations with our clerical colleagues over the years indicates that the conflict debated among the scholars and writers is found also out on the front-lines with the practicing clerics. As a rough (but accurate) generalization, we can say that clerical officials commonly ignore the legal mandates and follow their own conscience, if the situation is not life-threatening, and they have the discretion to do so. The brute fact is that a minuscule number of official reports come from clerics; whether ignorance of the law or a well-considered moral/ethical alternative produces it is not for the methodological sophistication of modern social science to know or discover.

Conclusion

This restudy of Johnson's 1982 survey shows small but still relatively little change concerning the church response to domestic violence problems during the 1980s. Clerics have little formal education about family violence— expressing ignorance or uncertainty concerning the policies of their church or denomination—and receive relatively significant numbers of reports—which they do not refer to more appropriate outside agencies or the mandated offi- cial authorities. While there are small signs that more individuals within the church are becoming concerned about the changing moral sentiments that are becoming widespread in society, the available evidence suggests that small changes take a very long time within the boundaries of the church.

Works Cited

Alsdurf, J.M. 1985. "Wife Abuse and the Church: The Response of Pastors." *Response to the Victimization of Women and Children* 8/1: 9–11.

Bok, S. 1983. "The Limits of Confidentiality." *The Hastings Center Report* 4 (February): 24–31.

Bondurant, D. M. 1989. *Family Violence and the Church Response.* Master's Thesis, School of Justice Studies, Arizona State University.

Bowker, L. H. 1982. "Battered Women and the Clergy." *The Journal of Pastoral Care* 36: 226–34.

Fortune, M. 1984. "The Church and Domestic Violence." *TSF Bulletin* 99 (November–December): 17–20.

———. 1986. "Confidentiality and Mandatory Reporting." *Christian Century* 18/25 (June): 582–83.

Garanzini, M. J. 1988. "Troubled Homes: Pastoral Responses to Violent and Abusive Families," *Pastoral Psychology* 36: 218–29.

Pagelow, M. D., and P. Johnson. 1988. "Abuse in the American Family: The Role of Religion." In *Abuse and Religion*, ed. A. C. Horton and J. A. Williamson. Lexington, Mass. Lexington Books, 1–12.

Straus, M. 1979. "Measuring Intrafamily Conflict and Violence: The Conflict Tactics Scale." *Journal of Marriage and the Family* 41 (February): 75–85.

"Reorganizing Victimization": The Intersection between Liturgy and Domestic Violence

MARJORIE PROCTER-SMITH

I can never romanticize language again
        never deny its power for disguise for mystification
but the same could be said for music
or any form created
        painted ceilings beaten gold worm-worn Pietàs
reorganizing victimization frescoes translating
violence into patterns so powerful and pure
        we continually fail to ask are they true for us.[1]

—Adrienne Rich

What do domestic violence and the liturgy have to do with one another? Certainly the relationship is not immediately manifest. The church's liturgy, after all, is public; domestic violence is domestic: that is, it takes place in what is regarded in our society as a private domain, the home.

But perhaps the distinction between "public" liturgy and "private" violence is too sharp. The Christian liturgy has its roots deep in the domestic liturgies of Judaism, especially the table blessings and the Passover meal. Until the Peace of Constantine and the development of Imperial Christianity, all of the church's liturgies were necessarily both domestic and private, with the church itself being understood as the new "family": the household of God. The fact that domestic violence occurs in the homes of "church-going" Christians, including the homes of Christian clergy, ought to make us wonder what is being heard, seen, said, and done in our Christian assemblies that allows the violence to continue.[2] How have we failed to make it clear that the physical, emotional, and sexual abuse of women, children, the elderly is an offense also against God and the Christian community? How can we do better? These two questions will guide this exploration of possible connections between the liturgy and domestic violence.

First, the perpetuation of domestic violence is a sin. The typical victims of domestic violence are those members of a family or household who are smaller, weaker or in some way dependent (i.e., financially) on the abuser. The presence of violence (whether physical, sexual, or psychological) violates the relationship of trust which is necessary for a healthy functioning of any family, community, or relationship. The use of violence or abuse eliminates the possibility of equality, mutuality, or cooperation. Alongside the casual, taken-for-granted attitude towards wife-battering must be set the society-wide silence about the reality and extent of the problem.[3] That silence and acceptance has been and continues to be terribly costly for the victims of violence and abuse. To name this violence as sin is to challenge both the silence and the acceptance, and to make it the concern of the whole church.

Second, domestic violence is a symptom of the more extensive social sin of sexism (and often, its companion, racism). Women stand a much greater chance of being victims of abuse than men (some estimate one out of two women are victims of physical, sexual, or psychological abuse; girl children are more likely to be sexually abused than boys [between one in five and one in three girls, one in seven boys, it is estimated, are sexually abused before age eighteen]), and their abuser is most likely to be a family member, primarily the father (94 percent of all incest cases reported are father-daughter incest).[4] The abuse of children and the elderly may be regarded in some sense as a corollary to the abuse of women, since they occupy a status comparable to that of women in our society in their marginality and enforced dependence on adult males. The hard reality of domestic abuse puts a face on those often rather vague concepts of sexism, patriarchy, and androcentrism. It may help us to recognize how deeply sexism is imbedded in our culture to recall that the origin of the expression "rule of thumb" was the English common law that a man may beat his wife with a stick no thicker than his thumb.

The liturgy is fundamentally the "work of the people," and therefore the primary business of all Christian people, including women, the young, and the old. "Liturgy," *leitourgia*, has its origins in the civil-political arena, as does the term *ekklesia*, "church." The *ekklesia* is "the actual assembly of free citizens gathering for deciding their own spiritual-political affairs."[5] The *leitourgia* is the public work done by them and, on their behalf, by their public servants.[6] At the same time, the tradition in which the liturgy has come to us is androcentric and patriarchal; it is a product of cultures which, however much they may have varied, have agreed in regarding women and children as marginal or invisible. By "patriarchal" is meant the social structure in which the basic social unit is the male-headed household, and the male head of such a household is the only full member of the political state. Thus the term "patriarchal" does not mean simply male rule of women, but a structure of interlocking patterns of dominance and submission in which not only gender but also age, class, race, and status become important factors.[7] Because women and children (together with the elderly, who in our present culture are also marginal or invisible) are the primary victims of domestic abuse, it is important to attend to elements of the liturgy which reflect androcentric or patriarchal assumptions. Second, the liturgy is the worship of God; it is not therapy, education, or social work. Any or all of these (and much more besides) may be needed in order to prevent domestic violence, but the liturgy can not do them. To admit ulterior motives, however well-intentioned, into our worship, will inevitably result in the failure of both our inappropriate intentions and our worship. To put it another way: this essay is concerned with the point at which domestic violence as a social reality and the church's liturgy intersect. Neither the root source nor the ultimate solution to the problem of domestic violence lies in our liturgy.[8]

Nevertheless, the liturgy is much like language. On the one hand it expresses what we believe and who we believe we are, in word and song and gesture. At the same time, it shapes our identity and self-understanding in relation to God and to the world, both by what is said and done, and by what is omitted. Because liturgy not only expresses what we believe but tells us what we ought to believe, and how we ought to act, it is a powerful shaper of human consciousness.

Christian liturgy, like any other "form created," can disguise and mystify domestic violence and its roots, making the abuse seem not only acceptable, but even divinely sanctioned. And because liturgy (again, like language) shapes us gradually and in tiny increments, words and gestures which are used regularly and repeatedly, although appearing small, have a powerful effect. The intersection between liturgy and the occurrence of domestic violence therefore, will be explored by examining the use of the Bible in liturgy, the implications of androcentric liturgical language, the church's marriage rites, and the non-verbal elements of the liturgy. Finally we will examine specific possibilities for change.

The Word of God

The central verbal element in most Christian liturgy is the Word: the proclamation of and exposition on the Scriptures of the Old and New Testaments. In this liturgical context, moreover, the reading of Scriptures is not presented, as it might be in a Bible study group or a class, as a text to be studied, discussed, and evaluated, but as the "Word of God."[9] Non-verbal gestures of deference to the Bible, the reader, or to the reading itself intensify this assumption. Since it is presented as the "Word of God," it is not a matter for debate or dispute; instead, the congregation is expected to sit (or stand) and listen passively, to "hear with joy what [God] say[s] to us today." It is presumed, then, that the texts read are not only undebatable, but also that they have a present authoritative claim on us.[10]

Therefore, the use of the Bible in liturgical proclamation immediately raises problems. The patriarchal and, in many cases, misogynist nature of the Bible has been thoroughly examined of late by such biblical scholars as Phyllis Trible, Phyllis Bird, and Elisabeth Schüssler Fiorenza. Schüssler Fiorenza sums up the findings of such research succinctly:

> Not only is scripture interpreted by a long line of men and proclaimed in
> patriarchal churches, it is also authored by men, written in androcentric
> language, reflective of religious male experience, selected and transmitted
> by male religious leadership. Without question, the Bible is a male book.[11]

Therefore, she wryly proposes that all biblical texts should carry a warning label addressed to women: "Caution! Could be dangerous to your health and survival."

People who work with battered women note the frequency with which abused women interpret their abuse as divinely ordained, and cite scriptural support for their interpretation. One woman said, "God punished women more," and cited Gen. 3:16. Another, who complained to her husband that she had sustained injuries after one of his attacks, was told by him: "your bones are my bones—just like it says in the Bible." Another, regularly beaten and raped by her husband, interpreted this abuse as God's correction of her tendency to rebel against her husband's authority.[12] In general, battered women who were strongly religious tended to interpret their experiences of abuse according to the Genesis stories of the creation and the fall; the New Testament "household code" admonitions to wives to be subject to their husbands; the saying of Jesus about divorce; and assorted other Gospel texts which urge meekness, self-abegnation, suffering, and sacrifice as marks of the Christian life. Based on her own experience of conducting Bible study groups for battered women, Thistlethwaite concludes that "the religious sanction in the household codes for the submission of women is a primary legitimation of wife abuse and must be challenged by women."[13] Schüssler Fiorenza's proposal is even more sweeping: "Patriarchal texts should not be allowed to remain in the lectionary but should be replaced by texts affirming the discipleship of equals."[14] Decisions about which texts justify the oppression of women and others in general and the abuse of women in particular, and which texts challenge or correct such abuse cannot be made without careful attention to the function and uses of Scripture in contemporary society.

An examination of current lectionaries, however, reveals that the two most frequently cited texts in the justification of violence against women— Genesis 1–2 and the houshold codes—are part of the three-year Sunday cycle:

> Episcopal, Lutheran: Gen. 2:4b–9, 15–17, 3:1–7
> (the second Creation story and the Fall, with the creation of woman omitted): 1st Sunday of Lent, Year A
> Episcopal, Lutheran, Revised Common Lectionary: Gen. 2:18–24 (the creation of woman from the rib of the man):
> Episcopal: Proper 22, Year B; Lutheran: Twentiethth Sunday after Pentecost, Year B; RCL: October 2–8, year B
> Episcopal: Eph. 5:21–33
> (the first element of the three-part household code; Lutheran has Eph. 5:21–31): Proper 16, Year B (Lutheran Fourteenth Sunday after Pentecost, Year B)

Including these texts in these lectionaries endows them with ecclesiastical authority. Furthermore, their relationship to the other texts for the day offers a particular interpretation of them. Thus, the text from Genesis 2 recounting the creation of woman is coupled in all three lectionaries with Mark 10:2–9, Jesus' saying on divorce, which concludes, "What God has joined together let not man [*sic*] put asunder," a text which has been frequently used to keep women in an abusive or life-threatening marriage. By joining it to the creation of woman the lectionary implies that there is a direct relationship between woman's created nature and the indissolubility of marriage. A listener might very well conclude not only that the marriage bond is forged by God, but also that to be married is part of woman's nature, rather than a state which she may choose or reject. If the psalm appointed for that Sunday is used, the picture is complete. Psalm 128 recounts the blessings a God-fearing man may expect, including:

> Your wife will be like a fruitful vine within your house;
> Your children will be like olive shoots around your table.
> Lo, thus shall the man be blessed who fears the Lord. (vv. 3–4)

Preaching, the application of the biblical "Word of God" to a specific community, is more difficult to analyze. It is of necessity localized and particularized, and defies generalities. Nevertheless, the importance and power of the sermon must never be underestimated. Sermons which speak without nuance of the virtue of "submitting to the will of God," for example, or of the way in which "God sends us suffering to test our faith" may have critical or even fatal consequences when heard and believed by a woman who may be considering leaving an abusive husband. Preachers tend to fail to recognize that people often take their sermons very seriously, perhaps more seriously than the preacher. They also sometimes fail to recognize that women may hear a sermon's message differently from men listeners. A sermon on "forgiveness" will resonate differently to an abusive husband than to his victimized wife. In spite of the fact that women are the majority in most church pews, sermons are almost always addressed to men.

The lectionary also proclaims by what it omits. Susan Thistlethwaite notes that "the text with which many abused women find the most identification is John 7:53–8:11"—the story of Jesus' defense of the woman taken in adultery. To these women, the powerful impact of the text comes from their recognition that Jesus defends a woman who is about to be physically battered.[15] The text is not in any of the three lectionaries under consideration. Also absent from the lectionary is Jesus' healing of the woman bent over (Luke 13:10–17), in which Jesus violates the Sabbath laws on the woman's behalf and defends her healing against the objections of religious leaders.

The Words of the Liturgy

While biblical texts form a significant and particularly authoritative verbal element of liturgy, there are also other words. The language of prayers, blessings, hymns, acclamations also carries its weight. Of concern here is the language about the human community and the church, language about God, and language which implies dominant-submissive relationships.

The problem of the use of androcentric language to speak of people in general has been thoroughly examined and assessed.[16] It may be sufficient here simply to note the two factors in the use of androcentric language which have bearing on our subject. First, androcentric language is bound to the androcentric and patriarchal social structures it both reflects and helps to sustain. Violence against women and children within the patriarchal family is subtly sustained by the use of language which presupposes that the male human being is the norm. Second, androcentric language renders women invisible, which not only makes it difficult for women to recognize their own needs for health and safety as legitimate, but also makes such recognition difficult for the entire community. Clearly the use of androcentric language carries these (and other) liabilities in all manner of discourse. But its significance is deepened when used in a liturgical context, as, for example, when a minister, presumably addressing the congregation in the name of God, calls them "brothers."

Language about God is certainly one of the most pressing theological issues facing the church in this day. The exclusively male language which is still predominant in most traditions and in most liturgies has been vigorously attacked and just as vigorously defended. We may ask, however, what significance this male image of God has for the perpetuation of domestic violence. It has often been assumed that for those whose experiences with their own fathers have been negative, as in an abusive relationship, the image of God as Father can have no positive value. Others, recognizing that religious symbols are more complex and operate far more subtly than this, have argued the opposite: that those who have been abused or abandoned by their fathers have a greater need for a heavenly Father. But this correlation would seem to be too simple, too. As Mary Pellauer notes, women who have been abused by men, particularly over a period of years, tend to generalize their fear and distrust from the abuser (or abusers) to all men. They become "simply unable to trust men any longer."[17] Women with religious convictions may extend this generalization yet further, and conclude that because God is male, "he" too, cannot be trusted, and feel that they have been abandoned by God.[18]

There is a still deeper problem with male God-language which has bearing on the perpetuation of domestic violence: the mirroring of patriarchal family/social structures and patriarchal father-God religion. Paul Tillich recognized this (without recognizing its implications) when he wrote, "If God is symbolized as 'Father,' he [sic] is brought down to the human relationship of father and child. But at the same time this human relationship is consecrated into a pattern of the divine-human relationship."[19] Mary Daly, in *Beyond God the Father*, recognizes the implications of this for women: "If God in 'his' heaven is a father ruling his people, then it is the 'nature' of things and according to divine plan and the order of the universe that society be male dominated. Within this context, a mystification of roles takes place: the husband dominating his wife represents God 'himself'."[20] One hundred years before Mary Daly, Antoinette Doolittle, a Shaker theologian, had put the same point even more succinctly: "As long as we have all male Gods in the heavens we shall have all male rulers on the earth."[21]

Thus women who are subject to all manner of life-threatening abuse by their husbands often interpet that abuse as punishment by a Father-God who is readily identifiable with the husband, or at least working through him.

Those who work with abused women report the difficulty such women have in accepting the idea that their abuse is neither deserved nor divinely sanctioned. To challenge such abuse is to challenge God. The effect of Father-God language, then, given our patriarchal social and familial structures, is to legitimate male dominance and violence and to inhibit women's legitimate anger and protest against such treatment.

Other forms of language which imply relationships of dominance and submission carry the same liabilities as Father-God language. Titles such as "Master" and "Lord" ("King," "Ruler," "Sovereign," and the like) presuppose that there are also servants and subjects. While it may be argued that the application of such titles to God implicitly subverts all earthly or human authority, it is also readily apparent from our everyday experience that the servants and subjects in our society are overwhelmingly women and children, primarily the women and children of color. Language of dominance and submission goes beyond titles for God to include expressions of the sort reflected in the prayer of confession in *The United Methodist Hymnal* which identifies sin with willful rebellion and repentance with obedience:

> Merciful God, we confess that we have not
> loved you with our whole heart.
> *We have failed to be an obedient church.*
> we have not *done your will,*
> we have *broken your law,*
> we have *rebelled against your love,*
> we have not loved our neighbors,
> and we have not heard the cry of the needy.
> Forgive us, we pray.
> Free us for *joyful obedience,*
> through Jesus Christ our Lord. Amen.[22]

The identification of sin with rebellion and repentance with obedience narrows our understanding of the meaning and manifestations of sin in our midst. It precludes or at least does not mention the possibility that sin might also be manifested in abuse of power, exploitation of the vulnerable, or patterns of oppression which violate the unity and health of the body of Christ. When such language is linked with Scriptural and hymn texts which image the Church as the obedient bride of Christ, a powerful chain is forged which prevents the abused woman from being able to break out of the cycle of violence in which she lives, without committing sin.

Marriage Rites

Do contemporary Christian marriage rites reinforce these patterns which inhibit the ability of women to reject violence against themselves? Unquestionably the "traditional" rites, which include the "giving away of the bride," the asymetrical marriage vows which demand obedience of the wife only, and the use of legal language from English common law for the transfer of property in the vows, provide powerful reinforcement for the assumption that the husband has "divine right" to rule over his wife. The newer reformed rites in the current Episcopalian, Lutheran, United Methodist, and Roman Catholic liturgies have taken some steps to eliminate these liabilities. For example, the giving away of the bride is absent from all of the new rites.[23] The asymmetry in the vows has been eliminated by dropping references to obedience. The legal language remains intact in the Episcopal and United Methodist revisions, but is much modified in the Lutheran rite.[24] Some elements openly affirm the equality and mutuality of Christian marriage, as in the prayers following the marriage vows in *The Book of Common Prayer* ("Give them grace, when they hurt each other, to recognize and acknowledge their fault, and to seek each other's forgiveness and yours," 429).

Given these relatively hopeful signs, it is discouraging to examine the proposed Scripture readings for the new rites. In the Episcopalian and Lutheran rites, the proposals include Gen. 2:18–24; Eph. 5:21–33; and Mark 10:6–9 (or the Matthean parallel, Matt. 19:4–6), the significance of which for the perpetuation of domestic violence has already been discussed. The Episcopal rites also suggest Eph. 3:14–19 ("the Father from whom every family in heaven and on earth is named"). An earlier version of the United Methodist rite included the following texts:

Isa. 54:5–8: "For your Maker is your husband, the Lord of Hosts is his name . . . For the Lord has called you like a wife forsaken and grieved in spirit. . . ."

Jer. 31:31–34: ". . . I was their husband, says the Lord."

I Peter 3:1–9: "Likewise you wives, be submissive to your own husbands. . . . So, once the holy women who hoped in God used to adorn themselves and were submissive to their husbands, as Sarah obeyed Abraham, calling him Lord. . . ."[25]

In addition, the suggested readings in all of the rites under consideration include texts such as 1 Corinthians 13, Col. 3:12–17, and Rom. 12:9–18, which enjoin such virtues as meekness, forbearance, and forgiveness. The intent of these latter texts may have been to foster mutuality and cooperation (and of course none of these texts are writing of the marriage relationship but of relationships within the Christian community). But as both Schüssler Fiorenza and Thistlethwaite point out, such texts are often intepreted as applying more specifically to women than to men, as the 1 Peter text does. The sermon may make this implicit cultural assumption explicit, as may other elements in the rite, such as the nuptial blessing in the Roman Wedding Mass, which is addressed to the woman only or predominantly. Rite B prays, "Give your blessings to N., your daughter, so that she may be a good wife (and mother), caring for the home, faithful in love for her husband, generous and kind."[26] The Lutheran, Episcopal, and United Methodist rites all follow the announcement of the marriage by the minister with the words from Matt. 19:6: "Those whom God has joined together let no one put asunder."[27]

At the heart of all Western Christian marriage rites is a simple legal transaction expressed in the exchange of vows between the two contracting parties. Recent rites acknowledge, implicitly at least, the equality of the two parties by the symmetrical wording of the vows exchanged. Although the contract is entered into "until death," the violation of the terms (i.e., "to love and to cherish") by one party, which violence surely is, must be considered a breach of contract.

Unfortunately, the equality and freedom of the two contracting parties is obscured in these rites by an emphasis on the indissolubility of the bond (which is, after all only *one* term in the contract) and by the use of language and scripture which identifies the husband with God or Christ.

Non-Verbal Language

Liturgy is more than words. It also includes a non-verbal element which is both powerfully influential and enormously difficult to analyze and assess. The non-verbal language of gesture, posture, vesture, and physical environment has been generally ignored or treated as a secondary matter of "ceremonial," detachable from liturgical texts and less significant than the texts themselves. It has taken anthropologists and social scientists to remind us that our liturgies communicate in more than words.[28] Because the application of this perspective to liturgy is so new, we can only suggest possible connections and relationships between non-verbal elements of liturgy and domestic violence.

The predominant presence of males as liturgical leaders has a definite connection with the use of androcentric and patriarchal language. It reinforces the implicit assumptions in such language, namely that adult males are simultaneously representative human beings and adequate representatives of God. The argument of the 1976 Vatican Declaration on the Admission of Women to the Ministerial Priesthood depends upon what might seem to be an extreme expression of this view: "The Christian priesthood is therefore of a sacramental nature: the priest is a sign. . . . [W]hen Christ's role in the Eucharist is to be expressed sacramentally, there would not be this 'natural resemblance' which must exist between Christ and his minister if the role of Christ were not taken by a man. In such a case it would be difficult to see in the minister the image of Christ."[29] While most Protestants probably would reject this *form* of the argument against women as liturgical ministers, they nevertheless are content to assume that men are more adequate representatives of God than women.[30] The reluctance of abused women to turn to male pastors for help, and conversely, their relative readiness to confide in a woman minister, may be construed, in part, at least, as evidence of both the complexity and significance of this representative function. The male liturgical minister, speaking words in an androcentric language shaped by patriarchal presuppositions, is a powerful combination of verbal and non-verbal elements which may continue to legitimate male authority by identifying it with divine authority.

Bodily attitudes and postures may do the same. A clergywoman whose husband is also ordained once told me, "I never take communion from my husband. I refuse to kneel before him." Certainly postures such as standing when the clergy enter the church, bowing one's head to them, or kneeling before them are not only signs of respect but also express relative social status.[31] Even when such are signs of respect for or reverence toward God, the Bible, or the presence of Christ in the Eucharist, when the human mediators are invariably or predominantly males, the same mystification process we observed in the case of language takes place.

Even in churches which do not employ many changes in posture it is often easy to observe the expression of relative social status. In these cases it is relative movement and posture which is eloquent. When one person (or a small group of persons) does virtually all of the speaking and moving, the power lies with the speaker and mover. The pastor who stands for most of the service and does most of the speaking makes the congregation into passive spectators and hearers. When the leaders are usually male and the passive, seated congregation mostly female, expressions about relative power and status are combined with gender identity to encourage female passivity and acceptance. For the woman who is or has been abused, such encouragement is dangerous and destructive.

Making a Free Place on Which to Land

> I curse you, I say.
> What that mean? he say.
> I say, Until you do right by me, everything you touch will crumble.
> He laugh. Who you think you is? he say. You can't curse nobody. Look at you. You black, you pore, you ugly, you a woman. Goddam, he say, you nothing at all.
> Until you do right by me, I say, everything you even dream about will fail. I give it to him straight, just like it come to me. And it seem to come to me from the trees.
> Whoever heard of such a thing, say Mr. __. I probably didn't whup you ass enough.
> Every lick you hit me you will suffer twice, I say. Then I say, You better stop talking because all I'm telling you ain't coming just from me. Look like when I open my mouth the air rush in and shape words. . . .
> A dust devil flew on the porch between us, fill my mouth with dirt. The dirt say, Anything you do to me already done to you. . . .
> I'm pore, I'm black, I may be ugly and can't cook, a voice say to everything listening. But I'm here.
> Amen, say Shug. Amen, amen.
> —The Color Purple by Alice Walker[32]

Alice Walker's Celie, the heroine of The Color Purple, suffers years of abuse first at the hands of her stepfather and then from her husband, whom she cannot bring herself to name in her letters to God and to her long-lost sister Nettie. The moment in the novel when she is at last able to draw on her own strength, and on a strength that comes from beyond her, and to curse her husband is the turning point both for Celie and for her abusive husband.

We have considered some of the ways in which the church has, in its liturgy, bound women to abusive relationships and restrained them from protesting against their own abuse. How might the church, in its liturgy, reverse the cycle of violence, loose the bonds, and enable women to reject relationships and environments which are dangerous to their health and well-being?

On the level of a general principle, we must work toward a recovery of the notion of the liturgy as "the work of the people." As long as liturgy is regarded as the proper domain only of (predominantly male) clergy, church bureaucrats, and academic theologians, it will never be the work of the people. On the contrary, liturgy as the people's work must recognize that the majority of the people in the pews in every tradition and denomination are women. Therefore the experiences of women and their struggles for survival and dignity must take a central place as the locus out of which the primary theology, which is the liturgy, grows. Elisabeth Schüssler Fiorenza has named this idea "womanchurch."[33] Similarly, Aidan Kavanagh has argued that "Mrs. Murphy and her pastor" are the primary theologians of the church, whose theology is expressed not in "concepts and propositions," but in the daily working out of faith.[34] The chances are good, statistically speaking, that Mrs. Murphy is or has been a victim of domestic violence or abuse. Thus, the way in which she has struggled with and survived that experience is of primary significance to the church and to its worship, as is the prevention of the continuation of that abuse in the lives of her daughters.

The liturgy as "work of the people" also means that the liturgy as event must be restored to the gathered community. It can no longer remain the performance of the clergy, making the community mere passive observers. The restoration of elements such as the prayers of the people and the kiss of peace in which the people of God exercise their priestly ministry is vitally necessary. Physical restraints, such as pews, and barriers, such as altar rails, must be removed in order to free the community to be active.

The relocation of the matrix of liturgical theology in the struggle of women for survival and dignity in the context of their own faith has implications for the doing of liturgy. If we take seriously the theological significance of the presence of domestic violence suffered by women, children, and the elderly, we must begin to do differently the elements in our liturgies which have permitted or perpetuated this suffering.

The interpretation of the Bible and the use of the Bible in liturgy must undergo a significant shift. The "intersection of the Bible with contemporary culture, politics and society" must become more important.[35] Preaching would have to be done out of the matrix of the struggles of women and others for justice and dignity. The lectionary needs to be reconstructed in such a way that oppressive texts which demand submission or devalue persons are excluded. At the same time, texts which contain painful stories of women's suffering, texts which Phyllis Trible calls "Texts of Terror," need to be included, so that the reality of such suffering will not be forgotten.[36]

The "household of God," unlike the patriarchal household of our culture, is characterized by cooperation, mutuality, and equality. It is a household without "fathers" (Mark 10:29-30), and without relationships based on dominance and submission. Relationships of dominance and submission reflected in verbal and non-verbal transactions must be eliminated, and transactions which reflect mutual respect, cooperation, and equality encouraged. Non-reciprocal actions, such as standing when the clergy enter, or receiving a blessing from clergy, for example, reinforce relationships based on patterns of dominance and submission, whether lay-clergy, male-female, or adult-child.[37] On the other hand, the liturgy already has within it seeds of reciprocal actions, such as, for example, the bow exchanged between presider and people, the kiss of peace (as long as it is not "clericalized" by being passed first among the clergy), and (verbally) the dialogue between presider and congregation at the beginning of the Eucharistic prayer. A reciprocal absolution after confession is now part of the official United Methodist Sunday service and the Lutheran daily office.

Social sins of sexism such as domestic violence must not continue, as they do now, protected by silence. The recognition, confession, and repentance of and restitution for such offenses is not a "private matter," but a concern of the whole household of God. Language of prayer, especially prayers of confession and intercession, must recognize and confront this form of sin as well as others. Prayers of confession should name complicity in the perpetuation of domestic violence, by failing to speak or act, as one of the sins to which we are prone. Prayers of intercession ought always to mention the victims and the perpetrators of violence in the home among the petitions for those in need or trouble.

The proclamation in the liturgy of the justice of God can not be allowed to remain vague and unspecific. The implicit critique of unjust social structures (both within and without the church) needs to be made explicit. The church needs to learn to say not only "Yes, Amen" to God's righteousness, but also "No, this must not be" to injustice. Although the use of curses (such as the "commination" of the 1552 *Book of Common Prayer*) is unfamiliar and alien to most of our present practices, curses can provide the opportunity for repentance and conversion.[38] In The Color Purple, Celie's prophecies about Mr. ___ are accomplished. He does suffer all of the ills which she promises. But Celie's curse also becomes the means by which he is able finally to repent and be transformed. A litany might be modeled either on the "Communications," taken chiefly from Deuteronomy 27 and focusing on offenses against the community, especially the vulnerable, or on the "Reproaches" of the Good Friday liturgy, focusing on offenses against God. Either type could be an opportunity for repentance and conversion.

The women who have been victims of violence must recognize their own need to gather for their own purposes to heal, to find support, to express anger at God, to curse. Such gatherings will require their own unique liturgies and rituals, born out of the suffering and the struggles of the women. Curses, blessings, healings (such as the laying on of hands and anointing), and rites of purification may be needed.[39] It is important for the church to recognize and legitimate these gatherings (although women ought not wait on such recognition). It is even more important for the church not to use such gatherings as an excuse to fail to deal with the issue of domestic violence in its mixed assemblies, or to marginalize the subject as a "woman's issue."

Exploring the intersection of liturgy and domestic violence is painful, wrenching, and costly. It is painful to acknowledge the depth of the social sin of sexism which expresses itself in violence against women, and the extent to which the church in its liturgy has abetted that violence, the dreadful price in distorted and destroyed lives paid by the Christian community. It is wrenching to contemplate the changes that are called for. The changes will be costly. The process of identifying domestic violence as a social ill, providing shelter and care for victims and accountability for abusers, doing the essential research and study of the roots and resolutions of such a disease has already begun, and will continue unless hindered by New Right political forces. Providing the necessary medical, legal, and psychological help is not all that is needed. As Aidan Kavanagh writes, "Liberators accomplish only half their task when they liberate. The other half of their labor is to provide a normal place, a free place, on which the liberation may land."[40] Those who are working at the terrible and courageous task of freeing themselves from the cycle of domestic violence need a free and normal place on which to land. Those who have not yet found the courage to begin need a place which can show them that such work is both possible and necessary. The liturgy can be that place, and the words of Alice Walker in "Remember?" can also be the works of the church:

> I am the woman
> offering two flowers
> whose roots
> are twin
> Justice and Hope
> Let us begin.[41]

Notes

1. Adrienne Rich, "The Images" in *A Wild Patience Has Taken Me This Far*, (New York: W.W. Norton, 1981), 3–7.

2. For statistics on domestic violence in the United Methodist context, see the study done by the National Division of the Board of Global Ministries' Program on Ministries with Women in Crisis, by Peggy Halsey and Lee Coppernoll: *Crisis: Women's Experience and the Church's Response. Final Report on a Crisis Survey of United Methodists*, March 1982.

3. See especially Marie Marshall Fortune, *Sexual Violence: The Unmentionable Sin* (New York: Pilgrim Press, 1983), and Mary Pellauer, "Moral Callousness and Moral Sensitivity," in *Women's Consciousness, Women's Conscience*, ed. Barbara Hilkert Andolsen, Christine E. Gudorf, and Mary D. Pellauer, (New York: Winston Press, 1985), for thorough discussions of the extent and results of this silence, especially for the church.

4. For the sources on these statistics and others, see Carol J. Adams, "Toward a Feminist Theology of the State," 15–35 in this volume; and Pellauer, "Moral Callousness and Moral Sensitivity," 7–41, cited above.

5. Elisabeth Schüssler Fiorenza, *In Memory of Her* (New York: Crossroad, 1983), 344.

6. See, for example, "Liturgies," *The Westminster Dictionary of Worship*, ed. J. G. Davies (Philadelphia: Westminster Press, 1972).

7. See Susan Moller Okin, *Women in Western Political Thought* (Princeton: Princeton University Press, 1979), 15–96; and Schüssler Fiorenza, *In Memory of Her*, 88–91, for an analysis of the relationship of this structure to Christianity.

8. The term "liturgy" is used throughout this essay to refer to the corporate worship of the church in whatever form it may appear. The worship of so-called "non-liturgical" churches is not excluded, although, practically speaking, the worship of churches which use published orders of worship and prayers is obviously more accessible for analysis.

9. The most recent liturgical commentaries and handbooks emphasize that during the reading of Scripture and preaching, "God's life-giving Word . . . comes to us through Scripture." See *The Service for the Lord's Day*, Supplemental Liturgical Resource 1, Joint Office of Worship for the Presbyterian Church (U.S.A.) and Cumberland Presbyterian Church (Philadelphia: Westminster Press, 1984), 16. See also: *Word and Table: A Basic Pattern of Sunday Worship for United Methodists* (Nashville: Abingdon, 1980), 29–32; Ray Lonergan, *A Well-Trained Tongue* (Chicago: Liturgy Training Publications, 1982), 5–6; and James A. Wallace, C.S.S.R., *The Ministry of Lectors* (Collegeville: Liturgical Press, 1981), 7–15.

10. On the feminist critique of traditional biblical authority, see Marjorie Procter-Smith, "Lectionaries: Principles and Problems—Alternative Perspectives," in *Studia Liturgica* 22/1 (1992), and "Feminist Interpretation and Liturgical Proclamation," in *Searching the Scriptures, Vol. I: A Feminist Introduction*, ed. Elisabeth Schüssler Fiorenza (New York: Crossroad, 1993).

11. "The Will to Choose or Reject; Continuing our Critical Work," in *Feminist Interpretation of the Bible*, ed. Letty Russell (Philadelphia: Fortress Press, 1985), 130.

12. Fortune, 194; Susan Brooks Thistlethwaite, "Every Two Minutes: Battered Women and Feminist Interpretation," in *Feminist Interpretation of the Bible*, 99, 106.

13. Thistlethwaite, 105.

14. Schüssler Fiorenza, "The Will to Choose or Reject," 132.

15. Thistlethwaite, 101–2. See also my analysis of the CCT lectionary, "Images of Women in the Lectionary," in *Women: Invisible in Church and Theology* ed. Elisabeth Schüssler Fiorenza and Mary Collins (Philadelphia: Fortress Press, 1986), *Concilium* 182.

16. See, for example, Casey Miller and Kate Swift, *Words and Women* (New York: Anchor Press, 1976), Robin Lakoff, *Language and Women's Place* (New York: Harper & Row, 1975), for general introductions. In relation to

Christianity see, for example, *The Liberating Word*, Letty Russell, ed. (Philadelphia: Westminster Press, 1976).

17. Pellauer, "Moral Callousness and Moral Sensitivity," 42.

18. See also Fortune, 202–4.

19. *Systematic Theology* I (Chicago: University of Chicago Press, 1951), 240.

20. *Beyond God the Father* (Boston: Beacon Press, 1973), 13.

21. *The Shaker* (June 1892).

22. *The United Methodist Hymnal* (Nashville: United Methodist Publishing House, 1989), 8. Emphasis mine.

23. Although it is allowed as an option in the 1979 *Book of Common Prayer*, it is forbidden in the *Lutheran Book of Worship* (Minister's Desk Edition, 36).

24. "Weddings consist essentially of a public contract freely and mutually assented to before witnesses. The traditional language—'to have and to hold'—is language still used in conveyance of property. 'From this day forward' dates the contract. Then follows the unconditional nature of said contract: 'for better or worse.' 'Til death us do part' terminates the above, and 'I give thee my troth' is the pledge of faithfulness to it. . . . Almost identical words appear in English in fourteenth century manuscripts, long before other liturgical documents were translated into the vernacular." James F. White, *Introduction to Christian Worship* (Nashville: Abingdon Press, 1980), 240.

25. *A Service of Christian Marriage* (Supplemental Worship Resource 5; Nashville: Abingdon, 1979). *The United Methodist Book of Worship* (Nashville: United Methodist Publishing House, 1992) includes a long list of recommended texts from which all of these texts are omitted, in part due to my recommendations.

26. *The Sacramentary*, (Collegeville: The Liturgical Press, 1971), 763; cf. 760–61, 766. Note, however, this phrase in the blessing of Rite A: "May her husband put his trust in her and recognize that she is his equal and the heir with him of the life of grace." The androcentrism of the prayer, however, while only implied here is made explicit in the beginning of the prayer: "You [i.e., God] gave man the constant help of woman."

27. This verse was not part of the medieval marriage rites. It first appeared in Luther's "Order of Marriage," in 1592. It has been adopted by most Protestants.

28. Ronald Grimes, *Beginnings in Ritual Studies* (Lanham, Md.: University Press of America, 1982). See Victor Turner, *The Ritual Process: Structure and Anti-Structure* (New York: Cornell University Press, 1977); Victor Turner and Edith Turner, *Image and Pilgrimage in Christian Culture* (Columbia University Press, 1978); Mary Douglas, *Natural Symbols* (New York: Pantheon, 1973).

29. For the complete text, see, for example, *Women Priests: A Catholic Commentary on the Vatican Declaration*, Arlene and Leonard Swidler, eds., (New York: Paulist Press, 1977), 37–49.

30. This representative function is certainly one of the major barriers encountered by women clergy, who find that people often fail to respond to them as clergy because they do not look, sound, or act like the "normal" male clergy.

31. See especially Erving Goffman, *Interactional Ritual: Essays on Face-to-Face Behavior* (New York: Anchor Books, 1967); *Encounters: Two Studies in the Sociology of Interaction* (New York: Bobbs-Merrill, 1961); and *Relations in Public: Microstudies of the Public Order* (New York: Basic Books, 1971).

32. Alice Walker, *The Color Purple* (New York: Harcourt Brace Jovanovich, 1982), 175–76.

33. Schüssler Fiorenza, 126–29. See also "Women-Church: the Hermeneutical Center of Feminist Biblical Interpretation," in *Bread Not Stone: The Challenge of Feminist Biblical Interpretation* (Boston: Beacon Press, 1984), 1–22; and "Toward a Feminist Biblical Spirituality: the *Ekklesia* of Women," in *In Memory of Her* (New York: Crossroad, 1983), 343–51.

34. Aidan Kavanagh, *On Liturgical Theology* (New York: Pueblo Press, 1984), 146–47.

35. Schüssler Fiorenza, "The Will to Choose or Reject," 133.

36. Phyllis Trible, *Texts of Terror* (Philadelphia: Fortress Press, 1984). See especially pages 1–7.

37. See J. Frank Henderson, "Discrimination Against the Laity in Liturgical Texts and Rites," paper presented at the North American Academy of Liturgy, January, 1985.

38. See also Mark Searle, ed., *Liturgy and Social Justice*, 28–29.

39. See Fortune, 221–24; Carolyn E. Shaffer, "Spiritual Techniques for Re-Powering Survivors of Sexual Assault," in *The Politics of Women's Spirituality*, Charlene Spretnak, ed. (New York: Doubleday/Anchor Press,1982), 462–69.

40. Kavanagh, 170.

41. Alice Walker, "Remember?" in *Horses Make A Landscape Look More Beautiful* (New York: Harcourt Brace Jovanovich, 1984).

Saving the Family:
When Is Covenant Broken?

MITZI N. EILTS

For those of us in the church, there are critical questions presented by the reality of domestic violence. Is maintaining the family unit more sacred than the well-being and safety of the individuals within it? Is there any spiritual reason for suffering or abuse to be endured which is perpetrated by one member of the family against another? Who is responsible for breaking up the family—the one who leaves home and partner or parent to escape the abuse *or* the one who is being abusive?

To find some answers to these questions requires that we reexamine what constitutes family in our faith traditions. What is the nature of the covenant around which we build family? What are the principles of covenant as established by God on which we pattern our covenants with each other? Is there any evidence or precedent in scripture or our faith traditions for the breaking of covenant? What are they? Is the only kind of family "to be saved" the nuclear family with father *and* mother and children? In this chapter these questions are examined so that the religious community and service providers might consider what a danger it is to apply a save-the-family ethic without equal consideration of other spiritual ethics and values.

Covenant Making

Covenant making is older than the Judeo-Christian tradition; there is evidence of this in the language used in the Old Testament that comes from treaty-making language of the nations and tribes occupying the territory into which the Israelites moved.[1] Covenant making is the establishment of an agreement between two parties defining the relationship (responsibilities and obligations) between them. It may be an agreement between equals (mutual, parity) or a unilateral agreement (suzerainty) in which one party must accept the conditions presented by the other due to favors owed or difference in power.

It is generally understood and accepted in the Jewish and Christian traditions that covenants with God are initiated by God. There is nevertheless some recognition of mutuality in God's covenant making with us in that God takes on promises and responsibilities to uphold as well as naming obligations to be upheld by those to whom the covenant is offered. (In other words, covenants are good for us *and* good for God.) A common thread in all of God's covenants is a promise of deliverance and well-being, liberation from suffering, persecution, or oppression (either already bestowed, to come, or to be continued), and in exchange God seeks loyalty and commitment—commitment of heart reflected in behavior.

Consider the covenants established with Noah (Gen. 9:1: out of chaos a promise never again to destroy the earth); with Abraham and Sarah (Gen. 17:1: out of barrenness the promise of generations to carry on); with Moses (out of bondage a promise of a home). Covenants made with the God of the Hebrew Scriptures and the Christian Testament have as their most basic element the offer of liberation from bondage or affliction—the offer of new life, life as God intended it to be for us.[2]

> For I the Lord love justice, I hate robbery and wrong; I will faithfully give them their recompense, and I will make an everlasting covenant with them. (Isa. 61:8)

> I call heaven and earth to witness against you this day, that I have set before you life and death, blessing and curse; therefore choose life, that you and your descendants may live. (Deut. 30:19)

> I came that they may have life and have it more abundantly. (John 10:10)

We should remember that as the people of God we are in a constant process of renewing and reestablishing the covenant between God and ourselves. It is common to speak and act as though God's covenant with us is a settled event. Yet the covenant with Moses was offered anew to the Hebrew people through Joshua as they entered the promised land. The original covenant with Moses was a revision of the ones made with Noah and Abraham and Sarah, then renewed with Jacob. The Davidic covenant was seen as new, yet it was related to the one made with Abraham and Sarah. Jeremiah and the New Testament authors represented the covenant as being reestablished in new ways. Renewal of covenant has been seen as necessary and has been practiced as new generations have emerged with different conditions in their lives, so that all covenants are relevant to the present circumstances.[3]

> Behold, the days are coming, says the Lord, when I will make a new covenant with the house of Israel and the house of Judah, not like the covenant which I made with their fathers when I took them by the hand to bring them out of the land of Egypt, my covenant which they broke. . . . But this is the covenant which I will make with the house of Israel after those days, says the Lord: I will put my law within them and I will write it upon their hearts; and I will be their God, and they shall be my people. (Jer. 31:31–33)

> Blessed be the Lord God of Israel, for God has visited and redeemed his people, and has raised up a horn of salvation for us in the house of his servant David . . . that we should be saved from our enemies, and from the hand of all who hate us; to perform the mercy promised to our ancestors,

and to remember his holy covenant, the oath which God swore to our
father Abraham, to grant that we, being delivered from the hand of our
enemies might serve God without fear. (Luke 1: 68–69, 71–73)

Consequences of Covenant Breaking

Additionally, there is history of covenants being broken between God and
God's people. The language of God's covenants acknowledges this possibility
by the use of blessings and curses.

> [BLESSINGS] If you walk in my statutes and observe my commandments
> and do them, then I will give you your rains in their season and the land
> shall yield its increase, and the trees of the field shall yield their fruit. . . .
> And I will give you peace in the land, and you shall lie down and none
> shall make you afraid; . . . And I will have regard for you and make you
> fruitful and multiply you, and will confirm my covenant with you. . . . And
> I will walk among you and will be your God and you shall be my people.

> [CURSES] But if you will not hearken to me, and will not do all these
> commandments, if you spurn my statutes, and if your soul abhors my
> ordinances, so that you will not do all my commandments, but break my
> covenant; I will do this to you: I will appoint over you sudden terror, con-
> sumption, and fever that waste the eyes and cause life to pine away . . .
> and I will break the pride of your power. (Leviticus 26; see also Psalm 78
> and Deuteronomy 29)

These verses illustrate that there are consequences for the breaking of
covenant—not so much wrath or vengeance, but the consequences of living life
without God. For once we have broken the covenant(s) we make with God,
we are in essence living in a world devoid of God and God's ways. Though it
has become clear over time that God has an unending ability and desire to forgive our unfaithfulness or breaking of covenant, it has also remained true that
there are consequences when we desert the ways of God. Change and amends
(repentance) are necessary to restore covenant relationships.

> And when all these things come upon you, the blessing and the curse,
> which I have set before you, and you call them to mind among all the
> nations where the Lord your God has driven you, and return to the Lord
> your God, you and your children, and obey his voice in all that I com-
> mand you this day, with all your heart and all your soul; then the Lord
> your God will restore your fortunes and have compassion upon you, and
> will gather you again from all peoples where the Lord your God has
> scattered you. (Deut. 30:1–3)

Who Decides When a Covenant Is Broken?

When a covenant is broken, who names the fact? Is it the covenant breaker,
the one who has ignored, forgotten, transgressed the promise made? Or is it

the one who is still living by the promises, the one who is attempting to keep covenant? Again and again, throughout the scriptures, it is God or one called by God (prophets such as Jeremiah, Isaiah, and John the Baptist) who calls attention to the fact that the covenant has been broken. It is God who says "if you want to be in a relationship with me you must change your ways—return to the promises you made with me." God, the one who has been faithful, is the one who says the covenant is broken; the covenant no longer stands. It is the one who is faithful to the covenant who calls attention to the fact it has been broken, and *that* makes common sense, does it not?

Covenant Making in Human Relationships

The idea of covenant between God and human beings was quickly picked up and applied to human relationships in the scriptures. In the book of Genesis we find Abraham making covenant with Abimelech, and then Jacob and Laban using the idea and language of covenant with each other. Their oaths of loyalty and promises of peace are bound in the language of covenant.

Similarly, as people of faith, we have continued to apply the model of covenant with God to our human relationships. A prime example of this is our understanding of marriage as a form of covenant—making and keeping promises with God as an essential witness. Historically, marriage has sometimes been understood as a mutual covenant between two equal parties, and other times as a covenant of protection/caretaking by one person in exchange for nurturing/obedience by the other. (Notice the parallel to the model of treaties—mutual/parity and suzerainty.) Evidence supports the mutual marriage covenant as the one that most closely resembles and fulfills the purpose of God in covenant making. It is the mutual/parity form of relationship which establishes a way of relating and a setting for the promotion of health and well-being (physical, emotional, and spiritual), a setting within which life as God intended it to be for us might be nurtured and sustained.

Rev. Joy Bussert in her book *Battered Women: From a Theology of Suffering to a Theology of Empowerment* examines some theological premises that have been instrumental in making the marriage covenant one of suzerainty. Her thesis is that ideas such as mind-body dualism (debasing the very nature of femaleness) or that men have a right and a spiritual duty to chastise women, have distorted the nature of relationships between women and men, setting the stage for domestic violence to occur.[4] Friar Cherubino in the Rules of Marriage adhered to in the city of Sienna in the middle to late fifteenth century, for example, expressed a rationale used today by some abusers.

> When you see your wife commit an offense, don't rush at her with insults and violent blows; rather first correct the wrong lovingly . . . but if your wife is of a servile disposition and has a crude shifty spirit, so that pleasant words have no affect, scold her sharply, bully and terrify her. And if this still doesn't work . . . take up a stick and beat her soundly . . . for it is better to punish the body and correct the soul than to damage

the soul and spare the body. . . . You should beat her . . . only when she commits a serious wrong; for example, if she blasphemes God or a saint, if she mutters the devil's name, if she likes being at the window and lends ready ear to dishonest men, or if she has taken to bad habits or bad company, or commits some other wrong that is a mortal sin. Then readily beat her, not in rage but out of charity and concern for her soul, so that the beating will resound to your merit and good.[5]

Any covenant of marriage based on the protector/provider and obeyer/nurturer model lends itself too easily to the idea that a man ought to, even has a duty to, keep his woman in line, for his sake and hers.[6] In contrast, a marriage covenant based on mutual respect and responsibility expects both parties to work on and uphold their promises to love, cherish, and obey—the command of God, not of each other.

Rev. Marie Fortune has outlined the elements necessary to a marriage covenant based on mutuality; these elements make possible the fulfillment of God's intentions for us in the relationship and are parallel to those in the covenant between God and God's people.

1. It is made in the full knowledge of the relationship.
2. It involves a mutual giving of self to the other.
3. It is assumed to be lasting.
4. It values mutuality, respect, and equality between persons.[7]

Such marriage does not leave room for abuse. If and when abuse does occur, it is clear that promises and vows have been broken and the covenant (trust) has been breached.

When physical violence or emotional abuse occurs within a marriage relationship, the very intent of the covenant is being broken. When abuse is occurring, marriage becomes a setting of bondage and affliction rather than a setting for God's ways of compassion, justice, and love to be practiced and lived out.

Yet a woman victimized in an abusive domestic relationship feels serious ethical/spiritual dilemmas about the marriage covenant. She has made promises that are still important and meaningful to her. One of those is that the relationship will be a lasting one. To stay in the relationship means to suffer further abuse, but to leave (temporarily or permanently) makes her feel as if she is breaking her promise. Many women thus stay and suffer the abuse, precisely because they take their commitment seriously. Seldom does it occur to the victim of the abuse (at least in the beginning)—or to friends, family or the church—that the covenant has already been broken by the behavior of her partner.

Saving the Family

There is a big problem with the concept of saving the family (keeping covenant or the appearance of covenant) when it is applied indiscriminately to families in which domestic abuse/violence is present. The problem is that meaningless suffering and sometimes even death are very real consequences. The victim holds on for many reasons, one of which is usually hope—hope that what the marriage is supposed to be might be restored. It is common for the victim to persist in the hope that her patience will last longer than his abuse. Often this attitude is reinforced by church teachings on long suffering which may apply in settings where one is *choosing* to make a stand on behalf of God's ideals in this world, but which do not apply when the suffering is perpetrated by another who has promised to live according to God's ways with her.

In abusive families, hope and patience without safety for the victims and intervention for the abuser are dangerous because unless he takes responsibility for his actions and seeks help, the cycle of abuse will continue and worsen. Any chance that the covenant relationship might be restored requires both confession (taking responsibility for wrongdoing) and serious repentance on the part of the abuser, achieved by consistent participation in an abuser's program.

Victims often remain long past the danger point for some other emotional and religious reasons as well. Guilt is a common reason. The world around us reinforces the notion that the marriage relationship is primarily the responsibility of the woman. In many Jewish and Christian traditions women are told that marriage is the domain in which they are to live out their service to God. Therefore, if something is going wrong it must be their fault.

Most battered women have been told by at least one person that she must have done something to deserve such treatment. Most women hear that message from many sources, including their religious leaders and communities. Too seldom is the belief voiced that covenant is a two-way street, a partnership with responsibilities and obligations for both people involved. Too seldom is the one who is really breaking covenant, the abuser, being called to account for creating a home environment that is so oppressive that his partner needs to seek safety and peace elsewhere.

Victims/survivors often stay on in an abusive relationship for years because of the idea that marriage is permanent. For some women separation or divorce from their partner will also mean separation from their religious community. The first decision is tough in itself; feelings of failure are strong. For those women for whom separation or divorce from the partner also means the censure of or expulsion from their faith community, the decision is excruciatingly painful. The victim who seeks safety, or eventually decides to seek separation or divorce, *is* acknowledging that the covenant which she had established with another no longer exists, *but she is not the one breaking the covenant.* In fact, she is taking steps toward the basic purpose of the marriage covenant: to provide a home where the ways of life intended by God might be practiced: the ways of justice, peace, and mutual caretaking.

While marriage is a covenant that is *meant* to be lasting, there is nothing in scripture that can be construed to justify a lifetime of meaningless suffering, and there is substantial evidence calling for covenants with God to be ended when their purpose has been forgotten, ignored, or transgressed. Should it not be the same with covenants between people? When the marriage covenant is treated as more sacred than the way of living that it is intended to provide, are we not then abusing the very purpose of the covenant?

Conclusion

The intent of family, or marriage, covenants is to provide a place where justice, mercy, and love are lived out in keeping with God's covenantal ways. But when the family environment deviates from this intention due to the presence of abuse or violence, then the saving grace is to release the victim from the obligation. In families afflicted by domestic abuse, the only way to save the family is to allow the victim the opportunity to rededicate herself to life abundant in an environment free of the abuse.

The definition of who makes up a family is different with different cultures, circumstances, and generations. It is time we began focusing on what is really important—and that is the promise that for each of us God wishes life in all its abundance. Saving the family means ending the violence that is destroying it.

Notes

1. For more detail on treaty language and form see George E. Mendenhall, "Covenant Form in Israelite Tradition," *The Biblical Archaeologist Reader*, 3rd ed., ed. E. F. Campbell, Jr. and D. N. Freedman (Garden City, N.Y.: Doubleday, 1970).

2. All scripture quotations are from the Revised Standard Version.

3. For further examples and discussion of covenant renewal see G. F. Mendenhall, "Covenant Forms in Israelite Tradition," in *Old Testament Theology*, Vol. 1, ed. Gerhard von Rad (New York: Harper & Row, 1962), 38.

4. For more in-depth discussion of these issues see Joy M. K. Bussert, *Battered Women: From a Theology of Suffering to an Ethic of Empowerment* (New York: Division for Mission in Northern America/Lutheran Church in America, 1986).

5. Cherubino da sienna, *Regole della Vita Matrimoniale*, cited in Bussert, 13–14, from O'Faolain and Martines, *Not in God's Image*, 177.

6. See Bussert, *Battered Women*, chapters 1 and 4 for further discussion.

7. Rev. Marie M. Fortune, "A Commentary on Religious Issues in Family Violence," in *Violence in the Family: A Workshop Curriculum for Clergy and Other Helpers* (Cleveland: Pilgrim Press, 1991), 137–51. Marie Fortune's writings and workshops have made immeasurable impact on my thinking as expressed in this chapter.

Calling to Accountability:
The Church's Response to Abusers

MARIE M. FORTUNE AND JAMES POLING

A girl in the youth group tells the pastor that her father is pressuring her to have sex with him.

Raped by the leader of a neighborhood boy's club, a ten-year-old boy tries to commit suicide.

A member of the congregation is hospitalized because her husband beat her.

Sexual involvement with several female parishioners leads to a pastor's dismissal from his charge.

Stories that only a few years ago were unusual have become commonplace. Increasing numbers of pastors and congregational leaders are coming face-to-face with survivors of physical and sexual abuse who are in need of the healing ministries of the church. Fortunately, the church is beginning to respond, and there are resources for counseling victims.[1] Still, much more needs to be done.

For every victim who is trying to escape a private hell, there is a perpetrator who has taken advantage of her or him during a period of vulnerability. As more and more victims come forward, pastors are discovering perpetrators of abuse in their congregations and in their local communities. While it is not useful to be overly fearful of offenders, the increasing prevalence of physical and sexual abuse places upon Christian leaders an imperative to confront this issue.

Specifically, the church can minister to victims by being willing to deal with abusers.

However, the church's mistaken understanding of God's love for all people has sometimes led Christian leaders to tolerate rather than stop abusers. Providing nurturing concern and healing resources is an appropriate response for victims of violence. However, for perpetrators, the most loving response may be the development of systems of accountability and consequences that stop their destructive behaviors.

For a congregation to face the reality that one of its own members or even its own pastor may have sexually or physically abused an adult or child can be devastating. At the point of disclosure by the victim(s), there are many temptations for a church, which can lead it to play the priest and Levite, passing by the wounded person on the side of the road:

1. THE TEMPTATION OF DISBELIEF: Abusers often are respected members of the church and community. They are the persons who teach Sunday School, or chair the board of trustees, or preach the sermon every Sunday. They are often well-known and liked and their public persona is totally contrary to the people's image of a sex offender or wifebeater. To believe that such a person is responsible for the abuse of another brings us face-to-face with our own failure of judgment. Yet this reluctance to believe has made the church slow to respond to the victims and survivors in its midst. In our naïveté about the behavior of abusers we may inadvertently contribute to the silence which perpetuates the suffering for many.

2. THE TEMPTATION TO PROTECT THE CHURCH'S IMAGE: Sometimes a church's reluctance to believe that one of its members or its pastor is an abuser arises out of its desire to protect its own image in the community. Even if there has been some private acknowledgment, there is often public denial or minimization. This refusal to deal openly with the reality of victimization is excruciating for victims who have come forward. It is yet another denial of their experience. It also allows the abuser to continue to minimize or deny responsibility.

3. THE TEMPTATION TO BLAME THE VICTIM: The most common reaction to someone who discloses that they have been victimized by sexual or domestic violence is to blame them for it. Churches are notorious for thinking that the victim brought the destruction on by his/her own behavior. As long as the church persists in blaming the victim(s), they can avoid holding the abuser accountable.

4. THE TEMPTATION TO SYMPATHIZE WITH THE ABUSER: This temptation is in tandem with blaming the victim: it focuses on the pain which the accusation causes the abuser, the possible damage which will be done to the abuser's career, etc. Again it ignores the real issue which is that this person is responsible for harm done to another. He or she avoids accountability for the harm done.

5. THE TEMPTATION TO PROTECT THE ABUSER FROM THE CONSEQUENCES OF HIS/HER BEHAVIOR: This temptation leads to the avoidance and secret-keeping which so often accompany any disclosure of abuse in a church setting. It also underlies a pastor's avoidance of reporting abuse to law enforcement. Some pastors seem to believe that their primary responsibility is to prevent a church member from ever encountering law enforcement. Unfortunately the protection from consequences only further supports the abuser's minimization and denial of responsibility which are not in anyone's best interest.

6. THE TEMPTATION OF CHEAP GRACE: If and when a congregation does acknowledge that a member or pastor is an abuser, there is an immediate move to forgive and forget. Not only is this bad psychology, it is even worse theology. It has no basis in either Hebrew or Christian scriptural teaching. The purpose of judgment is always to bring someone to confession and from confession to repentance. The substance of repentance is always ". . . a new heart and a new spirit" (Ezek. 18:31). Repentance always begins with acknowledgment to oneself, one's victim(s), and one's community of responsibility for

harm done. Jesus outlines the basics of accountability in the Gospels: "If your brother sins, rebuke him, and if he repents, forgive him; and if he turns to you seven times, and says, 'I repent,' you must forgive him" (Luke 17:1–4). Cheap grace shortcircuits the process that the abuser needs in order to repent.

A group of twenty-five incest offenders sat in a circle during their treatment. They said, "Tell the clergy for us that they should not forgive us so quickly." Each of them upon arrest had gone to their minister and had been prayed over, "forgiven," and sent home. Each of them said it was the worst thing that could have been done for them. That cheap grace had allowed them to continue to deny responsibility for their abuse of others. It in no way facilitated their repentance or their treatment.

If there is any hope of stopping physical and sexual abuse, leaders of the church need to join social workers, police, lawyers, psychologists, and judges in educating the public and developing systems of accountability. To this end, this chapter summarizes research on physical and sexual abusers and suggests some principles for stopping them.

What Is Abuse?

Abuse can best be understood in four categories:[2]

A. PHYSICAL VIOLENCE: This is the most overt form and includes slapping, punching, kicking, pushing, throwing objects at a person, using a weapon, and the like. Obviously this form has the highest probability of causing serious injury or death.

B. SEXUAL VIOLENCE: Included here are rape (marital, acquaintance, or stranger), child sexual abuse (incest or molestation), and sexual harassment and exploitation (in the workplace or in a professional relationship).

C. PSYCHOLOGICAL ABUSE: This is a persistent pattern of psychological pressure or brainwashing with the intent of instilling fear in the victim in order to control her/his behavior. This form of abuse includes verbal humiliation, threats, manipulation, and coercion usually over a period of time.

D. DESTRUCTION OF PROPERTY AND PETS: This form which is common in the family setting carries a psychological dimension. There is always an explicit or implicit threat toward the victim in the damage to property or pets: "This time it is the china; next time it will be you."

These types of behavior can occur between family members, between acquaintances, co-workers, or friends, or, least often, between strangers. They most likely occur between men and women, but also can occur between men, or between women. They can occur between persons of every age. They are most likely intraracial but can be interracial. They occur in public and in private.

Abusers are persons who use aggressive and/or manipulative behaviors to enhance their position of dominance in order to coerce or control another person for the abuser's own purposes. Abusers may use physical force, emotional assaults, psychological pressure, threats, and/or social privilege and position to exploit the vulnerability of another in order to control (as is the case with batterers and most rapists) or to seek sexual gratification (as is the case with molesters).

Abuse can occur betweens any two persons; regardless of who is the abuser and who is the victim, it is a matter to be taken very seriously. But those persons most likely to exploit the vulnerabilities of others are those with the resources, i.e., power, to do so. In a patriarchal society, this means that abuse is most likely to be male to female and adult to child. (Men of color who exercise less power due to race and class still retain the privilege of gender within their own racial and class groups.) Male violence against women and children in our society is not merely an individual experience but a social issue because it is socially sanctioned in many ways.

> Madison, Wis. (AP)—Amos Smith was sentenced to 14 years in prison for sexual assault yesterday despite his attorney's argument that violence against women is acceptable in American society. His attorney, Roger Merry of Belleville, argues that Smith, 30, should not be sent to prison "for being a victim of culture." "Hostility toward women, I think, is something that is culturally instilled in men." Merry said. "It's part of our culture that has been for hundreds of years, that violence against women is not unacceptable."[3]

Thus in dealing with individual male abusers who have victimized women and children, we are dealing not only with an individual's misconduct or pathology but with an entire set of social, cultural, and religious beliefs which serve to justify and support his conduct.[4]

Identifying these *behaviors* as abusive helps us to identify those who engage in these behaviors as abusers which then allows us to address their need for accountability and possible treatment.

Types of Abusers

Clinical and sociological research has focused on categories of abusers: child molesters, rapists, batterers, and men who use their profession and position to exploit others. (While there are women who abuse, research suggests that men are the most frequent perpetrators of interpersonal violence.[5]) Because abusers are members of our churches and of the communities in which we minister, we must be able to recognize their behavioral patterns.

CHILD MOLESTERS sexually exploit children. Researchers estimate that 35 to 38 percent of girls under eighteen years of age were molested by someone at least five years older than themselves,[6] and 5 to 10 percent of boys under eighteen were molested.[7] This usually includes attempted or actual sexual contact, but can include exhibitionism, pornography, inappropriate sexual references, and other behaviors that are clearly destructive of children at various stages of development. The defining characteristic of child sexual abuse is the use of an adult's superior power over a child to obtain the adult's sexual gratification. Child molesters fit into several subcategories.

a. Some molesters abuse girls and boys within the family and within other situations of trust. Fathers, step-fathers, grandfathers, uncles, cousins, and trusted community leaders who molest children form the largest group of molesters, making the family and other intimate groups one of the most dangerous places for children. Coerced and/or manipulated, children are forced to comply with adult sexual desires and threatened with consequences if they don't keep the secret. Their confusion and terror is often made worse when other adults in the family respond ineffectively to their disclosures and deny them the help they need for healing.

b. Adolescent molesters are usually abused children who act out sexually in relation to younger boys and girls with whom they have contact. Because they themselves are often seriously damaged, both the adolescents and the children they molest need help.

c. Pedophiles, men who target boys and girls of specific ages for sexual abuse, sometimes develop sophisticated plans of manipulation and coercion to entrap children. Pedophiles are especially dangerous when they hide in trusted leadership roles such as pastors, teachers, and leaders of children's organizations. They are also dangerous because they have multiple victims, sometimes numbering in the dozens. Contrary to stereotypes about dangerous strangers, pedophiles are often known and respected persons whose social position protects them from suspicion. They are predominantly heterosexual in their adult relationships even though they may molest young boys. They are often protected because boys are less likely than girls to report sexual abuse and because men who have been abused as children are slow to report their childhood trauma. Both of these hesitations are rooted in homophobia.

d. A small number of men brutally rape and sometimes murder children they do not know. Because of their especially gruesome nature, these cases often receive notorious attention from the press and public. Men in this category form a very small percentage of all molesters, yet the group often receives the most attention. The public hysteria about child rapists and murderers actually may serve to protect the majority of molesters who are known and trusted members of families and churches.

RAPISTS engage in coercive and exploitative sexual behaviors. Because rape also describes the sexual abuse of many children, this group overlaps with molesters. In a classic study Nicholas Groth defines rape as "all nonconsenting sexual encounters, whether the victim is pressured or forced."[8] Social pressure and physical assault are two primary methods that rapists use to coerce sexual activity. "In pressured situations, advantage is taken of a person's vulnerable status, so that refusal to engage in sexual activity may have serious social, economic, or vocational consequences. . . . The defining characteristic in forced assault is the risk of injury or bodily harm to the victim should she refuse to participate in sexual activity. Her physical safety is placed in jeopardy."[9]

It is difficult to estimate the prevalence of rape because our understanding of what constitutes it is changing so quickly. Diana Russell has done a landmark empirical study of 930 women (1982) which shows the prevalence of attempted and completed rape. Of her sample, "forty-four percent (44 percent) of the 930 women interviewed had been subjected to at least one rape or attempted rape in the course of their lives, but . . . 8 percent of the entire sample, which includes women who had never been married, had been raped by a husband."[10]

In trying to understand rapists, Groth suggests a distinction between an anger rape and a power rape. "In some cases of sexual assault, it is very apparent that sexuality becomes a means of expressing and discharging feelings of pent-up anger and rage. The assault is characterized by physical brutality."[11] In the power rape, "it is not the offender's desire to harm his victim, but to possess her sexually. Sexuality becomes a means of compensating for underlying feelings of inadequacy and serves to express issues of mastery, strength, control, authority, identity, and capability. His goal is sexual conquest, and he uses only the amount of force necessary to accomplish his objective."[12] A third pattern is sadism in which the pain and torture of the victim creates sexual gratification.[13]

Given this background, we can differentiate between types of rapists according to whom they victimize: men who rape women and children within the family (brothers, uncles, cousins); men who rape within marriage and other intimate relationships; men who rape dates and acquaintances; men who rape strangers.

BATTERERS inflict harm upon women and children in their families. Gelles and Straus estimate that 25 percent of married women will be abused sometime in their marriage.[14] Men Stopping Violence estimates that 50 percent of all men are violent or threaten violence with intimates at one time or another.[15] The physical abuse of children is all too common: "A national study of 2,143 intact [sic] families with children aged 3–17 found that . . . 8 percent were kicked, bitten, or punched, about nine times per year; 4 percent were beaten and this occurred about six times per year; and 3 percent had a gun or knife used on them."[16] Sibling violence is also widespread, as well as physical abuse of elders. Of course physical abuse can coexist with sexual abuse and rape; batterers can also be child molesters and rapists.[17]

One type of batterer physically, psychologically, and sexually abuses his wife or lover. Clinicians who work with wife batterers believe that the abusers act primarily out of an expression of the need for power and control. Feeling entitled to dominate wives or girlfriends, such men are willing to enforce their dominance with physical abuse. Highly dependent, often emotionally isolated from others, they try to control and possess their spouses: "One of the common expectations of a man who batters is that his partner must be available to him, when, where, and how he wishes her to be. When, for whatever reason, she isn't there for us to meet our needs, we act as though we will do anything to get her back."[18]

Another type of batterer physically abuses children. Sometimes he batters both wife and children, and sometimes, he batters only one or more children: "The most widely accepted incidence figures are those prepared by the National Committee for the Prevention of Child Abuse, which estimates that over 1 million children are 'seriously abused' and 2,000–5,000 deaths occur in the United States each year. In other words, it believes that 2 to 2.5 percent of the families in this country engage in physical child abuse."[19] Physical abuse of young children is the one area in which gender issues are less clear. "Gil found females to be responsible for the abuse in 51 percent of the cases and males in about 48 percent. Because children generally spend the vast majority of their time with females, however, such data may actually indicate that women are less likely to victimize children than are men."[20]

ABUSERS IN THE PROFESSIONS betray client's trust. In *Is Nothing Sacred?* Fortune reports a detailed case study of a pastor who manipulated and coerced over a dozen women in his parish into sexual relationships under the cloak of his religious office. When the women went to congregational and judicatory leaders with complaints of pastoral misconduct, the church was inept in understanding and dealing with this breach of ethics. The pastor's crimes were never made public and he was able to escape the consequences of his behavior.[21] In one of the first books on the subject of sexual misconduct by men in other professional relationships, Peter Rutter coined the term, "sex in the forbidden zone" to describe "men in power who betray women's trust."

> Almost 80 percent of the women I spoke with had an incident to recount about having been approached sexually by a man who was her doctor, therapist, pastor, lawyer, or teacher. In about half of the cases, an actual sexual relationship took place, with disastrous results. Those who did not become sexually involved reported feeling outraged, confused, or sickened by the man's erotic innuendos in ways that forever compromised a once-vital relationship. The 20 percent of women to whom this had never happened all knew two or three other women to whom it had.[22]

While this is a heuristic rather than a scientific study, it is suggestive of the growing wisdom of clinicians that sexual abuse by professional men is not unusual and that the ethical standards for such misconduct must be reexamined. The underlying pattern of abusing power in order to exploit the vulnerabilities of women is clear. Even though such behavior is not illegal in many places, it surely is unethical by Christian standards. The church needs to focus much research and other resources on this issue.

Principles for Intervention with Abusers

When the church and its leadership are willing to hear a victim's disclosure of abuse, they are then called upon to intervene on behalf of the victim. The Hebrew tradition of hospitality is one mandate for our action. The hospitality tradition called upon the community as a whole to protect the widow, the sojourner, and the orphan. These were the persons in the community who had the least resources and were most vulnerable to exploitation by others. In our communities, surely victims of sexual and domestic violence are vulnerable and in need of our assistance.

Both our Hebrew and Christian traditions place heavy emphasis on justice as the proper response to injustice and harm done to others. From the prophets to the Gospels we hear a word of judgment for those who cause harm to innocent people (e.g., Luke 17:1). That word of judgment is the basis of accountability for abusers from which may come confession and repentance and ultimately restoration to the community. The ultimate concern of our faith is genuine healing and restoration. But Jeremiah cautions against the pretense of healing: "[T]hey have healed the wound of my people lightly, saying, 'Peace, peace,' when there is no peace" (Jer. 6:14 RSV).

It is our task within the church to face the reality that some among us exploit and damage others among us and that as a faith community, in concert with the wider community, we have the resources to confront this evil with justice and bring genuine healing in its wake.

The goals of our efforts are as follows:[23]

1. Protect the vulnerable from further abuse [*hospitality*];

2. Call the abuser to accountability [*confrontation, confession, repentance*];

3. Restoration of the relationship (between victim and abuser) IF POSSIBLE [*restitution, healing*]. Often this restoration is not possible. The harm is too great, the damage too deep, the resistance of the abuser to change too formidable. IF NOT POSSIBLE, then mourn the loss of that relationship and work to restore the individuals [*comfort for the grieving*]. There is always a sense of grief, loss, and anger for the victim who was denied a genuine, healthy relationship because of the abuser's treatment of her or him.

The important thing for any pastor or lay leader to understand about these goals for intervention is that they are in chronological order. Goal 3 is the most worthy goal but it cannot be accomplished until goals one and two are complete. The successful completion of these two goals is the most effective means to helping achieve goal three.

In order to be effective in roles of pastoral care with abusers, the following principles should guide our efforts.

1. THE CHURCH'S FIRST PRIORITY MUST BE THE SAFETY OF AND PASTORAL CARE FOR VICTIMS OF ABUSE. The first priority, whenever a pastor learns about physical or sexual abuse, must be the protection of those who are most vulnerable, the victim(s). While this principle should be obvious, experience has shown that sympathy often goes first to the perpetrator, especially if he is a respected leader, because his reputation reflects on the identity of the community itself.

Those terrorized by physical or sexual violence are in danger and least able to protect themselves. Unless there is intervention, disclosure alone almost never ends the abuse, and the victim(s) continue to be in danger. Safety can be enhanced if there is no contact between perpetrator and victim in the immediate crisis. All future contact must be based on the needs of the victim, assessed with the help of trained caregivers. The victim must receive whatever medical care, crisis intervention, financial support, safe housing, and counseling necessary for creating a new context for living. Adequate care for victims is the first step in stopping abusers.

2. IN ORDER TO STOP ABUSERS, CHURCH LEADERS MUST USE WIDER COMMUNITY STRUCTURES OF ACCOUNTABILITY.[24] Clinical and legal research has shown

that abuse does not stop unless the abuser is subjected to accountability and consequences. Since many forms of abuse are illegal, effective accountability usually requires legal action. The moral authority of the pastor alone is useful but often insufficient to stop the patterns of abusers. In confronting an abuser privately and accepting reassurances from him/her that things will change, a pastor only enables the abuser to hide his/her actions better and to further threaten his/her victims. As a result there is no accountability in his/her community. In fact, rather than effecting any real change, the pastor may have inadvertently warned the abuser to lie low until the crisis blows over. Referral for counseling alone is likewise ineffective because there is no motivation for the abuser to tell the truth to the counselor about what has happened.[25]

In spite of the best intentions expressed by an abuser ("I'll never do it again. . . . I've found the Lord. . . . I'll go to counseling if she'll come back to me. . . ."), it is virtually impossible for true repentance to take place, i.e., a fundamental change of self, without expert help and a structure of accountability. If we carry a genuine concern for the well-being of the abuser, our best pastoral intervention is seeing that he/she is held accountable in a community or church structure with the power to enforce participation.

This often means that the pastor to whom a disclosure of abuse is revealed, either by a victim or through the confession of an abuser, should *assist* in reporting this allegation to the appropriate legal and/or church authorities for further investigation and possible action. *If the report involves the abuse of a child, the pastor should report on behalf of that child immediately to his or her state child protection service.* Some states legally require ministers to report child abuse while others do not. Regardless of the law's requirement, our pastoral mandate to protect the vulnerable from further harm requires that we act immediately to bring to bear all possible resources to assist that child.[26] Some states also provide for reporting abuse of the elderly and of persons with developmental disabilities. These persons are also extremely vulnerable to abuse and need our assistance.

In the case of an *adult* victim or survivor who chooses to report an abuser to either secular or church authorities, our pastoral task is to assist that person with support and information. In other words, it is finally the choice of that adult whether to report or confront their abuser, and they should decide the terms of their action.

Making such reports is often difficult for pastors or church leaders, especially if they know the persons involved. Often there is a wish to provide pastoral care and referral for counseling before taking what seems like such drastic action. However, this only increases the danger for victims and may even block the perpetrator from the help he needs to stop his destructive behaviors. What may seem to be harsh measures are actually the most appropriate and helpful forms of pastoral care for all involved.

3. CHURCH LEADERS MUST BE ABLE TO COMBAT THE SECRECY AND DECEPTION THAT ABUSERS USE TO HIDE THEIR CRIMES. When confronted, abusers will minimize, lie or deny responsibility for their actions. All abusers depend on deceiving others about the nature of their behaviors. Child molesters threaten and

manipulate their victims into silence. Batterers batter in the privacy of their homes while a "normal" facade is presented to the public. Rapists choose dark and private times and places to avoid confrontation. Abusive professionals use the privacy of counseling and other confidential settings to hide their exploitative behaviors.

Abusers often rely on the naïveté of Christians who believe that they would not lie to protect themselves from the consequences of their behaviors. Church leaders who would confront abusers must be alert to this web of lies even by those who hold positions of trust within the community. When scandals emerge, Christians sometimes find it hard to face their own gullibility and complicity.

4. THE CHURCH MUST NOT ALLOW A MISUSE OF CONFIDENTIALITY TO PREVENT IT FROM ACTING TO INTERVENE IN SITUATIONS OF ABUSE.[27] The purpose of confidentiality in the religious setting is to provide a safe place for persons to understand their suffering without the voyeuristic glare of the community's judgment. Because people are fragile and need confidence in their healing relationships, trust must remain a cornerstone of all religious and secular counseling. But counselors experienced in working with abusers agree that the rules of confidentiality must not jeopardize those who are least able to protect themselves. Confidentiality is too often equated with secrecy, i.e., pastors incorrectly believe that keeping a confidence means keeping a secret. Secrecy is the key to a pattern of abuse; the abuse thrives on secrecy and the only way to assist the abuser and the victim is to break the silence which sustains the secret. Confidentiality means that one does not share information received in confidence without legitimate reason, e.g., to seek consultation or to report suspected abuse. In seeking consultation from another professional, it is not necessary to disclose persons' names in order to get help on how to deal with them. In reporting child abuse, it is necessary to disclose the names of persons involved.

Some denominations retain the privilege of the seal of the confessional for their clergy. The primacy of this seal can be respected and the pastor can still intervene. If a penitent confesses under the seal to abuse, the pastor can direct the penitent to report him or herself to the authorities. If the abuser refuses, there is nothing the pastor can do to help the abuser but he or she can continue to assist the victim.

Rarely does the disclosure of an abusive situation occur in the formal confessional setting. It is more likely to come in counseling or conversation and most often with the victim rather than the abuser who is not usually very forthcoming. This information then is not subject to a confessional seal and hence this pastor is free to report. The right of children and women to protection from physical and sexual violence overrides the value of secrecy. In fact, inserting accountability for destructive behaviors into a counseling relationship is often the most healing intervention a counselor can make with a perpetrator.

5. IN ORDER TO STOP ABUSERS CHURCH LEADERS MUST WORK COOPERATIVELY WITH OTHER PROFESSIONALS. It should be obvious by this point that most pastors and church leaders are not qualified to confront and stop abusers by themselves. Rather, the stubbornness and severity of this problem require the

concerted effort of many community agencies and authorities. Pastors need to know the resources in their local communities and must be willing to cooperate with them in appropriate ways. Every community has a network of social workers, psychologists, and legal agencies which specialize in intervention, counseling and prevention in situations of abuse. Rape counseling centers can provide information and advocacy for rape victims. Battered women's shelters have expertise in providing safe havens for women and children in danger. Child protection agencies and family courts have authority to protect children by intervening in families. Finally, the police and criminal courts can bring misdemeanor and felony charges for some forms of abuse. One of the marks of adequately trained professionals, including pastors, is their willingness to call upon or cooperate with the specialized resources needed to protect those who are vulnerable to abuse and stop those who are responsible.

The church sometimes has the mistaken notion that Christian faith and community alone are adequate for all human problems. While problems of abuse have a spiritual and religious dimension, an adequate response to this manifestation of evil requires cooperation in the wider community.

6. CHURCHES MUST INSTITUTE EFFECTIVE STRUCTURES OF ACCOUNTABILITY AND CONSEQUENCES FOR LEADERS WHO ABUSE THEIR POWER.[28] The church has a long, sad history of covering up the sins of men in powerful positions who abuse women and children. Pastors who are perpetrators have quietly moved to other congregations where no one has been warned of the danger. Clergy who have abused wives and children have been supported for the sake of family unity while their victims have been deprived of truth and resources for healing. Regional and national religious leaders have been excused for their violations of others while their victims disappeared from public view.

Churches need to reassess their own policies and procedures for identifying and dealing with abuse among their leaders. Persons with specialized training should be authorized to conduct timely investigations when complaints are filed against clergy. Procedures must be fair not only to those who are charged but also to victims whose lives have already been damaged. Consequences must be severe enough that abusers will be held accountable and stop their destructive behaviors.

A note to ministerial professionals reading this: If you have been or are tempted to use your professional position for sexual contact with a parishioner or client, you should immediately seek help. Though you may not see the word *abuser* applying to your behavior, you must accept the truth that you are not the best judge. There are men and women in every community who are trained to help you evaluate the extent of your problem and begin a program of change and restitution. It is possible to change if you are willing to face yourself honestly and seek help.

Conclusion

This chapter suggests the need for a courageous and assertive response on the part of the church to abusers in its midst. In the face of the massive personal and social suffering of victims of sexual and domestic violence and in the face of a history of silence on the part of the church, this response is long overdue. Large numbers of children who have been sexually and physically abused carry life-long consequences because of their trauma. Large numbers of women and some men have experienced some form of sexual or physical violation. As these victims come forward, their stories lead us to reassess our understanding of ourselves as Christian communities.

The six principles outlined above should guide the church in its response to the problem of abuse. The church must respond more aggressively to the danger facing women and children by providing victims with safety and needed resources for healing. It must call for better societal structures of accountability and consequences for abusers, inform itself on the role of secrecy and deception in abuse, reevaluate its practice of confidentiality, cooperate with other professionals and agencies, and institute internal structures of accountability for leaders of its own community. In sum, the church must be much better informed about the dangers of abuse and much more assertive in establishing its vision of justice and mercy for all persons.

※

Notes

1. The following books deal with intervention and treatment issues for victims of abuse: Marie Fortune, *Sexual Violence* (New York: Pilgrim, 1982); Mary Pellauer et al., eds., *Sexual Assault and Abuse: A Handbook for Clergy and Religious Professionals* (San Francisco: Harper & Row, 1987); Suzanne Sgroi, ed., *Handbook of Clinical Intervention in Child Sexual Abuse* (Lexington, Mass.: Lexington Books, 1982); Ellen Bass and Laura Davis, *The Courage to Heal* (New York: Harper & Row, 1988); Linda Ledray, *Recovering from Rape* (New York: Henry Holt, 1986); P. Lynn Caesar and L. Kevin Hamburger, eds., *Treating Men Who Batter: Theory, Practice, and Programs* (New York: Springer, 1989).

2. Anne L. Ganley, "Integrating Feminist and Social Learning Analyses of Aggression," in Caesar and Hamburger, *Treating Men Who Batter: Theory, Practice, and Programs*. Ganley uses this descriptive paradigm to discuss spouse abuse only. We are applying it more broadly here.

3. *Seattle Times*, September 1, 1982.

4. For discussion of religious issues of abuse, see James Poling, *Abuse of Power: A Theological Problem* (Nashville: Abingdon, 1991).

5. Mary Lystad, ed., *Violence in the Home*. (New York: Brunner/Mazel, 1986), 55; Richard Gelles and Murray Straus, *Intimate Violence* (New York: Simon and Schuster, 1988), 90.

6. Diana Russell, *The Secret Trauma* (New York: Basic Books, 1986), 70.

7. David Finkelhor, *Child Sexual Abuse* (New York: Free Press, 1984), 150.

8. Nicholas Groth, *Men Who Rape* (New York: Plenum, 1979), 4.

9. Ibid., 3.

10. Diana Russell, *Rape in Marriage* (New York: Macmillan, 1982), 64.

11. Nicholas Groth, *Men Who Rape*, 13.

12. Ibid., 25.

13. Ibid., 44.

14. Gelles and Straus, *Intimate Violence*, 104.

15. Dick Bathrick, Kathleen Carlin, Gus Kaufman, Rich Vodde, *Men Stopping Violence: A Program for Change*. Men Stopping Violence. 1020 DeKalb Ave, Atlanta, GA 30307; 1.

16. Lystad, *Violence in the Home*, 56.

17. Ibid., 57.

18. *Men Stopping Violence*, 32.

19. Dante Cicchetti and Vicki Carlson, eds., *Child Maltreatment: Theory and Research on the Causes and Consequences of Child Abuse and Neglect* (Cambridge: Cambridge University Press, 1989), 48.

20. Ibid., 52.

21. Marie Fortune, *Is Nothing Sacred? When Sex Invades the Pastoral Relationship* (San Francisco: Harper & Row, 1989).

22. Peter Rutter, *Sex in the Forbidden Zone: When Men in Power—Therapists, Doctors, Clergy, Teachers and Others—Betray Women's Trust* (Los Angeles: Jeremy Tarcher, 1989), 11–12.

23. Marie M. Fortune, *Violence in Families: A Workshop Curriculum For Clergy and Other Helpers* (Cleveland: Pilgrim Press, 1991).

24. Bathrick, et al. *Men Stopping Violence*; Sgroi, *Handbook for Clinical Intervention in Child Sexual Abuse*; Groth, *Men Who Rape*; George Barnard, et al., ed., *The Child Molester: An Integrated Approach to Evaluation and Treatment* (New York: Brunner/Mazel, 1989).

25. Paul and Peter Isely, "The Sexual Abuse of Male Children by Church Personnel: Intervention and Prevention." *Pastoral Psychology* 39/2 (November 1990): 96.

26. See Marie M. Fortune, "Reporting Child Abuse: An Ethical Mandate for Ministry" in *Abuse and Religion*, ed. Anne L. Horton and Judith A. Williamson (Lexington, Mass.: Lexington Books, 1988).

27. Fortune, "Reporting Child Abuse"; Ronald Bullis, "When Confessional Walls Have Ears: The Changing Clergy Privileged Communications Law," *Pastoral Psychology* 39/2 (November 1990): 75–84; Ronald Bullis, "Child Abuse Reporting Requirements: Liabilities and Immunities for Clergy," *Journal of Pastoral Care* XLIV/3 (Fall, 1990): 244–49.

28. See Marie M. Fortune, *Is Nothing Sacred?* especially the appendix: "Sexual Misconduct by Clergy Within Pastoral Relationships," 135–53.

The Whole Loaf:
Holy Communion and Survival

MARJORIE PROCTER-SMITH

In Robin Morgan's poem, "The Two Gretels," Hansel stays at home while two Gretels explore the forest. They become afraid, sometimes one, sometimes the other suggesting that they turn back. But turning back is impossible: they forgot the breadcrumbs, and turning back in any case becomes unimaginable. So they go forward until they find the Gingerbread House, and the Witch (who is really the "Great Good Mother Goddess"). "The Moral of the story is," Morgan concludes:

> Those who would have the whole loaf,
> let alone the House,
> had better throw away their breadcrumbs.[1]

The "two Gretels" of Robin Morgan's poem are familiar: Have we gone far enough? Have we gone too far? Should we turn back? For those who struggle to remain within their faith tradition, particularly within the "House" of the church, while confronting the church's complicity in the violence suffered by women and children, these voices are eerily familiar. Fearful for our own safety, not wanting to get lost in the forest, we often settle for the crumbs, when what we truly need, for our deepest hunger, is the "whole loaf." The voices of the two Gretels argue in our own heads.

We who are Christians, who have been formed by Christian rhetoric about humility and suffering, have few spiritual resources which enable us to claim the whole loaf of survival and well-being, particularly if we are women.

Even one of the most daring women in the Gospel narratives is unable to ask for the whole loaf, but is forced to couch her claim in terms of fragments and leftovers. In Mark 7, a woman begs Jesus for healing for her daughter. Jesus responds negatively, denying her right, as a foreign woman, to his healing: "It is not fair to take the children's bread and throw it to the dogs." But the woman refuses to take no for an answer, and retorts, "Even the dogs under the table eat the children's crumbs." Jesus accepts her rejoinder: "For this saying you may go your way; the demon has left your daughter."[2] She asked for crumbs; she was given a loaf. But where is the model for Christians who need to ask for the whole loaf, for themselves and for their children? We need spiritual resources which empower us to ask for the whole loaf; we need a serious rethinking of our theology and practice of celebrating the Christian meal so that it both nourishes and empowers.

Contemporary Christian women and men who struggle with the church's complicity in violence against women and children frequently look to the church's central ritual of meaning, the Lord's Supper, or Holy Communion, for nourishment and strength for the struggle. But they often feel that they are given only crumbs. Why do so many people concerned with these issues find the communion meal so painful, so lacking in nourishment?

Identifying the Problems

The lack of spiritual nourishment in the communion meal for survivors of violence stems from three problems in current liturgical practice and theology: issues of authority, issues of sin and guilt, and issues of sacrifice. Each of these problems presents itself in many forms, and not all forms are present in all traditions of the communion meal. But in Christian traditions which celebrate the communion meal, all three problems are present in some way, and the churches are challenged to confront these ways in which they offer people not bread, but stone; not nourishment and strength, but pain and want.

Authority

Who gets to decides who receives the loaf, and how much each one receives? Who decides what we need? Traditional Christian rituals express power and authority in two modes: male authority and parental authority. Both of these expressions of authority have consequences for the participation of survivors of violence.

Historically, the clericalization of Christian ritual accompanied the masculinization of Christian leadership offices. Whereas in the earliest centuries of the Christian movement women held positions of leadership and authority, as the church became more institutionalized and adapted to the culture, structures of leadership became more rigid, more hierarchical, and limited to men. In this, the church did not differ significantly from the authority structures of the ancient world, in which social, political, and familial authority resided in men. The legacy of this history in Christian worship is the association of male power and authority with religious power and authority. The minister or priest represents (in some way) God, and speaks and acts with the authority and power of God, who is unvaryingly referred to as a male. The result is a ritual system which values men's bodies, men's wills, men's initiative, men's bonds with one another, remembers men's history, and legitimates men's power. Christian ritual is thus a male-defined and male-centered event. The voice of God is a male voice. Thus, as I argued in "'Reorganizing Victimization,'" male power and authority are mystified; rather than being seen for what it is, human male power is confused with divine, ultimate power and authority.

This ritual male dominance is often particularly apparent in the celebration of Holy Communion. In some mainline Christian churches women serve in some leadership roles (such as reading Scripture, leading prayer or music, and so on), but the power to preside at the communion table is the primary role which is restricted to ordained men. Even in denominations that ordain women, in practice one is most likely to see a man presiding at the table, since male clergy still outnumber women clergy, and women clergy are often relegated to associate or assistant roles. This male dominance is particularly valued and powerful in traditions which place the greatest emphasis on the importance of the rite of holy communion, such as the Roman Catholic, Anglican, and Lutheran. In these traditions, the presence of a woman presider at the table is controversial if not absolutely forbidden.

This identification of male power in ritual authority is buttressed by the preference in Christian liturgy for explicitly male referents to God, especially by titles of authority, such as Father, Lord, King, and Master. Thus the one presiding at the table is understood to be a representative (at least) of divine and absolute male power and authority. The meal becomes a reiteration and affirmation of male authority, both divine and human.

In every congregation are worshippers who are survivors of violence and abuse. Statistically, their abusers are most likely to be men in positions of authority over them: husbands, fathers, relatives, counselors, doctors, teachers, and ministers. The enacting of male authority and power at the communion table becomes for these survivors not only reiteration and affirmation of male authority, but also a reiteration and affirmation of their expected submission to that authority. Rather than a celebrative and nourishing meal, it becomes a painful reminder of powerlessness.

Related to the ritual enactment of male power and authority at the table is the enactment of parental authority. This form of authority is most often expressed in male terms: God is "Father"; the minister may also be called "Father." But even when such explicitly parental titles are not used of the clergy (as in most mainline Protestant churches), the clergy are most often still understood to stand in a parental relationship to parishoners. This mystification of parental authority reinforces the suffering of the child who is abused by a parent or parent figure. The minister's presidency at a meal further reinforces this familial image of the minister.

Related to all this, of course, is the absence of references to divine authority either as female or as child, the most likely persons to be subjected to intimate violence. Likewise, in most Christian traditions, women are rarely seen in positions of authority at the communion table (except in subsidiary roles, reinforcing rather than challenging traditional household roles) and children never. Women continue to make the bread, but eat last, if at all.

Sin and Guilt

What must one do to receive the loaf? Issues of male and/or parental authority and power are intensified by the association in most Christian traditions of the reception of communion with notions of individual worthiness. Logically, one might reasonably expect that requirements that participants in the holy meal be worthy would be enforced most clearly on offenders. However, the way in

which the church has defined sin and forgiveness work against the victim
rather than the offender, in four different but interlocking ways.

In most Christian communities reception of communion is preceded by
prayers or rituals of confession and forgiveness. In Protestant churches, this
most often takes the form of a brief congregational prayer of confession followed by a declaration of or prayer for forgiveness. In Roman Catholic communities, opportunity is offered for confession to a priest before the Mass.

The earliest accounts of Christian eucharistic rituals do not include congregational prayers of confession, but they do insist that all participants be
baptized for forgiveness of sins. The original form of prayers of confession
were not congregational but priestly prayers, intended to prepare the priest
for the appropriate handling of holy (and thus possibly dangerous) things. As
the eucharistic liturgy became increasingly clericalized, these priests' prayers
for forgiveness and purity, originally prayed by the clergy before the service,
became part of the public prayer. A medieval theological emphasis on human
sinfulness, picked up and elaborated on by the reformers, fed the development of prayers of confession as prerequisites to reception of communion.

The connection is by now so firmly made that many Protestants particularly associate the communion ritual with a penitential rite, in which they
confess their sins and receive forgiveness in the form of communion. But how
are sin and forgiveness presented in these prayers and rituals?

1. AGAINST WHOM IS SIN AN OFFENSE? The focus of all of the prayers and
rituals of confession is on offenses against God, and only secondarily, if at all,
on offenses against people.

> Merciful God,
> we confess that we have sinned *against you*
> in thought, word, and deed,
> by what we have done,
> and by what we have left undone. . . .
> —*Book of Common Prayer*, Episcopal Church, 360

> Holy and merciful God,
> in your presence we confess
> our sinfulness, our shortcomings,
> and our *offenses against you*. . . .
> —*Book of Common Worship*,
> Presbyterian Church [USA], 53

> My God,
> I am sorry for my sins with all my heart.
> In choosing to do wrong
> and failing to do good,
> *I have sinned against you*
> whom I should love above all things. . . .

> —*The Rites of the Catholic Church as Revised
> by the Second Vatican Ecumenical Council*, 382

Although most of these and other prayers of confession go on to name sins against the neighbor as an example of our sinfulness, nowhere in any of these rites of confession and forgiveness is any suggestion that acts of confession and reparation are due to anyone but God. Sins against other people are defined as sins against God, but only God is the subject of the act of repentance and confession. Batterers and rapists are not likely to see their sins against women named here. But even if they do see their violent or abusive behavior as sin (which they are not likely to do unless it has been defined that way by the church) no demands about asking the victim for forgiveness or for making reparations are placed on them. On the contrary, these prayers of confession are normally followed immediately in the liturgy by declarations of pardon which emphasize not God's demands for justice but God's mercy and readiness to forgive.

> The mercy of the Lord is from everlasting.
> I declare to you, in the name of Jesus Christ,
> you are forgiven.
> May the God of mercy,
> who forgives you all your sins,
> strengthen you in all goodness,
> and by the power of the Holy Spirit
> keep you in eternal life.
> —*Book of Common Worship*, Presbyterian
> Church U.S.A., 56

> God hears the confession
> of our hearts and lips.
> Through Jesus Christ
> we are forgiven all our sins,
> and by the power of the Holy Spirit
> we are empowered for new life.
> —*Book of Worship*, United Church of Christ, 38

> Almighty God, in his mercy,
> has given his Son to die for us and,
> for his sake, forgives us all our sins.
> As a called and ordained minister of the Church of Christ,
> and by his authority,
> I therefore declare to you the entire forgiveness
> of all your sins, in the name of the Father, and of the Son,
> and of the Holy Spirit.
> —*Lutheran Book of Worship*, 195

2. WHO IS THE FORGIVER, AND WHO RECEIVES FORGIVENESS? The divine model of God's unconditional forgiveness is often presented as a model for humans to emulate: "Bear with one another and, if anyone has a complaint against another, forgive each other; just as the Lord has forgiven you, so you must forgive" (Col. 3:13, NRSV). This imperative of forgiveness, based on the premise

that we have already been forgiven, contrasts with the understanding of forgiveness expressed in the Lord's Prayer: "forgive us our sins as we forgive those who sin against us," where our being forgiven is predicated on our having forgiven others. However, demanding forgiveness from the victim before confession and justice has been done by the offender is harmful. Marie Fortune suggests that "an act of forgiveness by a victim cannot be hurried; nor can it be orchestrated by those on the outside."[3] Nor can such forgiveness be coerced by liturgical text.

By defining sin as primarily an offense against God, and by offering forgiveness immediately following the confession, the message is given that even if violence and abuse of women and children are understood as sin, God will readily forgive. And if God will so readily forgive, the victim should also be willing to forgive. Some contemporary service books indicate that God has forgiven the sin even before the sinner has confessed it, let alone changed their behavior or made restitution to the victim.

> Hear the good news:
> Christ died for us while we were yet sinners;
> that proves God's love toward us.
> —*United Methodist Hymnal*, 8

Moreover, traditional Christian theology has not made a distinction between one who commits sin and one who is the victim of sin. It has instead insisted that "all have sinned" and assumes that all human beings are equally sinful and equally culpable. Andrew Sung Park has critiqued this leveling of sin, arguing that the church has failed to distinguish appropriately the difference between the pain of the sinner and the pain of the victim of sin:

> The victims of various types of wrongdoing express the ineffable experience of deep bitterness and helplessness. Such an experience of pain is called *han* in the Far East. *Han* can be defined as the critical wound of the heart generated by unjust psychosomatic repression, as well as by social, political, economic, and cultural oppression. It is entrenched in the hearts of the victims of sin and violence, and is expressed through such diverse reactions as sadness, helplessness, hopelessness, resentment, hatred, and the will to revenge.[4]

3. HOW IS SIN DEFINED OR EXEMPLIFIED? Another problem with the association between sin and reception of communion is the way in which sin is defined in prayers of confession.

> Merciful God,
> we confess that we have not loved you with our whole heart.
> We have failed to be an obedient church.
> We have not done your will,
> we have broken your law,
> we have rebelled against your love,
> we have not loved our neighbors,
> and we have not heard the cry of the needy.

> Forgive us, we pray.
> Free us for joyful obedience,
> through Jesus Christ our Lord.
> —*United Methodist Hymnal,* 8[5]

This prayer in particular, from the United Methodist Sunday service, defines sin primarily in terms of disobedience, and freedom from sin is defined in terms of obedience. For the woman battered by her husband, for the child abused by an adult, obedience does not equal freedom, but rather suffering, terror, and possible death. Because women who are battered or raped and children who are abused commonly blame themselves for their suffering, the presuppositions of this prayer are particularly dangerous. With disobedience defined as a sin (or as THE sin), sufferers have no spiritual resources for rejecting the abuse being inflicted on them by persons to whom, according to some readings of the Bible, they are to be obedient. The rebellion against their abuse, their refusal to accept victimization, and their willingness to claim well-being for themselves, which are the very things they must do in order to survive, these things are defined as sin in this prayer of confession.

4. WHAT ARE THE CONSEQUENCES OF SIN? Prayers of confession typically focus on the consequences of sin for the sinner, particularly in that sin separates the sinner from God in some way.

> Have mercy on us, O Lord,
> for we are ashamed and sorry
> for all we have done to displease you. . . .
> —*Book of Common Worship,* 54

> Almighty God, merciful Father,
> I, as a troubled and penitent sinner, confess to you
> all my sins and iniquities with which I have offended you
> and for which I justly deserve your punishment. . . .
> —*Lutheran Book of Worship,* 319

The prayers tend to emphasize the suffering and burden of sin for the sinner (and the threat of punishment by God). What these texts do not mention are the consequences of sin for the victims. Christine Gudorf argues that:

> Preferential option for the poor cannot be effectively taught—which means that the gospel cannot be effectively taught—unless we teach the consequences of sin for victims as an integral part of the meaning of sin. For too long the churches have taught the consequences of sin for the sinner only, and emphasized that damnation can always be avoided by repentance since God's love is gratuitous and merciful, bestowed upon all willing to accept it.[6]

Even if prayers of confession before communion included condemnations of violence against women and children, as long as these were presented only as sins against God, and as long as the terrible long-term consequences of such violence and abuse were neither acknowledged nor repaired in some way by the sinner, then the confession and declaration of pardon would still remain empty and unfulfilled.

For survivors of sexual or domestic violence, prayers of confession before communion also evoke anxiety about their unworthiness. A text from I Corinthinans is often cited in connection with communion, since it follows immediately on Paul's account of the institution of the Lord's Supper:

> Whoever, therefore, eats the bread or drinks the cup of the Lord in an unworthy manner will be answerable for the body and blood of the Lord. Examine yourselves, and only then eat of the bread and drink of the cup. For all who eat and drink without discerning the body, eat and drink judgement against themselves. For this reason, many of you are weak and ill, and some have died.
>
> —1 Cor. 11:27–30

Those who have suffered sexual, physical, or emotional abuse frequently blame themselves for their victimization, feel unclean or damaged, often keep the story of their suffering to themselves out of misplaced shame and guilt. This text encourages them to see their pain and suffering, and even their deaths, as signs of their unworthiness. The ritual of confession before communion thus serves not only to confirm survivors' self-image as unworthy and their suffering as just, but also to deny them access to a potentially nurturing and possibily liberating ritual.

Sacrifice

What does the loaf signifiy? What does it mean to be nourished from the one loaf? Sacrifice is related to the Christian eucharist in multiple forms, and has a complex history within Christian thought. The New Testament writers, on the whole, interpreted Jesus' tragic and unexpected execution for sedition in sacrificial terms, largely drawn from Jewish understandings of the meaning of sacrifice. In the chronology of John's gospel, the death of Jesus on the cross takes place at the same time that the Passover lamb is sacrificed in the Jewish temple. Liturgical texts reiterate this association by connecting First Testament texts about sacrifice with the ritual commemoration of the passion of Jesus. For example, the following text from Isaiah is read at the Good Friday service in all mainline denominations:

> He was oppressed, and he was afflicted, yet he opened not his mouth; like a lamb that is led to the slaughter, and like a sheep that before its shearers is silent, so he did not open his mouth.
>
> —Isa. 53:7

A recommended hymn at the beginning of the communion service in the *Lutheran Book of Worship* also refers to Christ as the sacrificial lamb, the text taken from the book of Revelation:

> Alleluia. This is the feast of victory for our God.
> Alleluia. Worthy is Christ, the Lamb who was slain, whose blood set us free to be people of God. . . .

The Lamb who was slain has begun his reign.
Alleluia.
—*Lutheran Book of Worship*, 273

This image of Jesus as the submissive, innocent victim, led lamblike to his own suffering and death, pervades the communion service in such overt ways as well as more subtle ones. The mainline denominations recommend prayer texts to be used at the celebration of communion which express this idea of innocent suffering as salvific.

> Obeying you, he took up his cross and died that we might live.
> We praise you that he overcame death and is risen to rule the world.
> —*Book of Common Worship*,
> Great Thanksgiving C, 131

> Through your prophets
> you renewed your promise;
> and, at this end of all the ages,
> you sent your Son,
> who in word and deeds
> proclaimed your kingdom
> and was obedient to your will,
> even to giving his life.
> —*Lutheran Book of Worship*, 221

> In the fullness of time
> you came to us
> and received our nature
> in the person of Jesus,
> who, in obedience to you,
> by suffering on the cross,
> and being raised from the dead,
> delivered us from the way of sin and death.
> —*Book of Worship*, United Church of Christ, 46

> By the baptism of his suffering, death and resurrection,
> you gave birth to your church,
> delivered us from slavery to sin and death,
> and made with us a new covenant
> by water and the Spirit.
>
> —*United Methodist Hymnal*, 9

> He stretched out his arms upon the cross,
> and offered himself, in obedience to your will,
> a perfect sacrifice for the whole world.
> —*Book of Common Prayer*,
> Eucharistic Prayer A, 363

Father, calling to mind the death your son endured for our salvation,
his glorious resurrection and ascension into heaven,
and ready to meet him when he comes again,
we offer you in thanksgiving this holy and living sacrifice.
Look with favor on the church's offering,
and see the Victim whose death has reconciled us to yourself.

—The Sacramentary, 515

It is the redemptive interpretation of Jesus' suffering which is most problematic about these prayers. The use of the phrase, "On the night before he gave himself up for us . . . ," found in the United Methodist rite, ties together the ideas that Jesus was a willing sacrifice, and that his suffering and death somehow benefit us. The sacrifical language used here and elsewhere suggests the mechanism of surrogacy, namely, that one person can suffer and die in the place of someone else. Such notions are commonly used by those who are being battered or abused to explain their inability to remove themselves from the violent situation.

Since Jesus is also held up as the primary model for Christian behavior, this interpretation of Jesus' death as a redemptive sacrifice is deeply problematic for survivors of violence, whose own suffering and death saves no one. Joanne Carlson Brown and Rebecca Parker identify this interpretation of Jesus' suffering and death as a primary source of the general acceptance of violence against women and children in Christian communities:

> Christianity is an abusive theology that glorifies suffering. Is it any wonder that there is so much abuse in modern society when the predominant image or theology of the culture is of "divine child abuse"—God the Father demanding and carrying out the suffering and death of his own son?[7]

Certainly the glorification of suffering in Christian thought and practice contributes to the difficulty of those who need to claim their own right and need to live without suffering inflicted on them by another. As Christine Gudorf notes, "It is certainly dangerous—and also cruel—to assume that suffering inevitably leads to real life, to joy, to meaning, to wholeness. For suffering destroys. It kills, it maims the body and the spirit, it produces despair and evil."[8]

Such a realistic interpretation of suffering is entirely absent from the communion prayers and piety of Christian churches. Instead, the texts quoted above suggest that life and salvation (the literal meaning of which is "health") come as a result of suffering and death. This theologizing of suffering is also expressed in the common visual symbols associated with communion, especially the crucifix with the bloody body of Jesus suspended from a cross, or even more so in the so-called "glorified cross" showing a regal, fully clothed and crowned Jesus rising above the cross.

The use of body and blood language and imagery intensifies the connection between human suffering and divine redemption. At the ritual action of breaking the bread and pouring the wine, the United Church of Christ *Book of Worship* offers the following explanation:

The bread is broken and the wine is poured as visible and audible reminders of the sacrificial self-giving of Jesus Christ. These actions call to mind the cost as well as the joy of Christian discipleship.[9]

Elsewhere the liturgical texts themselves make this connection between bodily suffering and redemption:

> Grant that we, who are nourished by his body and blood,
> may be filled with the Holy Spirit,
> and become one body, one spirit in Christ.
> —*The Sacramentary*, 515

> Eat this, for it is the body of Christ, broken for you.
> Drink this, for it is the blood of Christ, shed for you.
> —United Church of Christ *Book of Worship*, 73–74

> Almighty God, you gave your Son both as a sacrifice for sin and a model
> of the godly life. Enable us to receive him always with thanksgiving, and
> to conform our lives to his.
> —*Lutheran Book of Worship*, 229

The loaf thus interpreted becomes not a source of nourishment and pleasure, but an eating and drinking of suffering and death. The eating of broken bodies, and the drinking of spilled blood appears to spiritualize and justify the real life broken bodies and spilled blood of women and children.

Suggestions for Change

Like the two Gretels in Robin Morgan's poem, once we set our feet on the path of seeking well-being and justice for women in the church, we can no longer settle for the crumbs. We seek the whole loaf. Going beyond the challenge of the Syrophonecian woman in Mark's story, we speak out boldly for ourselves and women and children who are struggling for survival and dignity, both physically and spiritually. The liturgical changes we ask for are not minor, not crumbs that fall from the patriarchal table. Rather we ask for the whole loaf of a transformation of eucharistic piety and practice.

1. MAKE CONFESSION APPROPRIATE AND MEANINGFUL. Current communion liturgies include explicit and implicit references to human sinfulness, without distinguishing between the sinner and the victim of sin. Instead, they focus exclusively on the sinner, and when used by victims of sin, they contribute to the general tendency of church and culture to blame the victims. Prayers of confession which name sin as disobedience or pride, which assure forgiveness before confession and restitution, or which ignore the human consequences of sin are inadequate. In their place churches need to offer ritual processes for calling batterers and abusers to repentance, holding them accountable for their behavior, insisting on confession to those harmed by their behavior, overseeing the

necessary restitution, and only then offering rites of reconciliation. While many pastors assume that these steps are best done in the form of pastoral counseling, most pastors are in fact not trained to counsel men who batter, rape, or sexually abuse. Professional counseling by those who are so trained, however, can and should be supported by the church's ritual life. Those who work with violent men report that these men are most likely to change when they are confronted and challenged by many different authority figures. The church must not hesitate to use its authority in order to confront and challenge the violent man. A serious process of repentance and reconciliation might include denial of access to communion for the offender until the process of reconciliation is completed to the satisfaction of the church community and the offender's victims, as well as rituals marking stages in the violent man's life changes.

Pastors and church members must be informed, however, about the dynamics of the process of recovery for a batterer or abuser, lest they attempt to short-circuit the process by moving to the process of reconciliation before repentance, confession, and restitution have taken place. A model for this ritual process is suggested in the work of Andrew Sung Park on the Asian concept of *han*, the relational consequences of sin. He notes:

> It is my view that the guilt of the oppressor is not a matter to be resolved though the unilateral proclamation of forgiveness and absolution by a priest or pastor, without regard to their victims. Forgiveness must take place in cooperation with victims and must involve offenders' participation in the dissolution of their victim's *han*-ridden shame. The one-sided forgiveness proclaimed by any authority is not forgiveness, but false comfort.[10]

Lest the church and its representatives be guilty of offering false comfort, it must develop adequate ritual responses to the man who batters or abuses, and to his victims. As Park observes, "Forgiveness is not a mechanical process resulting from an offender's repentance, but a dynamic relational fruit yielded through the work of grace."[11]

On the other hand, the church must provide ritual opportunities for healing of the injury done to the victims. Healing rituals may be appropriate in this context, although published healing services and rituals sometimes imply that the person's suffering is due either to sin or to lack of faith. For example, the United Church of Christ *Book of Worship* service of healing includes a confession of sin and a reaffirmation of faith in Jesus Christ as possible elements.

More appropriate would be rituals and prayers which name the cause of the harm, allow the survivor to express anger and grief over the harm done to themselves and to others, claim their right to live free from fear, and receive the love and support of the Christian community. Many healing rituals allow for laying on of hands or anointing the head or body with oil. Such actions should be reviewed with the survivor before using them, since some survivors may find any physical contact painful or frightening. A non-traditional service of holy communion might be included in the service.

2. RECOVER A LIBERATIVE AND JOYFUL EMPHASIS IN THE COMMUNION SERVICE IN PLACE OF A PENITENTIAL OR SORROWFUL APPROACH. Newer liturgies of

communion attempt to make this shift, although the perception of worshippers who grew up with the penitential rites may be unchanged. Even where newer prayers and rituals have moved away from excessive emphasis on the suffering and death of Jesus, and of the sacrificial nature of his death, and the salvific benefits of his suffering, they still tend to draw to some extent on the older tradition, as the texts cited above indicate. As long as body and blood language is used, the pain and suffering of survivors is increased. As Elisabeth Schüssler Fiorenza observes, "How can we point to the eucharistic bread and say, 'This is my body,' as long as women's bodies are battered, raped, sterilized, mutilated, prostituted, and used to male ends?"[12] There are alternative interpretations of the bread and wine available from scripture. There is a need for communion prayers and rituals which draw from, for example, the miraculous feeding stories (Matt. 14:13–20 and parallels), or the stories of Jesus' meals with outcasts (Matt. 9:10–13 and parallels). There is a need for communion prayers which offer the communion meal as a model of the great messianic feast (Matt. 22:1–13, Luke 14:16–24), where people will come from all directions to feast in joy and peace. The communion food need not be identified with suffering, sacrifice and death, but with life, joy, abundance, and community.

3. REPLACE SACRIFICIAL LANGUAGE WITH LANGUAGE OF STRUGGLE AND LIBERATION. Present prayers and rituals of communion assume that God approves of undeserved suffering endured without protest. As Elisabeth Schüssler Fiorenza points out, "Such admonitions are not isolated aberrations, but go to the heart of Christian faith: trust in God the Father, and belief in redemption through the suffering and death of Christ."[13] Sacrificial language in communion prayers and rituals presents a harmful and dangerous model of Christian behavior. Suggestions that life comes out of suffering, that suffering itself is somehow redemptive, or "good for you" must be eradicated. With Carlson Brown and Parker, we must conclude that "suffering is never redemptive, and suffering cannot be redeemed."[14] Good does not come because of suffering, nor even out of suffering. *In spite of* suffering and death, God brings forth life. Instead of emphasizing verse 7 of Isaiah 53, in which the Suffering Servant is described as meekly accepting his suffering and death as a slaughtered lamb is imagined to do, we must emphasize the following verse: "By a perversion of justice he was taken away." Jesus' death can be seen not as God's will, but as a "perversion of justice." The resurrection thus becomes not the mark of God's *acceptance* of Jesus' sacrificial death, as in traditional theology, but a sign of God's *rejection* of the injustice of Jesus' death, a divine correction of human injustice. As such, the resurrection of Jesus becomes a resource for the ongoing activity of God in human actions which work to correct and end human violence and injustice, and to bring about communities of peace and justice, with bread and life for all.

Notes

1. Robin Morgan, "The Two Gretels," in *Lady of the Beasts: Poems* (New York: Random House, 1975).
2. Mark 7:24–30; a parallel story is found in Matt. 15:21–28, with different details.
3. Marie Fortune, *Sexual Violence: The Unmentionable Sin* (New York: The Pilgrim Press, 1983), 208.
4. Andrew Sung Park, *The Wounded Heart of God: The Asian Concept of Han and the Christian Doctrine of Sin* (Nashville: Abingdon Press, 1993).
5. See also the confession in the Episcopal *Supplemental Liturgical Texts, Prayer Book Studies 30*: "We confess that we have sinned against you, resisting your will in our lives . . ." for another example of the necessity of submission to the will of another as a religious principle. The Standing Liturgical Commission of the Episcopal Church (New York: Church Hymnal Corporation, 1987).
6. Christine Gudorf, *Victimization: Examining Christian Complicity.* (Philadelphia: Trinity Press International, 1992), 52.
7. Joanne Carlson Brown and Rebecca Parker, "For God So Loved the World?" in this volume, 36–59.
8. Gudorf, 72.
9. *Book of Worship*, 50.
10. Park, 84.
11. Ibid.
12. Elisabeth Schüssler Fiorenza, *In Memory of Her: A Feminist Theological Reconstruction of Christian Origins* (New York: Crossroad Press, 1983), 350.
13. Elisabeth Schüssler Fiorenza and Mary Shawn Copeland, eds., *Violence Against Women, Concilium* 1994. (London: SCM Press and Maryknoll: Orbis Books, 1994), "Introduction," xv.
14. Carlson Brown and Parker.

Liturgical Texts Cited

The Episcopal Church, U.S.A. *The Book of Common Prayer.* New York: The Church Hymnal Corporation, 1977.

The Episcopal Church, U.S.A. *Supplemental Liturgical Texts.* Prayer Book Studies 30. New York: The Church Hymnal Corporation, 1989.

The Inter-Lutheran Commission on Worship. *Lutheran Book of Worship.* Minneapolis, Minn.: Augsburg Publishing House, and Philadelphia: Board of Publication, Lutheran Church in America, 1978.

National Conference of Catholic Bishops. *The Sacramentary*. Collegeville, Minn.: The Liturgical Press, 1974.

The Presbyterian Church. *The Book of Common Worship*. Louisville: Westminster/John Knox Press, 1994.

Roman Catholic Church. *The Rites of the Catholic Church as Revised by Decree of the Second Vatican Council*. English translation prepared by The International Commission on English in the Liturgy. New York: Pueblo Publishing Company, 1976, 1983.

United Church of Christ. *Book of Worship*. New York: United Church of Christ Office of Church Life and Leadership, 1986.

United Methodist Church. *The United Methodist Hymnal*. Nashville: United Methodist Publishing House, 1989.

United Methodist Church. *The United Methodist Book of Worship*. Nashville: United Methodist Publishing House, 1992.

Hope Lies in "the Struggle Against It": Co-teaching a Seminary Course on Domestic Violence and Theology

MARVIN M. ELLISON AND KRISTINA B. HEWEY

The problem lies in the domination of women.
The answer lies in the struggle against it.
—R. Emerson and Russell Dobash

In the spring semester 1992–93 we taught a seminary course on domestic violence and theology as an elective offering in a Master of Divinity curriculum.[1] In this essay we reflect on that course and our experience of co-teaching.[2] We first describe how we developed this project and were able to gain the mutual respect and trust needed to work as colleagues. We then discuss the design and methodology of the course, relate some of what students said they learned, and finally identify some of our own learnings as instructors. We offer this analysis as a resource and encouragement for others to go and do likewise.

Our Locations and Commitments

MARVIN: I am a full-time, resident faculty member of Bangor Theological Seminary in Maine where I have taught Christian ethics since 1981. Three years ago, after relocating from Bangor to the Seminary's Portland campus, I approached my friend, Lois Reckitt, director of the Family Crisis Shelter, one of nine domestic violence projects in Maine. I was interested in developing educational resources on domestic violence for churches and the wider community. This interest fits with my professional commitments as a theological "educator for justice" and with some writing projects I've completed recently on men's responses to violence. I'm persuaded that men, as well as women, fear men's violence, but racist, capitalist patriarchy gives many men enough privilege—or at least the illusion of access to privilege—that we're less inclined to see feminist struggle as life-giving for us as men or to recognize the gains of investing our lives in the movement to end male violence, race and class violence, and violence against the earth and earth-creatures. I wanted to teach this course because I'm searching for allies and ways to become a stronger, more outspoken ally myself in resisting injustice inside and outside the church. Given what Lois knew of my commitments, she had little trouble identifying the right person on her staff to take up this collaborative project. She introduced me to Kristie.

In the process of developing and then teaching this course, both Kristie and I confirmed for each other the benefits of clarifying our respective social locations and how each of us enters these issues of men's violence against women and others. I ground some of my own convictions this way: as a gay man I'm especially indebted to feminist and womanist activists. When push comes to shove, they're the ones who most consistently show up to do the hard work whether that's about AIDS, welfare rights, sterilization abuse, or militarization of the economy. Women's courageous public advocacy around almost every justice issue, most recently Portland's Equal Protection campaign to secure this city's gay rights ordinance, models for me a very large moral vision of what it means to love generously and seek justice passionately. Over the years it's from my feminist friends and colleagues, men and women alike, that I've learned to take seriously that the "personal is political" and to make connections between intimate violence and heterosexism, racism, and other injustices.

Because I'm also a single parent of a teenaged daughter, I'm feeling new urgency for finding resources, in the religious community and beyond, to stop these patterns of abuse that deny especially women's safety and block any shared sense of well-being. I'm interested in teaching this course wearing my multiple hats—as an ethicist, an ordained clergyman, a man who is gay with white skin and class privilege, and as a father. I'm here as someone who teaches so that I can learn among colleagues how to think more creatively about matters that anger me, frighten me, puzzle me, and push me to "dream dreams" of a justice that begins at home. I do this *as a man* who takes pride in being *committed to justice* for myself and for women, children, and marginalized men. I'm getting clearer and clearer that unless we men pay greater attention to the justice struggles very close at hand in our intimacy relations, including our families, we will have precious little moral credibility as peace advocates elsewhere.

KRISTIE: I began my work in the domestic violence movement in 1984 when I became an on-call volunteer at the Family Crisis Shelter in Portland. In 1988 I became a staff member there, first as the house manager/shelter advocate and later as the shelter program coordinator. Through the years that I have spent with abused women and children, both at the shelter and on the hotline, I grew increasingly aware of difficulties many women had in gaining support from their religious communities in the midst of their struggles to be safe from an abusive relationship. Women told me that they felt blamed by their clergy for their abuser's behaviors. Others described being pressured to stay in a dangerous relationship because to do otherwise would betray their marriage and/or faith covenant. And many women saw that any attempt they made to talk about the abuse in their lives was met with fear or disregard by those in their religious community. Overwhelmingly, I understood that abused women's voices were being silenced, and their efforts to gain support and safety were often fruitless.

Over time I became interested in women's struggles to claim a faith for themselves, regardless of whether or not they found support in their community, and what this meant to them in the context of being abused. Questions of why her (why me?) arose and what does her faith (my faith?) say about this abuse. This struggle was of deep personal and political concern to me, not only as a battered women's advocate but as a woman who had frequently found it difficult to reconcile religious tenets with my own life experience. At one point I randomly interviewed women at the shelter and at support groups to listen more closely to their thoughts on faith and how (or whether) it sustained their reality. These conversations, and subsequent discussions with my colleagues and friends, nurtured my interest in the connections between domestic violence, theology, and survival.

I also came to my work at Bangor Theological Seminary with conviction based on my experiences as a community educator. This is, countless conversations with individuals and with groups had convinced me of the need all people have to think and talk about domestic violence in a safe environment that acknowledges how personal that discussion will be. As we try to understand and sort out the complexity of domestic violence, so too will we react based on who we are and how that discussion illuminates the world in which we live—our families, our relationships, our faith, our situation in life, our community, or our society as a whole. On a daily basis I saw how important it was for those of us who worked at the shelter to talk and think about the effects of abuse on all women in order to be able to be helpful in our role. I'd also had conversations with frantic pastors or lay leaders who needed to "minister to" a woman but who had never had the opportunity to think about domestic violence in a non-crisis environment, much less on a personal level. Eventually I began to see how essential it would be for members of the faith community to have that opportunity to think and read and listen and ask themselves about abuse and its meaning.

The timing was right for collaboration between shelter and seminary.

Getting Started

The two of us, a seminary professor and a shelter staff person, discovered early on that we shared a commitment, a conviction, and at least one reservation. We were both committed to working to stop domestic violence. We were also convinced that both church (and theological education) and the domestic violence movement have contributions to make toward that end. At the same time, we recognized, along with Joy Bussert in *Battered Women: From a Theology of Suffering to an Ethic of Empowerment*, that often "the churches and the shelters [are] two distinct worlds, divided by a deep chasm of suspicion on both sides."[3] On the church side of the chasm, too many deny or simply ignore the fact that women, children, and some marginalized men are routinely brutalized in their homes. On the shelter side of the chasm, too few believe that the churches either care about battered women or can offer much help. Bussert has described her own work this way: "My task was to walk the delicate line between these two worlds in order to find a common language and a common meeting ground."[4] Our reservation at least initially was how we would find our own way to walk that delicate line between seminary and shelter.

Finding our common ground was aided by two factors. First, we both arrived at this task as strong advocates of justice for women, gay men, and children—of all colors and classes—affected by societal violence and injustice. We were both quick to acknowledge a longstanding indebtedness to the grassroots feminist and womanist movements for their social analyses and activism, rooted in the diversity and complexity of women's lives. Each of us recognized, therefore, that the other spoke a familiar language, as well as communicated a similar passion for righting wrongs. We also acknowledged our particular debt to survivors of domestic violence. Their courage, truthtelling, and resistance have allowed many women to reclaim their lives while demonstrating that women are never only victims.

As a feminist woman and profeminist man, we recognized in each other a style of education and politics grounded in respect for persons and enlivened by advocacy for the disempowered and oppressed. We saw each other as persons living faithfully toward a vision of friendship and justice while yearning for a time, in the words of feminist ethicist Eleanor Haney, "when the structures of enemyhood will be broken." We trusted that each of our voices was valid and deserved to be heard, but we also knew, from friends and critics alike, that our voices were also limited and inevitably distorted. We had, therefore, intentionally chosen to position ourselves in communities of resistance, justice-making, and transformation. We write this essay very much, as Haney says, "*in media res*, in the middle of things, in the midst of struggles that are never ending, in the light of insights that are incomplete and blurred."[5] We do this work and write this essay because we want to make a difference, maintain our integrity, and be held accountable by those who will challenge and strengthen us in justice-making.

A second factor helped to bring us and our worlds of seminary and shelter closer together. Six months before we had to sit down and plan our course, we co-chaired a planning group to design a conference for clergy on domestic violence and the church. That "Turning the Tide" conference, co-sponsored by the Shelter and the Seminary, drew about sixty-five Protestant clergy and had several objectives: (1) to increase awareness among clergy and lay leaders of the nature and extent of domestic violence in Maine; (2) to increase clergy skills in responding to victims/survivors and to their religious needs, in particular; and (3) to increase cooperation between churches and synagogues and the domestic violence movement. From that planning process and the conference itself, we gained confidence in our ability to collaborate and solidified several learnings that would prove valuable for the course we would later teach.

First, our planning group consisted of shelter staff (all female) and clergy, the majority of whom were clergywomen. These women ministers had previously worked as staff at a domestic violence project (or, in one instance, had founded a project), continued to volunteer there, and/or were themselves formerly battered women. Kristie was not surprised and Marvin soon witnessed how women, including feminist clergywomen, are more likely than men to traverse the territory between church and shelter with regularity and relative ease. Although the clergywomen on the planning committee had managed to be highly creative in bridging the chasm between church and shelter, they were now in a privileged position to insist on formalizing more secure institutionalized pathways to maintain those connections, well beyond the personal strategies they had developed on their own. These women, as insiders to church and shelter, reinforced the urgency of addressing the faith issues and struggles of battered women and of domestic violence (DV hereafter) staff, as well.

A second insight is that battered women are the primary experts on domestic violence and that the appropriate response is to listen to and learn from them. That is, of course, not a position (male or female) ministers in a patriarchal church occupy either customarily or all that comfortably. For this reason, the conference we planned started by showing a video, *Just To Have a Peaceful Life*,[6] the story of Pat, an older woman and survivor of domestic assault, and then moving to a panel of formerly battered women telling their stories. Only after the silence was broken by women's truthtelling did the agenda turn to social analysis and discussion of why safety is the primary issue for battered women. Later in the day a panel of clergy, both men and women, was invited to tell their own stories about breaking the silence in congregations. They spoke about how seminary had not prepared them to address domestic violence, how they had to unlearn some stereotypes and misinformation about DV, and how they had to develop new knowledge and skills, in order to be useful to battered women, their families, and their communities.

For clergy to be perceived as allies and as resources useful to battered women, as Mary Pellauer has argued,

> [Clergy] must become convinced that violence against women is literally a life-and-death issue; they must learn to respond from the new knowledge of such abuses rather than from old stereotypes, and to engage in the social analysis that embeds our understanding of violence against women in larger understandings of sexism. Clergymen must be transformed, personally and theologically, as women have been.[7]

Such transformations will require clergy to honor, first of all, their moral obligation to "do no harm" by not compounding the suffering of DV victims and survivors, and then to work in alliance with shelters and other groups to promote women's concrete good by advocating their rights, including their right to lives free of violence. As Pellauer rightly notes, if clergy "learn nothing more than to refer to women's agencies, to support shelters and rape crisis lines, it will be a gain."[8]

Third, the planning group gained insights as it struggled with its own conflict. Some committee members were inclined to speak more than listen or stayed preoccupied with rescuing victims, preserving marriages, and "fixing" batterers rather than on learning from survivors, promoting women's safety, or holding batterers accountable. Because of these internal conflicts, Kristie had an opportunity to witness whether the men, including Marvin, were simply grandstanding on these issues or rather invested in contributing to justice-making for women. She looked to see how they handled their male privilege, whether they took responsibility to use it creatively, or whether they expected gratitude for their contributions. Kristie also observed how Marvin works with others while endeavoring to maintain his profeminist commitments. Marvin witnessed how Kristie works with a gender-mixed group and approaches conflict with directness, candor, and flexibility.

In an unplanned way, this planning group allowed both of us to check each other out in terms of knowledge, competence, and commitment, all indispensable elements for effective teaching and for effective advocacy for battered women among others. In addition, we found in each other a welcomed sense of humor and capacity to keep perspective. Trustworthiness was also particularly important, we found. The reason is simple. For men to become women's allies in the movement to end men's violence against women, children, and other men, men will need to establish good reasons that women can find them trustworthy and helpful. Trust, feminist philosopher Annette Baier writes, may be understood as "accepted vulnerability to another's possible but not expected ill will (or lack of good will) toward one." Trust, Baier suggests, is fragile, not easy to get started, but "never hard to destroy."[9] The pervasive societal patterns of men's violence against women is primary cause for mistrust, and so is men's insensitivity and indifference about these matters. Whether any particular man has ever struck a woman or not, as a man he shares in the privileges of patriarchal power and must examine how he may be perpetuating anti-woman abuse, if only by silence or unwillingness to "get it." Men must publicly demonstrate their moral seriousness about setting things right, no matter what their connection with DV, and that they care for justice and for women's well-being as much as they care for their own.

During the final stages of our preparing for the clergy training event, the dean of the Seminary asked Marvin to teach an elective in theology on the Portland campus during the following semester. Ethicists sometimes, but infrequently, have an opportunity to teach theology, so this invitation was tantalizing. Because of his current work with the Family Crisis Shelter, what intrigued Marvin even more was designing a theology course specifically contextualized in relation to domestic violence. What are the faith issues that victims and survivors, perhaps some abusers, and also clergy and congregations typically encounter? The possibility of sharing the teaching role with Kristie Hewey, for example, and thereby introducing the DV movement directly into the seminary classroom, *as a primary community of discourse and accountability*, was exactly the kind of innovation that theological educators committed to liberation and justice-making need to embrace. Marvin discussed the course possibility with Kristie; she signed on. The Seminary dean endorsed our plan, arranged for her standing as adjunct faculty, and happily, also made institutional funds available to compensate her for her work. Without knowing exactly what we were getting into, we proceeded to design a course on domestic violence and theology.

Course Design and Methodology

Course planning included establishing goals, clarifying our assumptions and methodology, and mapping out a syllabus with course requirements and readings. Marvin brought two models to our initial conversations. The first model was an ethics course on "Ministry with Persons with AIDS." During that half-semester course he had invited PWAs (persons living with AIDS) and staff from the local AIDS project to come into the classroom at several different times as resource people. As the course instructor, however, he had maintained his authority to finalize the design of the course, evaluate students' participation and written assignments, and assign final grades. A second model was provided by Martha Reineke, a professor of religion at the University of Northern Iowa, who had written an article about an undergraduate seminar she had taught on "Women and Christianity" which had focused exclusively on the theme of (men's) violence against women and children.[10] Reineke's essay, published by the American Academy of Religion's *Religious Studies News Spotlight on Teaching*, provided helpful suggestions about readings and assignments, insights about pedagogy and group process, and criteria for critical assessment of a course on this subject. However, the presence and voices of battered women and of shelter staff were not explicitly incorporated into the course methodology, nor was there a sharing of teaching role and authority between academia and the domestic violence movement. Although we found good ideas in both these resources, we discovered that, to a large extent, we needed to build the road as we travelled.

A major turning point in our planning came as we decided to share power and authority as co-teachers and co-learners. We decided, in contrast to Marvin's course on AIDS ministries, not to divide the course into two parts, say, with an initial six-week section on domestic violence (DV 101 and so forth), to be followed by a second six-week theology component, in which theology would occupy a privileged seat to "answer" a set of lived questions and dilemmas. Instead, we chose to follow a praxis model of weaving theology and life together and, further, to have both of us share responsibility for teaching the entire course from start to finish.

Although Kristie has particular expertise about domestic violence, she also has theological voice and knowledge to provide leadership around faith issues and theological discernment. (At the same time, Kristie was surprised to discover over the course of the semester the clarity of her theological voice and her ability to speak with insight and conviction, not only with battered women but to a larger audience, as well.) Likewise, Marvin has specialized training as a theologian and ethicist, but also has valuable knowledge, especially as a profeminist gay man, about the social realities of violence and oppression that needs to be offered alongside Kristie. By modelling a sharing of teaching role and of authority and power, we hoped to make explicit our commitments to feminist pedagogy, our investment in redistributing power and status in the classroom, and our mutual respect for the moral wisdom found among activists and social change agents, as well as among academic-based theorists. In other words, we intended to demonstrate a teaching model that would fit with the values of the "equality wheel" and transgress the values of the "power and control wheel."[11]

In a preliminary draft of this essay, Kristie articulated the pedagogical approach we followed this way: "My goal was to develop a course on domestic violence and theology with the same conviction and philosophy that I use in my work as a community educator or as an advocate with an individual woman. I did not want to dictate to students what they should say or believe; rather, I hoped to hold all of us accountable for what we said or meant from the point of view of an abused woman and to identify sources of our beliefs about DV, its victims, and its perpetrators. My experience has shown me that education and learning come from an environment of safety, support, and personal choice." In the same way, we are now offering this course plan not as the definitive model, but as our attempt to be responsive to the needs of battered women and their struggles, including their faith struggles. We believe there are many ways to teach a similar course. Therefore, our focus here has been as much on the politics of our collaboration and on issues of trust, collaboration, and shared authority as it has been on specific content.

In several respects the clergy training event we had designed, in company with shelter staff and local pastors, provided the most significant clues for shaping the content and method of our course. First, we identified course learning goals similar to those for the clergy conference: to increase knowledge about domestic violence, especially in our local communities; to build skills, as well as clarify limits, for responding to victims and survivors, as well as to abusers; to increase cooperation between religious communities and the domestic violence movement; and to explore strategies, both personal and social, for stopping family violence.

Second, we committed ourselves to a primary issue, that of battering. Although sexual assault, including rape and incest, and sexual harassment, for example, are serious problems, we decided to limit attention to battering and only address other forms of sexual and domestic violence insofar as they are employed by batterers to control their victims. Our judgment call, to limit the scope of inquiry in order to increase depth of reflection about battery, made sense to us, especially in light of Kristie's primary expertise and the work of the Family Crisis Shelter.

Third, in addition to the primary issue, we also chose a primary focus, namely, to identify a variety of religious and spiritual concerns that arise among victims and survivors and to reflect, over a sixteen week period, on ways to respond constructively and imaginatively to these concerns. In particular, we agreed that theological questions about suffering, fidelity, obedience, marriage and family, power, forgiveness, reconciliation, hope, and so forth would be addressed *as these questions are confronted by victims/survivors* of domestic violence and, secondarily, by those seeking to offer support and empowerment for change.

The voices of battered women (as the primary, not exclusive, group affected by family violence), we were clear, would be granted a privileged place in our discourse. Along with Joy Bussert, for example, we agreed that "battered women helped [us] to understand the urgency of addressing this issue in the church" and in the seminary, and further, that "it was in listening to their stories that [we] discovered the connection between some of the church's theology and the violence that governs battered women's lives and threatens the safety of all women."[12] However, we intended to do more than simply add battered women's voices to *our* theological conversation. We pledged to honor battered women *as theologians* and as exemplary moral agents whose insights would guide us in critiquing and reconstructing any and all theological claims we would be exploring.[13] They would be our teachers and not merely "objects" for our study.

In order to shift the authority structure in the classroom, we named explicitly that our own theological and ethical reflections would be evaluated in terms of how well we were able to listen to, be engaged by, and be of some use to battered women in their struggle for a violence-free life of safety and self-respect, for themselves and for other women, children, and men. Theological accountability would be, first and foremost, not to the church, the academic-based theological guild, or even the course instructors, but to battered women in their quest for freedom.

This decision placed us within the methodological bounds of liberation theologies, which exhibit some familiar characteristics: theological reflection (1) is an advocacy project, engaged in to serve the needs of oppressed and struggling peoples; (2) begins not with revelation or church traditions but with the concrete sufferings of peoples and with a commitment to join their struggle to reduce, and finally end, unjust suffering; (3) requires suspicion of the way the problem has been customarily interpreted and dealt with; and (4) relies upon critical social theory to analyze the problem, its dynamics and social roots, and to critique structures and ideological supports for the injustice. As Suzanne Toton argues, "only after we have analyzed the roots of the problem" in light of the experiential wisdom of those directly affected, "can we begin to interpret it in light of faith," and also formulate specific strategies for change. Such a methodology, Toton rightly notes, remains provisional in character. The knowledge gained, its truthfulness and benefits, "can be tested only by living out its full implications."[14]

The course design fits with these methodological assumptions. The first few sessions, for example, showed how breaking silences, gaining voice, and becoming "articulate listeners" (Langston Hughes) became important metaphors for our work during the entire semester. At the opening session, designed to introduce both the course and the participants to one another, we spoke first about our connections with domestic violence and the DV movement, identified our own learning agendas, and invited the students to engage in a similar sharing. As women and men introduced themselves, several identified themselves—somewhat cautiously—as survivors of battering, as well as other forms of sexual and/or domestic violence. Some spoke of needing to move beyond "snap judgments" about battered women ("why don't they just leave?"). Others admitted to their hesitation about enrolling in the course and to their fear of taking this "longer look" at family violence. Almost to a person, they spoke of being "left speechless" or nearly so when confronted with the need to articulate hope and peace in the midst of violence.

After these introductions, as a group we then discussed how to create an ethical classroom. What conditions would encourage all the participants to feel safe and encouraged to "show up" as strong contributors to the learning process? In developing their ground rules and expectations, class members identified what would facilitate their work and what would inhibit candid participation. Therefore, from the beginning, the issues of power and safety, of responsibility and mutual accountability were made explicit, and the group committed itself to a process that would be respectful and empowering, invite appropriate risk-taking, and allow for periodic check-ins to make mid-course corrections.

The first session also included time to discuss definitions of terms, such as domestic violence, battering, and abuse. We ended by showing the video, *Just to Have a Peaceful Life*, the story of a battered women named Pat and her struggle to leave her abusive husband. Pat's story is disheartening because she dies before she is able to find safety. In introducing Pat's voice, we asked students to keep her in mind throughout the course and especially as they read the course material and prepared for discussions. At the close of the video, a profound silence fell, one we respected and did not attempt to rush or push away. At this and other moments in this course, we found ourselves needing to honor silence and not plunge too hastily into conversation. Silence was a valuable resource for us, a place for quiet and soulful reflection as we were confronted by the pain and absurdity of domestic violence, by the sacredness of human lives, by a profound grief and anger about lives destroyed by cruelty and callousness, and in the midst of this by a remarkable human tenacity to resist evil. Throughout the semester students referred again and again to Pat's story, raising the question, "Where is God in all this?"

The second session, facilitated by Kristie and Juliet Holmes-Smith, one of her colleagues from the Family Crisis Shelter, provided a basic overview of battering and analysis of the power-and-control wheel. They placed a strong emphasis on exploring the issue of women's safety, as well as the concept of family in their social analysis. This analysis was followed, in a third session entitled "Breaking the Silence," by a panel of formerly battered women telling their stories and encasing the social analysis, literally, by flesh and blood. The students had, by this time, also read sufficiently in the literature to know that prevailing explanations of domestic violence were often victim-blaming and disrespectful of women's lives. By the time they heard this panel, they were feeling challenged by the stories they were hearing and also invested in asking difficult questions. The process of listening to *and learning from* victims/survivors was well underway.

The primacy given to battered women's voices and to their stories as essential theological speech was reinforced by the design of the written assignments throughout the course. For example, the session following the panel of survivors was called "Breaking the Silence in the Church." As an appendix to *Battered Women*, Joy Bussert includes a "Letter from a Battered Wife." Students were asked to write a letter to this woman in which, by way of honoring the wisdom and courage of survivors, they would communicate what they used to believe, mistakenly, about domestic violence, as well as what they now know. They were also asked to "share what that process of unlearning and relearning has been like for you, and why it is important." Similarly, when we discussed the use and misuse of the Bible with respect to violence against women, we read Phyllis Trible's *Texts of Terror*. Students were then asked to complete this assignment: "Write a 3–5 page letter to Tamar and/or the unknown woman of Judg. 19:1–10, in which you speak to her (them) of how you understand grace and healing in the midst of violence against women. Then write a brief response as if from Tamar and/or the unknown woman in which she (they) answer you." We wanted to give students the chance to develop their own voices and designed the writing assignments to be personal, in the hope that they would experience how to speak from their own viewpoint and yet also be answerable to another human being.

By insisting on the primacy of narrative in theological discourse, we honored not only the voices of battered women, but also the integrity and strength of our students' voices around the classroom table. As the course progressed, their voices gained confidence, timbre and passion. Because of the course structure, at the beginning they listened more to others' speech—to the panel, to Kristie and her colleague from the DV project, and to Marvin. Increasingly, students were encouraged, by the nature of their assignments and because of their own investment in the work, to claim a larger and larger share of the conversation. By the close of the course, they had assumed full responsiblity to make presentations on issues of interest to them. As one student observed, "Individual presentations"—on topics as diverse as gay male battering, domestic violence in the deaf community, and verbal abuse— "allowed flexibility and freedom for each class member to do some independent work, as well as express her/himself more fully. . . The pace and process of the course seemed to flow well, . . . and I felt a growing sense of community as people found they could trust the classroom to be a safe place" where their own voices would be heard and taken seriously, even when challenged.

The course was also designed in two parts, so that a student might complete the first half of the semester for credit but elect not to continue. (Several students had initially registered for the half-course only, but all the students, except one because of limited financial resources, ended up enrolling for the full semester's work. This option, however, gave people a choice about how much they wanted to "buy into" the course and an opportunity to "wait and see" if their interest was piqued.)

The first half of the course, once the social analysis of battering and the panel of formerly battered women had been presented, turned to consider the church's role and how religious traditions have either supported or challenged men's violence against women and children. Again, feminist theological critiques of patriarchal structures, including religious structures and theological claims about gender roles and power, received considerable attention. We read Trible's *Texts of Terror* and reflected on how the Bible has been misused against victims. Marie Fortune's *Keeping the Faith: Questions and Answers for the Abused Woman* provided some ways to reframe anti-female sentiments and draw on scriptural resources to support women's movement toward justice and freedom from violence. We also looked for other religious resources that promised some measure of "grace and healing," and read essays by Mary Pellauer[15] and Beverly Harrison, including the now classic, "The Power of Anger in the Work of Love."[16] Harrison's reevaluation of anger as a primary theological virtue excited men and women alike, but the women even more so as they found permission to give anger its due as an indispensable resource in personal and political resistance to violation. We concluded the first half of the course by reading Alice Walker's *The Color Purple*, sharing visions and resources for "survival, hope, and new life," and doing a mid-course evaluation.

In the second half, we looked at specific issues that have challenged feminist theory about domestic violence and have also created controversy among grassroots activists. We began with an examination of men and domestic violence. Unfortunately, too little published work is available about men's responses to domestic violence,[17] and we were also frustrated that we did not locate a male resource person to visit class. A staff person, for example, from EMERGE or a similar organization of men working to end men's violence against women could have addressed how some men perpetuate violence by their fists and others by their silence and unwillingness to hold themselves and other men accountable. What are signs of hope that some men are revoking patriarchal privilege and committing themselves to being "domestic pacifists"? As real as the cultural pressures are on men to keep women in line, men may choose, and some do, to challenge gender injustice and other interlocking oppressions. We addressed these concerns while acknowledging that men, as well as women, fear men's violence and strategize to avoid, contain, and/or control it. Nevertheless, a resource person working directly with men who batter may have been able to give us a candid assessment of the difficulties of men changing their abusive behavior and what that change process requires.

A second controversy addressed how gender oppression interplays with other dynamics in domestic violence. No analysis of domestic violence is adequate that fails to incorporate a feminist analysis of gender oppression, but we also struggled with the limitations of any single-factor analysis. Other factors complicate the struggles of victims/survivors. Within the DV movement significant debate is underway about the multiple factors at work, their relative primacy, and how to be accountable to all persons affected by DV, including lesbians, people of color, persons with disabilities, and so forth. By reading feminist analysis from Third World women, in particular, we gained some clarity about how race and class dynamics compound gender oppression, as well as why male socialization toward violence is a major, but nonetheless only one, contributing factor to the problem.[18] Homophobia and heterosexism are also complicating factors. To understand the reality of lesbian battering, for example, we asked students to read *Naming the Violence: Speaking Out About Lesbian Battering*, edited by Kerry Lobel, and also Suzanne Pharr's *Homophobia: A Weapon of Sexism*. We also invited a lesbian woman to speak to the class about her experience as a battered partner and her struggle to find community support and resources, from the police as well as from the domestic violence movement itself.

A third area of dissension is the nature and scope of Christian complicity in violence against women. We read essays from *Christianity, Patriarchy, and Abuse: A Feminist Critique*, edited by Joanne Carlson Brown and Carole R. Bohn, and debated what a non-patriarchal Christianity would look like and how to make movement possible in that direction. The written assignment for students was to write a letter to a pastor (male or female) or church leader in which they were to speak about how church teaching and practice have been a hindrance in the problem of domestic violence, and then also identify how the church might make proper amends and offer positive resources to victims and survivors. Along with Mary Pellauer, we agreed that "adequate ministry on sexual and domestic violence requires a theological reconstruction in a feminist vein,"[19] as it also requires steady pushing for social and economic justice for women, children, and marginalized men. One component of that reconstruction is the depatriarchalizing of language, including liturgical language and theological images, and we devoted a session to issues of language and power.

This segment of the course concluded with a panel of clergy, all women who had also worked in the DV movement, speaking on the topic of "Possibilities of Justice and Mercy in Church and Society." We then reserved the remainder of the course for students to present their research and ministry projects in class. The final requirement was the completion of a take-home examination and a self-evaluation. The exam asked simply that students discuss the most important learnings they acquired from the course about domestic violence and theology. For the self-evaluation, students were asked to assess the level of their work in terms of preparation, participation, written work, and class project. They were also invited to critique the course and suggest changes for the future.

Student Learnings

In their evaluations of the course and in their self-evaluations, students identified a variety of learnings, including insights about the demands of becoming better educated about domestic violence. Their learnings fall into three categories.

First, students reported that to study domestic violence was also to reflect critically on self and society. For example, one woman wrote about her gaining "ever-increasing awareness" about matters both external and internal to her. "By 'external'," she explained, "I mean that I am more aware of facts, people, stories, and statistics having to do with domestic violence." This external awareness also included "being able to see the way domestic violence fits with other, larger systems not only in the church but also in the culture." On the other hand, her increased internal awareness has meant, she continued, "that I am more aware of my own attitudes, thoughts, feelings, and reactions." During the course she was encouraged to become more in touch, for example, with her own pain, struggles, and anger as a white, relatively privileged, divorced single parent. Although not a battered woman herself, she gained insights about how to identify politically with other women while respecting real differences of social location and options. She spoke of a breakthrough in coming to discern how a patriarchal society (and church) encourages women generally to focus their attention on taking care of others, particularly fathers, husbands, and sons, while accepting powerlessness, dependency, and abuse as their due. At the same time, the course also encouraged her not to see herself "simply" as victim, but as a responsible moral agent with choices and a capacity to make changes in company with others. Again and again, this student and others expressed appreciation that this course did not focus on victimization, but rather on women's *resistance* and the remarkable political/spiritual movement by battered women and their allies to transform their lives, the church, and the culture.

Students also found that the educational process was a matter not only of connecting the personal and the political, but also of healing and liberation, their own and others'. Often this was painful work, accompanied by discomfort, confusion, and anger. Even so, several students emphasized their delight at being invited to come into the course as "whole persons" so that they could draw on both their feelings and their intellect as resources. Another student likened her learning process throughout the semester to the multidimensional awakening of many battered women as they confront the hard reality of their situation, gain confidence to "know what they know," muster their resources and options, and exercise courage to leave the abuse and claim a new life. There were things, the student wrote, that she needed to learn, as well as unlearn, about domestic violence, about theology, and about herself and society. She proceeded to identify specific ways she had been changed, including "becoming more discriminating" about power dynamics, claiming her right to respect and safety, and becoming more attentive to how homophobia is used to restrict women's power and freedom, across the boards.

These students' observations about education as healing and empowerment, as an ongoing process of critical reflection on their lives-in-relation, resonate with what ethicist Christine Gudorf has said about teaching as a form of therapy:

> . . . I object to any absolute separation between teaching and therapy. Teaching ethics *is* a kind of therapy—teaching *anything* is a kind of therapy. It broadens persons, makes them freer, helps them understand themselves, their relationships, their world, and their yearnings better.[20]

The two caveats Gudorf rightly offers are that disclosures should be discouraged that would make the student (or instructor) excessively vulnerable to harm and that "class time should be used in ways that are helpful to all" and not narrowly focused on some to the detriment of others.[21] Similarly, Martha Reineke assessed her undergraduate course on women, Christianity, and abuse by asking, in part, "Did the resources of my discipline [religious studies] serve to empower women to deal personally and professionally with violence?" Her experience was similar to our own, namely, that "several students confided that the course had changed their lives." Reineke experienced how "it became an integral part of a post-divorce healing process."[22] We saw how it altered, for example, the way some students were thinking about justice advocacy in ministry and how, as survivors themselves, they now claimed their own stories more centrally as an integral part of doing ministry.

A second area of learning for students is their willingness to question their religious traditions and employ a hermeneutic of suspicion with respect to church teaching and practice about violence against women, children, and gay/lesbian/bisexual persons. To study domestic violence is to reflect critically on church, Bible, tradition, and one's own operational faith. As we talked about family, marriage, and community, we struggled with theological claims about suffering, forgiveness, compassion, obedience, and fidelity as these support or undermine the integrity and safety of women and children. A student-pastor in the course shared that "until this class I only knew that clergy didn't understand the problem of domestic violence; now I am aware how clergy must share [responsibility for] the violence itself. Clergy have fostered domestic violence by rejecting the fact of its existence, and when it was given some credence, it was downplayed with comments like 'He didn't mean it,' or 'Maybe his day was hard,' and 'She should try to forgive him.'" Commenting on the misuse of the Bible, as well as the Bible's own patriarchal cast, this same student acknowledged that she "had not been aware of how [Paul's admonition of women's submission to their husbands] had been used against battered women. I'm now aware," she added, "that the church has a responsibility to be careful in the interpretation of scripture, to interpret them with the intent of allowing people to be freed from the powers that bind them."

Other class members were equally sobered by how Bible and Christian tradition have not unequivocally denounced men's violence against women and other kinds of abuse in families. In fact, several women spoke of the negative impact of Christian teachings on their own lives, including the glorification of suffering and the model of the "good woman" as obedient, other-directed, and silent. Another woman wrote: "I am increasingly aware of how my personal theology, my 'working' theology, deeply affects me and those touched directly or indirectly by me. My working theology is in the process of great change . . . as I become aware of theological outlooks I didn't even know I had, either affirming these or letting them go in favor of a shift into new positions" that honor the well-being of women and other marginalized groups. This student was also able to hold in tension some complex judgments, including the knowledge that theological claims significant to her may, at the same time, be offensive or even detrimental to others. For example, she admitted that "in reading *Christianity, Patriarchy, and Abuse* I was struck by how adversely certain theological positions have affected some women while helping others. The theology of atonement, for example, has been extremely helpful to me in my own journey, and therefore I would not want simply to throw it out. Yet I can certainly understand [the feminist critique of classical atonement theory as divine child abuse]. Holding these two judgments in close proximity is an example for me of what it means to 'live the questions'."

A third learning for students was that studying domestic violence requires rethinking ministry. For example, one student in her final presentation revisited ten years of her counseling work with couples in the deaf and hearing-impaired community and identified how she had denied, minimized, and trivialized battering because her own ignorance and unwillingness to acknowledge the extent of such violence in the deaf community. She spoke of the gift of "unlearning" as necessary for good ministry. Others spoke of the need to *earn* trust on these issues rather than assume that victims/survivors will somehow intuit a clergy person's knowledgeability, compassion, or trustworthiness to protect their safety and confidentiality. In fact, one student commented that he intended to admonish any congregation *not* to grant him trust too readily until he had demonstrated sufficient reasons for their confidence, especially by establishing a consistent public record as a pro-feminist advocate of justice for women and children. Often clergy are able to gain trustworthiness or their integrity as "trustworthy trustees," Karen Lebacqz' metaphor for competent and ethically sensitized professionals,[23] only as they enter into concrete accountability with those who are directly confronted by injustice and oppression. In the case of domestic violence, clergy especially need to learn how to network with their local DV projects, how to make referrals, and also how to ask for and appropriate critical feedback in order to make changes in their leadership style, theological outlook, or whatever else may block their constructive response to battered women and others.

Rethinking ministry in relation to domestic violence may also require innovative ways to minister with men, as well as women. While most DV projects work only with women and rarely have any men on staff, churches are places where a gender-mixed population is the norm. A clergywoman who visited the course as a resource person talked about her congregation's annual worship service to commemorate those women locally, nationally, and internationally who had died because of domestic violence. Men, as well as women, work to plan and lead that service. Students debated whether and how churches might work with men who batter. Everyone agreed that if a minister has access to a (male or female) batterer, it is critical that nothing be said or done to jeopardize the safety of his victim. Further, it is equally critical to communicate the wrongness of his violence and his responsibility to end it. At the same time, students saw the importance, but wrestled with the difficulty and with their own reluctance to affirm the humanity of batterers. If the way to affirm those who batter is by holding them accountable for righting their wrongs, we saw this change as only one component of a larger socio-cultural transformation needed. More than once we returned to this issue of the urgency and complexity of both personal and social change.

Students found themselves struggling with issues around cynicism, hope, and realism about domestic violence and the movement to end it. They often acknowledged how hard it is to have hope. On the one hand, they were often

impressed and encouraged by the strength and courage of women, perhaps especially by the survivors in their midst. They were also bouyed up by the energy
and accomplishments, the growth and momentum within the multi-racial,
multi-cultural battered women's movement. On the other hand, as one man
poignantly wrote in his final paper, "There were times it felt a bit odd, even
uncomfortable, being a male student in the class. . . . I wanted to scream out:
'All men aren't like that!' But then I had to ask myself: 'Where *were* the men?'"

Students also pressed where and how the church may offer good news to
battered women and others caught up in family violence. One student wrote,
"Hope arises in me when I see the church moving to make amends, to at last
believe women's stories, to educate its people about issues of power abuse and
control, and to commit to strong social justice advocacy." Another suggested
that hope comes from the emergence of a vision of possibilities not yet seen,
but longed-for, a vision of women's empowerment, safety, and well-being, of
the courage of men to share power with women and other men, and of the
church as a place of genuine sanctuary for the vulnerable and oppressed. This
all requires, as one student summed up, a "long-term commitment" and a
willingness to "hang in even though we won't likely see many signs in our lifetime of the Promised Land or the Promised Family of justice and peace."
Another wrote, "Violence, I have learned, is an area that . . . leaves the pastor
speechless many times. I realize that I have to question myself time after time
as to how, without being in a savior role, I can possibly ease the pain, not only
pain from domestic violence, but from rape, hunger, poverty, and the emotional needs of women in general, but not excluding men and children."

Instructors' Learnings

As with any new course, the instructors have an opportunity at almost every
turn to discover what works well and what does not. Basically, the course
"worked" if we mean that students acquired accurate information about
domestic violence; discovered that faith issues inevitably arise for many battered women in the midst of crisis and change; located constructive religious
resources for victims, survivors and their allies, as well as engaged in critique
of how church traditions and teachings reinforce violence against women and
children; and gained appreciation for the courage and moral wisdom of survivors. Many survivors display what Elizabeth Janeway calls "powers of the
weak" in their radical *disbelief* that violence—against themselves or others —
is somehow deserved or okay and in their resistance to abuse and determination to work with others to stop the violence.[24]

In looking back over the course, we have gained insights about how to
proceed the next time. The model of co-teachers, male and female, representing the two worlds of church and shelter, we would retain and recommend to
others. As Kristie put the matter, "I was not just a 'guest presenter' but an
instructor of equal stature." While personally affirming, this model of partnership was even more significant as a political and theological affirmation of
the battered women's movement by an academic religious institution.

Furthermore, it was important that we both participated in all class discussions because we brought different, but not necessarily exclusive or contradictory contributions to the issues. Our vantage points were different, but we operated very much as co-facilitators and partners. As Kristie added, "What I felt I could and did bring to the course was my understanding of the questions and concerns that abused women had brought me in my five or more years of work at the shelter. I was not teaching the course because I was grounded in a 'refined' understanding of theology or a particular commitment to religious doctrine. While I certainly felt capable of entering theological discussion and debate, I knew that my perspective would be grounded in my work with women and within the DV movement. This also meant that I could move outside discussions of Christianity, as well as move within that framework, because my central concern would be to advocate for the safety of all members of society and not necessarily for the retainment of any particular theology." As one student described her style, Kristie had a "down-in-the-trenches approach."

In our collaboration we were more than "two halves." As we played off and responded to each other in the course planning and in the classroom, we each listened to our own "stuff" in new ways, as well as learned how to ask our questions from a different vantage point. A male teacher alongside a female colleague, both of whom consistently expressed feminist commitments, also made it more difficult to dismiss feminist perspectives as male-bashing or to reduce domestic violence to a women's issue alone. One male student wrote, "I have learned that domestic violence is not a women's issue, but that it seems to be addressed mostly as if it were. It is a societal problem, and if any group 'owns' it more than another, it is much more a men's issue." As co-teachers we modelled the importance of men as well as women claiming these issues, personally and politically, as our own. Theology worth its salt begins with such commitment.

We believe the course methodology, especially the primacy of battered women's stories and our partnership model, fit with and facilitated attaining our educational goals. However, we continue to wrestle with issues of commitment, power, and community accountability in the classroom. For example, we question our selection of our primary audience and the decision to offer this course in a seminary setting. While we wanted to make academic credit available to seminarians, by locating the course at the seminary rather than at the shelter, we also limited its accessibility and appeal for survivors and shelter staff. Although we intended to model a new thing by bringing seminary and shelter together, in reality the primary audience was a seminary/church audience. As with Mohammed and the mountain, shelter came more to seminary than the other way around. Our primary responsibility was to provide educational resources to seminarians, but we held ourselves accountable to how our work benefitted or failed to benefit battered women and their struggles for freedom, safety, and well-being. What would we need to do differently and what would we need to keep the same if we were to move the course, say, to the Family Crisis Shelter in Portland? Would they even want us, and what or whose good would we be serving? How would we then understand our responsibility and accountability? What if we were geared more toward addressing the needs of shelter staff in working with victims/survivors and their faith concerns? How would academic-based feminist and womanist theologies be reshaped if their discourse was situated primarily in the community of "everyday" women moving into and out of battered women's shelters?

We are clear that battered women's stories provide profound theological data and fresh insights into a liberating faith that insists upon justice and actively seeks right-relatedness throughout the social order, including intimate relationships. We are also clear that many battered women draw on, even create their own faith in the process of gaining their lives back. Theologians would do well to figure out how to acknowledge and learn from that creative process, but we dare not presume, given the patriarchal cast of Western Christianity, that any seminary will be a genuinely hospitable, safe place for that work to proceed. We must create, as we did at the beginning of the course, the conditions for sustaining an ethical classroom, wherever that classroom is located. That requires attending in an ongoing way to dynamics of power, to self-respect, and to matters of accountability. In the process it might be possible to discover what women have to gain and lose by claiming their faith (whether Christian, Jewish, Buddhist, and so on). In the midst of this, we must also wrestle with how it is possible to support women in their faith without supporting questionable theology. But the burden, we feel, is on seminaries to demonstrate how they might be helpful to battered women.

Two other learnings are worth mentioning. First, we are more convinced than ever that domestic violence and, in particular, men's violence against women, must be named as a justice issue. We find that many seminarians operate with a privatized model of ministry as a "helping profession." Too many focus on offering services to "helpless victims" rather than developing a politically astute sense of ministry as shared empowerment for justice-making and liberation. As Karen Lebacqz has observed, the norm of beneficence— and especially a paternalistic notion of doing good for others—has become the overriding obligation among many clergy who thereby neglect the norm of justice and the demands of correcting distorted power imbalances. A justice ministry will aim to "bind up the wounds" of those victimized, but also on restoring power to those who have been wronged.[25]

We have learned in this course how important it is to move beyond a narrow service approach to meeting battered women's needs and to keep in place a structural analysis of women's oppression which calls for a politics of transformation. Clergy can contribute to women's safety and freedom by working diligently for women's empowerment. Empowerment, not rescue and not control, is the watchword.

We also discovered that while justice is also the fitting response to batterers, much more work is needed to address men's struggles with violence and to envision new models of manhood and community. Many men resist this work. Their defensiveness poses significant challenges to education on domestic violence. A consistent message we conveyed is that advocacy for ending male violence against women and children is not about condemning men or reversing patriarchal dualisms (e.g., men are bad/women are good; all men are victimizers, all women victims), but rather a call to men and women alike to moral accountability to end violence in all forms. If violence is a learned response, then violence may also be unlearned. We work in that hope, for men as well as for women. However, since (most) men have more social power than (most) women and have historically used that power to reinforce male privilege and control, they bear a particular responsibility to use their power to confront injustice and directly engage other men in stopping male violence. That work also requires that men collaborate with and be accountable to women in creating new patterns of shared power, in the family, in church and synagogue, and throughout the social order. We fantasize the possibility of a seminary course or courses making these issues the primary educational agenda for male seminarians.

The two of us are not yet sufficiently resolved ourselves about what all this may require (or even if male rehabilitation is likely), but some things seem particularly important to Marvin as he follows through with other men. For example, men who victimize others must be held accountable and supported to change their behavior so that they will pose no danger to any woman, child, or other man. Such demands are made not for the sake of retribution, but to make transformation and restoration possible for the one who has harmed another.[26] As David Adams and Isidore Penn have noted in their work with men who batter, batterers require more than improved communication skills or even better anger management, important as these changes are. They require resocialization into a new pattern of what it means to be a man without reliance on violence, control over others, or status as the privileged powerful. Men who batter need to craft a new masculinity centered on justice and respect for women, children, and other men.[27]

A second learning was that as instructors, we were tempted at times to rescue rather than empower and be challenged by students. More than we would like to admit, we yielded to that temptation at two junctures. First of all, we approached this course with an unspoken and yet deeply felt obligation to somehow shield students from questionable perspectives on domestic violence, especially victim-blaming and anti-female approaches. This sentiment stemmed from our concern that both clergy and laity are at risk of doing harm if they lack proper understanding of domestic violence and do not know how to respond appropriately to victims and abusers. Too few clergy have been educated at seminary about DV, and we were determined in our own small way to correct that deficiency. However, we erred on the side of being overly protective. We eliminated a set of readings that, in retrospect, we might well have retained. Although the course syllabus initially listed a recently published study on gay male battering as required reading, we omitted this assignment because the study seemed quite flawed and many of its assumptions unfounded. To our surprise, a student chose this book for his in-class presentation. Although students validated our assessment that the study is flawed, they were able to engage in a lively, quite constructive critique of the material. They demonstrated to us that they are quite able and willing to discern the strengths and weaknesses of various perspectives and that the teachers did not need to "manage" their learnings so scrupulously. Indeed, sometimes we register the strengths and credibility of our own hard-earned insights only as we have been challenged by skewed, even "dangerous" notions.

There is a second illustration of our attempts to over-manage the class. The panel of clergy we invited to class did not include a man, and students identified this as a serious weakness. Although we had both worked with male pastors with experience in this area, we were uncertain about how they would speak to the issues, and so we had decided not to invite any of them to class. Again, our fears were exaggerated. We learned to have more confidence in students' ability to separate "sheep from goats." So, too, we needed to be reminded of the formative insight which grounded the course, namely, that knowledge about DV remains truthful only insofar as it stays rooted in and accountable to the experiences of victims/survivors, of whatever gender, sexual orientation, age, race, class, or religion. Ann Russo puts the matter well:

> What has been most compelling has not been the rhetoric or dogmatism or even the abstract theories, but the movement's rootedness in women's lives. . . . I believe we have to challenge ourselves again to return to the truths of our lives, no matter how painful or disturbing, and to change our theories and perspectives when they don't fit with our realities.[28]

Chocolate and More Questions

We ended the course with an evaluation of our work and a discussion of our learnings during the semester. We also shared chocolate. We brought an assortment of chocolate cookies, cakes, and candies to our final session, and we feasted on that wondrous substance that in ancient Mexico had been reserved for the exclusive consumption of male elites and their gods. Here was another way to make way for justice by sharing pleasure and comraderie. As Beverly W. Harrison notes, a feminist theology of liberation aims to sustain resistance to evil, and it does so by commending "a spirit of conviviality and mutual vulnerability." Celebration, even in the form of sharing chocolate, is a way to "support the longing for justice that is nurtured or reborn in us, together."[29] We indulged with abandon in chocolate and in that longing for justice.

Our closing celebration also brought to mind Adrienne Rich's poem "Sources," inviting us, in the midst of struggle, to ask two questions of ourselves and of those we might trust to carry us through hard times. Rich writes: "With whom do you believe your lot is cast? From where does your strength come? I think, somehow, somewhere every poem of mine must repeat those questions."[30] In light of the struggles by countless women, children, and marginalized men for safety, freedom, and faith throughout this society, repeating these questions—the "with whom" and the "from where"—seems entirely appropriate for the beginning and the ending of any course on domestic violence and theology. However, we must do more than ask the right questions. To make a difference, we must find the courage and insight to answer these questions not with our words or theories alone, but with our lives, our integrity, and the hope gleaned in the "struggle against it." Nothing less will do.

❦

Notes

1. A copy of the course syllabus may be obtained by writing to Marvin Ellison at Bangor Theological Seminary, 159 State Street, Portland, Maine, 04101.

2. We wish to express our appreciation to participants in CT/ET 751–52, many of whose insights and written comments we have incorporated in this essay. Our thanks also go to Juliet Holmes-Smith, staff at Portland's Family Crisis Shelter, Larney Otis, M.Div. candidate at Bangor Theological Seminary, and Kathleen Morgan, director of New Hope for Women in Rockland, Maine, for their constructive feedback and encouragement during the writing process.

3. Joy M. K. Bussert, *Battered Women* (New York: Division for Mission in North America, Lutheran Church in America, 1986), xi.

4. Ibid.

5. Eleanor H. Haney, *Vision and Struggle: Meditations on Feminist Spirituality and Politics* (Portland, Maine: Astarte Shell Press, 1989), 3.

6. The video is produced and distributed by Terra Nova Films, Inc.

7. Mary D. Pellauer, "Violence Against Women: The Theological Dimension," in *Sexual Assault and Abuse: A Handbook for Clergy and Religious Professionals*, ed. Mary D. Pellauer, Barbara Chester, and Jane A. Boyajian (San Francisco: Harper & Row, 1987), 55.

8. Ibid.

9. Annette Baier, "Trust and Antitrust," *Ethics* (October 1985): 235, 242.

10. Martha J. Reineke, "Tales of Terror: On Building a Course Around the Theme of Women, Christianity, and Abuse," *Religious Studies News Spotlight on Teaching* (American Academy of Religion) 1/1 (November 1992): 3–4.

11. These educational tools are well known and frequently used by domestic violence projects in the United States and beyond. The "power and control wheel" maps out various components typically present in some, but not all, abusive relationships, including physical and sexual violence, the use of threats, emotional abuse, and male privilege, as well as their dynamic interaction to produce both victim and victimizer. Similarly, the "equality wheel" visualizes characteristics of non-violent, egalitarian relations. These charts were developed by the Domestic Abuse Intervention Project, 206 West Fourth Street, Duluth, Minnesota 55806. Telephone: (218) 722-4134.

12. Bussert, *Battered Women*, xi.

13. On this issue, see Allison Mauel Moore, "Moral Agency of Women in a Battered Women's Shelter," in this volume 172–84.

14. Suzanne C. Toton, "The Methodology of Liberation Theology," in *World Hunger: The Responsibility of Christian Education* (Maryknoll, New York: Orbis Books, 1982), 91–93.

15. Pellauer's "Violence Against Women: The Theological Dimension" first appeared in *Christianity and Crisis* 43/9 (May 30, 1983): 206–12. See also Mary D. Pellauer with Susan Brooks Thistlethwaite, "Conversation on Grace and Healing," in *Lift Every Voice: Constructing Christian Theologies from the Underside*, ed. Susan Brooks Thistlethwaite and Mary Potter Engel (San Francisco: Harper & Row, 1990), 169–85.

16. Beverly Wildung Harrison, "The Power of Anger in the Work of Love," in *Making the Connections: Essays in Feminist Social Ethics*, ed. Carol S. Robb (Boston: Beacon Press, 1985), 3–21.

17. On men's responsibilities to end violence, see Marvin M. Ellison, "Refusing to Be 'Good Soldiers': An Agenda for Men," in *Redefining Sexual Ethics: A Sourcebook of Essays, Stories, and Poems*, ed. Susan E. Davies and Eleanor H. Haney (Cleveland: The Pilgrim Press, 1991), 189–98. Also, see Ellison, "Holding Up Our Half of the Sky: Male Gender Privilege as Problem and Resource for Liberation Ethics," *Journal of Feminist Studies in Religion* 9/1–2 (Spring/Fall 1993): 95–113.

18. For example, see Nilda Rimonte, "Domestic Violence Among Pacific Asians, in *Redefining Sexual Ethics*, ed. Davies and Haney, 157–65. In that same volume, see Elizabeth M. Bounds, "Sexuality and Economic Reality: A First World and Third World Comparison," 131–43.

19. Pellauer, "The Theological Dimension," 59.

20. Christine Gudorf, "Presumption and Humility," *The Annual of the Society of Christian Ethics* 1989, ed. D.M. Yeager, 268.

21. Ibid.

22. Reineke, "Tales of Terror," 4.

23. Karen Lebacqz, *Professional Ethics: Power and Paradox* (Nashville: Abingdon Press, 1985), especially 77–91.

24. Elizabeth Janeway, *Powers of the Weak* (New York: Morrow Quill Paperbacks, 1981), especially 157–85.

25. Lebacqz, *Professional Ethics*, especially 126–31.

26. Howard Zehr, *Changing Lenses: A New Focus for Crime and Justice* (Scottdale, Pa.: Herald Press, 1990).

27. David Adams and Isidore Penn, "Men in Groups: The Socialization and Resocialization of Men Who Batter," unpublished manuscript from *EMERGE* (Boston, 1981), 13. See also John Stoltenberg, *Refusing to Be a Man: Essays on Sex and Justice* (Portland, Oregon: Breitenbush Books, Inc., 1989).

28. Ann Russo, "If Not Now, When? Obstacles to Outrage, Part II," *Sojourner: The Women's Forum* (December 1991): 13.

29. Beverly W. Harrison, *Making the Connections*, 261.

30. Adrienne Rich, "Sources," in *Your Native Land, Your Life: Poems* (New York: W.W. Norton and Company, 1986), 6.

Epilogue

MARIE M. FORTUNE AND CAROL J. ADAMS

On December 6, 1989, an armed man entered the School of Engineering at the University of Montreal. He went to a class of men and women and ordered the men to leave. He then ranted and raved about "bitches and feminists" and proceeded to murder fourteen women. There was no question that this man's misogyny drove his violence and resulted, not in a random act, but in an intentional, focused hate crime. This tragic, horrific event shook the conscience of most Canadians who had long believed that such things happen in the United States, but not in Canada. In the United States, the event stayed in the news for several days and then conveniently disappeared and is now long forgotten. In Canada, the day is commemorated annually as a time to remember how many women have died that year from sexual and domestic violence and as a time to reflect upon a society in which such a thing could ever happen.[1]

The murders and their annual commemoration challenge all of us in North America to consider why it is that such things do occur; to reflect on the fact that during the United States' involvement in the Vietnam War, the number of women murdered by their intimate partners equaled the number of U.S. military personnel killed in battle; to ponder the fact that statistically in the United States women and children are less safe at home than on the public street; to contemplate the fact that domestic violence, according to the American Medical Association, is the number one threat to women's health in the United States today.

All of this brings us to the painful but unavoidable conclusion that neither our churches nor our cultures genuinely support the notion that women and children have a right to bodily integrity and safety. We do not really believe that all women and children should feel physically safe at home and in public. If we did, the story of the Montreal massacre would not have faded so quickly from our consciousness. Some may say that we do not react with outrage anymore because we are so overwhelmed and numbed by the constancy of the news of abuse and violence done to women and children. In fact we, as a society, have never really reacted with outrage because, under patriarchy, we accept that violence against women and children is "just the way things are." Sad, unfortunate, painful when it happens to us or to people we love, but not the outrage that it is. We do not believe that women and children have the right to bodily integrity and safety.

So it is no surprise that as we approach the end of the twentieth century we find ourselves in the midst of a strong backlash within both church and society against a number of efforts all related to women's rights: freedom of choice, feminist/womanist theologizing, redefining sexuality and sexual ethics, and efforts to address sexual and domestic violence.

The backlash comes not only from the religious right that proposes to retain traditional "family values," which presuppose women's subordination, but also within mainline denominations that suddenly discover that feminist/womanist theology is one of the targets of their most conservative members. Meanwhile, those who advocate for survivors of sexual and domestic violence are now accused of engaging in "victim feminism," and the memories of adult survivors of abuse as children are automatically challenged as false. How do we talk about personal violence and Christian theology together when there is a backlash against women engaging in theologizing and against recognizing the victimization of women and children who have suffered violence?

We have focused our energies on naming the violence and organizing to stop it within our faith communities and on challenging the traditions, practices and teachings of our faith communities which have supported the violence for so long. Our efforts have not always been welcome within the secular movements to end violence against women because we were "religious" and therefore part of the problem. Our efforts have not always been welcome within our faith communities (including some feminist/womanist faith communities) because we are raising issues and naming experiences which few people want to examine. Our efforts have not always been welcome within our religious institutions because addressing issues such as clergy misconduct challenges those with power. So we have stood at the nexus of feminist/womanist theologies, the patriarchal church, and efforts to end violence against women. From this place we have tried to create the opportunity to address the concrete experiences of personal violence as they are experienced by those who have been shaped by the Christian tradition.

There are some in leadership in the church who have been able to be self-critical, even confessional, in acknowledging the ways that our faith traditions have promoted and sustained violence against women. For example, in 1989 the Roman Catholic Bishops of Quebec, Canada, issued a pastoral reflection on conjugal violence. In it they clearly name the problem of domestic violence, the need to respond appropriately to victims/survivors and abusers, and they offer a social analysis which challenges the patriarchal values of church and society. They also acknowledge with appreciation the role of the feminist movement: "We owe it to the feminist movement and to certain individual women to have first drawn attention to this reality, which saps the dignity of so many people and undermines marital relationships."[2] The report goes on to call for demystifying and supporting the feminist movement—a far cry from the backlash sentiments we hear within most of church and society today.

We assert that women and children deserve to have bodily integrity and to be safe from bodily harm. Such seemingly simple but radical ideas invariably stir strong reactions. The backlash in its myriad forms is but an indicator of the success of our efforts to name violence against women and children and to organize to stop it. We see those with power refusing to relinquish their prerogative to use force and the threat of force to control women and children. Indeed, the backlash is the predictable response of those who benefit from a patriarchal world order they now experience as threatened.

John Stuart Mill, in 1869, commented regarding suffrage for women, "If the principle is true, we ought to act as if we believed it." His words challenge the church and theological education today: if the principle of bodily integrity for women and children is true, we ought to act as if we believed it. If we believe it, then our curricula and training of ministers and teachers will reflect it. Let us continue the study, research, and reflection which can inform and transform our ministry and teaching. Let us insure that the insights and scholarly work regarding sexual and domestic violence in all the disciplines of theological education will not be lost to us. We will not forget and we will not go back.

🌺

Notes

1. See Louise Mallette and Marie Chalouh, *The Montreal Massacre*, trans. Marlene Wildeman (Charlottetown, Prince Edward Island, Canada: gynergy books, 1991).
2. Social Affairs Committee of the Assembly of Quebec Bishops, *A Heritage of Violence? A Pastoral Reflection on Conjugal Violence*, trans. Antoinette Kinlough (Montreal: Social Affairs Committee of the Assembly of Quebec Bishops, 1989), 7.

The Center for the Prevention of Sexual and Domestic Violence

The Center was founded in 1977, in Seattle, Washington, by the Rev. Marie M. Fortune as an educational resource working primarily with religious communities. From modest beginnings, the Center has become an organization committed to equipping religious institutions to minister effectively to both victims and offenders of sexual and domestic violence, helping them mobilize their resources to prevent the recurrence of these problems. Operating not only in the United States, but also internationally, it is engaged in the transformation of religious institutions and bodies of the faithful. Programs focus on prevention and treatment in the areas of domestic violence, sexual abuse, child abuse, and clergy misconduct.

The Center's Statement of Purpose

Our religious values of equality and justice call us to celebrate the dignity and worth of each human being, and to affirm the right of each person to live without fear or threat of violence. We recognize:

- that sexual and domestic violence violate the rights and dignity of all women, men, and children
- that to the extent that any person is violated by sexual and domestic violence, the dignity and worth of all persons are diminished
- that oppression is deeply ingrained in our society and that all forms of oppression—including racism, sexism, classism, anti-Semitism, ageism, heterosexism, and oppression of the differently-abled—increase the suffering caused by sexual and domestic violence. In fact, sexual and domestic violence are often instruments of these forms of oppression
- that all those without power and privilege are the most vulnerable to and the most likely to be victimized by sexual and domestic violence
- that ending sexual and domestic violence requires changing attitudes and practices of individuals, communities, and institutions

Therefore, we affirm that those who are vulnerable to sexual and domestic violence have the right to organize in order to achieve empowerment and self-protection.

Recognizing the importance of spiritual values for each individual, we affirm that all organized religious communities have an ethical responsibility to play a major role in bringing about an end to sexual and domestic violence within their own communities and within society at large. Therefore we will seek to:

- mobilize religious communities and institutions to support and advocate for victims of abuse and to call perpetrators of abuse to account
- utilize education and training as the means to mobilize and involve religious communities in the prevention of sexual and domestic violence
- address religious issues and spiritual needs of victims/survivors/offenders and their communities
- work cooperatively with the secular community in these efforts
- ensure that institutional forms of oppression are not perpetuated in the Center's policies, practices, services, staffing, and resources

In our efforts to end sexual and domestic violence, we acknowledge that we are accountable to victims and survivors. The emphasis of our program will be on seeking justice as a means for healing and restoration for individuals and those communities affected by sexual and domestic violence.

To carry out our purpose effectively, we must include persons representing all the communities with which we work and do our best to ensure that Center resources address the diverse needs of our interreligious and multicultural constituency.

Applied Feminist Theology and Ethics

The work of the Center is applied feminist theology and ethics. It derives three fundamental principles from liberation and feminist theologies: that theology must take account of the lived experience of persons, stand with the powerless, and take seriously the reality of embodiment. A multiracial and interreligious organization, the Center works to confront racism, homophobia, ageism, and anti-Semitism because these are realities which interfere with efforts to end sexual and domestic violence for all women. It draws on the resources of diverse persons and experiences in order to serve the needs of diverse communities. It is unapologetically feminist in its agenda and its way of work, and unapologetically religious in its orientation.

The Center begins with the experience of people experiencing violence in both private and public spheres, advocates for the victims rendered powerless by violence, and attends to the experience of violation of bodily integrity as primary. Specifically the experiences of physical and sexual violence inflicted by persons known and unknown are the common denominators for women and children, who are the most likely victims; these experiences cross race, class, sexual orientation, and religious persuasion. All women (and some men) live with either the fear or the memory of violence. Most of these women and men have some connection to a religious tradition. In the United States this is likely to be Judaism or Christianity but may well be any of a number of traditions. In any case, the fact of exposure to religious doctrine and practice means that many people will encounter religious concerns as they face victimization. These concerns may take precedence over other issues faced by victims and offenders, exacerbating their pain; hence the need for increased awareness and a more sensitve response from religious leaders. In addition, some of the teachings and practices of our religious institutions are used to justify or rationalize sexual and domestic violence. It is our responsibility to change such practices in order to insure that religion does not further harm those who have been victimized. Rather, religious resources should be used to bring justice and healing in the midst of brokenness.

Educational Resources and Videos

The Center offers training, consultation, videos, curricula, and publications. Center materials are interreligious in perspective, multicultural, and multiracial.

Educational videos, available for free preview from the Center and ideal for training clergy, laity, seminary faculty and students, include:

- *Not In My Church*: a docudrama designed to help people deal with the problem of clergy misconduct involving sexual abuse in the ministerial relationship. A complete study guide and awareness brochures are included. 45 minutes. $149.00 (U.S.)

- *Not In My Congregation*: Intended for Jewish audiences, this version of *Not In My Church* includes an introduction by a rabbi, stressing how the subject affects the Jewish community. 47 minutes. $149.00 (U.S.)

- *Hear Their Cries, Religious Responses to Child Abuse*: This documentary addresses the role of clergy, lay leaders and religious educators in preventing child abuse. Includes interviews with Jewish and Christian clergy and secular professionals, stories of adult survivors of physical and sexual abuse, and a dramatic vignette demonstrating appropriate responses to a disclosure of abuse. A complete study guide and awareness brochures are included. 48 minutes. $129.00 (U.S.)

- *Bless Our Children, Preventing Sexual Abuse*: This is a companion piece to *Hear Their Cries*, which tells the story of one congregation's efforts to include sexual abuse prevention in their children's religious education. It is designed to help churches and synagogues implement an abuse prevention curriculum. A complete study guide and awareness brochures are included. 40 minutes. Combination price for *Hear Their Cries* and *Bless Our Children*: $185.00 (U.S.). *Bless Our Children* separately: $99.00 (U.S.)

- *Broken Vows, Religious Perspectives on Domestic Violence*: A documentary presenting the stories of six formerly battered women from diverse religious traditions. Includes introductory information about domestic violence; interviews with clergy, psychologists and shelter workers; discussion of theological issues; and concrete ideas about how religious institutions can work to end domestic violence. A complete study guide and awareness brochures are included. *Broken Vows* is a two-part video: Part I, 37 minutes, Part II, 22 minutes. $139.00 (U.S.)

For more information about the work of the Center,
or to order free resource catalogs, contact:

CENTER FOR THE PREVENTION
OF SEXUAL AND DOMESTIC VIOLENCE

936 N. 34th Street, Suite 200
Seattle, WA 98103
(206) 634-1903
FAX: (206) 634-0115

Essential Readings

(Note: This list contains only books.)

Adams, Carol J. 1994. *Woman-Battering*. Minneapolis: Fortress Press.

Brown, Joanne Carlson and Carole R. Bohn, eds. 1989. *Christianity, Patriarchy, and Abuse: A Feminist Critique*. New York: The Pilgrim Press.

Buchwald, Emilie, Pamela Fletcher, and Martha Roth, eds. 1993. *Transforming a Rape Culture*. Minneapolis: Milkweed Editions.

Burns, Maryviolet, ed. 1986. *The Speaking Profits Us: Violence in the Lives of Women of Color*. (English and Spanish). Seattle, Wash.: The Center for the Prevention of Sexual and Domestic Violence.

Bussert, Joy. 1986. *Battered Women: From a Theology of Suffering to an Ethic of Empowerment*. Division of Mission in North America, Lutheran Church in America.

Dobash, R. E. and R. P. Dobash. 1979. *Violence Against Wives*. New York: Free Press.

Fortune, Marie M. 1983. *Sexual Violence; The Unmentionable Sin: An Ethical and Pastoral Perspective*. New York: The Pilgrim Press.

———. 1987. *Keeping the Faith: Questions and Answers for the Abused Woman*. San Francisco: Harper & Row.

———. 1989. *Is Nothing Sacred? When Sex Invades the Pastoral Relationship*. San Francisco: Harper & Row.

———. 1991. *Violence in the Family: A Workshop Curriculum for Clergy and Other Helpers*. Cleveland, Ohio: The Pilgrim Press.

———. 1995. *Sexual Abuse Prevention: A Study for Teenagers*. New edition by Rebecca Voelkel-Hauger. Cleveland: The Pilgrim Press.

Gillespie, Cynthia. K. 1989. *Justifiable Homicide: Battered Women, Self-defense and the Law*. Columbus, Ohio: Ohio State University Press.

Heggen, Carolyn Holderread. 1993. *Sexual Abuse in Christian Homes and Churches*. Scottsdale, Ariz.: Herald Press.

Herman, Judith Lewis. 1992. *Trauma and Recovery: The Aftermath of Violence— From Domestic Abuse to Political Terror*. New York: Basic Books.

Horton, Anne L. and Judith A. Williamson, eds. 1988. *Abuse and Religion: When Praying Isn't Enough*. Lexington, Mass.: Lexington Books.

Imbens, Annie and Ineke Jonker. 1992. *Christianity and Incest*. Minneapolis: Fortress Press.

Jones, Ann and Susan Schecter. 1992. *When Loves Goes Wrong: What To Do When You Can't Do Anything Right. Strategies for Women with Controlling Partners*. New York: HarperCollins Publishers.

Kaschak, Ellyn. 1992. *Engendered Lives: A New Psychology of Women's Experiences*. New York: Basic Books.

National American Indian Court Judges Association. *Child Sexual Abuse in Native American Communities*. Order from National Indian Law Library, 1506 Broadway, Butler, CO 80302.

Newsom, Carol A. and Sharon H. Ringe. 1992. *The Women's Bible Commentary*. Louisville: Westminster/John Knox Press.

Pellauer, Mary D., Barbara Chester, and Jane A. Boyajian, eds. 1987. *Sexual Assault and Abuse: A Handbook for Clergy and Religious Professionals*. San Francisco: Harper & Row.

Poling, James. 1991. *The Abuse of Power: A Theological Problem*. Nashville: Abingdon Press.

Reid, Kathryn Goering. 1994. *Preventing Child Sexual Abuse: A Christian Education Curriculum for Children Ages 5–8*. Cleveland: United Church Press.

Reid, Kathryn Goering with Marie M. Fortune. 1989. *Preventing Child Sexual Abuse: Ages 9–12*. New York: United Church Press.

Rush, Florence. 1981. *The Best Kept Secret: Sexual Abuse of Children*. New York: McGraw Hill.

Schecter, Susan. 1982. *Women and Male Violence*. Boston: South End Press.

Stoltenberg, John. 1989. *Refusing to Be a Man: Essays on Sex and Justice*. Portland, Oregon: Breitenbush Books, Inc.

Trible, Phyllis. 1984. *Texts of Terror: Literary-Feminist Readings of Biblical Narratives*. Minneapolis: Fortress Press.

Winters, Mary. S. 1988. *Laws Against Sexual and Domestic Violence*. New York: Pilgrim Press.

Notes on Contributors

CAROL J. ADAMS is the author of *Woman-Battering*. She founded a Hotline for Battered Women in 1978 and chaired the Housing Committee of New York Governor Mario Cuomo's Commission on Domestic Violence from 1983 to 1987. Since moving to Texas, she has been a consultant to churches on issues of sexual and domestic violence, and periodically teaches a course on "Sexual and Domestic Violence: Theological and Pastoral Concerns" at Perkins School of Theology.

KAREN BAKER-FLETCHER is Associate Professor of Theology and Culture at the School of Theology at Claremont and Assistant Professor of Religion at the Claremont Graduate School. She is the author of *A Singing Something: Womanist Reflections on Anna Julia Cooper* and has written on issues concerning women for several publications.

SARAH BENTLEY is a counselor and educator living in Austin, Texas. An ordained minister in the United Church of Christ, she is a graduate of Union Theological Seminary in New York City. Dr. Bentley's writings on feminism, family violence, women's holistic health, and spiritual growth have appeared in *Christian Century*, *Christianity and Crisis*, and *Daughters of Sarah*. Her varied professional experience includes work in national ecumenical agencies, seminary teaching, performance and teaching in the liturgical arts, and leadership in workshops and retreats.

DENISE M. BONDURANT earned her Master's degree at the Arizona State University School of Justice Studies. For her Master's thesis research, she replicated the earlier study on the church response to domestic violence which had been conducted by John Johnson and his ASU students. For the last four years she has worked as a probation officer, has continued her research interests with the church response to domestic violence, and recently conducted a survey of how rural ministers and pastors respond to these problems.

ROSEMARY L. BRAY is the author of a children's biography of Martin Luther King, Jr., published by Greenwillow Press, and the author of a forthcoming memoir, *Unafraid of the Dark*. She lives with her husband and two-year-old son in Detroit, Michigan.

RITA NAKASHIMA BROCK holds the Endowed Chair in the Humanities at Hamline University and is the author of *Journeys By Heart: A Christology of Erotic Power* and an editor and contributor for *Setting the Table: Women in Theological Conversation*. She is completing a book, with Susan Thistlethwaite, on the sex industries in the United States and Asia.

JOANNE CARLSON BROWN is Professor of Church History and Ecumenics at St. Andrew's College, Saskatoon, Saskatchewan, Canada, and a United Methodist minister.

MITZI N. EILTS, writer, scuba diver, singer, and gardener, is a staffperson with the United Church Board for Homeland Ministries, Education and Publication.

An ordained UCC clergyperson for fifteen years, she is called to ministries which bridge the church with faith concerns beyond its common boundaries; campus ministry and church-related higher education, battered women's programs, educating about sexuality and identity. Her partner of twelve years is Jann C. Weaver.

MARVIN M. ELLISON is Bass Professor of Christian Ethics at Bangor Theological Seminary in Portland, Maine. He is co-author of the Presbyterian study on human sexuality, *Keeping Body and Soul Together*, and is completing a book on sexual ethics entitled *When Justice and Love Embrace: Sexual Justice and the Reframing of Christian Sexual Ethics*.

MARY POTTER ENGEL is an independent scholar and freelance writer living in Walterboro, South Carolina. Formerly, she was tenured Professor of Historical and Constructive Theology at United Theological Seminary of the Twin Cities, New Brighton, Minnesota.

CHARLES ESS is Professor of Philosophy and Religion and Chair of the Department, Drury College (Springfield, Missouri). He has received awards for outstanding teaching and published in the area of computers in education and politics, philosophy of technology, feminist studies, and the history of philosophy.

TOINETTE M. EUGENE educates for a more peaceful, ecological society of diverse peoples—racial, cultural, gender, sexual, and differently-abled—for a genuinely pluralistic, cross-cultural existence. She holds a Ph.D. in Religion and Society and is currently an Associate Professor of Christian Social Ethics at Garrett-Evangelical Theological Seminary in Evanston, Illinois. Dr. Eugene is the author of the forthcoming *Lifting as We Climb: A Womanist Ethic of Care*, and co-author with James N. Poling, *Balm for Gilead: Pastoral Care for African American Families Experiencing Abuse*.

MARIE M. FORTUNE, a minister in the United Church of Christ, is the founder of the Center for the Prevention of Sexual and Domestic Violence where she serves as Executive Director. She is the author of *Violence in the Family: A Workshop Curriculum for Clergy and Other Helpers*; *Is Nothing Sacred? When Sex Invades the Pastoral Relationship*; *Keeping the Faith: Questions and Answers for Abused Women*; *Sexual Abuse Prevention: A Study for Teenagers*; *Sexual Violence; the Unmentionable Sin: An Ethical and Pastoral Perspective*; and *Love Does No Harm: Sexual Ethics for the Rest of Us*.

KRISTINA B. HEWEY has been involved with the domestic violence movement since 1984. Most recently she was employed as a Program Coordinator for the Family Crisis Shelter, working with women and children, supervising staff and a volunteer hotline program, and providing community education in order to promote awareness and change.

LINDA H. HOLLIES received a M.Div. from Garrett-Evangelical Theological Seminary and a D.Min. from United Theological Seminary. She is an ordained elder, in the Northern Illinois Conference of the Methodist Church, and she founded Woman to Woman Ministries, Inc.

PETER HORSFIELD is an ordained minister of the Uniting Church in Australia. He is currently Dean of the Uniting Church Theological Hall and Lecturer in Practical Theology in the United Faculty of Theology in Melbourne. He is a member of SHIVERS, a support, advocacy, and resource network for women who are survivors of assault by clergy.

John M. Johnson is Professor of Justice Studies and Women's Studies at Arizona State University, where he has taught since 1972. He has founded or co-founded seven non-profit organizations or agencies to serve the needs of domestic violence or crime victims in the Phoenix, Arizona, area. He served as President of the Society for the Study of Symbolic Interaction, and currently serves as the President of his local church in Chandler, Arizona, where he lives with his wife Beverly and children Kailey and Kyle.

Frederick W. Keene is a Ph.D. mathematician who has studied at the Pacific School of Religion and the Graduate Theological Union in Berkeley. He writes on biblical theology and interpretation. Occasionally, he joins his wife, Hannah Abigail Keene, in presenting workshops on biblical and liturgical issues, including issues of sexual violence. They live in California with their two daughters.

Catherine Clark Kroeger, an evangelical, is co-author of *I Suffer Not a Woman: Rethinking I Timothy 2:11–115 in Light of Ancient Evidence* (Baker, 1992) and is adjunct associate professor of classical and ministry studies at Gordon-Conwell Theological Seminary. She is the founder and the president of Christians for Biblical Equality, an organization affirming a biblical basis for the equality, worth, and ministry of all persons in Jesus Christ. Currently she is editing a set of papers given at a CBE-sponsored consultation on women, abuse, and the Bible.

Stan McKay is a member of the Cree Nation. He grew up on the Fisher River Indian Reservation in northern Manitoba. He has served as a minister of the United Church of Canada since 1971. He is the Director of the Dr. Jessie Saulteaux Resource Center, a training center for Native ministries in Beausejour, Manitoba. He is married to Dorothy McKay and they have three grown children.

Jennifer L. Manlowe received her M.Div. in systematic theology from Princeton Theological Seminary and her Ph.D. in Psychology and Religion from Drew University. Her first book, *Faith Born of Seduction: Sexual Trauma, Body Image, and Religion*, explores in much greater depth points raised in her essay in this collection. She is an Adjunct Professor of women's studies at Harvard University, Program Coordinator of The Brown University AIDS Program, and is working on her next book, which will bring together her own research as well as the work of others on identity politics and HIV/AIDS research and prevention.

Allison Mauel Moore is a social ethicist and an Episcopal priest living in New York City. The article in this volume was adapted from her Ph.D. thesis on "An Analysis of Moral Agency from the Perspectives of Women in a Battered Women Shelter" (Boston University, 1989).

Rebecca Parker is President of Starr King School for the ministry in Berkeley, California, and a United Methodist minister.

Mary Pellauer is in transition to a fourth career. In her previous incarnations, she has been a seminary teacher, a freelance writer, and a researcher for the Commission for Women at the Evangelical Lutheran Church in America. She is co-editor of *Women's Consciousness/Women's Conscience: A Reader in Feminist Ethics* and *Sexual Assault and Abuse: A Handbook for Clergy and Religious Professionals.*

JAMES POLING, Ph.D., is an ordained minister in the Presbyterian Church (USA), a seminary professor, and a pastoral psychotherapist. He is Professor of Pastoral Theology and Counseling at the Divinity School, Rochester, New York. He is the author of several articles and books including *The Abuse of Power: A Theological Problem* and *Deliver Us From Evil: Resisting Racial and Gender Oppression,* in which he challenges the church to make violence against women and children a priority for theological reflection and action.

MARJORIE PROCTER-SMITH is Associate Professor of Liturgy and Worship at Perkins School of Theology, Southern Methodist University, Dallas, Texas. She is the author of *In Her Own Rite: Constructing Feminist Liturgical Tradition* and numerous articles on feminist worship, and is co-editor with Janet Walton of *Women at Worship: Interpretations of North American Diversity.* She is currently writing a book on feminist prayer.

ANDY SMITH is a Southern Baptist and is a former board member of the National Coalition Against Sexual Assault. She is currently attending Union Theological Seminary.

ANN TAVES is Professor of History of Christianity and American Religion at the School of Theology at Claremont. She edited the memoirs of Abigail Bailey, reissued as *Religion and Domestic Violence in Early New England,* as well as a book on American Catholic devotional practices, *The Household of Faith* and numerous articles on women and religion. She is currently at work on a book entitled *The Making and Unmaking of Religious Experience: Psychological Theory and Religious Revivals, 1734–1906.*

EMILIE M. TOWNES is an ordained American Baptist clergywoman. She is associate professor of Christian social ethics at Saint Paul School of Theology. Townes is editor of *A Troubling in My Soul: Womanist Perspectives on Evil and Suffering* and author of *Womanist Justice, Womanist Hope* and *In a Blaze of Glory: Womanist Spirituality as Social Witness.*

TRACY TROTHEN is writing her doctoral dissertation, "A Feminist Critical Analysis of the United Church of Canada's Evolving Understanding of Violence Against Women," at Emmanuel College, Toronto School of Theology. She has experience in chaplaincy and is very involved in the United Church. She is dedicated to the pursuit of justice for women and plans to continue her justice work through teaching and pastoral ministry.

KATHLEEN ZUANICH YOUNG received her Ph.D. from Simon Fraser University. Her dissertation was entitled, "Croatian Ethnic Diversity in Northern Puget Sound." She teaches in the anthropology department of Western Washington University.

Copyright Acknowledgments